British Columbia
& the Canadian Rockies

Yukon Territory
p252

British Columbia
p110

Alberta
p42

THIS EDITION WRITTEN AND RESEARCHED BY

John Lee,

Brendan Sainsbury, Ryan Ver Berkmoes

Contents

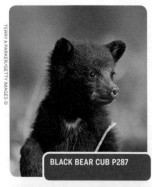

BLACK BEAR CUB P287

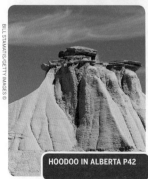

HOODOO IN ALBERTA P42

Contents

Welcome to BC & the Canadian Rockies

Soul-stirring mountains, mist-shrouded forests and epic tooth-and-claw wildlife – this is Canada's grand outdoor wonderland. And it's served alongside a full menu of cool, ever-welcoming communities.

Great Outdoors

Deep sighs are the usual response when encountering this region's sparkling diorama of sawtooth peaks, ethereally colored lakes and crenulated coastlines whipped by dramatic ocean waves. But it's the vast scale of this seemingly infinite wilderness that strikes most, triggering a humbled response in the face of nature's grand scheme. There has never been a more persuasive argument for tree-hugging, although when it comes to the area's astonishing wildlife, from whales and grizzlies to wolves and moose, it's best to keep the hugging to a minimum.

Adrenalin Rushes

Steely calved locals have been discovering ways to interact with the outdoors here for decades and there are hundreds of operators that can help you do the same. From skiing and snowboarding on Whistler's spectacular slopes to hiking the alpine meadows in Banff National Park or surfing with the West Coast beach bums in Tofino, there are more ways to work up a sweat here than you can swing a paddle at. Which reminds us: these are prime kayaking waters, with tree-lined lakes and rough-and-tumble ocean routes calling your name.

Dining & Drinking

The West Coast offers a cornucopia of charming farmers markets, juicy locally caught seafood, velvet-soft ranchland steaks and feast-triggering fruit and veggies. Restaurants fall over themselves to showcase the finest local ingredients, but it's Vancouver, possibly Canada's top dining city, that leads the way. And alongside the grape-tastic Okanagan Valley and its wine-producing satellite regions, there's been a tasty tidal wave of lip-smacking new microbreweries in recent years, making British Columbia a paradise for traveling beer nuts.

City Life

It's easy to be lured by the outdoors here but this region also has some great city action. Urbanites will enjoy the Edmonton arts scene and the Calgary cowboy vibe, but it's BC that offers the best city-based shenanigans with two very different approaches. Provincial capital Victoria frames its cool scene within a backdrop of historic buildings, while Vancouver, Western Canada's largest city, provides a full complement of distinctive neighborhoods ripe for exploration. From sophisticated Yaletown to hipster-haven Main Street and from cool-ass Gastown to the 'gayborhood' West End, you'll never run out of places to explore on foot here.

Why I Love BC & the Canadian Rockies

By John Lee, Author

Originally from the UK, my first visit to Western Canada included some spine-tingling sightings of deer, black bears and a gigantic moose that eyed me from the edge of a Rocky Mountains forest. I was smitten. And although I've now lived here for almost 20 years, I'm still deeply enthralled. Sliding along the coastline on a BC Ferries vessel; watching eagles whirl slowly overhead; or supping a craft beer in a tiny Vancouver Island town are constant reminders of why I live in the best place on earth.

For more about our authors, see page 336.

Above: Whistler (p155)

British Columbia & the Canadian Rockies

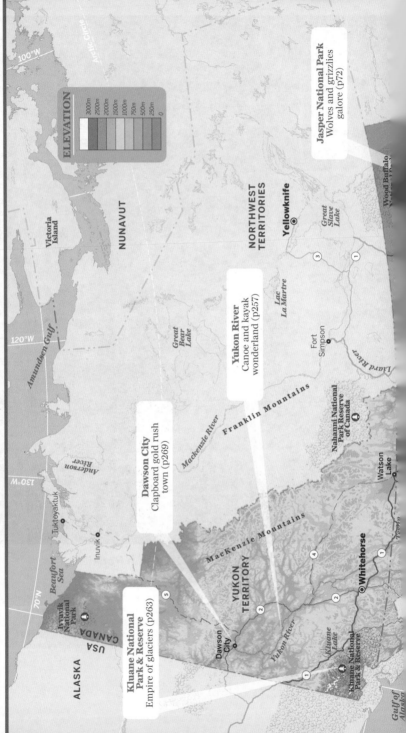

ELEVATION

3000m
2500m
2000m
1500m
1000m
750m
500m
250m
0

Kluane National Park & Reserve
Empire of glaciers (p263)

Dawson City
Clapboard gold rush town (p269)

Yukon River
Canoe and kayak wonderland (p257)

Jasper National Park
Wolves and grizzlies galore (p72)

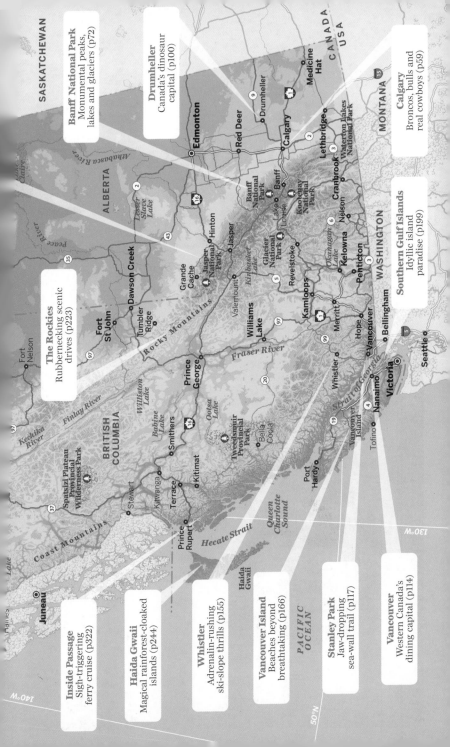

Banff National Park
Monumental peaks, lakes and glaciers (p72)

Drumheller
Canada's dinosaur capital (p100)

Calgary
Broncos, bulls and real cowboys (p59)

The Rockies
Rubbernecking scenic drives (p223)

Southern Gulf Islands
Idyllic island paradise (p199)

Inside Passage
Sigh-triggering ferry cruise (p322)

Haida Gwaii
Magical rainforest-cloaked islands (p244)

Whistler
Adrenalin-rushing ski-slope thrills (p155)

Vancouver Island
Beaches beyond breathtaking (p166)

Stanley Park
Jaw-dropping sea-wall trail (p117)

Vancouver
Western Canada's dining capital (p114)

SASKATCHEWAN

ALBERTA

BRITISH COLUMBIA

CANADA
USA

MONTANA

WASHINGTON

Coast Mountains

Rocky Mountains

PACIFIC OCEAN

Queen Charlotte Sound

Hecate Strait

Strait of Georgia

Fraser River

Athabasca River

Peace River

Finlay River

Kechika River

Edmonton
Red Deer
Drumheller
Calgary
Medicine Hat
Lethbridge
Cranbrook
Waterton Lakes National Park
Nelson
Kelowna
Penticton
Kamloops
Merritt
Hope
Revelstoke
Valemount
Jasper
Hinton
Grande Cache
Dawson Creek
Tumbler Ridge
Fort St John
Fort Nelson
Prince George
Williams Lake
Whistler
Vancouver
Bellingham
Seattle
Victoria
Nanaimo
Tofino
Port Hardy
Bella Coola
Smithers
Kitimat
Terrace
Kitwanga
Prince Rupert
Stewart
Juneau

Banff National Park
Lake Louise
Kootenay National Park
Glacier National Park
Spatsizi Plateau Provincial Wilderness Park
Tweedsmuir Provincial Park

Lesser Slave Lake
Lake Claire
Williston Lake
Babine Lake
Ootsa Lake
Kinbasket Lake
Okanagan Lake

Haida Gwaii

Vancouver Island

140°W

130°W

50°N

BC & the Canadian Rockies'
Top 15

Wildlife Watching in Jasper

1 Elk strut defiantly around the town's edge, nervous deer dart among the trees and giant bald eagles swoop overhead. Jasper National Park's (p72) dramatic mountain setting is enough to keep most camera-wielding visitors happy, but the surfeit of wandering wildlife makes you feel like you're part of a nature documentary. If you're lucky, you might even spot the show's stars: grizzly bears snuffling for berries alongside the highway or, across the other side of a river, a lone wolf silently tracking its next fresh-catch ungulate.

Stanley Park's Seawall Promenade

2 It's probably North America's finest urban park (p117) but some Vancouverites take it for granted; they may have grown up thinking everyone has a 404-hectare temperate rainforest lined with hiking and biking trails on their doorstep. It's only when they meet visitors that they realize how lucky they are. Stroll the 8.8km wave-licked, forest-backed seawall and you'll soon deplete your camera battery. But save some juice for the beady-eyed birdlife (especially blue herons) around Lost Lagoon and for a panoramic sunset at Third Beach.

JAMES ANDERSON/GETTY IMAGES ©

2

DOMINIK ECKELT/GETTY IMAGES ©

KARL WEATHERLY/GETTY IMAGES ©

Skiing at Whistler

3 This picture-postcard village is frosted with icicles and teeming with chatty visitors during the winter season; but it's the slopes that are the main attraction. Whistler (p155) was the host mountain for the 2010 Winter Olympic Games and you can emulate your Lycra-clad heroes on some of North America's most popular downhill runs. Then it's back to the village to compare your bruises, brag about your black-diamond abilities and imbibe a few hot chocolates. As the fireplace blazes nearby, watch the skiers outside and plan your next assault.

Hopping the Southern Gulf Islands

4 The islands (p199) off BC's mainland wink at you whenever you get close to the shoreline. But it's only when you take a short-hop ferry trip that you realize how different life is here. Your body clock will readjust to island time and you'll feel unexpectedly tranquil. If you have time, visit more than one. Start with the Saturday Market on Salt Spring Island, then consider a kayak excursion around Mayne Island or a cycling weave on Galiano. Mayne Island (p204)

Paddling the Yukon River

5 Relive the days of the craggy-faced frontier folk by canoeing (or kayaking) from Whitehorse to Dawson City. Not for the faint-hearted and certainly not for the uninitiated, the 16-day Yukon River paddle (p257) will glide you past rough-and-tumble rocky landscapes lined with critter-packed forests. Keep your eyes on the water; you might feel like panning for gold if you spot something glittery. For a less-intense taster, take a trip from Dawson City to Eagle City, Alaska: it's just three days.

ailing the Inside Passage

6 You're on the sunny deck on a BC Ferries' day-long service to Prince Rupert, breathtaking nautical odyssey guaranteed to slow heart rates to hibernation levels. With a gentle breeze licking your face, you let the Inside Passage (p322) diorama roll past: sharp peaks, tree-covered islands, red-capped lighthouses and tiny settlements with exotic names such as Namu and Dryad Point. Then the captain stirs you from your spa treatment with an announcement: grab your camera just in time to see a pod of passing orcas.

Vista Viewing in Banff

7 The colossal crags are like skyscrapers, while Banff's lakes are so ethereally colored you begin to wonder if Mother Nature has Photoshop. Banff National Park (p72) is so rich in jaw-dropping visuals, visitors can't help sighing almost everywhere they turn. And it's not just about the top attractions that lure tour groups: getting off the beaten path you'll stumble upon hidden waterfalls, alpine meadows studded with flowers and wildlife-packed valleys – all under domelike blue skies where the surrounding peaks peer down on you.

Calgary Stampede

8 When you arrive at North America's best rodeo (p64), you'll be greeted by belt buckles the size of saucers and Stetson cowboy hats that could house a small animal . But you'll soon be won over by this immersive introduction to cowboy culture; don your own hat and dive right in. Don't miss the zinging midway fairground, rootin'-tootin' live country music and the heart-stopping chuck-wagon races. When it comes to food, start with the barbecued steaks and then, if you're feeling adventurous, nibble on a prairie oyster or two.

Driving through the Rockies

9 Canada's most scenic driving route, the Icefields Parkway (p76), is handily located between Banff and Jasper. In an ideal world you'd have a designated driver so you could keep your eyes off the road: colossal peaks rise alongside, while the promise of spotting wildlife – especially bears and bighorn sheep – keeps things lively. There's even a celebrated attraction to lure you from your car: take a guided tramp on the Athabasca Glacier (p78) for an appreciation of how this mountainous region was cut and shaped.

DAVID WALL PHOTO/GETTY IMAGES ©

LILLISPHOTOGRAPHY/GETTY IMAGES ©

Aboriginal Culture in Haida Gwaii

10 Taking the ferry from Prince Rupert to this archipelago (p244) makes you feel like you're traveling to another country – a place like no other in British Columbia. Visit the Haida Heritage Centre and immerse yourself in the rich culture of the Aboriginal people who have called this area home for thousands of years. You'll find intricately carved artworks plus current practitioners illustrating the resurgence of Haida culture. Then visit the magical Gwaii Haanas National Park Reserve for ghostly reminders of ancient communities.

Digging the Dinosaurs in Drumheller

11 For kids who are in that wide-eyed dinosaur phase, there's no better place than this dusty Alberta town (p100). You'll find the planet's best dino museum to indulge children's insatiable need for facts (plus a chance to do their own fossil dig), as well as a photo op with the world's biggest T. rex – a 26m fiberglass fella who looms over the town like Godzilla. You're also in the heart of the Badlands here, an eerie, evocative landscape where imagining giant roaming reptiles is easy.

Dining in Vancouver

12 While fancy dining in Vancouver (p133) used to mean a steak and a baked potato, this taste-tripping metropolis has become the foodie capital of Canada in recent years. Start by trawling Granville Island Public Market for inspiration, lunch at one of the city's 100-plus food carts then enjoy dinner at one of the many great restaurants: from shimmering seafood to authentic *izakayas* and from Canada's best Chinese cuisine to fresh-picked farm-to-table joints, the choice is only limited by your belt buckle.

Dawson City

13 You're bouncing around for hours on some rickety old bus on the Klondike Hwy in the height of summer, not knowing whether it's three o'clock in the morning or afternoon, and suddenly you arrive in Dawson City (p269). Frilly-skirted ladies, straight out of a gambling hall, chat on wooden sidewalks, and a buzz of stories about gold can be heard everywhere – it's like stumbling into another world. True adventurers will try the infamous Sourtoe cocktail, and all who encounter Dawson City will brag about their experience forevermore.

Kluane National Park & Reserve

14 From the Alaska Hwy you get just a glimpse of the awesome beauty within the vast 22,015-sq-km Kluane National Park (p263). Hike for a day to the interior – or hop on a helicopter – and you'll witness an almost overwhelming, otherworldly beauty that has, not surprisingly, garnered Unesco World Heritage Site recognition. Huge icebergs break off glaciers and the water at the shoreline freezes – this is nature in all its grand, terrifying beauty and one of the largest protected wilderness areas in the world.

Beachcombing on Vancouver Island

15 The largest populated landmass off North America's west coast, Vancouver Island has some fantastic beaches. There's the golden expanses around Tofino (p189) and the wide, family-friendly bays around Parksville (p185). But it's the remote north coast that wins our vote. Pushing though the dense ferny undergrowth of Cape Scott (p198), you'll suddenly emerge blinking in the sunlight on an empty white-sand beach studded with tide pools and rocky outcrops. The waves lap gently and marine birds swoop around as if they own the place.

14

15

Need to Know

For more information, see Survival Guide (p312)

Currency
Canadian dollar ($)

Language
English

Visas
For many nationalities, a visa is not required for stays of up to 180 days; other nationalities will need a visa.

Money
ATMs widely available. Credit cards accepted in most hotels and restaurants.

Cell Phones
Local SIM cards can be used in European and Australian phones. Other phones must be set to roaming.

Time
Pacific Time in most of BC and the Yukon (GMT/UTC minus 8 hours); Mountain Time in Alberta (GMT/UTC minus 7 hours)

When to Go

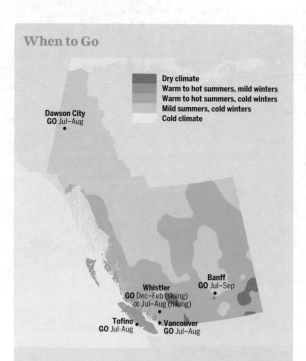

- Dry climate
- Warm to hot summers, mild winters
- Warm to hot summers, cold winters
- Mild summers, cold winters
- Cold climate

Dawson City
GO Jul–Aug

Banff
GO Jul–Sep

Whistler
GO Dec–Feb (skiing) or Jul–Aug (hiking)

Tofino
GO Jul–Aug

Vancouver
GO Jul–Aug

High Season
(Jul–Aug)

➡ Sunshine and warm weather prevail throughout the region

➡ Accommodation prices reach a peak, sometimes 50% above low season

➡ Festivals and farmers markets abound in communities large and small

Shoulder
(Apr & May, Sep & Oct)

➡ Temperatures are cool but comfortable; rain is typical

➡ Crowds and accommodation prices reduced

➡ Attraction hours outside cities are often cut

Low Season
(Nov–Mar)

➡ Snow and cold (below freezing) temperatures, especially in the north

➡ The year's best hotel rates, except in ski resorts

➡ Outside resorts and cities visitor attractions may be closed

Useful Websites

Destination British Columbia (www.hellobc.com) Formerly Tourism British Columbia, the province's official visitor website profiles regions, attractions and has an accommodation booking service.

Tourism Alberta (www.travel alberta.com) Official visitor site for the province, with download-able resources and accommoda-tion listings.

Tourism Yukon (www.travel yukon.com) Official visitor site, packed with inspiring images and suggested experiences for those planning a visit.

Lonely Planet (www.lonely planet.com/british-columbia) Destination information, hotel bookings, traveler forum and more for this region and beyond.

Important Numbers

Dial all 10 digits when making local calls. Add 1 to the front of the number if the call is long-distance, even if it's within the same region (eg calling Whistler from Vancouver).

Country code	☑1
International access code	☑011
Emergency	☑911
Local directory assistance	☑411

Exchange Rates

Australia	A$1 = $0.95
Euro zone	€1 = $1.04
Japan	¥100 = $1.06
New Zealand	NZ$1 = $0.81
UK	UK£1 = $1.63
US	US$1 = $1.04

For current exchange rates see www.xe.com.

Daily Costs

Budget: Less than $100

➡ Dorm bed: $25–$45

➡ Campsite: $20–$40

➡ Food court or street food vendor lunch: $8

➡ Transit day pass: $5–$10

Midrange: $100–$250

➡ Ensuite standard hotel room: $100–$150

➡ Meal in midrange local restaurant: $15–$25 (drinks extra)

➡ Admission to top local attraction: $15–$30

➡ Two drinks in local pub: $15–$20

Top End: More than $250

➡ Boutique hotel or posh B&B: $200

➡ Three-course meal in good restaurant: $50 (drinks extra)

➡ Car hire: up to $65 per day

➡ Ski day-pass: $60–$100

Opening Hours

Opening hours for attrac-tions can vary throughout the year, especially in smaller communities where hours are often decreased in shoulder and low seasons. The following are general guidelines to opening hours in this region - see listings for specific hours.

Banks 9am or 10am–5pm Monday to Friday

Restaurants breakfast 7am–11am, lunch 11:30am–2pm, dinner 5pm–9:30pm

Bars 11am–midnight, some only open from 5pm

Shops 10am–5pm Monday to Saturday, noon–5pm Sunday

Arriving in British Columbia & the Rockies

Vancouver International Air-port (p320) SkyTrain Canada Line trains run to the city center every few minutes from 5.10am to 12.57am ($7.75–$10.50). Travel time is around 25 min-utes. City center–bound hotels are $30 to $40 (30 minutes).

Calgary International Airport (p320) Sundog Tours run shut-tle buses every 30 minutes from 8.30am to 9.45pm. Downtown-bound taxis are around $35 (30 minutes).

Edmonton International Air-port (p320) Sky Shuttle airport buses run to city hotels ($18). They take around 45 minutes to reach downtown. Taxis from the airport cost around $50.

Getting Around

This is a vast region and while there are many transport options available, car travel is still the most popular way to get around beyond the cities.

Train Efficient commuter rail transit is available in Vancouver, Calgary and Edmonton, with limited VIA Rail and Rocky Mountaineer scenic services in other regions.

Car A good intercity highway system encourages road trips here. Vehicles are essential in many far-flung areas.

Bus Good public transit systems in big cities, with intercity serv-ices provided by Greyhound and smaller operators throughout the region.

Ferries Many short and long-haul routes provided by BC Ferries along the western coastline.

For much more on **getting around**, see p320

If You Like...

Fantastic Food

Vancouver dining Canada's top restaurant scene is also its most diverse – from the best seafood to authentic Asian adventures. (p133)

Cowboy cuisine Alberta beef is second to none but the food stands at the Calgary Stampede (p64) are the best places to dive in.

Farmers markets Dozens have sprouted here in recent years, with their tempting local fruits – from peaches to cherries – a must-have. (p138)

Cowichan Bay Artisan cheese and bread makers and restaurants serving locally sourced dishes and regional wines abound in Canada's favorite slow-food community. (p180)

Historic Sites

North Pacific Cannery National Historic Site You can feel the ghosts of canning workers past at this hulking, wood-built former plant near Prince Rupert. (p243)

Fort Langley National Historic Site The colonial outpost where BC was signed into existence offers a kid-friendly smorgasbord of activities and costumed 'residents.' (p151)

Head-Smashed-In Buffalo Jump With the region's most eye-popping name, this fascinating aboriginal interpretive center in Alberta recalls the local heritage. (p102)

Klondike National Historic Sites The gold-rush days are on every street corner in Dawson City, where frontier buildings stud the area like nuggets. (p271)

Barkerville Historic Town Stroll the streets of a pioneer town that once housed thousands of grubby frontiersmen, plus the occasional woman. (p239)

Adrenalin Rushes

Whistler Canada's favorite ski resort is also packed with summer activities, from zip-lining to white-water rafting. (p155)

Mt Washington Vancouver Island's ski resort transforms into a muscle-popping mountain-biking magnet in summer. (p194)

Tofino Idyllic beaches and a wave-whipped waterfront make this Canada's top surf spot. (p189)

Canmore Perfect for Rockies-region rock fans, the climbing here – including winter waterfall climbs – is spectacular. (p74)

Athabasca Glacier Avoid the too-easy bus tour and take a breathtaking guided hike on the icy surface, crampons included. (p77)

Arts & Culture

Vancouver Art Gallery This top museum with a keen eye for photoconceptualism stages blockbuster visiting shows in summer. (p117)

Whyte Museum of the Canadian Rockies Displays some fascinating pioneer-inspired artwork alongside its history exhibits. (p79)

Museum of Anthropology Its spectacular array of northwest coast aboriginal arts has recently broadened to represent other cultures. (p125)

Art Gallery of Alberta Edmonton's fancy new gallery is almost as striking as its mostly Canadian artworks. (p47)

Beer & Wine

Okanagan Valley This vine-striped, lakeside region is home to dozens of sample-happy wineries. (p207)

Cowichan Valley A Vancouver Island alternative to the Okanagan with boutique wineries and a great cidery. (p180)

Alibi Room Rather than traveling to BC's far-flung micro-breweries, just hit this friendly Vancouver bar and its dozens of tempting taps. (p139)

Banff Ave Brewing Co A brewpub in a national park? Oh yes. Go for a sampler or try the signature Head Smashed IPA. (p87)

Wildlife Watching

Khutzeymateen Grizzly Bear Sanctuary Near Prince Rupert, around 50 of the salmon-snaffling furballs call this area home. (p242)

Jasper National Park Often wandering across highways and stopping the traffic, the local elk – plus abundant deer, eagles and bears – make it perfectly clear who's in charge here. (p72)

Telegraph Cove Whale-watching operators line Victoria, the Lower Mainland and beyond but this Vancouver Island departure point is an evocative favorite. (p198)

Northern Lights Wolf Centre A Yoho National Park refuge for the lupine critters, this is a great spot to learn all about them. (p228)

PLAN YOUR TRIP IF YOU LIKE...

(Top) Art Gallery of Alberta (p47), designed by architect Randall Stout
(Bottom) Vineyards, Okanagan Valley (p207)

Month by Month

January

It's peak ski season, with winter-wonderland views and temperatures well below freezing in Alberta, the Yukon and much of British Columbia; it's warmer on the south coast with rain more likely.

 Winter Okanagan Wine Festival

BC's gable-roofed Sun Peaks Resort warms up with a taste-tripping tipple event (www.thewinefestivals.com) where ice wine is the major draw. Saturday night's progressive tasting weaves around the village and there are additional belt-busting dinners and tempting classes aplenty.

 Ice Magic Festival

The spectacular Lake Louise shoreline in Banff National Park is the snow-swathed backdrop for this annual ice-carving event (www.banfflakelouise. com/area-events). Wrap up warmly, take lots of pictures, then nip inside the nearby Fairmont Chateau Lake Louise for a hot toddy.

February

Spring may be in the air in southern coastal BC but winter dominates much of the region. Dressing for rain on the coast is a good idea, with thick coats (and hip flasks) advisable elsewhere.

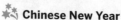 **Yukon Quest**

This legendary 1600km dog sled race (www.yukonquest. com) zips from Whitehorse in the Yukon to Fairbanks, Alaska through darkness and –50°C temperatures. It's a celebration of the tough north and a test of the relationship between musher and husky.

Chinese New Year

Depending on the calendar, this giant Vancouver celebration (www.vancouver-chinatown.com) can take place in January or February but it always includes plenty of color, great food and one of the region's biggest parades.

March

The ski season starts to wind down across parts of the region, although there are still plenty of great slopes to barrel down. Southern coastal cities and Vancouver Island are rainy.

Vancouver International Wine Festival

The city's oldest and finest wine party (www. vanwinefest.ca) makes grape fans of everyone here around the end of March, with jam-packed, slightly tipsy galas and tasting events.

April

Spring is budding across the region, but it's a good time to bag accommodation and snow-gear deals in ski resorts, now entering their shoulder period before summer's hiking and biking visitors.

✱ World Ski & Snowboard Festival

One of the biggest festivals in Whistler, this hugely popular nine-day celebration (www.wssf.com) includes daredevil demonstrations, outdoor concerts and a smile-triggering party atmosphere.

May

Blossoms are opening across Vancouver and beyond, while the bears are stirring from their hibernation in more remote climes. Expect warmish bouts of sun in the south plus rain and late-season snow elsewhere.

✗ BC Farmers Markets

Sprouting like post-thaw flowers, alfresco produce markets kick off this month, typically running to at least September. They're a great chance to sink your teeth into local apples, peaches and blueberries, and to check out crafts and bakery treats. Listings at www.bcfarmersmarket.org.

🍷 Vancouver Craft Beer Week

Celebrating the region's surging microbrew scene, Vancouver's top booze event (www.vancouvercraftbeer week.com) showcases the thirsty work of BC's best beer makers with tastings, parties, dinners and an awards night. Arrive parched and drink deep.

June

Even in the colder parts of BC and Alberta, the sun will be out this month, making this the time to lace up your hiking boots and embrace the great outdoors without freezing your extremities.

☆ Bard on the Beach

This joyously west coast approach to Shakespeare (www.bardonthebeach.org) features up to four plays staged in a lovely tented complex on Vancouver's mountain-framed waterfront. Runs to September but book ahead: it's a local favorite.

☆ Vancouver International Jazz Festival

Mammoth music celebration (www.coastaljazz.ca) staged in Gastown, Yaletown and around Vancouver over 10 days, with a generous helping of free outdoor shows complemented by superstar theater performances. Book in advance for top-drawer acts.

✱ Penticton Elvis Festival

Dozens of hip-swinging impersonators of The King invade this small Okanagan town for a three-day celebration of all-things Elvis (www.pentictonelvisfestival.com). It's a kitschtastic, eye-popping party whether or not you're a fan – although probably best not to tell anyone if you're not.

July

Summertime and the living is easy for visitors who enjoy warming their skin under sunny skies. It's also crowded, which means popular spots such as Banff and Jasper are at their busiest.

✱ Canada Day Celebrations

The Canadian version of July 4 in the US, this is the country's flag-waving annual birthday party. Expect to see community celebrations across the region, with the biggest, including fireworks, in downtown Vancouver's Canada Place.

🏃 Crankworx

It's definitely summer in Whistler when the ski slopes become a bike park and this massive annual celebration of mountain-bike shenanigans (www.crankworx.com) kicks off. Expect displays of saddle-crunching prowess, live music and mud-splattered partying.

✱ Calgary Stampede

North America's biggest rodeo event (www.calgary stampede.com) is a rocking cavalcade of cowboy culture where everyone finds their inner wearer of Stetson cowboy hats. Come along for raging bulls, frenetic chuck-wagon races and barbecued steak.

August

The region's summer peak, the crowds (and hotel prices) are now at their height. Interior areas in BC can be hot and humid, while the rest of the region is generally pleasantly warm and sunny.

☆ Edmonton International Fringe Theatre Festival

Canada's oldest and largest fringe fest (www.fringetheatre.ca) lures thousands to the city's Old Strathcona neighborhood for a 10-day buffet of short but eclectic comic and dramatic performances. It's Edmonton's biggest annual party.

☆ Discovery Days

The evocative pioneer-era streets of Dawson City are home to the Yukon's most popular annual event, a colorful week-long party of parades, games, races and movie shows that recall the region's gold-rush heyday. Look out for the naughty can-can dancers.

☆ Squamish Valley Music Festival

BC's biggest annual live music weekend (www.squamishfestival.com), with dozens of Canadian and international acts luring musos to a sunny farmland site between Vancouver and Whistler. Come with a tent and party hard.

☆ Pride Week

Canada's biggest pride event (www.vancouverpride.ca), this Vancouver party kicks off with a massive mardi gras–style parade that draws half-a-million oglers. Galas, live music, fashion shows and other saucy she-nanigans keep things lively.

September

One of the best months to visit: the crowds have gone home, there are still long stretches of sunny weather, and the colors are starting to turn to fall's golden hues.

☆ Rifflandia

Victoria's coolest music festival (www.rifflandia.com) lures local and visiting hipsters with dozens of live music happenings at venues throughout the city.

☆ Vancouver International Film Festival

Starting at the end of September, this is the city's favorite movie-watching event (www.viff.org). Book ahead for two weeks of the world's best new indie, international and documentary flicks; consider a multiaccess pass for maximum screen-time.

October

Fall foliage is in full blaze across the region but temperatures are cooling off, while rain is returning to coastal communities that have forgotten where they put their umbrellas.

☐ Fall Okanagan Wine Festival

The Okanagan's largest annual wine fest (www.thewinefestivals.com) encompasses 10 days of more than 150 events spread throughout the region's autumnal-hued rolling hills. Choose from vineyard tours, food-pairing seminars and gourmet dinners.

☆ Banff Mountain Film and Book Festival

One of the Rockies' biggest festivals, this annual celebration (www.banffcentre.ca/mountainfestival) draws the culturally inclined as well as world-renowned artists to readings, screenings and chin-stroking gatherings throughout the town.

November

The ski season starts to kick off for some resorts, while the southern cities unpack their waterproof jackets. Temperatures are just a taste of what's to come for winter, though.

✕ Cornucopia

November in Whistler means this indulgent multiday showcase (www.whistlercornucopia.com) of the region's great food and wine. It's also a chance to dress up at decadent parties throughout the village.

December

The region has a full advent calendar of Christmas events. Temperatures drop and the snow is back in many areas – go skiing in the Rockies, BC interior and beyond.

☆ Santa Claus Parade

The best reason to stand outside in the cold in Vancouver, this huge parade (www.rogerssantaclausparade.com) includes marching bands, floats, thousands of kids and an appearance by Santa.

Itineraries

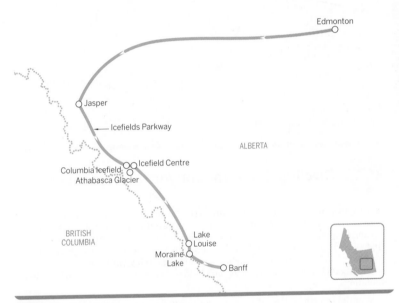

 The Epic Rockies Roll

Kick off your Canadian Rockies road trip in the gateway city of **Edmonton**, spending a couple of days shopping, perusing museums and puttering around Old Strathcona. Then hit Hwy 16 westward for your first big drive: a half-day weave to **Jasper**. Check in for three nights, grab a beer at the Jasper Brewing Co and plan your wildlife watching around the region's lakes and mountains. Next up, it's time to move on southwards via the **Icefields Parkway**, Canada's most scenic drive. It's shadowed by looming crags and studded with inquisitive bighorn sheep peering at you from the clifftops. Stop off en route at the Columbia Icefield and take a hike or truck tour on the Athabasca Glacier. After lunch at the nearby Icefield Centre, continue southwards to Lake Louise: take photos and wander the shoreline, saving time for a visit to the equally dazzling Moraine Lake a short drive away. Back in the car, you'll soon be in **Banff**. Treat yourself to a fancy hotel sleepover and spend the rest of your visit hiking flower-covered alpine trails and marveling at the epic Unesco-listed landscapes.

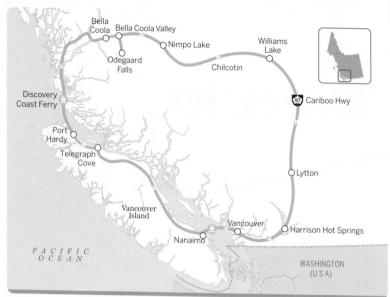

Circling BC – Vancouver to Vancouver

2 WEEKS

Start your journey of discovery in **Vancouver**. Catch the BC Ferries vessel from West Vancouver's Horseshoe Bay for the short ride to **Nanaimo**, where you can sink into 'island time' and start to enjoy Vancouver Island's laid-back culture – it's distinctly more independent and small-town than the mainland. After spending the night, head north on Hwy 19, taking an eastward detour to waterfront **Telegraph Cove**. Take a whale-watching tour here and check in for a night in one of the restored telegraph-station buildings.

Continue north on Hwy 16 the next morning and check in to **Port Hardy** for the night: if it's still daylight, consider an oceanfront hike. You'll have an early start to catch the **Discovery Coast Ferry** here the next morning (summer only) but it's well worth it: a languid 12 hours of coastline-gazing with the ever-present promise of spotting whales, seals and more from the sun-dappled deck.

Arriving in tiny **Bella Coola**, which sits at the end of a long fjord, find rustic retreat for a few nights in the **Bella Coola Valley**. Spend your days exploring trails past huge old cedars and make the hike to pounding **Odegaard Falls**. Go for a river float and lose count of the grizzlies wandering the shores. When you leave, tackle The Hill, a thrill-ride for cars, and head east through the lonely **Chilcotin**. Stop at the alpine waters of **Nimpo Lake** or just take any little tributary road and lose civilization – what little there is – altogether. At **Williams Lake** say yee-ha to cowboy country.

Turn south on the **Cariboo Hwy** (Hwy 97), otherwise known as the Gold Rush Trail. The road follows the route of the first pioneers and gold-seekers who settled in BC's un-forgiving interior. At **Lytton** go white-water rafting on the Fraser and Thompson Rivers. After these chilly waters, warm up with a soak in **Harrison Hot Springs**. From here, it's an easy drive back to Vancouver on Hwy 1.

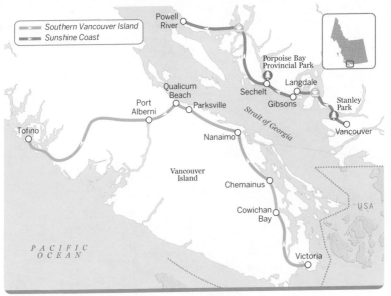

Southern Vancouver Island

1 WEEK

Start with two nights in **Victoria**, BC's provincial capital, giving yourself plenty of time to explore the museums, galleries and historic streets before departing northwards on day three via Hwy 1. Take your time weaving through the Malahat mountain region but save time for a long lunch in the idyllic waterfront community of **Cowichan Bay**. It'll be hard to tear yourself away (there are B&Bs in the area if you can't manage it) but worth it to continue north and reach **Chemainus**, a former logging town now adorned with dozens of murals. It's not far to your sleepover in **Nanaimo**, the island's second city, where there are some good restaurants and a popular museum. Next morning, you'll be off to check out the friendly oceanfront communities of **Parksville** and **Qualicum Beach** – ideal for beachcombing fans – before veering inland via Hwy 4 towards the dramatic west coast. **Port Alberni** is a handy en route lunch stop, but you'll likely be eager to thread through the winding mountain roads to **Tofino**. Spend several nights here soaking up BC's wild Pacific Ocean coastline.

Sunshine Coast

4 DAYS

Head north from **Vancouver** on Hwy 99 through Stanley Park and make for West Van's Horseshoe Bay ferry terminal. Take the Sunshine Coast vessel to **Langdale** and roll off onto Hwy 101, the region's main artery. After a few minutes you'll be in artist-studded **Gibsons**, an ideal lunch stop – fish tacos on the dock are recommended. Check into your local B&B, then take an early evening kayak tour on the glassy ocean. Rejoining Hwy 101 the next morning, continue on to **Sechelt** and consider a shoreline forest hike in Porpoise Bay Provincial Park. If you're lucky, you'll also catch the summertime Farmers & Artisans Market, a great way to hang with the locals. Stay in a waterfront B&B here then hit the road early the next morning. You'll have a short ferry hop before arriving in the area's top town. **Powell River** combines old-school heritage and a funky young population. Stick around for a day or two of hiking and mountain biking and be sure to toast your trip at Townsite Brewing.

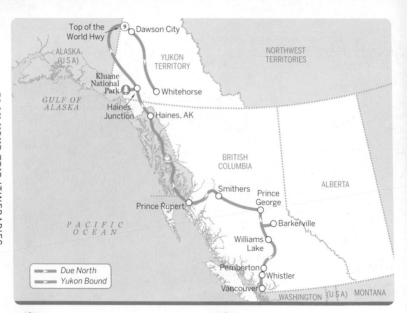

Legend:
- Due North
- Yukon Bound

 ## 6 DAYS Due North

 ## 2 WEEKS Yukon Bound

From downtown **Vancouver**, drive through Stanley Park on Hwy 1 then join Hwy 99 northwards to **Whistler**. Spend the afternoon hiking or biking the summer trails and sleep over at one of the resort's grand hotels. Next morning, continue north via **Pemberton** – keep your eyes peeled for towering Mt Currie. You're now in the heart of cowboy country but it's probably too late to swap your car for a horse. After a five-hour drive, stop for two nights in a **Williams Lake** motel: time your visit for the June–July rodeo and you'll have a blast, or book a white-water rafting tour with a local operator. Next, head off on Hwy 97 and you'll be en route to **Prince George**: the heart of northern BC's logging country is about three hours away but stop off – via Hwy 26 – at **Barkerville**, an evocative re-creation of an old pioneer town. After a Prince George layover, get an early start on the four-hour Yellowhead Hwy drive to **Smithers**, an arsty little town with some cool sleepover options. Your final four-hour drive the next day delivers you eastward to **Prince Rupert**, northern BC's loveliest town.

Spend a couple of days exploring **Prince Rupert** – the Museum of Northern BC and the North Pacific Cannery are must-sees – before rolling onto an Alaska Marine Highway ferry to **Haines, AK**. It's a two-day odyssey that the region's cruise ships will charge you a comparative arm and a leg for. Once you're back on dry land, spend a night in one of the many hotels in Haines. From here, you'll be (almost) on the doorstep of one of the world's largest protected wilderness. Accessed 249km away via the BC town of **Haines Junction**, **Kluane National Park** is a vast Unesco-recognized realm of glaciers and mountains. Weave through the park and cross over again into Alaska briefly to access the **Top of the World Hwy**. Continue on your merry way and you'll reach **Dawson City**, the Yukon's coolest old-school town and center of gold-rush heritage. Stick around for a couple of nights to enjoy the heritage ambience, then continue southwards on the Klondike Hwy for 538km to **Whitehorse**, the territory's capital. There are enough museums and galleries here to keep you occupied for another Yukon night.

Elk, Banff National Park (p72)

National & Regional Parks

Many Canada-bound visitors imagine towering sawtooth peaks, vast mirrored lakes and wildlife-packed forests. But what they're really imagining is BC, the Rockies and the Yukon – the region where the country's most awe-inspiring landscapes come to life. From Unesco World Heritage sites to breathtaking provincial gems, here's your guide to exploring the region's natural wonders.

Best of National & Regional Parks

Best for Hiking

Pacific Rim National Park Reserve; Banff, Jasper and Waterton Lakes National Parks.

Best for Skiing

Banff National Park; Strathcona, Seymour and Cypress Provincial Parks.

Best for Rock Climbing

Kootenay National Park; Horne Lake Caves Provincial Park.

Best for Wildlife Watching

Jasper, Banff, Wood Buffalo and Yoho National Parks.

Best for Kayaking

Gwaii Haanas and Gulf Islands National Park Reserves; Bowron Lake Provincial Park.

Best Unesco World Heritage Sites

Banff, Jasper and Yoho National Parks; Dinosaur Provincial Park.

Best National Historic Sites

Banff Park Museum; Head-Smashed-In Buffalo Jump; Gulf of Georgia Cannery Museum.

Where to Go

National Parks

These carefully protected parks of national and internationally-recognized importance are the region's must-see attractions. They typically have excellent visitor centers and do all they can to maintain a successful balance between wilderness preservation and enabling tourist access.

Banff, designated Canada's first national park in 1885, offers something for everyone, which is just as well given the number of visitors it draws. But its grand size means you can still escape into the backcountry and be wowed by its sheer-faced glacier-cut peaks. It is often compared to its smaller sibling Jasper to the north, and while it's best to visit both, there is one main difference if you only have time for a single visit: Banff offers close proximity to dramatic mountains lapped by ethereally blue lakes, while Jasper is the region's center for watching incredible wildlife in its natural setting. And by wildlife, we mean the big kind: bears, wolves, moose et al. That's not to say there isn't great mountain scenery in Jasper or wildlife aplenty in Banff. But if you have to choose your visit, that's the way to do it.

High alpine adventure awaits around Rogers Pass in BC's Glacier National Park, while among the highlights of craggy and uncrowded Yoho National Park are spectacular glacier-fed lakes such as O'Hara and Emerald.

In BC's Kootenays region, a multitude of microclimates are crammed into the comparatively tiny Kootenay National Park, which straddles the border between the two provinces. It's the ideal spot for a soak at Radium Hot Springs. Alternatively, consider Mt Revelstoke National Park, where you can hike wildlife-studded trails to the summit for breathtaking views over the Selkirks.

While Banff and Jasper draw the most visitors, the province's other three national parks are also visually thrilling: sublimely tranquil Waterton Lakes, with its off-the-beaten-path location and network of alpine day hikes; giant Wood Buffalo, where the world's last free-roaming herd of wood bison hang out; and Elk Island, a comparatively small park close to Edmonton and bristling with elk and plains bison.

TOP FIVE PROVINCIAL PARKS

Try to weave in a visit to some of these parks. You won't regret it... and you'll have major bragging rights when you get back home.

➡ Bowron Lake Provincial Park (p238)

➡ Dinosaur Provincial Park (p102)

➡ Garibaldi Provincial Park (p155)

➡ Kokanee Glacier Provincial Park (p235)

➡ Strathcona Provincial Park (p195)

Top: Takakkaw Falls, Yoho National Park (p229)

Bottom: Kootenay National Park (p231)

KAREN CROWE/GETTY IMAGES ©

Top: Bowron Lake
Provincial Park (p238)

Bottom: Bighorn
sheep, Banff National
Park (p72)

GREAT NATIONAL PARK HIKES

PARK	TRAIL	LENGTH (KM)	LEVEL
Banff	Lake Agnes	3.4	medium-hard
Jasper	Discovery Trail	8	easy
Pacific Rim	West Coast Trail	75	hard
Waterton Lakes	Carthew-Alderson Trail	19	medium
Yoho	Lake O'Hara Alpine Circuit	12	medium

The Yukon also has two remote national parks: Vuntut and Ivvavik.

There are also national park reserves in BC and the Yukon. These are areas that have been earmarked as national parks, pending the settlement of aboriginal land claims. They are managed in much the same way as national parks, with entry fees, visitor centers, and various environmental rules and regulations.

For more information on the region's national parks and national park reserves, visit the Parks Canada website (www.pc.gc.ca). And if you're Alberta-bound, pick-up Lonely Planet's *Banff, Jasper & Glacier National Parks*.

Provincial & Territorial Parks

Alberta has more than 500 provincial parks and protected areas (see www.albertaparks.ca for listings), while BC is home to almost double that number (visit www.bcparks.ca for further information). Among the highlights are Alberta's fossil-rich Dinosaur Provincial Park and Writing-On-Stone Provincial Park, with its fascinating 3000-year-old aboriginal artworks.

Since the Yukon is not a province, its large parks (described in detail at www.env.gov.yk.ca) are called 'territorial parks.' These include the rugged, bird-studded Herschel Island Territorial Park – which is also known as Qikigtaruk to the native people who still hold it sacred – and Tombstone Territorial Park, a wild and windswept area of broad tundra-cloaked valleys that plays host to jaw-dropping hiking trails.

Alongside the region's provincial and territorial parks systems, there are hundreds of city parks and some of them are among western Canada's must-see highlights. These include Calgary's Prince Island Park and, in Vancouver, the spectacular waterfront Stanley Park, which is one of North America's finest urban greenspaces.

Plan Ahead

When to Go

Summer is the most popular time to visit western Canada's parks, but that can mean rubbing shoulders with waves of camera-wielding tour groups at hotspots like Banff, Jasper and Lake Louise. There are three ways to deal with this and ensure the magic of your visit: when you arrive at the aforementioned must-see spots, head off the beaten path and onto a less-trafficked trail. Secondly, add some less-visited park gems to your visit – Yoho and Glacier, for example, are great Rockies parks with far fewer visitors. Thirdly, consider visiting outside the summer peak. Locals prefer late spring and early fall when there are no crowds, the colors are even more vibrant and the wildlife watching – from post-hibernation bears to rutting elk and big-horn sheep – is often spectacular.

Fees

National parks charge for entry, and you'll need to pay and display your pass in your car. Passes are purchased at toll-booth-style barriers in large parks like Banff and Jasper or at ticket machines or visitor centers in parks like Vancouver Island's Pacific Rim National Park Reserve. Daily fees go up to adult/child/family $9.80/4.90/19.60. If you're planning on visiting several parks over a number of days or weeks, the Parks Canada Discovery Pass is rec-

PARK TOUR OPERATORS

OPERATOR	ACTIVITIES	WHERE?	MORE INFORMATION
Athabasca Glacier Icewalks	guided glacier hikes	Columbia Icefield	www.icewalks.com
Brewster	bus tours	Banff, Jasper and Columbia Icefield	www.brewster.ca
Discover Banff Tours	guided tours of the region, including wildlife tours	Banff	www.banfftours.com
North Island Daytrippers	guided hikes to north Vancouver Island's remote parks	Northern Vancouver Island	www.islandday trippers.com
Queen Charlotte Adventures	single or multiday guided boat and kayak tours	Haida Gwaii	www.queencharlotte adventures.com
Tonquin Valley Adventures	multiday horseback riding tours	Jasper	www.tonquinadven tures.com
Up North Adventures	kayaking, guided bike trips and winter sports	Yukon	www.upnorthadven tures.com
Yamnuska Mountain Adventures	guided rock climbing	Lake Louise	www.yamnuska.com

ommended. It costs adult/child/family $67.70/33.30/136.40 and covers unlimited entry for 12 months to national parks and historic sites. The family passes include entry for groups of up to seven people (two adults only).

The BC Parks system does not charge admission. In addition, parking fees – which were first levied in 2002 – were scrapped across most BC parks in 2011.

The Yukon Parks system does not charge for entry to its parks.

On the Ground

Bears & Bugs

Wildlife attacks on humans in Canada's parks are rare but you need to be aware that you are going to be encroaching on areas that some scarily large critters call home. And while animals such as elk and deer may seem to be perfectly used to all the cameras pointing their way in busy parks like Banff and Jasper, Parks Canada works very hard to keep animals and humans from becoming too used to each other.

During spring and summer, black flies and mosquitoes blight the interior and northern reaches of BC, Alberta and the Yukon. The cumulative effect of scores of irritated, swollen bites can wreck your park trip. Bringing a liquid insect repellant and camping in a tent with a zippered screen is a necessity. In clearings, along shorelines or anywhere there's a breeze, you'll be safe from most bugs.

Driving Tips

Weather and driving conditions can change rapidly in the parks and wilderness areas of western Canada. If you're driving in winter, expect snow. In addition, when you see an animal by the side of the road, the etiquette here is to slow down and alert other drivers by using your hazard lights.

Plan Your Trip
Outdoor Activities

Even if you're a city visitor, you'll feel the region's wilderness – especially its gigantic forests, wild coastline and huge sawtooth mountains – impressing itself on your consciousness. Rather than shy away, jump right in. There's no shortage of world-class hiking, biking, skiing, kayaking, rafting or climbing here – and the experience will likely be one you'll brag about for years. Alternatively, rub shoulders with the friendly locals and watch someone else do all the work by taking in some popular spectator sports.

Cycling & Mountain Biking

Mountain biking is as huge as the mountains in BC and the Rockies. This is the birthplace of 'freeride,' which combines downhill and dirt-jumping.

Home to some of BC's best technical trails, Rossland and its West Kootenay surroundings are a hotspot of BC mountain biking. Vying for the 'mountain biking capital of Canada' moniker, Squamish offers dozens of off-road trails twisting around the mountain-framed region: expect a freerider's fantasy, with narrow boards and logs spanning lush, wet ferns. You'll find a similar set-up – and a burgeoning local scene – at Vancouver's North Shore area: see www.nsmba.ca for more information on this area or check out www.mountainbikingbc.ca for an introduction to the wider region.

Top Short Hikes

Discovery Trail, Jasper
An easy 8km circle around the townsite with a high possibility of elk and deer sightings.

Lake Louise, Banff
Stroll around the shoreline or hit the 1.6km uphill trail to the Big Beehive lookout for a grand panorama.

Stanley Park, Vancouver
A spectacular tree-lined seawall trail with ocean and mountain vistas.

Athabasca Glacier, Columbia Icefields
Uphill tramping on a crunchy glacier, complete with breathtaking views.

PEDALTASTIC NELSON

Freeriding pedalheads have plenty of favorite spots in BC and the Rockies, but many also enjoy the bikey ambiance of just hanging out in a cool community. In the heart of the Kootenay Rockies region, Nelson – which many locals will tell you is the coolest small town in British Columbia – fits the bill perfectly. The historic downtown area is lined with funky hangouts (an after-ride Nelson Brewing beer is recommended), while the surrounding area is striped with great trails, from the epic downhill of Mountain Station to the winding Svoboda Road Trails in West Arm Provincial Park.

Whistler has the province's best-organized mountain-bike park with jumps, beams and bridges winding through 200km of maintained downhill trails. In summer, the resort hosts the giant Crankworx festival (www.crankworx.com), a pedal-packed nirvana of contests, demos and live music.

Back in the urban sprawl, Victoria is one of Canada's best cycling cities, closely trailed by Vancouver, which has been carving out new citywide routes for cyclists in recent years.

In the Rockies region, Canmore and Banff are the biking hot spots, with the latter offering a good combination of road and off-road options and plenty of wildlife-spotting opportunities.

signature West Coast Trail is a challenge but it's one you'll never forget: rock-face ladders, stream crossings and wandering wildlife, plus the occasional passing whale, make it a rite of passage for serious hikers. It links to the lesser-known Juan de Fuca Marine Trail if you still need more. Atop Vancouver Island, the remote North Coast Trail is equally dramatic but far less crowded: ideal if you like hiking without other people around. You'll have a similar crowd-free ramble on the mainland's hidden gem: the Sunshine Coast Trail.

In contrast, the Okanagan's Kettle Valley Rail Trail meanders over towering wooden trestle bridges in Myra Canyon. It offers hikers the perfect chance to explore this beautiful valley without having to worry about traffic or steep hills. It's also a popular bike route.

In the Rockies, you'll find a hikers' paradise that even non-hikers will be blown away by. There are plenty of easy short walks at popular attractions like the impossibly azure Lake Louise. But once you turn your back on the tour bus crowds, you'll suddenly feel at one with the vastness of nature. Banff is the hot spot for Rockies hikers and its top routes include the Sawback Trail and the Hoodoos Trail.

In the northern Yukon region, those who like a challenge should check out the steep and difficult Chilkoot Trail, still lined with the detritus of those who desperately tried to seek their fortune in the gold rush. Elsewhere in the territory, Kluane National Park and Reserve and Tombstone Territorial Park offer world-class challenges and spectacles such as thousands of migrating caribou.

Hiking

Hiking in this region ranges from a leisurely wander around Vancouver's salt-sprayed Stanley Park seawall to tramping across glaciers under a cathedral-like blue sky at the Columbia Icefield between Banff and Jasper. Whatever your level, a walk through nature is a must-do highlight here.

On Vancouver Island, the spectacular Pacific Rim National Park Reserve offers some of Mother Nature's most dramatic vistas: swaying old-growth rainforest fringing white-sand beaches. The park's

Rock Climbing & Mountaineering

All those inviting crags you've spotted on your trip are an indication that western Canada is a major climbing capital, ideal for short scales or multiday crampon-picking jaunts.

Near Banff, the Rocky Mountain resort town of Canmore is an ideal first stop, no matter what your skill level. Climbing stores, a climbing school (www.yamnuska.com) and thousands of limestone sport climbs within a 30-minute radius make this a one-stop shop for rock fans.

Further west, BC's Squamish 'Chief' is the highlight – and one of the most challenging climbs – of a burgeoning local scene that includes dozens of area peaks. Tap into the local scene via Squamish Rock Guides (p154).

If mountaineering is more your thing, the Rockies are, not surprisingly, a hot spot. On the border with BC, the Matterhorn of Canada is Mt Assiniboine. Other western classics include Alberta's Mt Edith Cavell in Jasper; BC's Mt Robson; and Sir Donald in the Rockies. Closer to Vancouver, Garibaldi Peak, in Garibaldi Provincial Park, lures many city-based climbers for weekend jaunts.

If you need a guide, check in with the excellent **Alpine Club of Canada** (www.alpineclubofcanada.ca).

Skiing & Snowboarding

If you're staying in Vancouver, you can be on the slopes within a 30-minute drive from downtown, while Whistler (an additional hour away) is one of North America's most popular ski resorts.

But many would argue that even better skiing in BC is found in the east of the province, where vast swaths of mountains – especially in the Kootenays – are annually covered by 10 or more meters of snow. In fact this region now boasts the 'Powder Hwy,' a marketing moniker for a series of roads linking the major ski resorts.

Elsewhere in the province, the Okanagan has resorts like Sun Peaks, Apex and Big White boasting good snow year after year. Snowpack here ranges from 2m to 6m-plus, depending on how close the resort is to the Pacific Ocean.

You'll slide through stunning postcard landscapes in the Rockies, especially at Sunshine in Banff National Park. But for amazing cross-country skiing, head to Canmore: its popular trails were part of the Canadian Winter Olympics held in Calgary in 1988.

For insights and resources covering the region and beyond, check the website of the **Canadian Ski Council** (www.skicanada.org).

Diving

Justly famous for its superb, albeit chilly, conditions, BC features two of the top-ranked ocean dive spots in the world: Vancouver Island and the Gulf Islands. It's best to go in winter, when the plankton has decreased and visibility often exceeds 20m.

The water temperature drops to between 7°C and 10°C in winter; in summer, it may reach 15°C. At depths of more than 15m, visibility remains good throughout the year and temperatures rarely rise above 10°C. Expect to see a full range of marine life, including oodles of crabs, from tiny hermits to intimidating kings. If you're lucky you may also encounter seals and sea lions or bizarre creatures such as wolf eels and giant octopuses.

Popular dive areas include Comox and Campbell River but Nanaimo also lures many with its aquatic wildlife and sunk-to-order navy vessels. See www.divenanaimo.travel for information.

Paddle Sports

BC and beyond offers hundreds of opportunities for those who like messing about

PLAN YOUR TRIP OUTDOOR ACTIVITIES

HOOK, LINE & SINKER

Fishing – saltwater and freshwater – draws anglers from around the world to this region. Saltwater aficionados particularly like to cast their lines in the waters around Vancouver Island, where several places (particularly Campbell River) claim the title 'salmon capital of the world.' Also consider Prince Rupert and Haida Gwaii, known for their halibut fishing. You'll find good river and lake fishing in every region.

Ask at visitor centers and sporting goods stores for information on the profusion of fishing licenses. The **BC Ministry of Environment** (www.env.gov.bc.ca/fw) controls freshwater licenses. The federal **Department of Fisheries and Oceans** (www.pac.dfo-mpo.gc.ca) issues licenses for saltwater/tidal fishing.

on the water. Lakes, rivers and coastline abound, just waiting for the dip of an oar. Major paddling spots usually have stations where you can rent canoes, kayaks and gear.

Inland

The 116km Bowron Lake canoe circuit in Bowron Lake Provincial Park is one of the world's great canoe trips, covering 10 lakes with easy portages between each. Slightly less fabled – and less crowded – is the 116km-long circuit in Wells Gray Provincial Park.

During the short Yukon summer, scores of paddlers from around the world paddle the famed Yukon River and its tributaries – the route of the Klondike gold rush. You can still experience the stunning raw wilderness that the prospectors encountered, but from a modern canoe or kayak rather than a raft of lashed-together logs. Whitehorse is the center for guides and gear.

SKIING HOT SPOTS

Some of the region's best ski resorts:

➡ **Apex Mountain Resort** Known for its plethora of double-black-diamond and technical runs (the drop is over 600m), as well as gladed chutes and vast powdery bowls. Near Penticton.

➡ **Banff National Park ski resorts** Three excellent mountain resorts, Ski Banff@ Norquay, Sunshine Village and Lake Louise Ski Area, offer 250 runs of every description. Sunshine Village is the most popular.

➡ **Big White Ski Resort** BC's highest ski resort features 118 runs, and is excellent for downhill and back-country skiing. The drop is 777m and you can night ski. Near Kelowna.

➡ **Cypress Mountain** 2010's Winter Olympic snowboarding and freestyle skiing venue, with dozens of runs and 19km of cross-country runs. Near Vancouver.

➡ **Fernie Alpine Resort** With 114 runs across five large bowls, there's plenty of virgin powder where you can leave your mark. Near Fernie.

➡ **Grouse Mountain** A 30-minute drive from Vancouver, Grouse is a favorite for its night skiing.

➡ **Kicking Horse Mountain Resort** Many of the runs here are rated advanced or expert. A gondola gives you a great vantage over the 1260 vertical meters of this relatively snow-heavy location. Near Golden.

➡ **Kimberley Alpine Resort** A good all-round resort – especially if you like smaller ones with comparatively minimal nightlife. Near Kimberley.

➡ **Mt Seymour** Some 1000m up, this North Shore provincial resort offers popular runs including Brockton, Mystery Peak and Mushroom Junior Park. Also family-friendly tobogganing. Near North Vancouver.

➡ **Mt Washington Alpine Resort** Vancouver Island's main ski resort; there are 60 runs, plus cross-country trails and a snowshoe park. Near Comox.

➡ **Revelstoke Mountain Resort** BC's newest major resort has 52 runs with a focus on intermediate and advanced runs. Heli-skiing operators can take you out to track-free bowls across the ranges. Near Revelstoke.

➡ **Silver Star Mountain Resort** With 115 runs and a pioneer town aesthetic, there are 12 lifts and a 760m vertical drop. Near Vernon.

➡ **Sun Peaks Resort** BC's second-largest resort with three mountains and more than 100 runs. Snowshoeing, dog sledding and Nordic skiing also available. Near Kamloops.

➡ **Whistler-Blackcomb** This world-famous, dual-mountain paradise was the host resort for the 2010 Olympic Winter Games. Its lifts include the new 4.4km-long gondola linking Mts Whistler and Blackcomb. More than 200 runs and 29 sq km of bowls, glades and slopes keep the international crowds happy. Near Whistler.

For the ultimate adrenaline rush, try white-water rafting. Rugged canyons and seasonal melting snow make BC's rivers great for white-water action. You don't need to be experienced to have a go, as licensed commercial rafting operators offer guided tours for all abilities. Trips can last from three hours (average cost $100) up to a couple of weeks. Popular areas include the Thompson River near Lytton and the Kootenays – many consider the Kicking Horse River near Golden as one of province's best rafting trips. In the Yukon, Haines Junction is also a good base, while in the Rockies the Jasper region has several popular operators.

Coast

Although some people swear by their ocean-going canoes, the BC coast is truly the domain of kayaks. Since humans first stretched skin over a frame and deployed a double paddle some 4000 years ago, the little craft have been an excellent marriage of man and mode.

Options are as numerous as BC's endlessly crenulated coast and islands. The greatest concentration of outfitters is on Vancouver Island, which is one big paddling playground. The Broken Group Islands offer BC's best wilderness kayaking, revered for remoteness, rugged natural beauty and the opportunity to kayak to the little islands and camp overnight.

It's always safest to kayak with other people. Someone in the group should know how to plot a course by navigational chart and compass, pilot in fog, read weather patterns, assess water hazards, interpret tide tables, handle boats in adverse conditions and perform group- and self-rescues. Always check weather forecasts before setting out and don't expect your cell phone (mobile) to work.

If you have less time, you can rent a kayak for a few hours or take an introductory lesson in pretty much any of the island's coastal towns.

Urban paddlers can also take in Vancouver's cityscape from the waters of False Creek (rentals available on Granville Island), while in the Rockies, Banff has several operators if you'd like to paddle the region's glassy, mountain-backed lakes.

WINDSURFING & KITEBOARDING

The breeze-licked tidal flats around Vancouver are popular with windsurfers. On many a day you'll see scores of colorful sails darting around the shallows like flocks of birds – it's a signature photo from the Kitsilano coastline. But further north, Squamish is the real center of the region's kiteboarding and windsurfing frenzy: an hour from Vancouver, its wind-whipped Squamish Spit area is often studded with adrenaline-fueled locals. Stand-up paddle-boarding is also taking off in the region: consider Deep Cove, on Vancouver's North Shore, for an introduction.

Surfing

If you're aiming to become a temporary beach bum on your Canada trip, head to the wild west coast of BC's Vancouver Island and hang out around Tofino. Surfing schools and gear rentals stud the area: you'll have an awesome time riding the swells or just watching everyone else as you stretch out on the idyllic sand. Backed by verdant rainforest, this is a perfect spot to spend your time whether or not you plan to surf. June to September is the height of the season here but serious surfer dudes also like to drop by in winter to face down the lashing waves. Check **Surfing Vancouver Island** (www.surfingvancouver island.com) for a taste of what to expect.

Horseback Riding

Surveying the region's spectacular scenery from between the perky ears of a trusty steed is highly recommended: feel free to bring a costume and release your inner Mountie. BC's Cariboo and Chilcotin regions have long been horseback-riding areas: you can stay on a ranch here or climb into the saddle for a tour. Alternatively, in the midst of the Great Bear Rainforest, there are plenty of trails to explore in the Bella Coola Valley. Saddling up in Banff or Jasper is one of the best ways to feel at one with the region, while Calgary is the home of the cowboy: drop by in summer for the spectacular Calgary Stampede rodeo fest or check out your options on the region's cool Cowboy Trail (www.thecowboytrail.com).

Spectator Sports

Sport is the lifeblood of many western Canada communities, with hockey leading the way: mild-mannered locals can transform into fevered, face-painted nutbars on game night, especially if there's a chance of winning the Stanley Cup. But there's more to watching a game here than shelling out big bucks for NHL hockey: Canadian football (slightly different from American football) and soccer are the region's other top professionals sports, while a host of smaller grass-roots options ensure there are plenty of opportunities for visitors to hang out with sports-mad locals.

Hockey

While Canada is a multifaith country, there's one religion that rises above all others. Hockey – don't even bother calling it *ice* hockey here – rouses rabid emotions in die-hard fans and can trigger group hugging or uncontrollable sobbing at the drop of a puck, especially when the local team has just lost in the annual Stanley Cup play-offs.

BC and Alberta have three teams in the elite, US-dominated National Hockey League (NHL): the Vancouver Canucks, Calgary Flames and Edmonton Oilers.

While tickets can be hard to come by – Vancouver Canucks games routinely sell out, for example, and booking as far ahead as possible for the September to June season is essential – you don't have to hit a stadium to catch a game: head to a local pub on game night and you'll be swept up in the passion.

But it's not all about the pros: catching a game with lower league teams like the Kamloops Blazers, Prince George Cougars, Kelowna Rockets and Vancouver Giants is much cheaper and it's an entertaining glimpse at the sport's less-glamorous level.

Football

The Canadian Football League (CFL) is second only to hockey in the hearts and minds of many sport-mad locals. While it's similar to American Football – think hefty padding and crunching tackles that would stop a grizzly bear – the Canadian version involves larger teams and is fought on a larger pitch. And the trophy they all pursue? It's called the Grey Cup.

The region's teams are the BC Lions (www.bclions.com), Edmonton Eskimos (www.esks.com) and the Calgary Stampeders (www.stampeders.com). Tickets are usually easy to come by, except during Grey Cup time. Check their websites for schedules and ticket prices.

Regular season games run from June to November: expect a family atmosphere and a party-like vibe with cheerleaders and noisy crowd interaction. For more information on the league, peruse its official website at www.cfl.ca.

Soccer

Canada's most popular participation sport, soccer – you won't get far calling it football here – has traditionally mirrored the US experience by never quite reaching the heights of the continent's more established professional sports. But you can't keep a good pastime down and the game is on an upswing in Vancouver and beyond.

Canada's biggest pro soccer team, the Vancouver Whitecaps (www.whitecapsfc.com) was promoted to the top-level Major League Soccer (MLS) league in 2011. It now plays games against leading sides across North America and regularly attracts crowds of over 15,000 cheering fans.

Regions at a Glance

This guide encompasses three diverse areas: the adjoining provinces of British Columbia and Alberta – which straddle the Rocky Mountains – plus the Yukon Territory, a remote northern wilderness next to Alaska. Each offers spectacular outdoor vistas and some once-in-a-lifetime experiences. But they also have distinctions that you'll want to know about before you plan your trip.

Southern coastal BC and the Rockies region attract the lion's share of visitors: the first for Vancouver – cosmopolitan metropolis and gateway to Whistler, Victoria and wider Vancouver Island; and the latter for the iconic national parks of Banff and Jasper, with their picture-postcard, wildlife-packed mountains. But if your idea of communing with nature means not seeing anyone else, the vast and unremitting Yukon may be your nirvana: you'll certainly never forget your visit.

Alberta

Wildlife Watching
Cowboy Culture
Scenic Drives

Jasper Critters

There's wildlife throughout the Rockies but in Jasper you'll be closer than ever to a menagerie of elk, moose, bighorn sheep and, of course, bears (of the black as well as grizzly varieties). But it's a wolf sighting that will tingle your spine like nothing else.

Calgary Stampede

There's no better way to immerse yourself in cowboy culture than this giant summertime rodeo, a rip-roaring cavalcade of Stetson-donning Western culture, man-versus-beast contests and steaks as big as cars. Saddle up.

Rocky Roads

A drive-through diorama of towering peaks, mammoth forests and glacier-fed lakes, the Rockies are idyllic car country. Among the wide, wildlife-lined highway highlights is the Icefields Parkway, a smooth, leisurely ribbon linking Banff and Jasper.

p42

British Columbia

Coastline
Food & Drink
Activities

Ocean Vistas

The vast, multifjorded BC coastline defines this region, whether you're strolling the Stanley Park seawall, hiking Vancouver Island's rugged West Coast Trail or reclining on a BC Ferries deck watching for passing orcas.

Locavores United

From Vancouver's top restaurant tables to produce-packed farmers markets throughout the province, BC's local bounty is a foodie's delight. And seafood is the way to go, preferably coupled with regional wine or beer.

Adrenalin Rush

From ski resorts large and small to life-enhancing hiking, biking, kayaking and beyond, visitors will never run out of ways to challenge themselves in the great outdoors here. Start small with a forest stroll, and you'll be zip-lining through the valleys in no time.

p110

Yukon Territory

History
Raw Nature
Activities

Gold Rush

The imprint of the 1898 Klondike gold rush is indelible here, especially on the clapboard streets of old Dawson City. You wouldn't be surprised to see a wily-faced old geezer run down the main drag proclaiming his discovery here – although if you do, it's probably time to stop drinking.

Spectacular Beauty

You won't have to jostle with the kind of crowds that flock to the Rockies at remote Kluane National Park. And you'll be rewarded for your persistence with a vast, Unesco-recognized wonderland of glacier-sliced mountains. Humbling is the word.

Frontier Kayaking

Re-create the early days of gritty pioneer exploration by traveling the way they used to: via canoe or kayak along the Yukon River. Gold panning along the way is optional.

p252

On the Road

**Yukon
Territory**
p252

**British
Columbia**
p110

Alberta
p42

Alberta

Best Places to Eat

➡ Da-De-O (p54)

➡ Model Milk (p69)

➡ Bison Restaurant & Terrace (p86)

➡ Other Paw (p98)

Best Places to Stay

➡ Fairmont Banff Springs (p85)

➡ Metterra Hotel on Whyte (p50)

➡ Park Place Inn (p97)

➡ Hotel Alma (p65)

Why Go?

Alberta does lakes and mountains like Rome does churches and cathedrals, but without the penance. For proof head west to Jasper and Banff, two of the world's oldest national parks which, despite their wild and rugged terrain, remain well-trammeled and easily accessible. No one should leave this mortal coil without first laying eyes on Lake Louise and the Columbia Icefield. And think twice about dying before you've traveled east to the dinosaur-encrusted badlands around Drumheller, south to the Crypt Lake trail in Waterton Lakes National Park, and north to spot bison in the vast, empty northern parklands. Alberta's cities are of patchier interest. There are people still alive older than Calgary and Edmonton's downtowns. But, what these metropolises lack in history they make up for with their festivals. Edmonton's fringe theater festival is the world's second largest, while Calgary's July 'Stampede' is as unapologetically ostentatious as the city that hosts it.

When to Go
Edmonton

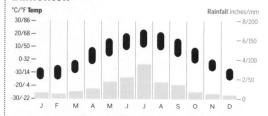

Jul Prime time for festivals, with Edmonton's Street Performers and the Calgary Stampede.

Jul–Sep Banff and Jasper trails are snow free, making a full range of hikes available.

Dec–Feb Winter-sports season in the Rocky Mountains.

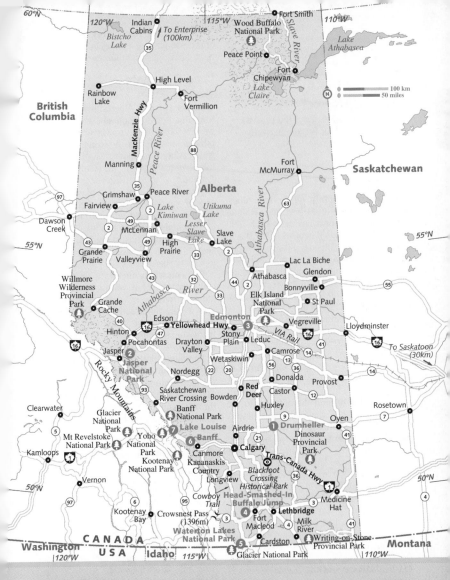

Alberta Highlights

1 Explore the Jurassic remnants of **Drumheller** (p100) and call into the Royal Tyrrell Museum of Palaeontology.

2 Make fresh tracks on a cross-country skiing trail in **Jasper National Park** (p72).

3 Attend the **Edmonton International Fringe Festival** (p50) and unlock the more bohemian side of the Albertan capital.

4 Decipher the foggy history of First Nations culture at **Head-Smashed-In Buffalo Jump** (p102).

5 Get above the tree line on the Carthew-Alderson Trail in **Waterton Lakes National Park** (p105).

6 Take afternoon tea after a morning hike in the **Fairmont Banff Springs** (p85) hotel.

7 Enjoy a brew in the **Lake Agnes Teahouse** (p91) high above bluer-than-blue Lake Louise.

ALBERTA FAST FACTS

➡ Population: 3,768,284

➡ Area: 642,317 sq km

➡ Capital: Edmonton

➡ Quirky fact: A relative of the T-rex, the Albertosaurus, was first discovered in the Horseshoe Canyon in 1884.

History

Things may have started off slowly in Alberta, but it's making up for lost time. Human habitation in the province dates back 7500 years – the Aboriginal peoples of the Blackfoot, Kainaiwa (Blood), Siksika, Peigan, Atsina (also called Gros Ventre), Cree, Tsuu T'ina (Sarcee) and Assiniboine tribes all settled here in prehistoric times, and their descendants still do. These nomadic peoples roamed the southern plains of the province in relative peace and harmony until the middle of the 17th century, when the first Europeans began to arrive.

With the arrival of the Europeans, Alberta began to change and evolve: the impact of these new arrivals was felt immediately. Trading cheap whiskey for buffalo skins set off the decline of both the buffalo and the traditional ways of the indigenous people. Within a generation, the Aboriginal peoples were restricted to reserves and the buffalo all but extinct.

In the 1820s the Hudson's Bay Company set up shop in the area, and European settlers continued to trickle in. By 1870 the North West Mounted Police (NWMP) – the predecessor of the Royal Canadian Mounted Police (RCMP) – had built forts within the province to control the whiskey trade and maintain order. And it was a good thing they did, because 10 years later the railway reached Alberta and the trickle of settlers turned into a gush.

These new residents were mostly farmers, and farming became the basis of the economy for the next century. Vast riches of oil and gas were discovered in the early 20th century, but it took time to develop them. At the conclusion of WWII there were 500 oil wells; by 1960, there were 10,000, by which time the petroleum business was the biggest in town.

From humble pastoral beginnings to one of the strongest economies in the world, Alberta has done alright for itself financially.

Land & Climate

The prairies that cover the eastern and southern parts of Alberta give way to the towering Rocky Mountains that form the western edge of the province. That mountainous spine forms the iconic scenery for which Alberta is known. The eastern foothills eventually peter out, melding into the flatland.

Alberta is a sunny sort of place; any time of year you can expect the sun to be out. Winters can be cold, when the temperature can plummet to a bone-chilling -20°C (-4°F). Climate change has started to influence snowfall, with the cities receiving less and less every year.

Chinook winds often kick up in the winter months. These warm westerly winds blow in from the coast, deposit their moisture on the mountains and give Albertans a reprieve from the winter chill, sometimes increasing temperatures by as much as 20°C in one day!

Summers tend to be hot and dry; the warmest months are July and August, when the temperature sits at a comfortable 25°C. The 'June Monsoon' is, as you'd expect from the nickname, often rain-filled, while the cooler temperatures and fall colors of September are spectacular.

❶ Getting There & Around

Alberta is easily accessible by bus, car, train and air. The province shares an international border with Montana, USA and provincial borders with the Northwest Territories (NWT), British Columbia (BC) and Saskatchewan.

AIR

The two major airports are in Edmonton and Calgary, and there are daily flights to both from major hubs across the world. Carriers serving the province include Air Canada, American Airlines, British Airways, Delta, Horizon Air, KLM, United Airlines and WestJet.

BUS

Greyhound Canada (www.greyhound.ca) has bus services to Alberta from neighboring provinces, and Greyhound has services from the USA. Times can vary greatly, based upon connections, and fares can be reduced by booking in advance.

Useful destinations, with one-way fares, from Edmonton:

Prince George ($100, 10 hours, daily)
Vancouver ($150, 17 hours, five daily)
Whitehorse ($214, 29 hours, one daily)
Winnipeg ($167, 18 hours, three daily)

Destinations from Calgary:
Kamloops ($99, 10 hours, four daily)
Regina ($82, 10 hours, two daily)
Saskatoon ($81, nine hours, four daily)
Vancouver ($104, 15 hours, five daily)
Winnipeg ($171, 20 hours, two daily)

Moose Travel Network (www.moosenetwork. com) runs a variety of trips in western Canada. Most start and finish in Vancouver, but along the way hit the highlights of the mountain parks and other Alberta must-sees. In winter it operates ski-focused tours that are a great option for carless ski bums. Trips depart daily during the summer months and a few times per week in the winter season.

CAR

Alberta was designed with the automobile and an unlimited supply of oil in mind. There are high-quality, well-maintained highways and a network of back roads to explore. Towns for the most part will have services, regardless of the population. Be aware that in more remote areas, especially in the north, those services could be a large distance apart. Fill up the gas tank where possible and be prepared.

TRAIN

Despite years of hard labor, countless work-related deaths, and a reputation for being one of the great feats of 19th-century engineering, Alberta's contemporary rail network has been whittled down to just two regular passenger train services. **VIA Rail** (www.via.ca) runs the thrice-weekly *Canadian* from Vancouver to To-ronto, passing through Jasper and Edmonton in both directions. Edmonton to Vancouver costs $225 and takes 27 hours; Edmonton to Toronto costs $405 and takes 55 hours. The Toronto-bound train stops in Saskatoon, Winnipeg and Sudbury Junction. VIA Rail also operates the train from Jasper to Prince Rupert, BC ($117, 32 hours, three weekly).

EDMONTON

POP 730,000

Modern, spread out and frigidly cold for much of the year, Alberta's second-largest city and capital is a demure government town that you're more likely to read about in the business pages than the travel

---

ALBERTA ITINERARIES

One Week

Spend the day in **Calgary** exploring the sites from the 1988 Winter Olympics and grab a meal on trendy 17th Ave. The next day, get into dino mode by taking a day trip to **Drumheller** and visiting the Royal Tyrrell Museum of Palaeontology (p101). Back in Calgary, go for a wander through the neighborhoods of Kensington and Inglewood and fight for a table at world-class Rouge (p69).

Wake early and head west. Stop first in **Canmore** before continuing into Banff National Park and arriving in **Banff Town**. Hike up Sulphur Mountain, ride back down on the Banff Gondola (p79) and finish off at the bottom with a soak in Banff Upper Hot Springs (p81).

After a stay in Banff, continue north to **Lake Louise**, stopping for the view outside the Chateau (p91). Find time for the short, steep hike to the Lake Agnes Teahouse (p91), then continue the drive to the Columbia Icefield (p76). Get ready to stop every five minutes to take yet another amazing photograph.

Roll into **Jasper** and splash out on the Park Place Inn (p97). After some much-needed sleep, stop off at Maligne Canyon (p93) on the way to Maligne Lake (p95), where a short hike might bag you a bear or a moose. Escape the mountains and head to **Edmonton**. Once there dive into the Old Strathcona neighborhood, finishing your Alberta adventure with a plate of smoking hot jambalaya at Da-De-O (p54).

The Complete Rockies

Follow the One Week itinerary, but include side trips into **Kananaskis Country**, the **Icefields Parkway** and north to **Grande Cache** to see the start of the mountains. Also tack on some time down south heading to **Waterton Lakes National Park**, experiencing this less-visited mountain paradise.

supplements. Maybe that's why the city's surprises, when (or if) you find them, are so delightful. Edmonton's annual fringe theater festival is the second largest in the world after Edinburgh, while the yawning fissure of a river valley that splits the city in half is less a park than its own self-contained ecosystem.

Despite all this, Edmonton acts more as a staging post than a destination in itself. Most non-Albertans pass through on their way to somewhere else – usually Jasper National Park, which lies four hours to the west, or, for a handful of visitors, the overhyped West Edmonton Mall, the largest mall in North America. Edmonton is also a frontier town: north of here the landscape is vast and empty, with practically no civilization to speak of until Yellowknife. If you're searching for the soul of the city, head south of the river to the university district and happy-go-lucky Whyte Avenue, home to small theaters, dive diners and a spirited Friday-night mood.

History

The Cree and Blackfoot tribes can trace their ancestry to the Edmonton area for 5000 years. It wasn't until the late 18th century that Europeans first arrived in the area. A trade outpost was built by the Hudson's Bay Company in 1795, which was dubbed Fort Edmonton.

Trappers, traders and adventurers frequented the fort, but it wasn't until 1870, when the government purchased Fort Ed and opened up the area to pioneers, that Edmonton saw its first real growth in population. When the railway arrived in Calgary in 1891, growth really started to speed up.

Meanwhile, the Aboriginal tribes had been severely weakened by disease and the near extinction of their primary food source, the bison. Increasingly vulnerable, they signed away most of their land rights to the Canadian government in a series of treaties

Edmonton

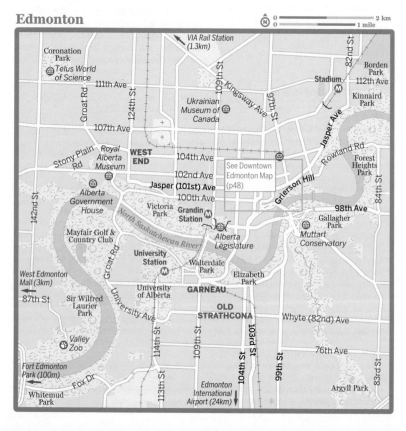

between 1871 and 1921 in return for money, reservation lands and hunting rights.

Gold was the first big boom for the area – not gold found in Alberta, but gold in the Yukon. Edmonton was the last stop in civilization before dreamers headed north to the Klondike. Some made their fortunes, most did not; some settled in Edmonton, and the town grew.

In the 1940s, WWII precipitated the construction of the Alaska Hwy, and the influx of workers further increased the population. Ukrainians and other Eastern European immigrants came to Edmonton in search of work and enriched the city.

Edmonton is again the hub for those looking to earn their fortune in the north. But it isn't gold or roads this time – it's oil.

◎ Sights & Activities

★ **Royal Alberta Museum**   MUSEUM
(Map p46; ☑ 780-453-9100; www.royalalberta-museum.ca; 12845 102nd Ave; adult/child $11/5; ⊙9am-5pm) Since getting its 'royal' prefix in 2005 when Queen Liz II dropped by, Edmonton's leading museum has successfully received funding – a cool $340 million – for a new downtown home which should be complete by 2015. For the time being, you can call in to these long-standing digs, on a bluff overlooking the river valley 2km west of downtown.

The museum is known for its enormous collection of insects (the world's largest) and a lauded display of Alberta's aboriginal culture. The highlight, however, is the 'Wild Alberta' gallery, which splits the province into different geographical zones and displays plants and animals from each.

★ **Art Gallery of Alberta**   GALLERY
(Map p48; ☑ 780-422-6223; www.youraga.ca; 2 Sir Winston Churchill Sq; adult/child $12.50/8.50; ⊙11am-5pm Tue-Sun, to 9pm Wed) With the opening of this maverick art gallery in 2010, Edmonton at last gained a modern signature building to counter the ubiquitous boxy skyscrapers. Looking like a giant glass-and-metal space helmet, the futuristic structure in Churchill Sq is an exhibit in its own right. Its collection comprises 6000 pieces of historical and contemporary art, many of which have a strong Canadian bias, including a couple of works by BC's master of green, Emily Carr.

However, this is Alberta not Paris. The gallery is relatively small and can't emulate

---

REGIONAL DRIVING DISTANCES

Calgary to Banff: 130km
Banff to Jasper: 290km
Edmonton to Calgary: 300km

---

its arty rivals in Toronto or Vancouver, although some decent temporary shows pass through. Additional facilities include a 150-seat theater, shop and restaurant.

Alberta Government House HISTORIC BUILDING
(Map p46; ☑ 780-427-2281; 12845 102nd Ave; ⊙11am-4:30pm Sun & holidays) **FREE** This opulent mansion was the former residence of the lieutenant governor. It's steeped in history and immaculately preserved – you'd never guess it's over 100 years old. The artwork alone is worth visiting: the walls are lined with stunning works by Alberta artists.

Alberta Legislature NOTABLE BUILDING
(Map p46; ☑ 780-427-7362; www.assembly.ab.ca; cnr 97th Ave & 107th St; ⊙8:30am-5pm) **FREE** Home to politicians, debate and some surprisingly good art is the Alberta Legislature. Where Fort Edmonton once stood, the Leg is a grand old building that, with its iconic dome and marble interiors, has grown to become a local landmark.

Free 45-minute tours (every hour) take you behind the scenes, and the grounds themselves are a splendid place to vegetate on a warm day. If you've less time, view the shop and **interpretive center** (pedway, 10820 98th Ave), which displays details of the building's architectural and political history.

Fort Edmonton Park HISTORIC SITE
(Map p46; ☑ 780-496-8787; www.fortedmontonpark.ca; cnr Fox & Whitemud Drs; adult/child $17.25/12.90; ⊙10am-6pm May-Sep; 🖝) Originally built by the Hudson's Bay Company in 1795, Fort Edmonton was moved several times before being finally dismantled in 1915. This newer riverside reconstruction began life in the 1960s and captures the fort at its 1846 apex. On site are very authentic mock-ups of Edmonton's city streets at three points of their historical trajectory: 1885, 1905 and 1920.

Come on a day devoid of school groups and you can almost imagine mildly inebriated emigrant Victorians prowling the unpaved streets on horseback. A vintage

Downtown Edmonton

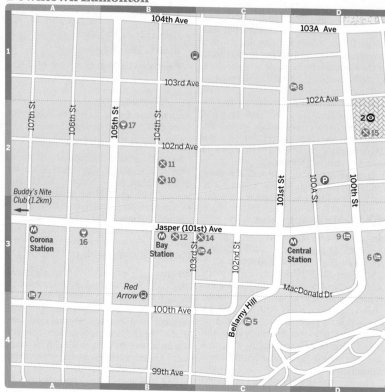

steam train links all the exhibits, and non-theatrical-costumed guides answer questions and add some flavor.

Muttart Conservatory GARDEN
(Map p46; ☎780-496-8755; www.muttartconservatory.ca; 9626 96A St; adult/child $12/6.50; ☺10am-5pm Fri-Wed, to 9pm Thu) Looking like some sort of pyramid-shaped, glass bomb shelter, the Muttart Conservatory is actually a botanical garden that sits south of the river off James MacDonald Bridge. Each of the four pyramids holds a different climate region and corresponding foliage. It's an interesting place to wander about, especially for gardeners, plant fans and those in the mood for something low-key.

Sir Winston Churchill Square SQUARE
(Map p48) The subject of a controversial 2005 face-lift, this pubic space, named a little bizarrely after a British prime minister, is a rather brutal treeless plaza where people

meet and hang out (assuming it's not -20°C degrees outside) and various festivals and public events kick off.

The square's former green areas have been replaced with a small amphitheater, a fountain and a cafe. Around the perimeter is a quadrangle of important buildings, including the City Hall, the Provincial Court and the impressive new Art Gallery of Alberta.

Alberta Railway Museum MUSEUM
(☎780-472-6229; www.albertarailwaymuseum.ca; 24215 34th St; adult/child $5/2; ☺10am-5pm May-Aug) This museum, on the northeast edge of the city, has a collection of more than 75 railcars, including steam and diesel locomotives and rolling stock, built and used between 1877 and 1950. It also has a collection of railway equipment, old train stations and related buildings.

On weekends, volunteers fire up some of the old engines, and you can ride along for $4 (the diesel locomotives run every Sunday

in season; the 1913 steam locomotive gets going only on holiday weekends). To get there, drive north on 97th St (Hwy 28) to Hwy 37, turn right and go east for 7km to 34th St, then turn right and go south about 2km.

Ukrainian Museum of Canada MUSEUM
(Map p46; www.umcalberta.org; 10611 110th Ave; ⊙10am-4pm May-Aug) FREE With a huge Ukrainian population and a long history of immigration, there are a few places around town to learn about the culture of the old country and its transplantation in Canada. This museum has its main branch in Saskatoon, but it retains a small collection of exhibits in Edmonton and has been in operation sine 1941.

In the pipeline is a new and more comprehensive Ukrainian museum on Jasper Ave. Plans are currently being launched by the Ukrainian Canadian Archives.

North Saskatchewan River Valley PARK
Edmonton has more designated urban parkland than any other city in North America, most of it contained within an interconnected riverside green belt that effectively cuts the metropolis in half. The green zone is flecked with lakes, bridges, wild areas, golf courses, ravines and approximately 160km worth of cycling and walking trails. It is easily accessed from downtown.

A fine way to get a glimpse of the downtown core from the river is to take a ride on the **Edmonton Queen** (Map p48; ☑780-424-2628; www.edmontonqueen.com; 9734 98th Ave; 1hr cruises from $19.95, dinner cruises $54.95; ⊙May-Sep). This modern stern-wheeler will take you for an hour-long cruise up- or downriver, depending on the mood of the captain. There is often onboard live entertainment to keep the mood festive.

West Edmonton Mall   SHOPPING MALL
(Map p46; www.westedmontonmall.com; 170th St; ⊙10am-9pm Mon-Fri, to 6pm Sat, noon-6pm Sun; 🖭) Kitsch lovers who can't afford the trip to Vegas will have a field day in West Edmonton Mall, while those less enamored by plastic plants and phony re-creations of 15th-century galleons will hate it.

Not content to simply be a shopping mall, Edmonton's urban behemoth has the world's largest waterslides, an equipped indoor wave pool, a full-size amusement park, a skating rink, two minigolf courses, a fake reef with real seals swimming around, a petting zoo, a hotel and 800 stores thrown in as a bonus. Stroll through Chinatown, grab a meal at an imitation Bourbon St or go for a skate or bungee jump. Then dive into the sea of retail shops – all of them chains.

🕭 Tours

Quirky free **walking tours** of downtown are offered in the summer months by students on vacation employed by the Downtown Business Association. They leave weekdays at 1pm from the corner of 104th St and 101st Ave.

Edmonton Ghost Tours   WALKING TOUR
(www.edmontonghosttours.com; tours per person $10; ⊙9.30pm Mon-Thu Jul & Aug) Spooky walking tours start from 10322 83rd Ave in Old Strathcona. No booking is required – just turn up 15 minutes early.

✯✯ Festivals & Events

Festivals are where Edmonton comes into its own. The city's identity is closely attached to its many annual festivals.

International Street Performers Festival   THEATER
(www.edmontonstreetfest.com) Sometimes the best theater is outside. International performers perform alfresco in this busker bonanza in the second week of July.

K-Days   CARNIVAL
(www.k-days.com; ⊙late Jul) For years, Capital Ex (Klondike Days) was the big summer festival in Edmonton. Since 2012, it has been known as K-Days, with less focus on gold-rush history and more on contemporary fun. Live music, rides and a nugget's worth of olden-days fun are the highlights of this evolving event.

Edmonton International Fringe Festival   THEATER
(www.fringetheatreadventures.ca; ⊙mid-Aug) The ultimate Edmonton experience is an 11-day program of live alternative theater on three outdoor stages in the parks and on the streets. Many shows are free and no ticket costs more than $15. There's no booking – you choose a theater and stand in line. The festival draws half a million people each year to Old Strathcona.

Canadian Finals Rodeo   RODEO
(www.canadianfinalsrodeo.ca; ⊙early Nov) The Canadian Finals Rodeo is the biggest indoor pro rodeo in Canada. With good bucking stock and the top cowboys there to test their skills, this is a great event to check out, especially if you missed the Calgary Stampede.

🛏 Sleeping

Edmonton has a better range of independent accommodations than some Canadian cities. Options include a centrally located B&B, a trio of boutique hotels and a couple of cheap hostels. Downtown is business-oriented, with more generic accommodations. If you are in town mainly to visit the West Edmonton Mall, then staying in or near it is feasible, but the digs there are definitely leaning toward the touristy side of the spectrum.

HI-Edmonton Hostel   HOSTEL $
(☏780-988-6836; www.hihostels.ca; 10647 81st Ave; dm/d $30/67; @🖭) Right in the heart of Old Strathcona, this busy hostel is a safe bet. The rooms are a bit jam-packed with bunks and it feels somewhat like a converted old people's home (it used to be a convent), but the location and price are hard to beat.

Rainbow Valley Campground & RV Park   CAMPGROUND $
(☏780-434-5531, 888-434-3991; www.rainbow-valley.com; 13204 45th Ave; campsites/RV sites $32/36; ⊙Apr-Oct) For an inner-city camping spot, this one is pretty good. It's in a good location to get to 'The Mall' and keep some distance from it at the same time.

★Metterra Hotel on Whyte   BOUTIQUE HOTEL $$
(☏780-465-8150; www.metterra.com; 10454 Whyte Ave; r from $150; @🖭) If you can wade through the uncreative hotel-brochure blurb ('urban oasis,' 'contemporary decor,'

'traditional hospitality'), you'll find that the Met is actually a decent place to stay and a fitting reflection of the happening entertainment district (Old Strathcona) in which it sits. The modern, luxurious interior is accented with Indonesian artifacts hinting at the owner's secret love for all things Eastern.

Matrix BOUTIQUE HOTEL **$$**
(Map p48; ☑780-429-2861; www.matrixedmonton.com; 10001 107th St; r from $150; @🛜) One of a triumvirate of Edmonton boutique hotels, the Matrix claims to serve the 'sophisticated traveler,' and largely succeeds, with cool minimalist architecture punctuated with woody color accents and plenty of handy modern gadgets. In keeping with its boutique image, there's free wine and cheese every evening at 5:30pm.

Varscona BOUTIQUE HOTEL **$$**
(☑780-434-6111; www.varscona.com; 8208 106th St, cnr Whyte Ave; r incl breakfast from $140; @🛜) Right in the heart of Old Strathcona, this charming hotel is elegant but not too hoity-toity, suggesting you can roll up either in a tracksuit or a business suit – or some kind of combination of the two. With the coolest neighborhood in town right on the doorstep, it's all the easier to stick your finger on the collective pulse of Edmonton. Breakfast, parking and evening wine and cheese are thrown in to sweeten the deal.

Chateau Lacombe HOTEL **$$**
(Map p48; ☑780-428-6611; www.chateaulacombe.com; 10111 Bellamy Hill; r from $120; ✱@🛜) Going defiantly against the grain, the spectacular Chateau was a chain hotel that, in 2013, was bought out by local private investors. There's some superficial work to do on this riverside behemoth, which has 24 floors, wonderful views and a revolving restaurant, but with an opulent lobby, fitness center and club-ish bar, it remains regally plush – and now at a bargain price!

Sutton Place Hotel HOTEL **$$**
(Map p48; ☑780-428-7111; www.suttonplace.com; 10235 101st St; r from $104; @🛜⊠) Part of a chain (albeit a small one) the upmarket Sutton Place lacks the intimacy of smaller hotels. Aside from classy rooms, replete with glitz and glamour, there are numerous additional facilities here. The indoor water park is fantastic, and there are res-

taurants, cocktail lounges and a casino on the grounds. Look out for cheap specials.

Hotel Selkirk HOTEL **$$**
(☑780-496-7227; www.hotelselkirk.com; 1920 St, Fort Edmonton Park; r from $124; ✱🛜) If you're into the idea of visiting the past at Fort Edmonton, why not take it to the next level and spend the night? This historic hotel has period-decorated rooms from the roaring 1920s, and staying here gives you free entry into the fort and its surrounds.

There's an on-site restaurant and English high tea ($19.50) on offer during the summer. The downside: it's isolated.

Glenora Inn B&B B&B **$$**
(☑780-488-6766; www.glenorabnb.com; 12327 102nd Ave; r with shared/private bathroom $100/130; @🛜) A B&B of the frilly Victorian variety, Glenora inhabits the burgeoning West End strip of 124th St. The building is of 1912 vintage, meaning it's 'historic' by Edmonton standards, though not technically 'Victorian.' It also houses a shop and a downstairs bistro where inn dwellers can procure breakfast.

There's a communal parlor and an outdoor patio for when the weather's less arctic.

Alberta Place Suite Hotel HOTEL **$$**
(Map p48; ☑780-423-1565; www.albertaplace.com; 10049 103rd St; studios/ste $144/174; @🛜⊠) What was once an apartment building is now a suite hotel with a range of room configurations from studios to one-bedroom suites to family suites. It's well located and refreshingly midpriced, and all rooms have private kitchen facilities, work desks and well-designed if austere furnishings. On the communal level, there's a pool and fitness center.

Fairmont Hotel Macdonald HOTEL **$$$**
(Map p48; ☑780-424-5181; www.fairmont.com; 10065 100th St; r from $210; @🛜⊠) Stealing the best nook in town (as Fairmont always does), Edmonton's historic Fairmont Hotel exhibits the usual array of intricate stucco, Italian marble, ornate chandeliers and lush carpets. In the early 20th century it was one in a luxurious chain of railway hotels that dotted the cross-continental line from east to west.

Preserved in all its regal glory, it's still fit for monarchs. The regularly renovated rooms with all the expected amenities are almost worth the premium price.

Canterra Suites Hotel
HOTEL **$$$**

(📞 780-421-1212; www.canterrasuites.com; 11010 Jasper Ave; suites from $199; ❈ 🛜) Catering to traveling businesspeople, the Canterra has large, efficient suites equipped with modern kitchenettes – and is close to downtown and right next to a supermarket. Ideal for long- or short-term stays.

Union Bank Inn
BOUTIQUE HOTEL **$$$**

(Map p48; 📞 780-423-3600; www.unionbankinn. com; 10053 Jasper Ave; r from $199; ❈ @ 🛜) This posh boutique hotel on Jasper Ave, in a former bank building dating from 1910, is an upmarket masterpiece. With just 34 rooms, the staff will be at your beck and call, and the in-room fireplaces make even Edmonton's frigid winters almost bearable. There's an equally fancy restaurant – Madison's – on the ground floor.

Fantasyland Hotel
HOTEL **$$$**

(📞 780-444-3000; www.fantasylandhotel.com; 17700 87th Ave; r from $278, themed rooms $448; ❈ @ 🛜 ▨) As if West Ed wasn't surreal enough, this adjoining hotel is something to behold. There are standard rooms, but the real draw is the themed rooms. With 13 themes to choose from – Africa, igloo, Roman, Polynesian – it's hard to pick one. Barely staying on the cool side of kitsch, it's a big hit with families.

It also has a wide variety of bedding options to suit any imaginable situation, plus plenty of giant Jacuzzis, thick carpets, ceiling mirrors and, above all, space.

🍴 Eating

Edmonton's food scene reflects its multiculturalism, though you're never far from the default dinner, Alberta beef. If you're willing to hunt around, you can get a quality meal at any price. The most varied and economical place to eat is in Old Strathcona on or around its arterial road, Whyte Ave. Here, you can traverse the globe gastronomically as well as choose from plenty of good vegetarian options. The best downtown nexus is Jasper Ave, the main road that slices through downtown. The up-and-coming option is the rejuvenated warehouse district centered north of Jasper Ave on 104th St.

🍴 Downtown & West End

⭐ Duchess Bake Shop
BAKERY, CAFE **$**

(📞 780-488-4999; www.duchessbakeshop.com; 10720 124th St; baked goods from $1.50; ⊙ 9am-

8pm Tue-Fri, 10am-6pm Sat, to 5pm Sun) Duchess is what you call a destination cafe/bakery. You'd cross town to eat here – on foot in the snow if necessary. It possesses a detectable French flavour in both taste and decor: the croissants and cakes are buttery, and the furniture is all marble tables and Louis XV–style chairs. Arrive early, before the queuing locals have stripped the cases bare.

There's an affiliated provisions shop next door.

Remedy Cafe
INDIAN **$**

(Map p48; 📞 780-433-3096; www.remedycafe.ca; 10279 Jasper Ave; mains $8-10; ⊙ 8am-midnight; 🛜) The 'remedy' here is cheap, authentic Indian food served in an ultracasual cafe setting – meaning you can wi-fi with one hand and dip your naan in curry sauce with the other. Everyone raves about the chai tea and the butter chicken, but you can also get good cakes (vegans are catered for) and excellent *masala dosas* (curried vegetables inside a crisp pancake).

There's another **branch** (8631 109 St) – the original – in Garneau on the south side of the river.

Three Bananas
CAFE **$**

(Map p48; www.threebananas.ca; Sir Winston Churchill Sq, 9918 102nd Ave; ⊙ 7am-7pm Mon-Fri, 10am-5pm Sat, 11am-5pm Sun) 🌿 This bookish coffee bar in Churchill Sq, with its mosaic walls and Warhol-esque banana prints, is a good place to grab a caffeine hit on the way to the new art museum.

Cavern
CAFE, DELI **$**

(Map p48; 📞 780-455-1336; www.thecavern.ca; 10169 104th St NW; plates $6-16; ⊙ 7am-8pm Mon-Thu, to 11pm Fri, 8am-11pm Sat, 10am-5pm Sun) 🌿 Edmonton doesn't often resemble a liberal Pacific Northwest city – except at this small cafe, an underground bastion of good taste in vogue 104th St, and particularly in the deli department. The clipboard menu suggests cheese plates (for two). Browse the glass cabinet before you choose and wash it down with a glass of wine.

If you're into good coffee, Cavern serves Coava, the small gourmet roasters from Portland, Oregon.

Tiramisu Bistro
ITALIAN **$$**

(📞 780-452-3393; www.cafetiramisu.ca; 10750 124th St; pastas $12-15; ⊙ 9am-8pm Mon, to 9pm Tue-Thu, to 10pm Fri & Sat; 🍴) If you just walked satiated out of Duchess Bake Shop, you'll be crushed or ecstatic (depending on your ap-

GO WEST

While Edmonton's downtown struggles to forge a collective personality, a small neighborhood 3km to the west centered on 124th St and sometimes referred to as the original 'West End' exhibits more charisma. Acting as a kind of quirky antidote to West Edmonton Mall, 124th St between Jasper Ave and 111th Ave is home to an abundance of small art galleries linked by occasional art walks, along with some interesting locally owned restaurants, the cutting-edge Roxy Theatre and two of the best European bakery/cafes this side of Winnipeg – Duchess Bake Shop and Tiramisu Bistro. More recently, a small street market has taken root: **124 Grand Market** (www.124grandmarket. com; 108th Ave btwn 123rd St & 124th St; ⊙4-8pm Thu) ✐ plies organic wares sold by local producers. It's a classic case of local businesses and businesspeople claiming back their community.

room is elegant, the service is top-notch and the wine-pairing menu goes for a wallet-stretching $50.

Corso 32 ITALIAN $$$
(Map p48; ☑780-421-4622; www.corso32.com; 10345 Jasper Ave; mains $21-32; ⊙5-11pm Tue-Sun) This new-wave Italian restaurant seems as if it was plucked from a far larger, trendier city (it wasn't). The quirks? Narrow minimalist decor, with at least one communal table, homemade pasta, an ultrasimple, ultraeffective menu and the best wine list in Edmonton (if you're Italian).

Hardware Grill STEAKHOUSE $$$
(Map p48; ☑780-423-0969; www.hardwaregrill. com; 9698 Jasper Ave; mains $36-48; ⊙5pm-late Mon-Sat) When you really want to impress even yourself, head to this plush oasis high on a bluff above the river in what is traditionally thought of as the seedier part of town. The Hardware occupies an old (for Edmonton) redbrick building that has retained its more elegant features and had the rest spruced up.

Try the expertly prepared duck breast, rack of lamb or Alberta beef.

✖ Old Strathcona & Garneau

★**Transcend Coffee** COFFEE $
(www.transcendcoffee.ca/garneau; 8708 109th St; ⊙7:30am-9pm Mon-Sat, to 5pm Sun; 🕾) ✐ In a city where cafes that produce their own microroasted coffee beans are lacking, Transcend should be treated like the gold dust that it is. Expert baristas on first-name terms with their Guatemalan farmer-producers concoct cups of their own roasted coffee with enough precision to satisfy a severely decaffeinated Seattleite. This spot in Garneau is hip but not remotely pretentious.

High Level Diner DINER $
(☑780-433-1317; www.highleveldiner.com; 10912 88th Ave; mains $6-15; ⊙8am-10pm Mon-Thu, to 11pm Fri & Sat, 9am-9pm Sun; ☑) When you head south of the river crossing the High Level Bridge from downtown you start to enter a noticeably cooler universe, starting with this cheap and cheerful diner popular with students, neighborhood types and the odd hipster. The menu challenges the normal Albertan meat obsession with some decent vegetarian options and staff make their own ketchup in house.

petite) to discover another vision of sweet deliciousness a few doors down. Tiramisu complements its cakes with simple Italian plates and panini. The setting's more cafe than bistro, with a special kids' room.

Blue Plate Diner VEGETARIAN $$
(Map p48; ☑780-429-0740; www.blueplatediner. ca; 10145 104th St; mains $12-18; ⊙11am-10pm, 9am-10pm Sat & Sun; ☑) ✐ In one of the redbrick buildings in Edmonton's warehouse district, this vegetarian-biased diner serves healthy food in hearty portions. And there's style too. Cool colored lighting and exposed brickwork embellish the atmospheric interior, meaning you can eat your tofu and lentils without feeling as if you've joined a hippy commune.

Try the tofu stir-fry or steak sandwich and enjoy larger-than-average plates of crisp, locally grown vegetables.

Madison's Grill FUSION $$$
(Map p48; ☑780-401-2222; www.unionbankinn. com; 10053 Jasper Ave; mains $26-42; ⊙8am-10pm Mon-Thu, to 11pm Fri & Sat, to 8pm Sun) Located in the Union Bank Inn and practicing the same high standards of service and quality, Madison's Grill prepares delicate meats and seafood with flair. The dining

Block 1912
CAFE **$**

(www.block1912.com; 10361 Whyte Ave; snacks $3-12; ⊘9am-midnight Mon-Sat, 10am-11pm Sun) A regal attempt at a genuine Torinese coffee bar on Whyte Ave, this inviting place allows you to recline on European-style sofas and armchairs and enjoy your coffee with a range of snacks – or even a gelato. There's a small bar open evenings.

Café Mosaics
VEGETARIAN **$**

(☑780-433-9702; www.cafemosaics.com; 10844 Whyte Ave; mains $6-12; ⊘9am-9pm Mon-Sat, 11am-2:30pm Sun; ☑🖶) ⯅ A Strathcona institution, this artsy, activist-frequented vegetarian-vegan haunt is a meat-free zone that has taken a page out of San Francisco's book: it makes vegetable dishes both interesting and tasty. As a litmus test, check the number of carnivores who take a day off meat to come here.

Try the tofu curry, cowgirl breakfast or Moroccan chickpea soup. There's even a special meat-free kids' menu.

Tokyo Noodle Shop
JAPANESE **$**

(☑780-430-0838; 10736 Whyte Ave; mains $7-12; ⊘11:30am-9:30pm Mon-Thu, to 10:30pm Fri & Sat, noon-9pm Sun) Good sushi and noodles by the gallon. Nothing fancy, but that's the point.

★Da-De-O
CAJUN **$$**

(☑780-433-0930; www.dadeo.ca; 10548A Whyte Ave; mains $10-16; ⊘11:30am-11pm Mon, Tue & Thu-Sat, noon-10pm Sun) Wave goodbye to cloth serviettes and serious waitstaff and say hello to retro jukeboxes, art-deco lighting and jazz etchings on the wall. This dive diner serving Cajun food could well be Edmonton's best eating establishment. The key lies in the food – an unexpected summoning up of the Big Easy in the frozen north.

The oysters, gumbo and jambalaya are all done well, but plucked straight out of Louisiana legend are the spice-dusted sweet-potato fries and the ginormous po'boys (especially the blackened catfish). Save your New Orleans airfare and eat here.

Three Boars Eatery
TAPAS **$$**

(☑780-757-2600; www.threeboars.ca; 8424 109th St; small plates $13-21; ⊘4pm-late) ⯅ Three Boars is part of the burgeoning farm-to-table food movement, in which the owners retain cordial relations with most of their suppliers (who are all local). It specializes in small plates, cool local ambience and fine Edmonton microbrews on draught.

If you have an appetite for a large Alberta steak, this isn't your bag. If you're up for tasting pork terrine and smoked quail, it definitely is.

Origin India
INDIAN **$$**

(☑780-436-0556; www.theoriginindia.com; 10511 Whyte Ave; mains $13-16; ⊘11:30am-10:30pm Sun-Thu, to 3am Fri & Sat) Jumping on the burgeoning Indian fusion bandwagon, Origin India embraces a chic modern look while staying true to its origins – *dal makhani,* butter chicken and spicy *paneer.*

🍷 Drinking & Nightlife

The best nightlife scene has traditionally centered on or around Whyte Ave in Old Strathcona. Recently, things have gotten more interesting on Jasper Ave, particularly on its western section between 108th and 118th Sts. Clubs open and close in a blink; bars tend to stay longer. Some host music and/or DJs.

Yellowhead Brewery
BREWERY

(Map p48; www.yellowheadbrewery.com; 10229 105th St NW; ⊘11am-6pm Mon-Fri) Last things first. This isn't a pub. It's just a tasting room next door to a brewery where you can sup on Yellowhead's one and only offering: Yellowhead amber ale – a light, not unpleasant lager, brewed in the big vats visible through a glass partition. It also serves small snacks and offers brewery tours if you book in advance.

Black Dog Freehouse
PUB

(☑780-439-1089; www.blackdog.ca; 10425 Whyte Ave; ⊘2pm-2am) Insanely popular with all types, the Black Dog is essentially a pub with a couple of hidden extras: a rooftop patio, known as the 'wooftop patio,' with heaters (naturally: this is Alberta), a traditional ground-floor bar (normally packed cheek to jowl on weekday nights), and a basement that features live music, DJs and occasional parties. The sum of the three parts has become a rollicking Edmonton institution.

Public House
BAR

(www.yourpublichouse.com; 10765 Jasper Ave; ⊘11am-2am Wed-Fri, 2pm-2am Sat, noon-10pm Sun) In the era of Amazon and ebooks, it appears to have become fashionable to furnish your bar/coffee shop with plush floor-to-ceiling bookshelves – especially in the parts of town that consider themselves hip. Thus, new-bar-on-the-block Public House on Jasper Avenue offers a pleasing perch for bibliophiles, beer-drinkers and casual diners as well.

Beers on tap include a couple of local microbrews. Food is American pub grub.

Elephant & Castle   PUB
(www.elephantcastle.com; 10314 Whyte Ave; ⊗11:30am-midnight Mon-Fri, 9am-2am Sat & Sun) What passes for damn ordinary in London (where the Elephant & Castle is a rather grotesque shopping center) is strangely exotic in Edmonton. A red phone box, velvety bar stools and the smell of beer emanating from the thick, carpeted floor add British authenticity to this sporty drinking nook where you're more likely to see Manchester United than the Oilers.

Fluid Lounge   CLUB
(www.thefluidlounge.com; 10888 Jasper Ave; ⊗8pm-2am Thu-Sat) An upscale club on Jasper Ave's burgeoning nightlife strip west of 108th St. Join the line and compete with the beautiful people for dancing space, cocktails and how well you know the DJ.

O'Byrne's   PUB
(☑780-414-6766; www.obyrnes.com; 10616 Whyte Ave; ⊗11:30am-2am) Get lost in the labyrinth of rooms in this popular Irish pub – Edmonton's oldest. There's a variety on tap, including the obligatory stout. Live music (from 8:30pm) keeps the place interesting in the evenings.

Pub 1905   PUB
(Map p48; ☑780-428-4711; 10525 Jasper Ave; ⊗11am-midnight) A popular local watering hole with a happening happy hour, billiards

and a plethora of TVs usually tuned in to the latest Oilers game.

Next Act   PUB
(www.nextactpub.com; 8224 104th St NW; ⊗11am-1am Sun-Thu, to 2am Fri & Sat) Theater district pub just off Whyte Avenue with a good quotient of arty types. There are well-selected ales, including local stalwarts Yellowhead and Alley Kat, plus decent burgers, and mac-and-cheese.

Buddy's Nite Club   GAY
(www.buddysedmonton.com; 11725B Jasper Ave; ⊗9pm-3am) The font of wet T-shirt comps, drag shows and ominous-sounding 'dance-your-pants-off' nights, Buddy's is ever popular with gay men.

☆ Entertainment

Theater! Don't leave Edmonton without trying some. *See* and *Vue* are free local alternative weekly papers with extensive arts and entertainment listings. For daily listings, see the entertainment section of the *Edmonton Journal* newspaper.

★New Varscona Theatre   THEATER
(www.varsconatheatre.com; 10329 83rd Ave; tickets from $14) There are only 176 precious seats at the Varscona, a cornerstone of the Old Strathcona theater district that puts on edgy plays, late-night comedy and morning kids' shows. A $6-million renovation may or may not be underway by the time you read this.

Garneau Theatre   CINEMA
(www.metrocinema.org; 8712 109th St NW) Edmonton's only surviving art-deco-era cinema has operated under various guises

EDMONTON FOR CHILDREN

With its wallet-lightening mall, Edmonton likes to think of itself as kid friendly, but if you can pry your offspring away from the fake plastic trees, there are plenty more family-oriented things to do. **Telus World of Science** (Map p46; www.edmontonscience.com; 11211 142nd St; adult/child $13.95/11.95; ⊗10am-7pm; 📷) is an obvious starting point. With an emphasis on interactive displays, it has a million things to do, all under one roof. Fight crime with the latest technology, see what living on a spacecraft is all about, go on a dinosaur dig and explore what makes the human body tick. The center also includes an IMAX theater (extra cost) and an observatory with telescopes (no extra cost).

The **Valley Zoo** (Map p46; ☑780-496-8787; www.valleyzoo.ca; 13315 Buena Vista Rd; adult/child $10.50/5.25; ⊗9:30am-6pm; 📷), with more than 100 exotic, endangered and native animals, is another option. Kids will enjoy the petting zoo, camel and pony rides, miniature train, carousel and paddleboats. If you want to brave the zoo in the frigid winter, admission costs are reduced.

Fort Edmonton Park (p47) has a small amusement park for kids, while West Edmonton Mall (p50) could keep even the most hyperactive seven-year-old distracted for days.

since 1940, changing hands most recently in 2011. It's affectionately described as 'vintage,' meaning the seats could be more comfortable, but who cares when you roll in for a *Trainspotting* matinee and the concession stand is open for beer?

Citadel Theatre   THEATER
(Map p48; www.citadeltheatre.com; 9828 101A Ave; tickets from $45; ⊙ Sep-May) Edmonton's foremost company is based right in downtown's Winston Churchill Sq. Expect glowing performances of Shakespeare and Stoppard, Dickens adaptations, and the odd Sondheim musical.

Princess Theatre   CINEMA
(☑ 780-433-0728; www.rainbowcinemas.ca; 10337 Whyte Ave; tickets adult/child $8/6) The Princess is another grand old theater that defiantly sticks her finger up at the multiplexes that are dominant elsewhere. Dating from the pretalkie days (1915), it screens first-run, arthouse and cult classics. Tickets for Mondays and weekend matinees are $5.

Roxy Theatre   THEATER
(☑ 780-453-2440; www.theatrenetwork.ca; 10708 124th St NW) Another unexpected thespian surprise, this one hidden in the trendy 'West End,' the Roxy is intimate (198 seats), historic (since 1938) and eclectic, showing burlesque, live bands and comedy.

Blues on Whyte   LIVE MUSIC
(☑ 780-439-981; www.bluesonwhyte.ca; 10329 Whyte Ave) This is the sort of place your mother warned you about: dirty, rough, but still somehow cool. It's a great place to check out some live music; blues and rock are the standards. The small dance floor is a good place to shake a leg.

Jubilee Auditorium   THEATER
(www.jubileeauditorium.com; 11455 87th Ave) The place to check out the Edmonton Opera (☑ 780-424-4040; www.edmontonopera.com; tickets from $24; ⊙ Oct-Apr). Otherwise, this is a great venue for live performances of every kind.

Edmonton Oilers   SPECTATOR SPORT
(www.edmontonoilers.com; tickets from $38.50) To avoid any embarrassing situations, wise up on the Oilers before you arrive in Edmonton. The local National Hockey League (NHL) team dominated the game in the 1980s thanks to a certain player named Wayne Gretsky – aka 'The Great One' – but hasn't won much since. Games are played at oft-renamed Rexall Place (7424 118th Ave NW) in the northeast of town. The season runs from October to April.

Edmonton Eskimos   SPECTATOR SPORT
(www.esks.com; adult/child from $43/21.50) The Eskimos take part in the Canadian Football League (CFL) from July to October at Commonwealth Stadium (11000 Stadium Rd).

 Shopping
=========

Old Strathcona is the best area for unique independent stores – vintage magazines, old vinyl, retro furnishings and the like. If you're in search of the opposite – ie big chains selling familiar brands – sift through the 800-plus stores in West Edmonton Mall.

FRINGE BENEFITS

Edmonton becomes a different city in August, when thespians, buskers, food vendors and unorthodox local performers – with names like Three Dead Trolls in a Baggie, and Mump and Smoot – rev up the crowds at the annual Edmonton International Fringe Festival (p50). Using Edinburgh's famous festival as its inspiration, the fringe was launched in 1982 in the Old Strathcona district, where small theater venues provided performance space for self-produced indie artists to showcase their alternative, low-budget, uncensored shows. The idea was a hit, and the fringe evolved in the ensuing years to become the world's second largest, with 600 artists entertaining up to half a million visitors. As well as being uniquely Edmontonian in its humor and atmosphere, it has gone on to inspire countless other fringe festivals across Canada.

The Fringe usually kicks off in mid-August, with tickets going on sale around 10 days beforehand. True to its DIY ethos, prices are kept low (around $10 to $15 per performance), or you can buy one of a limited number of Frequent Fringer festival passes. Most of the best small venues are in and around Whyte Avenue, including the Waterdale Theatre and the New Varscona Theatre. Creating a buzz in the surrounding neighborhood are myriad street performers and buskers, as well as an outlandish street carnival.

Avenue Guitars MUSIC
(www.avenue-guitars.com; 10550 Whyte Ave; ☺10am-6pm Mon-Sat) You can warm your fingers plucking opening stanzas to 'Stairway to Heaven' in Old Strathcona's premier music store. It sells custom-made and collectors' guitars and all the usual suspects.

Decadence VINTAGE
(www.divineplanet.com; 10760 Whyte Ave NW; ☺11am-8pm Mon-Fri, to 7pm Sat, noon-6pm Sun) Come here to see what you won't find in 800 stores in West Edmonton Mall.

Old Strathcona Farmers Market FOOD
(✆780-439-1844; 10310 83rd Ave, at 103rd St; ☺noon-5pm Tue, 8am-3pm Sat Jul & Aug) ✐ This not-to-be-missed indoor market offers everything from organic food to arts and crafts, and hosts some 130 vendors. Everyone comes here on Saturday morning – it's quite the scene.

Junque Cellar ACCESSORIES
(10442 Whyte Ave; ☺10am-9pm Mon-Sat, to 6pm Sun) What is plain old junk to some is retro-cool to others. Sift through the typewriters, lava lamps, old phones, comics, clothes and other flashbacks of erstwhile pop culture.

ⓘ Information

Custom House Global Foreign Exchange
(10104 103rd Ave) Foreign currency exchange.
Edmonton Tourism (Map p48; 9797 Jasper Ave; ☺8am-5pm) Friendly place with tons of flyers and brochures.
Main Post Office (9808 103A Ave; ☺8am-5:45pm Mon-Fri)
Royal Alexandra Hospital (✆780-477-4111; 10240 Kingsway Ave) Has a 24-hour trauma center. Located 1km north of the downtown core.

ⓘ Getting There & Away

AIR

Edmonton International Airport (YEG; www.flyeia.com) is about 30km south of the city along the Calgary Trail, about a 45-minute drive from downtown.

BUS

The large **bus station** (Map p48; 10324 103rd St) has Greyhound Canada services to numerous destinations, including Jasper ($67, 4½ hours, four daily) and Calgary ($49, from 3½ hours, from 10 daily).

Red Arrow (Map p48; www.redarrow.ca) buses stop downtown at the Holiday Inn Express and serve Calgary ($70, 3½ hours, six daily) and

Fort McMurray ($86, 5½ hours, three daily). The buses are a step up, with wi-fi, sockets for your laptop, single or double seats, a free minibar and hot coffee.

CAR

All the major car-rental firms have offices at the airport and around town. **Driving Force** (www.thedrivingforce.com; 11025 184 St) will rent, lease or sell you a car. Check the website; it often has some good deals.

TRAIN

The small **VIA Rail station** (www.viarail.ca; 12360 121st St) is rather inconveniently situated 5km northwest of the city center near Edmonton City Centre Airport. The *Canadian* travels three times a week east to Saskatoon ($85, eight hours), Winnipeg ($181, 20 hours) and Toronto ($405, 55 hours) and west to Jasper ($117, 5½ hours), Kamloops ($172, 16½ hours) and Vancouver ($225, 27 hours). At Jasper, you can connect to Prince George and Prince Rupert.

ⓘ Getting Around

TO/FROM THE AIRPORT

Bus 747 leaves from outside the arrivals hall every 30 to 60 minutes and goes to Century Park ($5), the southernmost stop on Edmonton's Light Rail. From here regular trains connect to Strathcona and downtown.

Sky Shuttle Airport Service (www.edmontonskyshuttle.com; adult/child $18/10) runs three different routes that service hotels in most areas of town, including downtown and the Strathcona area. The office is by carousel 12. Journey time is approximately 45 minutes.

Cab fare from the airport to downtown is about $50.

CAR & MOTORCYCLE

There is metered parking throughout the city. Most hotels in Old Strathcona offer complimentary parking to guests. Visitors can park their car for the day and explore the neighborhood easily on foot. Edmonton also has public parking lots, which cost about $12 per day or $1.50 per half hour; after 6pm you can park for a flat fee of about $2.

PUBLIC TRANSPORTATION

City buses and a 16-stop Light Rail Transit (LRT) system cover most of the city. There are plans for four more LRT lines. The fare is $3.20. Buses operate at 30-minute intervals between 5:30am and 1:30am. Check out the excellent transit planning resources at www.edmonton.ca. Daytime travel between Churchill and Grandin stations on the LRT is free.

Between mid-May and early September you can cross the High Level Bridge on a streetcar

($5 round-trip, every 30 minutes between 11am and 10pm). The vintage streetcars are a great way to travel to the Old Strathcona Market (103rd St at 94th Ave), where the line stops. Or go from Old Strathcona to the downtown stop, next to the Grandin LRT Station (109th St between 98th and 99th Aves).

TAXI

Two of the many taxi companies are **Yellow Cab** (☑780-462-3456) and **Alberta Co-Op Taxi** (☑780-425-2525). The fare from downtown to the West Edmonton Mall is about $25. Flag fall is $3.60, then it's $0.20 for every 150m.

AROUND EDMONTON

East of Edmonton

When Edmontonians want to get away from it all and retreat back to nature, Elk Island National Park (www.pc.gc.ca/eng/pn-np/ab/elkisland/index.aspx; adult/child/senior $7.80/3.90/6.80, campsites & RV sites $25.50, campfire permits $8.80; ☉dawn-dusk) is often their first port of call. Just 45km east of Edmonton on the Yellowhead Hwy (Hwy 16), it's convenient for weekend getaways, meaning the campgrounds are quite popular. Some of the park's campgrounds close from early October to May.

The Ukrainian Cultural Heritage Village (☑780-662-3640; www.history.alberta.ca/ukrainianvillage; adult/child $9/4; ☉10am-5pm May-Aug), 50km east of Edmonton on Hwy 16 (3km east of Elk Island National Park), is an exact replica of a turn-of-the-century Ukrainian town, paying homage to the 250,000 Ukrainian immigrants who came to Canada in the late 19th and early 20th centuries. Many settled in central Alberta, where the landscape reminded them of the snowy steppes of home. Among the exhibits are a dozen or so structures, including a restored pioneer home and an impressive Ukrainian Greek Orthodox church. The staff are dressed in period garb and are in character, too, adding a slice of realism and fun to the day.

South of Edmonton

Halfway between Edmonton and Calgary on Hwy 2 is Alberta's third-largest city, Red Deer (population 97,000), a growing community fueled by agricultural production and, more recently, oil. Beyond being a rest stop and an all-else-fails place to stay during the tourist season, there is very little for the traveler here. Red Deer is about 1½ hours away from either Calgary or Edmonton, and accommodations will not be as tight or as expensive. For more information, contact the Red Deer Visitor & Convention Bureau (www.tourismreddeer.net; 30 Riverview Park), or just drive through the city, where you'll have your pick of chain establishments.

WORTH A TRIP

ELK ISLAND NATIONAL PARK

In case you hadn't noticed, there are five national parks in Alberta, and three of them *aren't* Jasper or Banff. Overshadowed by the gothic Rockies, tiny Elk Island National Park (adult/child $7.70/3.90) attracts just 5% of Banff's annual visitor count despite its location only 50km east of Edmonton. Not that this detracts from its attractions. The park – the only one in Canada that is entirely fenced – contains the highest density of wild hoofed animals in the world after the Serengeti. If you come here, plan on seeing the 'big six' – plains bison, wood bison, mule deer, white-tailed deer, elk and the more elusive moose. The wood bison live entirely in the quieter southern portion of the park (which is cut in two by Hwy 16), while the plains bison inhabit the north. Most of the infrastructure lies in the north, too, around Astotin Lake. Here you'll find a campground, a nine-hole golf course (with a clubhouse containing a restaurant), a beach and a boat launch. Four of the park's 11 trails lead out from the lakeshore through trademark northern Albertan aspen parkland – a kind of natural intermingling of the prairies and the boreal forests.

Public transport to the park is nonexistent. Either hire a car or join a guided tour from Edmonton with Watchable Wildlife Tours Group (☑780-405-4880; www.birdsandbackcountry.com), led by wildlife expert Wayne Millar. It's a lovely way to watch the sunset surrounded by animals on a long summer evening.

West of Edmonton

Heading west from Edmonton toward Jasper, Hwy 16 is a gorgeous drive through rolling wooded hills that are especially beautiful in fall. Accommodations are available along the way. Greyhound buses ply the route.

Hinton is a small, rough-around-the-edges town carved from the bush. The pervasive logging industry keeps the majority of the town's population gainfully employed. There is some good mountain biking to be found here; the info center has information on trails.

If there is snow on the ground, the **Athabasca Lookout Nordic Centre** offers winter visitors beautiful groomed ski trails up to 25km long. It also has illuminated night skiing on a 1.5km trail, plus a 1km luge run. There's a user fee of $5. For more information, contact the **Hinton Tourist Information Centre** (☑ 780-865-2777; 309 Gregg Ave), off Hwy 16.

Just northwest of Hinton lies the tiny settlement of **Grande Cache**. There is little of interest in this small industry town – only a few overpriced hotels aimed at expense-account-wielding natural-resources workers. However, the drive along Hwy 40 between Hinton and Grande Cache is spectacular, with rolling forested foothills, lakes and abundant wildlife.

CALGARY

POP 1,065,000

Calgary, to most non-Calagarians, is Canada in a Stetson with a self-confident American swagger and a seemingly insatiable thirst for business, especially if it involves oil. But like most stereotypes, the truth is more complex. Shrugging off its image as the city other Canadians love to hate, and standing strong despite serious flooding that caused havoc in June 2013, Alberta's largest metropolis continues to stride cool-headed toward the future with a thick skin and clear sense of its own destiny. Lest we forget, this is a city that hosted the highly successful 1988 Winter Olympics, produced Canada's current prime minister (Stephen Harper), elected North America's first Muslim mayor, and throws one of Canada's biggest parties. The famous July Stampede is subtitled, with typical Calgarian immodesty, 'the greatest outdoor show on earth.'

Overtaken sometimes by the pace of its own development, Calgary has often forsaken quality for quantity in the past, following a path more in tune with Dubai or Dallas than Austin or Portland, but there are signs that the trend may be changing. Community activists in emerging Calgary neighborhoods such as Inglewood and Kensington are finally waking up and smelling the single-origin home-roasted coffee, with new bars, boutiques, restaurants and entertainment venues exhibiting more color and experimentation. Before you know it, the city that to unaffiliated non-Calgarians has long served as an unloved and somewhat bland business center or a functional springboard for the wonders of Banff and the Rockies might actually become – ahem – interesting.

History

From humble and relatively recent beginnings, Calgary has been transformed into a cosmopolitan modern city that has hosted an Olympics and continues to wield huge economic clout. Before the growth explosion, the Blackfoot people called the area home for centuries. Eventually they were joined by the Sarcee and Stoney tribes on the banks of the Bow and Elbow Rivers.

By the time the 1870s rolled around, the NWMP built a fort and called it Fort Calgary after Calgary Bay on Scotland's Isle of Mull. The railroad followed a few years later, and, buoyed by the promise of free land, settlers started the trek west to make Calgary their home. The Blackfoot, Sarcee and Stoney Aboriginals signed Treaty 7 with the British Crown in 1877 that ushered them into designated tribal reservations and took away their wider land rights.

Long a center for ranching, the cowboy culture was set to become forever intertwined with the city. In the early 20th century, Calgary simmered along, growing slowly. Then, in the 1960s, everything changed. Overnight, ranching was seen as a thing of the past, and oil was the new favorite child. With the 'black gold' seeming to bubble up from the ground nearly everywhere in Alberta, Calgary became the natural choice of place to set up headquarters.

The population exploded, and the city began to grow at an alarming rate. As the price of oil continued to skyrocket, it was good times for the people of Cowtown. The '70s boom stopped dead at the '80s bust. Things slowed and the city diversified.

Calgary

KENSINGTON

11th St NW
10A St NW
10th St NW

C-Train

Memorial Dr

Bow River

Prince's
Island
Park

6

Eau Claire
Ave SW

18
7

1st Ave SW

16
38

4

2nd Ave SW

35

3rd Ave SW

33 14 49

Louise
Bridge

21

4th Ave SW

13

5th Ave SW

6th Ave SW

DOWNTOWN

7th Ave SW

C-Train

Greyhound Bus Station
(400m)

8th Ave SW

Stephen Ave Walk

3rd St SW

48

39 2 20

9th Ave SW

34

8

51

10th Ave SW

45

37 40

28

11th Ave SW

**DESIGN
DISTRICT**

12th Ave SW

6th St SW

BELTLINE

46

41 10

12th St SW
11th St SW
10th St SW
9th St SW
8th St SW

15

13th Ave SW

5th St SW

4th St SW

2nd St SW

1st St SW

27

14th Ave SW

24

15th Ave SW

11

19 29

42 44 43

16
16th Ave SW

23

32 31

17th Ave SW

**UPTOWN
17TH AVE**

18th Ave SW

18th Ave SW

7th St SW

19th Ave SW

19th Ave SW

20th Ave
SW

21st Ave
SW

**4TH ST -
MISSION
DISTRICT**

30

Prospect Ave

23rd Ave SW

24th Ave SW

Hillcrest Ave

25th Ave SW

17

The 21st century began with an even bigger boom. House prices have gone through the roof, there is almost zero unemployment and the economy is growing 40% faster than the rest of Canada. Not bad for a bunch of cowboys.

⊙ Sights

Calgary's downtown isn't particularly interesting unless you've got your finger in an oil well. More alluring are a handful of still-evolving city neighborhoods. **Uptown 17th Ave** is a rainbow of obnoxious hockey crowds, beer-hall-style bars, and emerging locavore restaurants. **Inglewood**, just east of downtown, is the city's hippest neighborhood, with antique shops, indie boutiques and some esoteric eating options. **Kensington**, north of the Bow River, is a little more upscale but has some decent coffee bars and a tangible community spirit. **4th St – Mission District** is an extension of 17th Ave that's a little more mellow and worth visiting for its Italian restaurants.

★ **Glenbow Museum** MUSEUM
(☑ 403-777-5506; www.glenbow.org; 130 9th Ave SE; adult/child $14/9; ⊙ 9am-5pm Fri-Wed, to 9pm Thu) For a town with such a short history, Calgary does a fine job telling it at the commendable Glenbow Museum, which traces the legacy of Calgary and Alberta from pre-to post-oil. Contemporary art exhibitions and story-worthy artifacts dating back centuries fill its halls and galleries.

With an extensive permanent collection and an ever-changing array of traveling exhibitions, there is plenty for the history buff, art lover and pop-culture fiend to ponder.

Fort Calgary Historic Park HISTORIC SITE
(☑ 403-290-1875; www.fortcalgary.com; 750 9th Ave SE; adult/child $12/7; ⊙ 9am-5pm) In 1875 Calgary was born at Fort Calgary. The site today is occupied by a replica of a military barracks that stood here in the 1880s (the original fort has long since disappeared). The barracks acts as a museum of Calgary history from 1875 to the 1920s, with more than a passing nod to the NUMP.

Granted, it's not particularly old, but this is fast-moving Calgary, where last week is considered ancient history.

Calgary Zoo ZOO
(☑ 403-232-9300; www.calgaryzoo.ab.ca; 1300 Zoo Rd NE; adult/child $22.50/14.50; ⊙ 9am-6pm; ⋒) More than 1000 animals from around the

ALBERTA CALGARY

Calgary

world, many in enclosures simulating their natural habitats, make Calgary's zoo one of the top rated in North America and almost on a par with Toronto's.

Besides the animals, the zoo has a **Botanical Garden**, with changing garden displays, a **tropical rain forest**, a good **butterfly enclosure** and the 6½-hectare **Prehistoric Park**, featuring fossil displays and life-size dinosaur replicas in natural settings. Picnic areas dot the zoo, and a cafe is on-site. During winter, when neither you nor the animals will care to linger outdoors, the admission price is reduced. To get here, take the C train east to the Zoo stop.

Heritage Park Historical Village HISTORIC SITE (☑403-259-1900; www.heritagepark.ab.ca; 1900 Heritage Dr SW, at 14th St SW; adult/child $21/15; ⊙9.30am-5pm daily May-Aug, Sat & Sun Sep & Oct) Want to see what Calgary used to look like? Head down to this historical park and step right into the past. With a policy that all buildings within the village are from

1915 or earlier, it really is the opposite of modern Calgary. There are 10 hectares of re-created town to explore, with a fort, grain mill, church, school and lots more.

You can ride on the steam train, catch a trolley and even go for a spin on the SS *Moyie*, the resident stern-wheeler, as it churns around the Glenmore Reservoir. Heritage Park has always been a big hit with the kiddies and is a great place to soak up Western culture. To get there, take the C train to Heritage station, then bus 20. The park is located 10km south of Calgary's downtown.

Bow   NOTABLE BUILDING
(500 Centre St) In the competition to be the tallest building in Calgary, the 58-storey, 236m-high Bow stole top honours in 2012, though its reign looks like it will be fleeting.

The shiny, curvaceous headquarters of the EnCana Corporation is certainly more aesthetically pleasing than some of the city's brutalist architecture. It's finished off nicely at its (main) southwest entrance by a huge mesh sculpture of a human head, called *Wonderland*, by Spanish artist Jaume Plensa.

Inglewood Bird Sanctuary   NATURE RESERVE

(☑403-268-2489; 2425 9th Ave SE; sanctuary & interpretive center donations appreciated; ☺dawn-dusk, interpretive center 10am-4pm) **FREE** Get the flock over here and look out for some foul play at this nature reserve. With more than 260 bird species calling the sanctuary home, you're assured of meeting some feathered friends. It's a peaceful place, with walking paths and benches to observe the residents.

There is a small **interpretive center** to give you some more information about the birds, complete with displays that are popular with the young ones.

Calgary Chinese Cultural Centre   CULTURAL BUILDING

(☑403-262-5071; 197 1st St SW; center admission free, museum adult/child $2/1; ☺9am-9pm, museum 11am-5pm) Inside this impressive landmark building, built by skilled Chinese artisans in 1993, you'll find a magnificent 21m-high dome ornately painted with 561 dragons and other imagery. Its design was inspired by Beijing's Temple of Heaven. The 2nd and 3rd floors frequently house changing art and cultural exhibitions. Downstairs, the **museum** holds Chinese art and artifacts, including a collection of replica terracotta soldiers.

Prince's Island Park   PARK

For a little slice of Central Park in the heart of Cowtown, take the bridge over to this island, with grassy fields made for tossing Frisbees, bike paths and ample space to stretch out. During the summer months, you can catch a Shakespeare production in the park's natural grass amphitheater.

Watch yourself around the river. The water is cold and the current is strong and not suitable for swimming; the island was badly flooded during the summer 2013 floods. The bridge to the island from downtown is at the north end of 3rd St SW, near the Eau Claire Market shopping area.

Fish Creek Provincial Park   PARK

(☑403-297-5293; ☺8am-dusk) Cradling the southwest edge of Calgary, this huge park is a sanctuary of wilderness hidden within the city limits. Countless trails intertwine to form a labyrinth, to the delight of walkers, mountain bikers and the many animals who call the park home.

Severe flooding in the park in the mid-2000s washed away many bridges and, in many cases, severely impacted the landscape. The park is slowly returning to normal with the assistance of the city and Mother Nature. There are numerous access points to the park, which stretches for 20km between 37th St in the west and Bow River in the east. From downtown, take bus 3 via Elbow Dr.

Calgary Tower   NOTABLE BUILDING

(☑403-266-7171; www.calgarytower.com; 101 9th Ave SW; adult/youth $15/7; ☺observation gallery 9am-9pm) This 1968 landmark tower is an iconic feature of the Calgary skyline, though it has now been usurped by numerous taller buildings and is in danger of being lost in a forest of skyscrapers. There is little doubt that the aesthetics of this once-proud concrete structure have passed into the realm of kitsch, but, love it or hate it, the slightly phallic 191m structure is a fixture of the downtown area.

The views from the top are fantastic, and, copying Seattle's Space Needle, there's a revolving restaurant.

Art Gallery of Calgary   GALLERY

(☑403-770-1350; www.artgallerycalgary.org; 117 8th Ave SW; adult/child $5/2.50; ☺10am-5pm Tue-Sat) Calgary isn't really an art city (yet), and this aspiring gallery is more an exhibition space than a weighty portfolio of art. Indeed, the Art Gallery of Calgary has no permanent collection like Vancouver or Edmonton, meaning you'll have to rely on getting lucky with a decent temporary expo of contemporary Canadian paintings.

Military Museums   MUSEUM

(☑403-974-2850; www.themilitarymuseums.ca; 4520 Crowchild Trail SW; adult/child $10/4; ☺9am-5pm Mon-Fri, 9:30am-4pm Sat & Sun) Those with an interest in the military will enjoy the Military Museums (essentially one museum), providing a very thorough overview of Calgary's military background – air force, army and navy – and its role in Canadian conflicts over the years, from British colonial escapades in the 1880s to Afghanistan. Follow Crowchild Trail to Flanders Ave about 3km south of Downtown.

✦ Activities

Canada Olympic Park
SPORTS

(☑403-247-5452; www.canadaolympicpark.ca; 88 Canada Olympic Rd SW; mountain biking hill tickets/lessons $22/99; ◷9am-9pm Mon-Fri, 10am-5pm Sat & Sun) In 1988 the Winter Olympics came to Canada for the first time. Calgary played host, and many of the events were contested at Canada Olympic Park. It's near the western edge of town along Hwy 1 – you won't miss the distinctive 70m and 90m ski jumps crowning the skyline.

Check out the **Sports Hall of Fame** (admission $12) and learn about some great Canadian athletes and the story of the Calgary games. If you're feeling more daring, go for a 60-second bobsled ride ($135) with a professional driver on a 120kmh Olympic course. It could be the most exhilarating and expensive minute of your life. Alternatively, you can take a trip along a zip line ($65) from the top of the ski jump. In winter you can go for a ski, or strap on a snowboard and hit the superpipe. Summer is for mountain biking, when you can ride the lift-serviced trails till your brakes wear out.

Olympic Oval
ICE SKATING

(☑403-220-7954; www.ucalgary.ca/oval; adult/child $6/4) Get the Olympic spirit at the University of Calgary, where you can go for a skate on Olympic Oval. Used for the speed-skating events at the Olympics, it offers public skating on the long track and has skates available to rent.

☞ Tours

Free two-hour **walking tours** led by local retirees leave from the Glenbow Museum every Wednesday at 10am between May and September. See www.walkaroundcalgary.com for bookings and more details.

Hammerhead Tours
CULTURAL TOUR

(☑403-590-6930; www.hammerheadtours.com; tours $45-135) Has a variety of tour options to choose from, including city tours and trips to the Columbia Icefield, Drumheller, Banff and more.

Legendary Tours
CULTURAL TOUR

(☑403-285-8376; www.legendarytravels.net; tours from $115) Gets you out to some of Alberta's lesser-known sites, including the new Blackfoot Crossing Historical Park.

★彡 Festivals & Events

For a year-round list of the city's events, go to www.visitcalgary.com/things-to-do/events-calendar. The big festival in Calgary is the annual Calgary Stampede.

Calgary International Children's Festival
CHILDREN'S

(www.calgarychildfest.org; Epcor Centre for the Performing Arts, 205 8th Ave SE; tickets $14-21; ◷late May) Kids have all the fun at this annual event, with music, performers and all sorts of kidding around.

Carifest
CARNIVAL

(www.carifestcalgary.com; Stephen Ave & Prince's Island Park; ◷early Jun) The Caribbean comes alive right here in Calgary. Concerts, food stalls, street parties and stuff for kids.

Calgary Stampede
RODEO

(www.calgarystampede.com; ◷2nd week Jul) Billed as the greatest outdoor show on earth and now over 100 years old, Calgary's Stampede is world-famous. Rodeos don't come much bigger than this, with daily shows featuring bucking broncos, steer wrestling, barrel racing and, of course, bull riding. At night there's a grandstand show and the ever-popular chuckwagon races. It's a great time to visit Calgary: civic spirits are on a yearly high, and there's live music, free stampede breakfasts and seemingly a cowboy hat on every head in the city. Book ahead for accommodations.

Calgary Folk Music Festival
MUSIC

(www.calgaryfolkfest.com; ◷late Jul) Grassroots folk is celebrated at this annual four-day event featuring great live music on Prince's Island. Top-quality acts from around the globe make the trek to Cowtown. It's a mellow scene hanging out on the grass listening to the sounds of summer with what seems like 12,000 close friends.

⌁ Sleeping

Calgary has found its independent spirit in the last few years and established a pleasant assortment of boutique hotels across different price ranges that promote individual quirks and design features.

Downtown hotels are notoriously expensive, although many run frequent specials. Business-oriented hotels are often cheaper over weekends. Hotels near the western edge of town are concentrated into an area called, appropriately, Motel Village (next to

CARLESS IN CALGARY

As the main operations center for Canada's oil industry, Calgary has a reputation for big, unsubtle automobiles plying endless low-rise suburbs on a network of busy highways. But, hidden from the ubiquitous petrol-heads is a parallel universe of urban parkways (712 kilometers of 'em!) dedicated to walkers, cyclists and skaters, and many of them hug the banks of the city's two mighty rivers, the Bow and the Elbow. Even better, this non-car-traffic network is propped up by a cheap, efficient light-rail system: the C-Train was significantly expanded in 2012 and carries a number of daily riders comparable to the Amsterdam metro. Yes, dear reader, Calgary without a car is not an impossible – or even unpleasant – experience.

Not surprisingly, the best trails hug the riverbanks. The Bow River through downtown and over into Prince's Island is eternally popular, with the new pedestrian-only Peace Bridge providing a vital link. If you're feeling strong, you can follow the river path 20km south to Fish Creek Provincial Park and plenty more roadless action. Nose Creek Parkway is the main pedestrian artery to and from the north of the city, while the leafy Elbow River Pathway runs from Inglewood to Mission in the south.

Bike Bike (www.bikebike.ca; 1501A 17th Ave SW; bicycles per day from $35; ⊙10am-5pm Tue, Wed & Sat, to 7pm Thu & Fri, noon-5pm Sun) rents nonsporty city bikes April to September. Abutting the downtown Bow River Pathway is **Rapid Rent** (www.outlawsports.ca; Barclay Parade; bikes/in-line skates per day from $30/15; ⊙10am-7pm Mon-Fri, to 6pm Sat, to 5pm Sun), an outlet of Outlaw Sports located next to the Eau Claire shopping center.

The city publishes an official Calgary Bikeways and Pathways map available from any local leisure center or downloadable from the City of Calgary website (www.calgary.ca). There's also a mobile app at www.calgary.ca/mobileapps.

the Banff Trail C-Train station). Every chain hotel you can think of has a property here, from shabby to chic. If you are looking for a deal, investigate this area.

During the Stampede (early July), demand causes rates to rise and availability to plummet. Be sure to book ahead.

HI-Calgary
HOSTEL $

(☑403-269-8239; www.hostellingintl.ca/Alberta; 520 7th Ave SE; dm/r from $30/75; @🛜) For the budget-minded, this pleasant hostel is one of your only options for the price in Calgary. Fairly standard bunk rooms and a few doubles are available. It has a kitchen, laundry, games room and internet facilities; it's a popular crossroads for travelers and a good place to make friends, organize rides and share recommendations.

Be careful at night in this area – you are only a couple of blocks from the roughest bar in town.

Calaway RV Park
CAMPGROUND $

(☑403-240-3822; www.calawaypark.com; Hwy 1; campsites/RV sites $27/33; 🛜) The youngsters will love camping at the amusement park, 25km west of downtown. During the Stampede it runs a shuttle into town.

Calgary West Campground
CAMPGROUND $

(☑403-288-0411; www.calgarycampground.com; Hwy 1; campsites/RV sites $36/44; @🛜▣) West of downtown Calgary on the Trans-Canada Hwy (Hwy 1), this campground is close to the city and has good facilities.

★Hotel Alma
BOUTIQUE HOTEL $$

(☑403-220-3203; www.hotelalma.ca; 169 University Gate NW; r from $129, apt $180; 🛜) Some cruel critics claim Calgary lacks *alma* (soul), and although this fashionable boutique establishment in – of all places – Calgary's university campus can't really be described as soulful, it *is* funky and arty. Supermodern rooms are either one- or two-bedroom apartments or 'Euro-style' rooms, which in Alberta means 'small,' although small by Alberta standards isn't that small.

Guests also get access to all on-campus facilities, including a proper fitness center, a pool and a fine lobby bistro. The university is 6km northeast of downtown, but easily accessible on the C-train.

Centro Motel
MOTEL $$

(☑403-288-6658; www.centromotel.com; 4540 16th Ave NW; r incl breakfast from $114; ✳@🛜) A 'boutique motel' sounds like an oxymoron until you descend on the misleadingly named Centro 7km northwest of Calgary's real 'centro' on the Trans-Canada Hwy (Hwy 1). Taking an old motel building in March 2010 and making it over with modern boutique features, the indie owners have left no detail missing, from light fittings to bathrobes to the flower baskets hanging from the walkways. Calls to anywhere in Canada and the US are free.

Nuvo Hotel Suites   HOTEL **$$**
(☑ 403-452-6789; www.nuvohotelsuites.com; 827 12th Ave SW; ste from $150; ✳ 🤚) Now this is more like it.... Large, comfortable studio apartments with full kitchens including washing machines, all for a decent price in the Beltline neighborhood. Handy for downtown and Uptown 17th action.

Twin Gables B&B   B&B **$$**
(☑ 403-271-7754; www.twingables.ca; 611 25th Ave SW; ste $99-175; @) In a lovely old home, this B&B features hardwood floors, stained-glass windows, Tiffany lamps and antique furnishings. The three rooms are tastefully decorated, and the location across from the Elbow River provides opportunities for serene walks.

International Hotel   HOTEL **$$**
(☑ 403-265-9600; www.internationalhotel.ca; 220 4th Ave SW; d from $135; @ 🤚 🏊) All 35 floors of this property were renovated a few years ago and the results are uplifting. Large living spaces with great city views are standard, while the sweet suites may have the comfiest beds you'll ever pay to sleep on.

Carriage House Inn   INN **$$**
(☑ 403-253-1101; www.carriagehouse.net; 9030 Macleod Trail S; r from $159; ✳ @ 🏊) When you arrive here, the boxlike exterior is less than inspiring, but things perk up inside. Recent renovations have done wonders in bringing the Carriage House back up to speed. The rooms are tidy and it's close to lots of eating and shopping options. The inn is 8km south of downtown Calgary on the arterial MacLeod Trail.

★**Hotel Le Germain**   BOUTIQUE HOTEL **$$$**
(☑ 403-264-8990; www.germaincalgary.com; 899 Centre St SW; d from $329; ✳ @ 🤚) 🍴 At last, a posh boutique hotel to counteract the bland assortment of franchise inns that service downtown Calgary. Germain is actually a member of a franchise, albeit a small French-Canadian one, but the style (check out the huge glass wall in reception) verges

on opulent, while the 24-hour gym, in-room massage, complimentary newspapers and funky lounge add luxury touches.

Even better, the hotel is efficiently built and has a long list of conservation policies.

Hotel Arts   BOUTIQUE HOTEL **$$$**
(☑ 403-266-4611; www.hotelarts.ca; 119 12th Ave SW; ste from $269; ✳ @ 🤚 🏊) Setting a new standard in Calgary, this boutique hotel plays hard on the fact that it's not part of an international chain. Aimed at the modern discerning traveler with an aesthetic eye, there are hardwood floors, thread counts Egyptians would be envious of and art on the walls that should be in a gallery.

Fairmont Palliser   HOTEL **$$$**
(☑ 403-262-1234; www.fairmont.com/palliser; 133 9th Ave SW; r from $319; @ 🤚 🏊) Cut from the same elegant cloth as other Fairmont hotels, the Palliser is easily the most stunning place to bed down in Calgary. With crystal chandeliers, marble columns, wood-inlaid arched ceiling domes and antique furniture, the interior has a deep regal feel to it, unlike anything else within the city limits. Classic, beautiful and worth every penny.

Hotel Elan   BOUTIQUE HOTEL **$$$**
(☑ 403-229-2040; www.hotelelan.ca; 1122 16th Ave SW; r/ste $419/629; ✳ 🤚) Elan is a luxury boutique hotel that opened in 2013 in a fancily refurbished Uptown condo building. For a slightly inflated price, you get rooms with personal internet routers, rainfall showerheads, heated toilet seats and heat-controlled floors. There's also a small gym. Parking costs $18 extra. If you're not the sultan of Brunei, come off-season, when prices fall to a more reasonable $200-ish a night.

Kensington Riverside Inn   BOUTIQUE HOTEL **$$$**
(☑ 403-228-4442; www.kensingtonriversideinn. com; 1126 Memorial Dr NW; r from $269; 🤚) This impressive hotel in Kensington is a delight; a refined attitude permeates the smart-looking, beautifully finished property. The rooms are elegant and have river views. Highly recommended.

Sheraton Suites Calgary Eau Claire   HOTEL **$$$**
(☑ 403-266-7200, 800-325-3535; www.sheraton.com; 255 Barclay Pde SW; ste from $379; ✳ @ 🤚 🏊) With a great location and overflowing with amenities, this business-oriented all-suite hotel should satisfy even the fussiest of travelers. The staff love to go

the extra mile. Valet parking, a pool and a beautiful interior top it all off.

Eating

If Calgary is a fast-moving city, then its burgeoning restaurant scene is supersonic. Eating establishments come and go here like thieves in the night, making gastronomic Top 10s out of date before critics can even tweet them. The overall culinary trend is one of constant improvement in terms of both quality and eclecticism. Where solitary cows once roamed, vegetables and herbs now prosper, meaning that the trusty old stalwart, Alberta beef, is no longer the only thing propping up the menu.

You will find good eat streets in the neighborhoods of Kensington, Inglewood, 4th St – Mission District and Uptown 17th Ave, and downtown on Stephen St.

✗ Downtown

1886 Buffalo Cafe
BREAKFAST **$**

(187 Barclay Pde SW; ☺6am-3pm Mon-Fri, from 7am Sat & Sun) A salt-of-the-earth diner in the high-rise-dominated city center that the realty lords forgot to knock down, this wooden shack construction is famous for its brunches fortified by huevos rancheros.

Peter's Drive-In
BURGERS **$**

(☑403-277-2747; www.petersdrivein.com; 219 16th Ave NE; mains $2.50-5; ☺9am-midnight) In 1962 Peter's opened its doors and locals have been flocking here ever since to a largely unchanged menu of superthick shakes, burgers off the grill and fries that make no pretense of being healthy. It's a true drive-in, so either bring the car along or be happy to eat on the lawn out front. Peter's is handily located on 16 Ave NE, aka the Trans-Canada Hwy, 3km north of downtown.

Catch
SEAFOOD **$$**

(☑403-206-0000; www.catchrestaurant.ca; 100 8th Ave SW; mains $17-27; ☺11:30am-2pm Mon-Fri & 5-10pm Mon-Sat) The problem for any saltwater fish restaurant in landlocked Calgary is that, if you're calling it fresh, it can't be local. Overcoming the conundrum, Catch, situated in an old bank building on Stephen Ave Walk, flies its 'fresh catch' in daily from both coasts (BC and the Maritimes).

You can work out the carbon offsets for your lobster, crab and oysters on one of three different floors: an oyster bar, a dining room or an upstairs atrium.

Blink
FUSION **$$**

(☑403-263-5330; www.blinkcalgary.com; 111 8th Ave SW; mains from $20; ☺11am-2pm Mon-Fri & 5-10pm Mon-Sat) 🖉 Blink multiple times but you still won't miss this trendy city-center gastro haven where an acclaimed British chef oversees an ever-evolving menu of fine dishes that yell out that well-practised modern restaurant mantra of 'fresh, seasonal and local.'

The decor is all open-plan kitchens and exposed brick, and you can delve even deeper into the culinary process through regular cooking classes (last Sunday of the month; $125).

Home Tasting Room
CANADIAN, FUSION **$$**

(☑403-262-8100; www.hometastingroom.ca; 110 8th Ave SW; tasting plates $14-23; ☺11am-10pm Mon-Fri, 5-11pm Sat, noon-10pm Sun) Sure, there's no accounting for taste, but if you can whip up food as good and as varied as Home Tasting Room, then you've got most bases covered. Wine pairing and shared plates of experimental Euro-influenced food are the order of the day at this new downtown perch where quality reigns over quantity.

Drop by and take the sting out of your midmorning appetite.

King and I
THAI **$$**

(☑403-264-7241; www.kingandi.ca; 822 11th Ave SW; mains from $12; ☺11:30am-10:30pm Mon-Thu, to 11:30pm Fri, 4:30-11:30pm Sat, to 9:30pm Sun) Not just a movie with Yul Brynner, but Bangkok-good Thai food too. This downtown classic with an exotic atmosphere is popular with groups. Try the curries or the pad thai – both are fantastic.

Rush
FUSION **$$$**

(☑403-271-7874; www.rushrestaurant.com; 207 9th Av SW; mains from $25; ☺11:30am-2pm Mon-Fri & 5-10pm Mon-Sat) Not to be confused with the so-bad-they're-almost-good Canadian rock band of the same name, Rush the restaurant is a decidedly cooler affair, with glass walls, gold millwork and not a head banger in sight. Foodwise, this is gastronomy from the top drawer, with intelligent wine pairings and a chef's tasting menu winning almost universal plaudits.

Opt for the foie gras or the halibut and enjoy the complimentary canapés and petit fours.

Teatro
ITALIAN, FUSION **$$$**

(☑403-290-1012; www.teatro.ca; 200 8th Ave SE; mains $32-45, 8-course tasting menus $135;

CALGARY FOR CHILDREN

Calgary is a very kid-friendly destination, with most attractions having a portion aimed at the younger set.

Encased in new digs east of downtown, **Telus Spark** (☑817 6800; www.sparkscience. ca; 220 St George's Drive NE; adult/child $19.95/12.95; ⊙9am-5pm; ☷) is the obligatory science center for kids. There is a dome theater, a kids' museum and exhibits on space, energy and science. On the same side of town is the highly rated Calgary Zoo (p61), which has a kids club, kids' camp and various youth programs.

The Heritage Park Historical Village (p62) is one of the best ways to teach a child about history, with costumed actors roaming wonderful re-creations of Calgary's early-20th-century streets.

Children of all ages enjoy **Calaway Park** (☑403-240-3822; www.calawaypark.com; admission/family $35.95/89; ⊙10am-7pm Jul-early Sep, 11am-6pm Sat & Sun early Sep-early Oct, 5-9pm Fri, 10am-7pm Sat & Sun late May–Jul), western Canada's largest outdoor family amusement park. It has 30 rides from wild to mild, live entertainment, food vendors, different carnival games, a trout-fishing pond and an interactive maze. To get there, head 10km west of the city on Hwy 1.

⊙noon-4pm Mon-Fri & 5-10pm daily) With performing waitstaff and Tony Award–worthy food, the aptly-named Teatro, in a regal bank building next to the Epcor Centre of Performing Arts, could quite easily be mistaken for a theater at first glance. This has long been one of Calgary's most discussed restaurants, and the dishes fuse Italian influences, French nouvelle cuisine and a bit of traditional Alberta.

The chef's eight-course tasting menu is an epic journey through the best parts of the fancy menu.

Caesar's Steak House　STEAKHOUSE $$$
(☑403-264-1222; www.caesarssteakhouse.com; 512 4th Ave SW; steaks from $35; ⊙11am-10:30pm) In Naples, you eat pizza. In Vancouver, you eat salmon. In Calgary, you eat prime Alberta AAA steak – right here.

✖ Uptown 17th Ave & 4th St – Mission District

Jelly Modern Doughnuts　BAKERY $
(☑403-453-2053; www.jellymoderndoughnuts. com; 1414 8th St SW; doughnuts from $2; ⊙7am-6pm Mon-Fri, 9am-6pm Sat, to 5pm Sun) A Calgary tradition in the making, Jelly Modern has grabbed the initiative on weird doughnut flavors. The maple and bacon, and carrot cake (with dried carrots) varietals won't help ward off any impending heart attacks, but they'll make every other doughnut you've ever tasted seem positively bland by comparison.

Everything's baked on-site, meaning once you've taken one sniff inside the glass door, you're putty in their hands.

Analog Coffee　COFFEE $
(www.fratellocoffee.com; 740 17th Ave SW; coffees $2-5; ⊙7am-10pm) The third-wave coffee scene is stirring in Calgary (at last!) led by companies like Fratello, which runs this new hipster-ish cafe on 17th Ave that displays the beans of the day on a clipboard and has rows of retro vinyl spread along the back wall.

Galaxie Diner　BREAKFAST $
(☑403-228-0001; www.galaxiediner.com; 1413 11th St SW; mains $5-9; ⊙7am-3pm Mon-Fri, to 4pm Sat & Sun) Classic no-nonsense 1950s-style diner that serves all-day breakfasts. Squeeze into one of the half-dozen tables, grab a pew at the bar or (more likely) join the queue at the door.

Mercato　ITALIAN $$
(☑403-263-5535; www.mercatogourmet.com; 2224 4th St SW; mains $16-22; ⊙11:30am-11pm) Attached to an open-plan Italian market/deli that sells everything from coffee to salami, Mercato is one of those local restaurants that gets everything right. Decor, service, atmosphere, food and price all hit the spot in a modern but authentic take on la dolce vita in the endearing Mission neighborhood.

Ox and Angela　TAPAS $$
(☑403-457-1432; www.oxandangela.com; 528 17th Ave; tapas $4-14; ⊙11:30am-late) Re-creating Spain in modern Calgary isn't an obvious business project – there's the lack of palm

trees, qualified matadors and Latin lovers, for starters – but the new Ox and Angela has a good shot at it, at least in the gastronomic sphere. Inside a gorgeous modern-meets-Euro-rustic interior, tapas are served with a strong Iberian bias. Order piecemeal from a menu of Manchego cheese, tortilla (Spanish omelette) and cured *jamón serrano.*

Farm FUSION $$

(☑403-245-2276; www.farm-restaurant.com; 1006 17th Ave SW; tasting plates $12-19; ☉11.30am-10pm Sun-Fri, 10.30am-11pm Sat) 🍴 Raising the excitement bar on 17th Ave, Farm is a 'tasting kitchen' for fine meats, beer, wine and particularly cheese. The menu is about attention to detail, back-to-the-land purity and a genuine love of good food.

Melrose Café & Bar CANADIAN $$

(☑403-228-3566; www.melrosecalgary.com; 730 17th Ave SW; mains $9-15; ☉11am-midnight Mon-Fri, 10am-1am Sat & Sun) Right in the epicenter of what passes for cool in Calgary on 17th Ave, Melrose is split into three sections: obligatory patio, casual sit-down restaurant and a sports bar with enough TV screens to make you feel like Winston Smith in *Nineteen Eighty-Four.* The scene alternates between boisterous post-hockey-game euphoria and unironic pre-Stampede cowboy antics. Count the 'yee-haws.'

★**Model Milk** CANADIAN $$$

(☑403-265-7343; www.modelmilk.ca; 108 17th Ave SW; mains $19-32; ☉5pm-1am) Model Milk has a revolving menu that changes before the ink's even dry, so it's impossible to predict what you'll get to eat at the former dairy turned hip restaurant. Grits and prawns with a fried egg on top was heading the 'starter' lineup at last visit.

More certain is the service (knowledgeable waitstaff), the decor (mezzanine floor, communal seating and open kitchen) and the ambience (cool without trying too hard).

🍴 Kensington

Higher Ground CAFE $

(☑403-270-3780; www.highergroundcafe.ca; 1126 Kensington Rd; snacks $5-8; ☉7am-11pm Mon-Thu, 8am-midnight Fri-Sun) 🍴 Giving Calgary's as-yet-uncrowded indie coffee-bar scene the shot of home-roasted caffeine it needs, Higher Ground is a delicious mix of art gallery, gossip shop, public theater and community resource. It is also where you come for

lunch-size panini and a damned fine cup of coffee.

Pulcinella ITALIAN $$

(☑403-283-1166; www.pulcinella.ca; 1147 Kensington Crescent NW; pizzas $15-20; ☉11:30am-11pm) So Italian that the pizza oven was – apparently – made with rocks quarried from Mt Vesuvius near Naples, Pulcinella specializes in thin crispy Neapolitan pies with purposefully simple toppings. The decor is silvery metallic, and a casual bar area out front offers sanctuary for lone diners or those stood up on a first date.

Sushi Club JAPANESE $$

(☑403-283-4100; 1240 Kensington Rd NW; mains from $10; ☉11:30am-2pm & 5-9pm Mon & Wed-Fri) This could well be the best sushi in town. It's perhaps a bit on the pricey side, but you get what you pay for. It has a great lunch special, where a massive spread costs less than $10.

🍴 Inglewood

★**Gravity Espresso & Wine Bar** CAFE $

(www.cafegravity.com; 909 10th St SE; light lunches $6-12; ☉8am-6pm Sun & Mon, to 10pm Tue-Thu, to midnight Fri & Sat) 🍴 More evidence that Calgary might be abandoning its bland race to modernity for more thoughtful community-led business is this hybrid cafe-bar, which alters its personality depending on the clientele and the time of day. The crux of the operation is the locally roasted Phil & Sebastian coffee beans, but that's just an overture for loads of other stuff, including live acoustic music, curry nights, home-baked snacks and fund-raisers.

★**Rouge** FUSION $$$

(☑403-531-2767; www.rougecalgary.com; 1240 8th Ave SE; mains $36-80; ☉11:30am-1:30pm Mon-Fri & 5-10pm Mon-Sat) Rouge is becoming the city's – and one of Canada's – most celebrated restaurants. Located in a historic 1891 mansion in Inglewood, it's expensive and hard to get into, but once inside you're on hallowed ground. Enjoy the inspired, creative and sustainable food choices and exceptional fit-for-a-king service.

🍷 Drinking & Nightlife

For bars hit 17th Ave NW, which has a slew of martini lounges and crowded pubs, and 4th St SW, which has a lively after-work scene. Other notable areas include Kensington Rd NW and Stephen Ave Walk (a six-block downtown stretch of 8th Ave). You can see the money walking Calgary's streets after dark in the form of beautiful, well-dressed 20-somethings in stretch limos and noisy stag nights in corporate bars.

For more on gay and lesbian nightlife, pick up a copy of *Outlooks* (www.outlooks.ca), a monthly newspaper distributed throughout the province. The website has an extensive gay resource guide to Calgary and beyond.

Hop In Brew   PUB
(☑ 403-266-2595; 213 12th Ave SW; ☺ 4pm-late) An old Craftsman-style house clinging on for dear life amid the spanking-new condos of the Victoria Park district, the Hop still gets hopping on a good night, with good tunes, a grungy atmosphere and plenty of beers on tap.

National   BAR
(www.ntnl.ca; 550 17th Ave SW; ☺ 11am-midnight) A new bar with old-school Calgary pretensions, the National blends seamlessly into the 17th Ave action. On its outdoor patio, office bods in Stetsons cluster loudly around communal tables and you'll hear the odd unashamed cry of 'yee-haw' (especially during Stampede). There's loads of beer choice, including some microbews on tap, plus typical pub grub.

Barley Mill   PUB
(☑ 403-290-1500; www.barleymill.net; 201 Barclay Pde SW; ☺ 11am-late) This freestanding structure next to Eau Claire Market is a favorite after-work stop for the downtown working stiffs who hug the outdoor patio when the temperature pulls itself out of its deathly winter chill.

Ship & Anchor   PUB
(☑ 403-245-3333; www.shipandanchor.com; 534 17th Ave SW; ☺ 11am-2am) The frankly ugly Ship is a classic Calgary institution – an all-time favorite of university students, people who think they're hip, and indie music fans. With an abundance of beers on tap, the shadowy interior is a cozy winter hideaway, while the picnic-table-filled patio is Posing Central come summertime.

Flames Central   BAR
(☑ 403-935-2637; www.flamescentral.com; 219 8th Ave SW; ☺ 9am-5pm Mon, 11am-5pm Tue-Thu, 11am-2am Fri, 4pm-2am Sat) The huge interior of what used to be a cinema has been transformed into the sports bar to end all sports bars. With more TVs than an electronics shop, it'll definitely give you a good view of the beloved Calgary Flames hockey team, even when they're playing avowed rival the Oilers. There is an on-site restaurant, and concerts are held from time to time.

Rose & Crown   PUB
(☑ 403-244-7757;   www.roseandcrowncalgary.ca; 1503 4th St SW; ☺ 11am-late) A popular, multi-level British-style pub located in the Beltline neighborhood.

HiFi Club   CLUB
(www.hificlub.ca; 219 10th Ave SW; ☺ 9pm-2:30am Wed-Sun) The HiFi is a hybrid. Rap, soul, house, electro, funk – the dance floor swells nightly to the sounds of live DJs who specialize in making you sweat. Check out Sunday Skool, the weekly soul and jazz session, or Saturday night's showcase for touring bands and DJs.

Twisted Element   GAY, LESBIAN
(www.twistedelement.ca; 1006 11th Ave SW) Consistently voted the best gay dance venue by the local community, this club has weekly drag shows, karaoke nights and DJs spinning nightly.

Back Lot   GAY
(209 10th Ave SW; ☺ 9pm-2:30am) This one's for boys mainly. There's a patio and drink specials while you take in the view.

☆ Entertainment

For complete entertainment guides, pick up a copy of *ffwd* (www.ffwdweekly.com), the city's largest entertainment weekly. The paper is free and found in numerous coffee bars, restaurants and street boxes in Calgary, Banff and Canmore.

Plaza Theatre   CINEMA
(☑ 403-283-3636; 1113 Kensington Rd NW) Right in the heart of Kensington, the Plaza shows art-house flicks and cult classics – it's where you'll end up doing the 'Time Warp' (again!).

Globe Cinema   CINEMA
(www.globecinema.ca; 617 8th Ave SW) Specializing in foreign films and Canadian cinema – both often hard to find in mainstream movie houses.

Epcor Centre for the
Performing Arts   THEATER
(www.epcorcentre.org; 205 8th Ave SE) This is the hub for live theater in Calgary, with four

theaters and one of the best concert halls in North America.

Loose Moose Theatre Company THEATER
(www.loosemoose.com; 1235 26th Ave SE) Guaranteed to be a fun night out, Loose Moose has recently transferred to new digs near the Inglewood neighborhood. It specializes in improv comedy and audience participation.

Pumphouse Theatres THEATER
(www.pumphousetheatres.ca; 2140 Pumphouse Ave SW) Set in what used to be, you guessed it, the pumphouse, this theater company puts on avant-garde, edgy productions.

Ironwood Stage & Grill LIVE MUSIC
(www.ironwoodstage.ca; 1229 9th Ave SE; ⊙ shows 8pm Sun-Thu, 9pm Fri & Sat) Cross over into the hipper universe of Inglewood to find the grassroots of Calgary's not-exactly-legendary music scene. Local bands alternate with bigger touring acts for nightly music in the woody confines of Ironwood. Country and folk are the staples.

Broken City LIVE MUSIC
(☑ 403-262-9976; www.brokencity.ca; 613 11th Ave SW; ⊙ 11am-2am) There's music here most nights – everything from jazz jams to hip-hop. There's also food and a patio.

Jubilee Auditorium CONCERT VENUE
(www.jubileeauditorium.com/southern; 1415 14th Ave NW) You can hang with the upper crust at the ballet or rock out to a good concert, all under the one roof.

Calgary Flames SPECTATOR SPORT
(☑ 403-777-0000; www.flames.nhl.com) Arch-rival of the Edmonton Oilers, the Calgary Flames play ice hockey from October to April at the Saddledome (Stampede Park). Make sure you wear red to the game and head down to 17th Ave or the 'Red Mile' afterwards as they call it during play-offs.

Calgary Stampeders SPECTATOR SPORT
(☑ 403-289-0258; www.stampeders.com; ⊙ Jul-Sep) The Calgary Stampeders, part of the CFL, play at McMahon Stadium (1817 Crowchild Trail NW) in the University District, 6km northwest of downtown.

🛍 Shopping

Calgary is shopping heaven or hell depending on your taste for modern mall ubiquity. There are several hot spots, but these districts are reasonably far apart. The Kensington area and 17th Ave SW have a good selection of interesting, fashionable clothing shops and funky trinket outlets. Stephen Ave Walk is a pedestrian mall with shops, bookstores and atmosphere. Inglewood is good for antiques, junk, apothocaries and secondhand books and vinyl.

Alberta Boot Co SHOES
(☑ 403-263-4605; www.albertaboot.com; 50 50th Ave SE; boots $235-1700; ⊙ 9am-6pm Mon-Sat) Visit the factory and store run by the province's only Western boot manufacturer and pick up a pair of your choice made from kangaroo, ostrich, python, rattlesnake, lizard, alligator or boring old cowhide.

Chinook Centre MALL
(☑ 403-259-2022; www.chinookcentre.com; 6455 Macleod Trail SW; ⊙ 9:30am-9pm Mon-Sat, 11am-7pm Sun) If you're in need of some retail therapy, Chinook, 6km south of downtown, is a good place to get your treatment. Chain retail shops, department stores, a movie theater and lots of greasy food are all present and accounted for.

Mountain Equipment Co-op OUTDOOR EQUIPMENT
(☑ 403-269-2420; www.mec.ca; 830 10th Ave SW; ⊙ 10am-9pm Mon-Fri, 9am-6pm Sat, 11am-5pm Sun) MEC is the place to get your outdoor kit sorted before heading into the hills. It has a huge selection of outdoor equipment, travel gear, active clothing and books.

Smithbilt Hats CLOTHING
(☑ 403-244-9131; www.smithbilthats.com; 1103 12th St SE; ⊙ 9am-5pm Mon-Thu, 8am-4:30pm Fri) Ever wondered how a cowboy hat is made? Well, here is your chance to find out. Smithbilt has been shaping hats in the traditional way since you parked your horse out front.

ℹ Information

Banks seem to live at every corner downtown; look to 17th Ave or Stephen Ave Walk if one isn't within sight. Many branches are open on Saturday and bank machines are open 24/7.

Alberta Children's Hospital (☑ 403-955-7211; 2888 Shaganappi Trail NW) Emergency room open 24 hours.

Calforex (228 8th Ave SW; ⊙ 8:30am-7pm Mon-Fri, 10am-5pm Sat & Sun) Currency exchange facilities.

Main Post Office (207 9th Ave SW; ⊙ 8am-5:45pm Mon-Fri)

Rockyview General Hospital (☑ 403-943-3000; 7007 14th St SW) Emergency room open 24 hours.

Tourism Calgary (www.tourismcalgary.com; 101 9th Ave SW; ⊙8am-5pm) Operates a visitors center in the base of the Calgary Tower. The staff will help you find accommodations. Information booths are also available at both the arrivals and departures levels of the airport.

❶ Getting There & Away

AIR

Calgary International Airport (YYC; www. calgaryairport.com) is about 15km northeast of the center off Barlow Trail, a 25-minute drive away.

BUS

The Greyhound Canada **bus station** (877 Greyhound Way SW) has services to Banff ($29, 1¾ hours), Edmonton ($49, 3½ hours), Drumheller ($38, 1¾ hours) and Lethbridge ($48, 2½ hours). Note that discounts are available online.

For a more comfortable experience, go with the superluxurious **Red Arrow** (www.redarrow. pwt.ca; 205 9th Ave SE) buses to Edmonton ($70, 3½ hours, six daily) and Lethbridge ($49, 2½ hours, one daily).

Canmore and Banff ($54, 2¼ hours, eight daily) are served by the legendary **Brewster** (www.brewster.ca).

Red Arrow picks up downtown on the corner of 9th Ave SE and 1st Ave SE. Brewster buses pick up at various downtown hotels. Inquire when booking.

CAR

All the major car-rental firms are represented at the airport and downtown.

TRAIN

Inexplicably, Calgary welcomes no passenger trains (which bypass the city in favor of Edmonton and Jasper). Instead, you get **Rocky Mountaineer Railtours** (www.rockymountaineer. com), which runs expensive cruise-ship-like rail excursions (two-day tours per person from $1000).

❶ Getting Around

TO/FROM THE AIRPORT

Sundog Tours (☑403-291-9617; www.sundogtours.com; 1 way adult/child $15/8) runs every half hour from around 8:30am to 9:45pm between all the major downtown hotels and the airport.

You can also go between the airport and downtown on public transportation. From the airport, take bus 57 to the Whitehorn stop (northeast of the city center) and transfer to the C-Train; reverse that process coming from downtown. This costs only $3, and takes between 45 minutes and an hour.

A taxi to the airport costs about $35 from downtown.

CAR & MOTORCYCLE

Parking in downtown Calgary is an expensive nightmare – a policy designed to push people to use public transportation. Luckily, downtown hotels generally have garages. Private lots charge about $20 per day. There is also some metered parking. Outside the downtown core, parking is free and easy to find.

PUBLIC TRANSPORTATION

Calgary Transit (www.calgarytransit.com) is efficient and clean. You can choose from the Light Rapid Transit (LRT) rail system, aka the C-Train, and ordinary buses. One fare ($3) entitles you to transfer to other buses or C-Trains. The C-Train is free in the downtown area along 7th Ave between 10th St SW and 3rd St SE. If you're going further or need a transfer, buy your ticket from a machine on the C-Train platform. Most buses run at 15- to 30-minute intervals daily. There is no late-night service. The C-Train was recently expanded, and there are plans for more lines in the future.

TAXI

For a cab, call **Checker Cabs** (☑403-299-9999) or **Yellow Cab** (☑403-974-1111). Fares are $3 for the first 150m, then $0.20 for each additional 150m.

BANFF & JASPER NATIONAL PARKS

While Italy has Venice and Florence, Canada has Banff and Jasper, legendary natural marvels that are as spectacular and vital as anything the ancient Romans ever built. But don't think these protected areas have no history. Of the thousands of national parks scattered around the world today, Banff, created in 1885, is the third oldest, while adjacent Jasper was only 22 years behind. Situated on the eastern side of the Canadian Rockies, the two bordering parks were designated Unesco World Heritage sites in 1984, along with BC's Yoho and Kootenay, for their exceptional natural beauty coupled with their manifestation of important glacial and alluvial geological processes. In contrast to some of North America's wilder parks, they both support small towns that lure between 2 to 5 million visitors each year. Despite all this, the precious balance between humans and nature continues to be delicately maintained – just.

Visiting the Parks

Visitors come here for all sorts of reasons: to ski, climb and hike on the mountains, to raft and kayak the rivers, to camp among the trees, or explore on their mountain bikes. But most come simply to look, and to stand in awe of the sheer beauty of this amazing place.

As you pass through this special area, you are under the ever-watchful eye of the animals that call it home. This is the place to see the Canadian Rockies' Big Five: deer, elk, moose, wolf and bear. (But only if you're lucky: they don't pose for everyone's photos.)

The one-day park entry fee (for entry to both parks) is $9.80/4.90 per adult/child; the passes are good until 4pm the following day.

History

Banff National Park, Canada's first park, became the template for conservation. When Jasper joined the park system just over a century ago, this corridor of conservation was complete. Within that protected zone, the small towns of Banff and Jasper have emerged. These two towns, where development is frozen and the idea of ecotourism has been around since the 1880s, have lived in harmony with the surrounding wilderness for decades.

Banff is far from a secret these days: crowds are inevitable and you will have to share those scenic lookouts. But most will agree that that's a small price to pay for a part of this country that will remain in your thoughts long after you leave the mountains behind.

Kananaskis Country

Kananaskis, or K-Country as the locals call it, is a mountainous Shangri-la, with all the natural highlights of Banff National Park, but with almost no clamor. It abuts Banff National Park in the southeast, acting as both a buffer zone and a first-class wilderness area in its own right. At an impressive 4000 sq km, it's a hefty tract of landscape to try and take in. Luckily, there is a network of hiking trails to get you into the backcountry and away from the roads. Hikers, cross-country skiers, bikers and climbers – mainly in-the-know Albertans – all lust over these hills, which are the perfect combination of wild, accessible, unspoiled and inviting. If

you recognize anything, it's probably because you've seen it in one of a score of films made here, including *Brokeback Mountain*.

On the eastern edge of the mountains you can drive the scenic and sparsely trafficked Hwy 40 (south off Hwy 1, 20km east of Canmore) to the Kananaskis lakes, before turning down onto the unsealed Smith-Dorian Rd to complete the drive back to Canmore by a circuitous picturesque route. Or if you can, continue along Hwy 40 – which will treat you to blankets of pine forest interspersed with craggy peaks and the odd moose in the verge – all the way to Highwood House. This scenic drive is definitely the road less traveled and well worth exploring; be aware that this portion of the road is closed over winter.

🏃 Activities

K-Country is also C-Country. Cowboy-up and go for a ride with **Boundary Ranch** (☑ 403-591-7171; www.boundaryranch.com; Hwy 40; rides from $43.50; ☺ May-Oct), which will take you for a trail ride that could last anywhere from an hour to days.

Purpose-built to host the alpine skiing events in the 1988 Olympics, **Nakiska** (www.skinakiska.com; Hwy 40), five minutes' drive south of the region's main service center, Kananaskis Village, is a racer's dream. Top Canadian skiers still train here. K-Country's other ski resort, Fortress Mountain, has been closed on and off (mainly off) since 2004.

The Kananaskis River has grade II and III rapids and is popular with white-water rafting companies operating out of Banff.

🛏 Sleeping & Eating

Proof of Kananaskis' get-away-from-it-all ethos came when it was selected to host the 2002 G8 summit, with leaders hidden away at the **Delta Lodge at Kananaskis** (☑ 403-591-7711; www.deltahotels.com; 1 Centennial Dr, Kananaskis Village; r from $189). The amazing scenery, tip-top facilities and isolation were a big hit. Delta's pricey **Fireweed Grill** (Delta Lodge; mains $20-30) does baked river fish and AAA Alberta steak.

Alternatively, sleep under the stars at the **Boulton Creek Campground** (☑ 403-591-7226; Kananaskis Lakes Rd; campsites/RV sites $23/35; ☺ May-Oct).

ℹ Information

About 8km from Hwy 1 along Hwy 40 is the **Barrier Lake Information Centre** (☑ 403-

Banff National Park

673-3985; www.tpr.alberta.ca/parks; Hwy 40;
⊙ 9am-5pm), which has loads of info and sells
backcountry camping permits ($12).

Canmore

A former coal-mining town, Canmore was
once the quiet alternative to the mass tourism of Banff. Then, after one too many 'best-
kept secret' travel articles, everybody started
coming here for a little peace and quiet. Despite the commotion, the soul of the town
has remained intact, and Canmore, although
not national-park protected, has been developed sensibly and sustainably – so far. At
just 26km from Banff and on the cusp of
Kananaskis Country, it's at the crossroads of
some of the most magnificent scenery you
will ever see. For those seeking a mountain
holiday with slightly less glitz, more of a rugged feel and less pretension, Canmore can
still cut it.

⊙ Sights & Activities

Canmore excels in three mountain activities: cross-country skiing, mountain biking and rock climbing.

Cross-Country Skiing

Both winter and summer are prime times at the Canmore Nordic Centre (☑403-678-2400; www.canmorenordic.com; 1988 Olympic Way; day ski pass $10). Used for the cross-country skiing events at the 1988 Olympics, the Nordic Centre is arguably the best facility of its kind in Canada and the training ground for many national champions. It offers ski rentals and lessons for the uninitiated and a network of trails that would keep an Olympian busy for days.

Mountain Biking

Once the snow melts, the Nordic Centre's trails transform into some of the best mountain biking around, with over 80km of off-road to test your skills. On-site rentals cost $45 per day. Close to here, the Rundle Riverside and Spray River/Goat Creek trails both head north to Banff Town.

Rock Climbing

Canmore is one of the premier rock-climbing destinations in the Rockies. Not surprisingly, national mountaineering organization the Alpine Club of Canada has its HQ here. In the summer there are numerous climbing crags, such as Cougar Creek, Grassi Lakes and Grotto Canyon, all within a relatively short distance of each other. For those looking for multipitch rock, the limestone walls of Mt Rundle and Mt Yamnuska are local classics, with routes of all grades. In the colder months Canmore is the place to be for frozen waterfall climbing: learn at the Junkyards, practise on Grotto Falls or take the final exam on The Terminator.

If you're keen to give climbing in any of its forms a try, talk to Yamnuska Mountain Adventures (☑403-678-4164; www.yamnuska.com; Suite 200, Summit Centre, 50 Lincoln Park), which will provide expert instruction, qualified guides and all the gear you might need (two-day beginners' courses start from $325). Yamnuska also offers longer courses for those wanting to gain the skills necessary to spend some serious time in the hills.

🛏 Sleeping

Canmore Clubhouse HOSTEL **$**
(☑403-678-3200; www.alpineclubofcanada.ca; Indian Flats Rd; dm from $36) 🌢 Steeped in climbing history and mountain mystique, the Alpine Club of Canada's beautiful hostel sits on a rise overlooking the valley. You'll find all of the usual hostel amenities here, along with a sauna. The Alpine Club offers classes in mountaineering and maintains several backcountry huts.

The Clubhouse is a great place to find climbing partners or just soak up the spirit of adventure. Located 5km south of town, it's an inconvenient 45-minute walk or pleasant five-minute drive away.

Windtower Lodge & Suites HOTEL **$$**
(☑403-609-6600; www.windtower.ca; 160 Kananaskis Way; d/ste $139/239; @🗫) Named for the stunning rock feature only a few kilometers to the east, this modern and well-appointed hotel is a good option. The rooms are a bit small, so spending more on a suite is a good idea. Some rooms have fine views of the Three Sisters, and all have access to the hot tub and fitness center.

Falcon Crest Lodge HOTEL **$$$**
(☑403-678-6150; www.falconcrestlodge.ca; 190 Kananaskis Way; r from $209; ❄🗫) Of all the salubrious woody lodges in Canmore, Falcon Crest is perhaps the best. Ample deluxe rooms have balconies with views of Canmore's famous peaks, incuding Three Sisters, and there are various suite options. An exercise room and outdoor hot tub complement the Rocky Mountain experience.

✖ Eating

Bagels for breakfast, beer and burgers for lunch, and steak for dinner. Look no further than the following trio.

Rocky Mountain Bagel Co CAFE **$**
(☑403-678-9978; www.thebagel.ca; 829 8th St; bagels $6-8; ☉6am-6pm; 🗫) 🌢 Is there anything better in life than sitting under the flower baskets at Rocky Mountain Bagel Co, studying the morning shadows on the Three Sisters while enjoying a toasted maple bagel and a latte? Possibly not.

Grizzly Paw PUB **$$**
(☑403-678-9983; www.thegrizzlypaw.com; 622 Main St; mains $13-20; ☉11am-midnight) Shock horror exclusive. Alberta's best microbrewery (offering six year-round beers) is hiding in the mountains of Canmore. The veterans of raspberry ale and Grumpy Bear beer have just built a new brewery to support their legendary brewpub (tours and

tasters are promised). There's also a micro-distillery on the way. And, yes, the pub serves grub.

Wood STEAKHOUSE **$$**
(☑403-678-3404; www.thewood.ca; 838 8th St; mains $12-29; ⊙7:30am-11pm) Plenty of wood and a big fireplace create a relaxed, sophisticated vibe in this log building in Canmore's town center. If you're having a day off from AAA Alberta steak (not easy here), plump for the excellent salmon burger with a Dijon tartar relish.

❶ Information

Canmore Visitors Information Centre (www.tourismcanmore.com; 907A 7th Ave; ⊙9am-5pm) Just off the main drag.

❶ Getting There & Away

Canmore is easily accessible from Banff Town and Calgary from Hwy 1. The **Banff Airporter** (www.banffairporter.com) runs up to 10 buses a day to/from Calgary Airport ($55). **Brewster** (Map p80; ☑1-800-760-6934; www.explore-rockies.com) has connections with the airport and downtown Calgary for roughly the same price. **Roam** (www.roamtransit.com) buses connect every hour to Banff ($6, 20 minutes).

Icefields Parkway

Paralleling the Continental Divide for 230km between Lake Louise and Jasper Town, plain old Hwy 93 has been wisely rebranded as the Icefields Parkway (or the slightly more romantic 'Promenade des Glaciers' in French) as a means to somehow prepare people for the majesty of its surroundings. And what majesty! The highlight is undoubtedly the humungous Columbia Icefield and its numerous fanning glaciers, and this dynamic lesson in erosive geography is complemented by weeping waterfalls, aquamarine lakes, dramatic mountains and the sudden dart of a bear, an elk, or was it a moose?

The parkway was completed in 1940, and most people ply the asphalt by car, meaning it can get busy in July and August. For a clearer vision consider taking a bus or, even better, tackling it on a bike – the road is wide, never prohibitively steep, and sprinkled with plenty of strategically spaced campgrounds, hostels and hotels.

◉ Sights

There are two types of sights: static (lakes, glaciers and mountains) and moving (elk, bears, moose etc). If you don't see at least one wild animal (look out for the inevitable 'bear jams') you'll be very unlucky. Static sights are arranged here geographically from south to north.

Peyto Lake LAKE
(Map p74) You'll have already seen the indescribable blue of Peyto Lake in a thousand publicity shots, but there's nothing like gazing at the real thing; especially since the viewing point for this lake is from a lofty vantage point roughly 100m above the water. The lake is best visited in early morning, between the time the sun first illuminates the water and the first tour bus arrives.

From the bottom of the lake parking lot, follow a paved trail for 15 minutes up a steady gradual incline to the wooden platform overlooking the lake. From here you can continue up the paved trail, keeping right along the edge of the ridge. At the junction of three trails, follow the middle trail until you reach an unmarked dirt road; if you continue down it for about 2.5km you'll find yourself in a serene rocky bowl with a stream running through the center.

Weeping Wall WATERFALL
(Map p74) This towering rock wall sits just above the east side of the highway. In the summer months it is a sea of waterfalls, with tears of liquid pouring from the top creating a veil of moisture. Come winter, it's a whole different story. The water freezes up solid to form an enormous sheet of ice.

The vertical ice field is a popular playground for ice climbers, who travel from around the globe to test their mettle here. Scaling the wall is a feather in the cap for the alpinists lucky enough to clamber to the top. Be sure to observe the ice from the safety of the roadside lookout; falling chunks of ice the size of refrigerators are not uncommon.

★ Columbia Icefield OUTDOORS
About halfway between Lake Louise Village and Jasper Town is the only accessible section of the vast Columbia Icefield, which covers an area the size of the city of Vancouver and feeds eight glaciers. This remnant of the last ice age, which is up to 350m thick in places, stretches across the plateau between Mt Columbia (3747m) and Mt Athabasca (3491m).

It's the largest ice field in the Rockies and feeds the North Saskatchewan, Columbia, Athabasca, Mackenzie and Fraser River systems with its meltwaters. The mountainous sides of this vast bowl of ice are some of the highest in the Rockies, with nine peaks higher than 3000m.

Be sure to stop at the **Icefield Centre** (Map p74; ☑780-852-6288; ⊙9am-6pm May-Oct) **FREE**, where you can chat with the rangers from Parks Canada about camping options and climbing conditions; they can answer any questions you might have regarding the park. There's a fairly insipid cafeteria here, along with some equally bland hotel rooms at the Glacier View Inn (p78).

Athabasca Glacier   OUTDOORS
(Map p74) The tongue of the Athabasca Glacier runs from the Columbia Icefield almost down to the road opposite the Icefield Centre and can be visited on foot or in specially designed buses. The glacier has retreated about 1.6km in the last 150 years. To reach its toe (bottom edge), walk or drive 1km to a small parking lot and the start of the 0.6km **Forefield Trail**.

While it is permitted to stand on a small roped section of the ice, do not attempt to cross the warning tape. Many do, but the glacier is riddled with crevasses and there are fatalities nearly every year.

The best way to experience the Columbia Icefield is to walk on it. For that you will need the help of **Athabasca Glacier Icewalks** (Map p74; ☑780-852-5595; www.icewalks. com; Icefield Centre; 3hr tours adult/child $70/35, 6hr tours $85/45), which supplies all the gear you'll need and a guide to show you the ropes. It offers a three-hour tour (departing 10:40am daily June to September), and a six-hour option (Sunday and Thursday) for those wanting to venture further out on the glacier.

The other far easier (and more popular) way to get on the glacier is via a 'Snocoach' ice tour offered by **Brewster** (Map p74; ☑877-423-7433; www.brewster.ca; adult/child $49.95/24.95; ⊙tours 9am-5pm May-Oct). For many people this is the defining experience of their Columbia Icefield visit. The large hybrid bus-truck grinds a track onto the ice where it stops to allow you to go for a short walk in a controlled area on the glacier. Dress warmly and wear good shoes. Tickets can be bought at the Icefield Centre or online; tours depart every 15 to 30 minutes.

ALBERTA ICEFIELDS PARKWAY

CYCLING THE ICEFIELDS PARKWAY

With its ancient geology, landscape-altering glaciers, and lakes bluer than Picasso paintings from the blue period, the 230km-long Icefields Parkway is one of the world's most spectacular roads, and, by definition, one of the world's most spectacular bicycle rides – if your legs and lungs are up to it. Aside from the distance, there are several long uphill drags, occasional stiff headwinds and two major passes to contend with: namely Bow Summit (2088m) and Sunwapta Pass (2035m). Notwithstanding, the route is highly popular in July and August (don't even think about doing it in the winter), with aspiring cyclists lapping up its bicycle-friendly features. No commercial trucks are allowed on the parkway, there's a generous shoulder throughout, two-wheeled company is virtually guaranteed, and accommodations along the route (both campgrounds and hostels/hotels) are plentiful and strategically placed. Some ply the parkway as part of an organized tour (with back-up vehicles), others do it solo over two to five days. There's a choice of six HI hostels and four lodge/motel accommodations en route. Book ahead. Basic provisions can be procured at Saskatchewan River Crossing, 83km north of Lake Louise.

It's considered slightly easier to cycle from north to south, starting in Jasper and finishing in Lake Louise, but the differences aren't great. Some people tack on the extra 60km between Banff and Lake Louise at the start or finish proceeding along the quiet Bow Valley Parkway and avoiding the busy Trans-Canada (Hwy 1).

Sturdy road bikes can be rented from **Wilson Mountain Sports** (www.wmsll.com; Samson Mall; ⊙9am-7pm) in Lake Louise village. Brewster buses can sometimes transport bicycles, but always check ahead. **Backroads** (☑510-527-1555; www.backroads.com) runs a Canadian Rockies Bike Tour, a six-day organized trip that incorporates cycling along the parkway.

Athabasca Glacier to Jasper Town

SCENIC HIGHWAY

As you snake your way through the mountains on your way to Jasper, there are a few places worth stopping at. Sunwapta Falls (Map p92) and Athabasca Falls (Map p92), closer to Jasper, are both worth a stop. The latter is the more voluminous and is at its most ferocious in the summer when it's stoked with glacial meltwater.

A less-visited spot is idyllic blue-green Horseshoe Lake (Map p92), revered by ill-advised cliff-divers. Don't be tempted to join them.

At Athabasca Falls, Hwy 93A quietly sneaks off to the left. Take it. Literally the road less traveled, this old route into Jasper offers a blissfully traffic-free experience as it slips serenely through deep, dark woods and past small placid lakes and meadows.

🍴 Sleeping & Eating

The Icefields Parkway is punctuated by several well-camouflaged hostels. Most are close to the highway in scenic locations. More substantial hotels/lodges are available at Bow Lake, Saskatchewan Crossing, Columbia Icefield and Sunwapta Falls. There are also numerous primitive campgrounds (per night $16) in the area. Good options are Honeymoon Lake (Map p92), Jonas Creek (Map p92), Mt Kerkeslin (Map p92), Waterfowl Lakes (Map p74) and Wilcox Creek (Map p74) campgrounds.

Mosquito Creek International Hostel

HOSTEL $

(Map p74; ☑ 403-670-7589; www.hihostels.ca; dm member/nonmember $24/26) Don't let the name put you off. Mosquito Creek, 26km north of Lake Louise, is a perfect launching pad for backcountry adventures, the sauna is an ideal flop-down-and-do-nothing end to the day, and the adjacent river just adds to the atmosphere. The hostel sometimes closes in winter, so call ahead.

Rampart Creek International Hostel

HOSTEL $

(Map p74; ☑ 403-670-7589; www.hihostels.ca; dm member/nonmember $24/26) Rampart, 11km north of the Saskatchewan River Crossing, has long been a popular place with climbers, cyclists and other troublemakers. The tiny crag at the back is good fun for a bouldering session, and the 12 bunks and facilities are clean and cozy. Then there's the sauna –

for lethargy. Call ahead in winter in case it's closed.

Beauty Creek International Hostel

HOSTEL $

(Map p92; ☑ 780-852-3215; www.hihostels.ca; Icefields Parkway; dm member/nonmember $24/26; ⊗ check-in 5-10pm) 🌿 Forget the lack of electricity, propane-powered lights, outdoor loos and well-drawn water, and home in on the all-you-can-eat pancake breakfast and poetry-inspiring scenery.

Sunwapta Falls Resort

HOTEL $$$

(Map p92; ☑ 888-828-5777; www.sunwapta.com; r from $209; @) A handy Icefields pit stop 53km south of Jasper Town, Sunwapta offers a comfortable mix of suites and lodge rooms cocooned in pleasant natural surroundings. The home-style restaurant and gift shop on-site are popular with the tour-bus crowd.

Glacier View Inn

HOTEL $$$

(Map p74; ☑ 877-423-7433; Icefield Centre, Icefields Parkway; r from $249; ⊗ May-Oct) Panoramic views of the glacier are unbelievable at this chalet – if only the windows were a bit bigger. You are in the same complex as the madness of the Icefield Centre, so it can feel like you are staying in a shopping mall at times. But after all the buses go away for the night, you are left in one of the most spectacular places around. A nothing-to-write-home-about cafeteria shares the complex.

Num-Ti-Jah Lodge

INN $$$

(Map p74; ☑ 403-522-2167; www.sntj.ca; d from $233, mains from $14, 3-course dinners $45) Standing like a guardian of Bow Lake, the historic Num-Ti-Jah Lodge is full to the brim with character and backcountry nostalgia. Carved-wood interior decor, animal heads and photos from the golden age adorn the walls. The rooms are tidy, if a little small. The lodge restaurant has an extensive wine list.

Banff Town

Like the province in which it resides, Banff is something of an enigma. A resort town with souvenir shops, nightclubs and fancy restaurants is not something any national-park purist would want to claim credit for. But, looks can be misleading. First, Banff is no ordinary town. It developed not as a residential district, but as a service center for the park that surrounds it. Second, the commercialism of Banff Ave is delusory. Wander five minutes in either direction and (though you may not initially realize it) you're in wild country, a primeval food chain of bears, elk, wolves and bighorn sheep. Banff civilized? It's just a rumor.

History

While most mountain towns have their roots in the natural-resource industry, Banff was created in the late 1800s with tourism in mind. The railway arrived first, then the Cave and Basin hot springs were discovered, and the potential to make some money became evident. First came the hordes of wealthy Victorians, staying at the Banff Springs Hotel and soaking in the soothing waters. Everything changed in 1911 when the road finally reached the town and the doors were flung open to the masses.

Banff continued to grow as more tourists arrived and services aimed at not just the upper class began to take root. Town developers have long been frustrated by the inclusion of the town within the national park. This has meant that building restrictions are tight, new development has ceased and the future of building in Banff is both a political and ecological hot potato. Actually living in Banff is a challenge: the federal government owns all the land, only those employed can take up residence and businesses are obligated to provide accommodations for their employees.

Though the infrastructure and size of the town remains fixed, the number of tourists has continued to spiral skywards. For as long as the town has been incorporated, locals have bickered about tourism. While they may pay everyone's wages, the visitors overrun the town and move it away from the quiet mountain town it once was.

◎ Sights

Banff supports a healthy four museums, virtually unprecendented for a 'natural' national park.

★ **Whyte Museum of the Canadian Rockies** MUSEUM
(Map p80; www.whyte.org; 111 Bear St; suggested donation $5; ☉10am-5pm) The century-old Whyte Museum is more than just a rainy-day option. There is a beautiful gallery displaying some great pieces on an ever-changing basis. The permanent collection tells the story of Banff and the hardy men and women who forged a home among the mountains.

Attached to the museum is an archive with thousands of photographs spanning the history of the town and park; these are available for reprint. The museum also gives out leaflets for a self-guided Banff Culture Walk.

Banff Gondola CABLE CAR
(☑403-762-2523; Mountain Ave; adult/child $34.95/16.95; ☉8am-9pm) In summer or winter you can summit a peak near Banff thanks to the Banff Gondola; its four-person enclosed cars glide up to the top of Sulphur Mountain in less than 10 minutes. Named for the thermal springs that emanate from its base, this peak is a perfect viewing point and a tick-box Banff attraction.

There are a couple of restaurants on top plus an extended hike on boardwalks to Sanson Peak, an old weather station. Some people hike all the way up on a zigzagging 5.6km trail. You can travel back down on the gondola for half price and recover in the hot springs.

The gondola is 4km south of central Banff.

Cave & Basin National Historic Site HISTORIC SITE
(☑403-762-1557; Cave Ave; adult/child $3.90/1.90; ☉10am-5pm daily May-Oct, noon-4pm Wed-Sun Oct-May) Attention. National Historic Site ahead. The Canadian National Park system was effectively born at these hot springs, discovered accidently by three Canadian Pacific Railway employees on their day off in 1883, but known to Aboriginals for 10,000 years. Uncovering a thermal gold mine, the springs quickly became a bun fight for private businesses who offered facilities for bathers to enjoy the then trendy thermal treatments.

To avert an environmental catastrophe, the government stepped in, deciding to declare Banff Canada's first national park in order to preserve the springs. You can't swim here any more, but the site ropened as an impressive museum in May 2013 after a two-year restoration. Viewable is the original cave, the old outdoor springs and bathhouse (closed in 1971) and a lovingly curated cinematic display of Parks Canada's cache of 42 national parks. Leading out from the complex are two trails: an interpretive walk along boardwalks to the cave vent, and the 2.5km Marsh Loop Trail across the park's only natural river marsh.

Banff Town

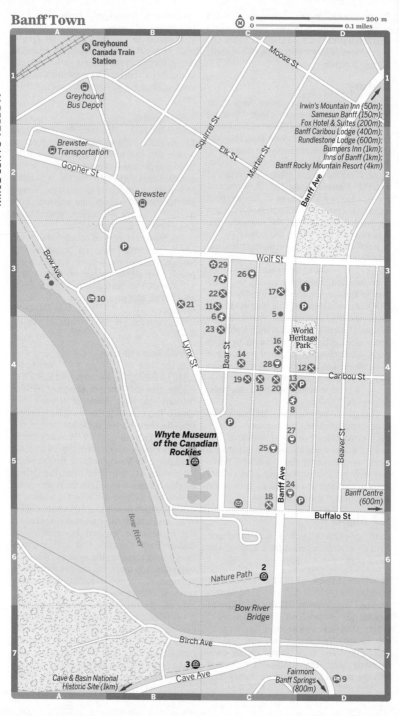

Greyhound Canada Train Station

Greyhound Bus Depot

Brewster Transportation

Gopher St

Brewster

Bow Ave

4

10

Lynx St

Bear St

Squirrel St

Elk St

Marten St

Moose St

Banff Ave

Irwin's Mountain Inn (50m);
Samesun Banff (150m);
Fox Hotel & Suites (200m);
Banff Caribou Lodge (400m);
Rundlestone Lodge (600m);
Bumpers Inn (1km);
Inns of Banff (1km);
Banff Rocky Mountain Resort (4km)

Wolf St

29
7
22
11
6
23

26

21

14

19   15   20

28

16

12

17

5

World Heritage Park

13
8

27

25

24

Whyte Museum of the Canadian Rockies

1

18

Caribou St

Beaver St

Banff Centre (600m)

Banff Ave

Buffalo St

Bow River

Nature Path   2

Bow River Bridge

Birch Ave

3

Cave Ave

Cave & Basin National Historic Site (1km)

Fairmont Banff Springs (800m)

9

Banff Town

Banff Upper Hot Springs SPA
(☏403-762-1515; Mountain Ave; adult/child $7.30/6.30; ⊙9am-11pm) Modern tourists use these soothing (if often crowded) hot pools, steam room and spa furnished with excellent mountain views near the Banff Gondola, 4km south of town. The water emerges from the spring at 47°C; in winter it has to be cooled to 39°C before entering the pool, but in spring the snowmelt does that job.

In addition to the pool, you can indulge in a massage or an aromatherapy wrap. Bathing suits, towels and lockers can be rented.

Lake Minnewanka LAKE
Lake Minnewanka, pronounced miniwonka, as in Willy Wonka (not miniwanker, as Australian visitors enjoy saying), sits 13km east of Banff Town, making it a popular escape from downtown. The scenic recreational area has plenty of hiking, swimming, sailing, boating and fishing opportunities.

The nonchallenging trail around the lake is a good option for a walk; the path is easy to follow and popular. **Minnewanka Lake Cruises** (www.explorerockies.com/minnewanka; adult/child $44.95/19.95; ⊙departures 10am-6pm May-Sep) offers a 60-minute interpretive cruise on the lake, giving plenty of insight into the region's history and geol-

ogy. You can also fish here or hike to the Alymer Lookout trail for spectacular lake and mountain views. A Brewster bus can transport you to the lake for an extra fee.

Banff Park Museum MUSEUM
(Map p80; ☏403-762-1558; 93 Banff Ave; adult/child $3.95/1.95; ⊙10am-6pm) Occupying an old wooden Canadian Pacific Railway building dating from 1903, this museum is a national historic site. Its exhibits – a taxidermic collection of animals found in the park, including grizzly and black bears, plus a tree carved with graffiti dating from 1841 – have changed little since the museum opened a century ago.

Buffalo Nations Luxton Museum MUSEUM
(Map p80; ☏403-762-2388; 1 Birch Ave; adult/child $10/6; ⊙11am-6pm) The Luxton Museum is essentially the story of the Alberta Aboriginal people, with a strong emphasis on the Cree, Blackfoot, Blood and Stony people. The displays, though a bit dusty, are pretty informative and contain some impressive eagle-feather headdresses and a life-size replica of a rather macabre sundance ceremony.

You'll probably learn an interesting fact or two here, but the museum won't delay you more than 30 minutes, making the $10 entrance fee a little steep.

🏃 Activities

Canoeing & Kayaking

Despite a modern penchant for big cars, canoe travel is still very much a quintessential Canadian method of transportation. The best options near Banff Town are Lake Minnewanka and nearby Two Jack Lake, both to the northeast, or – closer to the town itself – the Vermilion Lakes. Unless you have your own canoe, you'll need to rent one; try Blue Canoe (Map p80; ☑ 403-760-5007; www.bluecanoeing.com; cnr Wolf St & Bow Ave; canoes per hour/additional hours $36/20).

Cycling

There are lots of riding options around Banff, both on road and on selected trails. Popular routes around Banff Town include Sundance (7.4km round-trip) and Spray River Loop (12.5km); either is good for families. Spray River & Goat Creek (19km one way) and Rundle Riverside (14km one way) are both A to Bs with start/finish points near Canmore. The former is pretty straightforward; the latter is more challenging, with ups and downs and potential for thrills and spills.

Serious road cyclists should check out Hwy 1A between Banff and Lake Louise; the rolling hills and quiet road here are a roadie's dream. Parks Canada publishes the brochure *Mountain Biking & Cycling Guide – Banff National Park,* which describes trails and regulations. Pick it up at the Banff Information Centre.

Snowtips/Bactrax (Map p80; www.snowtips-bactrax.com; 225 Bear St; bicycles per hour/day from $12/42) has a barn full of bikes to rent and will also take you on a tour to one of the many bike trails in the Banff area ($20 per hour). Ask about shuttles to trailheads.

Hiking

Hiking is Banff's tour de force and the main focus of many travelers' visit to the area. The trails are easy to find, well signposted, and maintained enough to be comfortable to walk on, yet rugged enough to still get a wilderness experience.

In general, the closer to Banff Town you are, the more people you can expect to see and the more developed the trail will be. But regardless of where in the park you go walking, you are assured to be rewarded for your efforts.

Before you head out, check at the Banff Information Centre for trail conditions and possible closures. Keep in mind that trails are often snow-covered much later into the summer season than you might realize, and trail closures due to bears are a possibility, especially in berry season (June to September).

One of the best hikes from the town center is the Bow River Falls and the Hoodoos Trail, which starts by the Bow River Bridge and tracks past the falls to the Hoodoos, weird rock spires caused by wind and water erosion. The trail plies its way around the back of Tunnel Mountain through forest and some river meadows and is 10.2km return.

You can track the north shore of Lake Minnewanka for kilometers on a multi-use trail that is sometimes closed due to bear activity. The classic hike is to walk as far as the Alymer Lookout just shy of 10km one way. Less taxing is the 5.6km-return hike to Stewart Canyon, where you can clamber down rocks and boulders to the Cascade River.

Some of the best multiday hikes start at the Sunshine parking lot where skiers grab the gondola in winter. From here you can plan two- to four-day sorties up over Healy

---

LOCAL KNOWLEDGE

LEGACY TRAIL

After years of planning, Parks Canada opened the long-awaited Legacy Trail in 2010, a paved multiuse path for cyclists, skaters and pedestrians that runs between Canmore and Banff. The 19km trail extends from Banff National Park's eastern gate 6km west of Canmore all the way to Banff town closely shadowing Hwy 1. From the park gate you can then pick up the Canmore Trail, which crosses the highway to reach Canmore. For those not up to cycling/walking in both directions, Bike 'n' Hike Shuttle (☑ 403-762-4453; www.bikeandhikeshuttle.com; one-way from $10) offer a handy bus service between the trailheads to get you back to your starting point.

Banff and Canmore are linked by two additional trails, the rugged Rundle Riverside Trail (for experienced off-road cyclists) and the easier Goat Creek Trail. All of the trails were washed out in the June 2013 floods. Check with Parks Canada (www.pc.gc.ca) for current status.

Pass and down to Egypt Lake, or get a bus up to Sunshine Village where you can cross the border into BC and head out across Sunshine Meadows and Mount Assiniboine Provincial Park.

The best backcountry experience is arguably the Sawback Trail that travels from Banff up to Lake Louise the back way over 74km, six primitive campsites and three spectacular mountain passes.

Check out Lonely Planet's *Banff, Jasper & Glacier National Parks* guide for more details about single-day and multiday hikes.

Horseback Riding

Banff's first European explorers – fur traders and railway engineers – penetrated the region primarily on horseback. You can recreate their pioneering spirit on guided rides with Warner Guiding & Outfitting (Map p80; ☑ 403-762-4551; www.horseback.com; 132 Banff Ave; 1hr rides from $45), which will fit you out with a trusty steed and lead you along narrow trails for part of the day. Instruction and guiding are included; a sore backside is more or less mandatory for beginners. Grin and bear it. If you're really into it, opt for Warner's six-day Wildlife Monitoring Adventure Expeditions out to limited-access areas accompanied by a Parks Canada researcher.

Skiing & Snowboarding

Strange though it may seem, there are three ski areas in the national park, two of them in the vicinity of Banff Town. Large, snowy Sunshine Village is considered world-class. Tiny Norquay, a mere 5km from the center, is your half-day, family-friendly option.

Sunshine Village (Map p74; www.skibanff. com; day ski passes $75) straddles the Alberta–BC border. Though slightly smaller than Lake Louise in terms of skiable terrain it gets much bigger dumpings of snow, or 'Champagne powder' as Albertans like to call it (up to 9m annually). Aficionados laud Sunshine's advanced runs and lengthy ski season, which lingers until Victoria Day weekend in late May. A high-speed gondola whisks skiers up in 17 minutes to the village, which sports Banff's only ski-in hotel, the Sunshine Mountain Lodge.

Ski Banff@Norquay (Map p74; ☑ 522 3555; www.banffnorquay.com; Mt Norquay Rd; lift tickets $46), just 6km north of downtown Banff, has a long history of entertaining Banff visitors. The smallest and least visited of the three local hills, this is a good place to body-swerve

the major show-offs and hit the slopes for a succinct half day.

Local buses shuttle riders from Banff hotels to both resorts (and Lake Louise) every half hour during the season.

White-Water Rafting

The best rafting is outside the park (and province) on the Kicking Horse River in Yoho National Park, BC. There are grade IV rapids here, meaning big waves, swirling holes and a guaranteed soaking. Lesser rapids are found on the Kananaskis River and the Horseshoe Canyon section of the Bow River. The Bow River around Banff is better suited to mellower float trips.

The following companies all have representation in the park. They offer tours starting at around $79. Factor in $15 more for a Banff pickup.

Canadian Rockies Rafting Company RAFTING
(Map p80; ☑ 403-763-2007; www.chinookraft.com; Sundance Mall, 215 Banff Ave)

Hydra River Guides RAFTING
(Map p80; ☑ 403-762-4554; www.raftbanff.com; 211 Bear St)

Wild Water Adventures RAFTING
(☑ 403-522-2211; www.wildwater.com; Lake Louise Dr) Has a desk at the Chateau Lake Louise, but will pick up from Banff for a fee.

☞ Tours

GyPSy Guide DRIVING TOUR
(Map p80; ☑ 403-760-8200; www.gpstourscan-ada.com; Sundance Mall, 215 Banff Ave; per day $39) The GyPSy is a hand-held GPS device that you take in your car and guides you around the area. There is a lively running commentary that broadcasts through your stereo, pointing out highlights as you travel. All you have to do is follow the directions and you get a great self-guided tour of the area – Banff, Lake Louise, Columbia Icefield, Jasper and Calgary are all included on the tour. Best of all, if you get tired of the tour guide you can always turn it off.

Discover Banff Tours GUIDED TOUR
(Map p80; ☑ 403-760-5007; www.banfftours.com; Sundance Mall, 215 Banff Ave; tours from $54) Discover Banff has a great selection of tours to choose from: three-hour Banff Town tours, sunrise and evening wildlife tours, Columbia Icefield day trips and even a 10-hour

grizzly bear tour, where if you don't see a bear you get your money back.

✻ Festivals & Events

The town's biggest annual event is the **Banff Mountain Film and Book Festival** (www.banffcentre.ca/mountainfestival) in late October and early November. Attracting the cream of the mountain-culture aficionados, this event is a must-do for the armchair adventurer and mountain guru alike with film screenings and book readings.

🛏 Sleeping

Compared with elsewhere in the province, accommodations in Banff Town are fairly costly and, in summer, often hard to find. The old adage of the early bird catching the worm really holds true here, and booking ahead is strongly recommended.

The Banff/Lake Louise Tourism Bureau tracks vacancies on a daily basis; check the listings at the Banff Information Centre. You might also try **Enjoy Banff** (📞 1-888-313-6161; www.enjoybanff.com), which books rooms for more than 75 different lodgings.

Camping in Banff National Park is popular and easily accessible. There are 13 campgrounds to choose from, most along the Bow Valley Parkway or near Banff Town.

HI-Banff Alpine Centre   HOSTEL $
(📞 403-762-4122; www.hihostels.ca; 801 Hidden Ridge Way; dm/d from $45/143; @🛜) Banff's best hostel is near the top of Tunnel Mountain and well away from the madness of Banff Ave. Walkers will find the commute a good workout, and their efforts will not go unrewarded. The buildings are finished in classic mountain-lodge style but without classic mountain-lodge prices.

There are clean, comfortable accommodations in bunk rooms and a few doubles, fireplaces in the common areas, and good views top it all off. The public bus runs right by the front door, so don't let the location deter you. The hostel is located off Tunnel Mountain Rd, an extension of Banff's Otter St.

Samesun Banff   HOSTEL $
(📞 403-762-5521; www.banffhostel.com; 449 Banff Ave; dm/d incl breakfast $31.50/85; @🛜) 🏄 One of a half a dozen Canadian hostels, the Samesun is zanier, edgier and a little cheaper than the other local budget digs. Features include a large central courtyard with barbecue, compact four- or eight-person dorms,

an on-site bar, plus a selection of hotel-style rooms in an adjacent 'chalet' (they're billed as four-star standard though they're not quite there). The clientele is international, backpacker and young (or young at heart).

Banff Y Mountain Lodge   HOSTEL $
(Map p80; 📞 403-762-3560; www.ymountainlodge.com; 102 Spray Ave; dm $33, d with shared/private bathroom $115/135; @🛜) The YWCA is Banff's swankiest hostel option, offering dorm rooms along with private family-oriented accommodations down by the river.

Tunnel Mountain Village   CAMPGROUND $
(📞 877-737-3783; www.pccamping.ca; Tunnel Mountain Rd; campsites/RV sites $27/38) It's hard to imagine this campground filling its nearly 1000 sites, but come summer it's bursting at the seams with holidaymakers from around the globe. Located at the top of Tunnel Mountain with sites among the trees, it's not nearly as grim as it sounds.

Part of it is open during winter too, so if you want to sleep under canvas at -20°C, you can do it here.

★ Banff Rocky Mountain Resort   HOTEL $$
(📞 403-762-5531; www.bestofbanff.com; 1029 Banff Ave; r from $159; 🛜❄) Being 4km out of town at the far, far end of Banff Ave is a small price to pay for the preferential prices and excellent all-round facilities here (including a hot tub, pool, tennis courts and cafe-restaurant).

Added to this is the greater sense of detachment, quiet tree-filled grounds (it never feels like a 'resort') and generously sized bedrooms with sofas, desks and extra beds. There's a free shuttle into town (hourly) or you can walk or cycle 4km along the Legacy Trail.

Banff Caribou Lodge   HOTEL $$
(📞 403-762-5887; www.bestofbanff.com; 521 Banff Ave; d from $179; @🛜❄) One of the posher places in the locally run Banff Lodging Co empire (who don it three-and-a-half stars), the Caribou fits the classic stereotype of a mountain lodge, with its log and stone exterior, giant lobby fireplace and general alpine coziness.

Aside from 189 comfy rooms, you get free local bus passes here, a heated underground car park, an on-site Keg Steakhouse, and a hard-to-avoid spa with various pools and treatment rooms.

Irwin's Mountain Inn HOTEL $$

(☎403-762-4566; www.irwinsmountaininn.com; 429 Banff Ave; d inc breakfast from $174; @☎🏊) A marginal drop in price and quality on the upper echelons of Banff Ave lands you in Irwin's, where the rooms are verging on motel-like and the decor is more 'plastic' than granite. Not surprisingly, the place is popular with families who take advantage of the hot tub, steam room, fitness center and continental breakfast.

Bow View Lodge HOTEL $$

(Map p80; ☎403-762-2261; www.bowview.com; 228 Bow Ave; r from $144; ✳☎🏊) The Bow View is a journeyman Banff option – older than most of the attractive log inns that line Banff Avenue, but neat and tidy all the same. Without any surcharge you can use the fitness facilities and pool in the huge Banff Park Lodge next door.

Inns of Banff HOTEL $$

(☎403-762-4581; www.bestofbanff.com; 600 Banff Ave; r from $149; @☎🏊) Slightly out of the hustle and bustle, there are some good deals to be found here. Though the architecture is a little passé, there are loads of facilities, including both indoor and outdoor pools, ski and bike rentals, and a Japanese restaurant.

Bumpers Inn MOTEL $$

(☎403-762-3386; www.bumpersinn.com; 603 Banff Ave; r from $125; ☎) Banff provides a rare no-frills motel in bog-standard Bumpers, which offers zero pretension, but plenty of financial savings.

★ Fairmont Banff Springs HOTEL $$$

(☎403-762-2211; www.fairmont.com/banffsprings; 405 Spray Ave; r from $412; @☎🏊) Sitting at the top end of the 'lost-for-words' category comes this exquisite beauty. Imagine crossing a Scottish castle with a French chateau and then plonking it in the middle of one of the world's most spectacular (and accessible) wilderness areas.

Rising like a Gaelic Balmoral above the trees at the base of Sulphur Mountain and visible from miles away, the Banff Springs is a wonder of early 1920s revivalist architecture and one of Canada's most iconic buildings. Wandering around its museumlike interior, it's easy to forget that it's also a hotel.

Rimrock Resort Hotel HOTEL $$$

(☎403-762-3356; www.rimrockresort.com; 300 Mountain Ave; r $298-313; @☎🏊) Next door to the hot springs, the Rimrock is plush and spectacularly located, although it often gets overshadowed by Banff's crème de la crème hotel, the Fairmont. Controversially located in a wildlife corridor on the slopes of Sulphur Mountain, the views here are nonetheless inspiring.

Mountain decadence coats the chaletlike interior, the restaurant (Eden) is considered fine dining, and the rooms almost match the stunning outdoor vistas. Worth every penny.

Fox Hotel & Suites HOTEL $$$

(☎800-760-8500; www.bestofbanff.com; 461 Banff Ave; d from $229; @☎🏊) A relative newcomer opening in 2007, the Fox justifies its four-star billing with an eye for the aesthetic and great attention to detail. Bright, modern rooms have retro-patterned wallpaper and unique, interesting artworks, while the reception has enough trickling water to invoke flashbacks of Rome.

The highlight is the inspired re-creation of the Cave & Basin springs in the hot-tub area, with an open hole in the roof that gives out to the sky. The bar-restaurant is called Chilis and serves, among other things, excellent margaritas. The town is a 10-minute walk away.

Rundlestone Lodge HOTEL $$$

(☎403-762-2201; www.rundlestone.com; 537 Banff Ave; d/ste from $209/274; ☎🏊) This place is filled with pseudo old-English charm, complete with Masterpiece Theater chairs in the lobby. The standard rooms are fairly, well... standard, but family and honeymoon suites come with a kitchen, fireplace and loft.

The centrally located indoor pool is a nice feature, and the obligatory Banff hotel restaurant – this one's called Toloulous – makes a game attempt at food with a Creole twist.

✖ Eating

Banff dining is more than just hiker food. Sushi and foie gras have long embellished the restaurants of Banff Ave, and some of the more elegant places will inspire dirty hikers to return to their hotel rooms and take a shower before pulling up a chair. Aside from the following establishments, many of Banff's hotels have their own excellent on-site restaurants that welcome nonguests. AAA Alberta beef makes an appearance on even the most exotic à la carte menu.

Evelyn's Coffee Bar CAFE $

(Map p80; ☎403-762-0352; www.evelynscoffeebar.com; 201 Banff Ave; mains $6-10;

⊙6.30am-11pm; 🛜) Pushing Starbucks onto the periphery, Evelyn's parades four downtown locations all on or within spitting distance of Banff Ave. Dive in to any one of them for wraps, pies and – best of all – its own selection of giant homemade cookies.

Wild Flour
CAFE $
(Map p80; ☑ 403-760-5074; www.wildflourbakery. ca; 211 Bear St; mains $5-10; ⊙ 7am-7pm; 🛜 🍴) 🅿 Banff's antidote to Tim Hortons is heavy on organic, vegan and frankly strange-looking cakes, pastries and cinnamon buns backed up with free-trade, organic coffee. They also bake their own bread.

Cows
ICE CREAM $
(Map p80; ☑ 403-760-3493; www.cows.ca; 134 Banff Ave; ice cream $3.50-5; ⊙ 11am-9pm) A Prince Edward Island import, Cow's ice cream is legendary out east, but this is one of only two branches in western Canada. Bypass the tacky T-shirts and choose from 32 extracreamy flavors.

Bruno's Cafe & Grill
BREAKFAST, BURGERS $
(Map p80; ☑ 403-762-8115; 304 Caribou St; mains $10-16; ⊙ 8am-10pm) While other joints stop serving breakfasts at 11am, Bruno's keeps going all day, replenishing the appetites of mountain men and women as it once replenished its one-time Swiss guide owner, Bruno Engler. It's a kind of greasy spoon meets pub. The walls are decorated with antique ski gear, and the crowd at the next table could well be last night's live band refueling for tonight's gig.

The formidable Mountain Breakfast ($17) is served in a basket and requires a Mt Rundle-size appetite.

Coyote's Deli & Grill
FUSION $$
(Map p80; ☑ 403-762-3963; www.coyotesbanff. com; 206 Caribou St; lunch mains $8-14, dinner mains $20; ⊙ 7:30am-10:30pm) Coyote's is best at lunchtime, when you can bunk off hiking and choose a treat from the deli and grill menu, which is inflected with a strong southwestern slant. Perch on a stool and listen to the behind-the-bar banter as you order up flatbreads, seafood cakes, quesadillas or some interesting soups (try the sweet potato and corn chowder).

Eddie Burger & Bar
BURGERS $$
(Map p80; ☑ 403-762-2230; www.theeddieburgerbar.ca; Caribou St; burgers $13) Avoid the stereotypes. The Eddie might appear pretentious (black leather seats and mood lighting), and

its name may contain the word 'burger,' but it welcomes all types (including exhausted hikers and kids) and its gourmet meals-in-a-bun are subtler and far less greasy than your standard Albertan patty.

Try the Spicy Italian or the Mexican and wash it down with a Kokanee beer.

Melissa's Restaurant
STEAKHOUSE $$
(Map p80; ☑ 403-762-5511; www.melissasrestaurant.com; 218 Lynx St; mains $17-27; ⊙ 7am-10pm; 🍴) Melissa's is a casual ketchup-on-the-table type of place in a 1928 heritage building. It's huge in the local community and has an equally huge selection of food and price ranges. Nonetheless, its brunch, dinnertime steaks and deep-dish pizzas are probably its most defining dishes.

Giorgio's Trattoria
ITALIAN $$
(Map p80; ☑ 403-762-5114; www.giorgiosbanff. com; 219 Banff Ave; mains $16-30; ⊙ 5-10pm) Slightly fancier than your average salt-of-the-earth trattoria, Giorgio's nonetheless serves up authentic Italian classics like osso buco risotto and a fine pear-and-Gorgonzola pizza mixed with the odd Alberta inflection (buffalo pappardelle!). The interior is elegant and there are prices to go with it (especially the wines).

Saltlik
STEAKHOUSE $$
(Map p80; ☑ 403-762-2467; www.saltliksteakhouse. com; 221 Bear St; mains $16-27; ⊙ 11am-2am) With rib eye in citrus-rosemary butter and peppercorn New York striploin on the menu, Saltlik is clearly no 'plain Jane' steakhouse knocking out flavorless T-bones. No, this polished dining room abounds with rustic elegance and a list of steaks the length of many establishments' entire menu. In a town not short on steak-providers, this could be No 1.

Magpie & Stump
MEXICAN $$
(Map p80; ☑ 403-762-4067; 203 Caribou St; mains $9-14; ⊙ noon-2am) A classic musty cantina full of dreadlocked Sol-swigging snowboarders. You'll feel it's almost your dinnertime duty to demolish an overloaded plate of oven-finished chicken enchiladas with a tangy side relish.

⭐ Bison Restaurant & Terrace
CANADIAN, FUSION $$$
(Map p80; ☑ 403-762-5550; www.thebison.ca; 211 Bear St; mains $29-45; ⊙ 5pm-late) The Bison might look like it's full of trendy, well-off Calgarians dressed in expensive hiking gear,

but its a two-level affair, with a rustically elegant restaurant upstairs sporting a menu saturated with meat, and a cheaper, more casual terrace below, which serves big salads and weird starch-heavy pizzas with butternut squash and rosemary-potato toppings.

Maple Leaf Grille   CANADIAN $$$
(Map p80; 403-762-7680; www.banffmapleleaf. com; 137 Banff Ave; mains $20-40; 11am-10pm) With plenty of local and foreign plaudits, the Maple Leaf eschews all other pretensions in favor of one defining word: 'Canadian.' Hence, the menu is anchored by BC salmon, east coast cod, Albertan beef and Okanagan Wine Country salad...you get the drift. All very patriotic – and tasty.

Le Beaujolais   FRENCH $$$
(Map p80; 403-762-2712; www.lebeaujolaisbanff. com; Banff Ave, at Buffalo St; 3-/6-course meals $68/95; 6-10pm) Stick the word 'French' in the marketing lingo and out come the ironed napkins, waiters in ties, snails (billed as 'escargot' because it makes them sound so much more palatable) and elevated prices.

Beaujolais might not be everybody's post-hiking cup of tea, but if you just came here to gaze romantically at the mountains, why not do it over wild boar, bison and foie gras.

Drinking & Nightlife

Throw a stone in Banff Ave and you're more likely to hit a gap-year Australian than a local. For drinking and entertainment, follow the Sydney accents to local watering holes or look through the listings in the 'Summit Up' section of the weekly *Banff Crag & Canyon* newspaper.

★Banff Ave Brewing Co   PUB
(Map p80; www.banffavebrewingco.ca; 110 Banff Ave; 11:30am-2am) An offshoot of the excellent Jasper Brewing Co, this brewpub opened in Banff in 2010. It's best for a drink of craft beer, brewed on the premises and infused with Saskatoon berries and the like.

St James's Gate Olde Irish Pub   PUB
(Map p80; www.stjamesgatebanff.com; 205 Wolf St; mains from $10; 11am-1am Sun-Thu, to 2am Fri & Sat) As Celts pretty much opened up western Canada and gave their name to the town of Banff, it's hardly surprising to find an Irish pub in the park, and a rather good one at that. Aside from stout on tap and a healthy selection of malts, St James's offers classic pub grub such as burgers and stew.

Tommy's Neighbourhood Pub   PUB
(Map p80; www.tommysneighbourhoodpub.com; 120 Banff Ave; 11am-11pm) Tommy's pub-grub menu stretches to crab cakes and spinach-artichoke dip. More importantly for traditionalists there's good draft beer, a darts board, and plenty of opportunity to meet the kind of globe-trotting mavericks who have made Banff their temporary home.

Wild Bill's Legendary Saloon   BAR
(Map p80; www.wbsaloon.com; 201 Banff Ave; 11am-late) Cowboys – where would Alberta be without them? Check this bar out if you're into line dancing, calf-roping, karaoke and live music of the twangy Willy Nelson variety. The saloon is named after Wild Bill Peyto, a colorful 'local' character who was actually born and raised in that not-so-famous cowboy county of Kent in England.

Elk & Oarsman   PUB
(Map p80; www.elkandoarsman.com; 119 Banff Ave; 11am-1am) Upstairs with a crow's-nest view of Banff Ave, this is the town's most refined pub. The rooftop patio is prime real estate in the summer, and the kitchen will fix you up with some good food if you so desire.

Hoodoo Club   CLUB
(Map p80; 137 Banff Ave) If you came to Banff to go nightclubbing (silly you!) look no further than this joint, where you can drink, pose and dance in your sexy fleece not a mile from where wild animals roam.

☆ Entertainment

Banff Centre   THEATER
(www.banffcentre.ca; 107 Tunnel Mountain Dr) A cultural center in a national park? Banff never ceases to surprise. This is the cultural hub of the Bow Valley – concerts, art exhibitions and the popular Banff Mountain Film Festival are all held here.

Lux Cinema Centre   CINEMA
(Map p80; 229 Bear St) The local movie house screens first-run films.

ℹ Information

Banff Information Centre (Map p80; www. parkscanada.gc.ca/banff; 224 Banff Ave; 8am-8pm) Offices for Parks Canada.

Banff Warden Office Dispatch Line (403-762-1470) Open 24 hours for nonemergency backcountry problems.

Custom House Currency Exchange (211 Banff Ave; 9am-10pm) In the Park Ave Mall.

Main Post Office (Map p80; 204 Buffalo St; ⊙8:30am-5:30pm Mon-Sat)

Mineral Springs Hospital (☑403-762-2222; 301 Lynx St; ⊙24hr) Emergency medical treatment.

❶ Getting There & Away

The nearest airport is in Calgary.

Greyhound Canada (Map p80; ☑1-800-661-8747; 327 Railway Ave) operates buses to Calgary ($29, two hours, six daily), Vancouver ($130, 14 hours, five daily) and points in between.

Brewster Transportation (Map p80; www. brewster.ca) will pick you up from your hotel. It services Jasper ($69, 4¾ hours, daily) and Lake Louise ($20, one hour, several daily).

SunDog Tour Co (www.sundogtours.com) also runs transport between Banff and Jasper (adult/child $69/39, four hours, daily).

All of the major car-rental companies have branches in Banff Town. During summer all the cars might be reserved in advance, so call ahead. If you're flying into Calgary, reserving a car at the airport (where the fleets are huge) may yield a better deal than waiting to pick up a car when you reach Banff Town.

❶ Getting Around

Over 20 shuttle buses a day operate year-round between Calgary International Airport and Banff. Buses are less frequent in the spring and fall. Companies include Brewster Transportation and **Banff Airporter** (www.banffairporter.com). The adult fare for both is around $54 one way.

Banff Transit (☑403-762-1215) runs four hybrid 'Roam' buses on two main routes. Stops include Tunnel Mountain, the Rimrock Resort Hotel, Banff Upper Hot Springs, Fairmont Banff Springs and all the hotels along Banff Ave. Route maps are printed on all bus stops. Buses start running at 6:30am and finish at 11pm; the fare is $2.

Taxis can easily be hailed on the street, especially on Banff Ave. Otherwise call **Banff Taxi** (☑403-762-4444). Taxis are metered.

Lake Louise

Famous for its teahouses, grizzly bears, grand hotel, skiing, Victoria Glacier, hiking and lakes (yes, plural), Lake Louise is what makes Banff National Park the phenomenon it is, an awe-inspiring natural feature that is impossible to describe without resorting to shameless clichés. Yes, there is a placid turquoise-tinted lake here; yes, the natural world feels (and is) tantalizingly close; and

yes, the water is surrounded by an amphitheater of finely chiseled mountains that Michelangelo couldn't have made more aesthetically pleasing. Then there are the much commented-on 'crowds,' plus a strangely congruous (or incongruous – depending on your viewpoint) lump of towering concrete known as Chateau Lake Louise. But, frankly, who cares about the waterside claustrophobia? Lake Louise isn't about dodging other tourists. It's about viewing what should be everyone's god-given right to see.

When you're done with gawping, romancing or pledging undying love to your partner on the shimmering lakeshore, try hiking up into the mountainous amphitheater behind. Lake Louise also has a widely lauded ski resort and some equally enticing cross-country options. Thirteen kilometers to the southeast along a winding seasonal road is another spectacularly located body of water, Moraine Lake, which some heretics claim is even more beguiling than its famous sibling.

The village of Lake Louise, just off Hwy 1, is little more than an outdoor shopping mall, a gas station and a handful of hotels. The object of all your yearnings is 5km away by car or an equitable distance on foot along the pleasantly wooded Louise Creek trail, if the bears aren't out on patrol (check at the visitors center).

The Bow Valley Parkway between Banff Town and Lake Louise is slightly slower, but much more scenic, than Hwy 1.

⊙ Sights

★**Lake Louise**   LAKE

Named for Queen Victoria's otherwise anonymous fourth daughter (who also lent her name to the province), Lake Louise is a place that requires multiple viewings. Aside from the standard picture-postcard shot (blue sky, even bluer lake), try visiting at six in the morning, at dusk in August, in the October rain or after a heavy winter storm.

You can rent a canoe from the **Lake Louise Boathouse** (per hour $45; ⊙9am-4pm Jun-Oct) and go for a paddle around the lake. Don't fall overboard – the water is freezing.

Moraine Lake   LAKE

The scenery will dazzle you long before you reach the spectacular deep-teal colored waters of Moraine Lake. The lake is set in the Valley of the Ten Peaks, and the narrow winding road leading to it offers views of these distant imposing summits. As there is little hustle or bustle and lots of beauty,

Lake Louise Area

0 ——————— 4 km
0 ——————— 2 miles

To Golden (75km)

Trans-Canada Hwy

Icefields Pkwy

93

Bow River

Gondola Base Terminal

To Lake Louise Ski Area (4km)

Trail

1

Hi-Lake Louise

Whitehorn Rd

Lake Louise Station Restaurant

Lake Louise Inn

▲ Mt St Piran (2649m)

Little Beehive

Fairmount Chateau Lake Louise

Deer Lodge

Laggan's Bakery

Lake Louise Village

Bow Valley Pkwy

Lake Agnes Teahouse

Mirror Lake

Lake Louise Trailer Campground

▲ Mt Niblock (2976m)

Lake Agnes

Fairview Rd

1A

Big Beehive

Louise Creek Trail

Lake Louise Dr

To Banff (54km)

▲ Mt Whyte (2983m)

Lake Louise Boathouse

Lake Louise

To Banff (52km)

▲ Mt Fairview (2744m)

Saddle Mountain (2433m)

Trans-Canada Hwy

Plain of Six Glaciers

Paradise Creek

Moraine Lake Rd (closed Oct–Jun)

▲ Mt Sheol (2779m)

▲ Mt Aberdeen (3152m)

Paradise Valley

Banff National Park

The Mitre (2886m)

Lake Annette

▲ Mt Lefroy (3423m)

Ringrose Peak (3278m)

▲ Mt Temple (3453m)

Trail

Moraine Creek

Pinicle Mountain (3067m)

Sentinel Pass

▲ Mt Hungabee (3490m)

Eiffel Peak (3084m)

Larch Valley (2360m)

Moraine Lake Lodge

▲ Wenkchemna Peaks (3170m)

Wenkchemna Pass

Moraine Lake Boathouse

▲ Mt Bell (2910m)

Yoho National Park

Eiffel Lake

Trail

Valley of the Ten Peaks

Moraine Lake

Consolation Lakes

▲ Mt Neptuak (3233m)

Alberta

▲ Mt Tuzo (3245m)

Mt Bowlen (3072m)

Mt Fay (3235m)

▲ Mt Babel (3101m)

Kootenay National Park

British Columbia

▲ Mt Deltaform (3424m)

Mt Allen (3301m)

Mt Tonsa (3054m)

Mt Perren (3051m)

Mt Little (3088m)

many people prefer the more rugged and remote setting of Moraine Lake to Lake Louise.

There are some excellent day hikes from the lake, or rent a boat at the **Moraine Lake Boathouse** (per hour $40; ⊙9am-4pm Jun-Oct) and paddle through the glacier-fed waters.

Moraine Lake Rd and its facilities are open from June to early October.

Lake Louise Sightseeing Gondola CABLE CAR (www.lakelouisegondola.com; 1 Whitehorn Rd; round-trip adult/child $28.75/14.25, guided hikes per person $5; ⊙9am-5pm, guided hikes 11am, 1pm & 3pm) To the east of Hwy 1, this sightseeing gondola will lever you to the top of Mt Whitehorn, where the views of the lake and Victoria Glacier are phenomenal. At the top, there's a restaurant and a Wildlife Interpretive Centre where you can partake in 45-minute guided hikes.

🏃 Activities

Hiking
In Lake Louise beauty isn't skin-deep. The hikes behind the stunning views are just as impressive. Most of the classic walks start from Lake Louise and Moraine Lake. Some are straightforward, while others will give even the most seasoned alpinist reason to huff and puff.

From Chateau Lake Louise, two popular day walks head out to alpine-style teahouses perched above the lake. The shorter but slightly harder hike is the 3.4km grunt past **Mirror Lake** up to the Lake Agnes Teahouse on its eponymous body of water. After tea and scones you can trek 1.6km further and higher to the view-embellished **Big Beehive** lookout and Canada's most unexpectedly sited gazebo. Continue on this path down to the Highline Trail to link up with the **Plain of Six Glaciers**, or approach it independently from Chateau Lake Louise along the lakeshore (5.6km one way). Either way, be sure to get close enough for ice-crunching views of the Victoria Glacier. There's another teahouse on this route that supplements its brews with thick-cut sandwiches and spirit-lifting mugs of hot chocolate with marshmallows.

From Moraine Lake, the walk to **Sentinel Pass**, via the stunning **Larch Valley**, is best in the fall when the leaves are beginning to turn. A strenuous day walk with outstanding views of Mt Temple and the surrounding peaks, the hike involves a steep scree-covered last push to the pass. If you're lucky you might spy some rock climbers scaling The Grand Sentinel – a 200m-tall rock spire nearby.

Shorter and easier, the 6km out-and-back **Consolation Lakes Trail** offers that typical Banff juxtaposition of crowded parking lot disappearing almost instantly into raw, untamed wilderness.

In recent years there has been a lot of bear activity in the Moraine Lake area. Because of this, a minimum group size of four has been imposed by the park on some hikes during berry-gathering season (June to September). If you're arriving solo, check on the noticeboard in the information center in Lake Louise for other hikers looking to make up groups.

Skiing & Snowboarding
Lake Louise Ski Area (Map p74; www.skilouise.com; lift tickets from $75), 3km east of Lake Louise Village and 60km northwest of Banff, is marginally larger than Sunshine Village but gets less natural snow. The ample runs, containing plenty of beginner and intermediate terrain, are on four separate mountains, so it's closer to a European ski experience than anything else on offer in Canada. The front side is a good place to get your ski legs back with a good selection of simpler stuff and fantastic views. On the far side there are some great challenges, from the knee-pulverizing moguls of Paradise Bowl to the high-speed cruising of the Larch area. Make sure you grab a deck burger at the Temple Lodge – it's part of the whole experience.

🛏 Sleeping

Lake Louise has a campground, a hostel, a couple of midpriced inns, and a handful of places that fall into the 'special night' category for many travelers.

HI-Lake Louise   HOSTEL $
(☑403-522-2200; www.hihostels.ca; Village Rd; dm/d from $44/123) This is what a hostel should be – clean, friendly, affordable and full of interesting travelers. The building itself is a stunning example of Rockies architecture, with raw timber and stone melding to a rustic aesthetic masterpiece. The dorm rooms are fairly standard, but beware of the private rooms: they are on the small side and a bit overpriced.

Lake Louise Trailer
Campground
CAMPGROUND **$**

(☑ 403-522-3833; off Lake Louise Dr; RV sites $32; ☺ May-Oct) This is the closest campground to the village and your best option if you plan to sleep in a million-star hotel. It's a vast place that has great views of Mt Temple. Steer clear of the sites near the railroad tracks as the thundering trains do wonders for keeping you up all night. This campground is for RVs only.

Deer Lodge
HOTEL **$$**

(☑ 403-410-7417; www.crmr.com; 109 Lake Louise Dr; r from $175) Tucked demurely behind the Chateau Lake Louise, the Deer Lodge is another historic throwback dating from the 1920s. But, although the rustic exterior and creaky corridors can't have changed much since the days of bobbed hair and F Scott Fitzgerald, the refurbished rooms are another matter, replete with new comfy beds and smart boutiquelike furnishings.

TV addicts, beware – there aren't any.

Lake Louise Inn
HOTEL **$$**

(☑ 403-522-3791; www.lakelouiseinn.com; 210 Village Rd; d from $119; @ 🛜 🛋) A large, sprawling resort close to the village that has its merits, including a pool, restaurant and a tiny historic ice-cream chalet. Room quality is variable, with some of the older wings more downbeat and motel-like.

★ Fairmont Chateau
Lake Louise
HOTEL **$$$**

(Map p74; ☑ 403-522-3511; www.fairmont.com/lake-louise; Lake Louise Dr; d from $450; @ 🛜 🛋) This opulent Fairmont enjoys one of the world's most enviable locations on the shores of Lake Louise. Originally built by the Canadian Pacific Railway in the 1890s, the hotel was added to in 1925 and 2004.

While opinions differ on its architectural merits, few deny the luxury and romance of its facilities, which include a spa, fine dining, a mini-museum, fine views and unforgettably grandiose decor. Rooms are comfortable, if a little generic.

Moraine Lake Lodge
HOTEL **$$$**

(☑ 800-522-2777; www.morainelakelodge.com; d $345-599; ☺ Jun-Sep) Few people would shirk at an opportunity to hang around Moraine Lake for a day or three – and here's your chance. The experience here is intimate, personal and private, and the service is famously good.

While the lodge is billed as rustic (ie no TVs), the rooms and cabins offer mountain-inspired luxury with real fireplaces and balconies overlooking *that* view. There's a fine-dining restaurant on-site which wins equal plaudits.

✗ Eating

If you can't scrape together the $43 necessary for afternoon tea in the Lakeview Lounge at the Chateau Lake Louise, reconvene to one of the following.

★ Lake Agnes Teahouse
CAFE **$**

(Lake Agnes Trail; snacks $3-6; ☺ Jun-Oct) You thought the view from Lake Louise was good? Wait till you get up to this precariously perched alpine-style teahouse that seems to hang in the clouds beside ethereal Lake Agnes and its adjacent waterfall. The small log cabin runs on gas power and is hike-in only (3.4km uphill from the Chateau).

Perhaps it's the thinner air or the seductiveness of the surrounding scenery, but the rustic $6 tea and scones here taste just as good as the $43 spread at the Chateau Lake Louise.

Laggan's Bakery
BAKERY **$**

(☑ 403-522-2017; Samson Mall; mains $5-10; ☺ 6am-8pm) Laggan's (named after Lake Louise's original settlement) is a cafeteria/bakery with limited seating that's famously busy in the summer. The pastries and savories aren't legendary, but they're handy hiking snacks and tend to taste better the hungrier you get. The pizza bagels are worth a special mention.

Lake Louise Station Restaurant
CANADIAN **$$**

(mains $15-25; ☺ 11:30am-9:30pm) Restaurants with a theme have to be handled so carefully – thankfully this railway-inspired eatery, at the end of Sentinel Rd, does it just right. You can either dine in the station among the discarded luggage or in one of the dining cars, which are nothing short of elegant. The food is simple yet effective. A must-stop for train-spotters.

ℹ Information

Lake Louise Visitors Centre (Samson Mall, Lake Louise village; ☺ 9am-8pm) Has some good geological displays, a Parks Canada desk and a small film theater.

Jasper National Park

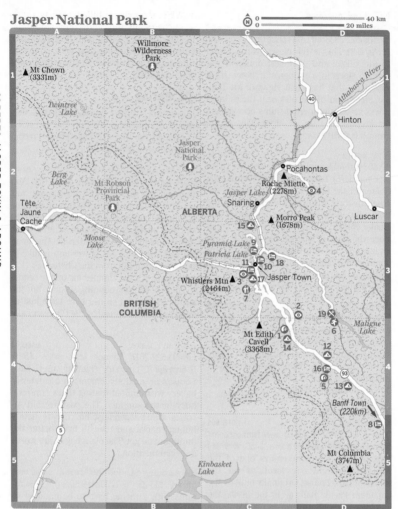

ⓘ Getting There & Around

The bus terminal is basically a marked stop at Samson Mall. The easiest way to get here from Banff is by car or Brewster bus.

Jasper Town & Around

Take Banff, half the annual visitor count, increase the total land area by 40%, and multiply the number of bears, elk, moose and caribou by three. The result: Jasper, a larger, less-trammeled, more wildlife-rich version of the other Rocky Mountains parks. Its rugged backcountry wins admiring plaudits for its vertiginous river canyons, adrenalin-charged mountain-bike trails, rampartlike mountain ranges and delicate ecosystems.

Most people enter Jasper Town from the south via the magnificently Gothic Icefields Parkway that meanders up from Lake Louise amid foaming waterfalls and glacier-sculpted mountains, including iconic Mt Edith Cavell, easily visible from the town. Another option is to take a legendary VIA train from either Edmonton or BC through foothills imbued with fur-trading and aboriginal history.

Jasper National Park

Stacked up against Canada's other national parks, Jasper scores high marks for its hiking, pioneering history (it's the country's eighth-oldest park), easy-to-view wildlife and hut-to-hut backcountry skiing possibilities. Similarly, bike enthusiasts consistently laud it as having one of the best single-track cycling networks in North America.

⊙ Sights

Jasper Tramway   CABLE CAR
(Map p92; ☑ 780-852-3093; www.jaspertramway.com; Whistlers Mountain Rd; adult/child $32/16; ⊙ 9am-8pm Apr-Oct) If the average, boring views from Jasper just aren't blowing your hair back, go for a ride up this sightseeing tramway. The vista is sure to take your breath away, with views, on a clear day, of the Columbia Icefield 75km to the south.

From the top of the tram you can take the steep 1.5km hike to the summit of Whistlers Mountain, where the outlook is even better. The tramway is about 7km south of Jasper Town along Whistlers Mountain Rd, off the Icefields Parkway.

Miette Hot Springs   SPA
(Map p92; www.parkscanada.gc.ca/hotsprings; Miette Rd; adult/child/family $6/5/18.50; ⊙ 8:30am-10:30pm) More remote than Banff's historic springs, Miette Hot Springs, 'discovered' in 1909, are 61km northeast of Jasper off Hwy 16, near the park boundary. The soothing waters are kept at a pleasant 39°C and are especially enjoyable when the fall snow is falling on your head and steam envelops the crowd.

There are a couple of hot pools and a cold one too – just to get the heart going – so it's best to stick a toe in before doing your cannonball.

You can hike 1km from the parking lot to the source of the springs, which is overlooked by the original aquacenter built in the 1930s.

Patricia & Pyramid Lakes   LAKE
There's nothing like seeing the mountains reflected in a small deserted alpine lake. These two lakes, a convenient 7km from town, fit that order nicely. Abundant activities are available on the water, with canoes, kayaks and windsurfers available for rent. For those wanting to stay dry, there are hiking and horseback-riding trails too.

Keep your eyes peeled for animals – these are prime spotting locations.

Lakes Annette & Edith   LAKE
On the opposite side of the highway to the town, Lakes Annette and Edith are popular for water activities in the summer and skating in the winter. If you're brave and it's very hot, Annette is good for a quick summer dip – just remember the water was in a glacier not too long ago! Edith is more frequented by kayakers and boaters.

Both are ringed by cycling/hiking trails and picnic areas. The trail that circumnavigates Lake Annette is wheelchair-accessible.

Jasper Town to Maligne Lake   SCENIC DRIVE
The inspiring 46km drive between Jasper and Maligne Lake is almost obligatory for anyone with a day to spare in Jasper. The road twists and turns and it would seem that at every corner there is an opportunity to see some wildlife. This is one of the best places in Jasper to look for deer, elk, moose and, if you're lucky, bear.

The ideal time to see wildlife is early in the morning.

Maligne Canyon   CANYON
A steep, narrow gorge shaped by a river flowing at its base, this canyon at its narrowest is only a few meters wide and drops a stomach-turning 50m beneath your feet.

Jasper Town

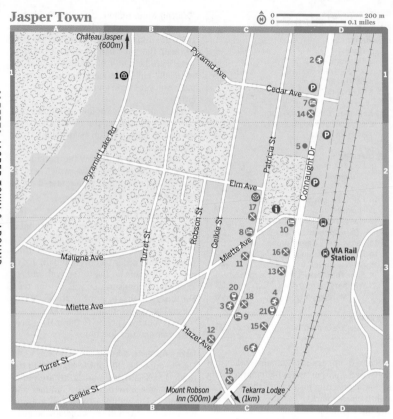

Jasper Town

◎ Sights
1 Jasper-Yellowhead Museum &
   Archives B1

⊕ Activities, Courses & Tours
2 Jasper Adventure Centre D1
  Jasper Walks & Talks ....(see 4)
3 Maligne Rafting Adventures.................C3
  Maligne Tours....................................(see 3)
4 Rocky Mountain River Guides.............. C3
5 SunDog Tour Company D2
6 Vicious Cycle C4

⊜ Sleeping
7 Astoria Hotel..D1
8 Athabasca Hotel C3
9 Park Place Inn...C4
10 Whistlers Inn..C3

⊗ Eating
11 Coco's Café C3
12 Evil Dave's Grill C4
13 Fiddle River Seafood Co C3
14 Jasper Pizza Place D1
15 Karouzo's..C4
16 Other Paw...C3
17 Raven Bistro...C2
18 Something Else......................................C3
19 Villa Caruso C4

⊝ Drinking & Nightlife
  Atha-B Nightclub..............................(see 8)
20 Horseshoe Club C3
21 Jasper Brewing Co C3

Crossed by six bridges, various trails lead out from the parking area on Maligne Lake Rd. In the winter waterfalls freeze solid into sheets of white ice and are popular with ice climbers.

Maligne Lake
LAKE

Almost 50km from Jasper at the end of the road that bears its name, 22km-long Maligne Lake is the recipient of a lot of hype. It is billed as one of the most beautiful lakes within the park and there's no denying its aesthetics: the baby blue water and a craning circle of rocky, photogenic peaks are feasts for the eyes.

Although the north end of the lake is heavy with the summer tour-bus brigade, most of the rest of the shoreline is accessible only by foot or boat – hence it's quieter. Numerous campgrounds are available lakeside and are ideal for adventurous kayakers and backcountry hikers. Moose and grizzly bears are also sometimes seen here.

The **Maligne Lake Boathouse** (Map p92; ☑780-852-3370; boats per hour/day $30/90) rents canoes for a paddle around the lake. Not many people paddle all the way to Spirit Island – the lake's most classic view; it would take you all day. If you are really keen to see it, **Maligne Tours** (Map p94; ☑780-852-3370; www.malignelake.com; 616 Patricia St; adult/child $59/35; ☑10am-5pm May-Oct) will zip you out there on its 1½-hour boat tours to the island.

Jasper-Yellowhead Museum & Archives
MUSEUM

(Map p94; ☑780-852-3013; www.jaspermuseum. org; 400 Pyramid Lake Rd; admission $6; ☑10am-5pm) Poke your head into this museum if it's raining, snowing or too hot. Even if the weather is nice, it does an ample job of telling the Jasper story and the stories of those who arrived here to make it into the town it is today.

🏃 Activities

Cycling

Jasper is way better than Banff for single-track mountain biking; in fact, it's one of the best places in Canada for the sport. Many routes are within striking distance of the town. Flatter, on-road options include the long-distance grunt along the Icefields Parkway. The holy grail for experienced off-road bikers is the **Valley of the Five Lakes**, varied and scenic with plenty of places where you can let rip. For more information, get a copy of *Mountain Biking Guide, Jasper National Park* from the Jasper Information Centre.

Vicious Cycle (Map p94; ☑780-852-1111; www.viciouscyclecanada.com; 630 Connaught Dr; per day from $32; ☑9am-6pm) can sort out bike rentals and offer additional trail tips.

Hiking

Even when judged against other Canadian national parks, Jasper's trail network is mighty, and with comparatively fewer people than its sister park to the south, you've a better chance of seeing more wildlife and fewer humans.

Initiate yourself on the interpretative **Discovery Trail**, an 8km easy hike that encircles the town and highlights its natural, historical and railway heritage.

Other short trails include the 3.2km **Mary Schäffer Loop** by Maligne Lake, named for one of the earliest European visitors to the area; the **Old Fort Loop** (3.5km) to the site of an old fur-trading post; and the 9km **Mina and Riley Lakes Loop** that leads out directly from the town.

Further away and slightly harder is the famous 9.1km **Path of the Glacier Trail** below the impressive face of Mt Edith Cavell, which takes you to the foot of the Angel Glacier through the wildflowers of the Cavell meadows.

The blue-ribbon multiday hike is the **Skyline Trail**, unusual in that almost all of its 46km are on or above the tree line, affording amazing cross-park views. The hike is usually split over two days, starting at Maligne Lake and emerging near Maligne Canyon on Maligne Lake Rd. You can pitch your tent in a campground or stay in the historic Shovel Pass Lodge.

The leaflet *Day-Hikers' Guide to Jasper National Park* has descriptions of most of the park's easy walks, while the backcountry visitors guide *Jasper National Park* details longer trails and backcountry campsites and suggests itineraries for hikes of two to 10 days. If you're hiking overnight, you must obtain a backcountry permit (per person per night $10, or buy a season pass for $69) from Parks Canada in the Jasper Information Centre.

Horseback Riding

Incredible fully guided summer pack trips head into the roadless Tonquin Valley where you are bivouacked in the backcountry (but comfortable) Tonquin Amethyst Lake Lodge. The trips are run by **Tonquin Valley Adventures** (☑780-852-1188; www.tonquinadventures.com; 3-/4-/5-day trips $795/1050/1295) and include accommodations, meals and complimentary fishing trips on Amethyst Lake.

JASPER IN WINTER

Half of Jasper shuts down in the winter; the other half just adapts and metamorphoses into something just as good (if not better) than its summertime self. Lakes become skating rinks; hiking and biking routes (and some roads) become cross-country skiing trails; waterfalls become ice climbs; and – last but by no means least – prices become far more reasonable.

The best natural outdoor skating rink is on Lac Beauvert in front of the Fairmont Jasper Park Lodge, an area that is floodlit after dark. More skating can be found 6km northeast of the town on Pyramid Lake.

The park has an incredible 200km of cross-country skiing trails. Routes less prone to an early snow melt are the **Pyramid Lake Fire Road**, the **Meeting of the Waters** (along a closed section of Hwy 93A), the **Moab Lake Trail** and the **Mt Edith Cavell Road**. Relatively safe, but dramatic, backcountry skiing can be found in the Tonquin Valley, where you can overnight in a couple of lodges. See www.tonquinvalley.com for more details.

Slightly less athletic is the iconic three-hour **Maligne Canyon Ice Walk** offered by **Jasper Adventure Centre** (Map p94; ☑780-852-5595; www.jasperadventurecentre.com; 618 Connaught Dr; adult/child $55/25), a walk through a series of frozen waterfalls viewable from December to April. Extremists tackle these slippery behemoths with rappels and ice axes.

Skiing & Snowboarding

Jasper National Park's only downhill ski area is **Marmot Basin** (Map p92; www.skimarmot.com; Marmot Basin Rd; day pass adult/child $72/58), which lies 19km southwest of town off Hwy 93A. Though not legendary, the presence of 86 runs and the longest highspeed quad chairlift in the Rockies, mean Marmot is no pushover, and its relative isolation compared to the trio of ski areas in Banff means shorter lift lines.

On-site are some cross-country trails and a predictably expensive day lodge, but no overnight accommodations. Regular shuttles link to Jasper Town in season. Seriously cold weather can drift in suddenly off the mountains, so be sure to dress appropriately.

White-Water Rafting

There's nothing like glacial waters to fight the summer heat. The Jasper area has lots of good rafting opportunities, from raging to relaxed, on the **Maligne, Sunwapta** and **Athabasca Rivers**. The season runs from May to September.

Maligne Rafting Adventures   RAFTING
(Map p94; ☑780-852-3370; www.raftjasper.com; 616 Patricia St; trips from $59) Everything from float trips to grade II and III adventures, plus overnight trips.

Rocky Mountain River Guides   RAFTING
(Map p94; ☑780-852-3777; www.rmriverguides.com; 626 Connaught Dr; trips from $64) Fun for beginners and also for more experienced river-runners.

Tours

There is a variety of tour companies and booking centers in Jasper. They run a plethora of tours, including horseback riding, boat trips, wildlife-watching, hiking, and other outdoor activities.

Jasper Walks & Talks   HIKING
(Map p94; ☑780-852-4994; www.walksntalks.com; 626 Connaught Dr) Walks & Talks Jasper leads small groups of people on personalized tours that include two-hour wildlife tours ($60) at 6.45am from June to October, and Mount Edith Cavell Meadows picnics ($85) departing at 9.30am from June to October.

SunDog Tour Company   GUIDED TOUR
(Map p94; ☑780-852-4056, 888-786-3641; www.sundogtours.com; Connaught Dr) SunDog Tour Company is one of many tour companies and booking centers in Jasper. It runs a whole host of tours, including trips to the icefields, train rides, boat rides, wildlife-viewing, rafting, horseback riding and more.

🛏 Sleeping

Despite its reputation as a quiet antidote to Banff, Jasper Town still gets busy in the summer. Book ahead or consider visiting in the less-crowded late winter/early spring shoulder season when the deserted mountainscapes (best accessed on cross-country skis) take on a whole new dimension.

Accommodations in Jasper are generally cheaper than Banff, but that's not really saying much. Jasper's 10 park campgrounds are open from mid-May to September/October. One (Wapiti) is partly open year-round. Four of them take reservations. For information, contact **Parks Canada** (☑780-852-6176; 500 Connaught Dr) at the Jasper Information Centre.

Several places outside the town proper offer bungalows (usually wooden cabins) that are only open in summer. There are considerable winter discounts.

YHA Maligne Canyon HOSTEL $
(Map p92; ☑1-877-852-0781; www.hihostels.ca; Maligne Lake Rd; dm $24.20) ✈ Well positioned for winter cross-country skiing and summer sorties along the Skyline Trail, this very basic hostel is poised a little too close to the road to merit a proper 'rustic' tag. Die-hards can get back to nature with six-bed dorms, outhouse toilets and regular visits to the water pump.

Whistlers Campground CAMPGROUND $
(Map p92; ☑780-852-6177; Whistlers Rd; campsites/RV sites $22.50/38; ☺May-Oct) Ever spent the night with 780 other campers? Well, here is your chance. This mini camping city isn't particularly private, but it is the closest option to Jasper Town. Unbelievably, it regularly fills up in the high season. There are interpretive programs, flush toilets and fire pits.

HI-Jasper HOSTEL $
(Map p92; ☑780-852-3215; www.hihostels.ca; Whistlers Mountain Rd; dm/d $30.80/78.10; @ 🛜) It would be easy not to like this hostel. With dorm rooms that sleep upward of 40 people, giving it that distinctive refugee-camp feel, and a location just far enough from town that the walk is a killer, it's already two strikes down. Despite all of this, though, it's a great place to stay.

The proximity of roommates and relative isolation foster a real community feel, and the nice interior, friendly staff and pristine surroundings make it that much better.

Snaring River Campground CAMPGROUND $
(Map p92; Hwy 16; campsites $15.70; ☺May-Sep) Situated 17km north of Jasper Town, this basic campground – the park's most primitive and isolated – is the perfect antidote to the busy campgrounds found elsewhere in the park.

Athabasca Hotel HOTEL $$
(Map p94; ☑780-852-3386; www.athabascahotel.com; 510 Patricia St; r with shared/pirvate bathroom $99/175; @ 🛜) If you can take the stuffed moose heads, noisy downstairs barnightclub and service that is sometimes as fickle as the mountain weather, you'll have no problems at the Athabasca (or Atha-B, as it's known). Centrally located with an attached restaurant and small, but comfortable, rooms (many with shared bathroom) it's been around since 1929 and is the best bargain in town.

★**Park Place Inn** BOUTIQUE HOTEL $$$
(Map p94; ☑780-852-9970; www.parkplaceinn.com; 623 Patricia St; r from $229; @) Giving nothing away behind its rather ordinary exterior among a parade of downtown shops, the Park Place is a head-turner as soon as you ascend the stairs to its plush open lobby. The 14 self-proclaimed heritage rooms are well deserving of their superior status, with marble surfaces, fine local art, claw-foot baths and a general air of refinement and luxury. The service is equally professional.

Tekarra Lodge HOTEL $$$
(☑780-852-3058; www.tekarralodge.com; Hwy 93A; d from $219; ☺May-Oct) The most atmospheric cabins in the park are set next to the Athabasca River amid tall trees and splendid tranquility. Hardwood floors, wood-paneled walls plus fireplaces and kitchenettes inspire coziness. It's only 1km from the town, but has a distinct backcountry feel.

Fairmont Jasper Park Lodge HOTEL $$$
(Map p92; ☑780-852-3301; www.fairmont.com/jasper; 1 Old Lodge Rd; r from $600; @ 🛜) Sitting on the shore of Lake Beauvert and surrounded by manicured grounds and mountain peaks, this classic old lodge is deservedly popular. With a country-club-meets-1950s-holiday-camp air, the amenity-filled cabins and chalets are a throwback to a more opulent era.

The lodge's gem is its main lounge, open to the public, with stupendous lake views. It's filled with log furniture, chandeliers and fireplaces and is the best place in town to write a postcard over a quiet cocktail. There are often off-season discounts.

Whistlers Inn HOTEL $$$
(Map p94; ☑780-852-9919; www.whistlersinn.com; cnr Connaught Dr & Miette Ave; r $195; @🗢🗶) A central location and above-standard rooms give Whistlers an edge over many of its rivals. The rooftop hot tub alone is worth spending the night for – watch the sun dip behind the hills as the recuperative waters soak away the stress of the day. What more could you ask for?

Astoria Hotel HOTEL $$$
(Map p94; ☑780-852-3351; www.astoriahotel.com; 404 Connaught Dr; d from $188; 🗢) With its gabled Bavarian roof, the Astoria is one of the town's most distinctive pieces of architecture and one of an original trio of Jasper hotels that has been owned by the same family since the 1920s. Journeyman rooms are functional and comfortable, and are bolstered by the presence of a downstairs bar (De'd Dog) and restaurant (Papa George's).

Coast Pyramid Lake Resort HOTEL $$$
(Map p92; ☑780-852-4900; www.coasthotels.com; Pyramid Lake Rd; d from $249; ☺May-Sep) This large property has fantastic views of the lake and great access to it. The design is a bit strange, with a huge swath of concrete driveway bisecting the hotel. The chalet-style buildings fan up the hill, giving most rooms an unencumbered view of the lake.

Ample opportunities for lake fun abound, with canoes for rent and a small beach to hang out on. The prices are a bit on the high side and it would do well to improve some of the finishing touches.

Mount Robson Inn MOTEL $$$
(☑780-852-3327; www.mountrobsoninn.com; 902 Connaught Dr; r incl breakfast from $255; ✴@🗢) A clean, plush place laid out motel-style on the edge of Jasper Town which offers hot tubs, on-site restaurant and a substantial breakfast.

Château Jasper HOTEL $$$
(☑780-852-5644; www.mpljasper.com; 96 Geikie St; r from $242; ✴@🗢🗶) The Château Jas-per is more conference hotel than castle, though with the right expectations, it shouldn't disappoint. It's a 700m stroll into the town center.

🍴 Eating

Jasper's cuisine is mainly hearty post-hiking fare. Inexplicably, there's an abundance of Greek-themed places. Most of the restaurants are located in the town around Connaught Dr and Patricia St. Outlying nexuses such as Maligne Lake and the Whistlers have cafeteria-style restaurants that close in the winter.

★Other Paw CAFE, BAKERY $
(Map p94; ☑780-852-2253; 610 Connaught Dr; snacks $2-6; ☺7am-6pm) An offshoot of The Bear's Paw, a larger cafe around the corner, the Other Paw offers the same insanely addictive mix of breads, pastries, muffins and coffee, but it stays open longer, plus it's right opposite the train station. The aromatic memory of its white chocolate and raspberry scones is enough to jerk your senses into action during the last few kilometers of a lengthy hike/bike/ski.

Coco's Café CAFE $
(Map p94; ☑780-852-4550; 608 Patricia St; mains $5-10; ☺8am-4pm) 🍃 Rating Jasper's best overall cafe is a toss-up for some punters, but few disagree that Coco's usually comes out on top on the breakfast front. There's not much room inside, but plenty of bodies are content to cram in to plan hikes, trade bear sightings or compare rucksack burns. Ethical eaters are well catered for, with tofu scrambles and fair-trade coffee.

View Restaurant FAST FOOD $
(Map p92; Maligne Lake Lodge; snacks $4-10; ☺9am-7pm) On first impressions this aptly named restaurant (behold the view!) at the head of Maligne Lake is just another overpriced cafeteria for tourists. But, beyond the sandwiches, soups and summer jobbers, this place serves up some of the best pastries, muffins and cinnamon buns in the park.

Jasper Pizza Place PIZZA $$
(Map p94; ☑780-852-3225; 402 Connaught Dr; pizzas $13-16; ☺11am-11pm) Ask a local (if you can find one) where to grab a cheap meal and they'll mention this place. There's a method to the queuing madness, if you're prepared to stick around long enough

to fight for a table. Not surprisingly, the much-sought-after pizzas are rather good.

Karouzo's STEAKHOUSE $$
(Map p94; 780-852-4640; www.karouzojasper. com; 626 Connaught Dr; mains $15-30; 11am-11pm Mar-Oct;) Flying the flag for simple, family-friendly restaurants serving big portions from internationally themed menus (with an inevitable Greek subsection), Karouzo's suceeds in numerous fields – especially steak.

Something Else MEDITERRANEAN, STEAKHOUSE $$
(Map p94; 621 Patricia St; mains $13-24; 11am-11pm;) Essentially a Greek restaurant, Something Else wears many hats (American, Italian, Cajun) and doesn't always succeed. What it *is* good for is space (even on a Saturday night), decent beer, menu variety, copious kids' options and the good old homemade Greek stuff. Try the lamb or chicken souvlaki.

Raven Bistro MEDITERRANEAN $$
(Map p94; 780-852-5151; 504 Patricia St; mains $10-28; 5-10pm;) It's not every day that Jasper sprouts a new restaurant, so make the most of this small, tastefully designed bistro that pushes vegetarian dishes, encourages shared plates and wouldn't be out of place in a small Spanish city.

Villa Caruso STEAKHOUSE $$$
(Map p94; 780-852-3920; 640 Connaught Dr; mains $22-36; 11am-11:30pm) Carnivore, pescatarian and vegetarian needs are all catered for here. Plush wood trimmings and great views are the perfect appetizer for a fine meal out.

Evil Dave's Grill CANADIAN, FUSION $$$
(Map p94; 780-852-3323; www.evildaves.com; 622 Patricia St; mains $22-29; 4-11pm) There's nothing evil about Dave's, one of a handful of local attempts to bury Jasper's dodgy image as a bastion of family-friendly, post-hiking grub that fills stomachs rather than excites taste buds. The excellent fusion food's all over the map, with Caribbean, Middle Eastern and Japanese influences lighting up the fish and beef.

Fiddle River Seafood Co SEAFOOD $$$
(Map p94; 780-852-3032; 620 Connaught Dr; mains $22-32; 5-10pm) Being almost 1600km from the sea makes some customers understandably leery, but Jasper's premier seafood joint is no slouch. Pull up a seat near the window and tuck into one of the innovative creations, such as pumpkin-seed-crusted trout.

Drinking & Nightlife

Jasper Brewing Co BREWERY, PUB
(Map p94; 780-852-4111; www.jasperbrewingco. ca; 624 Connaught Dr; 11:30am-1am) Open since 2005, this brewpub, the first of its type in a Canadian national park, uses glacial water to make its fine ales, including the signature Rockhopper IPA or – slightly more adventurous – the Rocket Ridge Raspberry Ale. It's a sit-down affair, with TVs and a good food menu.

Atha-B Nightclub BAR, CLUB
(Map p94; 780-852-3386; Athabasca Hotel, 510 Patricia St; 4pm-2am) Nightclubbing in a national park is about as congruous as wildlife-viewing in downtown Toronto. Bear this in mind before you hit the Atha-B, a pub-slash-nightclub off the lobby of the Athabasca Hotel where mullets are still high fashion and the carpet's probably radioactive.

Horseshoe Club CLUB
(Map p94; 780-852-6262; www.thehorseshoe-club.ca; 610 Patricia St; 9pm-3am) Local hive of scary Led Zeppelin tribute bands.

Information

Jasper Information Centre (Map p94; 780-852-6176; www.parkscanada.gc.ca/jasper; 500 Connaught Dr; 8am-7pm) Informative office in historic 'parkitecture' building.

Post office (Map p94; 502 Patricia St; 9am-5pm Mon-Fri)

Seton General Hospital (780-852-3344; 518 Robson St)

Getting There & Around

BUS

The **bus station** (Map p94; www.greyhound. ca; 607 Connaught Dr) is at the train station. Greyhound buses serve Edmonton ($67, from 4½ hours, four daily), Prince George ($64, five hours, one daily), Kamloops ($70, six hours, two daily) and Vancouver ($115, from 11½ hours, two daily).

Brewster Transportation (www.brewster. ca), departing from the same station, operates express buses to Lake Louise village ($74, 4½ hours, at least one daily) and Banff Town ($84, 5½ hours, at least one daily).

The **Maligne Valley Shuttle** (www.maligne-lake.com) runs a May to October bus from Jasper Town to Maligne Lake via Maligne Canyon. Fares are one way/return $25/50.

CAR

International car-rental agencies have offices in Jasper Town.

If you're in need of a taxi, call **Jasper Taxi** (☑780-852-3600), which has metered cabs.

TRAIN

VIA Rail (www.viarail.ca) offers triweekly train services west to Vancouver ($125, 20 hours) and east to Toronto ($340, 62 hours). In addition, there is a triweekly service to Prince Rupert, BC ($102, 32 hours). Call or check at the **train station** (607 Connaught Dr) for exact schedule and fare details.

SOUTHERN ALBERTA

The national parks of Banff and Jasper and the cities of Calgary and Edmonton grab most of the headlines in Alberta, leaving the expansive south largely forgotten. Here, flat farmland is interrupted by deep coulees or canyons that were caused by flooding at the end of the last ice age. Another symbolic feature of the landscape is the towering hoodoos, funky arid sculptures that look like sand-colored Seussian realizations dominating the horizon. History abounds in both the recent Head-Smashed-In Buffalo Jump and the not so recent Dinosaur Provincial Park, two areas preserving the past that have attained Unesco World Heritage status.

Natural wonders are plentiful in this sleepy corner of the province. The dusty dry badlands around Drumheller open up into wide open prairies to the east that stretch all the way to the Cyprus Hills of western Saskatchewan. To the west there is Waterton Lakes National Park, with some of the most spectacular scenery in the Rockies – yet still under the radar of most visitors.

Drumheller

Founded on coal but now committed to another subterranean resource – dinosaur bones – Drumheller is a small (some would say 'waning') town set amid Alberta's enigmatic badlands. It acts as the nexus of the so-called Dinosaur Trail. While paleontology is a serious business here (the nearby Royal Tyrrell Museum is as much research center as tourist site), Drumheller has

cashed in on its Jurassic heritage – sometimes shamelessly. Aside from mocked-up stegosauruses on almost every street corner and dino-related prefixes to more than a few business names, there's the large matter of a 26m-high fiberglass T rex that haunts a large tract of downtown.

But don't let the paleontological civic pride deter you: once you get beyond the kitsch, the town itself is has a certain je ne sais quoi. The summers are hot and the deep-cut river valley in which Drumheller sits provides a much-needed break to the monotony of the prairies. Hoodoos dominate this badland landscape which has featured in many a movie, Westerns mainly.

◉ Sights & Activities

Horseshoe Canyon   CANYON
The baddest of the badlands can be seen at Hosreshoe Canyon, a spectacular chasm cut into the otherwise flat prairie located 17km west of Drumheller on Hwy 9. A large sign in the parking lot explains the geology of the area, while trails lead down into the canyon. There, stripey coloured rock reveals millions of years of geological history (beware: it's very slippery when wet). There are helicopter rides if you're flush ($50/100 for 5/10 minutes).

Dinosaur Trail & Hoodoo Drive   SCENIC DRIVE
Drumheller is on the Dinosaur Trail, a 48km loop that runs northwest from town and includes Hwys 837 and 838; the scenery is quite worth the drive. Badlands and river views await you at every turn.

The loop takes you past **Midland Provincial Park** (no camping), where you can take a self-guided hike; across the Red Deer River on the free, cable-operated **Bleriot Ferry**, which has been running since 1913; and to vista points – including the eagle's-eye **Orkney Viewpoint** – overlooking the area's impressive canyons.

The 25km Hoodoo Drive starts about 18km southeast of Drumheller on Hwy 10; the route is usually done as an out-and-back with Wayne as the turnaround point. Along this drive you'll find the best examples of **hoodoos**: weird, eroded, mushroomlike columns of sandstone rock. This area was the site of a once-prosperous coal-mining community, and the **Atlas Mine** is now preserved as a provincial historic site. Take the side trip on Hwy 10X (which includes 11 bridges in 6km) from Rosedale to the small community of

Wayne, population 27 and fast approaching ghost-town status.

★ Royal Tyrrell Museum of Palaeontology
MUSEUM

(☑403-823-7707; www.tyrrellmuseum.com; adult/child $11/6; ☺ 9am-9pm; 🖫) This fantastic museum is one of the preeminent dinosaur museums on the planet. It's not an overstatement to say that no trip to Alberta is complete without a visit to this amazing facility. Children will love the interactive displays and everyone will be in awe of the numerous complete dino-skeletons.

There are opportunities to get among the badlands on a guided tour and to discover your own dino treasures either on a guided hike or a dinosaur dig. You'll feel like you're behind the scenes of *Jurassic Park* – and in many ways this is the real Jurassic Park.

World's Largest Dinosaur
LANDMARK

(60 1st Ave W; admission $3; ☺10am-6pm; 🖫) Warning – cheesy tourist attraction ahead! In a town filled to the brim with dinosaurs, this T rex is the king of them all and features in the *Guinness Book of Records*. Standing 26m above a parking lot, it dominates the Drumheller skyline.

It's big, not at all scary and cost more than a million bucks to build, which explains the admission price to go up the 106 steps for the view from its mouth. Kids love it and, truth be told, the view *is* pretty good. Ironically, the dinosaur isn't even Jurassically accurate; at 46m long, it's about 4.5 times bigger than its extinct counterpart.

Dinosaur Discovery Museum
MUSEUM

(☑403-823-6666; www.fossilworld.com; 1381 North Dinosaur Trail; admission $6; ☺9:30am-7pm; 🖫) If the Tyrrell didn't satisfy your kids completely, this place ought to, while lightening your wallet in the process. On top of the admission fee, you'll pay extra for your kids to do a fossil dig ($12) or scale a climbing wall ($6). There *is* some real dino-related stuff here, but most of it isn't local.

🛏 Sleeping

The quality of accommodations is limited in Drumheller, so book ahead to ensure you're not stuck with something you don't like, or worse, nothing at all.

River Grove Campground & Cabins
CAMPGROUND $

(☑403-823-6655; www.camprivergrove.com; 25 Poplar St; campsites/RV sites/tepees/cabins from

$32/38/64/119; ☺May-Sep; 🐾) Right in town and close to the big dinosaur, this is a pleasant campground with lots of amenities. The tent facilities are alright, with a few shady trees to keep you cool in the hot summer sun. You can even rent a tepee for the night, although the Stoney people likely didn't have concrete floors in theirs.

Heartwood Inn & Spa
INN $$

(☑403-823-6495; www.innsatheartwood.com; 320 N Railway Ave E; d $149-275; @) Standing head and shoulders above most of the accommodations in town, this lovely country inn is awesome. The small rooms are luxurious, comfortable and tastefully done. It has an onsite spa facility that will welcome you like a queen or king.

All the rooms have Jacuzzis, and there are romance packages available: the staff decorate your room with candles and rose petals, draw you a bath made for two and let you handle the rest.

Taste the Past B&B
B&B $$

(☑403-823-5889; 281 2nd St W; s/d $100/125) This converted turn-of-the-century house has evolved into a cozy downtown B&B. All rooms have a private bathroom, and there is a shared facility downstairs. With only three rooms, this feels more like staying with friends – and by the end of your stay, that's often what it is.

✗ Eating & Drinking

Whif's Flapjack House
CANADIAN $

(☑403-823-7595; 801 N Dinosaur Trail; mains $6-10; ☺6am-2pm) The name is the menu: waffles, hamburgers, ice cream, flapjacks and salad. Big portions, a miniature train track suspended from the ceiling, and good value are all found at this local greasy spoon.

Bernie and the Boys Bistro
DINER $

(☑403-823-3318; www.bernieandtheboys.com; 305 4th St W; burgers $6-8; ☺11am-8:30pm Tue-Sat) Bistro it isn't. On the contrary, Bernie's is one of those small-town family-run diners that have replenished appetites on many a lengthy road trip. Join the queue (the place is small *and* popular!) for big, fresh Albertan burgers and legendary milkshakes.

Vietnamese Noodle House
VIETNAMESE $

(☑403-823-2000; 202 2nd St W; mains $9-12; ☺noon-11pm) If you're looking for something quick that isn't a burger the Noodle House might cut it. It's a long ways from Saigon in both geography and authenticity, but it's economical and cheerful and offers a couple of well-stacked Western food options.

★**Last Chance Saloon**   BAR
(☑403-823-9189; Hwy 10X, Wayne; ☺11:30am-midnight) In a land partial to fast-food franchises, the words 'there's nowhere else remotely like it' are a backhanded compliment. For a taste of something completely different, take the 15-minute drive from Drumheller to the tiny town of Wayne to find this former hell-raising bar-hotel turned Harley Davidson hangout.

Last Chance is a classic Western saloon, but without a hint of tourist kitsch. Check out the mining relics, Brownie cameras, old cigarette tins, fully functioning band-box, and the brick that somebody tossed through the window circa 1913. The food (mains from $4.50) is almost an afterthought – bog-standard burgers with optional beans or fries – but it'll fill you up and give you a little longer to ponder the unique offbeat atmosphere.

ⓘ Information

Tourist information center (☑403-823-1331; www.traveldrumheller.com; 60 1 Ave W; ☺9am-9pm) At the foot of the T rex. The entrance to the beast's entrails is in the same building.

ⓘ Getting There & Away

Greyhound Canada runs buses from the **bus station** (308 Centre St) to Calgary ($38, 1¾ hours, two daily) and Edmonton ($68, seven hours, two daily).

Hammerhead Tours runs a full-day tour ($90) from Calgary to the Drumheller badlands and Royal Tyrrell Museum.

Dinosaur Provincial Park

Where *The Lost World* meets *Little House on the Prairie*, **Dinosaur Provincial Park** (☑403-378-4344; www.dinosaurpark.ca; off Hwy 544; ☺8:30am-5pm Sun-Thu, to 7pm Fri & Sat) **FREE** isn't just the Grand Canyon in miniature – it's also a Unesco World Heritage site. The final resting place of thousands of dinosaurs, it's a stellar spot to check out some fossils. It's halfway between Calgary and Medicine Hat, and some 48km northeast of Brooks. From Hwy 1, take Secondary Hwy 873 to Hwy 544.

The park comes at you by surprise as the chasm in which it lives opens before your feet from the grassy plain. A dehydrated fantasy landscape, there are hoodoos and colorful rock formations aplenty. Where 75 million years ago dinosaurs cruised around a tropical landscape, it's now a hot and barren place to be. Make sure you dress for the weather with sunscreen and water at the ready.

The 81-sq-km park begs to be explored, with wildflowers, the odd rattler in the rocks and, if you're lucky, maybe even a T rex. This isn't just a tourist attraction, but a hotbed for science; paleontologists have uncovered countless skeletons, which now reside in many of the finest museums around the globe.

There are five short interpretive **hiking trails** to choose from and a **driving loop** runs through part of the park, but to preserve the fossils, access to 70% of the park is restricted. The off-limits areas may be seen only on **guided hikes** (adult/child $14/8) or **bus tours** (adult/child $12/8), which operate from late May to October. The hikes and tours are popular, and you should reserve a place.

The park's **visitors center** (☑403-378-4342; adult/child $3/2; ☺8:30am-5pm) has a small yet effective series of dino displays. Some complete skeletons and exhibits on the practicalities of paleontology are worthy of a look.

The park's **campground** (☑403-378-3700; campsites/RV sites $23/29, reservations $10) sits in a hollow by a small creek. The ample tree cover is a welcome reprieve from the volcanic sun. Laundry facilities and hot showers are available, as is a small shop for last-minute supplies. This is a popular place, especially with the RV set, so phone ahead.

Head-Smashed-In Buffalo Jump

The story behind the place with the strangest name of any attraction in Alberta is one of ingenuity and resourcefulness and is key to the First Nations' (and Canada's) cultural heritage. For thousands of years, the Blackfoot people used the cliffs near the town of Fort Macleod to hunt buffalo. **Head-Smashed-In Buffalo Jump** (☑403-553-2731; www.head-smashed-in.com; Secondary Hwy 785; adult/child $10/5; ☺10am-5pm) was a marvel of simple ingenuity. When the buffalo massed in the open prairie, braves from the tribe would gather and herd them toward the towering cliffs. As the animals got

BAR U RANCH & THE COWBOY TRAIL

Cowboy culture is woven into the cultural fabric of southern Alberta, but to experience it in its rustic purity you have to exit Calgary and its Stetson-wearing oil entrepreneurs and head south through the province's verdant rolling foothills on Hwy 22, aka the Cowboy Trail. What is today a smooth asphalt road frequented by shiny SUVs was once a dirt track used by dust-encrusted cow herders who drove their cattle north to the Canadian Pacific Railway in Calgary. Unperturbed by the modern oil rush, these rolling foothills are still punctuated by giant ranches, one of which, **Bar U Ranch** (www.friendsofthebaru. ca; adult/child $7.80/3.90; ⊘ 9am-5pm May-Sep), has been converted into a historic site by Parks Canada for posterity.

Founded in 1882, Bar U was once one of the largest commercial ranches in the world, covering 160,000 acres. John Ware, a freed African-American slave and, allegedly, Alberta's first cowboy, was an early visitor. A decade later, the ranch's horses were trained by Harry Longabaugh (known to history and Hollywood as the Sundance Kid) a dapper bank robber who worked at the ranch in 1891 before taking up a more lucrative career holding up banks with the Wild Bunch. The next visitor was more regal but no less notorious. The Prince of Wales, later Edward VIII, passed through in 1919 and was so taken with the place that he bought the EP Ranch next door. Edward visited the region five times, including twice after his abdication, and the EP was managed in his name until 1962.

Bar U Ranch is just off Hwy 22, 13km south of the town of Longview. Two dozen buildings, including a cookhouse, post office, corral, blacksmith's, and slaughterhouse, have been preserved in their Sundance Kid–era glory. Visitors can also partake in wagon rides, saddle up horses or even try to rope a steer.

---

closer, they would be funneled to the edge and made to stampede over it to their doom, thus ensuring the survival of the tribe. For the Blackfoot, the buffalo was sacred; to honor the fallen prey, every part of the animal was used.

The well-presented displays at the interpretive centre built cleverly into the hillside are befitting of a Unesco World Heritage site, and it's well worth the excursion from Calgary or Lethbridge. The site, about 18km northwest of Fort Macleod and 16km west of Hwy 2, also has a cafe, a shop staffed by Blackfoot First Nations and a couple of short walking trails.

Lethbridge

Right in the heart of southern Alberta farming country sits the former coal-mining city of Lethbridge, divided by the distinctive coulees of the Oldman River. Though there isn't a lot to bring you to the city, copious parkland, a couple of good historical sites and an admirable level of civic pride might keep you longer than you first intended. There are ample hiking opportunities in the Oldman River Valley, a 100m-deep coulee bisected by the proverbial Eiffel Tower of steel railway bridges, and the largest of its kind in the world. The downtown area, like many North American downtowns, has made a good stab at preserving its not-so-ancient history. To the east, less-inspiring Mayor McGrath Dr (Hwy 5) is a chain-store-infested drag that could be Anywhere, North America.

◉ Sights & Activities

Nikka Yuko Japanese Garden　GARDENS
(www.nikkayuko.com; cnr Mayor Mcgrath Dr & 9th Ave S; adult/child $8/5.50; ⊘ 9am-5pm) The Nikka Yuko Japanese Garden is the perfect antidote to the stresses of the road. The immaculate grounds, interspersed with ponds, flowing water, bridges, bonsai trees and rock gardens, form an oasis of calm amid the bustle of everyday life, and authentic Japanese structures sit among the grassy mounds.

Indian Battle Park　PARK
(3rd Ave S) In the coulee between the east and west sides of the city, Indian Battle Park, west of Scenic Dr and named after a famous 1870 battle between the Blackfoot and the Cree, is no ordinary manicured green space. Instead, this is an expansive, surprisingly wild place astride the Oldman River that is strafed with trails, wildlife and some unsung mining history.

Impossible to miss in the middle of it all is 96m-high, 1623m-long **High Level Bridge**, the largest trestle bridge in the world, built in 1909 to carry the railway across the deep coulee to the prairies on the other side.

Almost directly under the bridge, the **Helen Schuler Coulee Centre & Lethbridge Nature Reserve** (⊘10am-6pm) contains a small interpretive center and is the starting point for various nature trails on the reserve's 80 wooded hectares along the river. It runs special nature programs in the summer. At the other end of the car park is the Coalbanks Interpretive kiosk, an open-air shelter containing an impressive stash of information on Lethbridge's early mining history. Trails nearby lead to gazebos, picnic areas and viewpoints.

Fort Whoop-Up   FORT, MUSEUM
(☑403-329-0444; www.fortwhoopup.ca; 200 Indian Battle Park Rd; adult/child $7/5; ⊘10am-5pm) Inside expansive Indian Battle Park, bizarrely named Fort Whoop-Up is a replica of Alberta's first and most notorious illegal-whiskey trading post. Around 25 of these outposts were set up in the province between 1869 and 1874 to trade whiskey, guns, ammunition and blankets for buffalo hides and furs from the Blackfoot tribes.

Their existence led directly to the formation of the NWMP, who arrived in 1874 at Fort Macleod to bring law and order to the Canadian west. The fort has exhibits on the Blackfoot tribe, the mounties and, most notably, one of the largest firearms collections in Canada. It was open but undergoing renovations at last visit.

Galt Museum & Archives   MUSEUM
(www.galtmuseum.com; 320 Galt St; adult/child $6/3; ⊘10am-5pm Mon-Sat, 1-5pm Sun) The story of Lethbridge is continued at the Sir Alexander Galt Museum, encased in an old hospital building (1910) on the bluff high above the river. Interactive kid-oriented displays sit beside a small gallery with contemporary and historical art that will interest the bigger kids. The view from the lobby out onto the coulee is great and free.

🛏 Sleeping

A huge selection of chain hotels from fancy to thrifty can be found on Hwy 5. Take your pick.

Lethbridge Lodge   HOTEL $$
(☑403-328-1123; www.lethbridgelodge.com; 320 Scenic Dr S; r from $104; @🛇🛜) Like most Canadian hotels, the rooms here are clean if a little unmemorable; the atrium, on the other hand, is something else. All the rooms look down into the fake-foliage-filled interior, complete with winding brick pathways, a kidney-shaped pool and water features.

The Cotton Blossom Lounge sits among the jungle and is good fun – the piano player is stranded on a small island – and the pseudo Italian facade of the rooms completes the bizarre picture.

Holiday Inn   HOTEL $$
(☑403-380-5050; www.ihg.com; 2375 Hwy 5 S; r from $141; @🛜🛜) This slightly out-of-the-box Holiday Inn (formerly a Ramada hotel) has an indoor water park complete with dueling waterslides, wave pool and special kids' area. All the standard stuff is here too, and despite the wacky selling features, the hotel retains a sense of class. It was completely refurbished in 2011.

🍴 Eating

Round Street Café   CAFE $
(☑403-381-8605; 427 5th St S; sandwiches $7; ⊘7am-6pm Mon-Sat; 🛜) A simple but effective indie coffee bar near the Greyhound depot with a fine line in cinnamon buns and thick-cut sandwiches, plus free internet browsing rights.

Mocha Cabana Café   CAFE $$
(☑403-329-6243; www.mochacabana.ca; 317 4th St; lunches from $12; ⊘7am-9pm Sun-Thu, to 11pm Fri & Sat; 🛜) Austere from the outside, the multifunctional Mocha is anything but within. Billing itself as a coffee lounge, wine bar, patio and music venue, it grabs 'best in Lethbridge' prize in each genre. The bright interior has an appealing European ambience, and the substantial lunchtime salads are fantastic.

Ric's Grill   STREAKHOUSE $$$
(☑403-317-7427; www.ricsgrill.com; 103 Mayor McgGrath Dr; mains $19-40; ⊘11am-10pm) Ever eaten in a water tower – or an ex–water tower, to be more precise? Well, here is your chance. Ric's sits 40m high above the prairie in the old Lethbridge water tower (decommissioned in 1999). Turned into a restaurant in 2004, the curved interior affords great views of the city.

There is a lounge on one level and a classy dining room upstairs. The steaks are thick and the wine list long; best to reserve a good spot as it's deservedly popular.

ℹ Information

Chinook Country Tourist Association (www.chinookcountry.com; 2805 Scenic Dr S; ⊙9am-5pm)

Main Post Office (📠 403-382-4604; 704 4th Ave S)

ℹ Getting There & Around

AIR

The **Lethbridge airport** (📠 403-329-4474; 417 Stubb Ross Rd), a short drive south on Hwy 5, is served by commuter affiliates of Air Canada. Six or seven flights per day go to Calgary.

BUS

Greyhound Canada (📠 403-327-1551; 411 5th St S) goes to Calgary ($48, 2½ hours, five daily) and Regina ($103, from 14½ hours, two daily).

Luxurious **Red Arrow** (📠 1-800-232-1958; www.redarrow.ca; 449 Mayor Magrath Dr S) buses connect once daily with Calgary ($49, 2½ hours) and Fort MacLeod ($34, 45 minutes)

For detailed information about local bus services, call the **Lethbridge Transit Infoline** (📠 403-320-4978, 403-320-3885). The downtown bus terminal is on 4th Ave at 6th St. Local bus fares are $2.

Writing-on-Stone Provincial Park

Perhaps the best thing about this **park** (📠 403-647-2364; ⊙9am-6pm) **FREE** is that it really isn't on the way to *anywhere*. For those willing to get off the main thoroughfare and discover this hidden gem, all efforts will be rewarded. It's named for the extensive carvings and paintings made by the Plains Indians more than 3000 years ago on the sandstone cliffs along the banks of Milk River. There is an excellent self-guided interpretive trail that takes you to some of the more spectacular viewpoints and accessible pictographs.

The best art is found in a restricted area (to protect it from vandalism), which you can only visit on a guided tour with the park ranger. Other activities possible here include canoeing and swimming in the river in summer and cross-country skiing in winter. Park wildlife is ample, and a new **visitors center** (⊙9am-7pm), built in the shape of a traditional tepee, blends perfectly with the region's natural and cultural heritage. Pick up tickets for tours at the park entrance, from the naturalist's office. Tours generally run Saturday and Sunday at 2pm from May to October (adult/child $12/8), but check ahead. Beware: it can get exceedingly hot in the summer.

The park's riverside **campground** (📠 403-647-2877; campsites/RV sites from $20/26) has 64 sites, running water, showers and flush toilets and is popular on weekends.

The park is southeast of Lethbridge and close to the US border; the Sweetgrass Hills of northern Montana are visible to the south. To get to the park, take Hwy 501 42km east of Hwy 4 from the town of Milk River.

Waterton Lakes National Park

Who? What? Where? The name **Waterton Lakes National Park** (adult/child per day $7.80/3.90) is usually prefixed with a question rather than a sigh of recognition. While its siblings to the north – Canmore, Banff and Jasper – hemorrhage with tourists and weekend warriors, Waterton is a pocket of tranquility. Sublime. Established in 1895 and now part of a Unesco World Heritage site, Unesco Biosphere Reserve and International Peace Park (with Glacier National Park in the US), 525-sq-km Waterton Lakes lies in Alberta's southwestern corner. Here the prairies meet the mountains, and the relief from the flat land is nothing short of uplifting. The park is a sanctuary for numerous iconic animals – grizzlies, elk, deer and cougars – along with 800-odd wildflower species.

The town of **Waterton**, a charming alpine village with a winter population of about 40, provides a marked contrast to larger, tackier Banff and, to a lesser extent, Jasper. There is a lifetime's worth of outdoor adventure to discover here. Highlights include serene Waterton Lake, the regal 1920s-era Prince of Wales Hotel, and the immediacy of the high-alpine hiking terrain; you can be up above the tree line in less than one hour from leaving the town.

Sitting right on the US border and next to the immense **Glacier National Park**, this is a good spot to forge neighborly relations with the people to the south. You can even flash your passport and do a poly-country backcountry adventure. Together the two

OFF THE BEATEN TRACK

BLACKFOOT CROSSING HISTORICAL PARK

A First Nations reservation with a historical centre rather than a casino, the **Blackfoot Crossing Historical Park** (☑ 403-734-5171; www.blackfootcrossing.ca; adult/child $12/8; ⊙ 9am-5pm Tue-Sat) goes proudly against the grain, choosing to celebrate and embrace authentic Siksika (Blackfoot) culture with something that is both educational and inspiring.

The history of southern Alberta pre-1880 belongs to the Blackfoot confederacy, an amalgamation of the Peigan, Blood and Montana-based Blackfeet tribes. Blackfoot Crossing, long an important tribal nexus, was unique in that it was the only place where nomadic First Nations tribes built a semipermanent settlement (out of grassy earth-lodge). It was here that notorious Treaty 7 was signed by Chief Crowfoot in 1877, ceding land to the British crown and establishing the Siksika reservation. After a visit from Prince Charles in 1977, the idea for a historical site was hatched and, after 30 years of planning, the park finally opened in 2007.

It is anchored by a magnificent ecofriendly main building that incorporates elements of tepees and feathered headdresses into its creative design. Within its walls lie a 100-seat theater showcasing cultural dances, a set of exhibits chronicling Blackfoot history and guided tours with local Siksika interpreters and storytellers. Outside, you can enjoy various trails, prairie viewpoints, and a tepee village where traditional crafts are practiced and taught.

To get to the centre, head 100km east of Calgary on Hwy 1 and then 7km south on Hwy 842. Still in its infancy, the historical park remains curiously light on visitors who have yet to discover its latent glories.

parks comprise Waterton-Glacier International Peace Park. Although the name evokes images of binational harmony, in reality each park is operated separately, and entry to one does not entitle you to entry to the other.

For more information on Glacier National Park, see the excellent US National Park Service website at www.nps.gov/glac.

◉ Sights & Activities

A highlight for many visitors is a boat ride with **Waterton Shoreline Cruises** (☑ 403-859-2362; www.watertoncruise.com; 1 way adult/child $25/14; ⊙ May-Oct) across the lake's shimmering waters to the far shore of Goat Haunt, Montana, USA. The 45-minute trip is scenic, and there is a lively commentary as you go. Grab your passport before you jump on the often rather full boats, as they dock in the USA for about half an hour.

Those looking to stretch their legs are in luck – Waterton is a hiker's haven. With over 225km of walking tracks, you'll run out of time before you run out of trails. The trails are shared with bikes and horses (where permitted), and once the snow flies, cross-country skis will get you to the same places. The 17km walk to **Crypt Lake** is a standout: there's a 20m tunnel, a stream that material-

izes out of the ground and a ladder to negotiate. The only way to get to the trailhead is by boat. Waterton Shoreline Cruises leaves the town's marina in the morning and picks up the weary at the Crypt Lake trailhead in the afternoon (adult/child $18/9).

Another example of Waterton's 'small is beautiful' persona is the 19km **Carthew-Alderson Trail**, often listed as one of the best high alpine day hikes in North America. The **Tamarack Shuttle** (☑ 403-859-2378; 214 Mount View Rd) runs every morning in the summer to the trailhead by Cameron Lake (reservations recommended). From here you hike back over the mountains to the town.

⊨ Sleeping

The park has three Parks Canada vehicle-accessible campgrounds, none of which takes reservations. Backcountry campsites are limited and should be reserved through the visitors center.

Waterton Townsite Campground   CAMPGROUND $
(☑ 877-737-3783; Hwy 5; campsites/RV sites $22.50/38.20; ⊙ May-Oct) Dominating the southern end of Waterton village, the town campground isn't ideal, but it's a means to an end. Consisting mainly of an enormous gopher-hole-covered field aimed at RV

campers, it has all the charm of a camping area at a music festival. There are some treed sites near the edges, but by midsummer you'll be lucky to get anything.

Book ahead for this one.

Crandell Mountain Campground
CAMPGROUND $
(☑ 403-859-5133; Red Rock Pkwy; campsites & RV sites $21.50; ☺ May-Sep) For a more rustic alternative to the town, head out to this secluded camping spot a few minutes' drive from the park gates.

Aspen Village Inn
HOTEL $$
(☑ 403-859-2255; www.aspenvillageinn.com; 111 Windflower Ave; r $159-199; ☎) Aspen is a more economical, family-friendly version of the Bayshore. Rooms are in two main buildings and several cottage units. Bonuses include a kids' play area, a barbecue and picnic area, and the sight of wild deer grazing the grass outside your room.

Bear Mountain Motel
MOTEL $$
(☑ 403-859-2366; www.bearmountainmotel.com; 208 Mount View Rd; s/d from $105/130) Small, bog-standard motel rooms in a central location. Throw in friendly, knowledgeable owners, and you're laughing all the way to the ATM.

★ Prince of Wales Hotel
HISTORIC HOTEL $$$
(☑ 403-859-2231; www.princeofwaleswaterton.com; Prince of Wales Rd; r from $239; ☺ May-Sep; ☎) You can't come to Waterton and not check out this iconic alpine landmark. Situated to take full advantage of the best view in town, this hotel is nothing short of spectacular. When seen from a distance, the serene scene is perhaps the most photogenic in all the Canadian Rockies.

Up close, the old girl is starting to show her age, but she's aging like a fine wine. The grand lobby is illuminated with a chandelier worthy of a Scottish castle, and the elevator is the oldest working example in North America. The rooms are small but retain the classic feel of this historical hotel. There's antique porcelain in the bathrooms and views that justify the price.

Bayshore Inn
HOTEL $$$
(☑ 403-859-2211; www.bayshoreinn.com; 111 Waterton Ave; r $174-225; ☺ Apr-Oct; @ ☎) Taking the prize as the biggest hotel in the downtown area, the Bayshore is nothing if not centrally located. With rooms that back right onto the lake and a location only a couple of

steps away from the shops, this is a popular option. The lake views are great, but be sure to book early if you want to see them.

Waterton Glacier Suites
HOTEL $$$
(☑ 403-859-2004; www.watertonsuites.com; 107 Windflower Ave; ste from $239; @ ☎ ⚐) With amenities aplenty, these suites have two fireplaces, Jacuzzis, microwaves and fridges. The rooms are spotless, and the rock-and-log exterior looks the part too. It's open all year round – come winter you'll appreciate those dual fireplaces.

✕ Eating & Drinking

Waterton specializes in unsophisticated but filling cuisine, ideal for topping up your energy both pre- and posthike. Everything is contained within the town.

Waterton Bagel & Coffee Co
CAFE $
(☑ 403-859-2466; 309 Windflower Ave; bagels from $5; ☺ 10am-10pm) A godsend if you've just staggered out of the wilderness, this tiny caffeine stop has a handful of window stools, life-saving peanut-butter-and-jam bagels and refreshing frappuccinos.

Zum's Eatery
CANADIAN $$
(☑ 403-858-2388; 116B Waterton Ave; mains $13-18; ☺ 11am-10pm) Good home-style cooking of the burger, pizza, and fish-and-chips variety is brought to you by hard-up students working their summer breaks. The lack of sophisticated flavors is made up for by the character of the decor: several hundred North American license plates embellish almost every centimeter of wall.

Bel Lago Ristorante
ITALIAN $$$
(☑ 403-859-2213; www.bellagoristorante.com; 110 Waterton Ave; mains $19-32; ☺ noon-10pm) ⚐ Homemade-pasta-in-North-American-national-park shock! The decor's relatively simple, but this is probably Waterton's most ambitious eatery: the chef studied in Italy and creates tasty (but not gigantic) mains that embody that old Italian ethos of eating local where possible. The wine list's international with an Italian bias (Amarone anyone?).

Thirsty Bear Saloon
PUB
(☑ 403-859-2111; www.thirstybearsaloon.com; Main St; ☺ 4pm-2am Mon-Sat) Wild nights in the wilderness happen in this large pub/performance space aided by live music, karaoke and good beer.

❶ Information

Waterton Visitors Centre (✆403-859-5133; www.parkscanada.gc.ca/waterton; ☺8am-7pm May-Sep) Across the road from the Prince of Wales Hotel. It's the central stop for information.

❶ Getting There & Around

Waterton lies in Alberta's southwestern corner, 130km from Lethbridge and 156km from Calgary. The one road entrance into the park is in its northeastern corner along Hwy 5. Most visitors coming from Glacier and the USA reach the junction with Hwy 5 via Hwy 6 (Chief Mountain International Hwy) from the southeast. From Calgary, to the north, Hwy 2 shoots south toward Hwy 5 into the park. From the east, Hwy 5, through Cardston, heads west and then south into the park.

There is no public transportation from Canadian cities outside the park. However, a shuttle service (adult/child US$50/25) operated by **Glacier Park Inc** (www.glacierparkinc.com) offers daily transport from Prince of Wales Hotel to Glacier Park Lodge in Montana, USA from May to September. Here you can link up with the Amtrak train network.

A hikers' shuttle ($13.50) operates around the park in the summer, linking Cameron Lake with the town and the US border at Chief Mountain. It leaves from Tamarack Outdoor Outfitters (p106) in town.

Crowsnest Pass

West of Fort Macleod the Crowsnest Hwy (Hwy 3) heads through the prairies and into the Rocky Mountains to Crowsnest Pass (1396m) and the BC border. The Pass, as it's known, is a string of small communities just to the east of the BC border. Of note is the story of the town of **Frank**. In 1903, Frank was almost completely buried when 30 million cu meters (some 82 million tonnes' worth) of nearby Turtle Mountain collapsed and killed around 70 people. The coal mine dug into the base of the mountain was to blame, some say. But the mining didn't stop; this black gold was the ticket to fortune for the entire region some hundred years ago. Eventually the demand for coal decreased, and after yet more tragedy below the earth, the mines shut down for good.

Frank Slide Interpretive Centre (adult/child $10/5; ☺9am-6pm), 1.5km off Hwy 3 and 27km east of the BC border, overlooks the Crowsnest Valley. It's an excellent interpretive center that helps put a human face on the tragedy of the Frank landslide, with many interesting displays about mining, the railroad and the early days of this area. There's also a fantastic film dramatizing the tragic events of 1903. Most of the staff can trace their roots to the area and thus the slide.

NORTHERN ALBERTA

Despite the presence of the increasingly infamous oil sands, the top half of Alberta is little visited and even less known. Once you travel north of Edmonton, the population drops off to Siberian levels, and the sense of remoteness is almost eerie.

If it's solitude you seek, then this is paradise found. Endless stretches of pine forests seem to go on forever, nighttime brings aurora borealis displays that are better than any chemical hallucinogens, and it is here you can still see herds of buffalo.

This is also where the engine room of the Alberta economy lives. The oil sands near Fort McMurray are one of the largest oil reserves in the world. This helps to bring in workers from every corner of Canada, and the oil exported earns the province millions of dollars – per hour.

The Cree, Slavey and Dene were the first peoples to inhabit the region, and many of them still depend on fishing, hunting and trapping for survival. The northeast has virtually no roads and is dominated by Wood Buffalo National Park, the Athabasca River and Lake Athabasca. The northwest is more accessible, with a network of highways connecting Alberta with northern BC and the NWT.

Peace River & Around

Alaska, here we come! Heading northwest along Hwy 43 leads to the town of Dawson Creek, BC, and mile zero of the Alaska Hwy. Dawson is a whopping 590km from Edmonton, so it's a long way to go to check out this isolated section of northern Alberta. Along the way you'll pass through **Grande Prairie**, the base of operations for the local agricultural industry and home to chuckwagon legend Kelly Sutherland. If you decide to spend the night, most of the accommodations are centered on 100th St and 100th Ave.

Peace River is so named because the warring Cree and Beaver Indians made peace along its banks. The town of **Peace River** sits at the confluence of the Heart, Peace and Smoky Rivers. It has several motels and two campgrounds. Greyhound Canada buses leave daily for the Yukon and NWT. West out of town, Hwy 2 leads to the Mackenzie Hwy.

Mackenzie Highway

The small town of **Grimshaw** is the official starting point of the Mackenzie Hwy (Hwy 35) north to the NWT. There's not much here except for the mile-zero sign and a few shops. The relatively flat and straight road is paved for the most part, though there are stretches of loose gravel or earth where the road is being reconstructed.

The mainly agricultural landscape between Grimshaw and Manning gives way to endless stretches of spruce and pine forest. Come prepared as this is frontier territory and services become fewer (and more expensive) as the road cuts northward through the wilderness. A good basic rule is to fill your tank any time you see a gas station from here north.

High Level, the last settlement of any size before the NWT border, is a center for the timber industry. Workers often stay in the motels in town during the week. The only service station between High Level and Enterprise (in the NWT) is at Indian Cabins.

Lake District

From St Paul, more than 200km northeast of Edmonton, to the NWT border lies Alberta's immense lake district. Fishing is popular (even in winter, when there is ice fishing), but many of the lakes, especially further north, have no road access and you have to fly in.

St Paul is the place to go if you are looking for little green people. The **flying-saucer landing pad**, which is still awaiting its first customer, is open for business. Residents built the 12m-high circular landing pad in 1967 as part of a centennial project and as a stunt to try to generate tourism (it's billed as the world's largest, and only, UFO landing pad) to the remote region. It worked: UFO enthusiasts have been visiting ever since.

Hwy 63 is the main route into the province's northeastern wilderness interior. The highway, with a few small settlements and campgrounds on the way, leads to **Fort McMurray**, which is 439km northeast of Edmonton. Originally a fur-trading outpost, it is now home to one of the world's largest oilfields. The town isn't particularly interesting. Non-oil workers generally come here to see the aurora borealis (northern lights). The story of how crude oil is extracted from the vast tracts of sand is told at the **Oil Sands Discovery Centre** (515 MacKenzie Blvd; adult/child $7/4; ⏱ 9am-5pm May-Sep).

Wood Buffalo National Park

This huge park is best accessed from Fort Smith in the NWT. Covering an area the size of Switzerland, the park is known for its free-roaming herds of Wood buffalo (bison) and rare whooping cranes.

In Alberta, the only access is via air to Fort Chipewyan. In winter an ice road leads north to Peace Point (which connects to Fort Smith), and another road links the park to Fort McMurray.

British Columbia

Why Go?

British Columbia visitors need a long list of superlatives when describing their trips – the words spectacular, breathtaking and jaw-dropping only go so far. But it's hard not to be moved by towering mountains, wildlife-packed forests and dramatic coastlines that slow your heart like sigh-triggering spa treatments. Canada's westernmost province is more than just nature-hugging dioramas, though.

Cosmopolitan Vancouver fuses cuisines and cultures from Asia and beyond, while vibrant smaller cities like Victoria and Kelowna are increasingly creating their own intriguing scenes. For sheer character, it's hard to beat the kaleidoscope of quirky little communities from rustic northern BC to the ever laid-back Southern Gulf Islands.

Wherever you head, the great outdoors will always call. Don't just point your camera at it. BC is unbeatable for the kind of life-enhancing skiing, kayaking and hiking that can easily make this the trip of a lifetime.

Best Places to Eat

➡ Hawksworth (p133)

➡ Araxi Restaurant (p161)

➡ Flying Pig (p135)

➡ Red Fish Blue Fish (p173)

Best Places to Stay

➡ Wickaninnish Inn (p190)

➡ Rockwater Secret Cove Resort (p164)

➡ Free Spirit Spheres (p186)

➡ Nita Lake Lodge (p160)

When to Go
Vancouver

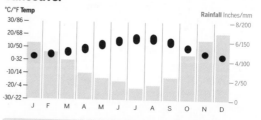

Dec–Mar Best powder action on the slopes of Whistler and Blackcomb mountains

Jul & Aug Beaches, patios and a plethora of outdoor festivals in sun-dappled Vancouver

Sep & Oct Dramatic surfing and the start of storm-watching season in beach-hugging Tofino

Getting There & Around

The sheer size of BC can overwhelm some visitors: it's a scary-sounding 1508km drive from Vancouver to Prince Rupert, for example. While it's tempting to simply stick around Vancouver – the main point of entry for most BC-bound visitors – you won't really have experienced the province unless you head out of town.

Despite the distances, driving remains the most popular method of movement in BC. Plan your routes via the handy DriveBC website (www.drivebc.ca) and check out the dozens of services offered by the extensive **BC Ferries** (www.bcferries.com) system.

VIA Rail (www.viarail.com) operates two BC train services. One trundles across the north from the coastline to Jasper. Pick up the second in Jasper for a ride back to Vancouver. A third line on Vancouver Island may also reopen in the coming years.

PARKS & WILDLIFE

BC's national parks include snow-capped **Glacier** and the Unesco World Heritage sites of **Kootenay** and **Yoho**. The newer **Gulf Islands National Park Reserve** protects a fragile coastal region. Visit the website of **Parks Canada** (www.pc.gc.ca) for information.

The region's almost 1000 provincial parks offer 3000km of hiking trails. Notables include **Strathcona** and remote **Cape Scott**, as well as the Cariboo's canoe-friendly **Bowron Lake** and the Kootenays' Matterhorn-like **Mt Assiniboine**. Check the **BC Parks** (www.bcparks.ca) website for information.

Expect to spot some amazing wildlife. Ocean visitors should keep an eye out for orcas, while land mammals – including elk, moose, wolves, grizzlies and black bears – will have most scrambling for their cameras. And there are around 500 bird varieties, including blue herons and bald eagles galore.

Raise a Glass: BC's Top Five Beers

➡ Back Hand of God Stout by Crannóg Ales: a rich, java-colored brew with a cult following.

➡ Red Racer ESB by Central City Brewing: a smooth, malty ale with nicely balanced hops.

➡ Fat Tug IPA by Driftwood Brewery: BC's best and most hoptastic Pacific Northwest IPA.

➡ Old Jalopy Pale Ale by Powell Street Craft Brewery: Canadian Brewery Awards' Beer of the Year winner, made by a tiny Vancouver nanobrewery.

➡ Zunga by Townsite Brewing: the Sunshine Coast's favorite quaff is a beautifully balanced blonde ale.

GUILT-FREE FISH & CHIPS

Seafood is BC's main dining choice. Support the sustainability of the region's aquatic larder by frequenting restaurants operating under the Ocean Wise banner; see www.oceanwise.ca.

BC Fast Facts

➡ Population: 4.6 million

➡ Area: 944,735 sq km

➡ Capital: Victoria

➡ Fact: BC is North America's third-largest film and TV production center.

It's Official

BC's provincial bird is the Steller's jay and its official mammal is the Kermode bear, a black bear with white fur.

Resources

➡ Destination British Columbia (www.hellobc.com)

➡ Cycling BC (www.cyclingbc.net)

➡ British Columbia Beer Guide (www.bcbeer.ca)

➡ BC Government (www2.gov.bc.ca)

➡ BC Wine Institute (www.winebc.com)

➡ Van Dop Arts & Cultural Guide (www.art-bc.com)

➡ Discover Camping (www.discovercamping.ca)

➡ Surfing Vancouver Island (www.surfingvancouverisland.com)

British Columbia Highlights

1 Stretch your legs on a seawall stroll around Vancouver's spectacular **Stanley Park** (p117).

2 Surf up a storm (or just watch a storm) in **Tofino** (p189) on Vancouver Island's wild west coast.

3 Slurp some celebrated tipples on an ever-winding **Okanagan Valley** winery tour (p211).

4 Ski the Olympian slopes at **Whistler** (p155), then enjoy a warming après-ski beverage in the village.

5 Explore the ancient and ethereal rainforest of **Gwaii Haanas National Park Reserve** (p244) and kayak the coastline for a fish-eye view of the region.

6 Putter around the lively Saturday Market on **Salt Spring Island** (p199) and scoff more than a few treats.

7 Indulge in some lip-smacking Asian hawker food at the two night markets in **Richmond, Vancouver** (p152).

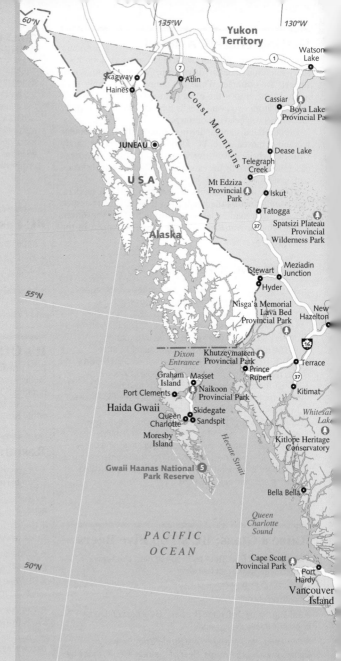

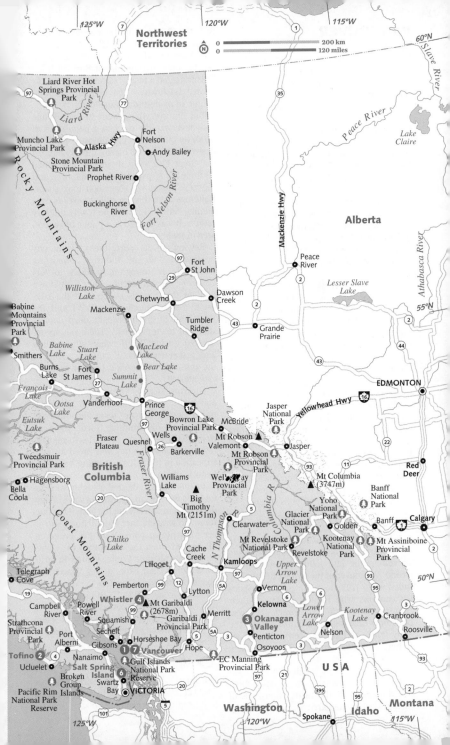

VANCOUVER

POP 666,500

Swooping into Vancouver International Airport on a cloud-free summer's day, it's easy to appreciate the idea that this is a nature-bound utopia that deserves to be recognized as one of the world's best places to live. Gently rippling ocean crisscrossed with ferry trails, the crenulated shorelines of dozens of forest-green islands and the ever-present sentinels of snow-dusted crags glinting on the horizon give this city arguably the most spectacular setting of any metropolis on the planet.

While the city's twinkling outdoor backdrop means you're never far from great skiing, kayaking or hiking, there's much more to Vancouver than appearances. Hitting the streets on foot means you'll come across a kaleidoscope of distinctive neighborhoods, each one almost like a village in itself. There's bohemian, coffee-loving Commercial Dr; the cool indie shops of hipster-hugging Main St; the character-packed bars of old Gastown and flare-topped roofs of adjoining Chinatown; and the colorful streets of the West End's 'gayborhood.' All that's before you even get to the bustling artisan nest otherwise known as Granville Island and the forested seawall vistas of Stanley Park, Canada's finest urban green space.

This diversity is Vancouver's main strength and a major reason why visitors keep coming back for more. If you're a first timer, soak in the breathtaking views and hit the verdant forests whenever you can, but also save time to join the locals and do a little exploring off the beaten track; it's in these places that you'll discover what really makes this beautiful metropolis special.

History

The First Nations lived in this area for up to 16,000 years before Spanish explorers arrived in the late 1500s. When Captain George Vancouver of the British Royal Navy sailed up in 1792, he met a couple of Spanish captains who informed him of their country's land claim. The beach they met on is now called Spanish Banks. But by the early 1800s, as European settlers began arriving, the British crown had an increasing stranglehold.

Fur trading and a feverish gold rush soon redefined the region as a resource-filled Aladdin's cave. By the 1850s, thousands of fortune seekers had arrived, prompting the Brits to officially claim the area as a colony. Local entrepreneur 'Gassy' Jack Deighton seized the initiative in 1867 by opening a bar on the forested shoreline of Burrard Inlet. This triggered a rash of development – nicknamed Gastown – that became the forerunner of modern-day Vancouver.

But not everything went to plan. While Vancouver rapidly reached a population of 1000, its buildings were almost completely destroyed in an 1886 blaze – quickly dubbed the Great Fire, even though it only lasted 20 minutes. A prompt rebuild followed and the new downtown core soon took shape. Buildings from this era still survive, as does Stanley Park. Originally the town's military reserve, it was opened as a public recreation area in 1888.

Relying on its port, the growing city became a hub of industry, importing thousands of immigrant workers to fuel economic development. The Chinatown built at this time is still one of the largest in North America. But WWI and the 1929 Wall St crash brought deep depression and unemployment. The economy recovered during WWII, when shipbuilding and armaments manufacturing added to the traditional economic base of resource exploitation.

Growing steadily throughout the 1950s and 1960s, Vancouver added an NHL (National Hockey League) team and other accoutrements of a midsize North American city. Finally reflecting on its heritage, Gastown – by now a slum – was saved for gentrification in the 1970s, becoming a national historic site in 2010.

In 1986 the city hosted a highly successful Expo world's fair, sparking a wave of new development and adding the first of the mirrored skyscrapers that now define Vancouver's downtown core. A further economic lift arrived when the city staged the Olympic and Paralympic Winter Games in 2010. Even bigger than Expo, it was Vancouver's chance to showcase itself to the world. But for many locals, 2013's 125th birthday party for Stanley Park was just as important: big events come and go, but Vancouverites aim to ensure the city's greatest green space is here forever.

⊙ Sights

Vancouver's most popular attractions are easily accessible on foot or by a short transit hop from the city center. Also save time for

Vancouver

0 — 4 km
0 — 2 miles

Coquitlam River

Noons Creek

Mossom Creek

Indian Arm Provincial Park

Mt Seymour Provincial Park

Lynn Canyon Park

Grouse Mountain (1km)

Indian Arm

BELCARRA

ANMORE

Belcarra Regional Park

Maplewood Farm

Mt Seymour Pkwy

Dollarton Hwy

Second Narrows Bridge

Barriston Island

Douglas Island

Fort Langley (8km)

Tynehead Regional Park

176th St

181st St

PORT COQUITLAM

COQUITLAM

Como Lake Ave

Mundy Park

Austin Ave

Simon Fraser University

Burnaby Mountain Conservation Area

Lougheed Hwy

Green Timbers Urban Forest

SURREY

88th Ave

152nd St

(1A)

King George Hwy

96th Ave

128th St

72nd Ave

120th St

Fraser River Discovery Centre

NEW WESTMINSTER

10th Ave

Canada Way

River Market

Kingsway

Marine Way

BURNABY

Deer Lake Park

Central Park

Burnaby Central Park

Burnaby Lake Regional Nature Park

Burnaby Village Museum

Kerr St

Boundary Rd

Rupert St

Nanaimo St

Commercial Dr

E Hastings St

Confederation Park

Burrard Inlet

Vancouver Harbour

First Narrows

Stanley Park

Lions Gate Bridge

Capilano Suspension Bridge

Marine Dr

NORTH VANCOUVER

Lonsdale Quay

Upper Levels Hwy

Horseshoe Bay (2km); Bowen Island (7km); Whistler (105km)

Lighthouse Park

Bowen Island

Burrard Inlet

Sandy Cove Bay

West Bay

Point Grey

Spanish Banks Beach Park

Jericho Beach

UNIVERSITY OF BRITISH COLUMBIA

Museum of Anthropology

Wreck Beach

UBC Botanical Garden

Marine Drive Foreshore Park

Pacific Spirit Regional Park

English Bay

KITSILANO

W Broadway

16th Ave W

WEST SIDE

W 41st Ave

Granville St

Oak St

Cambie St

Main St

Knight St

Kingsway

SOUTH MAIN

Queen Elizabeth Park

See Downtown Vancouver Map (p118)

Musqueam Indian Reserve 2

Iona Island

Sea Island

Vancouver International Airport

Richmond Night Market

Bridgeport Rd

Mitchell Island

Summer Night Market

Richmond Hwy Nature Park

Westminster Hwy

RICHMOND

Blundell Rd

No 1 Rd

Steveston Hwy

STEVESTON

Gulf of Georgia Cannery

Britannia Shipyard

Kuan Yin Temple

North Arm Fraser River

Fraser River

River Rd

DELTA

Annacis Island

Annacis Hwy

(91)

George Massey Tunnel

(99)

Delta Nature Reserve

Nordel Way

Tsawwassen (15km); Seattle (USA; 190km)

Richmond Fwy

Strait of Georgia

Lynn Creek

Capilano River

some urban exploring off the beaten path: the neighborhoods here – especially Gastown, Chinatown, Commercial Dr, Main St and Kitsilano – are well worth an afternoon of wandering and all have great places to eat when it's time for a break.

◉ Downtown

Lapped by ocean on two sides and with Stanley Park on its tip, downtown Vancouver combines shimmering glass apartment and business towers with the shop-lined attractions of Robson St, the city's central promenade.

Canada Place
LANDMARK

(Map p118; www.canadaplace.ca; 999 Canada Place Way; Ⓜ Waterfront) Vancouver's version of the Sydney Opera House, this iconic landmark is shaped like a series of sails. A cruise-ship terminal, it's also a pier where you can stroll the waterfront for camera-triggering North Shore mountain vistas. The adjoining grass-roofed convention center expansion opened in 2010. The nearby plaza houses the tripod-like Olympic Cauldron from the 2010 Games.

Fly Over Canada
AMUSEMENT RIDE

(Map p118; www.flyovercanada.com; 999 Canada Pl; adult/child $20/15; ⊙10am-9pm; Ⓜ Waterfront) The newest attraction in Canada Pl, this breathtaking movie-screen simulator ride makes you feel like you're swooping across the entire country, waggling your legs over landmark scenery from coast to coast. En route, your seat will lurch, your face will be sprayed and you'll likely have a big smile on your face. Once the short ride is over, you'll want to do it all again.

Jack Poole Plaza
PLAZA

(Map p118; Canada Pl; Ⓜ Waterfront) The heart of Vancouver's 2010 Olympic Games hosting duties, this handsome waterfront public space is the permanent home of the tripod-like Olympic Cauldron. The flame is lit for special occasions or you can pay $5000 to have it switched on. The plaza offers great views of the mountain-backed Burrard Inlet and you can follow the shoreline walking trail around the convention center West Building for public artworks and historic plaques.

If you fancy a further taste of the 2010 Games, nip along the subterranean pedestrian tunnel between the two convention buildings. You'll find a small display of medals, Olympic torches and even a podium from the event where you can pretend you won the skeleton.

Marine Building
HISTORIC BUILDING

(Map p118; 355 Burrard St; ⊙9am-5pm Mon-Fri; Ⓜ Burrard) Vancouver's best art-deco building, this graceful, 22-story beauty celebrates the city's maritime past with an elaborate exterior of sea horses, lobsters and streamlined ships. Nip into the lobby where a walk-through artwork of stained-glass panels and a polished floor inlaid with signs of the zodiac await – peruse the inlaid wood interiors of the brass-doored elevators as well.

VANCOUVER IN...

One Day

Begin with a heaping breakfast at the **Templeton** (p133) before strolling south to the **Vancouver Art Gallery** (p117). Next, take a window-shopping wander along **Robson St**, then cut down to the waterfront for panoramic sea and mountain vistas. Walk west along the **Coal Harbour** seawall and make for the dense trees of **Stanley Park** (p117). Spend the afternoon exploring the beaches, totem poles and **Vancouver Aquarium** (p117) here before ambling to the **West End** for dinner.

Two Days

Follow the one-day itinerary, then, the next morning, head to clamorous **Chinatown**. Stop at the towering **Millennium Gate** and duck into the nearby **Dr Sun Yat-Sen Classical Chinese Garden & Park** (p122) for a taste of tranquility. Check out the colorful stores (and tempting pork buns) around the neighborhood before strolling south along Main St towards **Science World** (p122) for some hands-on fun. Afterwards hop on the SkyTrain at the nearby station, trundle to Waterfront Station, and then take the scenic SeaBus to North Vancouver's **Lonsdale Quay Public Market** (p148). On your return, hit Gastown's **Alibi Room** (p139) for some craft beers.

Vancouver Art Gallery　GALLERY

(Map p118; ☑604-662-4700; www.vanartgallery.
bc.ca; 750 Hornby St; adult/child $20/6; ☺10am-
5pm Wed-Mon, to 9pm Tue; ☐5) The VAG has
dramatically transformed in recent years,
becoming a vital part of the city's cultural
scene. Contemporary exhibitions – often
showcasing Vancouver's renowned photo-
conceptualists – are now combined with
blockbuster international traveling shows.
Check out kid-friendly activities and **Fuse**,
a late-night party every few months where
you can hang with the city's young arties
over wine and live music.

Bill Reid Gallery of Northwest
Coast Art　GALLERY

(Map p118; www.billreidgallery.ca; 639 Hornby St;
adult/child $10/5; ☺11am-5pm Wed-Sun; Ⓜ Bur-
rard) Showcasing carvings, paintings and
jewelry from Canada's most revered Haida
artist, this gallery is lined with exquisite
works, plus handy touch screens to tell you
all about them. Check out the Great Hall,
where there's often a carver at work; then
hit the mezzanine level, where you'll be face-
to-face with an 8.5m-long bronze of intertwined magical creatures with impressively
long tongues.

Vancouver Lookout　LOOKOUT

(Map p118; www.vancouverlookout.com; 555 W
Hastings St; adult/child $15.75/7.75; ☺8:30am-
10:30pm; Ⓜ Waterfront) Expect your stomach
to make a bid for freedom as the glass elevator whisks you 169m to the apex of this
needle-like viewing tower. Up top, there's
not much to do but admire the awesome
360-degree vistas of city, sea and mountains
unfurling around you. Tickets are pricey but
are valid all day – return for a soaring sunset
view.

BC Place Stadium　STADIUM

(Map p118; www.bcplacestadium.com; 777 Pacific
Blvd; Ⓜ Stadium-Chinatown) With its fancy new
roof, BC Place is now an even bigger downtown landmark. But it's not all about size:
the city's main stadium is home to the BC
Lions Canadian Football League team and
the Vancouver Whitecaps soccer team. Also
check out the stadium's family-friendly BC
Sports Hall of Fame & Museum for a glimpse
at the region's sporty history.

Rogers Arena　STADIUM

(Map p118; www.rogersarena.ca; 800 Griffiths Way;
tours adult/child $12/6; ☺tours 10:30am, noon
& 1:30pm Wed, Fri & Sat; Ⓜ Stadium-Chinatown)

TOP FIVE MUSEUMS

➡ Museum of Anthropology (p125)

➡ Museum of Vancouver (p125)

➡ Beaty Biodiversity Museum (p126)

➡ Vancouver Police Museum (p122)

➡ Roedde House Museum (p121)

Vancouver's other stadium hosts the National Hockey League's Vancouver Canucks.
On game nights, when the 20,000-capacity
venue heaves with fervent fans, you'll enjoy
the atmosphere even if the rules are a mystery. Behind-the-scenes tours last 75 minutes
and take you into the hospitality suites and
the nosebleed press box up in the rafters and
are popular with visiting sports fans.

◉ Stanley Park

The magnificent 404-hectare **Stanley Park**
(Map p118; www.vancouver.ca/parks; ♿; ☐19)
combines attractions with a mystical natural aura. Don't miss a stroll or cycle around
the 8.8km seawall: a kind of visual spa treatment fringed by a 150,000-tree temperate
rainforest. The path takes you right alongside the park's camera-luring totem poles.
There are bike rentals near the W Georgia
St entrance.

★Vancouver Aquarium　AQUARIUM

(☑604-659-3474; www.vanaqua.org; 845 Avison
Way; Jul & Aug adult/child $27/17; ☺9:30am-6pm;
♿; ☐19) Stanley Park's biggest draw houses
9000 water-loving critters, including sharks,
beluga whales and a rather shy octopus.
There's also a small rainforest of birds, tur-
tles and a statue-still sloth. Peruse the mesmerizing iridescent jellyfish and consider an
Animal Encounter tour, where you'll learn
about being a trainer. Expansion was under-
way on our visit, so look out for changes.

Miniature Railway　MINIATURE RAILWAY

(adult/child from $5; ☺hours vary; ☐19) A short
walk from the aquarium, this beloved
family-friendly attraction – a replica of the
first passenger train that trundled in from
Montréal in 1887 – takes on several incarna-
tions throughout the year. In summer, it's a
First Nations–themed ride; in winter, it becomes a Christmas train; and, at Halloween,
it takes on a spooky, haunted ghost-loving
allure.

BRITISH COLUMBIA VANCOUVER

Downtown Vancouver

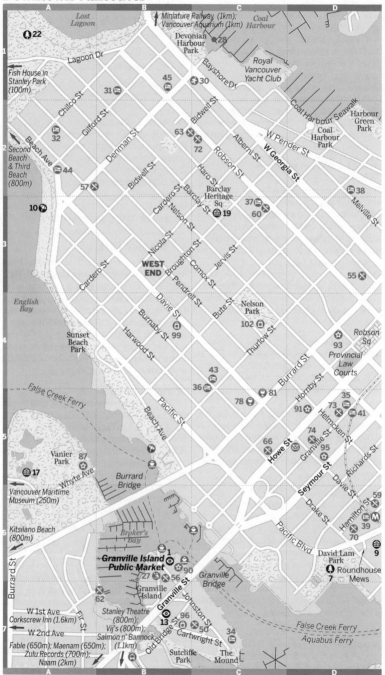

Lost Lagoon

Coal Harbour

22

Devonian Harbour Park

28

Royal Vancouver Yacht Club

Lagoon Dr

Fish House in Stanley Park (100m)

Miniature Railway (1km); Vancouver Aquarium (1km)

Bayshore Dr

Chilico St

31

45

30

Bidwell St

W Pender St

Coal Harbour Seawalk

Harbour Green Park

Gilford St

32

63

72

Alberni St

W Georgia St

Coal Harbour Park

Second Beach & Third Beach (800m)

Beach Ave

44

Denman St

Bidwell St

Haro St

Robson St

38

57

Cardero St

Barclay St

Nelson St

Barclay Heritage Sq

19

37

60

Melville St

10

WEST END

Nicola St

Broughton St

Jervis St

55

Cardero St

Comox St

Bute St

English Bay

Davie St

Burnaby St

Nelson Park

102

Thurlow St

93

Robson Sq

Sunset Beach Park

Harwood St

Burrard St

Provincial Law Courts

False Creek Ferry

Pacific St

43

36

78

81

Hornby St

35

73

41

91

Vanier Park

87

17

Whyte Ave

Burrard Bridge

Beach Ave

66

74

Howe St

95

Seymour St

Davie St

Richards St

Vancouver Maritime Museum (250m)

Kitsilano Beach (800m)

Drake St

Hamilton St

59

39

70

Pacific Blvd

David Lam Park

9

Burrard St

Broker's Bay

1

Granville Island Public Market

90

27

56

Granville Island

Granville St

Granville Bridge

7

Roundhouse Mews

62

W 1st Ave

Corkscrew Inn (1.6km)

W 2nd Ave

Fable (650m); Maenam (650m); Zulu Records (700m); Naam (2km)

Stanley Theatre (800m); Vij's (800m); Salmon n' Bannock (1.1km)

13

Old Bridge St

96

50

Johnston St

Cartwright St

34

Sutcliffe Park

The Mound

False Creek Ferry

Aquabus Ferry

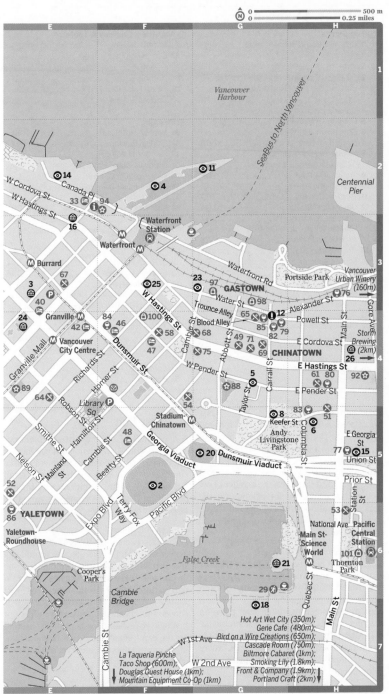

N 0 ——— 500 m
0 ——— 0.25 miles

Vancouver Harbour

SeaBus to North Vancouver

Centennial Pier

14
4
11

W Cordova St
Canada Pl
33 94
W Hastings St
16
Waterfront Station
Waterfront

Waterfront Rd

Portside Park
Vancouver Urban Winery (160m)
76
Vancouver

Burrard
67
3
40
Granville
24
42 46
Vancouver City Centre
Dunsmuir St
Richards St
Homer St

25
23
97
GASTOWN
Water St
98
Alexander St
Trounce Alley
65
12
Powell St
Blood Alley
85
82 79
68
49 71
E Cordova St
75
69
CHINATOWN
W Pender St
E Hastings St
61 80
5
E Pender St
88
54
83
Taylor St
51
8
6
Keefer St
Andy Livingstone Park
E Georgia St
77
15
Union St

84
100
58
47
Storm Brewing (2km)
26
92

89
64
Robson St
Library Sq
Smithe St
Hamilton St
Cambie St
48
Beatty St
Georgia Viaduct
20
Dunsmuir Viaduct

Prior St
Station St
53

Nelson St
Mainland St
52
86
YALETOWN

Yaletown-Roundhouse

Expo Blvd
Terry Fox Way
Pacific Blvd
2

National Ave
Main St-Science World
Pacific Central Station
101
Thornton Park

Cooper's Park

False Creek
21
Quebec St

Cambie Bridge
29
18
Main St

Cambie St

W 1st Ave

La Taqueria Pinche Taco Shop (600m);
Douglas Guest House (1km);
Mountain Equipment Co-Op (1km)

W 2nd Ave

Hot Art Wet City (350m);
Gene Cafe (480m);
Bird on a Wire Creations (650m);
Cascade Room (750m);
Biltmore Cabaret (1km);
Smoking Lily (1.8km);
Front & Company (1.9km);
Portland Craft (2km)

Downtown Vancouver

Lost Lagoon   LAKE

(www.stanleyparkecology.ca; ☐19) This forested lagoon near the park entrance is Vancouver's downtown nature sanctuary. Its perimeter pathway makes for a wonderful stroll – keep your eyes peeled for beady-eyed blue herons and duck into the excellent Lost Lagoon Nature House for exhibits on the park's multitudinous flora and fauna. Check ahead for their guided park walks and you'll spot even more.

Second Beach & Third Beach   BEACH

(☐19) Second Beach is a busy, family-friendly area on the park's western side, with a grassy playground, waterfront swimming pool and nearby Ceperley Meadow, where free outdoor movie screenings often take place on summer nights (see www.freshaircinema. ca). Alternatively, Third Beach is possibly Vancouver's best sunset-viewing spot, where the sky often comes alive with pyrotechnic color – hence the picnicking locals.

◎ **West End**

A dense nest of older apartment buildings and handsome wooden heritage homes on dozens of well-maintained residential streets, the West End has beaches, seawall promenades, plenty of midrange dining (especially on Davie and Denman Sts) and BC's largest gay community.

English Bay Beach   BEACH

(Map p118; cnr Denman St & Beach Ave; ☐5) Wandering south on Denman St, you'll suddenly spot a rustle of palm trees announcing one of Canada's best urban beaches. There's a party atmosphere here in summer as West Enders catch the rays, crowd the busker shows and check out artwork vendors...or just ogle volleyball players prancing around on the sand. Snap some pics of the laughing bronze figures – Vancouver's fave public artwork.

Roedde House Museum   MUSEUM

(Map p118; www.roeddehouse.org; 1415 Barclay St; admission $5; ⏱1-4pm Tue-Fri & Sun; 🚌5) For a glimpse of what the West End used to look like, drop by this handsome 1893 mansion, now a lovingly preserved museum. The house is packed with antiques and the surrounding gardens are planted in period style. The abode is the showpiece of **Barclay Heritage Sq**, a one-block site containing nine historic West End houses dating from 1890 to 1908.

◉ Yaletown

An evocative, brick-lined former warehouse district transformed into swanky bars, restaurants and boutiques, pedestrian-friendly Yaletown is where the city's chichi socialites come to see and be seen. Roughly bordered by Nelson, Homer and Drake Sts and Pacific Blvd, the area's gritty past is recalled by the old rail tracks still embedded in many of its roads.

Engine 374 Pavilion   MUSEUM

(Map p118; www.roundhouse.ca; Roundhouse Community Arts & Recreation Centre, 181 Roundhouse Mews; Ⓜ Yaletown-Roundhouse) FREE May 23, 1887 is an auspicious date in Vancouver's history. It was the day when Engine 374 pulled the first transcontinental passenger train into the fledgling city, symbolically linking the country and kick-starting the eventual metropolis. Retired in 1945, the engine was (after many years of neglect) finally restored and placed in this lovely free-entry pavilion. Drop by for a chat with the friendly volunteers.

David Lam Park   PARK

(Map p118; www.vancouverparks.ca; cnr Drake St & Pacific Blvd; Ⓜ Yaletown-Roundhouse) A crooked elbow of landscaped waterfront at the neck of False Creek, this is Yaletown's main green space. A popular spot for free shows at the Vancouver International Jazz Festival (p129), it's also sometimes used for alfresco summer movie screenings and is the perfect launch point for a 2km seawall stroll along the north bank of False Creek to Science World (p122).

On your walk, you'll pass intriguing public artworks, glass condo towers foresting the old Expo '86 site and the stadium where the Vancouver Canucks NHL team plays. Look out for beady-eyed birdlife along the route.

◉ Gastown

Now a national historic site, Vancouver's brick-paved old town area is where the city began. Many heritage buildings remain, most now housing cool bars, restaurants or trendy shops.

Steam Clock   LANDMARK
(Map p118; cnr Water & Cambie Sts; Ⓜ Waterfront) Halfway along Water St, this oddly popular tourist magnet lures the cameras with its tooting steam whistle. Built in 1977, the clock's mechanism is actually driven by electricity while only the pipes on top are fueled by steam, although this information might cause a riot if you reveal it to the patiently waiting tourists. Sounding every 15 minutes, it marks each hour with little whistling symphonies.

Once you have taken the required photo, spend some time exploring the rest of cobbled Water St, one of Vancouver's most historic thoroughfares.

Gassy Jack Statue   MONUMENT
(Map p118; Maple Tree Sq; ▣4) It's amusing to think that Vancouver's favorite statue is a testament to the virtues of drink. At least that's one interpretation of the jaunty 'Gassy' Jack Deighton bronze, perched atop a whiskey barrel in Maple Tree Sq. Erected in 1970, it recalls Deighton's 1867 arrival, after which he built a bar, triggering development that soon became Vancouver.

Vancouver Police Museum   MUSEUM
(Map p118; ☎604-665-3346; www.vancouverpolice-museum.ca; 240 E Cordova St; adult/child $12/8; ◎9am-5pm Tue-Sat; ▣4) Contextualizing the city's crime-colored history, this quirky little museum is lined with confiscated weapons, counterfeit currency and a grizzly former mortuary room where the walls are studded with preserved slivers of human tissue – spot the bullet-damaged brain slices. If your interest in crime is triggered, take their excellent Sins of the City walking tour around the area.

◉ Chinatown

Adjoining Gastown, North America's third-largest Chinatown is a highly wanderable explosion of sight, sound and aromas. Start your exploration at the **Chinatown Millennium Gate** (Map p118; cnr W Pender & Taylor Sts; Ⓜ Stadium-Chinatown) and don't miss the bustling newly reinvigorated summertime night market.

Dr Sun Yat-Sen Classical
Chinese Garden & Park   GARDENS
(Map p118; www.vancouverchinesegarden.com; 578 Carrall St; adult/child $12/9; ◎9:30am-7pm; Ⓜ Stadium-Chinatown) A tranquil break from clamorous Chinatown, this intimate 'garden of ease' illustrates Taoist symbolism through the placing of gnarled pine trees, winding covered pathways and limestone formations. Entry includes a 45-minute guided tour, where you'll learn that everything in the garden reflects balance and harmony. Look out for the lazy turtles bobbing in the jade-colored water.

If you're on a budget, check out the free park next door: not quite as elaborate as its sister, it's still a pleasant oasis of whispering grasses, a large fishpond and a small pagoda.

Chinatown Night Market   MARKET
(Map p118; www.vancouverchinatownnightmarket. com; Keefer St, btwn Columbia & Main Sts; ◎6-11pm Fri-Sun mid-May–early Sep; Ⓜ Stadium-Chinatown) Recently reinvented to compete with the success of larger night markets in Richmond, Chinatown's version is well worth a summer evening visit. Cheap and cheerful trinkets still feature, but the highlight is the food – it's like a walk-through buffet of fish balls, bubble tea and tornado potatoes. Check ahead: there's an eclectic roster of entertainment, including alfresco movie screenings.

Jimi Hendrix Shrine   NOTABLE BUILDING
(Map p118; 207 Union St; ◎1-6pm Mon-Sat Jun-Sep; ▣3) FREE Said to occupy the building that formerly housed Vie's Chicken and Steak House – the 1960s restaurant where Hendrix' grandmother cooked and the young guitarist frequently strummed – this is worth a quick look. A quirky, homemade attraction, the red-painted shack is lined with old photos and album covers and is staffed by a chatty volunteer or two.

Science World   MUSEUM
(Map p118; www.scienceworld.ca; 1455 Quebec St; adult/child $22.50/15.25; ◎10am-5pm Mon-Fri, to 6pm Sat & Sun; ☝; Ⓜ Main St-Science World) Nes-

VANCOUVER FOR CHILDREN

Family-friendly Vancouver is stuffed with things for vacationing kids. Pick up a copy of the free *Kids' Guide Vancouver* flyer from racks around town and visit www.kids-vancouver.com for tips, resources and family-focused events. Car-hire companies rent car seats – legally required for young children here – for a few dollars per day, but you'll need to reserve in advance. If you're traveling around the city without a car, make sure you hop on the SkyTrain or SeaBus transit services or the miniferry to Granville Island: kids love 'em, especially the newer SkyTrain cars, where they can sit up front and pretend they're driving. Children under five travel free on all transit.

Stanley Park (p117) can keep most families occupied for a full day. If it's hot, make sure you hit the water park at Lumberman's Arch or try the swimming pool at Second Beach; also consider the **Miniature Railway** (p117) for a fun trundle. The park is a great place to bring a picnic, and its beaches especially are highly kid-friendly. Save time for the **Vancouver Aquarium** (p117) and, if your kids have been good, consider a behind-the-scenes trainer tour. Kids who are into nature and critters will also enjoy the Nature House at **Lost Lagoon** (p120) and the **Capilano Suspension Bridge** (p147) with its forest walks – take them to nearby **Grouse Mountain** (p148) and they can also spot grizzly bears close-up.

The city's other educational family-friendly attractions – the kind where your moppets get educated without even noticing – include **Science World** (p122) and the **HR MacMillan Space Centre** (p125). If it's raining, you can also duck inside **Bloedel Conservatory** (p127) and hang with exotic birds.

If you time your visit right, the city has an array of family-friendly festivals, including the **Pacific National Exhibition** (p129), the **Vancouver International Children's Festival** (p129) and the fireworks fiesta known as the **Celebration of Light** (p129).

BRITISH COLUMBIA VANCOUVER

tled under the city's favorite geodesic dome (OK, its only one), this recently revamped hands-on science and nature showcase brings out the kid in almost everyone. Expect to spend a half-day here as your squirts run themselves ragged learning scientific principles, especially in the new outdoor park area.

Also consider checking out a movie in the on-site Omnimax Theatre or hanging out without the kids at one of the regular After Dark social events – there's also a teen-only version if you're looking for ways to entertain a sullen adolescent or two.

⊙ Main Street & Commercial Drive

Vancouver's indie crowd has colonized an area of town that used to be a byword for down-at-the-heels. Radiating south from the Main St-Science World SkyTrain Station (and easily accessed by the number 3 bus that runs along its length), Main St is the city's hippest hood: think skinny jeans and cool-ass coffeehouses, plus great independent shops (especially past the intersection with 18th Ave).

But Main isn't the city's first alternative district. Further east, Commercial Dr – just called 'the Drive' by locals – has a long counterculture history and was also settled by generations of Italian immigrants. It has great indie shops, patio-fronted restaurants and arguably the city's best family-run coffeehouses.

The 99 B-Line express bus along Broadway links both areas in 10 minutes.

Hot Art Wet City   GALLERY
(www.hotartwetcity.com; 2206 Main St; ⊙noon-5pm Wed-Sat; ▣3) **FREE** Possibly the most fun you can have at a private gallery in Vancouver, trip up the stairs at this funky little space and you're guaranteed some eye-popping art to look at. Mostly local artists are showcased and there's a new exhibition every month. Past themes have ranged from bizarre paintings of doll heads to art on beer bottles.

Check the retail space in the corner for quirky souvenir ideas and peruse the calendar before you arrive: there's a lively roster of artist talks, workshops and show openings.

Portobello West   MARKET
(Map p118; www.portobellowest.com; 1 Athletes Way, Creekside Community Recreation Centre; adult/child $2/free; ⊙11am-5pm Sat & Sun, 4 times per year; ▦; Ⓜ Main St-Science World) This weekend-long arts, crafts and fashion market runs four times a year – once each season – in the cavernous Creekside Community Recreation

Centre in the Olympic Village. Expect to find an eclectic blend of handmade, one-of-a-kind goodies and locally designed togs to take back home, or just enjoy the live music and fresh-made bakery and lunch treats.

Punjabi Market
NEIGHBORHOOD
(💻3) Located on Main St, past 48th Ave, and also known as 'Little India,' this enclave of sari stores, bhangra music shops and some of the region's best-value curry buffet restaurants is a good spot for a spicy all-you-can-eat lunch followed by a restorative walkabout. Plans are afoot to possibly add a gate, like the one in Chinatown.

Grandview Park
PARK
(Commercial Dr, btwn Charles & William Sts; 💻20) The Drive's alfresco neighborhood hub is named after the smashing views peeking between its trees: to the north are the North Shore mountains, while to the west is a city-scape vista of twinkling towers. Teeming with buskers, dreadlocked drummers, impromptu sidewalk sales and a waft or two of naughty cigarette smoke, the park is a big summertime lure for nearby locals.

◉ Granville Island

Fanning out under the giant iron arches of Granville Bridge, this gentrified former indus-trial peninsula – it's not actually an island – is one of the best spots to spend a lazy afternoon. Studded with restaurants, bars, theaters and artisan businesses, it's often crowded in sum-mer, as visitors chill out with the buskers and wrestle the seagulls for their fish and chips.

★ Granville Island Public Market
MARKET
(Map p118; www.granvilleisland.com/public-market; Johnston St; ⊙9am-7pm; 💻50, ⛴miniferries) Gran-ville Island's highlight is the covered Public Market, a multisensory smorgasbord of fish, cheese, fruit and bakery treats. Pick up some fixings for a picnic at nearby Vanier Park (a 10-minute walk west along the seawall) or hit the little international food court (dine off-

---

FERRY HOPPING

If you don't arrive or depart from Granville Island via one of the tiny miniferries operated by Aquabus Ferries (p146) or False Creek Ferries (p146), you haven't really conducted your visit correctly. But these signature little boats – the Aquabus vessels tend to be rainbow hued while the False Creek Ferries are blue – don't only transport passengers from the north side of False Creek to the market on the south side. Both have several additional ports of call around the shoreline and, if you have time, a 'cruise' of the area is a great way to see the city from the water. An all-day pass on each service costs $10 to $15 (tickets are not interchangeable between the operators, who remain cutthroat rivals) and there are several highlight stop-offs to consider along the way.

Aquabus can get you to Yaletown's David Lam Park (p121), a waterfront green space that's ideal for watching the gently lapping waters of False Creek from a grassy promon-tory, preferably with a picnic. On the opposite shoreline, you can step off at **Stamps Landing**, one of Vancouver's first urban waterfront housing developments: there's a pub here in the delightfully medieval-sounding **Leg-in-Boot Sq**. Back on the northern shoreline, there's a stop at the bottom of Davie St, which is a short stroll from the heart of Yaletown. You'll find the fascinating Engine 374 Pavilion (p121) here, home of the loco-motive that pulled the first passenger train into Vancouver in 1887.

You can see how things have transformed around False Creek in recent years at one final stop. The shoreline here used to be crammed with grungy industry, but in 2010 the **Olympic Village** opened. Providing housing for the athletes at the 2010 Winter Games, this swanky development is now a slick new city neighborhood. It's also just a short stroll to Science World (p122), one of Vancouver's most popular family-friendly attractions.

False Creek Ferries covers many of the same locations but also includes a unique stop at another popular – and appropriate – Vancouver attraction. From Granville Island and via a stop at the Aquatic Centre in the West End, it takes 25 minutes to voyage to the Vancouver Maritime Museum (p125). On the shoreline of verdant Vanier Park, it's a great spot to dive into the region's seafaring past, from historic vessels to scale models. And since you're now a veteran sea dog, you'll fit right in.

peak and you're more likely to snag a table). In summer, there's also a farmers market outside.

This is a great spot to pick up unusual souvenirs for home and – if you're a true foodie – market tours are available, with samples included.

Granville Island Brewing   BREWERY
(Map p118; ☑604-687-2739; www.gib.ca; 1441 Cartwright St; tours $9.75; ☺tours noon, 1:30pm, 3pm, 4:30pm & 5:30pm; ☑50) Canada's oldest microbrewery offers half-hour tours where smiling guides walk you through the tiny brewing nook, before depositing you in the Taproom for some tasty samples, often including the summer-favorite *Hefeweizen*. You can also buy takeout in the adjoining store – look for special-batch seasonals, like smooth Irish Red and hoppy Imperial IPA. Production has mostly shifted to larger premises.

◉ Kitsilano

A former hippie haven where the counter-culture flower children grew up to reap professional jobs, 'Kits' is a pleasant neighborhood of wooden heritage homes, cozy coffee bars and highly browsable shops. Store-lined W 4th Ave is especially recommended for a lazy afternoon stroll. A short seawall amble from Granville Island, Vanier Park houses three museums and is ideal for picnicking.

Museum of Vancouver   MUSEUM
(Map p118; www.museumofvancouver.ca; 1100 Chestnut St; adult/child $12/8; ☺10am-5pm Fri-Wed, to 8pm Thu; ⚐; ☑22) One of Vanier Park's three well-established educational attractions, the MOV has been upping its game in recent years with cool temporary exhibitions and regular late-opening parties for adults. It hasn't changed everything, though. There are still colorful displays on local 1950s pop culture and 1960s hippie counterculture, plus plenty of hands-on stuff for kids, including scavenger hunts and fun workshops.

HR MacMillan Space Centre   MUSEUM
(Map p118; www.spacecentre.ca; 1100 Chestnut St; adult/child $15/11; ☺10am-5pm; ⚐; ☑22) Popular with packs of marauding schoolkids – expect to have to elbow them out of the way to push the flashing buttons – this high-tech science center illuminates the eye-opening world of space. There's plenty of fun to be had battling aliens and designing a space-craft. There's also an observatory and planetarium; check ahead for the schedule of openings and events.

Vancouver Maritime Museum   MUSEUM
(www.vancouvermaritimemuseum.com; 1905 Ogden Ave; adult/child $11/8.50; ☺10am-5pm Tue-Sat, noon-5pm Sun; ☑22) The final member of Vanier Park's museum triumvirate combines intricate model ships with detailed re-created boat sections and some historic vessels. The main draw is the *St Roch,* a 1928 Royal Canadian Mounted Police Arctic patrol sailing ship that was the first vessel to navigate the legendary Northwest Passage in both directions. Evocative free tours of the vessel are offered.

Kitsilano Beach   BEACH
(cnr Cornwall Ave & Arbutus St; ☑22) Facing English Bay, Kits Beach is one of Vancouver's fave summertime hangouts. The wide, sandy expanse attracts buff Frisbee tossers and giggling volleyball players, as well as those who just like to preen while catching the rays. The water is fine for a dip, though serious swimmers should dive into the heated 137m Kitsilano Pool, a giant outdoor saltwater pool.

Old Hastings Mill Store Museum   MUSEUM
(☑604-734-1212; www.hastings-mill-museum.ca; 1575 Alma St; admission by donation; ☺1-4pm Tue-Sun; ☑4) Built near Gastown in 1865, this historic wooden structure is Vancouver's oldest surviving building. Originally a store for sawmill workers, it survived the Great Fire of 1886 and was used as a makeshift morgue on the fateful day. Saved from demolition by locals, it was relocated here by barge in the 1930s and now houses an eclectic array of pioneer-era and First Nations exhibits.

◉ University of British Columbia

West from Kits on a 400-hectare forested peninsula, the **University of British Columbia** (UBC; ☑604-822-2211; www.ubc.ca) is the province's largest university. Its concrete campus is surrounded by the University Endowment Lands, complete with accessible beach and forest areas and a smattering of visitor attractions.

★Museum of Anthropology   MUSEUM
(Map p115; ☑604-822-3825; www.moa.ubc.ca; 6393 NW Marine Dr; adult/child $14/12; ☺10am-5pm Wed-Mon, to 9pm Tue; ☑99 B-Line) Newly renovated and expanded, Vancouver's best

BRITISH COLUMBIA VANCOUVER

ℹ SAVE YOUR DOSH

There are two handy ways to save money on attractions admission in Vanier Park and at UBC. The Vanier Park Explore Pass costs $30/24 per adult/child and covers entry to the Museum of Vancouver (p125), HR Macmillan Space Centre (p125) and Vancouver Maritime Museum (p125). It's available at any of the three and saves around $10 on individual adult entries. You can also save with the UBC Museums and Garden Pass. Costing $33/28 per adult/child, it covers the Museum of Anthropology (p125), Beaty Biodiversity Museum (p126), Botanical Garden (p126) and Nitobe Memorial Garden (p126). It also includes discounts on campus parking, shopping and dining and is available from any of the listed attractions.

museum houses northwest coast aboriginal artifacts, including Haida houses and totem poles, plus non–First Nations exhibits, such as European ceramics and Cantonese opera costumes. The free guided tours are highly recommended, as is the excellent artsy gift shop. Give yourself a couple of hours at this museum.

Morris & Helen Belkin Gallery   GALLERY
(www.belkin.ubc.ca; 1825 Main Mall; ⊙10am-5pm Tue-Fri, noon-5pm Sat & Sun; 🚌99 B-Line) **FREE** This excellent little gallery specializes in contemporary and often quite challenging pieces. This explains the billboard-style depiction of an Iraqi city outside, complete with the caption 'Because there was and there wasn't a city of Baghdad.' Inside, you can expect a revolving roster of traveling shows, plus chin-stroking exhibits from a permanent collection of Canadian avant-garde works.

Beaty Biodiversity Museum   MUSEUM
(www.beatymuseum.ubc.ca; 2212 Main Mall; adult/child $12/8; ⊙10am-5pm; 🚌99B-Line) UBC's newest museum is also its most family-friendly. Start with the giant blue whale skeleton in the entrance lobby, then descend to the main exhibition hall showcasing more than two million natural-history exhibits. Check ahead for kid-friendly storytelling, puppet shows and hands-on events. Hit the

on-site cafe if you need a rest from all that knowledge.

UBC Botanical Garden   GARDENS
(Map p115; www.ubcbotanicalgarden.org; 6804 SW Marine Dr; adult/child $8/4; ⊙9:30am-5pm; 🚌99 B-Line, then C20) You'll find a giant collection of rhododendrons, a fascinating apothecary plot and a winter green space of off-season bloomers in this 28-hectare complex of themed gardens. The recently added Greenheart Canopy Walkway lifts visitors 17m above the forest floor on a 308m guided ecotour. Walkway tickets include garden entry. If here in October, hit the annual Apple Festival.

Nitobe Memorial Garden   GARDENS
(www.nitobe.org; 1895 Lower Mall; adult/child $6/3; ⊙9:30am-5pm; 🚌99 B-Line, then C20) Exemplifying Japanese horticultural philosophies, this verdant, tranquil oasis includes the Tea Garden – complete with ceremonial teahouse – and the Stroll Garden, which reflects a symbolic journey through life, with its little waterfalls and languid koi carp. The gardens are named after Dr Inazo Nitobe, a scholar whose mug appears on Japan's ¥5000 bill. Consider a springtime visit for the florid cherry-blossom displays.

Pacific Spirit Regional Park   PARK
(Map p115; www.pacificspiritparksociety.org; cnr Blanca St & W 16th Ave; 🚌99 B-Line) This stunning 763-hectare park stretches from Burrard Inlet to the North Arm of the Fraser River. A smashing spot to hug some trees and explore, you'll also find Camosun Bog wetland – accessed by a boardwalk at 19th Ave and Camosun St – a haven for native bird and plant species. There are 54km of walking, jogging and cycling trails.

◉ West Side

A large, catch-all area covering City Hall, the heritage homes of Fairview, the neighborhood eateries of Cambie Village and the strollable stores and restaurants of South Granville, there are several good reasons to visit this part of the city. And it's just a few minutes away from downtown by Canada Line SkyTrain (along the Cambie corridor) or number 10 bus (along South Granville).

Queen Elizabeth Park   PARK
(Map p115; www.vancouverparks.ca; entrance cnr W 33rd Ave & Cambie St; 🚌15) This 52-hectare park claims to house specimens of every tree

native to Canada. It's also the city's highest point, at 167m above sea level, and has panoramic views of the mountain-framed downtown skyscrapers. Sports fields, manicured lawns and two formal gardens keep locals happy, and you'll likely also see wide-eyed couples posing for wedding photos.

If you want to be taken out to the ball game, the recently restored Nat Bailey Stadium is a popular summer-afternoon haven for baseball fans.

Bloedel Conservatory GARDENS
(☑ 604-257-8584; www.vancouverparks.ca; Queen Elizabeth Park; adult/child $6.50/3.25; ⊙9am-8pm Mon-Fri, 10am-8pm Sat & Sun; ☐15) Cresting the hill in Queen Elizabeth Park, this Triodetic domed conservatory is an ideal indoor warm-up spot on a rainy day. It has three climate-controlled zones with 400 plant species, dozens of koi carp and many free-flying tropical birds, including noisy parrots and macaws: ask for a free brochure to help you identify the flora and fauna.

VanDusen Botanical Garden GARDENS
(www.vandusengarden.org; 5251 Oak St; adult/child $10.75/5.75; ⊙9am-9pm; ☐17) Vancou-

ver's favorite ornamental green space, this 22-hectare idyll is a web of paths weaving through small, specialized gardens: the Rhododendron Walk blazes with color in spring, while the Korean Pavilion is a focal point for a fascinating Asian plant collection. There's also a fun Elizabethan maze. A popular Christmastime destination, expect twinkling fairy lights illuminating the dormant plant life in December.

🏃 Activities

With a reputation for steely calved locals who like nothing better than an early morning 20km jog and a lip-smacking rice cake for breakfast, Vancouver is all about being active. Popular pastimes include running, biking and kayaking, while you're also just a short hop from some serious winter-sport action on the North Shore.

Walking & Running

For arm-swinging strolls or heart-pounding runs, the 8.8km **Stanley Park seawall** is mostly flat – apart from a couple of hills, where you could hang onto a passing bike. UBC's Pacific Spirit Regional Park is also a popular running spot, with tree-lined trails

BRITISH COLUMBIA VANCOUVER

STROLLING VANCOUVER'S PAST

Just a few weeks after renaming itself Vancouver (no one liked the original name 'Granville' or the insalubrious 'Gastown' slang name that preceded it), the fledgling city of around 1000 homes burnt almost to the ground in minutes in what was accurately termed the Great Fire. But locals weren't about to jump on the next boat out of town. Within days, plans were drawn up for a new city. This time, brick and stone would be favored over wood. The first buildings to be erected radiated from Maple Tree Sq – in particular along Carral St. This thoroughfare, one of the shortest streets in Vancouver, still exists today and links the historic center of Gastown to Chinatown. Take a stroll south on this street from Maple Tree Sq and you'll spot some grand buildings from the early days of the city. Perhaps due to an abundance of caution, they are also some of the sturdiest structures around and will likely survive for many years to come, whether or not there's a fire.

If you'd visited 30 years ago, however, you would have seen many of these buildings seemingly on their last legs. This part of Vancouver hadn't attracted any new development or investment for years and Carrall St's old, paint-peeled taverns, hotels and storefronts were spiraling into skid-row degradation. Two things changed the inevitable: historians and heritage fans banded together to draw attention to the area's important role in the founding years of the city, a campaign that finally culminated in a National Historic Site designation in 2010. Secondly, gentrification took hold. Developers had all but abandoned this part of the city for much of the last century. But with few neighborhoods left to enhance, they finally came back. While gentrification has many detractors here – worried that new development will change the area's old-school character – an undeniable positive is that it has preserved and protected Gastown's historic old buildings for decades to come. The brick and stone landmarks that once lined Carrall have, for the most part, been sympathetically restored and renovated, giving the entire area a new lease on life beyond its heritage designation.

marked throughout the area. If you really want a workout, try North Vancouver's Grouse Grind, a steep, sweat-triggering slog up the side of Grouse Mountain that's been nicknamed 'Mother Nature's StairMaster.' You can reward yourself at the top with free access to the resort's facilities – although you'll have to pay $10 to get down on the Skyride gondola.

South False Creek Seawall WALKING

(Map p118; end of Terminal Ave; Ⓜ Main St-Science World) Starting a few steps from Science World, this popular waterfront trail can take you all the way along the shoreline to Granville Island (about 3km). Or you can just take it easy and view a few sights along the way: look out for the giant bird sculptures in Olympic Village and Habitat Island, where visiting birdlife frequently perches.

Cycling

Joggers share the busy Stanley Park seawall with cyclists (and in-line skaters), necessitating a one-way traffic system to prevent bloody pileups. The sea-to-sky vistas are breathtaking, but the exposed route can be hit with crashing waves and icy winds in winter. Since slow-moving, camera-wielding tourists also crowd the route in summer, it's best to come early in the morning or late in the afternoon.

After circling the park to English Bay, energetic cyclists can continue along the north side of False Creek towards Science World, where the route heads up the south side of False Creek towards Granville Island, Vanier Park, Kitsilano Beach and, finally, UBC. This extended route, including Stanley Park, is around 25km. If you still have some energy, UBC's Pacific Spirit Regional Park has great forested bike trails, some with challenging uphill stretches.

There's a plethora of bike- and blade-rental stores near Stanley Park's W Georgia St entrance, especially around the inter section with Denman St. One of these, **Spokes Bicycle Rentals** (Map p118; www. vancouverbikerental.com; 1798 W Georgia St; adult per hr/7hr from $8.60/34.30; ◎8am-9pm; 🚌5), can also arrange guided tours. At time of writing, the city was planning to introduce a public bike-share scheme in addition to its expanding network of urban bike trails – check the City of Vancouver website for the latest info and resources (www.vancouver. ca/cycling).

Watersports

It's hard to beat the joy of an early evening paddle around the coastline here, with the sun sliding languidly down the mirrored glass towers that forest the city like modern-day totem poles. With its calm waters, Vancouver is a popular spot for both veteran and novice kayakers.

Ecomarine Paddlesport Centres KAYAKING

(Map p118; ☑604-689-7575, 888-425-2925; www. ecomarine.com; 1668 Duranleau St; single kayak rental per 2/24hr $39/94; ◎9am-6pm Sun, Mon, Wed & Thu, to 9pm Tue, Fri & Sat; 🚌50) With headquarters on Granville Island, the friendly folk at Ecomarine Paddlesport Centres offer equipment rentals and guided tours.

Windsure Adventure
Watersports WATER SPORTS

(☑604-224-0615; www.windsure.com; 1300 Discovery St; ◎9am-8:30pm Apr-Sep; 🚌4) For those who want to be at one with the sea breeze, Windsure Adventure Watersports specializes in kiteboarding, windsurfing and skimboarding and offers lessons and equipment rentals from its Jericho Beach base.

☞ Tours

★Forbidden Vancouver WALKING TOUR

(www.forbiddenvancouver.ca; adult/concession $22/19; ◎Apr-Nov) This quirky company offers two core, highly entertaining, tours: a delve into Prohibition-era Vancouver and a poke around the seedy underbelly of historic Gastown. Not recommended for kids. Book ahead: they fill up quickly. At the time of research, a third tour covering Granville St's colorful nightlife history was being introduced.

★Vancouver Foodie Tours GUIDED TOUR

(☑877-804-9220; www.foodietours.ca; tours $49-69; ◎year-round) The perfect way to dive into the city's food scene, the two belt-busting guided tours include a street-food crawl ($49) and a gourmet drink-and-dine tour ($69).

Architectural Institute of
British Columbia WALKING TOUR

(☑604-683-8588; www.aibc.ca; tours $10; ◎Tue-Sun Jul & Aug) Local architecture students conduct these excellent one- to two-hour wanders, focusing on the buildings, history and heritage of several key Vancouver neighborhoods. There are six tours in all and areas covered include Gastown, Strathcona,

Yaletown, Chinatown, downtown and the West End.

Accent Cruises BOAT TOUR
(Map p118; ☑604-688-6625; www.accentcruises.ca; 1698 Duranleau St, Granville Island; dinner cruise $89; ⊘May-Oct; ▣50) Popular salmon buffet cruise along the coastlines of English Bay, Stanley Park and Ambleside Beach in West Vancouver. Departures are from Granville Island and it's a relaxing way to spend your evening after a long day spent trawling the sights.

Vancouver Trolley Company BUS TOUR
(☑604-801-5515, 888-451-5581; www.vancouvertrolley.com; adult/child from $40/22; ⊘year-round) This company operates jolly replicas of San Francisco trolley cars (without the tracks), providing a hop-on, hop-off service to attractions around the city. The circuit takes 80 minutes and you buy your tickets from the driver – attraction tickets are also sold on board.

Harbour Cruises BOAT TOUR
(Map p118; ☑800-663-1500, 604-688-7246; www.boatcruises.com; Denman St; adult/child $30/10; ⊘May-Oct) View the city – and some unexpected wildlife – from the water on a 75-minute narrated harbor tour. Tours weave past Stanley Park, Lions Gate Bridge and the North Shore mountains. There's also a 2½-hour sunset dinner cruise ($79/69 per adult/child), with West Coast cuisine (ie salmon) and live music.

⭐ Festivals & Events

Dine Out Vancouver FOOD
(www.tourismvancouver.com; 3-course menus $18, $28 or $38; ⊘mid-Jan) Two weeks of three-course tasting menus at area restaurants.

Chinese New Year CULTURE
(www.vancouver-chinatown.com; ⊘Jan or Feb) Festive kaleidoscope of dancing, parades and great food held in January or February.

Winterruption PERFORMING ARTS
(www.winterruption.com; ⊘mid-Feb) Granville Island brushes off the winter blues with a music and performance festival.

Vancouver International Wine Festival WINE
(www.vanwinefest.ca; ⊘late Mar) The city's oldest and best annual wine celebration takes place in late March.

Vancouver Craft Beer Week BEER
(www.vancouvercraftbeerweek.com; ⊘late May) A boozy roster of tastings, pairing dinners and tipple-fueled shenanigans.

Vancouver International Children's Festival CHILDREN'S
(www.childrensfestival.ca; ⊘late May) Storytelling, performance and activities on Granville Island.

Bard on the Beach THEATER
(☑604-739-0559; www.bardonthebeach.org; ⊘Jun-Sep) A season of four Shakespeare and Bard-related plays in Vanier Park tents.

Vancouver International Jazz Festival MUSIC
(www.coastaljazz.ca; ⊘Jun & Jul) FREE City-wide cornucopia of superstar shows and free outdoor events.

Car Free Day Vancouver STREET CARNIVAL
(www.carfreevancouver.org; ⊘mid-Jun) Neighborhoods across the city turn over their streets for food, music and market stalls. Main St's is usually the biggest.

Dragon Boat Festival CULTURE
(www.dragonboatbc.ca; ⊘3rd week Jun) A two-day splashathon of boat-racing fun in False Creek.

Vancouver Folk Music Festival MUSIC
(www.thefestival.bc.ca; ⊘mid-Jul) Folk and world-music shows at Jericho Beach.

Celebration of Light FIREWORKS
(www.hondacelebrationoflight.com; ⊘late Jul) Free international fireworks extravaganza in English Bay.

Pride Week CARNIVAL, PARADE
(www.vancouverpride.ca; ⊘late Jul) Parties, concerts and fashion shows culminating in a giant pride parade.

Pacific National Exhibition CULTURE, CHILDREN'S
(www.pne.bc.ca; Hastings Park, East Vancouver; ⊘mid-Aug–Sep) Family-friendly shows, music concerts and a fairground.

Vancouver International Fringe Festival PERFORMING ARTS
(www.vancouverfringe.com; ⊘mid-Sep) Wild and wacky theatricals at mainstream and unconventional Granville Island venues.

Vancouver International Film Festival FILM
(www.viff.org; ⊘late Sep–Oct) Popular two-week showcase of Canadian and international movies.

BRITISH COLUMBIA VANCOUVER

Vancouver Writers Fest   LITERATURE
(www.writersfest.bc.ca; ☉ Oct) Local and international scribblers populate literary seminars, galas and public forums.

Eastside Culture Crawl   CULTURE
(www.eastsideculturecrawl.com; ☉ late Nov) East Vancouver artists open their studios for three days of wandering visitors.

Santa Claus Parade   CHRISTMAS
(www.rogerssantaclausparade.com; ☉ early Dec) Christmas procession, complete with the great man himself.

🛏 Sleeping

With more than 25,000 metro Vancouver hotel, hostel and B&B rooms, this region has options for all tastes and budgets. While rates peak in July and August, there are good deals available in fall and spring, when the weather is often amenable and the tourist crowds reduced. The **Tourism Vancouver** (www.tourismvancouver.com) website lists options and packages, while the province's **Hello BC** (☎ 800-435-5622; www.hellobc.com) service provides further information and bookings. Be aware that hotels charge up to $40 for overnight parking, while parking at B&Bs is typically free.

🛏 Downtown

Samesun Backpackers Lodge   HOSTEL $
(Map p118; ☎ 604-682-8226, 877-972-6378; www. samesun.com; 1018 Granville St; dm/r incl breakfast $35/95; ❂ @ 🛜; 🖳 10) Vancouver's party hostel, the brightly painted Samesun is on the city's nightlife strip – ask for a back room if you fancy a few hours of sleep – or just head down to the on-site bar (naughtily called the Beaver) to join the beery throng. Dorms are comfortably small and there's a large kitchen for your mystery-meat pasta dishes.

★ **St Regis Hotel**   BOUTIQUE HOTEL $$
(Map p118; ☎ 604-681-1135, 800-770-7929; www. stregishotel.com; 602 Dunsmuir St; d incl breakfast $220; ❂ ✳ @ 🛜; 🅼 Granville) Transformed in recent years, the St Regis is now an art-lined boutique sleepover in a 1913 heritage shell. The rooms – which, befitting its age, almost all seem to be a different size – exhibit a loungey élan, complete with leather-look wallpaper, earth-tone bedspreads, flatscreen TVs and multimedia hubs. Rates include cooked breakfast, nearby gym access and free international phone calling.

HI Vancouver Central   HOSTEL $$
(Map p118; ☎ 866-762-4122, 604-685-5335; www. hihostels.ca/vancouver; 1025 Granville St; dm/r incl breakfast $40/113; ❂ ✳ @ 🛜; 🖳 10) This warren-like sleepover is more of a party joint than its HI Downtown sibling. Enjoying some of the benefits of its past hotel incarnation – air-conditioning and small dorms – there are dozens of two-bed rooms for privacy fans (some en suite). There are Granville St noise issues, so snag a back room.

Victorian Hotel   HOTEL $$
(Map p118; ☎ 877-681-6369, 604-681-6369; www. victorianhotel.ca; 514 Homer St; r incl breakfast with shared/private bathroom $99/159; ❂ @ 🛜; 🅼 Granville) The high-ceilinged rooms at this popular heritage-building Euro-style hotel combine glossy hardwood floors, a sprinkling of antiques, an occasional bay window and plenty of historical charm. The best rooms are in the renovated extension, where raindrop showers, marble bathroom floors and flatscreen TVs add a slice of luxe. Rooms are provided with fans in summer.

Urban Hideaway Guesthouse   GUESTHOUSE $$
(Map p118; ☎ 604-694-0600; www.urban-hideaway.com; 581 Richards St; ste $109/159; ❂ @; 🅼 Granville) This cozy but fiendishly well-hidden home away from home is a budget word-of-mouth favorite in the heart of the city. Tuck yourself into one of the comfy rooms – the loft is recommended – or spend your time in the lounge areas downstairs. There are laundry facilities, a free-use computer and loaner bikes are also gratis. Bathrooms are mostly shared, although the loft's is private.

Rosewood Hotel Georgia   HOTEL $$$
(Map p118; ☎ 604-682-5566; www.rosewoodhotels. com; 801 W Georgia St; d $410; ❂ ✳ @ 🛜 ✳ ✳; 🅼 Vancouver City Centre) Vancouver's current 'it' hotel underwent a recent spectacular renovation that brought the 1927-built landmark back to its golden-age glory. Despite the abstract modern art lining its public areas, the rooms take a classic, elegant approach with warming earth and coffee tones alongside pampering treats, such as deep soaker tubs and sparkling downtown cityscape views (in some rooms).

Save time for the lobby-level restaurant. Alongside the hotel's successful resurrection, Hawksworth (p133) has become the place to be seen for the city's movers and shakers – and you, if you look the part.

Loden Hotel
BOUTIQUE HOTEL **$$$**

(Map p118; ☑877-225-6336, 604-669-5060; www. theloden.com; 1177 Melville St; r $300; ❋@�❄❆; ⒨Burrard) The stylish Loden is the real designer deal – and one of the first boutique properties in years to give Yaletown's Opus a run for its money. The chic, chocolate-hued rooms combine a knowing contemporary élan with luxe accoutrements, like marble-lined bathrooms and those oh-so-civilized heated floors. Service is top-notch – make sure you try the complimentary London taxicab limo service.

Fairmont Pacific Rim
HOTEL **$$$**

(Map p118; ☑877-900-5350, 604-695-5300; www.fairmont.com/pacificrim; 1038 Canada Pl; d $249; ❄❋�❄❆; ⒨Waterfront) Near the convention center, this chic 377-room property is Vancouver's newest Fairmont. While many rooms have city views, the ones with waterfront vistas will blow you away, especially as you sit in your jetted tub or cube-shaped Japanese bath with a glass of bubbly. Flourishes include iPod docks and Nespresso machines, but the rooftop swimming pool should monopolize your time.

🛏 West End

HI Vancouver Downtown
HOSTEL **$**

(Map p118; ☑866-762-4122, 604-684-4565; www. hihostels.ca/vancouver; 1114 Burnaby St; dm/r incl breakfast $42/108; ❄@❄; ▢6) It says 'downtown' but this purpose-built hostel is on a quiet residential West End side street. Popular with older hostelers and families, the dorms are all mercifully small – private rooms are also available. There's also bike storage, a full kitchen, and TV and games rooms, plus twice-weekly April to November tours with legendary local guide Erik.

Buchan Hotel
HOTEL **$$**

(Map p118; ☑800-668-6654, 604-685-5354; www.buchanhotel.com; 1906 Haro St; d with private/shared bathroom $139/99; ❄@❄; ▢5) The cheap and cheerful, 1926-built Buchan has bags of charm and is steps from Stanley Park. Along corridors lined with old prints of yesteryear Vancouver, its budget rooms – most with shared bathrooms – are clean, cozy and well maintained, although some furnishings have seen better days. The pricier rooms are correspondingly prettier, while the east-side rooms are brighter. Friendly front desk staff.

Sunset Inn & Suites
HOTEL **$$**

(Map p118; ☑800-786-1997, 604-688-2474; www. sunsetinn.com; 1111 Burnaby St; ste incl breakfast $175; ❄❋@❄; ▢6) A generous cut above most of the West End's self-catering suite hotels, the popular Sunset Inn offers larger-then-average rooms with full kitchenettes. Each has a balcony, while some rooms – particularly those on south-facing higher floors – have partial views of English Bay. Rates include rare-for-Vancouver free parking and the attentive staff are among the best in the city.

Times Square Suites Hotel
APARTMENT **$$$**

(Map p118; ☑877-684-2223, 604-684-2223; www. timessquaresuites.com; 1821 Robson St; ste $225; ❄❋❄❆; ▢5) Superbly located just steps from Stanley Park, this excellent West End hidden gem (even the entrance can be hard to spot) is the perfect apartment-style Vancouver sleepover. Rooms – mostly one-bedroom suites – are spacious, with tubs, laundry facilities, full kitchens and superbly well-maintained, if slightly 1980s, decor. Rates include nearby gym access and there's a supermarket just across the street.

Sylvia Hotel
HOTEL **$$**

(Map p118; ☑604-681-9321; www.sylviahotel.com; 1154 Gilford St; r $189; ❄❆; ▢5) Built in 1912, the ivy-covered Sylvia enjoys a prime location overlooking English Bay. Generations of guests keep coming back – many request the same room every year – for a dollop of old-world charm plus a side order of first-name service. There's a wide array of comfortable room configurations, but the best are the bed-sitting suites, with kitchens and waterfront views.

English Bay Inn
B&B **$$**

(Map p118; ☑866-683-8002, 604-683-8002; www. englishbayinn.com; 1968 Comox St; r incl breakfast $175; ❄❄; ▢6) Each of the six, antique-lined rooms in this Tudoresque B&B near Stanley Park has a private bathroom and two have sumptuous four-poster beds: you'll think you've arrived in Victoria, BC's determinedly traditional-English capital, by mistake. There's complimentary port in the parlor, a secluded garden for hanging out and a three-course breakfast – arrive early for the dining room alcove table.

Listel Hotel
BOUTIQUE HOTEL **$$**

(Map p118; ☑800-663-5491, 604-684-8461; www.thelistelhotel.com; 1300 Robson St; d $180; ❄❋@❄; ▢5) A sophisticated, art hotel, the

Listel attracts grown-ups with its on-site installations and package deals with local art galleries. There's original artwork – including contemporary installations and First Nations creations – in many rooms, which all have a relaxing, mood-lit West Coast feel. Artsy types should also check out the adjoining private gallery, plus Forage (p134), the hotel's new farm-to-table on-site restaurant.

Yaletown

★ YWCA Hotel
HOSTEL $

(Map p118; ☑ 604-895-5830, 800-663-1424; www.ywcahotel.com; 733 Beatty St; s/d/tr with shared bath $73/90/117; ⊗ ❋ @ ☎; Ⓜ Stadium-Chinatown) This good value, well-located option offers well-maintained, if spartan, rooms of the student accommodation variety. There's a wide range of configurations, from singles to five-bed rooms that are ideal for groups. Some rooms have shared bathrooms while all have access to communal kitchens – each room also has a minifridge. Rates include access to the **YWCA Health & Fitness Centre**, a 10-minute walk away.

Opus Hotel
BOUTIQUE HOTEL $$$

(Map p118; ☑ 604-642-6787, 866-642-6780; www.opushotel.com; 322 Davie St; r $299; ❋ @ ☎ ❋; Ⓜ Yaletown-Roundhouse) The Opus kick-started Vancouver's boutique-hotel scene and, with its recent full-on revamp, it's still high up on the city's most-stylish-sleepovers list. The spruced-up rooms have contemporary-chic interiors – think bold colors, mod furnishings and feng-shui bed placements – while the luxe bathrooms have clear windows overlooking the streets (visiting exhibitionists take note).

Granville Island & Kitsilano

HI Vancouver Jericho Beach
HOSTEL $

(☑ 866-762-4122, 604-224-3208; www.hihostels.ca/vancouver; 1515 Discovery St, Kitsilano; dm/r with shared bathroom $36/88; ⊙ May-Sep; ⊗ @ ☎; ☐ 4) One of Canada's largest hostels looks like a Victorian hospital from the outside but has a great location if you're here for the sun-kissed Jericho Beach vibe (downtown is a 40-minute bus ride away). Basic rooms make this the least palatial Vancouver HI, but there's a large kitchen, bike rentals and a recently revamped cafe. Dorms are also larger here: book ahead for private rooms.

Granville Island Hotel
BOUTIQUE HOTEL $$

(Map p118; ☑ 800-663-1840, 604-683-7373; www.granvilleislandhotel.com; 1253 Johnston St; r $220; ⊗ ❋ @ ☎ ❋; ☐ 50) This gracious boutique property hugs Granville Island's quiet eastern tip, enjoying tranquil views across False Creek to Yaletown's mirrored towers. You'll be a five-minute walk from the Public Market (p124), with shopping and theater options on your doorstep. Rooms have an elegant, West Coast feel with some exposed wood flourishes. There's also a cool rooftop Jacuzzi, while the on-site brewpub-restaurant has a great patio.

Corkscrew Inn
B&B $$

(☑ 877-737-7276, 604-733-7276; www.corkscrewinn.com; 2735 W 2nd Ave, Kitsilano; d incl breakfast $180; ⊗ ☎; ☐ 84) This immaculate, gable-roofed property appears to have a drinking problem: it houses a little museum, available only to guests, that's lined with quirky corkscrews and antique vineyard tools. Aside from the boozy paraphernalia, this lovely century-old Craftsman home has five artsy rooms – we like the art deco room – and is just a short walk from the beach. Sumptuous breakfast included.

University of British Columbia & West Side

University of British Columbia Accommodation
ACCOMMODATION SERVICES $$

(☑ 888-822-1030, 604-822-1000; www.ubc-conferences.com; 5961 Student Union Blvd, UBC; r $35-199; ⊙ May-Aug; ⊗ @; ☐ 99 B-Line) Pretend you're still a student with a UBC campus sleepover. Well-maintained accommodation options include good-value college-dorm units at Pacific Spirit Hostel; private rooms, most with great views, in shared apartments at Gage Towers; and impressive, hotel-style West Coast Suites with flatscreen TVs and slick interiors, which are the only accommodations available year-round and also include breakfast and wi-fi.

Douglas Guest House
GUESTHOUSE $$

(☑ 888-872-3060, 604-872-3060; www.dougwin.com; 456 W 13th Ave; r incl breakfast $125-195; ☐ 15) A tangerine-hued Edwardian B&B in a quiet characterful neighborhood near City Hall, the Douglas offers good rates, especially in winter, and the kind of laid-back feel where you don't have to worry about creaky floors and knickknacks being knocked over. Its six rooms – comfortable and old-school rather than antique lined – include flowery singles with shared bathrooms, larger doubles with en-suite bathrooms and two family-friendly suites. Free off-street parking is included.

Eating

Vancouver is one of Canada's top dine-out cities, with a huge menu of authentic ethnic dining, a recent renaissance in locally sourced West Coast cuisine and a miniwave of new vegetarian restaurants. You can have the best sushi outside Japan for lunch, then follow up with lip-smacking Fraser Valley duck and for-aged morels for dinner. Whatever you go for, don't miss the city's flourishing food truck scene and consider a craft beer or two to go with your dinner: BC is arguably Canada's microbrewery capital.

✕ Downtown

Finch's CAFE **$**

(Map p118; www.finchteahouse.com; 353 W Pender St; mains $5-10; ⊙9am-5pm Mon-Fri, 11am-4pm Sat; ☐4) For a coveted seat at one of the dinged old tables, arrive off-peak at this sunny corner cafe that has a 'granny chic' look combining creaky wooden floors and junk-shop bric-a-brac. You'll be joining in-the-know hipsters and creative types who've been calling this their local for years. They come for the well-priced breakfasts (eg egg and soldiers for $2.95), plus freshly prepared gourmet ba-guette sandwiches and house-made soups.

★ Mario's Coffee Express COFFEE **$**

(Map p118; 595 Howe St; mains $4-8; ⊙7am-4pm Mon-Fri; Ⓜ Burrard) A java-lover's favorite that only downtown office workers seem to know about, you'll wake up and smell the coffee long before you make it through the door here. The rich aromatic beverages served up by the man himself are the kind of ambrosia brews that should make Starbucks drinkers weep – you might even forgive the 1980s Italian pop percolating through the shop.

Hidden in plain view, this is arguably downtown's best cup of coffee.

Japadog JAPANESE **$**

(Map p118; www.japadog.com; 530 Robson St; mains $5-8; ⊙11am-10pm Mon-Thu, to 11pm Fri & Sat, to 9pm Sun; ☐10) You'll have spotted the lunch-time lineups at the Japadog hotdog stands around town, but these celebrated, ever-*genki* Japanese expats opened a storefront here in 2010. The menu is almost the same – think turkey smokies with miso sauce and

bratwursts with onion, daikon and soy – but there are also naughtily seasoned fries; try the wasabi version.

Templeton DINER **$$**

(Map p118; www.thetempleton.ca; 1087 Granville St; mains $10-14; ⊙9am-11pm Mon-Wed, to 1am Thu-Sun; ⊛; ☐10) A chrome-and-vinyl '50s-look diner with a twist, Templeton cooks up giant organic burgers, addictive fries, vegetarian quesadillas and perhaps the best hangover cure in town, the 'Big Ass Breakfast'. Sadly, the mini jukeboxes on the tables don't work but you can console yourself with a waistline-busting chocolate ice-cream float. Avoid week-end peak times or you'll be queuing for ages.

La Bodega SPANISH **$$**

(Map p118; www.labodegavancouver.com; 1277 Howe St; tapas $3-13; ⊙5pm-midnight; ☐10) It's all about the tasting plates at this rustic, checked-tablecloth tapas bar, arguably Vancouver's most authentic Spanish restaurant. Pull up a chair, order a jug of sangria and decide on a few shareable treats from the extensive menu. If you're feeling spicy, the chorizo sausage hits the spot and the Spanish meatballs are justifi-ably popular.

Twisted Fork Bistro FRENCH **$$**

(Map p118; www.twistedforkbistro.ca; 1147 Granville St; mains $20-22; ⊙10am-2pm Fri-Sun & 5:30-11pm daily; ☐10) The best place to park your appetite among Granville St's greasy pub-grub options, this narrow, art-lined bistro feels like it should be somewhere else. But even clubbers need to eat well sometimes. The menu of rustic French classics includes mussels, lamb shank and an excellent beef bourguignon, but there are also smaller tasting plates if you want to share.

Coast SEAFOOD **$$**

(Map p118; ☎604-685-5010; www.coastrestaurant.ca; 1054 Alberni St; mains $18-42; ⊙11:30am-1am Mon-Thu, to 2am Fri, 4pm-2am Sat, 4pm-1am Sun; ☐5) A buzzing seafood joint where Vancou-ver movers and shakers like to be seen scoff-ing a wide array of aquatic treats. Knowing reinventions of the classics include prawn or salmon flatbread pizzas, but it's the mighty seafood platter of salmon, cod, scallops and tiger prawns that sates true fish nuts. Lunch-time fish and chips to go is $14 and there's an excellent raw bar with oysters aplenty.

★ Hawksworth WEST COAST **$$$**

(Map p118; ☎604-673-7000; www.hawksworth-restaurant.com; 801 W Georgia St; mains $29-39;

⊙7am-11pm) A top spot for the city's movers and shakers, this is the fine-dining anchor of the top-end Rosewood Hotel Georgia (p130). But unlike most hotel restaurants, this one has a starry-eyed local following. Created by and named after one of the city's top local chefs, the menu fuses contemporary West Coast approaches with clever international influences, hence dishes such as soy-roasted sturgeon. The seasonal tasting menu is also heartily recommended.

Chambar
EUROPEAN $$$

(Map p118; ☎604-879-7119; www.chambar.com; 562 Beatty St; mains $23-33; ⊙5pm-midnight; MStadium-Chinatown) This candlelit, brick-lined cave is a great place for a romantic night out. The sophisticated Belgian-influenced menu includes delectable *moules-frites* (mussels and fries) and a braised lamb shank with figs that's a local dining legend. An impressive wine and cocktail list – try a Blue Fig Martini – is coupled with a great Belgian beer menu dripping with *tripel* and *lambic* varieties to tempt drinkers.

✕ West End & Stanley Park

Sushi Mart
JAPANESE $

(Map p118; www.sushimart.com; 1686 Robson St; sushi combos $7-18; ⊙11:30am-3pm & 5-9pm Mon-Sat;

🍴5) You'll be rubbing shoulders with chatty young ESL students at the large communal dining table, one of the best spots in town for an extra-fresh sushi feast in a casual setting. Check the ever-changing blackboard showing what's available and then tuck into expertly prepared and well-priced shareable platters of all your fave *nigiri, maki* and sashimi treats. Udon dishes are also available.

★ Guu with Garlic
JAPANESE $$

(Map p118; www.guu-izakaya.com; 1689 Robson St; small plates $4-9, mains $8-16; ⊙11:30am-2:30pm Tue-Sun & 5:30pm-midnight daily; 🍴5) Arguably the best of Vancouver's many authentic *izakayas*, this welcoming, wood-lined joint is a cultural immersion. Hot pots and noodle bowls are available but it's best to experiment with some Japanese-bar tapas, such as black cod with miso mayo, deep-fried egg pumpkin balls or finger-lickin' *tori-karaage* fried chicken. Garlic is liberally used in most dishes, and it's best to arrive before opening time for a seat.

★ Forage
WEST COAST $$

(Map p118; ☎604-661-1400; www.foragevancouver. com; 1300 Robson St; mains $17-21; ⊙6:30-10am & 5pm-midnight Mon-Fri, 7am-2pm & 5pm-midnight Sat & Sun; 🍴5) ✦ A champion of the local farm-to-table scene, this sustainability-loving

---

FOOD-TRUCK FRENZY

Keen to emulate the legendary street-food scenes of Portland and Austin, Vancouver jumped on the kitchen-equipped bandwagon in 2010, launching a pilot scheme with 17 carts. Things took off quickly and by mid-2013, there were 114 tasty trucks dotted around the city, serving everything from halibut tacos to Korean sliders and from pulled pork sandwiches to French stews. The downtown core is home to many of the four-wheeled takeouts and, while there are lots of experimental fusion trucks, several have quickly risen to the top table: look out for local favorites **TacoFino**, **Re-Up BBQ**, **Roaming Dragon**, **Feastro**, **Fresh Local Wild**, **Yolk's Breakfast**, **Pig on the Street** and **Vij's Railway Express**. And don't miss one of the **JapaDog** locations: the nori-and-miso-flavored hotdog vendors arguably kicked off the scene by nudging the original rules that limited street food in the city to hotdogs and hot chestnuts – those were *not* the days.

There are usually a few vendors around the Vancouver Art Gallery complex (p117), but downtown arteries like Howe St, Burrard St, Georgia St and Seymour St are also good bets. The city has recently moved to address one concern: since they are so spread out, the carts can sometimes be hard to find, unlike those in Austin and Portland, which are typically grouped together into multicart pods. A proposed grouping of carts on Hamilton St aims to provide several dining options in one strollable spot.

For up-to-the-minute listings, opening hours and locations for street food carts, go to www.streetfoodapp.com/vancouver. And keep your eyes peeled for special appearances by the carts at events around the city. If you want some extra help, Vancouver Foodie Tours (p129) offers the tasty Street Eats Tour.

restaurant is the perfect way to sample the flavors of the region. Brunch has become a firm local favorite – the turkey sausage hash is recommended – but for dinner the idea is to sample an array of tasting plates. Though the menu is innovative and highly seasonal, look out for the delectable pork tongue ravioli and roast bison bone marrow.

Espana   SPANISH $$

(Map p118; www.espanarestaurant.ca; 1118 Denman St; tapas plates $5-12; ⊙5pm-1am Sun-Thu, to 2am Fri & Sat; ⊕5) Reservations are not allowed but it's worth the line-up to get into Vancouver's best new Spanish tapas joint. The tables are crammed close and the atmosphere is warm and welcoming, triggering a hubbub of chat that's mostly centered on the great grub. The crispy squid and cod and potato croqettes are delish, while the crispy chickpeas dish is a bit of a revelation.

Fish House in Stanley Park   SEAFOOD $$$

(☑877-681-7275, 604-681-7275; www.fishhouse-stanleypark.com; 8901 Stanley Park Dr; mains $22-42; ⊙11:30am-10pm; ⊕19) 🍴 The park's fanciest dine out, this double-patioed joint serves some of the city's best seafood. The menu changes based on seasonality but typical favorites include salmon Wellington and smoked-cod linguine, while fresh oysters are ever popular with visiting shuckers. Weekend brunch is a highlight – the smoked-salmon Benedict is recommended. The restaurant is committed to serving sustainable seafood and locally sourced beef, duck and chicken dishes are also available.

If you haven't eaten enough already come back for a rich treat-focused afternoon tea, served 2pm to 4pm, then run around the park four times to work it off.

✕ Yaletown

★ Flying Pig   WEST COAST $$

(Map p118; www.theflyingpigvan.com; 1168 Hamilton St; mains $18-24; ⊙11:30am-midnight Mon-Fri, 10:30am-midnight Sat & Sun; Ⓜ Yaletown-Roundhouse) Yaletown's best midrange restaurant has mastered the art of friendly service and excellent, savor-worthy dining. But since everyone else knows that, too, it's a good idea to dine off peak to avoid the crowds. A warm, woodsy bistro, the dishes focus on seasonal local ingredients and are virtually guaranteed to make you smile: scallops and halibut are perfect, and the roasted chicken is the city's best.

Reservations are not accepted for dinner. At the time of writing, a new, much bigger Flying Pig had just opened in Gastown.

Rodney's Oyster House   SEAFOOD $$

(Map p118; ☑604-609-0080; www.rohvan.com; 1228 Hamilton St; mains $16-32; ⊙11:30am-11pm; Ⓜ Yaletown-Roundhouse) Vancouver's favorite oyster eatery for many years, Rodney's always has a buzz about it. And it's not just because of the convivial room with its nautical flourishes: these guys really know how to do seafood. While the fresh-shucked oysters with a huge array of sauces – try the spicy vodka – never fail to impress, there's everything from sweet mussels to superb Atlantic lobster available.

Blue Water Café + Raw Bar   SEAFOOD $$$

(Map p118; ☑604-688-8078; www.bluewatercafe.net; 1095 Hamilton St; mains $25-44; ⊙5pm-midnight; Ⓜ Yaletown-Roundhouse) Under expert chef Frank Pabst, this has become one of Vancouver's best high-concept seafood restaurants and is a highlight of Yaletown fine dining. Music gently percolates through the brick-lined, blue-hued interior, while seafood towers, Arctic char and BC sablefish grace the tables inside and on the patio. Consider the semicircular raw bar and watch the whirling blades prepare delectable sushi and sashimi.

✕ Gastown

★ Rainier Provisions   WEST COAST $

(Map p118; www.rainierprovisions.com; 2 W Cordova St; mains $8-12; ⊙11am-8pm Mon-Fri, 9am-8pm Sat & Sun; ⊕4) Revitalizing a former Gastown hotel building, this great-value cafe-bistro is a perfect fuel-up spot. Drop in for Stumptown coffee or dive into a hearty menu, ranging from hot-sandwich specials served with soup or salad to a heaping roast with all the extras. The locally made sausages with roast potatoes is the winner though.

Meat & Bread   SANDWICHES $

(Map p118; www.meatandbread.ca; 370 Cambie St; mains $7-9; ⊙11am-5pm Mon-Sat; ⊕14) Arrive early to avoid the lunchtime queue at Vancouver's favorite gourmet sandwich shop and you might even snag one of the four tiny window perches. If not, you can hang with the hip locals at the chatter-filled long table, tucking into the daily changing special, usually featuring slices of perfectly roasted local lamb, pork or chicken. The grilled cheese sandwich is ace, too.

Wash it down with a $6 craft beer and expect to come back: this place has a cult-like

BRITISH COLUMBIA VANCOUVER

following and it's hard not to return when your next sandwich craving rears its savory head.

Save On Meats
DINER $

(Map p118; www.saveonmeats.ca; 43 W Hastings St; mains $4-14; ⊙7am-10pm Mon-Wed, 7am-midnight Thu-Sat, 8am-10pm Sun; ⊛; ☐14) A former old-school butcher shop, Save On Meats has been transformed into the Downtown Eastside's fave hipster diner, though it's not just about looking cool. Slide into a booth or take a perch at the long counter and tuck into comfort dishes, including great-value all-day breakfasts and a menu of basic faves such as macaroni and cheese, and chicken pot pie.

Acme Cafe
DINER $$

(Map p118; www.acmecafe.ca; 51 W Hastings St; mains $9-13; ⊙8am-9pm Mon-Fri, 9am-9pm Sat & Sun; ☐14) The black-and-white, deco-style interior here is enough to warm up anyone on a rainy day – or maybe it's the comfy booths and retro-cool U-shaped counter. The hipsters have been flocking here since day one for hearty breakfasts and heaping comfort-food lunches flavored with a gourmet flourish: the meatloaf, chicken club and shrimp guacamole sandwiches are worth the trip.

Judas Goat Taberna
TAPAS $$

(Map p118; www.judasgoat.ca; 27 Blood Alley; tapas $4-12; ⊙5pm-midnight Mon-Sat; ☐4) Named after the goats used to lead sheep off slaughterhouse trucks, this tiny backstreet tapas nook has nailed the art of simply prepared small plates, such as duck confit, beef brisket meatballs, and beet and goat-cheese terrine. Like its Salt Tasting Room brother next door, you'll also find a good, although shorter, wine and Spanish sherry drinks list.

Wildebeest
WEST COAST $$$

(Map p118; www.wildebeest.ca; 120 W Hastings St; mains $13-42; ⊙5pm-midnight Tue-Sun; ☐14) This mood-lit, bi-level joint is a carnivore's dream dinner destination. In fact, they eat vegetarians here – just kidding, there are choices for vegetarians, too. Find a table among the chattering classes – or better still at the communal long table downstairs – and tuck into short ribs, pork jowl or the juiciest roast chicken you'll ever eat.

✗ Chinatown

★ Bao Bei
CHINESE $$

(Map p118; ☏604-688-0876; www.bao-bei.ca; 163 Keefer St; small plates $9-18; ⊙5:30pm-midnight

TOP FIVE ASIAN RESTAURANTS

➡ Bao Bei (p136)

➡ Guu With Garlic (p134)

➡ Maenam (p138)

➡ Gam Gok Yuen (p136)

➡ Sushi Mart (p134)

Mon-Sat; ✍; ☐3) Reinventing a Chinatown heritage building interior with funky flourishes, this hidden-gem Chinese brasserie is the area's most seductive dinner destination. Enjoying a local cult following, it brings a contemporary edge to Asian-style, tapas-sized dishes such as *shao bing,* octopus salad and crispy pork belly. There's also a tasty commitment to inventive cocktails, so don't despair if you have to wait at the bar for your table.

Campagnolo
ITALIAN $$

(Map p118; www.campagnolorestaurant.ca; 1020 Main St; mains $12-25; ⊙11:30am-2:30pm & 5-10pm; ☐3) Eyebrows were raised when this contemporary Italian restaurant opened in a hitherto sketchy part of town, but intimate, minimalist Campagnolo has lured locals into making the effort to get here. They've been rewarded with some of the city's best Italian cuisine: share some dishes but don't miss the truffle sausage rigatoni or the citrusy local octopus salad.

Gam Gok Yuen
CHINESE $$

(Map p118; 142 E Pender St; mains $7-14; ⊙10:30am-8pm; ☐3) Try to block out the faded, 1980s decor in this unassuming Chinatown dining room: the carnivorous, Hong Kong–style food is what keeps this place humming, especially the barbecued pork and duck dishes – the clammy front window of roasted meats probably gives the game away. Order at will, but make sure you include a hearty bowl of noodle soup.

✗ Main Street & Commercial Drive

Gene Cafe
COFFEE $

(2404 Main St; baked goods $3-6; ⊙7:30am-7pm Mon-Fri, 8:30am-7pm Sat & Sun; ☎; ☐3) Colonizing a flatiron wedge of concrete floors and expansive windows, slide onto a chunky cedar bench with your well-thumbed copy of *L'Étranger* and you might catch the eye of an available local. If not, console yourself with a perfectly made cappuccino and a chunky home-baked cookie. The fruit pies are highly recommended for additional consolation.

Café Calabria COFFEE $

(1745 Commercial Dr; sandwiches $4-9; ☺6am-10pm Mon-Thu to midnight Fri & Sat; ☐20) When Vancouverites tell you the Drive is the city's best coffee street, this is one of the places they're thinking about. It tops a healthy cupful of cafes founded here by Italian immigrants. Don't be put off by the chandeliers-and-statues decor – not everyone likes a side order of statuesque genitalia with their drink. Just order an espresso, sit outside and watch the Drive slide by.

★Cannibal Café BURGERS $$

(www.cannibalcafe.ca; 1818 Commercial Dr; main $12-15; ☺11:30am-midnight; ☒; ☐20) A punkish diner for fans of seriously real burgers, the jaw-dislocating treats are the real deal here. Expect to drown in a pool of your own drool as you wait for your aromatic meal to arrive, then enter burger heaven. Made with real love, the service here is ever friendly and you'll find an inventive array from classics to the highly recommended Korean-BBQ burger.

Acorn VEGETARIAN $$

(www.theacornrestaurant.ca; 3995 Main St; mains $17-19; ☺5:30pm-1am Tue-Thu, to 2am Fri & Sat, to midnight Sun; ☒; ☐3) Quickly becoming one of Vancouver's hottest vegetarian restaurants soon after its 2012 opening – hence the sometimes long wait for a table – the Acorn has since settled into being a dependable, diner-inspired joint for vegetarians looking for something more upscale than a mung-bean soup kitchen. Consider artfully presented dishes such as beet ravioli and the excellent, crunch-tastic kale caesar salad.

Sun Sui Wah Seafood Restaurant CHINESE $$

(www.sunsuiwah.com; 3888 Main St; mains $8-22; ☺10:30am-3pm & 5-10:30pm; ☐3) One of the best places in the city for dim sum, this large, chatty Hong Kong–style joint has been a deserved local favorite for years. Order an array of treats, then sit back for the feast, although you should expect to be fighting over the lazy Susan to see who gets the last mouthful. Seafood is a huge specialty here, hence the live tanks.

Via Tevere PIZZERIA $$

(www.viateverepizzeria.com; 1190 Victoria Dr; mains $12-19; ☺5-10pm Tue-Thu, to 11pm Fri & Sat, to 9pm Sun; ☐20) Just two blocks east from the Drive, it's worth the five-minute walk for what may well be East Van's best pizza. Which is saying something, since the Drive is studded like an over-packed pepperoni pie with good pizza joints. Run by a family with true Neapolitan roots, check out the mosaic-tiled wood-fired oven, then launch yourself into a feast. The *capricciosa* is highly recommended.

✕ Granville Island

★Go Fish SEAFOOD $

(Map p118; 1505 W 1st Ave; mains $8-14; ☺11:30am-6:30pm Tue-Sun; ☐50) A short stroll westwards along the seawall from the Granville Island entrance, this almost too-popular seafood stand is one of the city's fave fish-and-chips joints, offering halibut, salmon or cod encased in crispy golden batter. The smashing, lighter fish tacos are also recommended, while ever-changing daily specials, brought in by the nearby fishing boats, often include scallop burgers or ahi tuna sandwiches.

Agro Café CAFE $

(Map p118; www.agrocafe.org; 1363 Railspur Alley; mains $5-8; ☺8am-7pm Mon-Fri, 9am-7pm Sat & Sun; ☎; ☐50) This slightly hidden cafe on Railspur Alley is a smashing coffee stop. It also serves the best value breakfast on Granville Island – go for the $7 eggs, hash browns and turkey sausage. Lunch delivers soups, salads, sandwiches and wraps and there's always a BC craft beer or two if you need to crank it up from coffee.

★Edible Canada at the Market WEST COAST $$

(Map p118; ☎604-682-6681; www.ediblecanada.com/bistro; 1596 Johnston St; mains $18-29; ☺11am-9pm Mon-Thu, to 10pm Fri-Sun; ☐50) Granville Island's most popular bistro delivers a short but tempting menu of seasonal dishes from across Canada, often including perfectly prepared Alberta beef, Newfoundland fish and several BC treats – look out for slow-roasted pork belly. Consider sharing some small plates if you're feeling adventurous, perhaps topped with a naughty maple-sugar pie and a glass of ice wine. Book ahead.

✕ Kitsilano & West Side

★ La Taqueria Pinche Taco Shop   MEXICAN $

(www.lataqueria.ca; 2549 Cambie St; 4 tacos $7-9.50; ☺11am-8:30pm Mon-Sat; ✐; Ⓜ Broadway-City Hall) Vancouver's fave taco spot expanded from its tiny Hastings St location (which is still there) with this much larger storefront. It's just as crowded but, luckily, many of the visitors are going the takeout route. Snag a brightly painted table perch, then order at the counter from a dozen or so meat or veggie soft tacos (take your pick or ask for a selection), washed down with a cheap-ass beer.

Service is warm and friendly here and the prices and quality ingredients are enough to keep you coming back: the tacos are $2.50 each or four for $9.50 (or just $7 if you take the vegetarian option).

★ Fable   WEST COAST $$

(✐604-732-1322; www.fablekitchen.ca; 1944 W 4th Ave; mains $18-28; ☺11:30am-2pm Mon-Fri, 5:30-10pm Mon-Sat, brunch 10:30am-2pm Sat & Sun; ☐4) One of Vancouver's favorite farm-to-table restaurants is a lovely rustic-chic room of exposed brick, wood beams and prominently displayed red-rooster logos, but looks are just part of the appeal. Expect perfectly prepared bistro dishes showcasing local seasonal ingredients, often including duck, chicken or halibut. It's great gourmet comfort food with little pretension, hence the packed room most nights. Reservations recommended.

Salmon n' Bannock   WEST COAST $$

(www.salmonandbannock.net; 1128 W Broadway; mains $14-24; ☺11am-3pm Mon-Fri, 5-9pm Mon-Thu, 5-11pm Fri & Sat; ☐9) Vancouver's only First Nations restaurant is a delightful little art-lined bistro among an unassuming strip of Broadway shops. It's worth the bus trip, though, for freshly-made aboriginal-influenced dishes made with local ingredients. If lunching, tuck into the juicy signature salmon-and-bannock burger, made with their popular aboriginal flat-bread. If you're planning dinner, go for the velvet-soft braised deer shank.

Naam   VEGETARIAN $$

(www.thenaam.com; 2724 W 4th Ave; mains $9-16; ☺24hr; ✐; ☐4) An evocative relic of Kitsilano's hippie past, this vegetarian restaurant has the feel of a comfy, highly chatty farmhouse. It's not unusual to have to wait for a table here at peak times, but it's worth it for the hearty stir-fries, Mexican platters and sesame-fried potatoes with miso gravy. This is the kind of veggie spot where carnivores are happy to dine.

Maenam   THAI $$

(✐604-730-5579; www.maenam.ca; 1938 W 4th Ave; mains $15-19; ☺noon-2:30pm Tue-Sat & 5-10pm Mon-Sat; ✐; ☐4) At this contemporary reinvention of the Thai-restaurant model, subtle and complex traditional and

---

FARMERS MARKETS

A tasty cornucopia of BC farm produce hits the stalls around Vancouver from June to October. Seasonal highlights include crunchy apples, lush peaches and juicy blueberries, while home-baked cakes and treats are frequent accompaniments. Don't be surprised to see zesty local cheese and a few arts and crafts added to the mix. To check out what's on offer, visit www.eatlocal.org.

➡ **East Vancouver Farmers Market** (Commercial Dr, north parking lot of Trout Lake Park; ☺9am-2pm Sat mid-May–mid-Oct; ☐20)

➡ **Kitsilano Farmers Market** (Kitsilano Community Centre, 2690 Larch St; ☺10am-2pm Sun mid-May–mid-Oct; ☐4)

➡ **Main Street Station Farmers Market** (Map p118; Thornton Park, 1100 Station St; ☺3-7pm Wed Jun-Sep; Ⓜ Main St-Science World)

➡ **UBC Farmers Market** (6182 South Campus Rd, UBC; ☺9am-1pm Sat mid-Jun–Sep; ☐99B-Line)

➡ **West End Farmers Market** (Map p118; Nelson Park, btwn Bute & Thurlow Sts; ☺9am-2pm Sat Jun–mid-Oct; ☐6)

➡ **Winter Farmers Market** (Wise Hall, 1882 Adanac St, off Commercial Dr; ☺10am-2pm 2nd & 4th Sat of month Nov-Apr; ☐20)

international influences flavor the menu in a room with a modern lounge feel. Inviting exploration, you can start with the familiar – although even the pad thai here is eye-poppingly different – but save room for something new: the *geng pa neua* beef curry is a sweet, salty and nutty treat.

Vij's   INDIAN $$$
(www.vijsrestaurant.ca; 1480 W 11th Ave; mains $24-30; ⊙ 5:30-10pm; ⬚ 10) Just off southern Granville St, this Vancouver favorite is the highwater mark of contemporary East Indian cuisine, fusing regional ingredients, subtle global flourishes and classic Indian flavors to produce an array of innovative dishes. The unique results range from signature wine-marinated 'lamb popsicles' to savorworthy meals, such as halibut, mussels and crab in a tomato-ginger curry. Reservations are not accepted, which sometimes means a very long wait.

🍸 Drinking & Nightlife

Distinctive new lounges and pubs are springing up in Vancouver like persistent drunks at an open bar. Wherever you end up imbibing, sip some of the region's excellent craft brews, including tasty tipples from Driftwood Brewing, Howe Sound Brewing and Central City Brewing. Granville St, from Robson to Davie Sts, is a party district of mainstream haunts, but Gastown, Main St and Commercial Dr offer superior options loved by the savvy locals.

★Alibi Room   PUB
(Map p118; www.alibi.ca; 157 Alexander St; ⊙ 5-11:30pm Mon-Fri, 10am-11:30pm Sat & Sun; ⬚ 4) Vancouver's best craft-beer tavern, this exposed brick bar stocks an ever-changing roster of around 50 drafts from celebrated BC breweries, such as Phillips, Driftwood and Crannóg. Adventurous taste trippers – hipsters and old-lag beer fans alike – enjoy the $9.50 'frat bat' of four sample tipples: choose your own or ask to be surprised. And always check the board for ever-changing guest casks.

★Railway Club   PUB
(Map p118; www.therailwayclub.com; 579 Dunsmuir St; ⊙ 4pm-2am Mon-Thu, noon-3am Fri, 3pm-3am Sat, 5pm-midnight Sun; Ⓜ Granville) A local-legend, pub-style music venue, the upstairs 'Rail' is accessed via an unobtrusive wooden door next to a 7-Eleven. Don't be put off: this is one of the city's friendliest bars and you'll

fit right in as soon as you roll up to the bar – unusually for Vancouver, you have to order at the counter, since there's no table service. Live music nightly.

★Shameful Tiki Room   BAR
(www.shamefultikiroom.com; 4362 Main St; ⊙ 5pm-midnight Wed-Mon; ⬚ 3) Slip through the curtains into this windowless snug and you'll be instantly transported to a Polynesian beach. The lighting – including glowing puffer-fish lamp shades – is permanently set to dusk and the walls are lined with Tiki masks and rattan coverings under a straw-shrouded ceiling, but it's the drinks that rock: seriously well-crafted classics from zombies to scorpion bowls.

★Brickhouse   PUB
(Map p118; 730 Main St; ⊙ 8pm-2am Mon-Sat, to midnight Sun; ⬚ 3) Possibly Vancouver's most original pub, this old-school hidden gem is a welcoming, windowless tavern lined with Christmas lights, fish tanks and junk-shop couches. Popular with artsy locals and in-the-know young hipsters, it's like hanging out in someone's den. Grab a Storm Scottish Ale at the bar, slide onto a perch and start chatting: you're bound to meet someone interesting.

★Storm Crow Tavern   PUB
(www.stormcrowtavern.com; 1305 Commercial Dr; ⊙ 4pm-1am Mon-Thu, 11am-1am Fri & Sat; ⬚ 20) Knowing the difference between Narnia and *Neverwhere* is not a prerequisite for enjoying this smashing Commercial Dr nerd pub but, if you do, you'll certainly make new friends. It has displays of *Dr Who* figures and steampunk ray guns, plus a TV that seems to be always screening *Game of Thrones*. Dive into the craft beer and settle in for a fun evening.

Portland Craft   BAR
(www.portlandcraft.com; 3835 Main St; ⊙ 4pm-1am Mon-Thu, 11:30am-2am Fri & Sat, 10am-midnight Sun; ⬚ 3) With its unique-for-Vancouver 20-strong draft list of mostly Western US beers, this convivial new restaurant-bar is tapping into the popularity of craft brews from Portland and beyond. You'll find Rogue, Hopworks, Elysian and Deschutes well represented, so if you're a fan of superhoppy IPAs, you'll soon be puckering your lips with pleasure. Arrive early on weekend evenings to snag a table.

OFF THE BEATEN TRACK

VANCOUVER'S OTHER BREWS

If you're a true beer nut, consider checking out a round of little, off-the-beaten-path East Vancouver microbreweries that even some locals don't know about. Start on Commercial Drive and walk north from the intersection with Venables St for about 10 minutes. You'll soon be in a light industrial part of town – don't worry, it's perfectly safe. You'll come to **Storm Brewing** (☎604-255-9119; www.stormbrewing.org; 310 Commercial Dr; 🚌20), a legendary local brewery that's been crafting great ales since 1995. Call ahead for an impromptu tour – Wednesday is brewing day, so that's the best time to come. With any luck, you'll be able to sample their excellent **Black Plague Stout**. Continue north for two blocks and turn right onto Powell St. A few minutes along, you'll find the lovely **Powell Street Craft Brewery** (www.powellbeer.com; 1830 Powell St; ⏰1-7pm Wed-Sat; 🚌4). This art-lined, gable-roofed nanobrewery is one of the city's smallest beer producers. Consider a sample of the lip-smacking **Dive Bomb Porter**, and pick up a growler to go. Despite its diminutive stature, this producer stunned beer fans across the country in 2013 when its **Old Jalopy Pale Ale** was named the nation's Beer of the Year at the annual Canadian Brewing Awards. Continue east on Powell, turn right onto Victoria Dr and then left on Triumph St. Within a couple of minutes, you'll hit the storefront of **Parallel 49 Brewing Company** (www.parallel49brewing.com; 1950 Triumph St; ⏰noon-9pm; 🚌14). Nip into the tasting room here and sample their array of quirky tipples, including **Hoparazzi India Pale Lager** and **Gypsy Tears Ruby Red Ale**.

Diamond
COCKTAIL BAR

(Map p118; www.di6mond.com; 6 Powell St; ⏰5:30pm-1am Wed & Thu, to 2am Fri & Sat, to midnight Sun; 🚌4) Head upstairs via the unassuming entrance and you'll find yourself in one of Vancouver's warmest little cocktail bars. A renovated heritage room studded with sash windows – try for a view seat – it's popular with local coolsters but is rarely pretentious. A list of perfectly nailed, though not cheap, cocktails helps, coupled with a tasty tapas menu.

Six Acres
BAR

(Map p118; www.sixacres.ca; 203 Carrall St; 5pm-1am Mon-Sat; 🚌4) Gastown's coziest tavern, you can cover all the necessary food groups via the extensive, mostly bottled, beer menu. There's a small, animated summer patio out front, but inside is great for hiding in a candlelit corner and working your way through the brews, plus a shared small plate or three – the sausage platter is recommended.

Keefer Bar
COCKTAIL BAR

(Map p118; www.thekeeferbar.com; 135 Keefer St; ⏰5pm-midnight Mon, to 1am Tue-Thu & Sun, to 2am Fri & Sat; Ⓜ Stadium-Chinatown) A dark, narrow and atmospheric Chinatown bar, it's been claimed by local cocktail-loving coolsters from day one. Drop in for a full evening of liquid taste-tripping and you'll have a blast. From perfectly prepared rosemary gimlets and Siamese slippers to an excellent whis-

key menu and a side dish of tasty tapas – go for the late-night Keefer dog – this is a great night out.

Irish Heather
PUB

(Map p118; www.irishheather.com; 210 Carrall St, Gastown; ⏰11:30am-midnight Mon-Thu & Sun, to 2am Fri & Sat; 🚌4) Belying the clichés about expat Irish bars, with the exception of its reclaimed-Guinness-barrel floor, the Heather is one of Vancouver's best gastropubs. Alongside lovingly prepared sausage and mash, and steak-and-ale pie, you'll find top craft beers and some well-poured Guinness. Best time to come? The seasonal Sunday to Wednesday long-table nights: dinner and a pint is around $18.

Cascade Room
BAR

(www.thecascade.ca; 2616 Main St; ⏰5pm-1am Mon-Thu, to 2am Fri & Sat, to midnight Sun; 🚌3) The perfect contemporary reinvention of a trad neighborhood bar, this is arguably Mount Pleasant's merriest watering hole. The top-drawer craft beer list runs from Fullers to Phillips and includes own-brand Main Street Pilsner, soon to be produced in a nearby new brewery building. Indulge in Main St's best Sunday roast or hang with the locals at Monday's funtastic quiz or 'name that tune' night.

Vancouver Urban Winery
WINE BAR

(www.vancouverurbanwinery.com; 55 Dunlevy Ave; ⏰11am-6pm Mon-Wed, to 11pm Thu & Fri, noon-

5pm Sun; 📕4) Vancouver's only winery is actually a barrel-lined warehousing business storing tipples from BC and beyond, but there's also a large public tasting bar that's one of the city's hidden gems. Roll up for an afternoon tasting during the week (a five-glass tasting flight is $12) or, better still, drop by on Friday night when the place is a hopping nightlife spot for those in the know.

St Augustine's   PUB

(www.staugustinesvancouver.com; 2360 Commercial Dr; ⊙11am-1am Sun-Thu, to 2am Fri & Sat; Ⓜ Commercial-Broadway) It looks like a regular neighborhood sports bar from the outside, but step inside St Aug's and you'll find more than 40 on-tap microbrews – one of the largest selections in the city. Most are from BC – look out for beer from Russell Brewing, Howe Sound Brewing and Storm Brewing – but there's also an intriguing selection from south of the border.

Yaletown Brewing Company   BREWERY

(Map p118; www.drinkfreshbeer.com; 1111 Mainland St; ⊙11:30am-midnight Sun-Wed, to 1am Thu, to 3am Fri & Sat; Ⓜ Yaletown-Roundhouse) There's a brick-lined brewpub on one side and a giant dining room on the other. Both serve pints of beer made on site, and the restaurant adds a long menu of comfort foods. Check to see if there's an unusual small-batch beer on offer, otherwise hit one of the mainstays: Brick & Beam IPA is recommended. Beer nuts should drop by 4pm Thursdays for cask night.

Fortune Sound Club   CLUB

(Map p118; www.fortunesoundclub.com; 147 E Pender St; ⊙Wed-Sat; 📕3) The city's best club has transformed a tired Chinatown spot into a slick space with the kind of genuine staff and younger, hipster-cool crowd rarely seen in Vancouver venues. Slide inside and you'll find a giant dance floor bristling with party-loving locals out for a good time. Expect weekend queues and check-out Happy Ending Fridays, when you'll possibly dance your ass off.

☆ Entertainment

Pick up the free *Georgia Straight* or check www.straight.com for local happenings. Event tickets are available from **Ticketmaster** (☑604-280-4444; www.ticketmaster.ca) but **Tickets Tonight** (Map p118; ☑604-684-2787; www.ticketstonight.ca) also sells half-price day-of-entry tickets. Live music shows are listed at www.livevan.com; cinema listings, at www.cinemaclock.com.

Live Music

★**Commodore**   LIVE MUSIC

(Map p118; www.commodoreballroom.ca; 868 Granville St; 📕10) Local bands know they've made it when they play Vancouver's best mid-sized venue, a restored art-deco ballroom that still has the city's bounciest dance floor, courtesy of tires placed under its floorboards. If you need a break from your moshing, collapse at one of the tables lining the perimeter, catch your breath with a bottled Stella and then plunge back in.

GAY & LESBIAN VANCOUVER

Vancouver's gay and lesbian scene is part of the city's culture rather than a subsection of it. The legalization of same-sex marriages has resulted in a huge number of couples using Vancouver as a kind of gay Vegas for their destination nuptials. For more information on tying the knot, visit www.vs.gov.bc.ca/marriage/howto.html.

Vancouver's West End district – complete with its pink-painted bus shelters, fluttering rainbow flags and hand-holding locals – houses western Canada's largest 'gayborhood,' while the city's lesbian contingent is centered more on Commercial Dr.

Pick up a free copy of *Xtra!* for a crash course on the local scene, and check www. gayvancouver.net, www.gayvan.com and www.superdyke.com for pertinent listings and resources. In the evening, start your night off at the **Fountainhead Pub** (Map p118; www.thefountainheadpub.com; 1025 Davie St; ⊙11am-midnight Sun-Tue, to 1am Wed-Sat; 📕6), the West End's loudest and proudest gay bar, with its sometimes-raucous patio. Later, move on to the scene's biggest club, **Celebrities** (Map p118; www.celebritiesnightclub.com; 1022 Davie St; ⊙8pm-3am Wed, 10pm-3am Thu, 9pm-3am Tue, Fri & Sat; 📕6). For an even bigger party, don't miss the giant annual Pride Week (p129) in late July, which includes Vancouver's biggest street parade. You can also drop in and tap the local community at the popular **Little Sister's Book & Art Emporium** (Map p118; www.littlesisters.ca; 1238 Davie St; ⊙10am-11pm; 📕6).

★ **Biltmore Cabaret**   LIVE MUSIC
(www.biltmorecabaret.com; 2755 Prince Edward St; 🚇9) One of Vancouver's best alternative venues, the Biltmore is a firm favorite on the local indie scene. A low-ceilinged, vibe-tastic spot to mosh to local and touring musicians, there are also regular event nights: check their online calendar for upcoming happenings or hit the eclectic monthly Talent Time, Wednesday's rave-like dance night or Sunday's ever-popular Kitty Nights burlesque show.

Rickshaw Theatre   LIVE MUSIC
(Map p118; www.liveatrickshaw.com; 254 E Hastings St; 🚇14) Revamped from its grungy 1970s incarnation, the funky Rickshaw shows that Eastside gentrification can be positive. The stage of choice for many punk and indie acts, it's an excellent place to see a band, with a huge mosh area near the stage, and rows of theater-style seats at the back. Head to the front for a mega moshpit experience with plenty of sweat-triggering action.

Cinemas

Scotiabank Theatre   CINEMA
(Map p118; www.cineplex.com; 900 Burrard St; tickets $12.50; 🚇2) Downtown's shiny multiplex was big enough to attract its own corporate sponsor when it opened in 2005 and it's the most likely theater to be screening the latest must-see *Avengers* sequel. In contrast, it also shows occasional live broadcast performances from major cultural institutions, like London's National Theatre and New York's Metropolitan Opera. Note that there are no matinee or Tuesday discounts.

Pacific Cinémathèque   CINEMA
(Map p118; www.cinematheque.bc.ca; 1131 Howe St; tickets $11, double bills $14; 🚇10) This beloved repertory cinema operates like an ongoing film festival with a daily changing program of movies. A $3 annual membership is required – pick it up at the door – before you can skulk in the dark with the chin-stroking movie buffs.

Vancity Theatre   CINEMA
(Map p118; www.viff.org; 1181 Seymour St; tickets $11, double bills $14; 🚇10) The state-of-the-art headquarters of the Vancouver International Film Festival (p129) screens a wide array of movies throughout the year in the kind of auditorium that cinephiles dream of: generous legroom, wide arm rests and great sight lines from each of its 175 seats. It's a place where you can watch a four-hour sub-titled epic about a dripping tap and still feel comfortable.

Rio Theatre   THEATER, CINEMA
(www.riotheatre.ca; 1660 E Broadway; Ⓜ Commercial-Broadway) A recently restored 1980s movie house with very comfy seats, the Rio is like a community repertory theater staging everything from blockbuster and art-house movie screenings to live music, spoken word and saucy burlesque nights. Check the highly eclectic calendar to see what's on: Friday's midnight cult movies (from *Donny Darko* to *The Rocky Horror Picture Show*) are always popular.

Cineplex Odean International Village   CINEMA
(Map p118; www.cineplex.com; 88 W Pender St; Ⓜ Stadium-Chinatown) Incongruously located on the 3rd floor of a usually half-empty Chinatown shopping mall, this popular Vancouver theater combines blockbuster and art-house offerings. Comfy stadium seating is the norm here and it's ideal for sheltering on a rainy Vancouver day with a bottomless cup of coffee. Often used as a venue for the city's many film festivals, there's free mall parking for patrons.

Theater & Classical Music

★ **Cultch**   THEATER
(Vancouver East Cultural Centre; www.thecultch.com; 1895 Venables St; 🚇20) This once-abandoned 1909 church has been a gathering place for performers and audiences since being officially designated a cultural space in 1973. Following a comprehensive recent renovation, the beloved Cultch, as everyone calls it, is now one of Vancouver's entertainment jewels with a busy roster of local, fringe and visiting theatrical shows, from spoken word to touring Chekhov productions.

★ **Bard on the Beach**   PERFORMING ARTS
(Map p118; 📞604-739-0559; www.bardonthebeach.org; Vanier Park, Kitsilano; ⊙ Jun-Sep; 🚇22) Watching Shakespeare performed while the sun sets against the mountains through the open back of a tented stage is a Vancouver summertime highlight. There are usually three Bard plays, plus one Bard-related work (*Rosencrantz and Guildenstern are Dead*, for example) to choose from during the run. Question-and-answer talks are staged after Tuesday-night performances, along with regular opera, fireworks and wine-tasting nights throughout the season.

Arts Club Theatre Company
THEATER

(www.artsclub.com) Musicals, international classics and works by contemporary Canadian playwrights are part of the mix at Vancouver's leading theater company. If you're curious about West Coast theatrics, look out for plays by Morris Panych, BC's favorite playwright son. The company's three performance spaces are the **Granville Island Stage** (Map p118; 1585 Johnston St; ☐50), the nearby and more intimate **Revue Stage** (Map p118; 1601 Johnston St; ☐50) and the refurbished 1930s **Stanley Theatre** (2750 Granville St; ☐10).

Vancouver Symphony Orchestra
PERFORMING ARTS

(☑604-876-3434; www.vancouversymphony.ca) Led by popular maestro Bramwell Tovey, the city's stirring symphony orchestra serves up accessible classics and 'pops.' Shows to look out for include Symphony Sundays and film nights (when live scores are performed to classic movies), plus visits from revered soloists. Concerts often take place at the Orpheum Theatre, but the orchestra frequently unpacks its kettledrums at auditoriums across the Lower Mainland.

Sports

Vancouver Canucks
HOCKEY

(Map p118; www.canucks.com; Rogers Arena, 800 Griffiths Way; Ⓜ Stadium-Chinatown) The city's National Hockey League (NHL) team toyed with fans in 2011's Stanley Cup finals before losing Game 7 to the Boston Bruins, triggering riots and looting across Vancouver. But love runs deep and 'go Canucks, go!' is still boomed out from a packed Rogers Arena at every game. Book your seat early or just head to a local bar for some raucous game-night atmosphere.

Vancouver Whitecaps
SOCCER

(Map p118; www.whitecapsfc.com; BC Place Stadium, 777 Pacific Blvd; tickets $25-150; ⊘Mar-Oct; Ⓜ Stadium-Chinatown) Now using BC Place Stadium as its home, Vancouver's leading soccer team plays in North America's top-tier Major League Soccer (MLS) arena. They've struggled a little since being promoted to the league in 2011, but have been finding their feet (useful for soccer players) in recent seasons. A fun couple of hours; save time for a souvenir soccer shirt purchase to impress everyone back home.

BC Lions
FOOTBALL

(Map p118; www.bclions.com; BC Place Stadium, 777 Pacific Blvd; tickets $32-112; ⊘Jun-Nov; Ⓜ Stadium-Chinatown) The Lions are Vancouver's Canadian Football League (CFL) team, a game that's arguably more exciting than its US NFL counterpart. They've had some decent showings over the past few years, winning the all-important Grey Cup championship most recently in 2011. Tickets are easy to come by – unless the boys are laying into their arch enemies, the Calgary Stampeders.

🛍 Shopping

Robson St is ideal for wanton chain-store browsing, but if you're aiming your credit cards at independent retailers, you'll have to do a little sleuthing. If you prefer an edgier look, it's hard to beat Gastown and the quirky Main St boutiques south of 18th Ave. For window shopping, try Granville Island, South Granville (especially from Broadway southwards) and Kitsilano's W 4th Ave.

★Regional Assembly of Text
ARTS & CRAFTS

(www.assemblyoftext.com; 3934 Main St; ⊘11am-6pm Mon-Sat, noon-5pm Sun; ☐3) This ironic antidote to the digital age lures ink-stained locals with its journals, handmade pencil boxes and T-shirts printed with typewriter motifs. Check out the tiny under-the-stairs gallery showcasing zines from around the world, and don't miss the monthly letter-writing club (7pm, first Thursday of every month), where you can sip tea, scoff cookies and hammer away on vintage typewriters.

One of Vancouver most original stores, check out the array of handmade self-published minibooks near the front window – where else can you read *One Shrew Too Few* and *Secret Thoughts of a Plain Yellow House*?

★Smoking Lily
CLOTHING

(www.smokinglily.com; 3634 Main St; ⊘11am-6pm Mon-Sat, noon-5pm Sun; ☐3) Art-school cool rules here, with skirts, belts and halter tops whimsically accented with prints of ants, bicycles and the periodic table. Men's clothing is a smaller part of the mix, with fish, skull and tractor T-shirts. It's hard to imagine a better souvenir than the silk tea cozy printed with a Pierre Trudeau likeness – ask the friendly staff for more recommendations.

★Mountain Equipment Co-Op
OUTDOOR EQUIPMENT

(www.mec.ca; 130 W Broadway; ⊘10am-7pm Mon-Wed, to 9pm Thu & Fri, 9am-6pm Sat, 11am-5pm Sun; ☐9) Grown hikers weep at the amazing selection of clothing, kayaks, sleeping bags and clever camping gadgets at this cavernous outdoors store: MEC has been encouraging fully fledged outdoor enthusiasts for years. You'll have to be a member to buy, but that's easy to arrange for just $5. Equipment – canoes, kayaks, camping gear etc – can also be rented here.

★ **Gallery of BC Ceramics**   ARTS & CRAFTS
(Map p118; www.bcpotters.com; 1359 Cartwright St; ☺10:30am-5:30pm; ☐50) The star of Granville Island's arts-and-crafts shops, the public face of the Potters Guild of BC exhibits and sells the striking works of its member artists. You can pick up one-of-a-kind ceramic tankards or swirly-painted soup bowls – the hot items are the cool ramen noodle cups, complete with holes for chopsticks. Well-priced art for everyone.

Macleod's Books   BOOKS
(Map p118; 455 W Pender St; ☺11am-6pm Mon-Sat, noon-5pm Sun; ☐Granville) From its creaky floorboards to those scuzzy carpets and ever-teetering piles of books, this legendary locals' fave is the best place in town to peruse a cornucopia of used tomes. From dance to the occult, it's the ideal spot for a rainy-day browse. Check the windows for posters of local readings and artsy happenings around the city.

John Fluevog Shoes   SHOES
(Map p118; www.fluevog.com; 65 Water St; ☺10am-7pm Mon-Wed, to 8pm Thu & Fri, to 7pm Sat, noon-6pm Sun; ☐Waterfront) Like an art gallery for shoes, this alluringly cavernous store showcases the famed footwear of local designer Fluevog, whose men's and women's boots and brogues are what Doc Martens would have become if they'd stayed interesting and cutting edge. Pick up that pair of thigh-hugging dominatrix boots you've always wanted or settle on some designer-twisted loafers that would make anyone walk tall.

Zulu Records   MUSIC
(www.zulurecords.com; 1972 W 4th Ave; ☺10:30am-7pm Mon-Wed, to 9pm Thu & Fri, 9:30am-6:30pm Sat, noon-6pm Sun; ☐4) It's easy to spend a rainy afternoon in Kitsilano's fave indie music store sifting the racks of new and used vinyl and hard-to-find imports, including some of those newfangled CDs. There's an old-school *High Fidelity* ambience here – the scuffed blue carpet and Death Race vintage video game help. Ask the music nerd

staff for tips on the local live scene: they know their stuff.

Bird on a Wire Creations   ARTS & CRAFTS
(www.birdonawirecreations.com; 2535 Main St; ☺10am-6pm Mon-Sat, noon-5pm Sun; ☐3) Eminently browsable and highly tempting, there's a surprisingly diverse array of tasteful handmade goodies at this cute and ever-friendly store. Your credit cards will start to sweat as you move among the printed purses, flower-petal soaps, artsy T-shirts and grinning monster kids' toys that adults always want, too. It's not just for show: there are regular craft classes here too.

Hill's Native Art   ARTS & CRAFTS
(Map p118; www.hills.ca; 165 Water St; ☺9am-9pm; ☐Waterfront) Launched in 1946 as a small trading post on Vancouver Island, Hill's flagship store has many First Nations carvings, prints, ceremonial masks and cozy Cowichan sweaters, plus traditional music and books of historical interest. Artists are often found at work in the 3rd-floor gallery and it's a great spot to pick up some authentic aboriginal artworks for savoring at home.

Front & Company   CLOTHING, ACCESSORIES
(www.frontandcompany.ca; 3772 Main St; ☺11am-6:30pm; ☐3) A triple-fronted store where you could easily spend a couple of hours, its largest section contains trendy consignment clothing – where else can you find that vintage velvet smoking jacket? Next door houses new, knowingly cool house wares, while the third area includes must-have gifts and accessories, such as manga figures, peace-sign ice trays and nihilist chewing gum (flavorless, of course).

Barefoot Contessa   CLOTHING
(www.thebarefootcontessa.com; 1928 Commercial Dr; ☺11am-6pm; ☐20) Vintage-look dresses and sparkling costume jewelry , plus a 1920s-style flapper hat or two , are the mainstays of this popular women's clothing boutique aimed at those who never want to be a clone of a chain-store mannequin. You'll find cute tops and accessories from Canadian and international designers, plus artsy-craftsy purses and laptop bags trimmed with lace.

Attic Treasures   VINTAGE
(www.attictreasuresvancouver.com; 944 Commercial Dr; ☺11am-6pm Tue & Thu-Sat, noon-5pm Sun; ☐20) One of Vancouver's favorite antiques stores, this retro-cool double-room

shop specializes in mid-century furniture and treasures, which means you'll likely spot items that recall something you remember from an elderly relative's house. Peruse the candy-colored coffee pots and cocktail glasses and save time for the clutter room at the back, where bargains sometimes live.

ℹ️ Information

INTERNET ACCESS

Vancouver Public Library (☑604-331-3603; 350 W Georgia St; ⊙10am-9pm Mon-Thu, to 6pm Fri & Sat, noon-5pm Sun; Ⓜ Stadium-Chinatown) Free internet access on library computers, as well as free wi-fi access with guest card from the information desk.

MEDIA & INTERNET RESOURCES

CBC Radio One 88.1 FM (www.cbc.ca/bc) Canadian Broadcasting Corporation's commercial-free news, talk and music station.
CKNW 980AM (www.cknw.com) News, traffic and talk radio station.
City of Vancouver (www.vancouver.ca) Resource-packed official city site with downloadable maps.
Georgia Straight (www.straight.com) Alternative weekly providing Vancouver's best entertainment listings. Free every Thursday.
Inside Vancouver (www.insidevancouver.ca) Stories on what to do in and around the city.
Miss 604 (www.miss604.com) Vancouver's favorite blogger.
Tyee (www.thetyee.ca) Award-winning online local news source.
Vancouver Magazine (www.vanmag.com) Upscale lifestyle, dining and entertainment monthly.
Vancouver Sun (www.vancouversun.com) Main city daily, with Thursday listings pullout.

MEDICAL SERVICES

St Paul's Hospital (☑604-682-2344; 1081 Burrard St; ☐22) Downtown accident and emergency hospital.
Shoppers Drug Mart (☑604-669-2424; 1125 Davie St; ⊙24hr; ☐6) Pharmacy chain.
Ultima Medicentre (☑604-683-8138; www.ultimamedicentre.ca; Bentall Centre Plaza Level, 1055 Dunsmuir St; ⊙8am-5pm Mon-Fri; Ⓜ Burrard) Appointments not necessary.

MONEY

RBC Royal Bank (www.rbc.com; 1025 W Georgia St; ⊙9am-5pm Mon-Fri) Main bank branch with money-exchange services.
Vancouver Bullion & Currency Exchange (☑604-685-1008; www.vbce.ca; 800 W Pender St; ⊙9am-5pm Mon-Fri; Ⓜ Granville) Currency exchange with competitive rates.

POST

Canada Post Main Outlet (Map p118; ☑604-662-5723; 349 W Georgia St; ⊙8:30am-5:30pm Mon-Fri; Ⓜ Stadium-Chinatown) There is no separate poste-restante counter, so you must join the queue, show some identification and the person behind the counter will look for your mail. The post office will keep poste-restante mail marked 'c/o General Delivery' for two weeks and then return it to sender.
Howe St Postal Outlet (Map p118; ☑604-688-2068; 732 Davie St; ⊙9am-7pm Mon-Fri, 10am-5pm Sat; ☐6)

TOURIST INFORMATION

Tourism Vancouver Visitors Centre (Map p118; ☑877-826-1717, 604-683-2000; www.tourismvancouver.com; 200 Burrard St; ⊙8:30am-6pm; Ⓜ Waterfront) The Tourism Vancouver Visitors Centre is a large repository of resources for visitors, with a staff of helpful advisors ready to assist in planning your trip. Services include free maps, visitor guides, half-price theater tickets, accommodation and tour bookings.

ℹ️ Getting There & Away

AIR

Vancouver International Airport (YVR; Map p115; www.yvr.ca) is the main West Coast hub for airlines from Canada, the US and international locales. It's in Richmond, a 13km (30 minute) drive south of downtown.

Domestic flights arriving here include regular **Westjet** (☑888-937-8538; www.westjet.com) and **Air Canada** (www.aircanada.com) services. Linked to the main airport by free shuttle bus, the tiny South Terminal receives BC-only flights from smaller airlines and floatplane operators.

Several handy floatplane services can also deliver you directly to the Vancouver waterfront's **Seaplane Terminal** (☑604-647-7570; www.vhfc.ca; 1055 Canada Place; Ⓜ Waterfront). These include frequent Harbour Air Seaplanes (p163) services from downtown Victoria and beyond.

BOAT

BC Ferries (www.bcferries.com) services arrive at **Tsawwassen** – an hour's drive south of downtown – from Vancouver Island's Swartz Bay (passenger/vehicle $15.50/51.25, 1½ hours) and Nanaimo's Duke Point (passenger/vehicle $15.50/51.25, two hours). Services also arrive here from the Southern Gulf Islands.

Ferries arrive at West Vancouver's **Horseshoe Bay** – 30 minutes from downtown – from Nanaimo's Departure Bay (passenger/vehicle $15.50/51.25, 1½ hours), Bowen Island (passenger/vehicle $11.10/31.65, 20 minutes) and

Langdale (passenger/vehicle $14.55/49.05, 40 minutes) on the Sunshine Coast.

BUS

Most out-of-town buses grind to a halt at Vancouver's **Pacific Central Station** (1150 Station St). **Greyhound Canada** (www.greyhound.ca) services arrive from Whistler (from $18, 2¾ hours), Kelowna (from $29, five hours) and Calgary (from $57, 14 to 17 hours), among others.

Traveling via the BC Ferries Swartz Bay–Tsawwassen route, frequent **Pacific Coach Lines** (PCL; www.pacificcoach.com) services also trundle in from downtown Victoria (from $44, 3½ hours). PCL also operates services between Whistler, Vancouver and Vancouver International Airport. **Snowbus** (☑888-794-5511; www.snowbus.com) also offers a winter-only ski bus service to and from Whistler ($38, 3 hours).

Quick Coach Lines (www.quickcoach.com; ☎) runs an express shuttle between Seattle and Vancouver, departing from downtown Seattle (US$43.85, four hours) and the city's Sea-Tac International Airport (US$58.50, 3½ hours).

CAR & MOTORCYCLE

If you're coming from Washington State in the US, you'll be on the I-5 until you hit the border town of Blaine, then on Hwy 99 in Canada. It's about an hour's drive from here to downtown Vancouver. Hwy 99 continues through downtown, across the Lions Gate Bridge to Horseshoe Bay, Squamish and Whistler.

If you're coming from the east, you'll probably be on the Trans-Canada Hwy (Hwy 1), which snakes through the city's eastern end, eventually meeting with Hastings St. If you want to go downtown, turn left onto Hastings and follow it into the city center, or continue on along the North Shore toward Whistler.

If you're coming from Horseshoe Bay, Hwy 1 heads through West Vancouver and North Vancouver before going over the Second Narrows Bridge into Burnaby. If you're heading downtown, leave the highway at the Taylor Way exit in West Vancouver and follow it over the Lions Gate Bridge toward the city center.

All the recognized car rental chains have Vancouver branches. **Avis** (☑604-606-2847, 800-230-4898; www.avis.ca), **Budget** (☑604-668-7000, 800-219-3199; www.budgetbc.com), **Hertz** (☑604-606-4711, 800-654-3131; www.hertz.ca) and **Thrifty** (☑604-606-1655, 800-847-4389; www.thrifty.com) also have airport branches.

TRAIN

Trains trundle in from across Canada and the US at Pacific Central Station (p146). The Main Street-Science World SkyTrain station is just across the street for connections to downtown and the suburbs.

VIA Rail (www.viarail.ca) services arrive from Kamloops North (from $77.70, 10 hours), Jasper (from $162.75, 20 hours) and Edmonton (from $219.45, 27 hours), among others.

Amtrak (www.amtrak.com; ☎) US services arrive from Eugene (from US$64, 11 hours), Portland (from US$47, eight hours) and Seattle (from US$30, three hours).

❶ Getting Around

TO/FROM THE AIRPORT

SkyTrain's 16-station Canada Line (adult one-way fare to downtown $7.50 to $9) operates a rapid-transit train service from the airport to downtown. Trains run every few minutes and take around 25 minutes to reach downtown's Waterfront Station.

If you prefer to cab it, budget $30 to $40 for the 30-minute taxi ride from the airport to your downtown hotel.

BICYCLE

With 300km of dedicated routes, Vancouver is a good cycling city. Pick up a *Metro Vancouver Cycling Map* ($3.95) at convenience stores; it's also free to downlaod from www.translink.bc.ca. Cyclists can take their bikes for free on SkyTrain and SeaBus services and rack-fitted transit buses. Additional maps and resources are available at the **City of Vancouver** (www.vancouver.ca/cycling) website.

BOAT

Aquabus Ferries (www.theaquabus.com; adult/child from $3/1.50) runs mini-vessels (some big enough to carry bikes) between the end of Hornby St and Granville Island, and services spots along False Creek as far as Science World. Its rival is **False Creek Ferries** (Map p118; www.granvilleislandferries.bc.ca; adult/child from $3/1.50), which operates a similar Granville Island service from the Vancouver Aquatic Centre near the end of Thurlow St, plus additional ports of call around False Creek.

CAR & MOTORCYCLE

The rush-hour vehicle lineup to cross the Lions Gate Bridge to the North Shore frequently snakes far up W Georgia St. Try the alternative Second Narrows Bridge. Other peak-time hot spots to avoid are the George Massey Tunnel and Hwy 1 to Surrey.

Parking is at a premium downtown: there are few free spots available on residential side streets and traffic wardens are predictably predatory. Some streets have metered parking, but pay-parking lots (from $4 per hour) are a better proposition – arrive before 9am at some for early-bird discounts. Underground parking at either the Pacific Centre (entrance at Robson and Howe St intersection) or the Vancouver

Public Library (entrance at Hamilton and Robson intersection) will have you in the heart of the city.

PUBLIC TRANSPORTATION

The website for **TransLink** (www.translink.bc.ca) bus, SkyTrain and SeaBus services has a trip-planning tool. A ticket bought on any of its three services is valid for 1½ hours of travel on the entire network, depending on the zone you intend traveling in. The three zones become progressively more expensive the further you journey.

One-zone tickets are adult/child $2.75/1.75, two-zone tickets $4/2.75 and three-zone tickets $5.50/3.75. An all-day, all-zone pass costs $9.75/7.50. If you're traveling after 6:30pm or on weekends or holidays, all trips are classed as one-zone fares and cost $2.75/1.75. Children under five travel free on all transit services. At the time of writing, a new swipeable fare card system called Compass was being introduced: check the TransLink website for the latest information.

Bus

The bus network is extensive in central areas and many vehicles have bike racks. All are wheelchair accessible. Exact change is required since all buses use fare machines and change is not given.

The 99 B-Line express buses operate between the Commercial-Broadway SkyTrain station and UBC. These buses have their own limited arrival and departure points and do not use the regular bus stops.

There is also a handy night-bus system that runs every 30 minutes between 1:30am and 4am across the Lower Mainland. The last bus leaves downtown Vancouver at 3:10am. Look for the night-bus signs at designated stops.

SeaBus

The aquatic shuttle **SeaBus** (Map p118) operates every 15 to 30 minutes throughout the day, taking 12 minutes to cross the Burrard Inlet between Waterfront Station and Lonsdale Quay. At Lonsdale there's a bus terminal servicing routes throughout North Vancouver and West Vancouver (take bus 236 to Grouse Mountain and Capilano Suspension Bridge). Vessels are wheelchair accessible and bike friendly.

SkyTrain

The SkyTrain rapid-transit network consists of three routes and is a great way to move around the region: consider taking a spin on it, even if you don't have anywhere to go. A fourth route, the Evergreen Line, is scheduled for 2016 completion.

The original 35-minute Expo Line goes to and from downtown Vancouver and Surrey, via stops throughout Burnaby and New Westminster. The Millennium Line alights near shopping malls and suburban residential districts in Coquitlam and Burnaby. Opened in late 2009, the new Canada Line links the city to the airport and Richmond.

While SkyTrain ticket prices mirror the zones used across the TransLink network, there is one notable exception: passengers departing on Canada Line trains from the airport are charged an extra $5 AddFare when purchasing their ticket from station vending machines. You do not have to pay this extra charge when traveling to the airport from downtown.

TAXI

Flagging a downtown cab shouldn't take long, but it's easier to get your hotel to call one. Operators include **Vancouver Taxi** (☑ 604-871-1111) and **Yellow Cab** (☑ 604-681-1111). Many taxis take credit cards.

LOWER MAINLAND

Stretching from coastal Horseshoe Bay as far inland as the Fraser Valley, this region encompasses the towns and suburbs within an hour or so by car from downtown Vancouver, including the communities immediately adjoining the city that are also known as Metro Vancouver. Ideal for day-tripping from the city, the area is chock-full of looming mountains, crenulated coastal parks, wildlife sanctuaries and historic attractions.

North Vancouver

POP 52,000

A commuter burb for downtown professionals, the city of 'North Van' rises from the waterfront at the Lonsdale Quay SeaBus dock, where you'll also find a popular public market. The area is home to two of the region's most popular attractions. For more visitor information on North Vancouver and adjoining West Vancouver, see www.vancouversnorthshore.com.

◎ Sights & Activities

Capilano Suspension Bridge   PARK
(Map p115; www.capbridge.com; 3735 Capilano Rd; adult/child $34.95/12; ⊗8:30am-8pm; ⓐ; ☐236 from Lonsdale Quay) As you walk gingerly onto one of the world's longest (140m) and highest (70m) suspension bridges, swaying gently over the roiling Capilano Canyon, remember that its thick steel cables are embedded in concrete. That should steady your feet – unless there are teenagers stamping

across. Added park attractions include a glass-bottomed cliffside walkway and an elevated canopy trail through the trees.

A hugely popular attraction (hence the summer tour buses), try to arrive early during peak months and you'll be able to check out the historic exhibits, totem poles and tree-shaded nature trails on the other side of the bridge in relative calm. From May to September, Capilano makes it very easy to get here from downtown by running a **free shuttle** from Canada Pl and area hotels. Check their website for details.

Grouse Mountain OUTDOORS

(off Map p115; www.grousemountain.com; 6400 Nancy Greene Way; Skyride adult/child $39.95/13.95; ⊙9am-10pm; ⛄; ⮾236 from Lonsdale Quay) Calling itself the 'Peak of Vancouver,' this mountaintop playground offers smashing views of downtown, shimmering in the water below. In summer, **Skyride** gondola tickets include access to lumberjack shows, alpine hiking, movie presentations and a grizzly-bear refuge. Pay extra for zip lining and Eye of the Wind, a 20-story, elevator-accessed turbine tower with a panoramic viewing pod that will have your camera itching for action.

There are also restaurants up here if you fancy dining: it's an ideal sunset-viewing spot. You can reduce the gondola fee by hiking the ultra-steep Grouse Grind (p148) up the side of the mountain – you have to pay $10 to get back down on the Skyride, though. Like Capilano, Grouse lures visitors from downtown in summer by offering a **free shuttle** from Canada Pl. In winter, it's all about skiing and snowboarding as Grouse become the locals' fave powder playground.

Lynn Canyon Park PARK

(Map p115; www.lynncanyon.ca; Park Rd; ⊙7am-9pm; ⛄; ⮾229 from Lonsdale Quay) Amid a dense bristling of ancient trees, the main feature of this provincial park is its **suspension bridge**, a free alternative to Capilano. Not quite as big as its tourist-magnet rival, it provokes the same jelly-legged reaction as you sway over the river 50m below, and is always far less crowded. Hiking trails, swimming areas and picnic spots will keep you busy.

The **Ecology Centre** (www.dnv.org/ecology; 3663 Park Rd; entry by $2 donation; ⊙10am-5pm) houses interesting displays on the area's rich biodiversity, including dioramas and video presentations. It stages regular talks and events for kids, especially in summer.

Lonsdale Quay Public Market MARKET

(www.lonsdalequay.com; 123 Carrie Cates Ct; ⊙9am-7pm) As well as being a transportation hub, this waterfront facility houses a colorful public market. Look for fresh fruit and glassy-eyed whole fish on the main floor, plus trinkets and clothing on the 2nd floor. There's also a lively food court; **Montgomery's Fish & Chips** is recommended. The SeaBus from downtown docks here and you can pick up transit buses to Capilano, Grouse and beyond.

Mt Seymour Provincial Park OUTDOORS

(Map p115; www.bcparks.ca; 1700 Mt Seymour Rd; ⊙dawn-dusk) A popular, rustic retreat from the clamor of downtown, this giant, tree-lined park is suffused with more than

---

MOTHER NATURE'S STAIRMASTER

If you're finding your vacation a little too relaxing, head over to North Vancouver and join the perspiring throng snaking almost vertically up the **Grouse Grind** trail. The entrance is near the parking lot, across the street from where slightly more sane visitors to Grouse Mountain (p148) pile into the Skyride gondola and trundle up to the summit without breaking a sweat. Around 3km in total, the steep, rock-studded forest trek will likely have your joints screaming for mercy within 15 minutes as you focus on the feet of the person in front of you. Most people take around an hour to reach the top, where they collapse like gasping fish on the rocks. If you're feeling energetic, you might want to try and beat the record of Vancouverite Sebastian Albrecht who nailed the trail 14 times in one day in 2010. Things to keep in mind if you're planning to join the 110,000 who hike the Grind every year: take a bottle of water, dress in thin layers so you can strip down, and bring $10 with you: the trail is one way, so when you reach the summit you have to pay a special rate to take the Skyride back down – your consolation is that you get to enjoy the summit's many attractions for free in exchange for your exploding calf muscles.

a dozen summertime hiking trails that suit walkers of most abilities; the easiest path is the 2km Goldie Lake Trail. Many trails wind past lakes and centuries-old Douglas firs and offer a true break from the city. This is also one of the city's three main winter playgrounds. Drivers can take Hwy 1 to the Mt Seymour Pkwy (near the Second Narrows Bridge) and follow it east to Mt Seymour Rd.

Maplewood Farm   FARM
(Map p115; www.maplewoodfarm.bc.ca; 405 Seymour River Pl; adult/child $7.50/4.50; ⊙10am-4pm; 🚗; 🚌239 from Lonsdale Quay, then C15) A popular family-friendly site, this farmyard attraction includes plenty of hands-on displays plus a collection of over 200 domestic animals. Your wide-eyed kids can pet some critters, watch the daily milking demonstration and feed some squawking, ever-hungry ducks and chickens. The highlight is the daily 'running of the goats' at around 3:30pm, when the starving hair balls streak from the paddock to their barn for dinner.

🛏 Sleeping & Eating

Pinnacle Hotel at the Pier   HOTEL $$
(☎877-986-7437, 604-986-7437; www.pinnaclehotelatthepier.com; 138 Victory Ship Way; d $169; ⊛❄@🐾🐕🐾; 🚌230) North Van's new Pinnacle is an excellent option if you want to stay on this side of the water and hop to the city center on the nearby SeaBus. The hotel balances itself between business and leisure travelers, and rooms are furnished with contemporary elegance, with calming hues favored over bold colors. Harbor views are recommended but typically cost $10 to $20 extra.

★Tomahawk Restaurant   DINER $$
(www.tomahawkrestaurant.com; 1550 Philip Ave; mains $8-16; ⊙8am-9pm Sun-Thu, to 10pm Fri & Sat; 🚌240) A colorful blast from North Van's pioneering past, the family-run Tomahawk has been heaping its plates with comfort food since 1926. A bustling weekend brunch spot – if the massive Yukon bacon and eggs grease fest or the frightening Skookum Chief burger don't kill your hangover, nothing will – it's also fun for lunch or dinner, when bulging burgers and chicken potpies hit the menu.

Grab a spot at the counter, with its swivel stools, and check out the surfeit of First Nations artifacts lining the walls: it's like stuffing your face in a museum.

Burgoo Bistro   WEST COAST $$
(www.burgoo.ca; 3 Lonsdale Ave; mains $10-18; ⊙11am-10pm Sun-Wed, to 11pm Thu-Sat; 🚌230) With the feel of a cozy, rustic cabin, complete with a large stone fireplace, Burgoo's menu of comfort foods with a twist aims to warm up North Van's winter nights: the spicy apricot lamb tagine or smile-triggering butter chicken would thaw a glacier from 50 paces. There's also a wide array of house-made soups and heaping salads. As for drinks, try the tasty craft beers.

Observatory   WEST COAST $$$
(☎604-980-9311; www.grousemountain.com; Grouse Mountain; mains $39; ⊙5-10pm; 🚌236 from Lonsdale Quay) Crowning Grouse Mountain, the fine-dining Observatory serves its chorizo scallops and lamb medallions alongside breathtaking views over Stanley Park and Vancouver's twinkling towers far below. A perfect venue for a romantic dinner – you wouldn't be the first to propose here – there's an excellent wine list if you suddenly need to console yourself. Reserve in advance and you'll get free Skyride passes.

The atmosphere is more laid-back at the adjacent, pub-like **Altitudes Bistro**, which offers comfort grub of the burgers and fish-and-chips variety in a casual ski-lodge ambience.

ℹ Getting There & Around

SeaBus vessels arrive at Lonsdale Quay from Vancouver's Waterfront Station ($4, 12 minutes) every 15 to 30 minutes throughout the day. From the bus terminal at the quay, bus 236 runs to Capilano Suspension Bridge then on to the base of Grouse Mountain.

Rocky Mountaineer Vacations runs its popular Whistler Sea to Sky Climb (p162) train into North Vancouver from Whistler (from $169, three hours, daily May to mid-October).

West Vancouver

POP 44,000

Adjoining North Vancouver, the considerably wealthier 'West Van' is studded with multilevel mansions that cling to the cliff tops and look down – in more ways than one – across the region. It's a stop-off point on the drive from downtown to the Horseshoe Bay ferry terminal and other points north on the way to Whistler.

BRITISH COLUMBIA WEST VANCOUVER

◉ Sights

Cypress Provincial Park OUTDOORS
(www.bcparks.ca; Cypress Bowl Rd; ⊙ dawn-dusk)
Around 8km north of West Van via Hwy
99, Cypress offers great summertime hikes,
including the Baden-Powell, Yew Lake and
Howe Sound Crest trails, which plunge
through forests of cedar, yellow cypress and
Douglas fir and wind past little lakes and
alpine meadows. Also a popular area for
mountain bikers, Cypress becomes a snowy
playground in winter.

If you're driving from downtown Vancouver, cross the Lions Gate Bridge to the Upper Levels Hwy via Taylor Way in West Vancouver. Then, follow the signs to the park
entrance.

Lighthouse Park PARK
(Map p115; www.lighthousepark.ca; cnr Beacon
Lane & Marine Dr; ⊙ dawn-dusk; ☐ 250) Some
of the region's oldest trees live within this
accessible 75-hectare park, including a rare
stand of original coastal forest and plenty of
those gnarly, copper-trunked arbutus trees.
About 13km of hiking trails crisscross the
area, including a recommended trek that
leads to the rocky perch of **Point Atkinson
Lighthouse**, ideal for shimmering, camera-
worthy views over Burrard Inlet.

If you're driving from downtown, turn left
on Marine Dr after crossing the Lions Gate
Bridge to reach the park.

☞ Tours

Sewell's Sea Safari BOAT TOUR
(☑ 604-921-3474; www.sewellsmarina.com; 6409
Bay St, Horseshoe Bay; adult/child $83/53; ⊙ Apr-
Oct; ☐ 250) West Vancouver's Horseshoe Bay
is the departure point for this two-hour
marine-wildlife-watching boat tour. Orcas
are always a highlight but, even if they're not
around, you'll almost certainly spot harbor
seals lolling on the rocks pretending to ignore you. Seabirds are also a common sight,
while bald eagles are frequent contributors
to the show as well.

🛏 Sleeping & Eating

Lighthouse Park B&B B&B $$
(☑ 604-926-5959, 800-926-0262; www.lighthouse-
park.com; 4875 Water Lane; ste from $175) This
elegant two-suite sleepover, complete with
private entrances and a flower-decked court-
yard, will have you feeling like a West Van
aristo in no time. Each suite has a fridge and
DVD player, as well as a decanter of sherry

for that essential alfresco evening tipple. You
can sober up with a stroll to nearby Point
Atkinson Lighthouse.

Savary Island Pie Company BAKERY, CAFE $$
(www.savaryislandpiecompany.com; 1533 Marine
Dr; mains $8-14; ⊙ 6am-9pm; ☐ 250) Ask North
Shore locals where to get a great slice of
pie and they'll point you to this popular
bakery cafe, opened in 1989. The bulging,
fresh-baked pies are the mainstay of the
business – don't miss the raspberry rhubarb
– though the extended menu, with breakfasts, soup and sandwiches, suggests dessert
is not the only meal.

Fraîche WEST COAST $$
(☑ 604-925-7595; www.fraicherestaurant.ca; 2240
Chippendale Rd; mains $18-42; ⊙ 11am-3pm &
5-10pm Tue-Sun; ☐ 256) It's worth tearing your
gaze from the mesmerizing shoreline vistas
here to focus on your plate. Perfect Cana-
dian gourmet is the approach, with typical
highlights on the seasonal menu including
charred octopus and juicy roast duck. If you
fancy a taste of the high life without the
price, drop in for lunch or weekend brunch
when many dishes hover around $20.

Salmon House on the Hill SEAFOOD $$$
(☑ 604-926-3212; www.salmonhouse.com; 2229
Folkestone Way; mains $30-40; ⊙ 5-9:30pm Sun-
Thu, 6-10pm Fri & Sat, brunch 10:30am-2:30pm Sat
& Sun; ☐ 256) West Vancouver's old-school
destination restaurant, this landmark has
been luring locals for special-occasion dinners for years. But Salmon House doesn't
rest on its laurels – if laurels can be defined
as a gable-roofed wooden interior and floor-
to-ceiling windows with sunset cliff-top city
views. Instead, you'll find a menu of delectable seasonal BC seafood with serious gourmet credentials.

Burnaby

POP 232,000
Immediately east of Vancouver and accessible via SkyTrain from the city, Burnaby is
a residential suburb with a half-day's worth
of attractions.

The pathways of tranquil **Deer Lake Park**
(Map p115) crisscross meadows and wood-
lands, circling a lake where fowl and other
wildlife hang out. In summer, it's the home
of the annual **Burnaby Blues + Roots Festival** (www.burnabybluesfestival.com). The adjoining **Burnaby Village Museum** (Map p115;

IDYLLIC ISLAND JAUNT

Just because you've found yourself running out of road in shoreline West Vancouver, doesn't mean you have to end your adventures. You can hit the Horseshoe Bay ferry terminal – with or without your car (transit bus 257 will also get you here from downtown Vancouver) – for a quick hop to **Bowen Island** (off Map p115). Once a favored summertime retreat for colonials looking for a seaside escape, it's now populated by a friendly clutch of writers and artists.

Once you alight in Snug Cove – the breathtaking crossing over the glassy, tree-lined water takes around 20 minutes – you'll find yourself in a rustically charming little community that suddenly feels a million miles from big-city life. Drop into the **visitors center** (www.bowenchamber.com; 432 Cardena Rd; ⏰10am-3pm) for a crash course on what to do...then set about doing it.

Scenic paddle tours are offered by **Bowen Island Sea Kayaking** (☑800-605-2925, 604-947-9266; www.bowenislandkayaking.com; Snug Cove; rentals 3hr/day $45/70, tours from $65), but just strolling the forest trails – and stopping for a picnic overlooking the waterfront – is always a good idea. You'll likely also spend a lot of time clattering along the boardwalk area near the ferry dock. This is where you'll find **Doc Morgan's Restaurant & Pub** (www.docmorgans.com; 439 Bowen Island Trunk Rd; mains $10-12; ⏰11am-midnight Sun-Thu, to 1am Fri & Sat), where the chatty patios overlook the park and harbor. Pub grub is the main focus here and the fish and chips are popular – along with BC craft beer. On summer weekends, local artisans gather beside the marina to showcase their wares at the **Summer Market**. If you miss it, climb the hill to **Artisan Square** for little shops of the gallery and jewelery-store variety.

www.burnabyvillagemuseum.ca; 6501 Deer Lake Ave; ⏰11am-4:30pm May-Aug) **FREE** colorfully re-creates a BC pioneer town, complete with replica homes, businesses and a handsome 1912 carousel. To get directly there by car, take the Sperling Ave exit off Hwy 1 and follow the museum signs.

Topping Burnaby Mountain, **Simon Fraser University** (Map p115; www.sfu.ca; 8888 University Dr) is the Lower Mainland's second-biggest campus community. Small visitor attractions here include the free-admission **SFU Gallery** and the **Museum of Archaeology & Ethnology**.

For information on the area, visit the **Tourism Burnaby** (www.tourismburnaby.com) website.

New Westminster

A 30-minute SkyTrain ride from downtown Vancouver, New West is one of BC's most historic communities – it was briefly designated the capital of the new Colony of British Columbia in 1859. Its star faded during much of the last century but recent years have seen attempts at revival. It's easily worth a couple of hours of your time if you're looking for an easy excursion from Vancouver.

Hop off at the New Westminster SkyTrain station and stroll downhill to the Fraser River waterfront. The newly revitalized covered **River Market** (Map p115; www.rivermarket.ca; 810 Quayside Dr; ⏰10am-6pm) is a good place for lunch – **Re-Up BBQ** is recommended – and you'll also spot what claims to be the **world's largest tin soldier** looming over the boardwalk. If you have time, nip into the **Fraser River Discovery Centre** (Map p115; www.fraserdiscovery.org; 788 Quayside Dr; entry by $6 donation; ⏰10am-4pm) to uncover the story of the mighty river flowing alongside. Hit nearby **Front St** for shops and historic buildings and then hop back on the SkyTrain at Columbia Station for your return to Vancouver.

For more information on the area, visit the **Tourism New Westminster** (www.tourismnewwestminster.com) website.

Fort Langley

Little Fort Langley's tree-lined streets and 19th-century storefronts make it one of BC's most picturesque historic villages, ideal for an afternoon jaunt from Vancouver. Its highlight is the colorful **Fort Langley National Historic Site** (☑604-513-4777; www.pc.gc.ca/fortlangley; 23433 Mavis Ave; adult/

child $7.80/3.90; ⊙10am-4pm; 🚌501, then C62), the region's most important old-school landmark.

A fortified trading post since 1827, it's where James Douglas announced the creation of BC in 1858, giving the site a legitimate claim to being the province's birthplace. With costumed reenactors, re-created artisan workshops and a gold-panning area that's a kid-friendly must-do (they also enjoy charging around the wooden battlements), this is an ideal destination for families aiming to add a little education to their trips.

If you need an introduction before you start wading into the buildings, there's a surprisingly entertaining time-travel-themed movie presentation on offer. Make sure you check the website before you arrive: there's a wide array of events that evocatively bring the past back to life, including a summertime evening campfire program that will take you right back to the 1800s pioneer days.

If you're driving from Vancouver, take Hwy 1 east for 40km, then take the 232nd St exit north. Follow the signs along 232nd St until you reach the stop sign at Glover Rd. Turn right here, and continue into the village. Turn right again on Mavis Ave, just before the railway tracks. The fort's parking lot is at the end of the street.

Richmond & Steveston

POP 200,000

Hop aboard the Canada Line and head down to the region's Chinatown for a half-day of Asian shopping malls – centered on the Golden Village area – followed by a taste-trip through Chinese, Japanese and Vietnamese restaurants.

Don't miss the city's charming historic waterfront Steveston village, a popular destination for sunset-viewing locals with a penchant for great fish and chips. For more information on both areas, check www.tourismrichond.com.

◎ Sights & Activities

Richmond Night Market   MARKET
(Map p115; www.richmondnightmarket.com; 8351 River Rd, Richmond; admission $2; ⊙7pm-midnight Fri & Sat, 6pm-11pm Sun mid-May–mid-Oct; Ⓜ Bridgeport) One of two Asian-style night markets in Richmond – the other is called the International Summer Night Market – this seasonal bonanza is alive with steaming food stalls serving everything from sizzling fish balls to dragon's beard candy. Come hungry and don't forget to take a break from filling your face via the shiny trinket vendors and live entertainment.

Of the two markets, this one is easiest to reach on transit.

International Summer Night Market   MARKET
(Map p115; www.summernightmarket.com; 12631 Vulcan Way, Richmond; ⊙7pm-1am Fri & Sat, to midnight Sun mid-May–early Oct; 🚌407) Much larger than downtown Chinatown's version, thousands of hungry locals are lured here every weekend to check out the tacky vendor stands and, more importantly, the dozens of hawker food stalls. Don't eat before arriving and you can taste-trip through steaming Malaysian, Korean, Japanese and Chinese treats.

Gulf of Georgia Cannery   MUSEUM
(Map p115; www.gulfofgeorgiacannery.com; 12138 4th Ave, Steveston; adult/child $7.80/3.90; ⊙10am-5pm Feb-Oct; Ⓜ Richmond-Brighouse, then 🚌401) Once you've perused the boats hawking the day's fresh catch, check out Steveston's excellent cannery museum, illuminating the sights and sounds of the region's bygone era of labor-intensive fish processing. Most of the machinery remains and there's an evocative focus on the people who used to work here. Take one of the free tours, sometimes run by former cannery workers.

Britannia Shipyard   MUSEUM
(Map p115; www.britannia-hss.ca; 5180 Westwater Dr, Steveston; ⊙10am-6pm Tue-Sun; Ⓜ Richmond-Brighouse, then 🚌410) FREE After you've done the cannery, hit Steveston's lovely waterfront boardwalk – complete with art installations evoking the area's bustling fishing sector – and within 15 minutes you'll stroll into the area's other national historic site. Not as slick as the cannery, it's nevertheless a fascinating complex of creaky old sheds housing dusty tools, boats and reminders of the region's maritime past.

🍴 Sleeping & Eating

Fairmont Vancouver Airport   HOTEL $$$
(☎866-540-4441, 604-207-5200; www.fairmont.com/vancouverairport; Vancouver International Airport, Richmond; d from $250; ❈@🛜❈; Ⓜ YVR Airport) You can wave from the overhead walkway to the harried economy-class plebs below as you stroll toward the lobby of this

luxe airport hotel in the US departure hall. This is a great option for boarding long-haul flights in a Zen-like state of calm. The rooms are elegantly furnished with high-end flourishes including remote-controlled curtains and marble-lined bathrooms.

★ **Pajo's** SEAFOOD $
(www.pajos.com; The Wharf, Steveston; mains $6-9; ⊙ 11am-dusk; Ⓜ Richmond-Brighouse, then 🚌 402) It's hard to find a better spot to enjoy fish and chips than the boat-bobbing wharf at Steveston. Luckily, this floating, family-run local legend fully delivers. After perusing the fresh catches on the backs of the nearby fishing boats, descend the ramp to Pajo's little ordering hatch. Go the fresh-fried salmon or halibut route or mix things up with a yellowfin tuna burger.

Parker Place FOOD COURT $
(www.parkerplace.com; 4380 No 3 Rd, Richmond; mains $5-10; ⊙ 11am-7pm Sun-Thu, to 9pm Fri & Sat; Ⓜ Aberdeen) There are several popular Asian shopping malls in Richmond but, while Aberdeen Centre and Lansdowne Centre are bigger, Parker Place's highly authentic food court feels like a Singaporean hawker market. Beloved of Asian-Canadian locals, dive in for good-value noodle, fishball and dragon's-beard-candy dishes: buy a few plates and share 'em at your table.

Once you're full, peruse the labyrinth of surrounding international-flavored retailers or nip outside to the food court's adjoining parking lot for a surprise: a shimmering shrine.

Cattle Cafe ASIAN $
(www.cattlecafe.ca; 8580 Alexandra Rd, Richmond; mains $6-14; ⊙ 11am-1am; Ⓜ Lansdowne) Richmond's lip-smacking Asian dining scene is it's main lure and, if you want to get to the heart of the matter, head straight to Alexandra Rd, also called 'Eat Street', where dozens of restaurants await. Among the funkiest, this Hong Kong–style joint is great for trying barbecued-eel sandwiches, washed down with some delectable bubble tea.

Shanghai River Restaurant CHINESE $$
(7381 Westminster Hwy, Richmond; mains $6-18; ⊙ 11am-2:30pm & 5:30-11pm; Ⓜ Richmond-Brighouse) Grab a seat overlooking the kitchen window at this cavernous northern-Chinese eatery and you'll be mesmerized by the handiwork that goes into preparing the area's best dim sum. Order plates to share – one dish per person is the usual ratio – and

be careful not to squirt everyone with the delicate but juicy pork or shrimp dumplings.

Jang Mo Jib ASIAN $$
(www.jangmojib.com; 8230 Alexandra Rd, Richmond; mains $12-24; ⊙ 10am-1am Mon-Thu, to 2am Fri & Sat; Ⓜ Lansdowne) If you're in the mood for a spot of Korean hot pot and barbecue, this friendly, large restaurant is the one for you. Just look for the wacky carved poles outside, then nip into this gable-roofed restaurant for a host of immersive, mostly meaty dishes. The must-have specialty is the pork-blood sausage, which divides the table between real and pretend carnivores.

❶ Getting There & Away

The Canada Line SkyTrain link has made the region's modern-day Chinatown much easier to reach from downtown Vancouver.

SEA TO SKY HIGHWAY

Otherwise known as Hwy 99, this picturesque cliffside roadway links a string of communities between West Vancouver and Lillooet and is the main route to Whistler from Vancouver. Recently upgraded, the winding road has several worthwhile stops – especially if you're an outdoor-activity fan, history buff or lover of BC's variegated mountain landscape. **Mountain FM radio** (107.1) provides handy traffic and road-condition updates en route.

Squamish & Around
POP 18,500

An hour north of Vancouver and another hour to Whistler, Squamish sits at the meeting point of ocean, river and alpine forest. Originally just a grungy logging town, it's now a popular base for outdoor activities, especially in summer.

◉ Sights & Activities

The dozens of tree-fringed trails around Squamish draw plenty of mountain-bike enthusiasts. The **Cheekeye Fan trail** near Brackendale has some easy rides, while downhill thrill seekers prefer the **Diamond Head/Power Smart area**. Check the website of the **Squamish Off Road Cycling Association** (www.sorca.ca) for an intro to *'* area's two-wheeled scene.

If you prefer to hit the water, **Squamish Spit** is a kiteboarding (and windsurfing) hot spot. The season runs May to October and the website of the **Squamish Windsports Society** (www.squamishwindsports.com) is your first point of contact for weather, water conditions and information on access to the spit.

At time of research a new sightseeing gondola attraction was also being built in the area; check http://seatoskygondola.com for the latest details.

Britannia Mine Museum　　　　MUSEUM
(www.britanniaminemuseum.ca; adult/child $21.50/13.50; ⊙9am-5pm) Around 10 minutes before Squamish on Hwy 99, the Britannia Mine Museum is a recommended stop. Once the British Empire's largest copper mine, it's been restored as an impressive industrial museum. The underground mine-tunnel train tour is a highlight and there are plenty of additional kid-friendly exhibits, including gold panning, plus a large artsy gift shop.

Shannon Falls Provincial Park　　WATERFALL
(www.bcparks.ca) About 4km before you reach Squamish, you'll also hear the rushing waters of Shannon Falls Provincial Park. Pull into the parking lot and stroll the short trail to BC's third-highest waterfall, where water cascades down a 335m drop. A few picnic tables make this a handy spot for an alfresco lunch.

West Coast Railway Heritage Park MUSEUM
(www.wcra.org; 39645 Government Rd; adult/child $15/10; ⊙10am-5pm) Historic-train nuts should continue just past town to the smashing West Coast Railway Heritage Park. This large, mostly alfresco museum is the final resting place of BC's legendary Royal Hudson steam engine and has around 90 other historic railcars, including 10 working engines and the original prototype SkyTrain car. Check out the slick new Roundhouse building, housing the park's most precious trains and artifacts.

Stawamus Chief Provincial Park　　PARK
(www.bcparks.ca) On the way into Squamish from Vancouver, you'll see a sheer, 652m-high granite rock face looming ahead. Attracting hardy climbers, it's called the 'Chief' and it's the highlight of Stawamus Chief Provincial Park. You don't have to gear up to experience the summit's breathtaking vistas: there are hiking routes up the back for anyone who wants to have a go. Consider

Squamish Rock Guides (☑604-892-7816; www.squamishrockguides.com; guided rock climbs half-day/day from $75/115) for climbing assistance or lessons.

✦✦ Festivals & Events

Squamish Valley Music Festival　　MUSIC
(www.squamishfestival.com; ⊙Aug) If you're here in August, consider the giant Squamish Valley Music Festival, the region's biggest outdoor music event.

🍴 Sleeping & Eating

Alice Lake Provincial Park　　CAMPGROUND $
(☑800-689-9025; www.discovercamping.ca; Hwy 99; campsites from $30) This large, family-friendly campground, 13km north of Squamish, has more than 100 sites. There are two shower buildings with flush toilets, and campers often indulge in activities like swimming, hiking and biking (rentals available). Consider an interpretive ranger tour through the woods (July and August only). Reserve far ahead – this is one of BC's most popular campgrounds.

Howe Sound Inn & Brewing Company　　INN $$
(☑604-892-2603; www.howesound.com; 37801 Cleveland Ave; d from $99; 🕾🐾) Quality rustic is the approach at this comfortable sleepover: rooms are warm and inviting with plenty of woodsy touches. There's an outdoor climbing wall where you can train for your attempt on the nearby Stawamus Chief and a sauna for recovering afterwards. The downstairs brewpub serves some of BC's best house-made beers – guests can request free brewery tours.

Even if you're not staying, it's worth stopping at the restaurant here for great pub grub with a gourmet twist.

Sunflower Bakery Cafe　　CAFE $
(www.sunflowerbakerycafe.com; 38086 Cleveland Ave; mains $5-9; ⊙7:30am-5:30pm Mon-Sat) Just look for the bright yellow exterior and then nip inside for hearty, handmade lunches, often of the organic or vegetarian variety. Soups and sandwiches abound but the quiches are recommended if you fancy a change. On the way out, fill your car with chunky cakes and bulging fruit pies to keep you going until Whistler.

Galileo Coffee　　COFFEE $
(www.galileocoffee.com; 173 Hwy 99; baked goods $3-5; ⊙7am-3pm) Across from the entrance

to Britannia Mine Museum, Galileo Coffee is everyone's fave fuel-up spot en route to Whistler.

ℹ Information

Head to the slick visitors center, **Squamish Adventure Centre** (📞604-815-4994, 866-333-2010; www.tourismsquamish.com; 38551 Loggers Lane; ⊕8am-8pm), to see what's on offer. It has lots of good info on area hiking and biking trails.

ℹ Getting There & Away

Greyhound Canada (www.greyhound.ca) buses arrive in Squamish from Vancouver (from $10, 80 minutes, six daily) and Whistler (from $7, 55 minutes, five daily). Slightly more salubrious **Pacific Coach Lines** (www.pacificcoach.com) buses also arrive here from downtown Vancouver ($49, 70 minutes, five daily).

Garibaldi Provincial Park

Visiting outdoors types should make a beeline for the 1950-sq-km **Garibaldi Provincial Park** (www.bcparks.ca), justly renowned for hiking trails colored by diverse flora, abundant wildlife and panoramic wilderness vistas. Summer hikers seem magnetically drawn here but the trails also double as cross-country ski routes in winter. There are five main trail areas – directions to each are marked by the blue-and-white signs you'll see off Hwy 99.

Among the park's most popular trails, the **Cheakamus Lake hike** (3km) is relatively easy with minimal elevation. The **Elfin Lakes trail** (11km) is a lovely, relatively easy day hike. The **Garibaldi Lake hike** (9km) is an outstanding introduction to 'Beautiful BC' wilderness, fusing scenic alpine meadows and breathtaking mountain vistas.

Brandywine Falls Provincial Park

A few kilometers north of Squamish and adjacent to Hwy 99, this tree-lined 143-hectare **park** (www.bcparks.ca) is centered on a spectacular 70m waterfall. A short stroll through the forest leads to a leg-jellying platform overlooking the top of the falls, where water drops suddenly out of the trees like from a giant faucet. There are also great vistas over Daisy Lake and the mountains of Garibaldi Provincial Park. A 7km looped trail leads

further through the dense forest and ancient lava beds to Cal-Cheak Suspension Bridge.

WHISTLER

POP 10,600

Named for the furry marmots that populate the area and whistle like deflating balloons, this gabled alpine village – and 2010 Olympic and Paralympic Winter Games venue – is one of the world's most popular ski resorts. Nestled in the shade of the formidable Whistler and Blackcomb Mountains, the wintertime village has a frosted, Christmas-card look. But summer is now even more popular, with Vancouverites and visitors lured to the region's natural charms by everything from mountain biking to scream-triggering zipline runs.

There are several neighborhoods and smaller enclaves, including Function Junction, but Whistler Village is the key hub for hotels, restaurants and shops. You'll find humbler B&B-type accommodations in the quieter Village North, while the Upper Village is home to some swanky hotels, clustered around the Blackcomb base. Don't be surprised if you get lost when you're wandering around on foot: Whistler is a bit of a labyrinth until you get used to it.

◉ Sights

Squamish Lil'wat Cultural Centre   MUSEUM
(www.slcc.ca; 4584 Blackcomb Way; adult/child $18/8; ⊕9:30am-5pm) 🌿 This handsome, wood-beamed facility showcases two quite different First Nations groups – one coastal and one interior based. Take a tour for the vital context behind the museum-like exhibits, including four newly carved totem poles and a new upstairs gallery that includes a 1200-year-old ceremonial bowl. Ask about the summer barbecue dinners ($58) or nip into the downstairs cafe for delicious venison chili with traditional bannock.

Whistler Museum   MUSEUM
(www.whistlermuseum.org; 4333 Main St; adult/child $7.50/4; ⊕11am-5pm) Tracing Whistler's development from wilderness outpost to Olympic resort, quirky exhibits include a stuffed hoary marmot, a toilet-seat sailing trophy and a 2010 Olympic torch you can hold. A new permanent exhibit on skiing history was also being developed on our visit. Check ahead for events – October's adult Lego party is a must – and consider their

Whistler

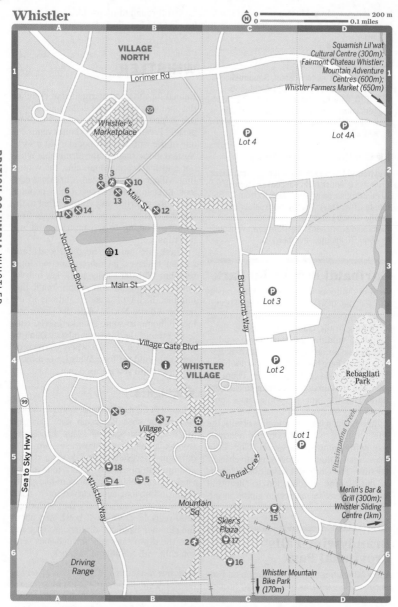

excellent by-donation village tours (held 1pm daily, from June to August).

Whistler Farmers Market MARKET
(www.whistlerfarmersmarket.org; Upper Village; ⏱11am-4pm Sun Jun-Oct) If you're here in summer, head to the Upper Village and the plaza in front of the Fairmont Chateau Whistler for the lively Whistler Farmers Market, where you can peruse more than 50 tent-topped stands hawking everything from arts and crafts to stuff-your-face sea-

Whistler

sonal fruits and bakery treats. A Whistler summer highlight, arrive early for the best selection of goodies.

Whistler Sliding Centre   ADVENTURE SPORTS (www.whistlerslidingcentre.com; 4910 Glacier Lane; ⊙10am-5pm Dec-Mar) Perched just above the village on Blackcomb, Whistler Sliding Centre hosted 2010's Olympic bobsled, luge and skeleton events and is now open to the public. You can wander exhibits, check out video footage from the track and take a self-guided tour. True sports fans should also consider trying bobsled and skeleton: gear, training and runs costs $159.

♯ Activities

Skiing & Snowboarding
Comprising 37 lifts and crisscrossed with over 200 runs, the **Whistler-Blackcomb** (www.whistlerblackcomb.com; 1-day winter lift ticket adult/child $98/52) sister mountains were physically linked for the first time when the resort's mammoth 4.4km Peak 2 Peak gondola opened in 2009. It takes 11 minutes to shuttle wide-eyed powder hogs between the two high alpine areas, so you can hit the slopes on both mountains on the same day. More than half the runs are aimed at intermediate-level skiers.

The winter season kicks off here in late November and typically runs to April on Whistler and June on Blackcomb; December to February is the peak. If you want to emulate your fave Olympic ski heroes, Whistler Creekside was the setting for the downhill skiing events at the 2010 Games.

You can beat the crowds with an early morning Fresh Tracks ticket ($18) which must be bought in advance at Whistler Village Gondola Guest Relations. With your regular lift ticket, it gets you an extra hour on the slopes and the ticket includes breakfast at the Roundhouse Lodge up top. Night owls might prefer the evening Night Moves program, operated via Blackcomb's Magic Chair lift after 5pm.

Snowboard fans should also check out the freestyle terrain parks, mostly located on Blackcomb, including the Snow Cross and the Big Easy Terrain Garden. There's also the popular Habitat Terrain Park on Whistler.

If you didn't bring you own gear, **Mountain Adventure Centres** (☎800-766-0449, 604-967-8950; www.whistlerblackcomb.com/rentals; 4599 Chateau Blvd) has several equipment rental outlets around town. It offers online reservations – choose your favorite gear before you arrive – as well as lessons for ski and snowboard first timers.

Cross-Country Skiing & Snowshoeing
A pleasant stroll or free shuttle bus away from the village, Lost Lake is a hub of wooded cross-country ski trails, suitable for novices and experts alike. Around 4km of the trail is lit for nighttime skiing until 10pm and there's a handy 'warming hut' providing lessons and equipment rentals. Snowshoers are also well served in this area: you can stomp off on your own on 10km of trails or rent equipment and guides.

The **Whistler Olympic Park** (www.whistlerolympicpark.com; 5 Callaghan Valley Rd, Callaghan Valley) is 16km southwest of the village via Hwy 99. It hosted several 2010 Olympic events and is now a prime wilderness area for cross-country skiing and snowshoeing, plus summertime bike tours.

FUNCTION JUNCTION

Take bus number 1 southbound from the village and within 20 minutes you'll be in the heart of the locals' fave neighborhood. **Function Junction** started life as a hidden-among-the-trees area where industrial businesses carried on without affecting the Christmas card visuals of the village. But things have changed in recent years and this area now resembles the early days of Vancouver's Granville Island, its industrial units now slowly colonized by galleries and cafes. It's ideal for an afternoon of leisurely browsing, especially if you plan to dine. The are a couple of streets to explore, but the best is **Millar Creek Rd**.

Start with a late breakfast at **Wild Wood Cafe** (www.wildwoodrestaurants.ca; 1085 Millar Creek Rd; mains $6-12; ⊙6:30am-2pm Mon-Thu, to 3pm Fri & Sat, 9am-3pm Sun; 🖘), a folkie, ever-friendly neighborhood haunt where the eggs Benedict is recommend; they also chef up great burgers if it's lunchtime. Then wander past the yarn-bombed trees en route to **White Dog Whistler Studio Gallery** (www.whitedogwhistler.com; 1074 Millar Creek Rd; ⊙11am-6pm). Luna, the white dog in question, will be waiting to welcome you at the door of this smashing gallery where artist Penny Eder works. As well as her own work, the snob-free spot showcases the eclectic creations of dozens of local artists: look out for pottery, paintings and a glass kaleidoscope or two and ask Eder about her guided village art tours – also check to see whether one of her regular workshops is running if you fancy being creative.

If you need inspiration first, nip across the street to **Whistler Brewing Company** (www.whistlerbeer.com; 1045 Millar Creek Rd; tours $13.95; ⊙1-8pm Mon-Thu, to 10pm Fri, noon-7pm Sat & Sun). The area's very own beer maker is responsible for challenging the choke hold of factory-made suds at bars in the village. You can take a tour of the facilities and try a few brews in the taproom – with any luck, the sought-after winter-only Chestnut Ale will be available. Finally, sober up with a coffee and some of Whistler's best bakery treats at nearby **Purebread** (www.purebread.ca; 1040 Millar Creek Rd; baked goods $3-5; ⊙9am-5pm), where pudgie pies and and lemon sugar buns are essential. There are lots of nearby hiking routes if you suddenly need to work off 1000 calories.

Mountain Biking

Taking over the melted ski slopes in summer and accessed via the lift at the village's south end, **Whistler Mountain Bike Park** (http://bike.whistlerblackcomb.com; 1-day pass adult/child $53/31; ⊙May-Oct) offers barreling downhill runs and an orgy of jumps, beams and bridges twisting through 200km of well-maintained forested trails. You don't have to be a bike courier to stand the knee-buckling pace: easier routes are marked in green, while blue intermediate trails and black-diamond advanced paths are offered if you want to **Crank It Up** – the name of one of the park's most popular routes. Those with calves of steel should also hit the spectacular **Top of the World Trail**.

Outside the park area, winding trails around the region include the gentle **Valley Trail**, an easy 14km loop that encircles the village and its lake, meadow and mountain-château surroundings – recommended for first timers.

Hiking

With more than 40km of flower-and-forest alpine trails, most accessed via the Whistler Village Gondola, the region is ideal for those who like nature of the strollable variety. Favorite routes include the **High Note Trail** (8km), which traverses pristine meadows and has stunning views of the blue-green waters of Cheakamus Lake. Route maps are available at the visitors center. Guided hikes are also offered by the friendly folk at **Whistler Alpine Guides Bureau** (☑604-938-9242; www.whistlerguides.com; 207B, 4368 Main St; adult/child from $79/59), who can also help with rock-climbing and rap-jumping excursions.

Rafting

Tumbling waterfalls, dense forest and a menagerie of wildlife are some of what you might see as you lurch along the Elaho or Squamish Rivers on an adrenalin-charged half- or full-day rafting trip. **Wedge Rafting** (☑604-932-7171, 888-932-5899; www.wedge-rafting.com; 4293 Mountain Sq; tours adult/child

$99/69) offers paddle-like-crazy-or-you'll-never-make-it excursions, plus more gentle jaunts for the less energetic.

✦✦ Festivals & Events

Winterpride COMMUNITY
(www.gaywhistler.com; ⊘ early Feb) A week of gay-friendly snow action and late-night partying.

World Ski & Snowboard Festival SKIING
(www.wssf.com; ⊘ mid-Apr) A nine-day showcase of pro ski and snowboard competitions, plus partying.

Crankworx MOUNTAIN BIKING
(www.crankworx.com; ⊘ mid-Aug) An adrenalin-filled celebration of bike stunts, speed contests and mud-splattered shenanigans.

Cornucopia FOOD & WINE
(www.whistlercornucopia.com; ⊘ Nov) Bacchanalian food and wine fest crammed with parties.

Whistler Film Festival FILM
(www.whistlerfilmfestival.com; ⊘ Dec) Four days of Canadian and independent movie screenings, plus industry schmoozing.

🛏 Sleeping

Winter, especially December and January, is the peak for prices, but last-minute deals can still be had if you're planning an impromptu overnight from Vancouver – check the website of **Tourism Whistler** (www.whistler.com) for room sales and packages. Most hotels extort parking fees of up to $40 daily and some also slap on resort fees of up to $25 daily, so confirm these before you book.

★ HI Whistler Hostel HOSTEL $
(☑ 866-762-4112, 604-962-0025; www.hihostels. ca; 1035 Legacy Way; dm/r $36/95; @ 🖳) Built as athlete accommodation for the 2010 Winter Olympics, this sparkling hostel is 7km south of the village near Function Junction. Transit buses to/from town stop right outside. Book ahead for private rooms (with en-suite bathrooms and TVs) or save by staying in a small dorm. Eschewing the sometimes institutionalized HI hostel feel, this one has IKEA-style furnishings, art-lined walls and a licensed cafe. There's also a great TV room for rainy-day hunkering.

If it's fine, hit the nearby biking and hiking trails or barbecue on one of the two mountain-view decks. When it's time to hit the

village, the bus will have you there in around 15 minutes.

Riverside Resort CAMPGROUND, CABINS $$
(☑ 604-905-5533; www.riversidewhistler.com; 8018 Mons Rd; campsites/yurts/cabins $35/89/157; 🖳) Beloved of in-the-know BC residents and just a few minutes past Whistler on Hwy 99, this facility-packed, family-friendly campground has elevated itself in recent years by adding cozy cabin and yurt options. The yurts, with basic furnishings and electricity, and bedding provided, are especially recommended. The resort's on-site Junction Café serves great breakfasts.

Adara Hotel HOTEL $$
(☑ 604-905-4009, 866-502-3272; www.adarahotel. com; 4122 Village Green; r from $149; ❋ 🖳🖳) Unlike all those lodges now claiming to be boutique hotels, the sophisticated and centrally located Adara is the real deal. Lined with designer details, including fake antler horns in the lobby, accommodations have spa-like bathrooms and fireplaces that look like TVs. Despite the ultra-cool aesthetics, service is warm and relaxed. Check ahead for the popular summertime bike packages.

Crystal Lodge & Suites HOTEL $$
(☑ 800-667-3363, 604-932-2221; www.crystal-lodge.com; 4154 Village Green; d/ste from $130/175; ❋ 🖳🖳) Not all rooms are created equal at the Crystal, forged from the fusion of two quite different hotel towers. Cheaper rooms in the South Tower are standard style – baths and fridges are the highlight – but those in the Lodge Wing match the handsome rock-and-beam lobby, complete with small balconies. Both share excellent proximity to restaurants and ski lifts.

Chalet Luise B&B Inn B&B $$
(☑ 800-665-1998, 604-932-4187; www.chaletluise. com; 7461 Ambassador Cres; d from $125; 🖳) A five-minute trail walk from the village, this Bavarian-look pension has eight bright and sunny rooms – think pine furnishings and crisp white duvets – and a flower garden that's ideal for a spot of evening wine quaffing. Or you can just hop in the hot tub and dream about the large buffet breakfast coming your way in the morning. Free parking.

Edgewater Lodge HOTEL $$$
(☑ 604-932-0688, 888-870-9065; www.edgewater-lodge.com; 8020 Alpine Way; d incl breakfast from $189; 🖳🖳) A few minutes' drive past Whistler on Hwy 99, this 12-room waterside lodge

is a nature lover's idyll and has a celebrated on-site restaurant. Each room overlooks the glassy waters of Green Lake through a large picture window – sit in your window alcove and watch the ospreys or hit the surface with a kayak rental. Rates include parking.

Pinnacle Hotel Whistler
HOTEL **$$**
(☎888-999-8986, 604-938-3218; www.whistler-pinnacle.com; 4319 Main St; d from $159; 🖥🚭♨) Just across the street from the museum, this friendly, well-established, adult-oriented lodge has the perfect extra in almost every room: a large jetted soaker tub that dominates proceedings. Balconies and full kitchens are also de rigueur and there's an on-site restaurant if it's too cold to stray far from your room.

Nita Lake Lodge
HOTEL **$$$**
(☎604-966-5700, 888-755-6482; www.nita-lakelodge.com; 2135 Lake Placid Rd; d from $199; 🖥♨) Adjoining Creekside railway station – very handy if you're coming up on the **Rocky Mountaineer train** (www.rockymountaineer.com; tickets from $129; ☺May to mid-Oct) – this swanky timber-framed lodge is perfect for a pampering retreat. Hugging the lakeside, the chic but cozy rooms feature individual patios, rock fireplaces and bathrooms with heated floors and large tubs; some also have handy kitchens. Creekside lifts are a walkable few minutes away.

There's an excellent on-site West Coast restaurant but a free shuttle can whisk you to the village if you want to dine further afield. Summer rates also include free-use bikes and fishing rods.

Fairmont Chateau Whistler
HOTEL **$$$**
(☎800-606-8244, 604-938-8000; www.fairmont.com/whistler; 4599 Chateau Blvd; d from $289; ❄🖥♨) Combining dramatic baronial lodge lobbies and comfortably palatial rooms, many with mountain views, the Fairmont is a handsome reproduction of the high-end chain's Canadian 'castle hotels.' Close enough to enjoy ski-in, ski-out privileges on Blackcomb, it's tempting just to stay indoors trawling the lower-level shops and hopping from restaurant to bar. The heated outdoor pool is a highlight.

🍴 Eating

★ Purebread
BAKERY **$**
(www.purebread.ca; 4338 Main St; baked goods $3-5; ☺8:30am-7pm) When this Function Junction legend finally opened a village branch,

the locals came running, and they've been queuing ever since. They're here for the cornucopia of eye-roll-worthy bakery treats, including salted caramel bars, sour-cherry choc-chip cookies and the amazing Crack, a naughtily gooey shortbread cookie bar. There's savory here, too; go for the hearty homity pie.

Service is ever friendly and, if you arrive just after the early morning bakeathon, you can expect the aromas to lure you into at least tripling your purchase. Wash it all down with a large coffee from Portland-based Stumptown.

Gone Village Eatery
CAFE **$**
(www.gonevillageeatery.com; 4205 Village Sq; mains $6-12; ☺6:30am-9pm; 🖥) Aim for the only booth at this well-hidden locals' fave and tuck into a wide range of hearty, good-value comfort grub of the chili, chicken-curry and steak-and-potatoes variety. This is where many fuel up for a calorie-burning day on the slopes and have a Mars-bar coffee when they return. There are also internet terminals ($1 per 10 minutes).

Mount Currie Coffee Co
CAFE **$**
(www.mountcurriecoffee.com; 4369 Main St; ☺6:30am-5:30pm) A Pemberton fave recently opened this toe-hold in the village. Though off the beaten path, this coffee nook is worth searching out for its perfectly prepped Intelligentsia java. Extras include hearty Pemberton beef wraps and, when you've reached your Americano limit, 'green machine smoothies.' Consider a mason-jar travel mug as a cool souvenir. Follow Main St and you'll soon find it.

Splitz Grill
BURGERS **$**
(www.splitzgrill.com; 4369 Main St; mains $9-13; ☺11am-8pm Mon-Thu & Sun, to 9pm Fri & Sat) Whistler's best burgers are served up at this unassuming storefront, which opens onto a surprisingly large seating area inside, plus a hidden tree-framed patio. The hand-rolled cannonballs of meat make for tasty burgers, served with perfect crunchy fries, that are far from regular fast food. Buffalo, salmon and turkey join the classic beef patties, but the juicy Salt Spring lamb burger is highly recommended.

★ Rimrock Cafe
WEST COAST **$$**
(☎604-932-5565; http://rimrockcafe.com; 2117 Whistler Rd; mains $16-28; ☺5:45-9:30pm) On the edge of Creekside and accessible just off Hwy 99, the menu at this locals' favorite

includes highlights such as seared scallops, venison tenderloin and a recommended seafood trio of grilled prawns, ahi tuna and nut-crusted sablefish. All are served in an intimate room with two fireplaces and a large, flower-lined patio where you can laugh at the harried highway drivers zipping past.

Mexican Corner
MEXICAN $$

(http://themexicancorner.ca; 4340 Lorimer Rd; mains $14-22; ⊘11am-9:30pm) Bringing authentic Mexican dishes to Whistler for the first time, this chatty little corner spot is the real deal for fans of perfect, fresh-made taco, enchilada and quesadilla dishes. Go for the four-taco *pastor* plate (roasted pork tacos topped with a pineapple sliver), coupled with a pleasingly sour tamarind margarita. An additional larger location was being eyed during our visit.

Crêpe Montagne
FRENCH $$

(http://crepemontagne.com; 4368 Main St; mains $8-24; ⊘8am-10:30pm) This small, authentic and highly cozy *crêperie* – hence the French accents percolating among the staff – offers a bewildering array of sweet and savory buckwheat crepes with fillings including ham, brie, asparagus, banana, strawberries and more. Fondues are also available. A good breakfast spot, go the waffle route and you'll be perfectly set up for a calorie-burning day on the slopes.

Christine's Mountain Top Dining
WEST COAST $$

(☑604-938-7437; Rendezvous Lodge, Blackcomb Mountain; mains $12-22) The best of the handful of places to eat while you're enjoying a summertime summit stroll or winter ski day on the slopes of Blackcomb Mountain. Socked into the Rendezvous Lodge, try for a patio table with a view and tuck into a seasonal seafood grill or a lovely applewood-smoked-cheddar grilled-cheese sandwich. Reservations recommended.

Sachi Sushi
JAPANESE $$

(www.sachisushi.com; 106-4359 Main St; mains $8-22; ⊘5:30-10pm) Whistler's best sushi spot doesn't stop at California rolls. It serves everything from crispy popcorn shrimp to seafood salads and stomach-warming udon noodles – the tempura noodle bowl is best. This bright and breezy eatery is a relaxing après-ski hangout and is good for a glass of hot sake on a cold winter day.

Araxi Restaurant & Bar
WEST COAST $$$

(☑604-932-4540; www.araxi.com; 4222 Village Sq; mains $24-41; ⊘5-11pm daily, plus brunch 10am-2pm Sat & Sun) Whistler's best splurge restaurant, Araxi cooks up an inventive and exquisite Pacific Northwest menu and has charming and courteous service. Try the BC halibut and drain the 15,000-bottle wine selection but save room for a dessert: a regional cheese plate or the amazing Okanagan apple cheesecake...or both.

🍷 Drinking & Entertainment

Merlin's Bar & Grill
PUB

(4553 Blackcomb Way; ⊘11am-1am) The best of Whistler's cavernous ski pubs, this Upper Village local also looks the part: log-lined walls, ceiling-mounted lift cars, bra-draped moose head and a large slope-facing patio. Menus, mounted on snowboard tips, cover the pub-grub classics and, although the beer is mostly of the generic Kokanee-like variety, there are usually some tasty Whistler Brewing ales available. There is regular live music during peak season.

Dubh Linn Gate
PUB

(☑604-905-4047; www.dubhlinngate.com; 4320 Sundial Cres; ⊘8am-1am) Whistler's archetypal pub, this dark, wood-lined joint would feel just like an authentic Ireland watering hole if not for the obligatory heated patio. Tuck yourself into a shady corner table and revive your inner leprechaun with a stout – there's Guinness as well as Murphy's. Even better is the slightly pricey BC-craft-brew menu and regular live music, often of the trad Irish variety.

Garibaldi Lift Company
PUB

(4165 Springs Lane, Whistler Village Gondola; ⊘11am-1am) The closest bar to the slopes, you can smell the sweat of the skiers or mountain bikers as they hurtle past the patio at this cavernous bar that everyone calls the GLC. The furnishings have the scuffs and dings of a well-worn pub, but the best time to come is when DJs or bands turn the place into a clubbish mosh pit.

Longhorn Saloon & Grill
PUB

(www.longhornsaloon.ca; 4284 Mountain Sq; ⊘9am-1am) Across from lifts at the base of Whistler Mountain, the sprawling patio at this raucous joint sometimes threatens to take over the village. Popular with twenty-somethings, it's all about downing jugs of fizzy lager and eyeing up potential partners

BRITISH COLUMBIA WHISTLER

DETOUR TO COWBOY COUNTRY

The next town north of Whistler on Hwy 99, **Pemberton** has a welcoming vibe and a distinctive provenance as a farming and cowboy region, which explains why its kitsch-cool mascot is a potato in a neckerchief called Potato Jack. But there's more to the region's top tubers than great fries.

Pemberton Distillery (www.pembertondistillery.ca; 1954 Venture Pl; ⊙ noon-6pm Wed-Sat) started making great artisan vodka from local potatoes several years back. The smooth, organic liquor was such a success that more booze was added to the roster and the company now also makes gin, apple brandy and one of BC's only absinthe concoctions. In total, they use up to 100,000lb of local spuds every year.

On our visit, the owners were close to bottling their first whiskey and were also planning to add beer to the lineup, made from their own-grown hops. A visit to the friendly little distillery, located on an unassuming industrial strip on the edge of town, includes a generous free sample or two at the **tasting bar**. The best time to visit is on Saturdays at 4pm (year-round) when $5 buys you a **guided tour** followed by some well-informed tastings. If you're suddenly inspired to take a bottle home, prices range from $24 to $58.

If you end up indulging a little too much and suddenly need something more substantial to ingest, don't leave town without visiting the locals' other fave hangout. The ever-animated **Pony** (☎ 604-894-5700; www.thepony.ca; 1392 Portage Rd; mains $10-22; ⊙ 8am-10pm) is the kind of bistro-style restaurant that effortlessly combines smiley service with excellent gourmet comfort nosh, from triple-decker shrimp clubs to perfect pizzas and heaping salads, plus a carefully curated craft-beer list. Aim for a patio table and, even better, drop by on Thursday evening for beer and pizza night: you'll likely meet every Pembertonian in the vicinity.

For more information on visiting Pemberton, head to www.tourismpembertonbc.com.

---

from your plastic lawn chair. The food is nothing special, but it's hard to beat the atmosphere on a hopping winter evening.

Moejoe's CLUB
(www.moejoes.com; 4155 Golfer's Approach; ⊙ 9pm-2am Tue-Sun) Popular with the kind of under-30s that work in Whistler shops and coffeehouses, this is the best place in town if you like dancing yourself into a drooling heap. It's always crowded on Friday and Saturday nights but, if you want to mix it up with those locals, drop by on twice-a-month Wednesdays when Whistler workers roll in for free.

Village 8 Cinema CINEMA
(www.village8cinema.com; 4295 Blackcomb Way) Shows first-run flicks in the heart of the village. Discounts on Tuesdays.

🛈 Information

Pick up the weekly *Pique* or *Whistler Question* newspapers for local happenings.

Northlands Medical Clinic (☎ 604-932-8362; www.northlandsclinic.com; 4359 Main St; ⊙ 9am-5:30pm) Walk-in medical center.

Post Office (www.canadapost.ca; 4360 Lorimer Rd; ⊙ 8am-5pm Mon-Fri, to noon Sat)

Public Library (☎ 604-935-8433; www.whistlerlibrary.ca; 4329 Main St; ⊙ 11am-7pm Mon-Thu, to 5pm Fri-Sun; 🛜) Free 24-hour wifi, including around the building, outside opening hours. Also has internet-access computers (free for up to one hour per person per day).

Whistler Visitors Centre (☎ 800-944-7853, 604-935-3357; www.whistler.com; 4230 Gateway Dr; ⊙ 8am-10pm) Flyer-lined visitors center with friendly staff.

Whistler Inside Blog (www.whistler.com/blog)

Whistler is Awesome (www.whistlerisawesome.com)

🛈 Getting There & Around

While most visitors arrive by car from Vancouver via Hwy 99, **Greyhound Canada** (www.greyhound.ca) buses also service the route, arriving at Creekside and Whistler Village from the city (from $14, two to 2½ hours, six daily). Most buses are equipped with free wi-fi.

Pacific Coach Lines (www.pacificcoach.com) services also arrive from Vancouver (from $49, two hours, five daily) and Vancouver International Airport and drop off at Whistler hotels. **Snowbus** (www.snowbus.com) operates a winter-only service from Vancouver (adult/child $38/22, two to three hours, two to three daily).

Train spotters can trundle into town on Rocky Mountaineer Vacations' **Whistler Sea to Sky**

Climb (www.rockymountaineer.com), which winds along a picturesque coastal route from North Vancouver (from $169, three hours, one daily May to mid-October).

Whistler's **WAVE** (www.busonline.ca) public buses (adult/child/one-day pass $2.50/2/7) are equipped with ski and bike racks. In summer, there's a free service from the village to Lost Lake.

SUNSHINE COAST

Stretching 139km along the water from Langdale to Lund, the Sunshine Coast – separated from the Lower Mainland by the Coast Mountains and the Strait of Georgia – has an independent, island-like mentality that belies the fact it's only a 40-minute ferry ride from Horseshoe Bay. Hwy 101 links key communities Gibsons, Sechelt and Powell River, plus tiny Roberts Creek, and it's an easy and convivial region to explore. There are also plenty of activities to keep things lively: think ocean kayaking and spectacular wilderness hiking with a side order of artists' studios. Peruse the website of **Sunshine Coast Tourism** (www.sunshinecoastcanada.com) for information and get a copy of the *Recreation Map & Activity Guide* ($3) – available in upper- and lower-region versions – for outdoorsy suggestions throughout the area.

❶ Getting There & Around

BC Ferries (www.bcferries.com) Services arrive at Langdale, 6km northeast of Gibsons, from West Vancouver's Horseshoe Bay (passenger/vehicle $14.55/49.05, 40 minutes, eight daily).

Sunshine Coast Transit System (www.busonline.ca; adult/child $2.25/1.75) Runs buses from the ferry terminal into Gibsons, Roberts Creek and Sechelt.

Malaspina Coach Lines (www.malaspina-coach.com) Buses arrive daily from Vancouver, via the ferry, in Gibsons ($35, two hours), Sechelt ($45, three hours) and Powell River ($66, five to six hours). Rates include ferry fares.

Harbour Air Seaplanes (www.harbour-air.com) Flies floatplanes from downtown Vancouver to Sechelt three times a day (from $78, 20 minutes).

Pacific Coastal Airlines (www.pacific-coastal.com) Flies into Powell River from the South Terminal of Vancouver International Airport up to five times daily (from $117, 35 minutes).

Gibsons

POP 4400

Your first port of call after docking in Langdale and driving or busing into town, the pretty waterfront strip here is called Gibsons Landing. A rainbow of painted wooden buildings overlooking the marina, it's famous across Canada as the setting for *The Beachcombers,* a TV show from the 1970s that fictionalized a town full of eccentrics. You can soak up the TV nostalgia with breakfast at the landmark **Molly's Reach** (www.mollysreach.ca; 647 School Rd; mains $8-19; ☺8am-9pm) restaurant.

Once you're fully fueled, putter around the rows of galleries and artisan stores, especially along Marine Dr and Molly's Lane. Be sure to drop into the **Gibsons Public Art Gallery** (www.gibsonspublicartgallery.ca; 431 Marine Dr; ☺11am-4pm Thu-Mon), where monthly exhibitions showcase local artists; check the website for show openings. As for activities, hit the water with a rental or guided tour via the friendly folks at **Sunshine Kayaking** (☑604-886-9790; www.sunshinekayaking.com; Molly's Lane; rentals 2/24hr $29/75; ☺hours vary, book ahead), whose guided sunset tours ($85) are recommended.

Your best bet for a sleepover is the lovely **Bonniebrook Lodge** (☑604-886-2887; www.bonniebrook.com; 1532 Ocean Beach Esplanade; d from $200; � ❀ ❁), a historic wood-built inn overlooking a quiet waterfront stretch. The area also abounds with B&Bs, including the homely, family-friendly **Arcturus Retreat Bed & Breakfast** (☑877-856-1940, 604-886-1940; www.arcturusretreat.ca; 160 Pike Rd; d from $160; ❀ ❁), handily located just up the hill

---

SUNSHINE COAST GALLERY CRAWL

Pick up the free *Sunshine Coast Purple Banner* flyer from area visitors centers for the location of dozens of studios and galleries throughout the region. Many are open for drop-in visitors – look out for the purple flags along the road on your travels – and they're a great way to meet the locals and find unique souvenirs. For further information, see www.suncoastarts.com. And, if you're here in October, check out the weekend-long **Sunshine Coast Art Crawl** (www.sunshinecoastartcrawl.com).

from the ferry dock. They can also point you to the nearby **Sprockids Mountain Bike Park**. For other B&Bs in the vicinity, see www.gibsonsgetaways.com.

Gourmet seafood fans shouldn't miss **Smitty's Oyster House** (www.smittysoysterhouse.com; 643 School Rd; mains $9-23; ☺noon-late Tue-Sat, to 8pm Sun), which faces the boat-bobbling marina, for perfect fresh-catch treats. Alternatively, amble along the pier at the nearby Government Dock and you'll find a local fave: the friendly, shack-like **Shed** (mains $6-12; ☺11am-4pm & 6-8pm) serves tasty tacos and burritos, with ingredients of the fish variety sourced from nearby boats. Snag a seat alongside for a side order of mesmerizing waterfront views.

Drop by the **visitors center** (☑604-886-2374, 866-222-3806; www.gibsonschamber.com; 417 Marine Dr; ☺9am-5pm Sat-Thu, to 7pm Fri) for more information and resources.

Roberts Creek

POP 3100

Just off Hwy 101 via Roberts Creek Rd, the funky 'downtown' here looks like a little hobbit community, if hobbits had gone through a hippie phase. Poke around the wood-built, shack-like stores and eateries and then tootle downhill onto **Roberts Creek Pier**, overlooking the Strait of Georgia. Backed by a large waterfront park, with a beach at low tide, it's an idyllic spot to watch the natural world float by.

The Sunshine Coast's best hostel, the effortlessly welcoming **Up the Creek Backpacker's B&B** (☑877-885-8100, 604-837-5943; www.upthecreek.ca; 1261 Roberts Creek Rd; dm/r $28/80; @☎) has small dorms, one family-friendly private room and a recommended cozy cabin in the fruit-tree-lined garden. Organic breakfast costs $6 extra and there are free loaner bikes for exploring the many area trails. Transit buses from the Langdale ferry terminal stop nearby.

On hot days, pick up an icy treat at cute **Batchworks Sorbet** (www.batchworkssorbet.com; Gumboot Gardens; ☺noon-5pm Thu & Fri, 11am-5pm Sat & Sun) or join the locals for coffee and baked goodies at the wood-floored **Gumboot Cafe** (1057 Roberts Creek Rd; mains $4-8; ☺7am-5pm Mon-Fri, 8am-5pm Sat, 10am-4pm Sun), where the pizza slices are recommended. For heartier fare, the recently revamped **Gumboot Restaurant** (1041 Roberts Creek Rd; mains $11-18) is a great spot

to slide onto a veranda table, catch a live band most Wednesdays and indulge in locally sourced, West Coast dishes from lamb to seafood; check the chalkboard for daily specials.

Sechelt

POP 9900

The second-largest Sunshine Coast town, Sechelt isn't as funky as Gibsons or Powell River, but there are lots of outdoor activity options, plus some good spots to fuel up.

With a good kayak launch site and a sandy, stroll-worthy beach, the fir-and cedar-forested **Porpoise Bay Provincial Park** (www.bcparks.ca) is 4km north of Sechelt along East Porpoise Bay Rd. There are trails throughout the park and a large **campground** (www.discovercamping.ca; campsites $25) with handy hot showers.

For visiting paddlers (and pedalers), **Pedals & Paddles** (☑604-885-6440; www.pedalspaddles.com; 7425 Sechelt Inlet Rd; rentals 2/24hr $32/80) organizes kayak rentals and can take you on tours of the inlet's wonderfully tranquil waters.

Alternatively, chat with local artists and growers at the summertime **Sechelt Farmers & Artisans Market** (www.secheltmarket.org; ☺9am-2:30pm Sat Apr-Sep) on Cowrie St. There's also a night market nearby on Thursdays from June to August. If you have an artsy itch to scratch, check out mid-August's **Sunshine Coast Festival of the Written Arts** (www.writersfestival.ca).

If you like the idea of a secluded waterfront retreat, check out the two designer suites and the cottage at **Beachside by the Bay** (☑604-741-0771; www.beachsidebythebay.com; 5005 Sunshine Coast Hwy; d $199-$239; ☎). You'll be waking up to spectacular Davis Bay panoramas, while facilities include full kitchens, covered outdoor hot tub and a huge private beach deck where you can spend the evening barbecuing and watching passing eagles. Alternatively, drive along Hwy 101 past Sechelt to swanky **Rockwater Secret Cove Resort** (☑877-296-4593, 604-885-7038; www.rockwatersecretcoveresort.com; 5356 Ole's Cove Rd; r/cabin/ste/tent $209/209/249/419; ☎☎), where the highlight accommodations include luxury tent suites perched like nests on a steep cliff. For a wealth of area B&B options, visit www.bbsunshinecoast.com.

If it's time to eat, join the locals and dive into a fresh-baked maple cinnamon bun at ever-buzzing **Wheatberries Bakery** (www. wheatberriesbakery.com; 5500 Wharf St; baked goods from $2; ⊙7am-5pm; 🐾). Alternatively, go for a curry or pizza – yes, they've mastered both – at **Saffron** (www.saffronrestaurant. ca; 5755 Cowrie St; mains $11-18; ⊙11:30am-9pm), a friendly but fiendishly well-hidden restaurant behind the Trail Bay Centre mall. Save time for the **Lighthouse Pub** (www. lighthousepub.ca; 5764 Wharf Rd; mains $12-22), a quality neighborhood haunt where you can eavesdrop on Sunshine Coast gossip while feasting on boat-bobbling waterfront views and hearty pub grub; fish and chips plus the incredible banana cheesecake churro are recommended.

For information, drop by the **Sechelt Visitors Centre** (☑877-885-1036, 604-885-1036; www.secheltvisitorcentre.com; 5790 Teredo St; ⊙9am-5pm).

Powell River

POP 13,600

Founded as a paper-mill town more than a century ago, the largest Sunshine Coast community has been busily reinventing itself in recent years, luring many from Vancouver and beyond to move in and set up cool businesses. The result is an increasingly funky town – especially in the historic Townsite area – that's also a gateway to splendid outdoor activities.

Pick up a free flyer from the **visitors center** (☑877-817-8669, 604-485-4701; www. discoverpowellriver.com; 4670 Joyce Ave; ⊙9am-6pm) and explore the Townsite's heritage buildings, many of them century-old Arts and Crafts constructions, on a self-guided stroll. Highlights include the **Henderson House**, now open to the public after a five-year renovation, and the lovely **Patricia Theatre** (www.patriciatheatre.com; 5848 Ash Ave), Canada's oldest continually operating cinema. Step inside for a chat with Ann the owner and she'll tell you some stories and let you snap shots of the art-painted interior. The **Townsite Heritage Society** (www. powellrivertownsite.com; 6211 Walnut Ave, Henderson House; $5; ⊙tours 2pm Wed & 10am Sat Jul & Aug) runs summer guided tours of the neighborhood, starting at Henderson House.

End your exploration with a free tour at **Townsite Brewing** (www.townsitebrewing.com; 5824 Ash Ave; ⊙11am-7pm daily, tours 3pm Thu & Sat), plus a $5 sampling of all the top tipples and seasonal specials. Zunga Golden Blonde

---

THE 'OTHER WEST COAST TRAIL'

Vancouver Island's West Coast Trail is so popular it's hard not to run into other hikers en route – that's if you can get one of the coveted daily access spots in the first place. But the Sunshine Coast offers its own under-the-radar version that many BC locals have only just started discovering. Running from Sarah Point to Saltery Bay, the 180km-long **Sunshine Coast Trail** is a wilderness paradise of ancient forests, stirring waterfronts and snow-capped vistas. Unlike the West Coast Trail, this one is free and reservations are not required – there are free-use sleeping huts dotted along the route. For more information, visit www.sunshinecoast-trail.com.

Ale is the top seller, but fans of the dark side will savor Pow Town Porter. If you're here on the third Friday of the month, look out for the ever-changing 'experimental cask.' If you need to blow away a few cobwebs the next morning, hit the water for a paddle with **Powell River Sea Kayak** (www.bcseakayak. com; 10676 Crowther Rd; 3/12hr rental $35/44).

When it's time to rest your weary noggin, it's hard to beat the highly welcoming **Old Courthouse Inn** (☑604-483-4000, 877-483-4777; www.oldcourthouseinn.ca; 6243 Walnut St; d from $89; 🐾), a transformed, immaculately preserved historic court building where recent new owners have lined the rooms with period knickknacks and spruced things up with mod flourishes like a jazzy new restaurant, serving cooked breakfasts (included with rates), lunches and dinnertime tapas – aim for a summertime patio table.

Alternatively, drop in for tacos at the tiny, bright-painted **Costa del Sol** (www.costadel-solcuisine.com; 4578 Marine Ave; mains $9.50-14; ⊙11:30am-9pm Sun, Mon, Wed & Thu, to 10pm Fri & Sat); the 'meaty maverick' is recommended. Or hang with the locals over fish and chips and a Townsite Brewing beer or three at the chatty **Hub** (www.thehub101.ca; 6275 Marine Ave; mains $11-15). For something fancier, try the **Alchemist Restaurant** (www.alchemist-restaurant.com; 4680 Marine Ave; mains $21-28; ⊙from 5pm Tue-Sat), where local seasonal ingredients are fused with Mediterranean approaches to produce mouthwatering dishes.

Vancouver Island

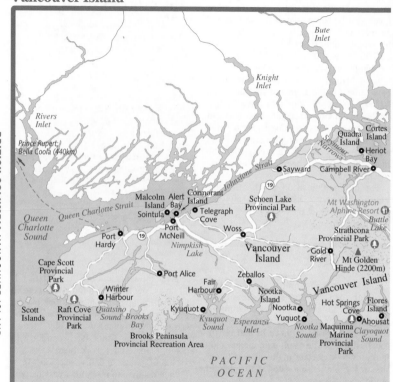

VANCOUVER ISLAND

The largest populated landmass between western North America and New Zealand – it's around 500km long and 100km wide – Vancouver Island is laced with colorful, often quirky communities, many founded on logging or fishing and featuring the word 'Port' in their name.

The locals are generally a friendly bunch, proud of their region and its distinct differences. Traveling around, you'll find a wide range of attractions, experiences and activities that feel many miles away from the bustle of mainland Vancouver. Which reminds us: if you want to make a good impression, don't mistakenly refer to the place as 'Victoria Island.'

While the history-wrapped BC capital Victoria is the first port of call for many, it should not be the only place you visit. Food and wine fans will enjoy weaving through the verdant Cowichan Valley farm region; those craving a laid-back, family-friendly enclave should hit the twin seaside towns of Parksville and Qualicum; outdoor-activity enthusiasts shouldn't miss the surf-loving west-coast area of Tofino and beyond; and those who fancy remote backcountry far from the madding crowds should make for the north, an undiscovered gem that's among BC's most rewarding wilderness areas.

ℹ Information

For an introduction to the island, contact **Tourism Vancouver Island** (☏250-754-3500; www.vancouverisland.travel) for listings and resources.

Victoria

POP 84,000

With a wider metro population approaching 360,000, this picture-postcard provincial capital was long-touted as North America's most English city. Thankfully, the tired theme-park version of old-fashioned England has faded in recent years. Fueled by an increasingly younger demographic, a quiet revolution has seen lame tourist pubs, eateries and stores transformed into the kind of brightly painted bohemian shops, coffee bars and innovative restaurants that would make any city proud. It's worth seeking out these enclaves on foot, but activity fans should also hop on their bikes: Victoria has more cycle routes than any other Canadian city. Once you've finished pedaling, there's BC's best museum, a park fringed by a windswept seafront and outdoor activities from kayaking to whale watching.

Sights

Royal BC Museum
MUSEUM

(Map p170; www.royalbcmuseum.bc.ca; 675 Belleville St; adult/child from $16/10; ⊙10am-5pm Sun-Wed, to 10pm Thu-Sat) Start in the natural-history gallery on your visit to the province's best museum. Fronted by a beady-eyed woolly mammoth, it's lined with evocative dioramas – the elk peeking through trees is a favorite. Next, head up to the First Peoples exhibit with its fascinating mask gallery – look out for a ferret-faced white man. The highlight is the walk-through colonial street with its chatty Chinatown and detailed storefronts.

The museum hosts regular special exhibitions and also has a popular IMAX theater screening documentaries and Hollywood blockbusters.

Robert Bateman Centre
GALLERY

(Map p170; www.batemancentre.org; 470 Belleville St; adult/child $12.50/8.50; ⊙10am-6pm Sun-Wed, to 9pm Thu-Sat) Victoria's newest cultural attraction isn't just a gallery showcasing the photo-realistic works of Canada's most popular nature painter, it's also a testament to Bateman's commitment to environmental issues. Start with the five-minute intro movie, then move through a series of small exhibit areas with 160 achingly beautiful paintings and

Victoria

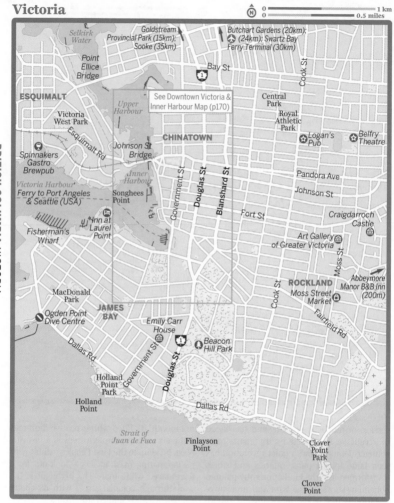

prints showing animals in nature from BC and beyond.

Use your smart phone or a loaner available at the front desk to scan QR codes near many works and you'll get the story behind them from the man himself. Better still, check the website ahead of your visit: Bateman lives on Salt Spring Island and gives talks and presentations here whenever possible; book ahead.

Parliament Buildings HISTORIC BUILDING
(Map p170; www.leg.bc.ca; 501 Belleville St; ⏲ tours 9am-5pm) **FREE** Across from the museum,

this handsome confection of turrets, domes and stained glass is the province's working legislature and is open to history-loving visitors. Peek behind the facade on a colorful (and free) 30-minute tour led by costumed Victorians, then stop for lunch at the 'secret' politicians' restaurant. Return in the evening when the elegant exterior is illuminated like a Christmas tree.

Art Gallery of Greater Victoria GALLERY
(Map p168; www.aggv.bc.ca; 1040 Moss St; adult/child $13/2.50; ⏲ 10am-5pm Mon-Wed, Fri & Sat, to 9pm Thu, noon-5pm Sun) Head east of down-

town on Fort St and follow the gallery street signs to one of Canada's best Emily Carr collections. Aside from Carr's swirling nature canvases, you'll find an ever-changing array of temporary exhibitions. Check online for events, including lectures, presentations and monthly late-night Urbanite socials, when artsy coolsters roll in to mingle. Admission is by donation on the first Tuesday of every month.

Craigdarroch Castle MUSEUM
(Map p168; www.thecastle.ca; 1050 Joan Cres; adult/child $13.75/5; ⊙9am-7pm) If you're in this part of town checking out the gallery, don't miss this elegant turreted mansion a few minutes' walk away. A handsome, 39-room landmark built by a 19th-century coal baron with money to burn, it's dripping with period architecture and antique-packed rooms. Climb the tower's 87 steps, checking out the stained-glass en route, for views of the snowcapped Olympic Mountains.

Victoria Bug Zoo ZOO
(Map p170; www.bugzoo.com; 631 Courtney St; adult/child $10/7; ⊙10:30am-5:30pm Mon-Sat, 11am-5pm Sun) The most fun any kid can have in Victoria without realizing it's educational, step inside the brightly painted main room for a cornucopia of show-and-tell insect encounters. The excellent young guides talk about critters such as frog beetles, dragon-headed crickets and the disturbingly large three-horned scarab beetles. There are plenty of chances to snap shots of your kids handling the goods (under supervision).

Beacon Hill Park PARK
(Map p168; www.beaconhillpark.ca; Douglas St) Fringed by crashing ocean, this waterfront park is ideal for feeling the wind in your hair – check out the windswept trees along the cliff top. You'll also find a gigantic totem pole, Victorian cricket pitch and a marker for Mile 0 of Hwy 1, alongside a statue of Canadian legend Terry Fox. If you're here with kids, consider the popular children's farm as well; see www.beaconhillchildrensfarm.ca.

Emily Carr House MUSEUM
(Map p168; www.emilycarr.com; 207 Government St; adult/child $6.75/4.50; ⊙11am-4pm Tue-Sat May-Sep) The birthplace of BC's best-known painter, this bright-yellow gingerbread-style house has plenty of period rooms, plus displays on the artist's life and work. There's an ever-changing array of local contemporary works on display, but head to the Art Gallery of Greater Victoria if you want to see more of

STROLLABLE CHINATOWN

Start your exploration of Canada's oldest, and possibly smallest, **Chinatown** at the handsome gate near the corner of Government and Fisgard Sts. From here, Fisgard is studded with neon signs and traditional grocery stores, while **Fan Tan Alley**, a narrow passageway between Fisgard St and Pandora Ave, is a small warren of traditional and trendy stores hawking cheap and cheerful trinkets, cool used records and funky artworks. If you crave company, consider a guided Chinatown amble with **Discover the Past** (www.discoverthepast.com; adult/child $15/13; ⊙10:30am Tue, Thu & Sat).

Carr's paintings. On your visit here, look out for the friendly house cats.

🏃 Activities

Whale-watching
Raincoat-clad tourists head out by the boatload throughout the May-to-October viewing season. The whales don't always show, so most excursions also visit the local haunts of lolling sea lions and portly elephant seals.

Prince of Whales BOAT TOUR
(Map p170; ☑888-383-4884, 250-383-4884; www.princeofwhales.com; 812 Wharf St; adult/child from $110/85) Long-established local operator.

Springtide Charters BOAT TOUR
(Map p170; ☑800-470-3474, 250-384-4444; www.springtidecharters.com; 1119 Wharf St; adult/child from $105/75) Popular local operator.

Water Sports
Paddling around the coastline is the perfect way to see this region, especially if you spot soaring eagles and starfish-studded beaches. If you like what you see on the surface, consider a dive below.

Ocean River Adventures KAYAKING
(Map p170; ☑800-909-4233, 250-381-4233; www.oceanriver.com; 1824 Store St; rental per 2hr $40, tours from $75; ⊙9:30am-6pm Mon-Wed & Sat, to 8pm Thu & Fri, 10am-5pm Sun) Rentals and popular three-hour harbor tours.

Ogden Point Dive Centre DIVING
(Map p168; ☑250-380-9119; www.divevictoria.com; 199 Dallas Rd; ⊙9am-6pm) Dive courses

Downtown Victoria & Inner Harbour

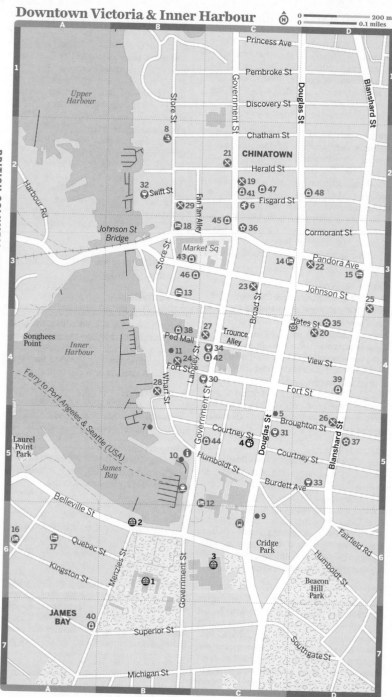

0 ——————— 200 m
0 ——————— 0.1 miles

Upper Harbour

Princess Ave
Pembroke St
Discovery St
Chatham St

Store St

Government St

Douglas St

Blanshard St

8

21

CHINATOWN
Herald St

32 Swift St

19 **47**
41
Fisgard St

6

48

Fan Tan Alley

29

45

18

36

Harbour Rd

Johnson St Bridge

Store St

Market Sq

43

46

13

Cormorant St

14

Pandora Ave
22
15

Johnson St

23

Broad St

25

Songhees Point

Inner Harbour

38

Ped Mall

27

Trounce Alley

11

24

Fort St

34

42

Yates St **35**
20

View St

39

28

Wharf St

Langley St

30

Fort St

7

Government St

26

Douglas St **5**
Broughton St

31

Blanshard St

Ferry to Port Angeles & Seattle (USA)

Laurel Point Park

James Bay

10

Courtney St

44

4

Humboldt St

Courtney St

37

Burdett Ave

33

12

9

Belleville St

2

Cridge Park

Fairfield Rd

16

17

Quebec St

Kingston St

Menzies St

Government St

3

Humboldt St

Beacon Hill Park

1

JAMES BAY

40

Superior St

Michigan St

Southgate St

Downtown Victoria & Inner Harbour

Sights
1 Parliament Buildings B6
2 Robert Bateman Centre....................... B6
3 Royal BC Museum C6
4 Victoria Bug Zoo C5

Activities, Courses & Tours
5 Architectural Institute of BC C5
  CVS Cruise Victoria .... (see 12)
6 Greater Victoria Cycling Coalition C2
7 Harbour Air B5
8 Ocean River Adventures B2
9 Pedaler C6
10 Prince of Whales B5
11 Springtide Charters.............................. B4

Sleeping
12 Fairmont Empress Hotel....................... C5
13 HI Victoria Hostel................................. B3
14 Hotel Rialto C3
15 Ocean Island Inn D3
16 Oswego Hotel A6
17 Royal Scot Hotel & Suites.................... A6
18 Swans Suite Hotel................................ B3

Eating
19 Brasserie L'École C2
20 Hernandéz D4
21 Jam Cafe C2
22 John's Place... D3
  Legislative Dining Room .... (see 1)
23 Lotus Pond Vegetarian
  Restaurant C3

24 Picnic... B4
25 Pig BBQ Joint D3
26 Pink Bicycle D5
27 ReBar C4
28 Red Fish Blue Fish B4
29 Ulla B2

Drinking & Nightlife
30 Bard & Banker C4
31 Big Bad John's C5
32 Canoe Brewpub B2
33 Clive's Classic Lounge D5
34 Garrick's Head C4

Entertainment
35 Cineplex Odeon D4
  IMAX Theatre .... (see 3)
36 McPherson Playhouse C3
37 Royal Theatre....................................... D5

Shopping
38 Bastion Square Public Market B4
39 Ditch Records D4
40 James Bay Market................................ A7
41 Milkman's Daughter C2
42 Munro's Books C4
43 Regional Assembly of Text................... B3
44 Rogers' Chocolates C5
45 Silk Road... C3
46 Smoking Lily B3
47 Victoria Downtown Farmers
  Market.. C2
48 Victoria Public Market D2

BRITISH COLUMBIA VICTORIA

and rentals a few minutes from the Inner Harbour.

Tours

Architectural Institute of BC WALKING TOUR
(Map p170; ☎800-667-0753, ext 333, 604-683-8588; www.aibc.ca; 1001 Douglas St; tours $10; ☺10am & 1pm Tue-Sun Jul & Aug) Six great-value, building-themed walking tours, covering angles from art deco to ecclesiastical.

Harbour Air SCENIC FLIGHTS
(Map p170; ☎800-665-0212, 250-385-9131; www.harbour-air.com; tours from adult/child $104/52) For a bird's-eye Victoria view, these breathtaking floatplane tours from the Inner Harbour are fab, especially when they dive-bomb the water on landing.

Pedaler BICYCLE TOUR
(Map p170; ☎778-265-7433; www.thepedaler.ca; 719 Douglas St; tours from $59; ☺9am-6pm) Guided bike tours weave around local breweries, plus there are history-themed and coffee-and-cake tour alternatives.

CVS Cruise Victoria BUS TOUR
(Map p170; ☎877-578-5552, 250-386-8652; www.cvscruisevictoria.com; 721 Government St; tours from adult/child $30/16) With its fleet of bio-diesel coaches, CVS offers a hop-on, hop-off city tour, plus shuttles to Butchart Gardens.

Festivals & Events

Victoria Tea Festival FOOD
(www.victoriateafestival.com; ☺Feb) Huge showcase of tea and tea-making paraphenalia in North America's cuppa-loving capital.

Victoria Day Parade PARADE
(☺mid-May) Street fiesta, with dancers, marching bands and 50,000-plus spectators.

**Victoria International
Buskers Festival** PERFORMING ARTS
(www.victoriabuskers.com; ☺mid-Jul) Ten days of street performing action from local and international artists.

Victoria Ska Fest
MUSIC

(www.victoriaskafest.ca; ⊙ mid-Jul) Canada's largest skank-filled music festival.

Victoria International JazzFest
JAZZ

(www.jazzvictoria.ca; ⊙ late Jun) Toe-tapping jazz shows over 10 days.

Victoria Fringe Theater Festival
THEATER

(www.victoriafringe.com; ⊙ late Aug) Two weeks of quirky short plays and stand-up performances throughout the city.

Rifflandia
MUSIC

(www.rifflandia.com; ⊙ Sep) Victoria's coolest music festival sees indie bands playing around the city.

🛏 Sleeping

From heritage B&Bs to cool boutiques and swanky high-end sleepovers, Victoria is stuffed with accommodation for all budgets. Off-season sees great deals. Tourism Victoria's **room reservation service** (☑ 800-663-3883, 250-953-2033; www.tourismvictoria.com/hotels) can show you what's available.

HI Victoria Hostel
HOSTEL $

(Map p170; ☑ 888-883-0099, 250-385-4511; www.hihostels.ca; 516 Yates St; dm/d $30.80/88; @ 🛜) A quiet downtown hostel with two large single-sex dorms, three small coeds and a couple of private rooms. There are also movie nights, a large games room and a book-lined reading area to keep you occupied. Free city tours are also scheduled.

Ocean Island Inn
HOSTEL $

(Map p170; ☑ 888-888-4180, 250-385-1788; www.oceanisland.com; 791 Pandora Ave; dm/s/d from $28/40/46; @🛜) This funky, multicolored sleepover is a labyrinth of small dorms and private rooms, some without windows. There's a large communal kitchen on the ground floor and a licensed lounge for breakfast, quiz nights and live music. They also have private, self-catering suites across town in a James Bay character house from $121; see www.oisuites.com for information.

Hotel Rialto
HOTEL $$

(Map p170; ☑ 250-383-4157; www.hotelrialto.ca; 653 Pandora Ave; d from $179; 🛜) Completely refurbished from the faded former budget hotel it once was, the Rialto is a well-located downtown option in an attractive century-old heritage building. Each of the mod-decorated rooms has a fridge, microwave and flatscreen TV and some have tubs as well as showers. The lobby's tapas lounge is popular, whether or not you're staying here. Highly solicitous staff.

Oswego Hotel
HOTEL $$$

(Map p170; ☑ 250-294-7500, 877-767-9346; www.oswegovictoria.com; 500 Oswego St; d $205; 🛜🖥) Well hidden on a residential side street a short stroll from the Inner Harbour, this contemporary boutique sleepover is an in-the-know favorite. Rooms come with granite floors, cedar beams and, in most units, small balconies. All have kitchens – think stainless steel – and deep baths, making them more like apartments than hotel rooms. Cleverly, the smaller studio rooms have space-saving high-end Murphy beds.

Inn at Laurel Point
HOTEL $$

(Map p168; ☑ 800-663-7667, 250-386-8721; www.laurelpoint.com; 680 Montreal St; d from $169; ✴@🛜🖥) Tucked along the Inner Harbour a short seaside stroll from the downtown action, this friendly, art-lined and ever-comfortable sleepover is all about the views across the waterfront. Spacious rooms come with private balconies for drinking in the mesmerizing sunsets. Still owned by a local family, there's a resort-like level of calm relaxation.

Abbeymoore Manor B&B Inn
B&B $$$

(Off Map p168; ☑ 888-801-1811, 250-370-1470; www.abbeymoore.com; 1470 Rockland Ave; d from $199; 🛜) A romantic 1912 Arts and Crafts mansion, Abbeymoore's handsome colonial exterior hides seven antique-lined rooms furnished with Victorian knickknacks. Some units have kitchens and jetted tubs and the hearty breakfast will fuel you up for a day of exploring: Craigdarroch Castle and the Art Gallery of Greater Victoria are nearby.

Royal Scot Hotel & Suites
HOTEL

(Map p170; ☑ 250-388-5463, 800-663-7515; www.royalscot.com; 425 Quebec St; d from $175; 🛜🖥🖥) The best of several midrange options crowding the banks of the Inner Harbour near the Parliament Buildings, rooms at the Royal Scot are spotlessly maintained. Expect a friendly welcome and lots of cruise-ship seniors in the lobby. Rooms come in a variety of configurations, some with full kitchens. A free local shuttle service is available.

Fairmont Empress Hotel
HOTEL $$$

(Map p170; ☑ 866-540-4429, 250-384-8111; www.fairmont.com/empress; 721 Government St; d $250; ✴@🛜🖥) Rooms at this ivy-covered, century-old Inner Harbour landmark are elegant but conservative and some are quite small, but the overall effect is grand and classy, from the raj-style curry and cocktail restaurant to the sumptuous high tea sipped while overlooking the waterfront. Even if you don't stay, make sure you stroll through and soak up the Old World charm.

Swans Suite Hotel   HOTEL **$$$**
(Map p170; ☎800-668-7926, 250-361-3310; www.swanshotel.com; 506 Pandora Ave; d incl breakfast $185; ☎✿❄) This former brick-built warehouse has been transformed into an art-lined boutique sleepover. Most rooms are spacious loft suites where you climb upstairs to bed in a gabled nook, and each is decorated with a comfy combination of wood beams, rustic chic furniture and deep leather sofas. The full kitchens are handy but continental breakfast is included. There's a brewpub downstairs.

🍴 Eating

Victoria's dining scene has been radically upgraded in recent years. Pick up the free *Eat Magazine* to check out the latest foodie happenings.

⭐**Red Fish Blue Fish**   SEAFOOD **$**
(Map p170; www.redfish-bluefish.com; 1006 Wharf St; mains $6-20; ⊙11:30am-7pm Mon-Thu, to 8pm Fri-Sun) On the waterfront boardwalk at the foot of Broughton St, this freight-container takeout shack serves a loyal clientele who just can't get enough of its fresh-made sustainable seafood. Highlights like scallop *tacones*, wild-salmon sandwiches, tempura-battered fish and chips and chunky Pacific Rim chowder all hit the spot. Find a waterfront perch to enjoy your nosh, but watch for hovering seagull mobsters.

Picnic   CAFE **$**
(Map p170; www.picniccoffee.com; 506 Fort St; mains $8-10; ⊙7:30am-4pm Mon-Fri) Downtown's funkiest little cafe is easy to miss, but it's worth the hunt. There's a Canadiana feel to the interior, hence the artwork moose head, but there's nothing kitsch about the menu: fresh-made sandwiches, salad and soup as daily specials, plus beverages from great coffee to tasty lavender lemonade. Ask about their new place: plans were afoot on our visit for a larger additional venue.

Hernandéz   MEXICAN **$**
(Map p170; www.hernandezcocina.com; 735 Yates St; mains $5-8; ⊙noon-8pm; ♨) Fiendishly well-hidden in an office building lobby between Yates and View Sts, this Mexican hole-in-the-wall is a local favorite. Vegetarian options abound but the *huarache de pollo* (thick tortilla with chicken) is legendary. Despite a recent expansion, there are never enough peak-time tables, so consider packing your butcher-paper parcel to Beacon Hill Park for a picnic. Cash only.

Pig BBQ Joint   BARBECUE **$**
(Map p170; www.pigbbqjoint.com; 1325 Blanshard St; mains $7.50-15; ⊙11am-10pm) Started as a hole-in-the wall but now in larger new digs, this joint is all about the meat, starting with bulging, Texas-style pulled-pork sandwiches (beef-brisket and smoked-chicken variations are also offered). Go for the 'pig size' serving if you're starving and make sure you add a side of crispy-fried mac 'n' cheese plus a draft of local Phillips Brewing beer.

⭐**Jam Cafe**   BREAKFAST **$$**
(Map p170; www.jamcafevictoria.com; 542 Herald St; mains $8-16; ⊙8am-3pm) The locals won't tell you anything about this slightly off-the-beaten-path place. But that's not because they don't know about it; it's because they don't want you to add to the lineups for the best breakfast in town. The delectable eggs Benedict varieties are ever popular, but we also recommend the amazing, and very naughty, chicken French toast.

Their main social occasion, Victorians are passionate about their brunches and this place is always humming. Arrive off-peak as there are no reservations and waiting for a table is common.

Legislative Dining Room   WEST COAST **$$**
(Map p170; ☎250-387-3959; www.leg.bc.ca; room 606, Parliament Bldgs, 501 Belleville St; mains $9-15; ⊙hours vary) One of Victoria's best-kept dining secrets, the Parliament Buildings have their own subsidized, old-school restaurant where both MLAs and the public can drop by for a silver-service menu of regional dishes, ranging from salmon salads to velvety steaks and a BC-only wine list. Entry is via the security desk just inside the building's main entrance; photo ID is required.

John's Place   DINER **$$**
(Map p170; www.johnsplace.ca; 723 Pandora Ave; mains $7-16; ⊙7am-9pm Mon-Fri, 8am-4pm & 5-9pm Sat & Sun) This ever-friendly, wood-floored local hangout is lined with quirky memorabilia, while its menu is a cut above standard diner fare. They'll start you off with

a basket of addictive house-made bread, but save room for heaping pasta dishes or an eggs Benedict brunch. Don't leave without trying a thick slab of pie from the case at the front. Perfect breakfast spot.

Lotus Pond Vegetarian Restaurant   CHINESE $$

(Map p170; www.lotuspond.webs.com; 617 Johnson St; mains $9-16; ◎11am-3pm & 5-9pm Mon-Sat, noon-3pm & 5-8:30pm Sun; ☑) This unassuming downtown spot was satisfying local vegetarians long before meat-free diets became fashionable. Far superior to most Chinese eateries and with a menu that easily pleases carnivores as well as veggie types, the best time to come is lunch, when the busy buffet lures everyone in the vicinity. Don't miss the turnip cakes, a house specialty.

Pink Bicycle   BURGERS $$

(Map p170; www.pinkbicycleburger.com; 1008 Blanshard St; mains $12-15; ◎11:30am-9pm Mon-Sat) Look for the bubble-gum-pink bike hanging in the window, then nip inside to the city's best gourmet burger joint. You'll be joining chatty locals, who'll never go back to regular fast food again. Spend time perusing the menu of more than a dozen made-with-love varieties, then dive into a blue-cheese lamb burger or Pacific halibut burger. Feeling naughty? Go for a side of truffle fries.

ReBar   VEGETARIAN, FUSION $$

(Map p170; www.rebarmodernfood.com; 50 Bastion Sq; mains $8-16; ◎11am-9pm Mon-Thu, to 10pm Fri, 8:30am-10pm Sat, to 8pm Sun; ☑) A laid-back downtown fixture, ReBar mixes colorful interiors with a mostly vegetarian menu. Carnivores will be just as happy to eat here, though, with hearty savory dishes such as shrimp quesadilla, mushroom-based curries and heaping weekend brunches – the salmon-topped bagel melt is great. There's also a wholesome specialty juice selection – try the orange, pear and cranberry.

Ulla   WEST COAST $$$

(Map p170; ☑250-590-8795; www.ulla.ca; 509 Fisgard St; mains $24-30; ◎5:30-10pm Tue-Sat; ☑) Hidden at the quiet end of Chinatown's Fisgard St, this is the best restaurant in the city to dive into perfectly prepared West Coast dining. In a wood-floored but contemporary room studded with local artworks and cookbooks, you'll find a seasonal menu often including BC halibut or lamb plus a bounty of organic veggies. If you're a vegetarian, the options for you are top-notch.

Brasserie L'École   FRENCH $$$

(Map p170; ☑250-475-6260; www.lecole.ca; 1715 Government St; mains $18-26; ◎5:30-11pm Tue-Sat) Preparing West Coast ingredients with French bistro flare, this warm and ever-popular spot is perfect for an intimate night out. The dishes constantly change to reflect seasonal highlights, like figs, salmonberries and heirloom tomatoes, but we recommend any seafood you find on the menu, or the ever-available *steak frites* with a red wine and shallot sauce. Great cocktail spot, too.

🍷 Drinking & Nightlife

One of BC's best beer towns, look out for local-made craft brews at pubs around the city. Repeated first-hand research was undertaken for this section.

★ Garrick's Head   PUB

(Map p170; www.bedfordregency.com; 1140 Government St; ◎11am-11pm Mon-Thu, to midnight Fri & Sat, to 10pm Sun) A huge overhaul has transformed this once humdrum downtown pub into Victoria's best spot for trying local-made brews. Pull up a perch at the long bar and you'll be faced with 40-plus taps serving a comprehensive menu of beers from Driftwood, Phillips, Hoyne and beyond. Once or twice a month, there are guest casks to keep things lively.

A good spot to fill up on pub grub before hitting the beer list, the fish and chips are recommended. You can also find the remnants of the old pub in the back room if you're feeling nostalgic.

★ Spinnakers Gastro Brewpub   PUB

(Map p168; www.spinnakers.com; 308 Catherine St; ◎11am-10:30pm) One of Canada's first craft brewers, this wood-floored smasher is a short hop from downtown via Harbour Ferry. Sail in for copper-colored Nut Brown Ale and hoppy Blue Bridge Double IPA and check out the daily casks to see what's on special. Save room to eat: the menu here is true gourmet gastropub grub.

Clive's Classic Lounge   LOUNGE

(Map p170; www.clivesclassiclounge.com; 740 Burdett Ave; ◎11am-midnight Mon-Wed, to 1am Thu & Fri, 5pm-1am Sat, to midnight Sun) Tucked into the lobby level of the Chateau Victoria Hotel, this has been the best spot in town for perfectly prepared cocktails as long as anyone can remember. Completely lacking the snobbishness of big-city cocktail haunts, this ever-cozy spot is totally dedicated to its mixed drinks menu, which means timeless classic cocktails, as well as cool-ass fusion tipples that are a revelation.

Canoe Brewpub
PUB

(Map p170; www.canoebrewpub.com; 450 Swift St; ⊙11:30am-11pm Sun-Wed, to midnight Thu, to 1am Fri & Sat) The cavernous brick-lined interior is great on rainy days, but the patio is also the best in the city with its usually sunny views over the harbor. Indulge in on-site-brewed treats, like the hoppy Red Canoe Lager and the summer-friendly Siren's Song Pale Ale. Grub is also high on the menu, with roasted halibut recommended.

Big Bad John's
PUB

(Map p170; www.strathconahotel.com; 919 Douglas St; ⊙noon-2am) Easily missed from the outside, this grungy little hillbilly-themed bar feels like you've stepped into the backwoods. But rather than some dodgy banjo players with mismatched ears, you'll find good-time locals enjoying the cave-like ambience of peanut-shell-covered floors and a ceiling dotted with dusty bras. A good spot to say you've been to, at least once.

Bard & Banker
PUB

(Map p170; www.bardandbanker.com; 1022 Government St; ⊙11am-1am) This cavernous Victorian reproduction pub is handsomely lined with cut-glass lamps, open fireplaces and a long granite bar topped with brass beer taps. Pull up a stool and taste test Phillips Blue Buck, Nova Scotia's Alexander Keith's and the house-brand Robert Service Ale. There's nightly live music, plus a nosh menu ranging from pub standards to fancier fare.

☆ Entertainment

Check the weekly freebie *Monday Magazine* for the lowdown on local happenings. Entertainment resources online include Live Victoria (www.livevictoria.com) and Play in Victoria (www.playinvictoria.net).

Logan's Pub
LIVE MUSIC

(Map p168; www.loganspub.com; 1821 Cook St; ⊙3pm-1am Mon-Fri, 10am-1am Sat, 10am-midnight Sun) A 10-minute walk from downtown, this no-nonsense pub looks like nothing special from the outside, but its roster of shows is a fixture of the local indie scene. Fridays and Saturdays are your best bet for performances but other nights are frequently also scheduled; check the online calendar to see what's coming up.

McPherson Playhouse
THEATER

(Map p170; ☑250-386-6121; www.rmts.bc.ca; 3 Centennial Sq) One of Victoria's main stages, McPherson Playhouse offers mainstream visiting shows and performances.

Royal Theatre
THEATER

(Map p170; www.rmts.bc.ca; 805 Broughton St) With a rococo interior, the Royal Theatre hosts mainstream theater productions, and is home to the Victoria Symphony and Pacific Opera Victoria.

Belfry Theatre
THEATER

(Map p168; www.belfry.bc.ca; 1291 Gladstone Ave) A 20-minute stroll from downtown, the celebrated Belfry Theatre showcases contemporary plays in its lovely former-church-building venue.

Cineplex Odeon
CINEMA

(Map p170; www.cineplex.com; 780 Yates St) The city's main first-run cinema.

IMAX Theatre
CINEMA

(Map p170; www.imaxvictoria.com) The IMAX Theatre at the Royal BC Museum (p167) shows larger-than-life documentaries and Hollywood blockbusters.

🛍 Shopping

While Government St is a souvenir shopping magnet, those looking for more original purchases should head to the Johnson St stretch between Store and Government, which is lined with cool independent stores.

Regional Assembly of Text
STATIONERY

(Map p170; www.assemblyoftext.com; 560 Johnson St; ⊙11am-6pm Mon-Sat, noon-5pm Sun) Vancouver's hipster stationery store has finally opened its much-anticipated Victoria branch, socked into a quirky space that resembles a hotel lobby from 1968. You'll find the same array of clever greeting cards and cool-ass journals, plus the best Victoria postcards you'll ever find; postage is available. Add the button-making table and typewriter stations ($2 for 20 minutes) and you'll be as happy as a shiny new paper clip.

Smoking Lily
CLOTHING

(Map p170; www.smokinglily.com; 569 Johnson St; ⊙11am-5:30pm Tue-Sat, noon-5pm Sun & Mon) LoJo's smallest shop is an almost-too-tiny boutique stuffed with eclectic garments and accessories that define art-school chic. Tops and skirts with insect prints are hot items, but there are also lots of cute handbags, socks and brooches to tempt your credit

BRITISH COLUMBIA VICTORIA

card. Two's a crowd here, though – it really is *that* small.

Silk Road   TEA
(Map p170; www.silkroadtea.com; 1624 Government St; ⊘10am-6pm Mon-Thu, to 8pm Fri & Sat, 11am-5pm Sun) A pilgrimage spot for regular and exotic tea fans, you can pick up all manner of leafy paraphernalia here. Alternatively, sidle up to the tasting bar to quaff some adventurous brews. There's also a small on-site spa, where you can indulge in oil treatments and aromatherapy.

Munro's Books   BOOKS
(Map p170; www.munrobooks.com; 1108 Government St; ⊘9am-9pm Mon-Sat, 9:30am-6pm Sun) Like a cathedral to reading, this high-ceilinged local legend lures browsers who just like to hang out among the shelves. There's a good array of local-interest tomes, as well as a fairly extensive travel section at the back on the left. Check out the piles of bargain books, too – they're not all copies of *How to Eat String* from 1972.

Ditch Records   MUSIC
(Map p170; www.ditchrecords.com; 784 Fort St; ⊘10am-6pm Mon-Sat, 11am-5pm Sun) In its larger new location for a couple of years now, Ditch is the locals' fave record store. Lined with tempting vinyl and furtive musos perusing releases by bands like the Meatmen and Nightmares on Wax, it's an ideal rainy-day hangout. If it suddenly feels like time to socialize, you can book gig tickets here, too.

Milkman's Daughter   CLOTHING, ARTS & CRAFTS
(Map p170; www.smokinglily.com; 1713 Government St; ⊘11am-6pm Tue-Sat, noon-5pm Sun & Mon) The larger offshoot of Johnson St's tiny Smoking Lily, this enticing shop carries the full range of men's and women's togs and mixes in must-have arts and crafts from both local artisans and those from further afield, mostly from the West Coast. It's an eclectic mix, from jewelry to pottery and from buttons to notebooks, but it's easy to find something to fall in love with.

Rogers' Chocolates   FOOD
(Map p170; www.rogerschocolates.com; 913 Government St; ⊘10am-10pm Mon-Sat, to 7pm Sun) This charming, museum-like confectioner has the best ice-cream bars in town, but repeat offenders usually spend their time hitting the menu of rich Victoria Creams, one of which is usually enough to substitute for lunch. Varieties range from peppermint to seasonal specialties and they're good souvenirs, so long as you don't scoff them all before you get home.

ⓘ Information

Downtown Medical Centre (☑250-380-2210; 622 Courtney St; ⊘8:30am-5pm) Handy walk-in clinic.

Main Post Office (Map p170; 709 Yates St; ⊘9am-5pm Mon-Fri) Near the corner of Yates and Douglas Sts.

Victoria Visitors Centre (Map p170; www.tourismvictoria.com; 812 Wharf St; ⊘8:30am-8:30pm) Busy, flyer-lined visitors center overlooking the Inner Harbour.

ⓘ Getting There & Away

AIR

Victoria International Airport (www.victoria-airport.com) is 26km north of the city via Hwy 17. **Air Canada** (www.aircanada.com) services arrive from Vancouver (from $87, 25 minutes, up to 16 daily), while **Westjet** (www.westjet.com) flights arrive from Calgary (from $161, 1½ hours,

---

TO MARKET, TO MARKET

The much-anticipated **Victoria Public Market** (Map p170; www.victoriapublicmarket.com; 1701 Douglas St; ⊘9:30am-6:30pm Tue-Sat, to 5pm Sun; ▣4) opened in 2013 with various food-focused vendors – from Silk Road Tea to Salt Spring Island Cheese – in this refurbished spot in downtown's heritage Hudson Building.

Outside the building, the **Victoria Downtown Farmers Market** (Map p170; www.victoriapublicmarket.com; 1701 Douglas St, back carriageway; ⊘11am-3pm Wed; ▣4), which runs all year, sells locally made and farmed food.

If you want more alfresco shopping, downtown's **Bastion Square Public Market** (Map p170; www.bastionsquare.ca; Bastion Sq; ⊘from 11am Thu-Sun May-Sep) houses art-and-craft stalls all summer, while **James Bay Market** (Map p170; www.jamesbaymarket.com; 494 Superior St; ⊘9am-3pm May-Oct; ▣27) and the large **Moss Street Market** (Map p168; www.mossstreetmarket.com; cnr Moss St & Fairfield Rd; ⊘10am-2pm May-Oct; ▣7) offer a community-focused combo of both arts and food.

WORTH A TRIP

HIT THE TRAILS

Easily accessed along the Island Hwy just 16km from Victoria, **Goldstream Provincial Park** (off Map p168; www.goldstreampark.com), at the base of Malahat Mountain, makes for a restorative nature-themed day trip from the city. Dripping with ancient, moss-covered cedar trees and a moist carpet of plant life, it's known for its chum-salmon spawning season from late October to December. Hungry bald eagles are attracted to the fish and bird-watchers come ready with their cameras. Head to the park's **Freeman King Visitors Centre** (☑250-478-9414; 2390 Trans-Canada Hwy; ⊙9am-4:30pm) for area info and natural history exhibits.

Aside from nature watching, you'll also find great hiking: marked trails range from tough to easy and some are wheelchair accessible. Recommended treks include the hike to 47.5m-high Niagara Falls (not *that* one) and the steep, strenuous route to the top of Mt Finlayson, one of the region's highest promontories. The visitors center can advise on trails and will also tell you how to find the park's forested **campground** (☑800-689-9025, 604-689-9025; www.discovercamping.ca; campsites $30) if you feel like staying over.

four daily). Both offer cross-Canada connections.

Harbour Air (www.harbour-air.com) flies into the Inner Harbour from downtown Vancouver ($185, 35 minutes) throughout the day. Similar **Helijet** (www.helijet.com) helicopter services arrive from Vancouver (from $199, 35 minutes).

BOAT

BC Ferries (www.bcferries.com) arrive from mainland Tsawwassen (adult/vehicle $15.50/51.25, 1½ hours) at Swartz Bay, 27km north of Victoria via Hwy 17. Services arrive frequently throughout the day in summer, less often off-season.

Victoria Clipper (www.clippervacations.com) services arrive in the Inner Harbour from Seattle (adult/child US$88/44, three hours, up to three a day). **Black Ball Transport** (www.ferrytovictoria.com) boats also arrive here from Port Angeles (adult/child/vehicle US$17/8.50/$60.50, 1½ hours, up to four daily).

BUS

Buses rolling into the city's main **bus depot** (Map p170; 700 Douglas St) include **Greyhound Canada** (www.greyhound.ca) services from Nanaimo (from $13.50, 2½ hours, three daily) and across the island, along with frequent **Pacific Coach Lines** (www.pacificcoach.com) services, via the ferry, from Vancouver (from $38, 3½ hours) and Vancouver International Airport ($44, four hours).

❶ Getting Around

TO/FROM THE AIRPORT

AKAL Airporter (www.victoriaairporter.com) minibuses run between the airport and area hotels ($21, 30 minutes). In contrast, a taxi to downtown costs around $50, while airport-serving transit buses 83, 86 and 88 take around

35 minutes, run throughout the day and cost $2.50 – you may need to change buses at McTavish Exchange.

BICYCLE

Victoria is a great cycling capital, with routes crisscrossing the city and beyond. Check the website of the **Greater Victoria Cycling Coalition** (Map p170; www.gvcc.bc.ca) for local resources. Bike rentals are offered by **Cycle BC Rentals** (☑866-380-2453, 250-380-2453; www.cyclebc.ca; 685 Humboldt St; ⊙9am-5pm; ▣1).

BOAT

Victoria Harbour Ferry (Map p170; www.victoriaharbourferry.com; fares from $5) covers the Inner Harbour and beyond with its colorful armada of little boats.

PUBLIC TRANSPORTATION & TAXI

Victoria Regional Transit (www.busonline.ca) buses (fare/day pass $2.50/5) cover a wide area from Sidney to Sooke, with some routes served by modern-day double-deckers. Children under five travel free.

Established taxi providers:

BlueBird Cabs (☑800-665-7055, 250-382-2222; www.taxicab.com)

Yellow Cab (☑800-808-6881, 250-381-2222; www.yellowcabofvictoria.ca)

Southern Vancouver Island

Not far from Victoria's madding crowds, southern Vancouver Island is a laid-back region of quirky little towns that are never far from tree-lined cycle routes, waterfront hiking trails and rocky outcrops bristling

ON YER BIKE

Bring your bike across on the ferry from the mainland and, when you arrive in Swartz Bay, you can hop onto the easily accessible and well-marked **Lochside Regional Trail** to downtown Victoria. The 29km, mostly flat route is not challenging – there are only a couple of overpasses – and it's an idyllic, predominantly paved ride through small urban areas, waterfront stretches, rolling farmland and forested countryside. There are several spots to pick up lunch en route and, if you adopt a leisurely pace, you'll be in town within four hours or so.

with gnarly Garry oaks. The wildlife here is abundant and you'll likely spot bald eagles swooping overhead, sea otters cavorting on the beaches and perhaps the occasional orca sliding silently by just off the coast.

Saanich Peninsula & Around

Home to Vancouver Island's main airport and busiest ferry terminal, this north-of-Victoria peninsula has plenty to offer day-trippers from the city.

SIDNEY

At the peninsula's northern end, seafront Sidney is studded with 10 or so bookshops, enabling it to call itself BC's only 'Booktown.'

It takes an hour to get here by transit bus from Victoria ($2.50, number 70 or 72) and the heart of the town is Beacon Ave. Drop into the friendly **chamber of commerce** (☎250-665-7362; www.sidney.ca; 2281 Beacon Ave; ☺9am-5pm) when you arrive for tips.

You can spend a leisurely afternoon ducking into the likes of **Tanner's Books** (www.tannersbooks.com; 2436 Beacon Ave; ☺8am-9pm), with its massive magazine and large travel-book sections; and **Beacon Books** (2372 Beacon Ave; ☺10am-5:30pm Mon-Sat, noon-4pm Sun), where the used tomes are guarded by store cat Rosabelle. See www.sidneybooktown.ca for additional page-turning options.

The popular **Shaw Ocean Discovery Centre** (www.oceandiscovery.ca; 9811 Seaport Pl; adult/child $15/5; ☺10am-5pm) is Sidney's kid-luring highlight. Enter through a dramatic Disney-style entrance – it makes you think you're descending below the waves –

then step into a gallery of aquatic exhibits, including alien-like jellyfish, a large touch tank with purple starfish and an octopus that likes to unscrew a glass jar to snag its fresh crab dinner. Continue your marine education aboard a whale-watching boat trek with **Sidney Whale Watching** (www.sidneywhalewatching.com; 2537 Beacon Ave; adult/child $109/89), located a few steps away.

If you decide to stick around, the swish **Sidney Pier Hotel & Spa** (☎866-659-9445, 250-655-9445; www.sidneypier.com; 9805 Seaport Pl; d from $175; @ ☎) on the waterfront fuses West Coast lounge cool with beach pastel colors. Many rooms have shoreline views, some side on, and each has local artworks lining the walls. If you're missing your pooch back home, there's a resident dog available for walkies.

If it's time to eat, duck into **Carlos Cantina & Grill** (www.carloscantina.ca; 9816 4th St; mains $10-14; ☺11:30am-8:30pm) for authentic Mexican grub in a colorful, friendly setting; the fish tacos and $7.95 lunch special are recommended. Crank it up a notch with dinner at local fave **Sabhai Thai** (www.sabhai.ca; 2493 Beacon Ave; mains $12-18; ☺11:30am-2pm & 5-10pm), a cozy, wood-floored room with a bonus patio and a good line in authentic curry and *phad* dishes. The lunch combos are good value.

When you just need to fuel up on java, join the gossiping locals at the art-lined **Red Brick Café** (2423 Beacon Ave; mains $4-9; ☺6:30am-5pm), where coffee and a large ginger snap make for an ideal pit stop. Light lunches are also available.

BRENTWOOD BAY

A 30-minute drive from Victoria via West Saanich Rd, the rolling farmlands of waterfront Brentwood Bay are chiefly known for **Butchart Gardens** (off Map p168; www.butchartgardens.com; 800 Benvenuto Ave; adult/child $30.20/10.30; ☺9am-10pm; ☐75), Vancouver Island's leading visitor attraction. The immaculate grounds are divided into separate gardens where there's always something in bloom. Summer is crowded, with tour buses rolling in relentlessly, but evening music performances and Saturday night fireworks in July and August make it all worthwhile. Tea fans take note: the **Dining Room Restaurant** serves a smashing afternoon tea, complete with quiches and Grand Marnier truffles; leave your diet at the door.

If you have time, also consider nearby **Victoria Butterfly Gardens** (www.butterfly-gardens.com; 1461 Benvenuto Ave; adult/child $15/5; ⊙9am-7pm), which offers a kaleidoscope of thousands of fluttering critters, from around 75 species, in a free-flying environment. As well as watching them flit about and land on your head, you can learn about ecosystem life cycles, and eyeball exotic fish, plants and birds. Look out for Spike, the long-beaked puna ibis, who struts around the trails as if he owns the place.

Sooke & Around

Rounding Vancouver Island's rustic southern tip towards Sooke, a 45-minute drive from Victoria, Hwy 14 is lined with twisted Garry oaks and unkempt hedgerows, while the houses – often artisan workshops or homely B&Bs – seem spookily hidden in the forest shadows.

Sharing the same building and hours as the visitors center, the fascinating **Sooke Region Museum** (www.sookeregionmuseum.com; 2070 Phillips Rd; ⊙9am-5pm) `FREE` illuminates the area's rugged pioneer days. Check out Moss Cottage in the museum grounds: built in 1869, it's the oldest residence west of Victoria.

If you're craving some thrills, find your inner screamer on the forested zip-line tours operated by **Adrena LINE** (www.adrenaline-zip.com; 5128 Sooke Rd; adult/child from $80/70; ⊙8am-5pm). Its full-moon zips are the most fun and, if you don't have your own transport, they'll collect you from Victoria.

A more relaxed way to encounter the natural world is the **Sooke Potholes Provincial Park** (www.bcparks.ca), a 5km drive from Hwy 14 (the turnoff is east of Sooke). With rock pools and potholes carved into the river base during the last ice age, it's ideal for swimming and tube floating. Camping is available through the website of the **Land Conservancy** (www.conservancy.bc.ca; campsites $25; ⊙May-Sep).

You'll find B&Bs dotted along the route here but, for one of the province's most delightful and splurge-worthy sleepovers, head to Whiffen Spit's **Sooke Harbour House** (☑250-642-3421; www.sookeharbourhouse.com; 1528 Whiffen Spit Rd; d from $299; ☎▣♨). Paintings, sculptures and carved wood line its interiors. Some of the 28 rooms have fireplaces and steam showers and all have views across the wildlife-strewn waterfront – look for gamboling sea otters and swooping cranes. The restaurant is also a great place for fine West Coast dining, whether or not you're staying here.

Port Renfrew

Conveniently nestled between the Juan de Fuca and West Coast Trails, Port Renfrew is a great access point for either route.

If you've had enough of your sleeping bag, try **Port Renfrew Resorts** (☑250-647-5541; www.portrenfrewresorts.com; 17310 Parkinson Rd; r from $190), a waterfront miniresort with motel-style rooms and some luxurious, wood-lined cabins.

For respite from campground pasta, the **Coastal Kitchen Café** (17245 Parkinson Rd; mains $8-16; ⊙8am-9pm Fri-Wed) serves fresh

---

JUAN DE FUCA PROVINCIAL PARK

The 47km **Juan de Fuca Marine Trail** (www.juandefucamarinetrail.com) in **Juan de Fuca Provincial Park** (www.bcparks.ca) rivals the West Coast Trail as a must-do trek. From east to west, its trailhead access points are China Beach, Sombrio Beach, Parkinson Creek and Botanical Beach.

It takes around four days to complete the route, but you don't have to go the whole hog if you want to take things easier. Be aware that some sections are often muddy and difficult to hike, while bear sightings and swift weather changes are not uncommon. The most difficult stretch is between Bear Beach and China Beach.

The route has several basic backcountry campsites and you can pay your camping fee ($10 per adult) at any of the trailheads. The most popular spot to pitch your tent is the more salubrious, family-friendly **China Beach Campground** (☑800-689-9025, 604-689-9025; www.discovercamping.ca; campsites $30; ⊙May-Sep), which has pit toilets and cold-water taps but no showers. There's a waterfall at the western end of the beach and booking ahead in summer is essential.

Booking ahead is also required on the **West Coast Trail Express** (☑888-999-2288, 250-477-8700; www.trailbus.com; fares from $30; ⊙May-Sep) minibus that runs between Victoria, the trailheads and Port Renfrew.

salads and sandwiches, plus burgers and pizzas. The seafood is the star attraction, especially Dungeness crab and chips.

Cowichan Valley

A swift Hwy 1 drive northwest of Victoria, the farm-filled Cowichan Valley region is ripe for discovery, especially if you're a traveling foodie or an outdoor activity nut. Contact **Tourism Cowichan** (☎888-303-3337, 250-746-4636; www.tourismcowichan.com) for more information.

Duncan

POP 5000

Developed as a logging-industry railroad stop – the gabled little station now houses a museum – Duncan is the valley's main community. A useful base for regional exploration, it's known for its dozens of totem poles, which dot downtown like sentinels.

If your First Nations curiosity is piqued, head to the **Quw'utsun' Cultural & Conference Centre** (www.quwutsun.ca; 200 Cowichan Way; adult/child $13/6; ⊙10am-4pm Mon-Sat Jun-Sep) to learn about carving and traditional salmon runs. Its on-site **Riverwalk Café** serves First Nations–inspired cuisine.

Alternatively, drive 3km north of town to the **BC Forest Discovery Centre** (www.bcforestdiscoverycentre.com; 2892 Drinkwater Rd; adult/child $16/11; ⊙10am-4:30pm), complete with its pioneer-era buildings, logging machinery and a working steam train.

The area's chatty hub, **Duncan Garage Cafe** (www.communityfarmstore.ca; 3330 Duncan St; mains $4-9; ⊙7:30am-6pm Mon-Sat, 9am-5pm Sun) is in a refurbished heritage building that also houses a bookshop and an organic grocery store. Libations of the boozy variety are on the menu at **Craig Street Brew Pub** (www.craigstreet.ca; 25 Craig St; mains $11-16; ⊙11am-11pm Mon-Thu, to midnight Fri & Sat, to 10pm Sun), where comfort grub and own-brewed beer lure the locals; the pizzas are recommended.

But the town's newest restaurant has really cranked Duncan dining up a notch. Housed in an immaculately restored former music-school building, the delightful **Hudson's on First** (www.hudsonsonfirst.ca; 163 First St; mains $16-26; ⊙11am-2.30pm & 5-8.30pm Tue-Sun) would be a top table option in far bigger cities. Farm-to-table local produce is the approach on an ever-changing seasonal menu that fuses West Coast ingredients

CANADA'S ONLY TEA FARM

Hidden in bucolic farmland 8km north of Duncan, you'll find one of Canada's rarest agricultural operations. Tucked into the hillside, the oasis-like **Teafarm** (www.teafarm.ca; 8530 Richards Trail, North Cowichan; ⊙10am-5pm Wed-Sun) has been growing its own tea plants for several years. The main harvest is coming soon, but until that time its contemporary, winery-like tasting room – or, better still, its flower-framed outdoor seating area – is the perfect spot to indulge in one of dozens of excellent tea blends – Sweet Morocco recommended – along with some decadent sweet treats. The tea is served in lovely pottery teapots made by owner Margit, while husband and tea guru Victor will be on hand to tell you about the operation. One of the most relaxing and surprisingly good-value ways to spend an hour or two in the region. It's not well signposted, so deploy your GPS.

with subtle European influences. For lunch, the red-snapper fish and chips is a regular, while weekend brunch lures locals with the region's best eggs Benedict. If you come for dinner, start with a cocktail in the tin-ceilinged bar.

Cowichan Bay

'Cow Bay' to the locals, the region's most attractive pit stop is a colorful string of wooden buildings perched over a mountain-framed ocean inlet. It's well worth an afternoon of your time, although it might take that long to find parking on a busy summer day. Arrive hungry and drop into **Hilary's Artisan Cheese** (www.hilaryscheese.com; 1737 Cowichan Bay Rd; ⊙9am-6pm) and **True Grain Bread** (www.truegrain.ca; 1725 Cowichan Bay Rd; ⊙8am-7pm Mon-Sat, to 5pm Sun) for the makings of a great picnic.

Alternatively, let someone else do all the work with fish and chips from **Rock Cod Café** (www.rockcodcafe.com; 1759 Cowichan Bay Rd; mains $10-14; ⊙11am-9pm). Or push out the boat – not literally – on the patio deck of the charming **Masthead Restaurant** (☎250-748-3714; www.themastheadrestaurant.com; 1705 Cowichan Bay Rd; mains $24-37; ⊙5-10pm), where the three-course BC-sourced tasting menu is good value.

Before you leave, duck into Cow Bay's **Maritime Centre** (www.classicboats.org; 1761 Cowichan Bay Rd; admission by donation; ☺ dawn-dusk) to peruse some salty boat-building exhibits and intricate models.

Carmanah Walbran Provincial Park

Home to some of BC's eldest residents, the old-growth spruce and cedar trees in this magnificent but remote **park** (www.bcparks.ca) frequently exceed 1000 years of age. With an ancient and mythical ambience, it's a half-hour walk down the valley to commune with the tallest trees. Be aware that the trails are primitive and not suitable for the unprepared.

For those without a map looking for the main Carmanah Valley trailhead, follow South Shore Rd from Lake Cowichan to Nitinat Main Rd and bear left. Then follow Nitinat Main to Nitinat Junction and turn left onto South Main. Continue to the Caycus River Bridge and, just south of the bridge, turn right and follow Rosander Main (blue-and-white BC Parks signs reassuringly point the way) for 29km to the trailhead. These are active logging roads, which means bumpy, often narrow tracks and the promise of a rumbling approach from a scary log truck – they have the right of way, so don't give them a hard time.

Chemainus

POP 4500

After the last sawmill shut down in 1983, tiny Chemainus became the model for BC communities dealing with declining resource jobs. Instead of submitting to a slow death, town officials commissioned a giant wall mural depicting local history. More than three dozen artworks were later added and a tourism industry was born.

Stroll the Chemainus streets on a mural hunt and you'll pass artsy boutiques and tempting ice-cream shops. In the evening, the surprisingly large **Chemainus Theatre** (www.chemainustheatrefestival.ca; 9737 Chemainus Rd) stages professional productions, mostly popular plays and musicals, to keep you occupied.

Nearby, the town's **Chemainus Inn** (🕿 877-246-4181, 250-246-4181; www.chemainushotel.com; 9573 Chemainus Rd; d from $169; ✵ 🕸 ✿) is like a midrange business hotel from a much larger community. Rooms are slick and comfortable and many include kitchens. Rates include breakfast.

Drop by the charming, heritage building housing **Willow Street Café** (www.willowstreetcafe.com; 9749 Willow St; mains $5-12; ☺ 8:30am-5pm) for a chat with the locals and a side order of hearty, house-made wraps, pizzas and sandwiches. In summer aim for a patio perch.

Check in at the **visitors center** (🕿 250-246-3944; www.chemainus.bc.ca; 9796 Willow St;

VANCOUVER ISLAND BOOZE TRAIL

Vancouver Island's burgeoning local food movement has spread to booze in recent years, with wineries, cideries and distilleries popping up across the island and giving regional craft-beer producers a run for their tipsy money. But unless you know where to go, many of these artisan operators can be hard to find. Here are some thirst-slaking recommendations for visitors.

In the Cowichan region, check out **Cherry Point Vineyards** (www.cherrypointvineyards.com; 840 Cherry Point Rd, Cobble Hill; ☺ 10am-5pm), with its lip-smacking blackberry port; **Averill Creek** (www.averillcreek.ca; 6552 North Rd, Duncan; ☺ 11am-5pm), with its patio views and lovely pinot noirs; and the smashing **Merridale Estate Cidery** (www.merridalecider.com; 1230 Merridale Rd, Cobble Hill; ☺ 10:30am-7pm), an inviting apple-cider producer that also makes brandy and has a great patio bistro.

But it's not all about the Cowichan. Further south in Saanich – and just a short drive from Victoria – organic apples are also on the taste-tripping menu at **Sea Cider** (www.seacider.ca; 2487 Mt St Michael Rd, Saanichton; ☺ 11am-4pm). While booze of a stronger hue is the approach at nearby **Victoria Spirits** (www.victoriaspirits.com; 6170 Old West Saanich Rd, Victoria; ☺ 10am-5pm Sat & Sun Apr-Sep), where the lovely Oaken Gin is recommended). Both offer tours and tastings.

For more information on wineries, cideries and distilleries throughout Vancouver Island, check www.wineislands.ca.

9am-5pm) for mural maps and further information.

Nanaimo

POP 87,000

Vancouver Island's 'second metropolis,' Nanaimo will never have the allure of tourist-magnet Victoria, but the Harbour City has undergone a quiet upgrade since the 1990s, with the emergence, especially on Commercial St and in the Old City Quarter, of some good shops and eateries, plus a slick new museum. With dedicated ferry services from the mainland, the city is also a handy hub for exploring the rest of the island.

◉ Sights

Nanaimo Museum   MUSEUM
(www.nanaimomuseum.ca; 100 Museum Way; adult/child $2/75¢; ⊗10am-5pm) Just off the Commercial St main drag, this excellent museum showcases the region's heritage, from First Nations to colonial, maritime, sporting and beyond. Highlights include a strong Coast Salish focus and a walk-through evocation of a coal mine that's popular with kids. Ask at the front desk about summer-only city walking tours and entry to the nearby Bastion, an 1853 wooden tower fortification.

**Newcastle Island Marine
Provincial Park**   PARK
(www.newcastleisland.ca) ✎ Nanaimo's rustic outdoor gem offers 22km of hiking and biking trails, plus beaches and wildlife spotting. Traditional Coast Salish land, it was the site of shipyards and coal mines before becoming a popular summer excursion for locals in the 1930s when a tea pavilion was added. Accessed by a 10-minute ferry hop from the harbor (adult/child return $9/5), there's a seasonal eatery and regular First Nations dancing displays.

Old City Quarter   NEIGHBORHOOD
(www.oldcityquarter.com; cnr Fitzwilliam & Wesley Sts) A steep hike uphill from the waterfront on Bastion and Fitzwilliam Sts delivers you to a strollable heritage hood of independent stores, galleries and eateries in brightly painted old buildings. Highlights include McLeans Specialty Foods; A Wee Cupcakery; and Fibber Magees, a handsome large pub that has taken over the town's old train station. Look out for the heritage plaques on buildings in this area.

Wild Play Element Parks   AMUSEMENT PARK
(🕿250-716-7874, 888-716-7374; www.wildplay.com; 35 Nanaimo River Rd; adult/child from $43/23; ⊗10am-6pm) The perfect spot to tire your kids out, this tree-lined adventure playground is packed with adrenalin-pumping fun, from bungee jumping to scream-triggering zip-lining. Along with its fun obstacle courses, there's plenty of additional action to keep the family occupied, from woodsy walking trails to busy volleyball courts. Bring a picnic and come for at least half a day.

🛏 Sleeping

Painted Turtle Guesthouse   HOSTEL $
(🕿250-753-4432, 866-309-4432; www.paintedturtle.ca; 121 Bastion St; dm/r $27/80; @ 🕷) This beautifully maintained heart-of-downtown budget property combines small dorms with very popular private rooms (book ahead). An HI affiliate, its hardwood floors and IKEA-style furnishings line a large and welcoming kitchen-lounge combo. You can book tours from the front desk if you've had enough of strumming the hostel's loaner guitar.

Buccaneer Inn   MOTEL $$
(🕿250-753-1246, 877-282-6337; www.buccaneer-inn.com; 1577 Stewart Ave; d/ste from $80/140; 🕷) Handy for the Departure Bay ferry terminal, this friendly, family-run motel has a gleaming white exterior that makes it hard to pass by. It's worth stopping though, as the neat-and-tidy approach is carried over into the maritime-themed rooms, many of which have kitchenettes. Splurge on a spacious suite and you'll have a fireplace, full kitchen and flatscreen TV.

Coast Bastion Hotel   HOTEL $$
(🕿250-753-6601, 800-716-6199; www.coast-hotels.com; 11 Bastion St; d from $157; ❋@🕷🕿) Downtown's best hotel has an unbeatable location overlooking the harbor, with most guests enjoying sparkling waterfront views, when it's not foggy. Rooms have been well refurbished with a modern élan in recent years, adding flatscreen TVs and, in most rooms, small fridges. The lobby restaurant-bar is a popular hangout and there's a spa if you want to chillax. The front desk staff are excellent.

Dorchester Hotel   HOTEL $$
(🕿800-661-2449, 250-754-6835; www.dorchester-nanaimo.com; 70 Church St; d from $119; 🕷) The cheaper of downtown's two waterfront ho-

Nanaimo

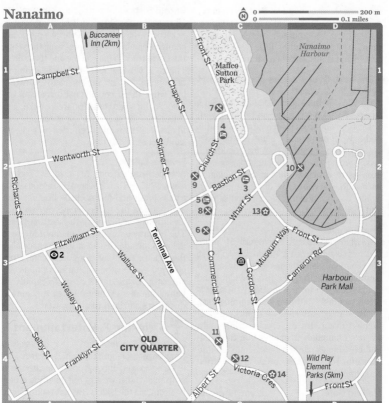

Nanaimo

◉ Sights

1 Nanaimo Museum C3
2 Old City Quarter A3

⌂ Sleeping

3 Coast Bastion Hotel............................... C2
4 Dorchester Hotel C2
5 Painted Turtle Guesthouse C2

⊗ Eating

6 2 Chefs Affair... C3
7 Corner Bistro C1

8 Gabriel's Café.. C2
9 Modern Cafe C2
10 Penny's Palapa D2
11 Pirate Chips... C4
12 Thirsty Camel Café C4

✪ Entertainment

13 Port Theatre.. C2
14 Queen's Hotel C4

tels, the Best Western–affiliated Dorchester is not as slick as its neighbor and has an unusual labyrinthine layout. Rooms, some with refrigerators, have a standard business-hotel look. Give yourself plenty of time to get here: the clunky elevator may be the slowest in Nanaimo. There are often good last-minute and off-season rate deals.

✗ Eating

★ **Gabriel's Café**   INTERNATIONAL $
(183 Commercial St; mains $6-9; ⊙ 8am-7pm Mon-Fri, 9am-5pm Sat & Sun; ⊘) This perfectly located downtown hole-in-the-wall is like a static food truck. Chat with the man himself behind the counter, then tuck into made-from-scratch treats, such as pulled-pork breakfast

wraps or the ever-popular Thai-green-curry rice bowl. Vegetarians are well looked after; try the black-bean burger. There's not much room to sit in this sunny little nook and it's best to arrive off-peak to avoid lineups.

2 Chefs Affair
WEST COAST $

(www.twochefsaffair.com; 123b Commercial St; mains $8-15; ⊗8am-4:30pm Mon-Fri, to 3pm Sat & Sun; 🐾) Focused on great comfort food, with a fresh, made-from-scatch approach, this highly welcoming locals' haunt in the heart of downtown is a great spot for breakfast – go the French toast route. Lunch is arguably even more enticing: ask for the 'ménage à trois' and you won't be disappointed – it comes with crab fish cake, candied salmon and garlic prawns.

Pirate Chips
FAST FOOD $

(www.pirate-chips.com; 1 Commercial St; mains $5-16; ⊗11am-8pm Wed & Thu, to 3am Fri & Sat, noon-8pm Sun) Nanaimoites originally started coming here for the great fish and chips and the best fries in town – the curry topping is recommended – but they keep coming back for the funky ambience and quirky pirate-themed decor. It's an excellent late-night weekend hangout: snag a spot on the skull-and-crossbones-painted bench outside and dive into your naughty order of deep-fried Nanaimo bars.

Modern Cafe
INTERNATIONAL $$

(www.themoderncafe.ca; 221 Commercial St; mains $15-23; ⊗11am-11pm Mon-Wed, to midnight Thu-Sat, 10am-11pm Sun) This reinvented old coffee shop has cool, loungy interiors combining exposed brick and comfy booths and, for when it's sunny, a ray-warmed street-side patio. The menu has risen up a notch or two in recent years and now includes gourmet comfort food with international influences – go for the Caribbean-jerk-chicken dish. Excellent burgers are also served up.

Thirsty Camel Café
MIDDLE EASTERN $$

(www.thirstycamelcafe.ca; 14 Victoria Cres; mains $8-14; ⊗11am-3pm Mon-Wed, to 7pm Thu & Fri, noon-4pm Sat; 🥗) Partake of a lip-smacking Middle Eastern feast at this sunny little family-owned joint, tucked into an elbow of Victoria Cres. Everything's prepared from scratch, which makes for addictive hummus, spicy soups and the region's best falafel. The shareable platters, especially the spice-encrusted Persian chicken, are recommended and there are several excellent vegetarian options that even meat eaters will love.

Corner Bistro
WEST COAST $$

(75 Front St; mains $14-24; ⊗11am-10pm Mon-Wed, to midnight Thu-Sat) Colonizing a spot that's changed hands several times over the years, the Corner Bistro may be the one that sticks. There's a pub-like feel inside – island craft beer helps – that invites chatty hanging out, while the street-side patio is a summer fave. As for grub, burgers are popular, but consider some shareable appetizers, including local scallops and deep-fried blue-cheese sandwiches.

Penny's Palapa
MEXICAN $$

(www.pennyspalapa.com; 10 Wharf St, Dock H; mains $8-16; ⊗11am-8:30pm May-Sep; 🥗) This tiny, flower-and-flag-decked floating hut and patio in the harbor is a lovely spot for an alfresco meal among the jostling boats. The inventive, well-priced menu of Mexican delights includes seasonal seafood specials – the signature halibut tacos are recommended – plus some good vegetarian options. Arrive early, as the dining area fills rapidly on balmy summer evenings. When it comes to drinks, it's all about the margaritas.

🍸 Drinking & Entertainment

Longwood Brewpub
BREWERY

(www.longwoodbrewpub.com; 5775 Turner Rd; ⊗11am-midnight) Incongruously located in a strip mall (northwest of the downtown harborfront, via the Island Hwy), this handsome stone and gabled restaurant-pub combines a surprisingly good menu with lip-smacking self-brewed beers. Try for a deck table and decide between recommended mains, like Cajun chicken quesadilla or halibut and prawn wraps; vegetarians should hit the roasted-vegetable lasagna. For drinks, try the four-glass tasting flight of beer.

Dinghy Dock Pub
PUB

(www.dinghydockpub.com; 8 Pirates Lane; mains $12-17; ⊗11:30am-11pm) Accessed via a mini-ferry hop, this lively but old-school pub and restaurant combo floating offshore from Protection Island is a salty local legend and a unique place to knock back a few malty brews on the deck. The menu doesn't stretch too far beyond fish and chips, but there's live music on weekends to keep your toes tapping. To get to the pub, take the 10-minute ferry (return $9) from the harbor.

Queen's Hotel
LIVE MUSIC

(📞250-754-6751; www.thequeens.ca; 34 Victoria Cres) The city's best live music and dance spot, hosting an eclectic roster of performances and club nights, ranging from indie to jazz and country.

Port Theatre THEATER
(☑ 250-754-8550; www.porttheatre.com; 125 Front St) Presenting local and touring live-theater shows.

❶ Information

Nanaimo Visitors Centre (☑ 800-663-7337, 250-751-1556; www.tourismnanaimo.com; 2450 Northfield Rd; ⊘ 9am-6pm) For tourist information, drop into the main visitors center or the summer-only satellite behind downtown's Nanaimo Museum (p182).

❶ Getting There & Away

AIR

Nanaimo Airport (www.nanaimoairport.com) is 18km south of town via Hwy 1. **Air Canada** (www.aircanada.com) flights arrive here from Vancouver (from $77, 25 minutes) throughout the day.

Frequent and convenient **Harbour Air** (www.harbour-air.com) floatplane services arrive in the inner harbor from downtown Vancouver ($105, 25 minutes).

BOAT

BC Ferries (www.bcferries.com) from Tsawwassen (passenger/vehicle $14.55/49.05, two hours) arrive at Duke Point, 14km south of Nanaimo. Services from West Vancouver's Horseshoe Bay (passenger/vehicle $15.50/51.25, 95 minutes) arrive at Departure Bay, 3km north of the city center via Hwy 1.

BUS

Greyhound Canada (www.greyhound.ca) buses arrive from Victoria (from $13.50, two hours, three daily), Campbell River (from $18.50, three hours, three daily), Tofino ($46, four hours, two daily) and beyond.

❶ Getting Around

Downtown Nanaimo, around the harbor, is highly walkable, but after that the city spreads out and a car or strong bike legs are required. Be aware that taxis are expensive here.

Nanaimo Regional Transit (www.busonline.ca; single trip/day pass $2.50/6.25) Buses stop along Gordon St, west of Harbour Park Mall. Bus 2 goes to the Departure Bay ferry terminal. No city buses run to Duke Point.

Nanaimo Airporter (www.nanaimoairporter.com; from $26) Provides door-to-door service to downtown from both ferry terminals, as well as handy airport drop-off and pick-up.

Parksville, Coombs & Qualicum Beach

This popular mid-island seaside region, which also includes rustic Coombs, has been a traditional destination for vacationing families for decades – hence the water parks and miniature golf attractions. It's a great spot to take a breather on your trip up or down island. For more information on the area, visit www.parksvillequalicumbeach.com.

◉ Sights

Coombs Old Country Market MARKET
(www.oldcountrymarket.com; 2326 Alberni Hwy, Coombs; ⊘ 9am-7pm) The mother of all pit stops, this sprawling food and crafts menagerie is stuffed with bakery and produce delectables. It attracts huge numbers of visitors on balmy summer days, when cameras are pointed at the grassy roof where a herd of goats spends the season. Nip inside for giant ice-cream cones, heaping pizzas and the deli makings of a great picnic.

Save some time to explore the attendant store and attractions clustered around the site.

World Parrot Refuge WILDLIFE RESERVE
(www.worldparrotrefuge.org; 2116 Alberni Hwy, Coombs; adult/child $14/10; ⊘ 10am-4pm) Rescuing exotic birds from captivity and nursing them back to health, this excellent educational facility preaches the mantra that parrots are not pets. Pick up your earplugs at reception and stroll among the enclosures, each alive with recovering, and very noisy, birds. Don't be surprised when some screech a chirpy 'hello' as you stroll past.

Milner Gardens & Woodland GARDENS
(www.milnergardens.org; 2179 W Island Hwy, Qualicum Beach; adult/child $11/free; ⊘ 10am-4:30pm) This idyllic summertime attraction combines rambling forest trails shaded by centuries-old trees with flower-packed gardens planted with magnificent rhododendrons. Meander down to the 1930s **tearoom** on a stunning bluff overlooking the water. Then tuck into a full afternoon tea ($17.95) on the porch and drink in views of the bird-lined shore and snowcapped peaks shimmering on the horizon.

Morningstar Farm FARM
(www.morningstarfarm.ca; 403 Lowry's Rd, Parksville; ⊘ 9am-5pm) **FREE** Check out the

region's 'locavore' credentials at this little working farmstead, which is a family-friendly visitor attraction. Let your kids run wild – most will quickly fall in love with the roaming pigs and goats – then hunt down some samples from the on-site Little Qualicum Cheeseworks and Mooberry Winery: blueberry, cranberry and gooseberry fruit wines are recommended.

Horne Lake Caves
PARK

(☑250-248-7829; www.hornelake.com; tours adult/child from $24/20; ⏰10am-5pm) Horne Lake Caves Provincial Park is a 45-minute drive from Parksville, but it's worth it for BC's best spelunking. Some caves are open to the public for self-exploration, though the excellent guided tours are recommended, from family friendly to 'extreme' – book ahead for these. To get there, take Hwy 19 towards Courtenay, then exit 75 and proceed for 12km on the gravel road.

🛏 Sleeping & Eating

★ Free Spirit Spheres
CABINS $$

(☑250-757-9445; www.freespiritspheres.com; 420 Horne Lake Rd, Qualicum Beach; cabins from $145) These unique spherical tree houses enable guests to cocoon themselves in the forest canopy. Compact inside, 'Eve' is small and basic, while 'Eryn' and 'Melody' are lined with built-in cabinets. It's all about communing with nature, with TVs replaced by books, and guests receive a basket of tasty snacks on arrival. There's also a ground-level facilities block with sauna, BBQ and hotel-quality showers. Book early for summer.

Blue Willow Guest House
B&B $$

(☑250-752-9052; www.bluewillowguesthouse. com; 524 Quatna Rd, Qualicum Beach; d from $140) A surprisingly spacious Victorian-style cottage, this lovely B&B has a book-lined lounge, exposed beams and a fragrant country garden. The two rooms and one self-contained suite are lined with antiques and each is extremely homely. The attention to detail carries over to the gourmet breakfast: served in the conservatory, it's accompanied by finger-licking home-baked treats.

Crown Mansion
BOUTIQUE HOTEL $$

(☑250-752-5776, 800-378-6811; www.crown-mansion.com; 292 E Crescent Rd, Qualicum Beach; d from $160; 🛜) A sumptuous family home built in 1912, this handsome white-painted mansion was restored to its former glory and opened as a unique hotel in 2009. Recall past guests Bing Crosby and John Wayne as you check out the family crest in the library fireplace, then retire to your elegant room. Rates include continental breakfast; arrive early to snag the window table.

Fish Tales Café
SEAFOOD $$

(336 W Island Hwy, Qualicum Beach; mains $8-24) This Qualicum fixture has the look of an old-school English tea shop, but it's been reeling in visitors with its perfect fish and chips for years. It's worth exploring the non-deep-fried dishes; the two-person platter of scallops, shrimp, smoked salmon and mussels is recommended. If you arrive early enough, you can grab a table in the lovely garden.

❶ Getting There & Away

Greyhound Canada (www.greyhound.ca) services arrive in Parksville from Victoria (from $18.50, from three hours, five daily) and Nanaimo (from $6.50, 40 minutes, five daily) among others. The same buses, with similar times and rates, serve Qualicum Beach.

Port Alberni

POP 17,500

With its fishing and forestry sectors declining, Alberni – located on Hwy 4 between the island's east and west coasts – has been ramping up its visitor appeal in recent years. A good location for outdoor exploration, there are also some intriguing historic attractions. For more on what to do in the region, visit www.albernivalleytourism.com.

◉ Sights

Cathedral Grove
PARK

(www.bcparks.ca) Between Parksville and Port Alberni, this spiritual home of tree huggers is the mystical highlight of MacMillan Provincial Park. It's often overrun with summer visitors – try not to knock them down as they scamper across the highway in front of you. The accessible forest trails wind through a dense, breathtaking canopy of vegetation, offering glimpses of some of BC's oldest trees, including centuries-old Douglas firs more than 3m in diameter. Try hugging that.

Alberni Valley Museum
MUSEUM

(www.alberniheritage.com; 4255 Wallace St; admission by donation; ⏰10am-5pm Tue, Wed, Fri, & Sat, to 8pm Thu) Studded with fascinating aboriginal and pioneer-era exhibits, the museum's intriguing section on the West Coast

Trail shows how the route was once a life-saving trail for shipwreck victims. History buffs should extend their visit by boarding the town's Alberni Pacific Railway heritage steam train (July and August) for a trundle to McLean Mill – a national historic site, it's Canada's only working steam-powered sawmill.

Tours

MV Frances Barkley   BOAT TOUR
(www.ladyrosemarine.com; 5425 Argyle St; return trip $52-74; ⊘May-Sep) This historic boat is a vital link for the region's remote communities, ferrying freight, supplies and passengers between Alberni and Bamfield thrice weekly. In summer, with its route extended to Ucluelet and the lovely Broken Group Islands, it lures kayakers and mountain bikers, but it's also open for those who just fancy an idyllic cruise up Barkley Sound.

Batstar Adventure Tours   ADVENTURE TOUR
(www.batstar.com; 4785 Beaver Creek Rd) If you're unsure about exploring the jaw-droppingly beautiful but undeniably remote Broken Group Islands by kayak on your own, these guys can sort you out. From long-weekend jaunts to multiday odysseys of the life-changing variety, all the details, including food and accommodations, are taken care of on these guided adventures.

Sleeping & Eating

Fat Salmon Backpackers   HOSTEL $
(☑250-723-6924; www.fatsalmonbackpackers.com; 3250 3rd Ave; dm $25; ⊘May-Sep; @🖸) Driven by its highly sociable owners, this funky, eclectic backpacker joint offers four-to eight-bed dorms (that means no private rooms) with names like 'Knickerbocker' and 'Mullet Room.' There are lots of books, free tea and coffee and a kitchen bristling with utensils. Say 'hi' to Lily, the world-famous house dog and she'll almost certainly let you take her for a walk.

Hummingbird Guesthouse   B&B $$
(☑888-720-2114, 250-720-2111; www.hummingbirdguesthouse.com; 5769 River Rd; ste $125-180; 🖸) With four large suites and a huge deck with its own hot tub, this modern B&B has a home-away-from-home feel – just ask Jasper, the laid-back house cat. There's a shared kitchen on each of the two floors and each suite has satellite TV; one has its own sauna. For families, there's a teen-friendly games room out back.

All Mex'd Up   MEXICAN $
(5440 Argyle St; mains $4-10) A funky and highly colorful little Mexican comfort food shack near the waterfront – it's decorated with chili-shaped fairy lights – this spot makes everything from scratch and focuses on local ingredients as much as possible. Pull up a stool and tuck into a classic array of made-with-love tacos, quesadillas and big-ass burritos and you'll be full for your day of exploring.

Getting There & Away

Greyhound Canada (www.greyhound.ca) buses arrive here from Victoria (from $46, four to five hours, three daily) and Tofino (from $28.40, two hours, two daily), among others.

Pacific Rim National Park Reserve

Dramatic, wave-whipped beaches and brooding, mist-licked forests make the **Pacific Rim National Park Reserve** (www.pc.gc.ca/pacificrim; park pass adult/child C$7.80/6.80) a must-see for anyone interested in experiencing BC's raw West Coast wilderness. The 500-sq-km park comprises the northern Long Beach Unit, between Tofino and Ucluelet; the Broken Group Islands Unit in Barkley Sound; and, to the south, the ever-popular West Coast Trail Unit. First timers should drop by the **Pacific Rim Visitors Centre** (☑250-726-4600; www.pacificrimvisitor.ca; 2791 Pacific Rim Hwy; ⊘10am-4:30pm) for maps and advice on exploring the region. If you're stopping in the park, you'll need to pay and display a pass, available from the visitors center or from the yellow dispensers dotted along the highway.

Long Beach Unit

Attracting the lion's share of visitors, Long Beach Unit is easily accessible by car along the Pacific Rim Hwy. Wide sandy beaches, untamed surf, lots of beachcombing nooks, plus a living museum of old-growth rainforest, are the main reasons for the summer tourist clamor. Cox Bay Beach alone is an ideal hangout for surfers and families. Seabirds, sand dollars, and purple and orange starfish abound.

For an introduction to the area's natural history and First Nations heritage, visit the **Kwisitis Centre** (Wick Rd; free with park pass admission; ⊘10am-4:30pm Mar-Aug) overlooking

Wickaninnish Beach. If you're suddenly inspired to plunge in for a stroll, try one of the following trails, keeping your eyes peeled for swooping bald eagles and giant banana slugs. Safety precautions apply: tread carefully over slippery surfaces and never turn your back on the mischievous surf.

Long Beach Great scenery along the sandy shore (1.2km; easy).

Rainforest Trail Two interpretive loops through old-growth forest (1km; moderate).

Schooner Trail Through old- and second-growth forests with beach access (1km; moderate).

Shorepine Bog Loops around a moss-layered bog (800m; easy and wheelchair accessible).

Broken Group Islands Unit

Comprising some 300 islands and rocks scattered across 80 sq km around the entrance to Barkley Sound, this serene natural wilderness is beloved of visiting kayakers – especially those who enjoy close-up views of whales, porpoises and multitudinous birdlife. Compasses are required for navigating here, unless you fancy paddling to Hawaii.

If you're up for a trek, **Lady Rose Marine Services** (www.ladyrosemarine.com) will ship you and your kayak from Port Alberni to its Sechart Whaling Station Lodge three hours away in Barkley Sound on the MV *Frances Barkley*. The lodge rents kayaks ($40 to $60 per day) if you'd rather travel light and offers accommodations (single/double $150/235, including meals).

From there, popular paddle destinations include Gibraltar Island, one hour away, with its sheltered campground and explorable beaches and tidal pools. Willis Island (1½ hours from Sechart) is also popular. It has a campground and, at low tide, you can walk to the surrounding islands. Remote Benson Island (four hours from Sechart) has a campground, grazing deer and a blowhole.

Camping fees are $9.80 per night, payable at Sechart or to the boat-based staff who patrol the region – they can collect additional fees from you if you decide to stay longer. The campgrounds are predictably basic and have solar composting toilets, but you must carry out all your garbage. Bring your own drinking water since island creeks are often dry in summer.

West Coast Trail Unit

The 75km West Coast Trail is BC's best-known hiking route. It's also one of the toughest. Not for the uninitiated, there are two things you'll need to know before tackling it: it will hurt and you'll want to do it again next year.

The trail winds along the wave-licked rainforest shoreline between trailhead information centers at Pachena Bay, 5km south of Bamfield on the north end, and Gordon River, 5km north of Port Renfrew on the southern tip. The entire stretch takes between six and seven days to complete. Open May to September, access to the route during the mid-June to mid-September peak season is limited to 60 overnight backpackers each day and **reservations** (✆877-737-3783, 250-726-4453; www.reservation.pc.gc.ca; nonrefundable reservation fee C$24.50) are required. All over-nighters must pay a trail-user fee ($127.50), plus $30 to cover the two short ferry crossings on the route. All overnighters must attend a 1½-hour orientation session before departing. If you don't have a reservation, some permits are kept back for a daily wait-list system.

If you don't want to go the whole hog (you wimp), you can do a day hike or even hike half the trail from Pachena Bay, considered the easier end of the route. Overnight hikers who only hike this end of the trail can exit from Nitinat Lake. Day hikers are exempt from the large trail-user fee, but they need to get a free day-use permit at one of the trailheads.

West Coast Trail walkers must be able to manage rough, slippery terrain, stream crossings and adverse, suddenly changing weather. There are more than 100 little, and some not-so-little, bridges and 70 ladders. Be prepared to treat or boil all water and cook on a lightweight camping stove; you'll be bringing in all your own food. Hikers can rest their weary muscles at any of the basic campsites along the route, most of which have solar-composting outhouses. It's recommended that you set out from a trailhead at least five hours before sundown to ensure you reach a campsite before nightfall – stumbling around in the dark is the prime cause of accidents on this route.

West Coast Trail Express (www.trailbus. com) runs a daily shuttle (May to September) to the trailheads. Book ahead in summer.

Tofino

POP 1900

Transforming from resource outpost to hippie enclave and now eco-resort town, Tofino is Vancouver Island's favorite outdoorsy retreat. It's not surprising that surf fans, families and city-escaping Vancouverites keep coming: packed with activities and blessed with stunning regional beaches, the funky community sits on Clayoquot Sound, where forested mounds rise from roiling, ever-dramatic waves.

◉ Sights & Activities

Tofino Botanical Gardens GARDENS
(www.tbgf.org; 1084 Pacific Rim Hwy; 3-day admission adult/child $10/free; ⊙9am-dusk) Ø Explore what coastal temperate rainforests are all about by checking out the frog pond, forest boardwalk, native plants and educational workshops at this smashing, bird-packed rustic attraction. There's a seasonal cafe onsite for that essential glass of wine, while classical music is piped through the gardens most evenings. There's a $1 discount if you arrive car free.

Maquinna Marine Provincial Park PARK
(www.bcparks.ca) Ø One of the most popular day trips from Tofino, the highlight here is **Hot Spring Cove**. Tranquility-minded trekkers travel to the park by Zodiac boat or seaplane, watching for whales and other sea critters en route. From the boat landing, 2km of boardwalks lead to the natural hot pools.

Meares Island PARK
Visible through the mist and accessible via kayak or tour boat from the Tofino waterfront, Meares Island is home to the Big Tree Trail, a 400m boardwalk through old-growth forest that includes a stunning 1500-year-old red cedar. The island was the site of the key 1984 Clayoquot Sound antilogging protest that kicked off the region's latter-day environmental movement.

Ahousat PARK
(www.wildsidetrail.com) Situated on remote Flores Island and accessed by tour boat or kayak, Ahousat is the mystical location of the spectacular Wild Side Heritage Trail, a moderately difficult path that traverses 10km of forests, beaches and headlands between Ahousat and Cow Bay. There's a natural warm spring on the island and it's also home to a First Nations band. A popular destination for kayakers, camping of the no-facilities variety is allowed.

Tofino Brewing Company BREWERY
(www.tofinobrewingco.com; 681 Industrial Way; ⊙noon-11pm) Hidden around the back of an unassuming industrial building, this smashing little brewery makes islanders very merry, which is why its brews are in restaurants around town and beyond. Roll up to the tasting bar and check out a few free samples. Always ask for the seasonal offering, but check out the excellent Tuff Session Ale, then consider a takeout growler.

Inkwis Arts & Culture GALLERY
(www.inkwis-portal.com; 368 Main St; ⊙11am-5pm Wed-Sun) The newest of several First Nations–focused galleries around Tofino's downtown drag, this spartan but friendly little space has a lively roster of ever-changing exhibitions; check the website for exhibition opening events. While the focus is contemporary First Nations, artists from other communities are also part of the mix, as are workshops and a growing art-for-sale section.

Pacific Surf School SURFING
(www.pacificsurfschool.com; 430 Campbell St; board rental 6/24hr $15/20) Offers rentals, camps and lessons for beginners.

STORMING TOFINO

Started as a clever marketing ploy to lure off-season visitors, storm-watching has become a popular pastime on the island's west coast. View spectacularly crashing winter waves, then scamper back inside for hot chocolate with a face freckled by sea salt. There are usually good off-peak deals to be had in area accommodations during storm-watching season (typically November to March) and most hotels can supply you with loaner 'Tofino tuxedos,' otherwise known as waterproof gear. The best spots to catch a few crashing spectacles are Cox Bay, Chesterman Beach, Long Beach, Second Bay and Wickaninnish Beach. Just remember not to get too close or turn your back on the waves: these gigantic swells will have you in the water within seconds if given half the chance.

Surf Sister SURFING
(www.surfsister.com; 625 Campbell St; lessons $79)
Introductory lessons for boys and girls, plus
women-only multiday courses.

👉 Tours

Remote Passages KAYAKING
(www.remotepassages.com; 51 Wharf St; tours
from $64) Gives short guided kayaking tours
around Clayoquot Sound and the islands.

Tofino Sea Kayaking KAYAKING
(www.tofino-kayaking.com; 320 Main St; tours from
$60) Evocative guided paddles; one-day
tours to the Freedom Cove floating gardens
are recommended.

Jamie's Whaling Station BOAT TOUR
(www.jamies.com; 606 Campbell St; adult/child
$99/69) Spot whales, bears and sea lions on
Jamie's boat jaunts.

Ocean Outfitters BOAT TOUR
(www.oceanoutfitters.bc.ca; 368 Main St; adult/
child $89/69) Popular whale-watching tours,
with bear and hot-springs treks also offered.

🛏 Sleeping

⭐**Tofino Inlet Cottages** CABIN $$
(☎250-725-3441; www.tofinoinletcottages.com;
350 Olsen Rd; ste from $130; 🛜) Located in a
pocket of tranquility just off the highway,
this hidden gem is perfect for waking up to
glassy-calm waterfront views. It consists of a
pairing of two 1960s-built A-frame cottages,
divided into two suites each, and a spacious
woodsy house, which has a lovely circular
hearth and is ideal for families.

**Whalers on the Point
Guesthouse** HOSTEL $$
(☎250-725-3443, 855-725-3443; www.tofinohostel.
com; 81 West St; dm/r from $37/93; @🛜) Close
to the town center, but with a secluded
waterfront location, this excellent HI hostel
is a comfy wood-lined retreat. The dorms are
mercifully small, and some double-bed private rooms are available. Facilities include
a granite-countered kitchen, BBQ patio,
games room and a wet sauna, plus you'll
spend plenty of time on the shoreline deck.
Reservations are essential in summer. Free
parking.

Ecolodge HOSTEL $$
(☎250-725-1220; www.tbgf.org; 1084 Pacific Rim
Hwy; r from $149; @🛜) In the grounds of the
botanical gardens, this immaculate and
quiet wood-built education center has a se-
lection of rooms, a large kitchen and an on-
site laundry. It's popular with families and
traveling groups – there's a bunk room that
works out at $40 each per night in summer
for groups of four. Rates include entry to the
surrounding gardens. A great sleepover for
nature lovers.

Ocean Village Beach Resort CABINS $$$
(☎866-725-3755, 250-725-3755; www.ocean-
villageresort.com; 555 Hellesen Dr; ste from $229;
🛜🍽🐾) Recently renovated, this immaculate
beachside resort of 53 beehive-shaped cedar
cabins – hence the woodsy aroma when you
step in the door – is a family favorite with a
Scandinavian look. Each unit faces a shoreline just a few steps away and all have handy
kitchens. If your kids tire of the beach, there
are surf lessons and a saltwater pool to keep
them occupied. No in-room TVs.

Pacific Sands Beach Resort RESORT $$$
(☎800-565-2322, 250-725-3322; www.pacific-
sands.com; 1421 Pacific Rim Hwy; d from $275;
🛜🐾) Combining comfortable lodge rooms,
all with full kitchens, plus spectacular three-
level beach houses, this family-friendly
resort hugs dramatic Cox Bay Beach. Wher-
ever you stay, you'll be lulled to sleep by
the sound of the nearby roiling surf. The
spacious, contemporary-furnished beach
houses are ideal for groups and have stone
fireplaces and top-floor bathtubs with views.
There are free summertime nature pro-
grams for kids.

Chesterman Beach B&B B&B $$$
(☎250-725-3726; www.chestermanbeach.net;
1345 Chesterman Beach Rd; d from $185; 🛜) Lo-
cated among a string of B&Bs, this classy,
adult-oriented spot has two main rooms,
each with a private entrance, and amazing access to the beach close at hand. The
smaller Lookout suite is our favorite, with
its cozy, wood-lined ambience and mesmerizing beach vistas. There's a separate cottage
at the back of the property that's great for
small groups.

Wickaninnish Inn HOTEL $$$
(☎800-333-4604, 250-725-3100; www.wickinn.
com; Chesterman Beach; d from $399; 🛜🐾) Cor-
nering the market in luxury winter storm-
watching packages, 'the Wick' is worth a
stay any time of year. Embodying nature
with its recycled wood furnishings, natu-
ral stone tiles and the ambience of a place
grown rather than constructed, the sump-
tuous guest rooms have push-button gas

DON'T MISS

PACIFIC RIM PIT STOP

Don't drive too fast in your rush to get to end-of-the-highway Tofino or you'll miss the locals' favorite stomping ground. Ostensibly known as the **Beaches Shopping Centre** area, 1180 Pacific Rim Hwy is home to dozens of funky little wood-built businesses where you could easily spend a happy half-day. Drop into the **Juicery** (⊙9am-6pm) for fresh-made fruit smoothies or grab a java at **Tofitian** (⊙7:30am-5pm; 🐦). While bike and surf rentals are available, forget the exercise and go straight for the treats.

TacoFino (www.tacofino.com; mains $4-12; ⊙11am-5pm Sun-Thu, to 6pm Fri & Sat) is one of BC's most legendary food trucks, serving the best fish tacos in the region. **Chocolate Tofino** (www.chocolatetofino.com; ⊙10am-9pm Mon-Sat) steps up to the plate for dessert, with heaping house-made ice cream and naughty chocolates to go, including amazing salted caramels. Go for the lavender-honey ice cream or ask them for the 'secret' flavors hidden in the back that only the locals know about.

fireplaces, two-person hot tubs and floor-to-ceiling windows. The region's most romantic sleepover.

✖ Eating

Shelter　　　　　　　　WEST COAST **$$**
(www.shelterrestaurant.com; 601 Campbell St; mains $12-30; ⊙11am-midnight) This woodsy, low-ceilinged haunt has kept expanding over the years, but has never lost its welcoming locals' hangout feel. The perfect spot to grab lunch; salmon surf bowls and a patio seat are recommended. Shelter becomes an intimate dinner venue every evening when the menu ratchets up to showcase finger-licking BC-sourced treats from seafood to gourmet burgers.

Sobo　　　　　　　　　WEST COAST **$$**
(www.sobo.ca; 311 Neill St; mains $15-30; ⊙11am-9pm) This local favorite started out as a still-remembered purple food truck and is now a popular sit-down eatery. The focus at Sobo – meaning Sophisticated Bohemian – is seasonal West Coast ingredients prepared with international influences. A brilliant place to dive into fresh-catch seafood for dinner, there's a hearty lunch menu if you need an early fill-up; the gourmet pizzas are highly recommended.

Schooner　　　　　　　　SEAFOOD **$$**
(www.schoonerrestaurant.ca; 331 Campbell St; mains $18-28) Family run for 50 years, this local legend has been reinvigorated recently by the return of the owner to cheffing duties. Start your evening with a cocktail, then launch your voyage into the region's seafood bounty; the giant, two-person Captain's Plate blowout of local salmon, scallops et al

is the way to go. Come back on the weekend for the excellent brunch.

❶ Information

Tofino Visitors Centre (📞250-725-3414; www.tourismtofino.com; 1426 Pacific Rim Hwy; ⊙9am-5pm) A short drive south of town, the visitors center has detailed information on area accommodations, hiking trails and hot surf spots. There's also a blue-painted Tourism Tofino VW van parked around the town center in summer that dispenses advice to out-of-towners.

❶ Getting There & Around

Orca Airways (www.flyorcaair.com) Flights arrive at Tofino Airport from Vancouver International Airport's South Terminal (from $174, one hour, up to five daily).

Greyhound Canada (www.greyhound.ca) Buses (operated by Tofino Bus) arrive from Port Alberni ($29, two hours), Nanaimo ($46, three to four hours), Victoria ($69, six to seven hours) and beyond.

Tofino Bus (www.tofinobus.com) 'Beach Bus' services roll in along Hwy 4 from Ucluelet ($17, 40 minutes).

Ucluelet

POP 1600

Threading along Hwy 4 through the mountains to the west coast, you'll arrive at a junction sign proclaiming that Tofino is 33km to your right, while just 8km to your left is Ucluelet. Sadly, most still take the right-hand turn, which is a shame, since sleepier 'Ukee' has more than a few charms of its own and is a good reminder of what Tofino was like before tourism arrived.

◉ Sights & Activities

Ucluelet Aquarium AQUARIUM
(www.uclueletaquarium.org; Main Street Waterfront Promenade; adult/child $12.50/6.25; ⊘10am-6pm) 🏊 Replacing the tiny waterfront shack that stood nearby, the excellent Ucluelet Aquarium opened this much larger facility in 2012. Retaining key approaches from the old place, the kid-luring touch tanks are still here, and the marine critters are local, with most on a catch-and-release program. But it's the enthusiasm of the young staff that sets this place apart, along with the ability to educate on issues of conservation without browbeating. Take your time to peer at the astonishing array of local aquatic life and, if you're lucky, you'll be here when a Pacific octopus is enjoying a live-crab feeding session. In summer, look out for family-friendly lab workshops (free).

Wild Pacific Trail HIKING
(www.wildpacifictrail.com) The 8.5km Wild Pacific Trail offers smashing views of Barkley Sound and the Broken Group Islands. Starting at the intersection of Peninsula and Coast Guard Rds, it winds around the wave-slapped cliffs past the lighthouse (get your camera out here) and along the craggy shoreline fringing the town. Seabirds are abundant and it's a good storm-watching spot – stick to the trail or the crashing waves might pluck you from the cliffs. Plans were in place on our visit to expand the route by another few kilometers; check the website for progress reports.

Majestic Ocean Kayaking KAYAKING
(www.oceankayaking.com; 1167 Helen Rd; tours from $67) Majestic Ocean Kayaking leads day trips around the area, plus multiday tours of the Broken Group Islands.

Relic Surf Shop SURFING
(www.relicsurfshop.com; 1998 Peninsula Rd; rentals from $30) If you want to practice the ways of surfing, check in with Relic Surf Shop.

Ukee Bikes CYCLING
(www.ukeebikes.com; 1559 Imperial Lane; bike rental 2/24hr $10/25; ⊘10am-6pm Tue-Fri, to 5pm Sat) Rent some wheels from the friendly folk at Ukee Bikes. They also sell kites.

🛏 Sleeping & Eating

C&N Backpackers HOSTEL $
(📞888-434-6060, 250-726-7416; www.cnnbackpackers.com; 2081 Peninsula Rd; dm/r $25/65; ⊘Apr-Oct; 🕾) They're very protective of their hardwood floors, so take off your shoes at the door of this calm and well-maintained hostel. The dorms are mostly small and predictably basic, but private rooms are available and there's a spacious downstairs kitchen. The highlight is the landscaped, nap-worthy garden overlooking the inlet, complete with hammocks and a rope swing.

Surfs Inn Guesthouse CABINS, HOSTEL $
(📞250-726-4426; www.surfsinn.ca; 1874 Peninsula Rd; dm/cottages from $28/139; 🕾) It's hard to miss this blue-painted house near the center of town, with its small, woodsy dorm rooms. But the real find is hidden out back: two cute cabins that are ideal for groups and families. One is larger and self-contained while the other is divided into two suites with kitchenettes. Each has a BBQ. Ask about surf packages if you fancy hitting the waves.

Black Rock Oceanfront Resort HOTEL $$$
(📞250-726-4800, 877-762-5011; www.blackrockresort.com; 596 Marine Dr; d from $269; 🕾🏊) Ucluelet's fanciest sleepover feels like a transplant from Tofino. This dramatic waterfront resort offers kitchen-equipped suites, all wrapped in a contemporary wood-and-stone West Coast look. Many rooms have great views of the often dramatically stormy surf. There's a vista-hugging restaurant specializing in regional nosh, plus a lobby-level bar shaped like a rolling wave.

Ukee Dogs CAFE $
(1576 Imperial Lane; mains $4-12; ⊘8:30am-3:30pm Mon-Fri, 10:30am-3:30pm Sat & Sun) Focused on own-baked treats and comfort foods, this bright and breezy, good-value eatery offers hot dogs of the gourmet variety (go for the Imperial), plus rustic pizzas, hearty breakfasts and great salmon sliders with fries or salad. Whatever you indulge in, aim for a sunny picnic table outside and pick up a sprinkle-topped coconut cookie to go.

★ Hank's WEST COAST $$
(www.hanksucluelet.com; 1576 Imperial Lane; mains $18-22; ⊘5-11pm Wed-Mon) Closed every Tuesday so they can forage island farms for ingredients, this smashing addition to Ukee's dining scene has quickly become a local fave. The fresh and local menu is divided between seafood and succulent barbecue; go for lamb. There's a brilliant array of BC craft beers, plus more than 50 bottles from further afield – look out for twice-monthly beer-cask nights.

Norwoods
WEST COAST $$$

(www.norwoods.ca; 1714 Peninsula Rd; mains $24-34; ⊙5-10pm) Showing how far Ucluelet's dining scene has elevated itself in recent years, this lovely candlelit room would easily be at home in Tofino. The ever-changing menu focuses on seasonal regional ingredients; think halibut and duck breast. All are prepared with a sophisticated international approach, plus there's a full menu of BC and beyond wines, many offered by the glass.

ℹ Information

Ucluelet Visitors Centre (☑250-726-2485; www.ucluelet.travel; 1604 Peninsula Rd; ⊙9am-5pm) For a few good reasons to stick around in Ukee, including a dining scene that finally has some great options, make for the new visitors center.

ℹ Getting There & Around

Greyhound Canada (www.greyhound.ca) Operated by Tofino Bus, services arrive from Port Alberni (from $26, 1½ hours, three daily), Nanaimo (from $46, three to four hours, three daily) and Victoria (from $34, six hours, four daily), among others.

Tofino Bus (www.tofinobus.com) The 'Beach Bus' comes into town along Hwy 4 from Tofino ($17, 40 minutes, up to three daily).

Denman & Hornby Islands

The main Northern Gulf Islands, Denman (www.denmanisland.com) and Hornby (www.hornbyisland.net) share laid-back attitudes, artistic flair and some tranquil outdoor activities. You'll arrive by ferry at Denman first from Buckley Bay on Vancouver Island, then hop from Denman across to Hornby. Stop at **Denman Village**, near the first ferry dock, and pick up a free map for both islands.

◎ Sights & Activities

Denman has three provincial parks: **Fillongley**, with easy hiking and beachcombing; **Boyle Point**, with a beautiful walk to the lighthouse; and **Sandy Island**, only accessible by water from north Denman.

Among Hornby's provincial parks, **Tribune Bay** features a long sandy beach with safe swimming, while **Helliwell** offers notable hiking. **Ford's Cove**, on Hornby's south coast, offers the chance for divers to swim with six-gilled sharks. The island's large **Mt Geoffrey Regional Park** is crisscrossed with hiking and mountain-biking trails.

Denman Hornby Canoes & Kayaks
KAYAKING

(www.denmanpaddling.ca; 4005 East Rd, Denman Island) For kayaking rentals in the area.

🛏 Sleeping & Eating

Blue Owl
B&B $$

(☑250-335-3440; www.blueowldenman.ca; 8850 Owl Cres, Denman Island; s/d incl breakfast $115/125; 🐾) An idyllically rustic retreat for those craving an escape from city life, this woodsy little cottage is a short walk from the ocean. Loaner bikes are freely available if you fancy exploring (there's a swimmable lake nearby), but you might want to just cozy up for a night in.

Sea Breeze Lodge
HOTEL $$

(☑888-516-2321, 250-335-2321; www.seabreezelodge.com; 5205 Fowler Rd, Hornby Island; adult/child $180/75) This 12-acre retreat, with 16 cottages overlooking the ocean, has the feel of a Spanish villa with a Pacific Rim twist. Rooms are comfortable rather than palatial and some have fireplaces and full kitchens. You can swim, kayak and fish or just flop lazily around in the cliffside hot tub. Rates are per person and include three daily meals.

Cardboard House Bakery
BAKERY $

(www.thecardboardhousebakery.com; 2205 Central Rd, Hornby Island; mains $4-10) It's easy to lose track of time at this old shingle-sided farmhouse that combines a hearty bakery, pizza shop and cozy cafe. It's impossible not to stock up on a bag full of oven-fresh muffins, cookies and croissants for the road. Stick around for an alfresco lunch in the adjoining orchard, which also stages live music Wednesday and Sunday evenings in summer.

Island Time Café
CAFE $

(3464 Denman Rd, Denman Island; mains $7-11) This village hangout specializes in fresh-from-the-oven bakery treats, such as muffins and scones, plus organic coffee, bulging breakfast wraps and hearty house-made soups. The pizza is particularly recommended, and is served with a side order of gossip from the locals. If the sun is cooperating, sit outside and catch some rays.

ℹ Getting There & Away

BC Ferries (www.bcferries.com) Services arrive throughout the day at Denman from Buckley Bay (passenger/vehicle $9.45/22.15, 10 minutes). Hornby Island is accessed by ferry from Denman (passenger/vehicle $9.45/22.15, 10 minutes).

Comox Valley

Comprising the towns of Comox and Courtenay and the village of Cumberland, this is a region of rolling mountains, alpine meadows and colorful communities. A good outdoor adventure base and mountain-biking hotbed, its activity-triggering highlight is Mt Washington.

◉ Sights & Activities

Save time for a poke around charming Cumberland, a town built on mining that's now luring artsy young residents from across BC to its clapboard shops and houses.

Courtenay & District Museum & Palaeontology Centre
MUSEUM
(www.courtenaymuseum.ca; 207 4th St, Courtenay; admission by donation; ⊙10am-5pm Mon-Sat, noon-4pm Sun) With its life-sized replica of an elasmosaur – a prehistoric marine reptile first discovered in the area – the excellent museum also houses pioneer and First Nations exhibits.

Cumberland Museum
MUSEUM
(www.cumberlandmuseum.ca; Dunsmuir Ave, Cumberland; ⊙10am-5pm) Get some historic context at the Cumberland Museum, with its little walk-through mine exhibit.

Mt Washington Alpine Resort
OUTDOORS
(www.mountwashington.ca; winter lift ticket adult/child $75/39) The main reason for winter visits, Mt Washington Alpine Resort is the island's skiing mecca, with its 81 runs, snowshoeing park and popular night skiing. There are also great summer activities, including some of the region's best hiking trails.

🛏 Sleeping & Eating

★ Riding Fool Hostel
HOSTEL $
(☑250-336-8250, 888-313-3665; www.ridingfool.com; 2705 Dunsmuir Ave, Cumberland; dm/r $25/60; @🖥) One of BC's top hostels colonizes a restored Cumberland heritage building with rustic wooden interiors, a large kitchen and lounge area and, along with its small dorms, the kind of neat and tidy private rooms often found in midrange hotels. Bicycle rentals are available downstairs: this is a great hostel to hang out with the mountain-bike crowd.

Cona Hostel
HOSTEL $
(☑877-490-2662, 250-331-0991; www.theconahostel.com; 440 Anderton Ave, Courtenay; dm/r $25/58; @🖥) It's hard to miss this orange-painted riverside hostel, a popular spot for families and young mountain-bike buddies gearing up for their next assault on the area's multitudinous trails. The friendly folks at the front desk have plenty of other suggestions for what to explore, but you might want to just stay indoors as there's a large kitchen, BBQ patio and board games to keep you busy.

Kingfisher Oceanside Resort
HOTEL $$
(☑250-338-1323, 800-663-7929; www.kingfisher-spa.com; 4330 Island Hwy, Courtenay; r/ste from $145/220; @🖥🏊🐕) At this boutique waterfront lodge, many of the rooms are oriented to focus on the waterfront, framed by islands and mountains. A good spot to take a break from your road trip, rooms are generally large and comfortable and many have full kitchens, so you can save on dining out – you'll likely blow it at the spa though. There are some good off-season deals.

Dark Side Chocolates
CHOCOLATE $
(www.darksidechocolates.com; 2722 Dunsmuir Ave, Cumberland; choc selections from $5; ⊙10am-4:30pm Tue-Sat) Drop into Dark Side Chocolates for treats; the mint melties are recommended.

Waverley Hotel Pub
BURGERS $$
(www.waverleyhotel.ca; 2692 Dunsmuir Ave, Cumberland; mains $9-15) If you're keen to meet the locals, hit this historic saloon for a pint of Blue Buck Ale. Food is of the hearty pub-grub variety – how many more reasons do you need to have a burger? There are often live bands on the kick-ass little stage.

Mad Chef Café
CANADIAN, FUSION $$
(www.madchefcafe.net; 492 Fitzgerald Ave, Courtenay; mains $8-20; ⊙11am-8pm Mon-Thu, to 9pm Fri & Sat) This bright and colorful neighborhood eatery serves a great selection of made-from-scratch meals, and is a good place for a salad, since they're heaping and crispy fresh. Sharers should go for the Mediterranean plate, piled high with olives, hummus, pita and lovely house-made bruschetta. Gourmet duck and salmon burgers are also popular.

Atlas Café
FUSION $$
(www.atlascafe.ca; 250 6th St, Courtenay; mains $12-24; ⊙8:30am-3:30pm Mon, to 9:30pm Tue-Sun) Courtenay's favorite dine-out has a pleasing modern bistro feel with a global menu, fusing Asian, Mexican and Mediterranean flourishes. Check out the gourmet fish tacos, plus ever-changing seasonal treats. Good vegetarian options, too.

❶ Information

Vancouver Island Visitors Centre (☑885-400-2882; www.discovercomoxvalley.com; 3607 Small Rd, Cumberland; ☺9am-7pm) Drop by the slick visitors center for tips on exploring the area.

Campbell River

POP 29,500

Southerners will tell you this marks the end of civilization on Vancouver Island, but Campbell River is a handy drop-off point for wilderness tourism in Strathcona Provincial Park and is large enough to have plenty of attractions and services of its own.

◉ Sights

Museum at Campbell River   MUSEUM
(www.crmuseum.ca; 470 Island Hwy; adult/child $8/5; ☺10am-5pm) This fascinating museum is worth an hour of anyone's time and showcases aboriginal masks, an 1890s pioneer cabin and video footage of the world's largest artificial, non-nuclear blast (an underwater mountain in Seymour Narrows that caused dozens of shipwrecks before it was blown apart in a controlled explosion in 1958). In summer, ask about their popular history-themed boat cruises around the area.

Discovery Pier   LANDMARK
(rod rentals per half-day $6) Since locals claim the town as the 'Salmon Capital of the World,' you should wet your line off the downtown Discovery Pier or just stroll along with the crowds and see what everyone else has caught. Much easier than catching your own lunch, you can buy fish and chips (and ice cream) here. The perfect sunset spot to hang with the locals.

🛏 Sleeping & Eating

Heron's Landing Hotel   HOTEL **$$**
(☑250-923-2848, 888-923-2849; www.heronslandinghotel.com; 492 S Island Hwy; d from $139; @🛜) Superior motel-style accommodation with renovated rooms, including large loft suites ideal for families. Rates include breakfast.

Shot in the Dark Cafe   CAFE **$$**
(940 Island Hwy; mains $8-14; ☺8am-5pm Mon-Sat; 🛜) Huge, freshly made sandwiches and soups are the way to go at this pastel-hued locals' fave. A good spot for cooked breakfast, especially if you haven't eaten for a couple of days.

❶ Information

Campbell River Visitors Center (☑877-286-5705, 250-830-0411; www.campbellriver.travel; 1235 Shoppers Row; ☺9am-6pm) Will fill you in on what to do here and on nearby Quadra Island.

❶ Getting There & Around

Pacific Coastal Airlines (www.pacific-coastal.com) Flights from Vancouver (from $88, 45 minutes, up to seven daily) arrive frequently.

Campbell River Transit (www.busonline.ca; adult/child $1.75/1.50) Operates buses throughout the area.

Strathcona Provincial Park

Driving inland via Hwy 28 from Campbell River, you'll find Vancouver Island's largest **park** (www.bcparks.ca) 🌿. Centered on Mt Golden Hinde (2200m), the island's highest point, Strathcona is a magnificent pristine wilderness crisscrossed with trail systems that deliver you to waterfalls, alpine meadows, glacial lakes and mountain crags.

On arrival at the main entrance, get your bearings at **Strathcona Park Lodge & Outdoor Education Centre** (www.strathcona.bc.ca). A one-stop shop for park activities, including kayaking, zip lining, guided treks and rock climbing, this is a great place to rub shoulders with outdoorsy types. All-in adventure packages are available, some aimed specifically at families. Head to the **Whale Room** or **Myrna's** eateries for a fuel up.

The lodge also offers good **accommodations** (☑250-286-3122; r/cabin from $139/175), ranging from rooms in the main building to secluded timber-framed cottages. If you are a true back-to-nature fan, there are several campsites available in the park. Alternatively, consider pitching your tent at **Buttle Lake Campground** (☑800-689-9025, 604-689-9025; www.discovercamping.com; campsite $24); the swimming area and children's playground make it a good choice for families.

Notable park hiking trails include **Paradise Meadows Loop** (2.2km), an easy amble in a delicate wildflower and evergreen ecosystem; and **Mt Becher** (5km), with its great views over the Comox Valley and mountain-lined Strait of Georgia. Around Buttle Lake, easier walks include

WORTH A TRIP

QUADRA ISLAND HOP

For a day out with a difference, take your bike on the 10-minute **BC Ferries** (www.bcferries.com; passenger/vehicle/bike $11.10/25.80/2) skip from Campbell River to rustic Quadra. There's an extensive network of trails across the island; maps are for sale in local stores. Many of the forested trails are former logging routes and the local community has spent a lot of time building and maintaining the trails for mountain bikers of all skill levels. If you didn't bring your wheels, you can rent on the island or in Campbell River. For more information on visiting the island, see www.quadraisland.ca.

Quadra's fascinating **Nuyumbalees Cultural Centre** (www.nuyumbalees.com; 34 Weway Rd; adult/child $10/5; ◷10am-5pm May-Sep) illuminates the heritage and traditions of the local Kwakwaka'wakw First Nations people, showcasing carvings and artifacts and staging traditional dance performances. But if you just want to chill out with the locals, head to **Spirit Square** where performers entertain in summer.

If you decide to stick aroud for dinner, go for the waterfront pub or restaurant at the handsome **Heriot Bay Inn & Marina** (☑888-605-4545, 250-285-3322; www.heriotbayinn.com; Heriot Bay; d/cabins from $109/229) where, if you have a few too many drinks, you might want to stay the night. The hotel has motel-style rooms and charming rustic cabins.

Lady Falls (900m) and the trail along Karst Creek (2km), which winds past sink-holes, percolating streams and tumbling waterfalls.

North Vancouver Island

Down islanders, meaning anyone south of Campbell River, will tell you, 'There's nothing up there worth seeing,' while locals here will respond, 'They would say that, wouldn't they?' Parochial rivalries aside, what this giant region, covering nearly half the island, lacks in towns, infrastructure and population, it more than makes up for in natural beauty. Despite the remoteness, some areas are remarkably accessible to hardy hikers, especially along the North Coast Trail. For further information on the region, check in with **Vancouver Island North** (www.vancouverislandnorth.ca).

Port McNeill

POP 2600

Barreling down the hill almost into Broughton Straight, Port McNeill is a useful supply stop for long-distance travelers heading to or from Port Hardy.

More a superior motel than a resort, the hilltop **Black Bear Resort** (☑866-956-4900, 250-956-4900; www.port-mcneill-accommodation.com; 1812 Campbell Way; d/cabin incl breakfast from $148/188; @�wifi☒) overlooks the town and is conveniently located across from shops and restaurants. The standard rooms

are small but clean and include microwaves and fridges; full-kitchen units are also available and a string of new cabins was recently added.

If you're still hungry, head for lunch or dinner at **Northern Lights Restaurant** (1817 Campbell Way; mains $12-22; ◷11am-9pm Mon-Sat). Alongside the usual burgers and pub-style grub, you'll find well-prepared seafood; the halibut is recommended.

Drop by the gabled **visitors center** (☑250-956-3131; www.portmcneill.net; 1594 Beach Dr; ◷9am-5pm Mon-Fri, 10am-3pm Sat) for regional info, then stop in at the **museum** (351 Shelley Cres; ◷10am-5pm) to learn about the area's logging-industry heritage.

Greyhound Canada (www.greyhound.ca) buses arrive from, among others, Port Hardy (from $6.50, 40 minutes, daily) and Nanaimo (from $36, six hours, daily).

Alert Bay

POP 500

Located on Cormorant Island, this visitor-friendly village has an ancient and mythical appeal, plus a lovely, walkable waterfront. Its First Nations community and traditions still dominate, but its blend with an old pioneer fishing settlement makes it an even more fascinating day trip from Port McNeill. Drop by the **visitors center** (☑250-974-5024; www.alertbay.ca; 116 Fir St; ◷9am-4:30pm Mon-Fri) for an introduction and a chat with manager Norine, who will tell you all you need to know about checking the place out –

and especially how to ensure you don't miss any of the area's amazing totem poles.

The highly recommended **U'mista Cultural Centre** (☑250-974-5403; www.umista.ca; 1 Front St; adult/child $8/1; ☺9am-5pm) showcases an impressive collection of Kwakwaka'wakw masks and other potlatch items originally confiscated by Canada's government. Singing, dancing and BBQs are often held here, while modern-day totem-pole carvers usually work their magic out front. One of the world's tallest totem poles was carved on site in the 1960s and is, appropriately, placed on the front lawn of the **Big House**, which hosts traditional dances in July and August. Also drop into the village's **Culture Shock Interactive Gallery** (www.cultureshockgallery.ca; 10 Front St; ☺9:30am-6pm) for some exquisite artwork souvenirs.

If the ocean is calling you, **Seasmoke Whale Watching** (www.seaorca.com; adult/child $100/90) offers a five-hour whale-watching trek on its yacht, including afternoon tea.

Port Hardy

POP 3700

This small north-island settlement is best known as the departure point for BC Ferries spectacular Inside Passage trips. It's also a handy spot for gearing up for the rugged North Coast Trail.

🏃 Activities

Odyssey Kayaking   KAYAKING
(www.odysseykayaking.com; from $50) For those who prefer to paddle, Odyssey Kayaking can rent you some gear and point you to local highlights – Malei Island and Alder Bay are recommended.

Catala Charters   DIVING
(www.catalacharters.net; dive trips from $150) For dive fans, Catala Charters can have you hanging with local octopus and wolf eels.

👉 Tours

North Island Daytrippers   HIKING
(www.islanddaytrippers.com) A great access point for exploring the north-island wilderness, hikers can book customized guided tours with the friendly folk here.

🛏 Sleeping & Eating

North Coast Trail Backpackers Hostel   HOSTEL $
(☑250-949-9441, 866-448-6303; www.porthardy-hostel.webs.com; 8635 Granville St; dm/r from

$25/60; ☎) Colonizing a former downtown storefront, this labyrinthine hostel is a warren of small and larger dorms, overseen by friendly owners with plenty of tips on how to encounter the region – they'll even pick you up from the ferry if you call ahead. The hostel's hub is a large rec room and, while the kitchen is small, the adjoining cafe can keep you well fueled.

Ecoscape Cabins   CABINS $$
(☑250-949-8524;   www.ecoscapecabins.com; 6305 Jensen Cove Rd; cabins $130-175; ☎) The clutch of immaculate cedar cabins are divided between compact units, with flatscreen TVs, microwaves and sunny porches, ideal for couples; and roomier hilltop units, with swankier furnishings, BBQs and expansive views. There's a tranquil retreat feel to staying here and you should expect to see eagles swooping around the nearby trees. Deer are not uncommon, too.

Café Guido   CAFE $
(7135 Market St; mains $5-8; ☺7am-6pm Mon-Fri, 8am-6pm Sat, 8am-5pm Sun; ☎) You'll easily end up sticking around for an hour or two at this friendly locals' hangout, especially if you hit the loungy sofas with a tome purchased from the bookstore downstairs. Grilled panini are the way to go for lunch – try the Nero – but there's always a good soup special. Afterwards, nip upstairs to the surprisingly large and diverse craft shop.

ℹ Information

Port Hardy Visitors Centre (☑250-949-7622; www.porthardy.travel; 7250 Market St; ☺9am-5pm) Lined with flyers and staffed by locals who can help you plan your visit in town and beyond, the visitors center should be your first port of call.

ℹ Getting There & Around

Pacific Coastal Airlines (www.pacific-coastal.com) Services arrive from Vancouver (from $170, 1¼ hours, up to four daily).

Greyhound Canada (www.greyhound.ca) Buses roll in from Port McNeill (from $6.50, 45 minutes, daily) and beyond.

BC Ferries (www.bcferries.com) Ferries arrive from Prince Rupert (passenger/vehicle $195/444, 15 hours, schedules vary) via the scenically splendid Inside Passage.

North Island Transportation (☑250-949-6300; nit@island.net; shuttle $8) Operates a handy shuttle to/from the ferry and area hotels.

WORTH A TRIP

TELEGRAPH COVE

Built as a one-shack telegraph station, this charming destination has since expanded into one of the north's main visitor lures. Its pioneer-outpost feel is enhanced by the dozens of brightly painted wooden buildings perched around the marina on stilts. Be aware that it can get very crowded in summer.

Head first along the boardwalk to the smashing **Whale Interpretive Centre** (www.killerwhalecentre.org; suggested donation adult/child $3/1; ⊙9am-5pm), bristling with hands-on artifacts and artfully displayed skeletons of cougars, sea otters and a giant fin whale.

You can also see whales of the live variety just offshore: this is one of the island's top marine-life viewing regions and **Stubbs Island Whale Watching** (www.stubbs-island.com; adult/child $99/84) will get you up close with the orcas on a boat trek – you might also see humpbacks, dolphins and sea lions. For a bear alternative, **Tide Rip Grizzly Tours** (www.tiderip.com; tours $299; ⊙May-Sep) leads full-day trips to local beaches and inlets in search of the area's furry locals.

The well-established **Telegraph Cove Resorts** (☑250-928-3131, 800-200-4665; www.telegraphcoveresort.com; campsites/cabins from $28/120) provides accommodations in forested tent spaces and a string of rustic cabins on stilts overlooking the marina. The nearby and much newer **Dockside 29** (☑877-835-2683, 250-928-3163; www.telegraph-cove.ca; d from $140) is a good, motel-style alternative. Its rooms have kitchenettes with hardwood floors and waterfront views.

The **Killer Whale Café** (mains $14-18; ⊙May-Sep) is the cove's best eatery – the salmon, mussel and prawn linguine is recommended. The adjoining **Old Saltery Pub** is an atmospheric, wood-lined nook with a cozy central fireplace and tasty Killer Whale Pale Ale. It's a good spot to sit in a corner and pretend you're an old salty dog – eye patch optional.

Cape Scott Provincial Park

It's more than 550km from Victoria to the nature-hugging trailhead of this remote park (www.bcparks.ca) ⚑ on the island's crenulated northern tip. This should be your number-one destination if you really want to experience the raw, ravishing beauty of BC, especially its unkempt shorelines, breeze-licked rainforests and stunning sandy bays animated with tumbling waves and beady-eyed seabirds.

Hike the well-maintained, relatively easy 2.5km San Josef Bay Trail and you'll stroll from the shady confines of the trees right onto one of the best beaches in BC, a breath-taking, windswept expanse of roiling water, forested crags and the kind of age-old caves that could easily harbor lost smugglers. You can camp right here on the beach or just admire the passing ospreys before plunging back into the trees.

One of the area's shortest trails (2km), in adjoining **Raft Cove Provincial Park** (www.bcparks.ca), brings you to the wide, crescent beach and beautiful lagoons of Raft Cove. You're likely to have the entire 1.3km expanse to yourself, although the locals also like to surf here – it's their secret, so don't tell anyone.

If you really like a challenge, consider the **North Coast Trail**, a 43km route opened in 2008. You can start on the western end at Nissen Bight, but you'll have to hike in 15km on the established and relatively easy Cape Scott Trail to get there. From Nissen Bight, the trail winds eastwards to Shush-artie Bay. You'll be passing sandy coves, deserted beaches and dense, wind-whipped rainforest woodland, as well as a couple of river crossings on little cable cars. The trail is muddy and swampy in places, so there are boardwalks to make things easier. The area is home to elk, deer, cougars, wolves and black bears; make sure you know how to handle an encounter before you set off.

Like its west-coast sibling, the North Coast Trail is for experienced and well-equipped hikers only. There are backcountry campsites at Nissen Bight, Laura Creek and Shuttleworth Bight and the route should take five to eight days.

For more infortmation on visiting Cape Scott Provincial park and the North Coast Trail, visit www.capescottpark.com.

SOUTHERN GULF ISLANDS

Stressed Vancouverites often escape into the restorative arms of the rustic, ever-relaxed Southern Gulf Islands, strung like a necklace between the mainland and Vancouver Island. Formerly colonized by BC hippies and US draft dodgers, Salt Spring, Galiano, Mayne, Saturna, and North and South Pender Islands deliver on their promise of idyllic, sigh-triggering getaways.

❶ Getting There & Around

BC Ferries (www.bcferries.com) Operates services, some direct, from Vancouver Island's Swartz Bay terminal to all the main Southern Gulf Islands. There are also services from the mainland's Tsawwassen terminal.

Gulf Islands Water Taxi (http://saltspring.com/watertaxi) Runs a myriad of handy walk-on boat services between some of the islands.

Salt Spring Air (www.saltspringair.com) Floatplanes service the area with camera-hugging short hops from the mainland.

Salt Spring Island

POP 10,500

The busiest and most developed of the islands, Salt Spring has a reputation for palatial vacation homes, but it's also lined with artist studios and artisan food and drink producers. Well worth a long weekend visit, the heart of the community is Ganges.

◉ Sights & Activities

Saturday Market   MARKET
(www.saltspringmarket.com; Centennial Park, Ganges; ⊙8am-4pm Sat Apr-Oct) Locals tell you they avoid the gigantic Saturday Market that animates the heart of Ganges; they claim to do their shopping at the smaller Tuesday and Wednesday versions. But everyone on the island seems to be here on the big day, checking out the stalls topped with goodies made, baked or grown on the island.

Salt Spring Island Cheese   FARM
(www.saltspringcheese.com; 285 Reynolds Rd; ⊙10am-5pm) Drop by for a wander around the idyllic farmstead, and a tasting or two in the winery-style shop. Consider some Ruckles goat cheese to go.

Mistaken Identity Vineyards   WINERY
(www.mistakenidentityvineyards.com; 164 Noxton Rd; ⊙11am-6pm) If you're on a picnic-gathering push and need an accompanying libation, consider a tasting visit, with designated driver, to Mistaken Identity Vineyards, where the Bianco is the big seller.

Saltspring Island Ales   BREWERY
(www.gulfislandsbrewery.com; 270 Furness Rd; ⊙hours vary) Hit Saltspring Island Ales, where the rustic upstairs tasting room serves little samples of great beers. Consider a takeout growler of Heatherdale Ale.

Ruckle Provincial Park   PARK
(www.bcparks.ca) Head to Ruckle Provincial Park, a southeast gem with ragged shorelines and gnarly arbutus forests. There are trails for all skill levels, with Yeo Point making an ideal pit stop.

Salt Spring Adventure Co   KAYAKING
(☑250-537-2764, 877-537-2764; www.saltspring-adventures.com; 124 Upper Ganges Rd, Ganges; tours from $50) When it's time to hit the water, touch base with Salt Spring Adventure Co. It can kit you out for a bobbling kayak tour around Ganges Harbour.

☞ Tours

Salt Spring Studio Tour   TOUR
(www.saltspringstudiotour.com) Art fans should hit the trail on Salt Spring by checking out gallery and studio locations via the free downloadable *Studio Tour Map*. Highlights include **Blue Horse Folk Art Gallery** (www.bluehorse.ca; 175 North View Dr; ⊙10am-5pm Sun-Fri Mar-Dec) and **Duthie Gallery** (www.duthie-gallery.com; 125 Churchill Rd, Ganges; ⊙10am-5pm & 9-11pm Thu-Mon Jul & Aug), which stages the popular summer Night Gallery in its art-lined woodland park.

🛏 Sleeping & Eating

Harbour House Hotel   HOTEL $$
(☑888-799-5571, 250-537-5571; www.saltspring-harbourhouse.com; 121 Upper Ganges Rd, Ganges; d from $149; 🞎) This smashing rustic-chic hotel with 17 rooms is just up the hill from the main Ganges action, but it feels like staying in a country cottage estate in England. The immaculate grounds are strewn with locally made artworks and the waterfront views will have your camera itching to be used. The restaurant is high-end gourmet; breakfast is recommended.

Wisteria Guest House   B&B $$
(☑888-537-5899, 250-537-5899; www.wisteria-guesthouse.com; 268 Park Dr; d/cottage from $120/180; 🞎) This home-away-from-home

Southern Gulf Islands

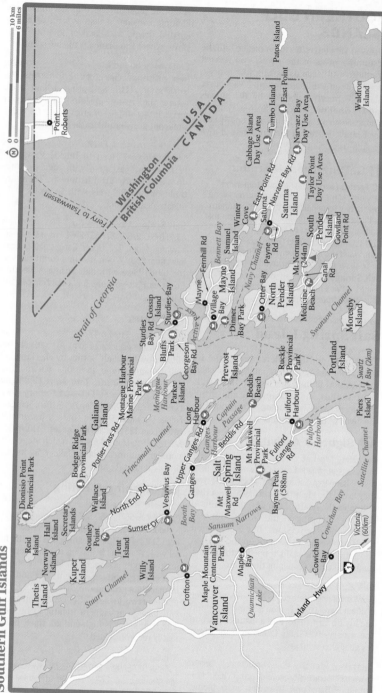

B&B has brightly painted guest rooms in the main building, some with shared bathrooms. There are also a pair of private-entrance studios and a small cottage with a compact kitchen – the immaculate studio 1 is our favorite. Breakfast is served in the large communal lounge, surrounded by a rambling, flower-strewn garden. A two-night minimum stay sometimes applies; check ahead.

Salt Spring Inn   HOTEL $$
(☑ 250-537-9339; www.saltspringinn.com; 132 Lower Ganges Rd, Ganges; d from $90; ☎) In the heart of Ganges and located above a popular bar, the seven small but well-maintained rooms at this friendly inn are popular with midrange travelers. The pricier deluxe rooms have sea views, en-suite bathrooms and fireplaces, while the standard rooms share bathrooms. All are well maintained and well located if you're stumbling up from the bar below after a few too many.

Salt Spring Coffee   CAFE $
(www.saltspringcoffee.com; 109 McPhillips Ave, Ganges; baked goods $3-8; ⊘ 6:30am-6pm Mon-Sat, 7am-5pm Sun) The perfect place to catch up on local gossip over some java – if you want to partake of the conservation, ask your neighbor whether or not they support expanding the Saturday Market. Cakes and wraps are also part of the mix at this ever-animated local legend.

★ Tree House Café   CAFE $$
(www.treehousecafe.ca; 106 Purvis Lane, Ganges; mains $10-16) At this magical outdoor dining experience in the heart of Ganges, you'll be sitting in the shade of a large plum tree as you choose from a menu of comfort pastas, Mexican specialties and gourmet burgers and sandwiches. The tuna melt is a local fave, perhaps washed down with a Saltspring Island Ales porter. There's live music every night in summer.

Gathering   FUSION $$
(115 Fulford Ganges Rd, Ganges; mains $8-16; ⊘ 11am-midnight Tue-Sun) Lined with sci-fi artworks and crammed with loaner board games, this new hangout is the perfect spot to spend a few hours. As for food, there's tapas, plus larger dishes combining local ingredients with international influences; think Moroccan spiced duck. Don't miss the crab-stuffed donuts, a menu standout perfect for fueling a leisurely evening of role-play gaming.

Restaurant House Piccolo   WEST COAST $$
(www.housepiccolo.com; 108 Hereford Ave, Ganges; mains $14-24; ⊘ 5-10pm Wed-Sun) White-tablecloth dining in a beaUtifully intimate heritage-house setting, this is the locals' top spot for a romantic night out. Focused on local seasonal ingredients prepared with knowing international flourishes, you'll find memorable seafood and duck dishes, as well as velvet-soft venison. For wine fans, you'll find the best drinks menu on the island.

❶ Information

Visitors Information Center (☑ 250-537-5252; www.saltspringtourism.com; 121 Lower Ganges Rd, Ganges; ⊘ 9am-5pm) The island has its own free app with a raft of resources for visitors; see www.hellosaltspring.com.

❶ Getting Around

The island's three ferry docks are at Long Harbour, Fulford Harbour and Vesuvius Bay. Water taxis and floatplanes arrive in Ganges Harbour.

If you don't have your own car, **Salt Spring Island Transit** (www.busonline.ca; adult/under 5yr $2/free) runs a five-route service around the island, connecting all three ferry docks. Bus 4 runs from Long Harbour to Ganges. Alternatively, **Amber Taxi Co** (☑ 250-537-3277) provides a local cab service. If you're flying in on Salt Spring Air, they provide free loaner bikes to passengers.

North & South Pender Islands

POP 2200

Once joined by a sandy isthmus, North and South Pender attract those looking for a quieter retreat. With pioneer farms, old-time orchards and dozens of coves and beaches, the islands – now linked by a single-lane bridge – are a good spot for bikers and hikers. For visitor information, check www.penderislandchamber.com.

❂ Sights & Activities

Enjoy the sand at **Medicine Beach** and **Clam Bay** on North Pender, as well as **Gowlland Point** on the east coast of South Pender. Just over the bridge to South Pender is **Mt Norman**, complete with a couple of hikes that promise grand views of the surrounding islands.

Farmers Market   MARKET
(www.pifi.ca; Pender Islands Recreation & Agriculture Hall, North Pender; ⊘ 9:30am-1pm Sat

Apr-Nov) The island has a regular Saturday farmers market in the community hall.

Pender Island Kayak Adventures KAYAKING
(www.kayakpenderisland.com; Otter Bay Marina; tours adult/child from $59/35) Hit the water with a paddle (and hopefully a boat) via the friendly folks here.

Tours

Pender Creatives WALKING TOUR
(www.pendercreatives.com) Many artists call Pender home and you can chat with them in their galleries and studios by downloading a pair of free maps from Pender Creatives that reveal exactly where they are. Most are on North Pender, where you can visit several within easy walking distance of each other.

Sleeping & Eating

Inn on Pender Island INN $$
(800-550-0172, 250-629-3353; www.innon-pender.com; 4709 Canal Rd, North Pender; d/cabins from $79/159) A rustic lodge with motel-style rooms and a couple of cozy, wood-lined cabins, you're surrounded by verdant woodland, which explains the frequent appearance of wandering deer. The lodge rooms are neat and clean and share an outdoor hot tub; the waterfront cabins have barrel-vaulted ceilings, full kitchens and little porches out front.

Shangri-La Oceanfront B&B B&B $$$
(250-629-3808, 877-629-2800; www.pender-islandshangrila.com; 5909 Pirate's Rd, North Pender; d from $199;) It's all about tranquility at this three-unit waterfront property, where each room has its own outdoor hot tub for drinking in the sunset through the trees. You'll have your own private entrance, plus pampering extrassuch as thick robes, large individual decks and a sumptuous breakfast. Our fave room is the Galaxy Suite, where the walls are painted with a glowing space theme.

Poet's Cove Resort & Spa HOTEL $$$
(250-629-2100, 888-512-7638; www.poetscove. com; 9801 Spalding Rd, Bedwell Harbour, South Pender; d from $250;) This luxurious harbor-front lodge has Arts and Crafts–accented rooms, most with great views across the glassy water. Extras include an activity center that books ecotours and fishing excursions; and an elegant West Coast restaurant, Aurora, where you can dine in style. As well as this, the resort offers kayak treks plus a full-treatment spa, complete with that all-important steam cave.

Pender Island Bakery Café CAFE $
(www.penderislandbakery.com; Driftwood Centre, 1105 Stanley Point Dr, North Pender; mains $6-16) At the locals' fave coffeehouse, the java is organic, as are many of the bakery treats, including some giant cinnamon buns, which will have you wrestling an islander for the last one. Gourmet pizzas are a highlight – the best is the Gulf Islander, with smoked oysters, anchovies, spinach and three cheeses. Heartier fare includes spinach and pine-nut pie and a bulging seafood lasagna.

Cafe at Hope Bay WEST COAST $$
(www.thecafeathopebay.com; 4301 Bedwell Harbour Rd, North Pender; mains $14-23; 11am-8:30pm Tue-Sun) West Coast ingredients with inter-national influences rule at this bistro-style spot, closely followed by the sterling views across Plumper Sound. Just a few minutes from the Otter Bay ferry dock, the fish and chips is predictably good, but dig deeper into the menu for less-expected treats, like the lip-smacking coconut curried mussels and prawns.

Getting Around

Ferries stop at North Pender's Otter Bay. Pender also has a cool 'public transit' system, where car-driving locals pick up at designated stops across the islands. If you're driving, you can pick up a green card at the ferry dock to indicate you're also willing to pick up passengers.

Galiano Island

POP 1100

With the most ecological diversity of the Southern Gulf Islands, this skinny landmass – named after a 1790s Spanish explorer – offers activities for marine enthusiasts and landlubbers alike.

The Sturdies Bay ferry end is markedly busier than the rest of the island, which becomes ever more forested and tranquil as you continue your drive from the dock. Drop into the **visitors info booth** (www.galianoisland.com; 2590 Sturdies Bay Rd; Jul & Aug) before you leave the ferry area, though. There's also a garage, post office and book-store nearby.

Once you've got your bearings – that is, driven off the ferry – head for **Montague Harbour Marine Provincial Park** for trails to beaches, meadows and a cliff carved by glaciers. In contrast, **Bodega Ridge Provincial Park** is renowned for its eagle and cormorant bird life and has spectacular drop-off viewpoints.

The protected waters of **Trincomali Channel** and the more chaotic waters of **Active Pass** satisfy paddlers of all skill levels. **Galiano Kayaks** (☑ 250-539-2442; www.seakayak.ca; 3451 Montague Rd; 2hr/day rental from $32/58, tours from $55) can help with rentals and guided tours. If you fancy exploring on land, rent a moped from **Galiano Adventures** (www.galianoadventures.com; Montague Harbour Marina; rental per hour from $20; ☺ May-Sep).

Among the places to sleep on the island, sophisticates will enjoy **Galiano Inn** (☑ 877-530-3939, 250-539-3388; www.galianoinn.com; 134 Madrona Dr; d from $249; ☎ ⚕), a Tuscan-style villa with 10 elegant rooms, each with a fireplace and romantic oceanfront terrace. It's close to the Sturdies Bay ferry dock. Those craving a nature-hugging retreat will also enjoy **Bodega Ridge** (☑ 877-604-2677, 250-539-2677; www.bodegaridge.com; 120 Manastee Rd; cabin from $250; ☎ ⚕), a tranquil woodland clutch of seven cedar cabins at the other end of the island.

Fuel up on breakfast, treats and local gossip at **Sturdies Bay Bakery Cafe** (2450 Sturdies Bay Rd; ☺ 7am-3pm Mon-Thu, to 5pm Fri-Sun; ☎). Once you're done exploring the island, drop in for beer and fish and chips at the venerable **Hummingbird Pub** (www.hummingbirdpub.com; 47 Sturdies Bay Rd; mains $8-12), where you'll likely spot some of the same people you saw at breakfast on the patio.

Ferries arrives at the Sturdies Bay dock.

Saturna Island

POP 325

Suffused with tranquility, tiny Saturna is a natural retreat remote enough to deter casual visitors. Almost half the island, laced with curving bays, stunning rock bluffs and towering arbutus trees, is part of the Gulf Islands National Park Reserve and the only crowds you'll see are feral goats that have called this munchable area home. If you've had enough of civilization, this is the place to be.

◉ Sights & Activities

On the north side of the island, **Winter Cove** has a white-sand beach that's popular for swimming, boating and fishing.

Great for a hike is **Mt Warburton Pike** (497m), where you'll spot wild goats, soaring eagles and restorative panoramic views of the surrounding islands: focus your binoculars and you might spy a whale or two sailing quietly along the coast.

Saturna Island Winery　　　WINERY
(www.saturnavineyards.com; 8 Quarry Rd; ☺ 11:30am-5pm) Wine fans can partake of tastings and tours at Saturna Island Winery, which also has an on-site bistro. The winery is south of the ferry terminal, via East Point Rd and Harris Rd.

✦✦ Festivals & Events

Lamb Barbeque　　　FOOD
(www.saturnalambbarbeque.com; adult/child $20/10; ☺ Jul 1) If you're here for Canada Day, you should also partake of the island's main annual event in the Hunter Field, adjoining Winter Cove. The communal event, complete with live music, sack races, beer garden and a carnivorous feast, is centered on a fire pit surrounded by staked-out, slow-roasting sheep.

⌖ Sleeping & Eating

Saturna Lodge　　　HOTEL $$
(☑ 250-539-2254, 866-539-2254; www.saturna.ca; 130 Payne Rd; d from $129; ☎) A peaceful respite from the outside world, this friendly lodge property is surrounded by a tree-fringed garden and offers six country-inn-style rooms – go for the spacious honeymoon suite. You're not far from the waterfront and rates include a hearty breakfast to keep you going for a full day of exploring.

★ **Wild Thyme Coffee House**　　　CAFE $
(www.wildthymecoffeehouse.com; 109 East Point Rd; mains $6-10; ☺ 6am-2pm Mon-Fri, 8am-4pm Sat & Sun; ☎) Located in and around a converted and immaculately preserved antique double-decker bus named Lucy, this charming local landmark is handily located not far from the ferry dock. Diners can snag seats inside the bus, where tables have been added, and tuck into wholesome breakfasts, soup and sandwich lunches, and baked treats all made with foodie love. There's a focus on local ingredients and fair trade coffee.

BRITISH COLUMBIA SATURNA ISLAND

ℹ Information

Saturna Island Tourism Association (www.saturnatourism.com) Visit the Saturna Island Tourism Association website for more information.

ℹ Getting Around

The ferry docks at Lyall Harbour on the west of the island. A car is not essential here since some lodgings are near the ferry terminal. Only bring your bike if you like a challenge: Saturna is a little hilly for casual pedalers.

Mayne Island

POP 900

Once a stopover for gold-rush miners, who nicknamed it 'Little Hell,' Mayne is the region's most historic island. Long past its importance as a commercial hub, it now houses a colorful clutch of resident artists.

The heritage **Agricultural Hall** in Miners Bay hosts the lively **farmers market** (⊘10am-1pm Sat Jul-Sep) of local crafts and produce. Among the most visit-worthy galleries and artisan studios on the island is **Mayne Island Glass Foundry** (www.mayneislandglass.com; 563 Aya Reach Rd), where recycled glass is used to fashion new jewelry and ornaments – pick up a cool green-glass slug for the road.

The south shore's **Dinner Bay Park** has a lovely sandy beach, as well as an immaculate **Japanese Garden**, built by locals to commemorate early-20th-century Japanese residents.

For kayakers and stand-up paddleboarders, **Bennett Bay Kayaking** (www.bennettbaykayaking.com; kayak rentals/tours from $33/65; ⊘Apr-Oct) can get you out on the water via rentals and tours.

If you're just too tired to head back to the mainland, **Mayne Island Beach Resort** (☑866-539-5399; www.mayneislandresort.com; 494 Arbutus Dr; d from $139; ☎✿☒☒) combines oceanview rooms in a century-old inn with swanky luxe beach cottages. There's a spa and large restaurant-bar.

If it's time to eat, head for a patio seat at the ever-friendly **Green House Bar & Grill** (454 Village Bay Rd; mains $8-16; ⊘noon-8pm Wed-Sun) and dive into fresh-made fries and heaping burgers.

For further visitor information, see www.mayneislandchamber.ca.

If you didn't bring your own car via the ferry, just stick out your thumb: most locals are always ready to pick up a passenger or two.

FRASER & THOMPSON VALLEYS

Vancouverites looking for an inland escape shoot east on Hwy 1 through the fertile plains of places like Abbotsford. Most just whiz past this farmland and you should too, unless you have a hankering to see a turnip in the rough. The Fraser Canyon thrills with stunning river gorge beauty while the Thompson River looks little changed in decades.

ℹ Information

About 150km east of Vancouver, Hope has a good **visitors center** (☑604-869-2021; www.hope.ca; 919 Water Ave; ⊘9am-5pm) with plenty of information about the local provincial parks and the region.

EC Manning Provincial Park

After the farmlands of the Lower Mainland, this 708-sq-km **provincial park** (☑604-795-6169; www.bcparks.ca), 30km southeast of Hope, is a hint of bigger – much bigger – things to come in the east; think Rocky Mountains. It packs in a lot: dry valleys; dark, mountainous forests; roiling rivers; and alpine meadows. It makes a good pause along Hwy 3, but don't expect solitude as there are scores of folk from the burgs west seeking the same.

The following hiking choices are easily reached from Hwy 3:

Dry Ridge Trail Crosses from dry interior to alpine climate; excellent views and wildflowers (3km round trip, one hour).

Canyon Nature Trail Nice loop trail with a river crossing on a bridge (2km, 45 minutes).

Lightning Lake Loop The perfect intro: a level loop around this central lake. Look for critters in the evening (9km, two hours).

Manning is a four-seasons playground. **Manning Park Resort** (☑800-330-3321, 250-840-8822; www.manningpark.com; 7500 Hwy 3; dm $35, r $80-300) offers downhill skiing and snowboarding (adult/child day pass $50/30) and 100km of groomed trails for cross-country skiing and snowshoeing. It also has the only indoor accommodations throughout the park. The 73 rooms are housed in the lodge and cabins. All provide use of the

Fraser & Thompson Valleys

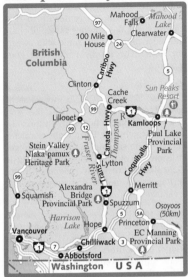

Just 2km north of Spuzzum, **Alexandra Bridge Provincial Park** (☑604-795-6169; www.bcparks.ca; off Hwy 1) makes for a scenic stop, where you can picnic while gazing up at the historic 1926 span. Further north, the ecologically diverse **Stein Valley Nlaka'pamux Heritage Park** (www.bcparks.ca; Stein Valley Rd, Lytton) is managed together with the Lytton First Nation. It offers some excellent long-distance hiking through dry valleys and snow-clad peaks amid one of the best-preserved watersheds in lower BC.

White-water rafting down the Fraser and its tributaries' fast-flowing rapids is popular and a number of companies near Lytton lead trips. One-day trips cost from $150 per adult. **Kumsheen Rafting Resort** (☑800-663-6667; www.kumsheen.com; Hwy 1, 5km east of Lytton; campsites/teepees from $35/130) offers a variety of trips and funky accommodations. **Fraser River Raft Expeditions** (☑604-863-2336; www.fraserraft.com; 30950 Hwy 1, Yale; trips from $150) covers all the main waterways.

requisite hot tub. In summer enjoy the Alpine splendor on day hikes.

You can pitch your tent at **Coldspring**, **Hampton** or **Mule campgrounds** (campsites $21) or the more popular **Lightning Lake campground** (☑reservations 800-689-9025; www.discovercamping.ca; campsites $28), which takes reservations. There are 10 **backcountry campgrounds** (campsites per person $5) for overnight hikers that are normally not accessible before late June.

The park's **visitors center** (Hwy 3; ⊙9am-6pm) is 30km inside the western boundary and has detailed hiking descriptions and a relief model of the park and nearby beaver ponds.

Greyhound Canada (☑800-661-8747; www.greyhound.ca) has buses from Vancouver ($46, 2½ to four hours, two daily).

Fraser River Canyon

The name alone makes Spuzzum a fun stop along Hwy 1 on its way to Cache Creek, 85km west of Kamloops. The road shadows the swiftly flowing Fraser River and, as you'd expect, white-water rafting is huge here. The grand scenery and several good provincial parks make this a winning trip.

Kamloops

POP 87,300

If you've opted to follow Hwy 1 from Vancouver east to the Rockies and Banff, Kamloops makes a useful break in the journey. Motels abound and there's a walkable heritage center. Historically, the Shuswap First Nation found the many rivers and lakes useful for transportation and salmon fishing. Traders set up camp for fur hunting in 1811.

The focus of the downtown area is tree-lined Victoria St, which is a lively place on sunny days; very busy train tracks separate the wide Thompson River from downtown. Franchises and malls line the highlands along Hwy 1.

◉ Sights

Using Victoria St as your anchor, stroll downtown, stopping at the art gallery and museum.

Kamloops Museum & Archives MUSEUM
(☑250-828-3576; www.kamloops.ca/museum; cnr Seymour St & 2nd Ave; adult/child $3/1; ⊙9:30am-4:30pm Tue, Wed, Fri & Sat, to 7:30pm Thu Jun-Aug) Kamloops Museum is in a vintage building and has a suitably vintage collection of historic photographs. Come here for the scoop on river-namesake David Thompson and an entire floor dedicated to kids.

ⓘ WHICH ROAD?

Coming from Vancouver and the Lower Mainland, Hwy 1 does a three-way split at Hope. Your choices:

Hwy 1 Continue north on one of the world's great scenic drives, literally through the vertical walls of the beautiful Fraser Canyon. From Lytton, it follows the Thompson River and the terrain slowly smooths out and becomes drier, foreshadowing the ranchlands of the Cariboo region to the north beyond Cache Creek, where you can turn east for Kamloops. Note that this entire route can get choked with traffic.

Hwy 5 A multilane marvel that shoots 200km northeast to the commercial center of Kamloops through steep and pretty mountain scenery.

Hwy 3 The Crowsnest Hwy takes a circuitous and scenic course east through rugged EC Manning Provincial Park and on to Osoyoos and the southern Okanagan Valley.

Kamloops Heritage Railway　　HISTORIC TRAIN
(☏250-374-2141; www.kamrail.com; 510 Lorne St) Across the train tracks from downtown, the Kamloops Heritage Railway runs steam-engine-powered excursions, although at the time of writing it was shut for maintenance.

Kamloops Art Gallery　　GALLERY
(☏250-377-2400; www.kag.bc.ca; 465 Victoria St; adult/child $5/3; ⊙10am-5pm Mon-Wed, Fri & Sat, to 9pm Thu) Suitably loft-like in feel, this gallery has an emphasis on contemporary Western and aboriginal works by regional artists.

BC Wildlife Park　　ZOO
(☏250-573-3242; www.bczoo.org; Hwy 1; adult/child $15/11; ⊙9:30am-5pm) This small zoo has examples of province natives such as bears and cougars.

Paul Lake Provincial Park　　PARK
(☏250-819-7376; www.bcparks.ca; Pinantan Rd; campsites $16) On the often-hot summer days, the beach at Paul Lake Provincial Park beckons and you may spot falcons and coyotes. There is a 20km mountain-biking loop. It's 24km northeast of Kamloops via Hwy 5.

🛏 Sleeping

Older and shabbier motels can be found along a stretch of Hwy 1 east of downtown. Columbia St, from the center up to Hwy 1 above town, has another gaggle of chain and older indie motels, some with sweeping views. The nearby parks have good camping.

★Plaza Hotel　　HOTEL $$
(☏877-977-5292, 250-377-8075; www.plazaheritagehotel.com; 405 Victoria St; r $90-250; ❄✳🖧) In a town of bland modernity in the lodging department, the Plaza reeks character. This 67-room six-story classic has changed little on the outside since its opening in 1928. Rooms are newly redone in a chic heritage style and it does excellent free breakfasts.

Scott's Inn　　MOTEL $$
(☏250-372-8221; www.scottsinn.com; 551 11th Ave; r $90-150; ✳@🖧🏊) Unlike many budget competitors, Scott's is close to the center and very well run. The 51 rooms are standard for a motel, but extras include an indoor pool, hot tub, cafe and rooftop sun deck.

South Thompson Inn Guest Ranch　　LODGE $$
(☏800-797-7713, 250-573-3777; www.stigr.com; 3438 Shuswap Rd; r $130-260; ✳🖧🏊) Some 20km west of town via Hwy 1, this ranch-like waterfront lodge is perched on the banks of the South Thompson and set amid rolling grasslands. Its 57 rooms are spread between the wood-framed main building, a small manor house and some converted stables.

🍴 Eating & Drinking

Look for the free booklet *Farm Fresh,* which details the many local producers you can visit. Local farmers markets are held Wednesday (corner of 5th Ave and Victoria St) and Saturday (corner of 2nd Ave and St Paul St). Victoria St is the place for nightlife.

★Art We Are　　CAFE $
(www.theartweare.com; 246 Victoria St; mains from $8; ⊙9am-9pm Mon-Fri, to 11pm Sat; 🖧🍴) Tea joint, local artist venue, hangout, bakery and more, this funky cafe is a great place to let some Kamloops hours slip by. The organic menu changes daily. Saturday night has live music.

Hello Toast
CAFE $

(☑250-372-9322; www.hellotoastkamloops.ca; 428 Victoria St; mains $5-9; ☺7:30am-3pm; ☑)
🍴 As opposed to Good Morning Croissant, this veggie-friendly, organic cafe offers whole grains for some, and fried combos of bacon and eggs or burgers for others. Nice open front and sidewalk tables.

Chapter's Viewpoint Restaurant
FUSION $$

(☑250-374-3224; www.chaptersviewpoint. com; 610 Columbia St; mains $12-26; ☺7-10am, 11:30am-2pm & 5-9pm) The patio overlooking Kamloops is the best place to be on a balmy summer evening. The menu features steaks and salmon, but the New Mexican route is recommended.

Commodore
PUB

(☑250-851-3100; www.commodorekamloops. com; 369 Victoria St; ☺11am-late Mon-Sat) An old-style pub with a long menu that highlights burgers and fondue (mains from $12), the Com is the place on Friday nights for live jazz and funk. Other nights, DJs spin pretty much anything.

🛈 Information

The **visitors center** (☑800-662-1994, 250-374-3377; www.tourismkamloops.com; 1290 W Hwy 1, exit 368; ☺8am-6pm; ☎) is just off Hwy 1, overlooking town.

🛈 Getting There & Around

Greyhound Canada (☑800-661-8747; www. greyhound.ca) is about 1km southwest of the center off Columbia St W.

TO	FARE	DURATION	FREQUENCY (PER DAY)
Calgary	$93	9hr	3
Jasper	$70	5½hr	1
Kelowna	$35	2½-5hr	3
Prince George	$93	7hr	2
Vancouver	$64	5hr	6

VIA Rail (☑888-842-7245; www.viarail.ca) serves Kamloops North Station, 11km from town, with the triweekly Canadian on its run from Vancouver (9½ hours) to Jasper (9½ hours) and beyond. Fares vary greatly by season and class of service.

Kamloops Transit System (☑250-376-1216; www.transitbc.com/regions/kam; adult/child $2.25/1.75) runs local buses.

Around Kamloops

The hills looming northeast of Kamloops are home to **Sun Peaks Resort** (☑800-807-3257; www.sunpeaksresort.com; 1280 Alpine Rd; lift tickets adult/child winter $79/40, summer $39/23). This ever-growing resort boasts 125 ski runs (including some 8km-long powder trails), 11 lifts and a pleasant base-area village. In summer, lifts provide access to more than two dozen mountain-bike trails.

Those saving their cash for the slopes and/or trails choose the **Sun Peaks Hostel** (☑250-578-0057; www.sunpeakshostel.com; 1140 Sun Peaks Rd; dm/d from $30/70; ☎) over the many lodges, B&Bs and luxury condos.

Past the resort road, Hwy 5 continues north toward the Alberta border and Jasper National Park (440km from Kamloops). Along the way, it passes near Wells Gray Provincial Park (125km from Kamloops), one of BC's finest and a haven for those who really want to get away from civilization.

OKANAGAN VALLEY

It is hard to know which harvest is growing faster in this fertile and beautiful valley: tourists or fruit. Certainly, bounty abounds in this ever-more-popular lovely swath midway between Vancouver and Alberta. The moniker 'Canada's Napa Valley' is oft repeated and somewhat apt. The 180km-long Okanagan Valley is home to dozens of excellent wineries, whose vines spread across the terraced hills, soaking up some of Canada's sunniest weather.

This emphasis on highbrow refreshments contrasts with the valley's traditional role as a summertime escape for generations of Canadians, who frolic in the string of lakes linking the Okanagan's towns. And while retirees mature slowly in the sun, so do orchards of peaches, apricots and other fruits that may not have the cachet of grapes, but which give the air a perfumery redolence at the peak of summer.

Near the US border, Osoyoos is almost arid, but things soon become greener heading north. Near the center, Kelowna is one of the fastest-growing cities in Canada. It's a heady mix of culture, lakeside beauty and fun. In July and August, however, the entire valley can seem as overburdened as a grapevine right before the harvest. For many, the best time to visit is late spring and early fall, when the crowds are manageable.

Summer days are usually dry and hot, with the nights pleasantly cool. Winters are snowy but dry, making nearby Big White an attraction for skiers and snowboarders.

Osoyoos

POP 4900

Once-modest Osoyoos is embracing an upscale and developed future. The town takes its name from the First Nations word 'soyoos,' which means 'sand bar across' and, even if the translation is a bit rough, the definition is not: much of the town is indeed on a narrow spit of land that divides Osoyoos Lake. It is ringed with beaches and the waters irrigate the lush farms, orchards and vineyards that line Hwy 97 going north out of town.

Nature's bounty aside, this is the arid end of the valley and locals like to say that the town marks the northern end of Mexico's Sonoran Desert; much of the town is done up in a manner that loses something across two borders. From the cactus-speckled sands to the town's cheesy faux-tile-and-stucco architecture, it's a big change from the BC image of pine trees and mountains found in both directions on Hwy 3.

◎ Sights & Activities

Osoyoos Lake is one of the warmest in the country. That, together with the sandy beaches, means great swimming, a huge relief when the summer temp hits 42°C (108°F). Many lakeside motels and campgrounds hire out kayaks, canoes and small boats.

For sweeping valley views, go just 3km east of town up Hwy 3. About 8km west of town on Hwy 3, look for Spotted Lake, a weird natural phenomenon that once would have made a kitschy roadside attraction. In the hot summer sun, the lake's water begins to evaporate, causing its high mineral content to crystallize and leave white-rimmed circles of green on the water.

★ Osoyoos Desert Centre   PARK
(☑250-495-2470; www.desert.org; off Hwy 97; adult/child $7/6; ☺9:30am-4:30pm May-Sep, call other times) Hear the rattle of a snake and the songs of birds at the Osoyoos Desert Centre,

3km north of town, which has interpretive kiosks along raised boardwalks that meander through the dry land. The nonprofit center offers 90-minute guided tours. Special gardens focus on delights like delicate wildflowers.

Nk'Mip Desert & Heritage Centre   MUSEUM
(☑250-495-7901; www.nkmipdesert.com; 1000 Rancher Creek Rd; adult/child $14/10; ☺9:30am-6pm Jul & Aug, call other times) Part of a First Nations empire, the Nk'Mip Desert & Heritage Centre, off 45th St north of Hwy 3, features cultural demonstrations and tours of the arid ecology. It also has a desert golf course, the noted winery Nk'Mip Cellars, a resort and more.

3 Phase Adventures   WATER SPORTS
(☑250-498-9989; www.3phaseadventures.com; Cottonwood Beach; board rental per hour from $25; ☺Jun-Sep) Osoyoos Lake is mirror flat, perfect for paddleboard high jinks. From this pretty beach location, rent or take lessons.

Double O Bikes   BICYCLE RENTAL
(☑250-495-3312; www.doubleobikes.com; 8905 Main St; bicycle rental per day from adult/child $24/20; ☺9:30am-5pm) Trails wander through the vineyards and along the lakes, making the valley a prime biking locale. There's a second location in Oliver.

🛏 Sleeping & Eating

The eastern edge of the lake is lined with campgrounds. More than a dozen modest motels line the narrow strip of land that splits Osoyoos Lake, but beware of shabby older properties. Many cluster around Hwy 3 and there's another clump on the southwest shore near the border. Chains can be found at the junction.

Nk'Mip Campground &
RV Resort   CAMPGROUND $
(☑250-495-7279; www.campingosoyoos.com; 8000 45th St; campsites/RV sites from $30/35) Over 300 sites at this year-round lakeside resort off Hwy 3.

Sandy Beach Motel   MOTEL $$
(☑866-495-6931, 250-495-6931; www.sandybeachmotel.com; 6706 Ponderosa Dr; r $90-280; ❄@) Free canoes, kayaks and a volleyball court set the cheery tone at this 27-unit beachside place just north of Hwy 3. Bungalows and two-story blocks surround a shady lawn with BBQs.

Okanagan Valley

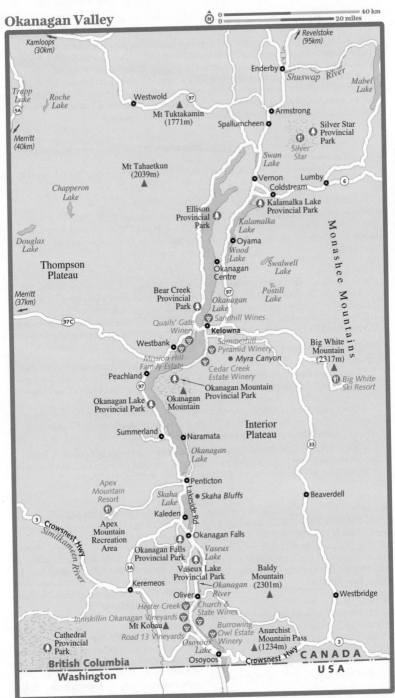

0 — 40 km
0 — 20 miles

Kamloops (30km)

Revelstoke (95km)

Trapp Lake

Roche Lake

Westwold

Enderby

Shuswap River

Mabel Lake

Mt Tuktakamin (1771m)

Spallumcheen

Armstrong

Silver Star Provincial Park

Silver Star

Merritt (40km)

Swan Lake

Chapperon Lake

Mt Tahaetkun (2039m)

Vernon

Coldstream

Lumby

Kalamalka Lake Provincial Park

Douglas Lake

Thompson Plateau

Ellison Provincial Park

Kalamalka Lake

Oyama

Wood Lake

Swalwell Lake

Monashee Mountains

Merritt (37km)

Okanagan Centre

Okanagan Lake

Bear Creek Provincial Park

Postill Lake

Quails' Gate Winery

Sandhill Wines

Kelowna

Big White Mountain (2317m)

Westbank

Summerhill Pyramid Winery

Myra Canyon

Mission Hill Family Estate

Cedar Creek Estate Winery

Big White Ski Resort

Peachland

Okanagan Mountain Provincial Park

Okanagan Lake Provincial Park

Okanagan Mountain

Interior Plateau

Summerland

Naramata

Okanagan Lake

33

Apex Mountain Resort

Penticton

Beaverdell

Skaha Lake

Skaha Bluffs

Lakeside Rd

Kaleden

Crowsnest Hwy

Simikameen River

Apex Mountain Recreation Area

Okanagan Falls

Okanagan Falls Provincial Park

Vaseux Lake

3A

Vaseux Lake Provincial Park

Baldy Mountain (2301m)

Keremeos

Okanagan River

Westbridge

Oliver

Hester Creek

Church & State Wines

Inniskillin Okanagan Vineyards

Cathedral Provincial Park

Mt Kobau

Road 13 Vineyards

Burrowing Owl Estate Winery

Anarchist Mountain Pass (1234m)

Osoyoos Lake

CANADA

British Columbia

Osoyoos

Crowsnest Hwy

USA

Washington

OKANAGAN VALLEY WINERIES

The abundance of sunshine, fertile soil and cool winters has allowed the local wine industry to thrive. Kelowna and the region north are known for whites, such as pinot grigio. South, near Penticton and Oliver, reds are the stars, especially the ever-popular merlots.

A majority of the more than 100 wineries are close to Hwy 97, which makes tasting a breeze. Most offer tours and all will gladly sell you a bottle or 20; in fact, many of the best wines are only sold at the wineries. Many feature excellent cafes and bistros that offer fine views and complex regional fare to complement what's in the glass.

Festivals

Okanagan seasonal **wine festivals** (www.thewinefestivals.com) are major events, especially the one in fall.

The usual dates are fall (early October), winter (mid-January), spring (early May) and summer (early August).

Information

Two good sources of information on Okanagan Valley wines are the **BC Wine Information Centre** in Penticton's visitors center (p216) and the BC Wine Museum & VQA Wine Shop (p217) in Kelowna. *John Schreiner's Okanagan Wine Tour Guide* is an authoritative guidebook.

Tours

There are numerous companies that let you do the sipping while they do the driving.

Club Wine Tours (☎866-386-9463, 250-762-9951; www.clubwinetours.com; 3-7hr tours $65-125) The 'signature' tour includes four wineries and lunch in a vineyard.

Distinctly Kelowna Tours (☎866-979-1211, 250-979-1211; www.wildflowersandwine.com; 3½-9hr tours $90-150) Offers winery tours by valley region; many include stops for lunch.

Visiting the Wineries

At wineries open for visitors, you can expect to taste wine, but the experience varies greatly. Some places have just a couple of wines on offer; others offer dozens of vintages. Some tasting rooms are just glorified sales areas; others have magnificent views of the vineyards, valley and lakes. Some charge; others are free.

Among the dozens of options, the following (listed north to south) are recommended. Summerhill Pyramid and Cedar Creek Estate are south of Kelowna along the lake's east shore. The rest of the wineries can be reached via Hwy 97.

Sandhill Wines (☎250-762-3332; www.sandhillwines.ca; 1125 Richter St, Kelowna; ⊗9am-6pm) Near Kelowna's Cultural District and one of BC's largest producers, Calona Vineyards (Sandhill's owner) was the first in the Okanagan Valley, starting in 1932.

Avalon Inn MOTEL $$
(☎800-264-5999, 250-495-6334; www.avaloninn.ca; 9106 Main St; r $90-180; ✳@⊚) Away from the lake but close to the best restaurants, this 20-unit motel has large rooms and gardens that get more ornate by the year. Some rooms have kitchens.

★ **Dolci Deli** CAFE $
(☎250-495-6807; www.dolcideli.com; 8710 Main St; mains $9-15; ⊗8am-4pm Mon-Fri, to 2pm Sat & Sun) Tucked into a small storefront mid-block, it's easy to miss this cafe, but that would be a mistake. Simple fare is transcendent thanks to their passionate flair for food provenance – even the bacon is smoked in house. Get a table on the terrace.

Osoyoos Gelato GELATO $
(☎250-495-5425; www.osoyoosgelato.com; 15 Park Pl, Watermark Beach Resort; gelato from $3; ⊗11:30am-9:30pm Jun-Sep) Downtown near the lake, there are always at least 24 splendid house-made flavors.

Wildfire Grill CANADIAN $$
(☎250-495-2215; 8526 Main St; mains $15-25; ⊗11am-10pm) Wildfire serves up sandwiches, pizzas, steaks and salmon with global accents. Tables in the courtyard are always in demand, especially on long summer nights.

Summerhill Pyramid Winery (☑250-764-8000; www.summerhill.bc.ca; 4870 Chute Lake Rd, Kelowna; ☉9am-7pm) On Kelowna's eastern shore, wines are aged in a huge pyramid. Noted for ice wine, it has a cafe.

Cedar Creek Estate Winery (☑250-764-8866; www.cedarcreek.bc.ca; 5445 Lakeshore Rd, Kelowna; ☉10am-7pm) Known for excellent tours, as well as Rieslings and Ehrenfelser, a refreshing fruity white wine. The **Vineyard Terrace** (mains $12-20; ☉11am-4pm Jun-Sep) is good for lunch.

Quails' Gate Winery (☑250-769-4451; www.quailsgate.com; 3303 Boucherie Rd, Kelowna; ☉10am-8pm) A small winery with a huge reputation, it's known for its pinot noir, chardonnay and chenin blanc. The **Old Vines Restaurant** (mains $20-30; ☉11:30am-9pm) is among the best.

★ **Mission Hill Family Estate** (☑250-768-7611; www.missionhillwinery.com; 1730 Mission Hill Rd, Westbank; ☉10am-6pm) Like a Tuscan hill town, this winery's architecture wows. Go for a taste of one of the blended reds (try the Bordeaux) or the excellent Syrah. **Terrace** (mains $25-33; ☉11am-9pm Jun-Oct) is one of the valley's finest restaurants and sources fine foods locally; book ahead.

Hester Creek (☑250-498-4435; www.hestercreek.com; 877 Road 8, Oliver; ☉10am-8pm Jul-Oct) Has a sweeping location and is known for its reds, especially is richly flavored cabernet franc. Terrafina (p212) has a Tuscan accent.

Inniskillin Okanagan Vineyards (☑250-498-6663; www.inniskillin.com; Road 11 W, Oliver; ☉10am-5pm) BC's first producer of zinfandel is also home to the elixirs known as ice wines; go for the golden-hued Riesling.

Road 13 Vineyards (☑250-498-8330; www.road13vineyards.com; 799 Ponderosa Rd, Road 13, Oliver; ☉10am-5:30pm) Its very drinkable reds (pinot noir) and whites (chenin blanc) win plaudits. The no-frills vibe extends to the picnic tables with gorgeous views and the motto 'It's all about dirt.'

Church & State Wines (☑250-498-2700; www.churchandstatewines.com; 31120 87th St, Osoyoos; ☉11am-6pm) This newcomer south of Oliver is making a big impression at its Coyote Bowl vineyards, especially with its full-bodied, luscious Syrahs.

Burrowing Owl Estate Winery (☑250-498-0620; www.bovwine.ca; 500 Burrowing Owl Pl, Oliver; ☉10am-5pm Mar-Dec) Wine with an eco-accent that includes organic farm techniques; try the Syrah. This Golden Mile landmark includes a hotel and the excellent Sonora Room (p212).

There's a stylish lounge area for enjoying the local wine bounty by the glass.

ℹ Information

The large **visitors center** (☑888-676-9667, 250-495-5070; www.destinationosoyoos.com; cnr Hwys 3 & 97; ☉9am-6pm; 🛜) has internet access, maps and books, and it can book bus tickets and accommodation.

ℹ Getting There & Away

Greyhound Canada (☑800-661-8747; www.greyhound.ca; cnr Hwys 3 & 97) runs to Vancouver ($80, 8½ hours, one daily) from outside the visitors center. There is no useful bus service north up the valley.

Around Osoyoos

West of Osoyoos, Hwy 3 follows the rugged Similkameen Valley for 47km to **Keremeos**, a cute town surrounded by orchards.

About 30km west of Keremeos is **Cathedral Provincial Park** (☑604-795-6169; www.bcparks.ca; Ashnola Rd; campsites $11), a 330-sq-km mountain wilderness that's a playground for the truly adventurous. The park offers excellent backcountry camping ($10) and hiking around wildflower-dappled alpine expanses and turquoise waters.

Oliver

POP 4900

Oliver is a center for organic produce and wine. Over the 20km drive between Oliver and Osoyoos, Hwy 97 plunges through orchard after orchard laden with lush fruits, earning it the moniker 'The Golden Mile.' Roadside stands display the ripe bounty and many places will let you pick your own.

◉ Sights & Activities

The small roads through the vineyards around Oliver are made for exploring on a bike. Local walking and biking routes include the excellent 10km **Golden Mile Trail**.

Pick up the heritage walking tour brochure from the tourist office to fully appreciate this traditional orchard town.

Double O Bikes   BICYCLE RENTAL
(☑ 250-498-8348; www.doubleobikes.com; 35653 Main St; bicycle rental per day from adult/child $24/20; ☺ 9:30am-5pm) Has good route advice and another store in Osoyoos.

🛏 Sleeping & Eating

Oliver's vibrant **farmers market** (Lion's Park, Hwy 97; ☺ 8-11am & 4-7pm Thu) showcases local foodstuffs and is just off Hwy 97.

Mount View Motel   MOTEL $$
(☑ 250-498-3446; www.mountviewmotel.net; 5856 Main St; r $80-120; ❄ 🤖) Close to the center of town, seven units sunbathe around a flower-bedecked motor court. All have kitchens – and corkscrews. The decor is simple and cute.

★**Burrowing Owl Guest House**   BOUTIQUE HOTEL $$$
(☑ 877-498-0620, 250-498-0620; www.bovwine.ca; off Black Sage Rd; r $170-300; ❄ @ 🤖 ☀) One of the Okanagan's best wineries has 10 rooms with patios facing southwest over the vineyards. There's a big pool, hot tub, king-size beds and corporate mission-style decor. The **Sonora Room** (mains $15-35; ☺ 11:30am-9pm) is noted for its fusion cuisine. It's 13km south of Oliver, off Hwy 97.

Hester Creek   INN $$$
(☑ 250-498-4435; www.hestercreek.com; 877 Road 8; r $200-300; ❄ 🤖) One of the valley's top wineries, Hester Creek has six rooms in a plush Mediterranean-style villa with a sweeping view over the vineyards. The trappings are plush, with fireplaces, soaking tubs

and more. **Terrafina** (☑ 250-495-3278; www.terrafinarestaurant.com; mains $18-34; ☺ 11:30am-9pm) has excellent Tuscan-accented fare, using foods from the region.

Medici's Gelateria   GELATO $
(☑ 250-498-2228; www.medicisgelateria.ca; 522 Fairview Rd; gelato from $3; ☺ 10am-6pm) Frozen delights so good you'll want to worship – and you easily can, given this is an old church. There's also good coffee, plus soups, panini and more, all made with local produce.

Firehall Bistro   BURGERS $$
(☑ 250-498-4867; www.thefirehallbistro.com; 34881 97th St; mains $12-25; ☺ 11am-9pm) You can't miss the fake hose tower of this family-friendly firehouse-themed restaurant. Eat inside or out on the patios, choosing from excellent burgers, pastas and other casual fare. Draft beers come from the on-site **Firehall Brewery** (www.firehallbrewery.com).

❶ Information

The **visitors center** (☑ 250-498-6321; www.winecapitalofcanada.com; 36250 93rd St; ☺ 9am-5pm), with its affable staff, is in the old train station near the center of town. It has excellent regional info, and walking and biking maps.

Oliver to Penticton

About 10km north of Oliver on Hwy 97, nature reasserts itself. **Vaseux Wildlife Centre** (Hwy 97; ☺ dawn-dusk) has a 300m boardwalk for viewing oodles of birds (it's not just humans migrating here), bighorn sheep, mountain goats and some of the 14 species of bat. You can also hike to the **Bighorn National Wildlife Area** and the **Vaseux Lake National Migratory Bird Sanctuary**, with more than 160 bird species. The lake itself is an azure gem, well framed by sheer granite cliffs.

If you're not in a hurry, small roads on the east side of Skaha Lake between Okanagan Falls and Penticton are much more interesting for their wineries and views than Hwy 97.

Penticton

POP 33,200

Not as frenetic as Kelowna, Penticton combines the idle pleasures of a beach resort with its own edgy vibe. It's long been a final stop in life for Canadian retirees, which added a certain spin to its Salish-derived name Pen-Tak-Tin, meaning 'place to stay forever.' The town today is growing fast, along with the rest of the valley.

Penticton makes a good base for your valley pleasures. There are plenty of activities and diversions to fill your days, even when you don't travel further afield. Ditch Hwy 97, which runs west of the center, for Main St and the attractively walkable downtown area, which extends about 10 blocks southward from the picture-perfect lakefront; avert your eyes from the long stretch of strip malls and high-rise condos further south.

⊙ Sights

Okanagan Beach boasts about 1300m of sand, with average summer water temperatures of about 22°C (72°F). If things are jammed, there are often quieter shores at 1.5km-long **Skaha Beach**, south of the center.

★SS Sicamous Inland Marine
Museum   HISTORIC SITE
(☑250-492-0405; www.sssicamous.ca; 1099 Lakeshore Dr W; adult/child $6/3.50; ⊙9am-6pm) Back when the best way to get around inland BC was by boat, the *SS Sicamous* hauled passengers and freight on Okanagan Lake from 1914 to 1936. Now restored and beached, a tour of the boat is an evocative self-guided ramble.

Penticton Museum   MUSEUM
(☑250-490-2451; www.pentictonmuseum.com; 785 Main St; admission by donation; ⊙10am-5pm Tue-Sat) Inside the library, the Penticton Museum has delightfully eclectic displays, including the de-rigueur natural-history exhibit with stuffed animals and birds, plus everything you'd want to know about the juicy fruits of the Peach Festival (p214).

Art Gallery of Southern Okanagan GALLERY
(☑250-493-2928; www.pentictonartgallery.com; 199 Marina Way; adult/child $2/free; ⊙10am-5pm Tue-Fri, noon-5pm Sat & Sun) The beachfront Art Gallery of Southern Okanagan displays a diverse collection of regional, provincial and national artists.

🏃 Activities

Aquatic fun abounds. Otherwise, classic cheesy resort diversions like miniature golf await at the west end of Okanagan Beach.

ℹ️ IT'S TIME FOR FRUIT

Roadside stands and farms where you can pick your own fruit (or just buy it) line Hwy 97 between Osoyoos and Penticton. Major Okanagan Valley crops and their harvest times:

Cherries Mid-June to late July

Apricots Mid-July to mid-August

Peaches Mid-July to mid-September

Pears Mid-August to late September

Apples Early September to late October

Table Grapes Early September to late October

Water Sports
Both Okanagan and Skaha Lakes enjoy some of the best sailboarding, boating and paddling conditions in the Okanagan Valley.

There are several water-sports places on Okanagan Lake. If it floats, you can rent it, including kayaks for $16 an hour and ski boats for $300 for four hours. Outlets include **Castaways** (☑250-490-2033; www.castawayswatersports.com; Penticton Lakeside Resort, 21 Lakeshore Dr; ⊙9am-7pm May-Sep) and **Pier Water Sports** (☑250-493-8864; www.pierwatersports.com; Rotary Park, Lakeshore Dr W; ⊙9am-7pm May-Sep).

The paved **Okanagan River Channel Biking & Jogging Path** follows the rather arid channel that links Okanagan Lake to Skaha Lake. But why pound the pavement when you can float?

★Coyote Cruises   WATER SPORTS
(☑250-492-2115; www.coyotecruises.ca; 215 Riverside Dr; rental & shuttle $10; ⊙10am-5pm Jun-Aug) Coyote Cruises rents out inner tubes that you can float on to a midway point on the channel. It then buses you back to the start near Okanagan Lake. If you have your own floatable, it's $5 for the bus ride.

Mountain Biking & Cycling
Long dry days and rolling hills add up to perfect conditions for **mountain biking**. Get to popular rides by heading east out of town, toward Naramata. Follow signs to the city dump and Campbell's Mountain, where you'll find a single-track and dual-slalom course, both of which aren't too technical. Once you get there, the riding is mostly on the right-hand side, but once you pass the

cattle guard, it opens up and you can ride anywhere.

For **cycling**, try the route through Naramata and onto the Kettle Valley Rail Trail (p221). Other good options are the small, winery-lined roads south of town and east of Skaha Lake.

Freedom – The Bike Shop   BICYCLE RENTAL
(☑ 250-493-0686; www.freedombikeshop.com; 533 Main St; bicycle rental per day $40; ⊙ 9am-5:30pm Mon-Sat) Rents bikes and offers a wealth of information. Can arrange transport to/from the Kettle Valley Rail Trail.

Rock Climbing

Propelled by the dry weather and compact gneiss rock, climbers from all over the world come to **Skaha Bluffs Provincial Park** (www.bcparks.ca; Smythe Dr; ⊙ Mar-Nov) to enjoy climbing on more than 400 bolted routes. The local climbing group, **Skaha.org** (www.skaha.org), has comprehensive info on the bluffs, which are off Lakeside Rd on the east side of Skaha Lake.

★**Skaha Rock Adventures**   ROCK CLIMBING
(☑ 250-493-1765; www.skaharockclimbing.com; 437 Martin St; 1-day intros from $135; ⊙ by appointment) Skaha Rock Adventures offers advanced technical instruction, as well as introductory courses for anyone venturing into a harness for the first time.

Skiing & Snowboarding

Apex Mountain Resort (☑ 877-777-2739, conditions 250-487-4848; www.apexresort.com; lift tickets adult/child $60/37), 37km west of Penticton off Green Mountain Rd, is one of Canada's best small ski resorts. It has more than 68 downhill runs for all ability levels, but the mountain is known for its plethora of double-black-diamond and technical runs; the drop is over 600m. It is usually quieter than nearby Big White (p221).

☞ Tours

Casabella Princess   BOAT TOUR
(☑ 250-492-4090; www.casabellaprincess.com; Penticton Marina; adult/child $20/10; ⊙ May-Sep) If the Penticton's *SS Sicamous* stimulates your inner seaman, enjoy a one-hour, open-air lake tour on a faux stern-wheeler. There are multiple daily sailings at summer's peak.

✯ Festivals & Events

It seems like Penticton has nothing but crowd-drawing festivals all summer long.

SCENIC DRIVE TO NARAMATA

On all but the busiest summer weekends, you can escape many of Penticton's mobs by taking the road less traveled, 18km north from town along the east shore of Okanagan Lake. The route is lined with more than 20 wineries, as well as farms producing organic lavender and the like. This is a good route for cycling and at several points you can access the Kettle Valley Rail Trail (p221). There are lots of places to hike, picnic, bird-watch or do whatever else occurs to you in beautiful and often secluded surroundings. **Naramata** is a cute little village.

Elvis Festival   MUSIC
(www.pentictonelvisfestival.com; ⊙ late Jun) Dozens of Elvis impersonators could be your idea of heaven or hound-dog hell, especially the afternoon of open-mike sing-alongs. Held in late June.

Peach Festival   FOOD
(☑ 800-663-5052; www.peachfest.com; ⊙ mid-Aug) The city's premier event is basically a party that has taken place since 1948, loosely centered on the ripe succulent orbs and crowning a Peach Queen.

Pentastic Jazz Festival   MUSIC
(☑ 250-770-3494; www.pentasticjazz.com; ⊙ early Sep) More than a dozen bands perform at five venues over three days.

🛏 Sleeping

Lakeshore Dr W and S Main St/Skaha Lake Rd are home to most of the local motels. The Okanagan Beach strip is the most popular area. The visitors center has a long list of B&Bs.

HI Penticton Hostel   HOSTEL $
(☑ 250-492-3992; www.hihostels.ca; 464 Ellis St; dm/r from $28/64; ❄ @ 🖥) This 47-bed hostel is near the center in a heavily used 1908 house. It arranges activities, including wine tours.

Tiki Shores Beach Resort   MOTEL $$
(☑ 866-492-8769, 250-492-8769; www.tikishores.com; 914 Lakeshore Dr W; condos $140-300; ❄ 🖥 🏊) This lively resort has 40 condo-style units with kitchens, most with separate bedrooms. Rooms have a light color scheme that seems ideal for a freshwater lakeside holiday.

Vancouver House Bed & Breakfast　B&B $$
(📞 250-276-3737; www.pentictonbedandbreakfast.
ca; 497 Vancouver Ave; r $100-170) This heritage-
listed home is only 500m from downtown
and is an easy walk to the beach. The
three rooms have their own HDTVs and
DVDs, plus other niceties. Breakfasts are
memorable.

Black Sea Motel　MOTEL $$
(📞 250-276-4040; www.blackseamotel.com; 988
Lakeshore Dr; r $100-275; ❇) As architecturally
challenged as its beachfront neighbors, the
Black Sea at least hints at a Soviet inspiration as you ponder its exterior. But it's what's
inside that counts and the hotel is a winner
for excellent service and large apartment-
style rooms.

Crooked Tree Bed & Breakfast　B&B $$$
(📞 250-490-8022; www.crooked-tree.com; 1278
Spiller Rd; ste $180-210; 🛜) All of Okanagan
Lake glistens below you from this moun-
tainside retreat that's 9km east of downtown
Penticton. The three large apartments each
have multiple decks amid this woodsy aerie
and are well stocked with luxuries.

🍴 Eating & Drinking

Penticton definitely has its share of good
eats. Stroll around Main and Front Sts in the
center and you will find numerous choices.
The **farmers market** (📞 250-583-9933; 100
Main St; ⏰ 8:30am-noon Sat May-Oct) hosts large
numbers of local organic producers and
runs a few blocks south of the lake.

Look for local Cannery Brewing beers on
tap around town; the seasonal Blackberry
Porter is fresh and smooth.

★ Burger 55　BURGERS $
(📞 778-476-5529; www.burger55.com; 85 West-
minster Ave E; mains $7-12; ⏰ 11am-8pm) Best
burger in Canada? It's your own damn fault
if it isn't, as you have myriad ways to cus-
tomize at this tiny outlet by the creek and
downtown. Six kinds of buns, eight kinds of
cheese, and toppings that include roasted
garlic and *pico de gallo* are just some of the
options. Sides like fries are equally superb.

Il Vecchio Deli　DELI $
(📞 250-492-7610; 317 Robinson St; sandwiches $6;
⏰ 10am-6pm Mon-Sat) The smell that greets
you as you enter confirms your choice. The
best lunch sandwiches in town can be con-
sumed at a couple of tables in this atmos-
pheric deli, but will taste better on a picnic.

Choices are amazing; we like the garlic sa-
lami with marinated eggplant sandwich.

Fibonacci　CAFE $
(📞 250-770-1913; www.fibonacci.ca; 219 Main St;
mains $7-10; ⏰ 7am-8pm Mon-Sat, to 6pm Sun; 🛜)
You see the large brass coffee roaster right
when you enter this downtown cafe that
serves up lots of healthy Mediterranean fare.
Thin-crust pizzas are made with local pro-
duce. Chillax on a sidewalk lounger; watch
for live events.

★ Dream Cafe　FUSION $$
(📞 250-490-9012; www.thedreamcafe.ca; 67 Front
St; mains $11-20; ⏰ 8am-late Tue-Sun) The heady
aroma of spices envelops your, well, head as
you enter this pillow-bedecked, upscale-yet-
funky bistro. Asian and Indian flavors mix
on the menu, which has many veggie options. On many nights there's live acoustic
music by touring pros; tables outside hum
all summer long.

Hillside Bistro　BISTRO $$
(📞 250-493-6274; www.hillsidewinery.ca; 1350
Naramata Rd; mains $16-27; ⏰ 11:30am-2pm &
5-9pm) Beautifully set among its namesake
vineyards, this casual eatery has great lake-
side views and upscale versions of burgers,
pasta and other dishes made from ingredi-
ents sourced locally. Enjoy a glass of Mosaic,
the house Bordeaux-style blended red.

Salty's Beach House　SEAFOOD $$
(📞 250-493-5001; www.saltysbeachhouse.com;
1000 Lakeshore Dr W; mains $12-25; ⏰ noon-10pm
Apr-Oct) You expect deep-fried but what
you get is a nuanced menu of seafood with
global accents. Typical is Cayman Island
chowder, which is rich and multifaceted.
Dine under the stars on the patio or enjoy
the lake views from the upper level.

Theo's　GREEK $$
(📞 250-492-4019; www.eatsquid.com; 687 Main
St; mains $10-25; ⏰ 11am-10pm) The place for
locals on match.com second dates, serving
up authentic Greek island cuisine in the at-
mospheric firelit interior or out on the patio.
The *garithes uvetsi* is a symphony of start-
ers that will please two.

Hooded Merganser　FUSION $$
(📞 250-493-8221; www.hoodedmerganser.ca; Pen-
ticton Lakeside Resort, 21 Lakeshore Dr; mains $12-
30; ⏰ 7am-midnight) Named for a small breed
of duck noted for its vibrant plumage, this
huge lakeside pub attracts plenty of birds of
a similar feather. On a summer afternoon its

waterfront terrace literally heaves. Food is designed for sharing, with some steaks and burgers tossed in.

🛍 Shopping

★ **Book Shop**   BOOKSTORE
(📞 250-492-6661; www.bookspenticton.com; 242 Main St; ⊙ 9:30am-8pm Mon-Fri, to 5:30pm Sat, 11am-5pm Sun) The perfect rainy day refuge, this used bookstore is one of Canada's largest and best.

ℹ Information

A whole room of the **visitors center** (📞 250-493-4055, 800-663-5052; www.tourismpenticton.com; 553 Railway St, cnr Hwy 97 & Eckhardt Ave W; ⊙ 8am-7pm; 🛜) is devoted to the BC Wine Information Centre, with regional wine information, tasting and sales of more than 600 varieties.

ℹ Getting There & Around

Greyhound Canada (📞 800-661-8747; www. greyhound.ca; 307 Ellis St) Services Vancouver ($73, seven hours, one daily) and Kelowna ($20, 1¼ hours, two daily).

Penticton Transit (📞 250-492-5602; www. bctransit.com; single trip/day pass $2/4) Runs between both waterfronts.

Penticton to Kelowna

A lakeside resort town 18km north of Penticton on Hwy 97, **Summerland** features some fine 19th-century heritage buildings on the hillside above the ever-widening and busy highway. The **Kettle Valley Steam Railway** (📞 877-494-8424; www.kettlevalleyrail.org; 18404 Bathville Rd; adult/child $22/13; ⊙ May-Oct) is an operating 16km remnant of the famous tracks. Ride behind an old steam locomotive in open-air cars and enjoy orchard views.

Hugging the lake below Hwy 97, some 25km south of Kelowna, the little town of **Peachland** is good for a quick, breezy stroll. Smart stoppers will pause longer at the **Blind Angler Grill** (📞 250-767-9264; 5899A Beach Ave; mains $8-25; ⊙ 7am-9pm), a shack-like place overlooking a small marina. What's lost in structural integrity is more than made up for in food quality: breakfasts shine, lobster wraps are a treat and nighttime ribs and halibut are tops.

Try not to lose your lunch on Canada's highest zip line at **Zipzone Peachland** (📞 855-947-9663; www.zipzone.ca; Princeton Ave; adult/child from $100/80; ⊙ 9am-5pm May-Oct), where you can sail high over Deep Creek Canyon.

Between Peachland and Kelowna, urban sprawl becomes unavoidable, especially through the billboard-lined nightmare of **Westbank**.

Kelowna

POP 117,800

A kayaker paddles past scores of new tract houses on a hillside: it's an iconic image for fast-growing Kelowna, the unofficial 'capital' of the Okanagan and the sprawling center of all that's good and not-so-good with the region.

Entering from the north, the everlengthening urban sprawl of tree-lined Hwy 97/Harvey Ave seems to go on forever. Once past the ceaseless waves of chains and strip malls, the downtown is a welcome reward. Museums, culture, nightlife and the parklined lakefront feature. About 2km south of the center, along Pandosy Ave, is **Pandosy Village**, a charming and upscale lakeside enclave.

Kelowna, an Interior Salish word meaning 'grizzly bear,' owes its settlement to a number of missionaries who arrived in 1858, hoping to 'convert the natives.' Settlers followed and, in 1892, the town was established. Industrial fruit production was the norm until the wine industry took off 20 years ago.

⊙ Sights

The focal point of the city's shoreline, the immaculate downtown **City Park** is home to manicured gardens, water features and **Hot Sands Beach**, where the water is a respite from the summer air.

Restaurants and pubs take advantage of the uninterrupted views of the lake and forested shore opposite. North of the marina, **Waterfront Park** has a variegated shoreline and a popular open-air stage.

Be sure to pick up the **Cultural District** walking-tour brochures at the visitors center and visit www.kelownamuseums.ca.

Public Art   PUBLIC ART
Among the many outdoor statues near the lake, look for the one of the **Ogopogo**, the lake's mythical – and hokey – monster. More prosaic is **Bear** (Water St), a huge, lacy confection in metal. The visitors center has a good public-art guide.

BC Orchard Industry Museum MUSEUM
(☑250-763-0433; 1304 Ellis St; admission by donation; ☺10am-5pm Mon-Sat) Located in the old
Laurel Packing House, the BC Orchard Industry Museum recounts the Okanagan Valley from its ranchland past, grazed by cows,
to its present, grazed by tourists. The old
fruit-packing-crate labels are works of art.

BC Wine Museum & VQA
Wine Shop MUSEUM
(☑250-868-0441; 1304 Ellis St; ☺10am-6pm Mon-
Fri, 11am-5pm Sat & Sun) FREE In the same
building as the BC Orchard Industry Museum, the knowledgeable staff at the BC Wine
Museum & VQA Wine Shop can recommend
tours, steer you to the best wineries for tastings and help you fill your trunk from the
selection of more than 600 wines on sale
from 90 local wineries.

Kelowna Art Gallery GALLERY
(☑250-979-0888; www.kelownaartgallery.com;
1315 Water St; adult/child $5/4; ☺10am-5pm Tue,
Wed, Fri & Sat, to 9pm Thu, 1-4pm Sun) The airy
Kelowna Art Gallery features local works.

Turtle Island Gallery GALLERY
(☑250-717-8235; www.turtleislandgallery.com; 115-
1295 Cannery Lane; ☺10am-5pm) Turtle Island
Gallery sells and displays works by Aboriginal artists.

Okanagan Heritage Museum MUSEUM
(☑250-763-2417; 470 Queensway Ave; admission by
donation; ☺10am-5pm Mon-Fri, to 4pm Sat) The
Okanagan Heritage Museum looks at centuries of local culture in an engaging manner that includes a First Nations pit house,
a Chinese grocery and a Pandosy-era trading
post.

Kasugai Gardens GARDENS
(Queensway Ave; ☺9am-6pm) FREE Behind the
Okanagan Heritage Museum, the exquisite
grounds of Kasugai Gardens are good for a
peaceful stroll.

🏃 Activities

The balmy weather makes Kelowna ideal for
fresh-air fun, whether on the lake or in the
surrounding hills.

You'll find great hiking and mountain-
bike riding all around town. The 17km **Mission Creek Greenway** is a meandering,
wooded path following the creek along the
south edge of town. The western half is a
wide and easy expanse, but to the east the
route becomes sinuous as it climbs into the
hills.

Knox Mountain, which sits at the northern end of the city, is another good place to
hike or ride. Along with bobcats and snakes,
the 235-hectare park has well-maintained
trails and rewards visitors with excellent
views from the top.

Cycling on the Kettle Valley Rail Trail and
amid the vineyards is hugely popular.

⭐ Monashee Adventure
Tours BICYCLE RENTAL
(☑250-762-9253; www.monasheeadventuretours.
com; bicycle rental per day from $40) Offers scores
of biking and hiking tours of the valley, parks,
Kettle Valley Rail Trail (from $80) and win-
eries. Many tours are accompanied by entertaining local guides. Prices usually include a
bike, lunch and shuttle to the route. The same
shuttle can also be used by independent riders looking for one-way transport. In winter,
snowshoe tours are offered.

Okanagan Rent A Boat BOATING
(☑250-862-2469; www.lakefrontsports.com; Grand
Okanagan Lakefront Resort; kayak rental per 2hr $30;
☺May-Sep) You can rent speedboats (starting at $110 per hour), canoes, kayaks, wake-
boards, pedal boats and much more from this
seasonal booth on the lakefront.

🛏 Sleeping

As in the rest of the Okanagan Valley, accommodations can be difficult to find on summer
weekends. The visitors center lists dozens of
area B&Bs. Chain motels dominate Harvey
Ave/Hwy 97 going east. Rates fall as you head
along the strip, but you pay the price by being
in less-than-salubrious surroundings.

Kelowna International Hostel HOSTEL $
(☑250-763-6024; www.kelowna-hostel.bc.ca; 2343
Pandosy St; dm/r from $25/60; ☺) About 1km
south of City Park, this small hostel is in a
'50s home on a tree-lined residential street.
Neighbors no doubt enjoy the regular keg
parties and other social events that keep this
cheery place hopping.

Kelowna Samesun
International Hostel HOSTEL $
(☑877-562-2783, 250-763-9814; www.samesun.
com; 245 Harvey Ave; dm/r from $33/70; ✳@☺)
Near the center and the lake, this purpose-
built hostel has 88 dorm beds plus private
rooms. Activities include various group
outings.

Kelowna

**Willow Creek Family
Campground** CAMPGROUND **$**
(☐ 250-762-6302; www.willowcreekcampground.
ca; 3316 Lakeshore Rd; campsites/RV sites from
$32/42; ☜) Close to Pandosy Village and a
beach, this shady 82-site facility has a laundry. Tent sites are on a grassy verge.

Abbott Villa MOTEL **$$**
(☐ 800-578-7878, 250-763-7771; www.abbottvilla.
com; 1627 Abbott St; r $90-180; ✳@☜☒) Per-
fectly located downtown and across from
City Park, this 52-room motel is as un-
adorned as a grapevine in winter. There is

a decent outdoor pool and a hot tub. Self-
cooked waffles are free for breakfast.

Royal Anne Hotel HOTEL **$$**
(☐ 250-763-2277, 888-811-3400; www.royalanne-
hotel.com; 348 Bernard Ave; r $90-200; ✳@☜)
Location, location, location are the three
amenities that count at this otherwise un-
exciting, older five-story hotel in the heart of
town. Rooms have standard modern decor,
fridges and huge, openable windows.

Prestige Hotel MOTEL **$$**
(☐ 877-737-8443, 250-860-7900; www.prestigeinn.
com; 1675 Abbott St; r $130-250; ✳@☜☒) This

Kelowna

67-room place has a great location across from City Park and, once you're inside, you can't see the rather hideous exterior. The rooms have a modern, unfussy style, in an upscale-motel sort of way.

★**Hotel Eldorado**   HOTEL **$$$**
(☑ 866-608-7500, 250-763-7500; www.hotel-eldoradokelowna.com; 500 Cook Rd; r $180-400; ❋ @ 🗢 ☲) This historic lakeshore retreat, south of Pandosy Village, has 19 heritage rooms where you can bask in antique-filled luxury. A modern low-key wing has 30 more rooms and six opulent waterfront suites. It's classy, artful and funky all at once. Definitely the choice spot for a luxurious getaway.

✖ Eating & Drinking

Many of Kelowna's restaurants take full advantage of the local bounty of foodstuffs. But don't let the feel of Vancouver East cause you to go all continental in your dining time: 8pm is late. The local microbrewer, **Tree Brewing**, has an excellent range of beers that are widely sold around town.

The **farmers market** (☑ 250-878-5029; cnr Springfield Rd & Dilworth Dr; ⊙ 8am-1pm Wed & Sat Apr-Oct) has more than 150 vendors, including many with prepared foods. Local artisans also display their wares. It's off Hwy 97, east of the center.

★**BC Fruit Market**   MARKET **$**
(☑ 250-763-8872; 816 Clement Ave; fruit from $1; ⊙ 9am-5pm Mon-Sat) Like a county fair right inside the local fruit-packing cooperative, dozens upon dozens of the Okanagan's best fruits are on display and available for tasting. Prices are half that in supermarkets.

Pulp Fiction Coffee House   COFFEE **$**
(☑ 778-484-7444; www.pulpfictioncoffeehouse. com; 1598 Pandosy St; coffee $2; ⊙ 7am-10pm) The blonde gave me the eye, her pneumatic... Ahem, the best of crime noir is sold here amid posters showing same. Buy a used book to go with your excellent coffee or tea at this sharp, category-busting cafe right downtown.

Bean Scene   CAFE **$**
(☑ 250-763-1814; www.beanscene.ca; 274 Bernard Ave; coffee $2; ⊙ 6:30am-11pm; 🗢) Has a great bulletin board to check up on local happenings while you munch on a muffin. The coffee's the best locally.

★**RauDZ**   FUSION **$$**
(☑ 250-868-8805; www.raudz.com; 1560 Water St; mains $12-25; ⊙ 5-10pm) Noted chef Rod Butters has defined the farm-to-table movement with his casual bistro that's a temple to Okanagan produce and wine. The dining room is as airy and open as the kitchen and the seasonal menu takes global inspiration

for Mediterranean-infused dishes good for sharing, as well as steaks and seafood. Suppliers include locally renowned Carmelis goat cheese.

★ Rotten Grape
TAPAS $$

(☑250-717-8466; www.rottengrape.com; 231 Bernard Ave; mains $10-20; ⊙5pm-midnight Wed-Sat) Enjoy flights of local wines (over 200 by the glass) without the froufrou in the heart of town. If you utter 'tannin, the hobgoblin of pinot' at any point, be quiet and eat some of the tasty tapas inside or out.

Sturgeon Hall
PUB

(☑250-860-3055; 1481 Water St; ⊙11am-late Mon-Sat) Fanatical fans of the Kelowna Rockets hockey team feast on excellent burgers and thin-crust pizza (mains $10 to $20) while quaffing brews at the bar or outside at sidewalk tables. In season, every TV shows hockey.

Micro
PUB

(www.microkelowna.com; 1500 Water St; ⊙5pm-late) This great small bar from the RauDZ team is a 10, meaning there are 10 wines, 10 superb microbrews and 10 artisan bites from the valley on the changing menu (snacks from $10). Gather at the beautiful wood-block bar.

Old Train Station Public House
PUB

(☑778-484-5558; www.thetrainstationpub.com; 1177 Ellis St; ⊙11am-late) The long-disused Canadian National train station has been reborn as an upscale pub with a fab selection of beers. The usual pub-food standards show color and flair (mains $11 to $20); enjoy the wide terrace on balmy days and live music Saturday nights.

Doc Willoughby's
PUB

(☑250-868-8288; 353 Bernard Ave; ⊙11:30am-2am) Right downtown, this pub boasts a vaulted interior lined with wood, as well as tables on the street. Perfect for a drink or a meal; the fish and chips are good (mains $10 to $20). The beer selection is excellent, including brews from Tree Brewing and Penticton's Cannery Brewing.

Rose's Waterfront Pub
PUB

(☑250-860-1141; www.rosespub.com; Delta Grand Okanagan Hotel, 1352 Water St; ⊙noon-late) Part of the upscale end of the waterfront, the vast lakeside terrace is the place for sunset drinks and snacks – from several hours before to several hours after. Rise above the masses at the rooftop cafe. Food is pub standard (mains $12 to $25).

☆ Entertainment

Downtown Kelowna's clubs are mostly at the west end of Leon and Lawrence Aves. Free summer nighttime concerts take place at various places along the waterfront.

Blue Gator
LIVE MUSIC

(☑250-860-1529; www.bluegator.net; 441 Lawrence Ave; ⊙3pm-late Tue-Sun) There's blues, rock, acoustic jam and more at the valley's sweaty temple of live music and cold beer.

Kelowna Rockets
HOCKEY

(☑250-860-7825; www.kelownarockets.com; tickets from $24; ⊙Sep-Mar) Kelowna Rockets is the much-beloved local WHL hockey team and a perennial contender, playing in the flashy 6000-seat **Prospera Place Arena** (☑250-979-0888; cnr Water St & Cawston Ave). Home games see the local pubs fill before and after the match.

Kelowna Actors Studio
THEATER

(☑250-862-2867; www.kelownaactorsstudio.com; 1379 Ellis St; tickets from $54) Enjoy works as diverse as *The Producers* and *Same Time Next Year* at this dinner theater with serious ambitions.

Rotary Centre for the Performing Arts
ARTS VENUE

(☑250-717-5304, tickets 250-763-1849; 421 Cawston Ave) There are galleries, a theater, cafe, craft workshops and live classical music.

🛍 Shopping

The many food purveyors offer locally produced items that make excellent gifts.

Mosaic Books
BOOKS

(☑250-763-4418; www.mosaicbooks.ca; 411 Bernard Ave; ⊙9am-6pm Sat-Wed, to 9pm Thu & Fri) Mosaic Books is an excellent independent bookstore, selling maps (including topographic ones) and travel guides, plus books on aboriginal history and culture.

ℹ Information

The **visitors center** (☑800-663-4345, 250-861-1515; www.tourismkelowna.com; 544 Harvey Ave; ⊙8am-7pm) is near the corner of Ellis St.

ℹ Getting There & Away

From **Kelowna airport** (YLW; ☑250-765-5125; www.kelownaairport.com), **Westjet** (www.westjet.com) serves Vancouver, Victoria, Edmonton, Calgary and Toronto. **Air Canada Jazz** (www.aircanada.com) serves Vancouver and Calgary.

> **DON'T MISS**
>
> ## KETTLE VALLEY RAIL TRAIL
>
> The famous **Kettle Valley Rail Trail** vies with wine drinking and peach picking as the attraction of choice for visitors – smart ones do all three.
>
> Once stretching 525km in curving, meandering length, the railway was built so that silver ore could be transported from the southern Kootenays to Vancouver. Finished in 1916, it remains one of the most expensive railways ever built on a per-kilometer basis. It was entirely shut by 1989, but it wasn't long before its easy grades (never over 2.2%) and dozens of bridges were incorporated into the Trans Canada Trail.
>
> Of the entire Kettle Valley Rail Trail, the most spectacular stretch is close to Kelowna. The 24km section through the **Myra Canyon** has fantastic views of the sinuous canyon from **18 trestles** that span the gorge for the cliff-hugging path. That you can enjoy the route at all is something of a miracle as 12 of the wooden trestles were destroyed by fire in 2003. But all are rebuilt; much credit goes to the **Myra Canyon Trestle Restoration Society** (www.myratrestles.com). The broad views take in Kelowna and the lake. Although fire damage remains, you can see alpine meadows reclaiming the landscape.
>
> To reach the area closest to the most spectacular trestles, follow Harvey Ave (Hwy 97) east to Gordon Dr. Turn south and then go east 2.6km on KLO Rd and then join McCulloch Rd for 7.4km after the junction. Look for the Myra Forest Service Rd, turn south and make a winding 8.7km climb on a car-friendly gravel road to the parking lot.
>
> Myra Canyon is just part of an overall 174km network of trails in the Okanagan that follow the old railway through tunnels, past Naramata and as far south as Penticton and beyond. You can easily access the trail at many points or book hiking and cycling tours. **Myra Canyon Bike Rentals** (☎250-878-8763; www.myracanyonrental.com; Myra Canyon; bicycle rental per half-day from adult/child $40/30; ☺9am-5:30pm May-Oct) has bike rentals; confirm by calling in advance.

Horizon Air (www.alaskaair.com) serves Seattle. The airport is 20km north of the center on Hwy 97.

Greyhound Canada (☎800-661-8747; www.greyhound.ca; 2366 Leckie Rd) is inconveniently located east of the downtown area, off Hwy 97. City buses 9 and 10 make the run from Queensway station in downtown (every 30 minutes between 6:30am and 9:45pm). Bus routes include Calgary ($93, 10 hours, daily), Kamloops ($35, 2½ to five hours, three daily), Penticton ($20, 1¼ hours, two daily) and Vancouver ($73, five to six hours, six daily).

ⓘ Getting Around

TO/FROM THE AIRPORT
Cabs cost about $36.

BUS
Kelowna Regional Transit System (☎250-860-8121; www.transitbc.com; adult/child $2.25/2) runs local bus services. A day pass costs $6. All the downtown buses pass through **Queensway station** (Queensway Ave, btwn Pandosy & Ellis Sts). Service is not especially convenient.

CAR & TAXI
All major car-rental companies are at Kelowna airport. Taxi companies include **Kelowna Cabs** (☎250-762-2222, 250-762-4444).

Big White Ski Resort

Perfect powder is the big deal at **Big White Ski Resort** (☎250-765-8888, 800-663-2772, snow report 250-765-7669; www.bigwhite.com; off Hwy 33; 1-day lift pass adult/child $79/43), located 55km east of Kelowna off Hwy 33. With a vertical drop of 777m, it features 16 lifts and 118 runs that offer excellent downhill and backcountry skiing, while deep gullies make for killer snowboarding. Because of Big White's isolation, most people stay up here. The resort includes numerous restaurants, bars, hotels, condos, rental homes and a hostel. The resort has lodging info and details of the ski-season shuttle to Kelowna.

Vernon

POP 38,400

The Okanagan glitz starts to fade before you reach Vernon. Maybe it's the weather. Winters have more of the traditional inland BC bite and wineries are few, but that doesn't mean the area is without its charms. The orchard-scented valley is surrounded by three lakes – Kalamalka, Okanagan and Swan – that attract fun seekers all summer long.

Most of the shops are found along 30th Ave, known as Main St. Confusingly, 30th Ave is intersected by 30th St in the middle of downtown, so mind your streets and avenues.

◉ Sights & Activities

Downtown Vernon is enlivened by more than 30 **wall murals**, ranging from schmaltzy to artistic.

The beautiful 9-sq-km **Kalamalka Lake Provincial Park** (☑250-545-1560; www.bcparks.ca; off Hwy 6) south of town lies on the eastern side of this warm, shallow lake. The park offers great swimming at Jade and Kalamalka Beaches, good fishing and a network of mountain-biking and hiking trails. **Innerspace Watersports** (☑250-549-2040; www.innerspacewatersports.com; 3103 32nd St; ◷10am-5:30pm Mon-Sat) operates a seasonal booth here, with canoe and stand-up paddleboard rentals; otherwise visit their store in town.

Two fun attractions make hay from local agriculture. **Davison Orchards** (☑250-549-3266; www.davisonorchards.ca; 3111 Davison Rd; ◷8am-6pm) **FREE** has tractor rides, homemade ice cream, fresh apple juice, winsome barnyard animals and more. Next door, **Planet Bee** (☑250-542-8088; www.planetbee.com; 5011 Bella Vista Rd; admission free; ◷8am-6pm) **FREE** is a working honey farm where you can learn all the sweet secrets of the golden nectar and see a working hive up close. Follow 25th Ave west, turn north briefly on 41st St, then go west on Bella Vista Rd and watch for signs.

🛏 Sleeping

Accommodations are available in all price ranges; chains are found at the north end of Hwy 97. Vacation rentals surround the lakes.

Ellison Provincial Park CAMPGROUND $
(☑800-689-9025, info 250-494-6500; www.discovercamping.ca; Okanagan Landing Rd; campsites $30; ◷Apr-Oct) Some 16km southwest of Vernon, this is a great place near the lake. The 71 campsites fill up early, so reserve in advance.

Beaver Lake Mountain Resort LODGE $$
(☑250-762-2225; www.beaverlakeresort.com; 6350 Beaver Lake Rd; campsites from $27, cabins $75-165; @) Set high in the hills east of Hwy 97, about midway between Vernon and Kelowna, this postcard-perfect lakeside resort has a range of rustic log and more luxurious cabins that sleep up to six people.

Tiki Village Motel MOTEL $$
(☑800-661-8454, 250-503-5566; www.tikivillage-vernon.com; 2408 34th St; r $70-150; ❇🐾📶🐕) Hide your brother's phone in the pool wall and he'll never find it again. An ode to the glory days of decorative concrete blocks, the Tiki has suitably expansive plantings and 30 rooms with a vaguely Asian-minimalist theme.

✖ Eating

The evening **farmers market** (☑250-546-6267; cnr 48th Ave & 27th St; ◷3-7pm Fri) adds class to the Village Green Mall parking lot at the north end of town. There are also morning **markets** (Kal Tire Place, 3445 43rd Ave; ◷8am-1pm Mon & Thu), just west of Hwy 97.

Main St (30th Ave) east of Hwy 97 (32nd St) is prime territory for browsing eateries.

Talkin Donkey CAFE $
(☑250-545-2286; www.talkindonkey.com; 5400 24th St; mains $7; ◷8am-10pm Mon-Thu, to 11pm Fri & Sat; 🐾) 🍃 When they talk about 'drinking responsibly' at this local institution, they mean ensuring that your coffee is fair trade. A good chunk of the proceeds at this funky coffeehouse with a spiritual edge goes to charity. Tap your Birkenstock-clad toes to regular live folk music.

★ Eclectic Med MEDITERRANEAN $$
(☑250-558-4646; 2915 30th Ave; mains $12-25; ◷noon-9pm) The name sums up the menu, which brings a Mediterranean accent to local standards such as Alberta steaks, lake fish and lots of valley veggies. Plates are artfully presented. The local wine list is long, with many choices by the glass.

Bamboo Beach Fusion Grille FUSION $$
(☑250-542-7701; 3313 30th Ave; mains $12-25; ◷noon-9pm; 🐾) Flavors from across Asia season popular local foods at this sprightly restaurant. Look for Japanese, Korean and Thai influences in the coconut halibut, the snapper fish and chips and much more. The curry soba noodles are good.

❶ Information

The **visitors center** (☑800-665-0795, 250-545-3016; www.tourismvernon.com; 701 Hwy 97 S; ◷9am-6pm) is 2km south of the town center.

ⓘ Getting There & Around

Greyhound Canada (☎800-661-8747; www.greyhound.ca; 3102 30th St, cnr 31st Ave) Services from Vernon include Kelowna ($17, 45 minutes, four daily) and Revelstoke ($35, 2¾ hours, one daily).

Vernon Regional Transit System (☎250-545-7221; www.transitbc.com; fares from $2) Buses leave downtown from the bus stop at the corner of 31st St and 30th Ave. For Kalamalka Lake, catch bus 1; for Okanagan Lake, bus 7.

North of Vernon

Attractions are few in this area, which is more notable for its major highway connections. Just north of Vernon, beautiful Hwy 97 heads northwest to Kamloops via tree-clad valleys punctuated by lakes.

Home to the O'Keefe family from 1867 to 1977, the **O'Keefe Ranch** (www.okeeferanch.ca; Hwy 97; adult/child $14/9; ⊙10am-5pm May-Sep) still has an original log cabin, plus lots of live displays of old ranching techniques. Before orchards – and later grapes – covered the valley, ranching as portrayed here was the way of life. It's 4km after Hwy 97 splits from Hwy 97A, which continues northeast to Sicamous and Hwy 1. **Armstrong**, 23km north of Vernon, is a cute little village.

Silver Star

Classic inland BC dry powder makes **Silver Star** (☎250-542-0224, snow report 250-542-1745; www.skisilverstar.com; 123 Shortt St; 1-day lift ticket adult/child $79/43) a very popular ski resort. The 115 runs have a vertical drop of 760m; snowboarders enjoy a half-pipe and a terrain park. In summer the lifts haul mountain bikers and hikers up to the lofty green vistas.

All manner of accommodations can be reserved through the resort. **Samesun Lodge** (☎877-562-2783, 250-545-8933; www.samesun.com; 9898 Pinnacles Rd; dm/r from $30/78; @ 🛜) runs a very popular and almost posh backpacker hotel.

To reach Silver Star, take 48th Ave off Hwy 97. The resort is 22km northeast of Vernon.

Shuswap Region

Rorschach-test-like **Shuswap Lake** anchors a somewhat bland but pleasing region of green, wooded hills, farms and two small towns, Sicamous and Salmon Arm. The latter has the area's main **visitors center**

(☎877-725-6667, 250-832-2230; www.shuswaptourism.ca; 20 Hudson Ave NE, Salmon Arm; ⊙8am-6pm).

The area is home to several lake-based provincial parks and is a popular destination for families looking for outdoor fun. The main attraction, though, is the annual spawning of sockeye salmon at **Roderick Haig-Brown Provincial Park** (☎250-851-3000; www.bcparks.ca; Saquilax), just off Hwy 1. This 10.59-sq-km park protects both sides of the Adams River between Shuswap Lake and Adams Lake, a natural bottleneck for the bright-red sockeye they run upriver every October. The fish population peaks every four years, when as many as four million salmon crowd the Adams' shallow riverbed – the next big spawn is due in 2014.

THE KOOTENAYS & THE ROCKIES

You just can't help sighing as you ponder the plethora of snow-covered peaks in the Kootenay Region of BC. Deep river valleys cleaved by white-water rivers, impossibly sheer rock faces, alpine meadows and a saw-tooth of white-dappled mountains stretching across the horizon inspire awe, action and mere contemplation.

Coming from the west, the mountain majesty builds as if choreographed from above. The roughly parallel ranges of the Monashees and the Selkirks striate the West Kootenays with the Arrow Lakes adding texture. Appealing towns like Revelstoke and Nelson nestle against the mountains and are centers of year-round outdoor fun. The East Kootenays cover the Purcell Mountains region below Golden, taking in Radium Hot Springs and delightful Fernie. The Rockies climb high in the sky to the border with Alberta.

BC's Rocky Mountains parks (Mt Revelstoke, Glacier, Yoho and Kootenay) don't have the – no pun intended – high profile of Banff and Jasper National Parks over the border, but for many that's an advantage. Each has its own spectacular qualities, often relatively unexploited by the Banff-bound hordes.

Across this richly textured region, look for grizzly and black bear, elk, moose, deer, beaver, mountain goats and much more. Pause to make your own discoveries.

Revelstoke

POP 7300

Gateway to serious mountains, Revelstoke doesn't need to toot its own horn – the ceaseless procession of trains through the center does that. Built as an important point on the Canadian Pacific transcontinental railroad that first linked eastern and western Canada, Revelstoke echoes not just with whistles but with history. The compact center is lined with heritage buildings, yet it's not a museum piece. There's a vibrant local arts community and most locals take full advantage of the boundless opportunities for hiking, kayaking and, most of all, skiing.

It's more than worth a long pause as you pass on Hwy 1, which bypasses the town center to the northeast. The main streets include 1st St and Mackenzie Ave.

Sights

Grizzly Plaza, between Mackenzie and Orton Aves, is a pedestrian precinct and the heart of downtown, where free live-music performances take place in the evenings throughout July and August.

While outdoor activities are Revelstoke's real drawcard, a stroll of the center and a pause at the museums is a must. Pick up the *Public Art* and *Heritage* walking tour brochures at the tourist office.

★ **Revelstoke Railway Museum**   MUSEUM
(☑250-837-6060; www.railwaymuseum.com; 719 Track St W; adult/child $10/2; ⊗9am-5pm) Revelstoke Railway Museum, in an attractive building across the tracks from the town center, contains restored steam locomotives, including one of the largest steam engines ever used on Canadian Pacific Railway (CPR) lines. Photographs and artifacts document the construction of the CPR, which was instrumental – actually essential – in linking eastern and western Canada.

Revelstoke Museum   MUSEUM
(☑250-837-3067; www.revelstokemuseum.ca; 315 1st St W; adult/child $5/free; ⊗10am-5pm Mon-Fri, 11am-5pm Sat) Furniture and historical odds and ends, including mining, logging and railway artifacts that date back to the town's establishment in the 1880s, line the rooms. The local skiing history displays are good.

🏃 Activities

Sandwiched between the vast but relatively unknown Selkirk and Monashee mountain ranges, Revelstoke draws serious snow buffs looking for vast landscapes of crowd-free powder. It's where North America's first ski jump was built, in 1915.

For **cross-country skiing**, head to the 22km of groomed trails at Mt MacPherson Ski Area, 7km south of town on Hwy 23; see www.revelstokenordic.org.

All that white snow turns into white water come spring and rafting is big. **Mountain biking** is also huge, as it is across the region; pick up trail maps from the visitors center.

Revelstoke Mountain Resort   SKIING
(☑888-837-2188; www.revelstokemountainresort.com; Camozzi Rd; 1-day lift ticket adult/child $80/28) Just 6km southeast of town, the Revelstoke Mountain Resort has ambitions to become the biggest ski resort this side of the Alps. But given its seemingly endless virgin slopes only opened in 2008, it has a way to go. In the meantime, you can, in one run (out of 59), ski both 700m of bowl and 700m of trees. At 1713m, the vertical drop is the greatest in North America.

Although the resort is making bowls accessible that were once helicopter or cat only, there are myriad more that are still remote. **Mica Heliskiing** (☑877-837-6191; www.

---

❶ AVALANCHE WARNING

The Kootenays are the heart of avalanche country, which kill more people in BC each year than any other natural phenomenon. The toll is stubbornly high every year.

Avalanches can occur at any time, even on terrain that seems relatively flat. Roughly half the people caught in them don't survive. It's vital that people venturing out onto the snow make inquiries about conditions first; if an area is closed, don't go there. Whether you're backcountry ski touring or simply hiking in the alpine region, you'll want to rent a homing beacon; most outdoor shops can supply one.

In Revelstoke, the Canadian Avalanche Centre is operated by the **Canadian Avalanche Association** (CAA; ☑250-837-2141, 24hr info 800-667-1105; www.avalanche.ca). It analyzes avalanche trends, weather patterns and issues forecasts for the Kootenays and beyond.

micaheli.com; 207 Mackenzie Ave; ⊗Dec-Apr) is one of several companies offering trips; costs begin at $1300 per day.

Free Spirit Sports SNOW SPORTS
(☑250-837-9453; www.freespiritsports.com; 203 1st St W; ⊗10am-5pm Mon-Sat) Rents a wide variety of winter gear, including essential avalanche equipment.

Apex Rafting Co RAFTING
(☑888-232-6666, 250-837-6376; www.apexrafting.com; 112 1st St E; adult/child $85/69; ⊗Jun-Aug) Runs kid-friendly two-hour guided trips on the Illecillewaet River in spring and summer.

Natural Escapes Kayaking KAYAKING
(☑250-837-7883; www.naturalescapes.ca; 1115 Pineridge Cres; rental per 2hr from $35; ⊗Jun-Sep) Leads tours, offers lessons and rents kayaks and canoes.

Skookum Cycle & Ski BICYCLE RENTAL
(☑250-814-0090; www.skookumcycle.com; 118 Mackenzie Ave; mountain-bike rental per day from $40; ⊗10am-5pm) Pick up trail maps and rent bikes.

Wandering Wheels CYCLING
(☑250-814-7609; www.wanderingwheels.ca; lessons per 1hr from $30; ⊗Jun-Oct) Offers bike shuttle services, lessons and tours.

🛏 Sleeping

Revelstoke has a good selection of places to stay right in the center. Only truck spotters will gravitate to those out on Hwy 1.

Samesun Backpacker Lodge HOSTEL $
(☑877-562-2783, 250-837-4050; www.samesun.ca; 400 2nd St W; dm/r from $25/60; @🐾🛜) Ramble though the numerous rooms in this perennial backpacker favorite. The 80 beds are often full, so book ahead. It has bike and ski storage, plus summer barbecues.

Blanket Creek Provincial Park CAMPGROUND $
(☑800-689-9025; www.discovercamping.ca; Hwy 23; campsites $21) This park, 25km south of Revelstoke, includes more than 60 campsites with flush toilets and running water. There's a playground, and a waterfall is nearby.

Courthouse Inn B&B $$
(☑250-837-3369; www.courthouseinnrevelstoke.com; 312 Kootenay St; r $120-200; ❄🛜) A posh 10-room B&B close to the center, extras include a lavish breakfast, boot- and glove-driers in winter and lots of personal service.

ℹ WATCH YOUR GAS

The closure of services at Rogers Pass means that there is no gas available along the 148km stretch between Revelstoke and Golden on Hwy 1.

You can't beat the quiet location; rooms have no TVs or phones.

Regent Inn HOTEL $$
(☑888-245-5523, 250-837-2107; www.regentinn.com; 112 1st St E; r $100-190; ❄🐾🛜) The poshest place in the center is not lavish, but is comfy. The 50 modern rooms (and exterior) bear no traces of the hotel's 1914 roots. The restaurant and lounge are justifiably popular. Many bob the night away in the outdoor hot tub.

Revelstoke Lodge MOTEL $$
(☑250-837-2181, 888-559-1979; www.revelstokelodge.com; 601 1st St W; r $70-160; ❄@🛜🏊) This 42-room, maroon-hued motel overcomes its inherent flaws – an all-encompassing parking area and stark cinder-block construction – thanks to its location. Check out a room or two, watch out for dark ones and take heed of their slogan: 'Your mom called and said to stay here.'

🍴 Eating & Drinking

The **farmers market** (⊗8:30am-1pm Sat May-Oct) sprawls across Grizzly Plaza. Mt Begbie Brewing makes good local microbrews that are available around town.

Modern Bakeshop & Café CAFE $
(☑250-837-6886; 212 Mackenzie Ave; mains from $5; ⊗7am-5pm Mon-Sat; 🛜) Try a *croque monsieur* (grilled ham-and-cheese sandwich) or an elaborate pastry for a taste of Europe at this cute art-moderne cafe. Many items, such as the groovy muffins, are made with organic ingredients.

★Woolsey Creek FUSION $$
(☑250-837-5500; www.woolseycreekbistro.ca; 604 2nd St W; mains $20-30; ⊗5-10pm; 🍴) The food at this lively and fun place is both artistic and locally sourced. There are global influences across the menu, which features meat, fish and a fine wine list. Excellent starters encourage sharing and lingering on the large patio.

Benoît's Wine Bar WINE BAR
(☑250-837-6606; www.benoitswinebar.com; 107 2nd St E; ⊗5pm-midnight Mon-Sat) Work on your French accent while munching on a

The Kootenays & The Rockies

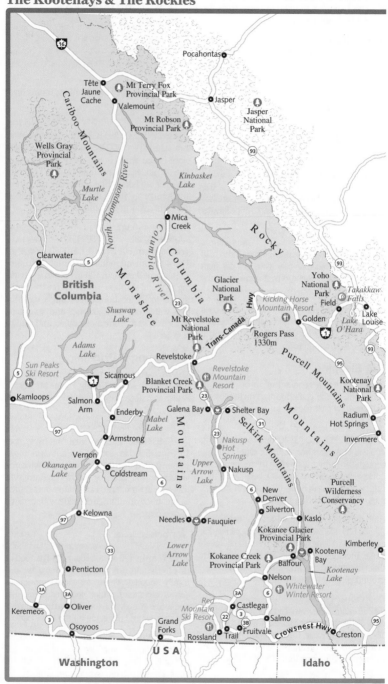

crepe or one of the many upscale sharing plates at this plush wine bar – or dig into some fondue (mains $8 to $20). Nightly specials include drinks; come for Scotch night.

Cabin BAR
(☑ 250-837-2144; www.cometothecabin.com; 200 1st St E; ☺ 5pm-midnight Tue-Sat) Bowling alley, bar, outdoor-gear store and art gallery, it's a funky chill spot with a few snacks to go with the beers.

ℹ Information

The **visitors center** (☑ 800-487-1493, 250-837-5345; www.seerevelstoke.com; cnr Victoria Rd & Campbell Ave; ☺ 9am-6pm) is set to open in a new building right in the center in 2014.

ℹ Getting There & Away

Greyhound Canada (☑ 800-661-8747; www. greyhound.ca; 1899 Fraser Dr) Located west of town, just off Hwy 1; it has storage lockers. Buses go east to Calgary ($63, six hours, four daily) via Banff, and west to Vancouver ($101, nine to 11 hours, two daily) via Kamloops or Kelowna.

Revelstoke Shuttle (☑ 888-569-1969; www. revelstokeconnection.com) Daily shuttle buses operate to/from Kelowna ($84, 2½ hours).

Mt Revelstoke National Park

Grand in beauty if not in size (only 260 sq km), this **national park** (www.pc.gc.ca/revelstoke), just northeast of its namesake town, is a vision of peaks and valleys – many all but untrodden.

From the 2223m summit of Mt Revelstoke, the views of the mountains and the Columbia River valley are excellent. To ascend here, take the 26km **Meadows in the Sky Parkway** (☺ 8am-5pm May-Oct), 1.5km east of Revelstoke off the Trans-Canada Hwy (Hwy 1). Open after the thaw, this paved road winds through lush cedar forests and alpine meadows and ends at Balsam Lake, within 2km of the peak. From here, walk to the top or take the **shuttle** (free; ☺ 10am-5pm).

There are several good hiking trails from the summit. You can camp only in designated backcountry campsites, and you must have a Wilderness Pass camping permit ($10; in addition to your park pass), which, along with lots of useful information, is available from **Parks Canada**

📧 250-837-7500; revglacier.reception@pc.gc.ca; 301 3rd St, Revelstoke; ☉ 8am-4:30pm Mon-Fri) or from the Rogers Pass Centre (p228) inside Glacier National Park. Admission to both Mt Revelstoke and Glacier National Parks (the two are administered jointly) is $8/4 per adult/child per day.

Glacier National Park

To be really accurate, this 1350-sq-km park (www.pc.gc.ca/glacier) should be called '430 Glaciers National Park'; the annual snowfall can be as much as 23m. Due to the sheer mountain slopes, this is one of the world's most active avalanche areas. For this reason, skiing, caving and mountaineering are regulated; you must register with park wardens before venturing into the backcountry. Call for a daily weather and avalanche report (📧 250-837-6867) in season. Admission to this and Mt Revelstoke National Park (the two are administered jointly) is $8/4 per adult/child per day.

Whether you travel by car, bus, trail or bicycle (more power to you), Rogers Pass will likely rank as one of the most beautiful mountain passes you'll ever traverse. Be sure to pause at the Hemlock Grove Trail, 54km east of Revelstoke, where a 400m boardwalk winds through an ancient hemlock rainforest.

Spend some time with the Canadian Pacific Railway dioramas at the informative Rogers Pass Centre (📧 250-814-5233; Hwy 1; ☉ 8am-7pm), 72km east of Revelstoke. The center shows films about the park and organizes guided walks in summer. As a bonus, there's an excellent bookstore run by the Friends of Mt Revelstoke & Glacier (www.friendsrevglacier.com).

Not far from here are the park's two campgrounds: Illecillewaet and Loop Brook (off Hwy 1; campsites $22; ☉ Jul-Sep). Both have running water and flush toilets.

Golden

POP 3800

Golden is well situated for the national parks – there are six nearby. For excitement even closer, like white-water rafting, the Kicking Horse River converges with the Columbia.

Don't just breeze past the strip of franchised yuck on Hwy 1 or you'll miss the tidy little town center down by the tumbling river.

TWO PERFECT WALKS

Easily accessible, Skunk Cabbage Trail, 28km east of Revelstoke on Hwy 1, is a 1.2km boardwalk along the Illecillewaet River. It is lined with its huge namesakes. Another 4km east, the Giant Cedars Boardwalk winds a 500m course up and down and all around a grove of huge old-growth cedars.

◉ Sights & Activities

Golden is the center for white-water rafting trips on the turbulent and chilly Kicking Horse River. Along with powerful grade III and IV rapids, breathtaking scenery along the sheer walls of the Kicking Horse Valley makes this rafting experience one of North America's best. Local operators include Alpine Rafting (📧 888-599-5299, 250-344-6778; www.alpinerafting.com; 101 Golden Donald Upper Rd; trips from $90; ☉ Jun-Sep), next to the visitors center.

Northern Lights Wolf Centre   NATURE PARK
(📧 250-344-6798; www.northernlightswildlife.com; 1745 Short Rd; adult/child $12/6; ☉ 9am-7pm) See wolves in nature and learn about bear conservation at the Northern Lights Wolf Centre. Visitors can expect to meet a resident wolf or two and learn about their complex and human-like family structure.

Kicking Horse Mountain Resort   SKIING
(📧 866-754-5425, 250-439-5400; www.kicking-horseresort.com; Kicking Horse Trail; 1-day lift pass adult/child from $80/26) Some 60% of the 120 ski runs at Kicking Horse Mountain Resort are rated advanced or expert. With a 1260m vertical drop and a snowy position between the Rockies and the Purcells, the resort's popularity grows each year. It's 14km from Golden.

🍴 Sleeping & Eating

There are scores of chain motels along Hwy 1. Check with the chamber of commerce (p229) for B&Bs and the municipal campground.

In the walkable center, 9th Ave N is good for cafes, bakeries and shops. The farmers market (10th Ave N; ☉ noon-5pm Wed Jun-Aug) is next to the chamber of commerce.

★ **Dreamcatcher Hostel**   HOSTEL $
(☑ 250-439-1090; www.dreamcatcherhostel.com;
528 9th Ave N; dm/r from $35/90) Run by two
veteran travelers, this centrally located hostel has everything a budget traveler could
hope for. There are 33 beds across eight
rooms, as well as a vast kitchen and a comfy
common room with a stone fireplace.

Mary's Motel   MOTEL $$
(☑ 866-234-6279, 250-344-7111; www.marysmotel.
com; 603 8th Ave N; r $80-130; ❉ ⚘ ⚐ ❇) In town,
right on the roaring river, Mary's has 81
rooms spread across several buildings; get
one with a patio. It's easy to get wet: there's
a large outdoor pool, an indoor one and two
hot tubs.

Chancellor Peak Chalets   LODGE $$$
(☑ 250-344-7038, 800-644-8888; www.chancellor-
peakchalets.com; 2924 Kicking Horse Rd; cabins
from $200; ⚐) The 11 log chalets at this riverside retreat have two levels and sleep up to
six. There are soaker tubs, full kitchens and
all the nature you can breathe in. The chalets are 25km east of Golden.

★ **Eleven22**   FUSION $$
(☑ 250-344-2443; www.eleven22.ca; 1122 10th Ave
S; mains $11-24; ⊙ 5-10pm; ✎) A cross between
a restaurant and a dinner party, this appealing restaurant has art on the walls of the
small dining rooms and all the stars you can
count out on the patio. Watch the kitchen
action from the lounge area while sharing small plates. Foods are mostly sourced
locally.

ℹ Information

Visitors Center (☑ 250-344-7711; 111 Golden
Donald Upper Rd; ⊙9am-6pm) The smiles are
as shiny as the building, 1km east on Hwy 1
from the Hwy 95 turnoff into Golden.

Kicking Horse Country Chamber of Commerce (☑ 800-622-4653, 250-344-7125;
www.goldenchamber.bc.ca; 500 10th Ave N;
⊙10am-5pm Mon-Fri) For lots of local info,
visit the chamber of commerce down near the
center.

ℹ Getting There & Away

Delays may offset improvements on Hwy 1 east
of Golden as the road is reconstructed from
scratch; see www.kickinghorsecanyon.ca.

Greyhound Canada (☑ 800-661-8747; www.
greyhound.ca; Husky Travel Centre, 1050 Hwy
1) serves Vancouver ($132, 10 to 13 hours, three
daily) and Calgary ($48, 3½ hours, four daily)
via Banff.

Yoho National Park

Fed by glaciers, the ice-blue Kicking Horse
River plows through the valley of the same
name. The surging waters are an apt image
for this dramatic **national park** (Map p74;
☑ 250-343-6783; www.pc.gc.ca/yoho; adult/child
$10/5), home to looming peaks, pounding
waterfalls, glacial lakes and patches of pretty
meadows.

Although the smallest (1310 sq km) of the
four national parks in the Rockies, Yoho is
a diamond in the (very) rough. This wilderness is the real deal; it's some of the continent's least tarnished.

East of Field on Hwy 1 is the **Takakkaw
Falls road**, open late June to early October.
At 254m, Takakkaw is one of the highest
waterfalls in Canada. From here **Iceline**, a
20km hiking loop, passes many glaciers and
spectacular scenery.

This World Heritage Site protects the
amazing Cambrian-age **fossil beds** on Mt
Stephen and Mt Field. These 515-million-
year-old fossils preserve the remains of
marine creatures that were some of the
earliest forms of life on earth. You can
only get to the fossil beds by guided hikes,
which are led by naturalists from the **Yoho
Shale Geoscience Foundation** (☑ 800-343-
3006; www.burgess-shale.bc.ca; tours from adult/
child $120/25; ⊙ Jul-Sep). Reservations are
essential.

Near the south gate of the park, you can
reach pretty **Wapta Falls** along a 2.4km
trail. The easy walk takes about 45 minutes
each way.

The four campgrounds within Yoho all
close from mid-October to mid-May. Only
the **Kicking Horse Campground** (off Hwy 1,
Field; campsites $28; ⊙May-Oct) has showers,
making its 88 sites the most popular. Appealing **Takakkaw Falls Campground** (Yoho
Valley Rd; campsites $18; ⊙ Jul-Oct), 13km along
a gravel road, has 35 walk-in (200m) campsites for tents only.

> ℹ **WINTER ROAD CONDITIONS**
>
> For up-to-date road conditions on the
> Hwy 1 and across the province, consult
> **DriveBC** (☑ 800-550-4997; www.drivebc.
> ca). This is essential in winter, when
> storms can close roads for extended
> periods.

BRITISH COLUMBIA YOHO NATIONAL PARK

The isolated **HI-Yoho National Park** (Whiskey Jack Hostel; ☑866-762-4122, 403-670-7580; www.hihostels.ca; Yoho Valley Rd; dm from $20; ☺Jul-Sep) offers 27 dorm-style beds. It's 13km off Hwy 1, just before the Takakkaw Falls Campground and close to the falls itself.

ℹ Information

At Yoho National Park Information Centre (☑250-343-6783; off Hwy 1, Field; ☺9am-7pm May-Oct), pick up maps and trail descriptions, however note that Parks Canada budget cuts mean that this vital resource is often closed. Rangers can advise on itineraries and conditions. Alberta Tourism staffs a desk here in summer.

Lake O'Hara

Perched high in the mountains east of Field, **Lake O'Hara** is worth the significant hassle involved in reaching the place, which is an encapsulation of the whole Rockies. Compact wooded hillsides, alpine meadows, snow-covered passes, mountain vistas and glaciers are all wrapped around the stunning lake. A basic day trip is worthwhile, but stay overnight in the backcountry and you'll be able to access many more trails, some quite difficult, all quite spectacular. The **Alpine Circuit** (12km) has a bit of everything.

To reach the lake, you can take the **shuttle bus** (Field; adult/child return $15/7.50; ☺mid-Jun–Sep) from the Lake O'Hara parking lot, 15km east of Field on Hwy 1. A quota system governs bus access to the lake and limits permits for the 30 backcountry campsites. You can freely walk the 11km from the parking area, but no bikes are allowed. The area around Lake O'Hara is usually covered with snow or very muddy until mid-July.

Make **reservations** (☑250-343-6433; reservation fee $12) for the bus trip or for **camping** (a permit costs $10 per night) three months in advance. Available spots often go the first hour lines are open, from 8am mountain time. Given the popularity of Lake O'Hara, reservations are basically mandatory, unless you want to walk. However, if you don't have advance reservations, six day-use seats on the bus and three to five campsites are set aside for 'standby' users. To try to snare these, call at 8am the day before.

Lake O'Hara Lodge (☑250-343-6418; www.lakeohara.com; r per person from $280) 🏌 has been leaving guests slack-jawed for over 80 years. The only place to stay at the lake without a tent, the lodge is luxurious in a rustic way. Its environmental practices are lauded. There's a two night minimum stay.

Field

Don't go past Field without stopping. Right off Hwy 1, this historic railroad town has a dramatic overlook of the river and is a quaint yet unfussy place. Many of its buildings date from the early days of the railways, when it was the Canadian Pacific Railway's headquarters for exploration and, later, for strategic planning when engineers were trying to solve the problem of moving trains over Kicking Horse Pass. See the results from the Hwy 1 **Spiral Tunnel Lookout** 8km east of Field.

Field has more than 20 B&Bs. **Fireweed Hostel** (☑877-343-6999, 250-343-6999; www.fireweedhostel.com; 313 Stephen Ave; dm $30-40, r $80-170; 🛜) has four spotless rooms.

Truffle Pigs Bistro (☑250-343-6303; www.trufflepigs.com; 100 Centre St; r from $170, mains $14-32; ☺7:30am-9pm; 🛜) is a legendary cafe serving inventive, high-concept bistro fare that's locally sourced and usually organic. Their inn across the street has 14 rooms with the same cheeky style as the bistro.

Greyhound Canada buses stop at the park info center on Hwy 1 on their trips west to Golden and east to Banff.

Mt Assiniboine Provincial Park

Between Kootenay and Banff National Parks lies this lesser-known and smaller (39 sq km) **provincial park** (Map p74; www.bcparks.ca), part of the Rockies' Unesco World Heritage site. The pointed peak of Mt Assiniboine (3618m), often referred to as Canada's Matterhorn, and its near neighbors have become a magnet for experienced rock climbers and mountaineers. Backcountry hikers revel in its meadows and glaciers.

The park's main focus is crystal-clear **Lake Magog**, which is reachable on a 27km trek from Banff National Park or by helicopter. At the lake, there's the commercially operated **Mt Assiniboine Lodge** (☑403-678-2883; www.assiniboinelodge.com; r per person $230-340), a **campground** (campsites adult/child $10/5) and some **huts** (per person from $25), which may be reserved through the lodge. Helicopter transport is $150 to $165 each way.

Kootenay National Park

Shaped like a lightning bolt, **Kootenay National Park** (Map p74; ☑ 250-347-9505; www.pc.gc.ca/kootenay; Hwy 93; entrance fee adult/child $10/5, campsites $22-39; ☺ camping May-Oct) is centered on a long, wide, tree-covered valley shadowed by cold, gray peaks. Encompassing 1406 sq km, Kootenay has a more moderate climate than the other Rocky Mountains parks and, in the southern regions especially, summers can be hot and dry, which is a factor in the frequent fires. It's the only national park in Canada to contain both glaciers and cacti. From BC you can create a fine driving loop via Kootenay and Yoho National Parks.

The interpretive **Fireweed Trail** (500m or 2km) loops through the surrounding forest at the north end of Hwy 93. Panels explain how nature is recovering from a 1968 fire. Some 7km further on, **Marble Canyon** has a pounding creek flowing through a nascent forest. Another 3km south on the main road is the easy 2km trail through forest to ochre pools known as the **Paint Pots**. Panels describe both the mining history of this rusty earth and its importance to Aboriginal people.

Learn how the park's appearance has changed over time at the **Kootenay Valley Viewpoint**, where informative panels vie with the view. Just 3km south, **Olive Lake** makes a perfect picnic or rest stop. A 500m lakeside interpretive trail describes some of the visitors who've come before you.

Radium Hot Springs

Lying just outside the southwest corner of Kootenay National Park, Radium Hot Springs is a major gateway to the whole Rocky Mountains national park area. The **Kootenay National Park & Radium Hot Springs Visitors Center** (☑ 250-347-9331; www.radiumhotsprings.com; 7556 Main St E, Hwy 93/95; ☺ visitors center 9am-5pm year-round, Parks Canada May-Oct) has internet access, an excellent display on the park and is staffed with Parks Canada rangers.

Radium boasts a large resident population of **bighorn sheep**, which often wander through town, but the big attraction is the namesake **hot springs** (☑ 250-347-9485; www.pc.gc.ca/hotsprings; off Hwy 93; adult/child $7/6; ☺ 9am-11pm), 3km north of town. The hot springs' pools are quite modern and can

get very busy in summer. The water from the ground at 44°C, ent... pool at 39°C and hits the final...

Radium glows with lodgin... motels at last count. Directly... park gate, **Misty River Lodge** ... 9912; www.mistyriverlodge.bc.ca; 5036 Hwy 93; r $60-100; @]) has six rooms and owners who are enthusiastic about the parks and ready to share their knowledge with guests; cyclists are welcomed.

Radium Hot Springs to Fernie

South from Radium Hot Springs, Hwy 93/95 follows the wide Columbia River valley between the Purcell and Rocky Mountains. It's not especially interesting, unless you're into the area's industry (building ski resorts), agriculture (golf courses) or wild game (condo buyers).

South of Skookumchuck, the road forks. Go left and after 31km you'll reach Hwy 3 for Fernie. Go left on Hwy 95A and you'll come to **Fort Steele Heritage Town** (☑ 250-426-7342; www.fortsteele.ca; 9851 Hwy 93/95; adult/child $12/5; ☺ 9:30am-6pm), a recreated 1880s town that's an order of magnitude less irritating than many of similar ilk.

From Fort Steele it's 95km to Fernie along Hwys 93 and 3.

Fernie

POP 4600

Surrounded by mountains on four sides – that's the sheer Lizard Range you see looking west – Fernie defines cool. Once devoted solely to lumber and coal, the town has used its sensational setting to branch out. Skiers love the 8m-plus of dry powder that annually blankets the runs seen from town. In summer, this same dramatic setting lures scores of hikers and mountain bikers.

Despite the town's discovery by pleasure seekers, it still retains a down-to-earth vibe, best felt in the cafes, bars, shops and galleries along Victoria (2nd) Ave in the historic center, three blocks south of Hwy 3 (7th Ave).

◎ Sights

One of many disasters, Fernie experienced a devastating fire in 1908, which

...ed in a brick-and-stone building ...e. So today you'll see numerous fine **early-20th-century buildings**, many of which were built out of local yellow brick, giving the town an appearance unique in the East Kootenays. Get a copy of *Heritage Walking Tour* ($5), a superb booklet produced by the impressively expanded **Fernie Museum** (☑250-423-7016; 491 2nd Ave; admission by donation; ☉10am-5:30pm).

🏃 Activities

Mountain biking is almost as big as skiing and Fernie has lots for riders. There are easy jaunts in **Mt Fernie Provincial Park** (www.bcparks.ca; Hwy 3), which is a mere 3km south of town; and legendary rides up and down the hills in and around the ski resort, which runs lifts in summer. Many come just to tackle the fabled **Al Matador**, which drops over 900m before finishing in the terrific Three Kings trail. Get a copy of the widely available *Fernie Mountain Bike Map* and check out the websites www.crankfernie.com and www.fernietrailsalliance.com.

Great hiking trails radiate in all directions from Fernie. The excellent and challenging **Three Sisters hike** (20km) winds through forests and wildflower-covered meadows, along limestone cliffs and scree slopes. Get directions at the visitors center.

★ Fernie Alpine Resort　　　　SKIING
(☑250-423-4655, 877-333-2339, snow conditions 250-423-3555; www.skifernie.com; 5339 Ski Area Rd; 1-day pass adult/child $80/26) In fall, eyes turn to the mountains for more than their beauty: they're looking for snow. A five-minute drive from downtown, fast-growing Fernie Alpine Resort boasts 142 runs, five bowls and almost endless dumps of powder. Most hotels run shuttles here daily.

Ski & Bike Base　　　　SKIING, CYCLING
(☑250-423-6464; www.skibase.com; 432 2nd Ave; bicycle rental per day from $45; ☉10am-6pm Mon-Sat) One of several excellent all-season gear sales and rental shops on 2nd Ave.

Mountain High River Adventures　　RAFTING
(☑877-423-4555, 250-423-5008; www.raftfernie.com; 100 Riverside Way; trips adult/child from $125/100; ☉May-Sep) The Elk River is a classic white-water river, with three grade IV rapids and 11 more grade III rapids. Besides rafting, Mountain High offers kayaking, floats and more on the surging waters.

Fernie Bike Guides　　　　CYCLING
(☑250-423-3650; www.ferniebikeguides.ca; guiding/instruction per hour $30/60) Raise your cycling game with experts or let them show you the far reaches of the Elk Valley.

🛏 Sleeping

Being a big ski town, Fernie's high season is winter. You'll have most fun staying in the center, otherwise **Fernie Central Reservations** (☑800-622-5007; www.ferniecentralreservations.com) can book you a room at the ski resort.

HI Raging Elk Hostel　　　　HOSTEL $
(☑250-423-6811; www.ragingelk.com; 892 6th Ave; dm/r from $29/75; ☉pub 4-11pm; @) Wide decks allow plenty of inspirational mountain gazing at this well-run central hostel that has good advice for those hoping to mix time on the slopes or trails with seasonal work. The pub is a hoot.

Mt Fernie Provincial Park　　CAMPGROUND $
(☑800-689-9025; www.discovercamping.ca; off Hwy 3; campsites $21; ☉May-Sep) Only 3km south from town, it has 40 sites, flush toilets, waterfalls and access to mountain-bike trails.

Park Place Lodge　　　　HOTEL $$
(☑888-381-7275, 250-423-6871; www.parkplacelodge.com; 742 Hwy 3; r $100-220; ❀@☀) The nicest lodging close to the center, its 64 comfortable rooms have high-speed internet, fridges, microwaves and access to an indoor pool. Some have balconies and views.

Snow Valley Motel & RV Park　　MOTEL $$
(☑250-423-4421; www.snowvalleymotel.com; 1041 7th Ave, Hwy 3; campsites $20-30, r $70-130; ❀@☎) Great value in the middle of town. The 20 motel units are large and come with microwaves and fridges, some with full kitchens. Nothing is fancy, but there is a barbecue deck with views.

🍴 Eating & Drinking

Get good produce year-round at **Cincott Farms Organic Market** (☑250-423-5564; www.cincott.com; 851 7th Ave; ☉11:30am-6pm Mon-Sat) 🍃. Look for the excellent ales of Fernie Brewing Co, including 'What the Huck!' berry beer, at local pubs.

Blue Toque Diner　　　　CAFE $
(☑250-423-4637; 500 Hwy 3; mains from $7; ☉9am-3pm Thu-Mon) Part of the Arts Station community gallery, this is *the* place for

breakfast. The menu features lots of seasonal and organic vegetarian specials.

Mug Shots Bistro   BAKERY $
(☑250-423-8018; 591 3rd Ave; mains $5; ☉8am-5pm; ☎) Always buzzing, it offers good coffee, baked goods, sandwiches and internet access.

★Yamagoya   JAPANESE $$
(☑250-430-0090; 741 7th Ave, Hwy 3 ; small dishes $4-8; ☉5-10pm) As compact as a California roll, this gem of a sushi place does a wide range of classics, from hot to tempura. Even the miso soup is good, especially after a day skiing. Besides sake, there's a great beer selection.

Bridge Bistro   CANADIAN $$
(☑250-423-3002; 301 Hwy 3; mains $10-20; ☉11am-10pm) Enjoy the views of the Elk River and surrounding peaks from the deck, but save some attention for the long menu of good burgers, steaks and pizza.

🔒 Shopping

Polar Peek Books   BOOKS
(☑250-423-3736; 592 2nd Ave; ☉10am-6pm) This eclectic mix of books has a good section of local interest. Great recommendations.

ℹ Information

The **visitors center** (☑250-423-6868; www.ferniechamber.com; 102 Commerce Rd; ☉9am-5pm) is east of town off Hwy 3, just past the Elk River crossing. It includes the **Fernie Nature Centre**, which has displays on local critters. The **Fernie Museum** also has tourist info.

ℹ Getting There & Around

Shuttles operate between town and the ski resort.

Greyhound Canada (☑250-423-6811; www.greyhound.ca; Husky Petrol Station, 2001 Hwy 3) runs buses west to Kelowna ($113, 11 hours, one daily) and Nelson ($65, 5½ hours, one daily), and east to Calgary ($63, six hours, one daily). The stop is a 1.5km truck-buffeted walk west of the center.

Kimberley

POP 6700

When big-time mining left Kimberley in 1973, a plan was hatched to turn the little mountain village at 1113m altitude into a tourist destination with a Bavarian theme. The center was turned into a pedestrian zone named the **Platzl**, locals were encouraged to prance about in lederhosen and dirndl, and sausage was added to many a menu. Now, more than three decades later, the shtick is fading. There's still a bit of fake half-timbering about, but mostly it's a diverse place that makes a worthwhile detour off Hwy 95 between Cranbrook and Radium Hot Springs.

The **visitors center** (☑250-427-3666; www.kimberleychamber.com; 270 Kimberley Ave; ☉10am-6pm) sits in the large parking area behind the Platzl.

Take a 15km ride on **Kimberley's Underground Mining Railway** (☑250-427-7365; www.kimberleysundergroundminingrailway.ca; Gerry Sorensen Way; adult/child $20/8; ☉tours 11am-3pm May-Sep, trains to resort 10am Sat & Sun), where the tiny train putters through the steep-walled Mark Creek Valley toward some sweeping mountain vistas. At the end of the line, you can take a chairlift up to the **Kimberley Alpine Resort** (☑877-754-5462, 250-427-4881; www.skikimberley.com; 1-day lift pass adult/child $68/22). In winter, the resort has over 700 hectares of skiable terrain, mild weather and 80 runs.

Cranbrook

POP 19,500

The area's main center, 31km southeast of Kimberley, **Cranbrook** is a dusty crossroads. Hwy 3/95 bisects the town, which is a charmless strip of motels.

However, it has one great reason for stopping: the **Canadian Museum of Rail Travel** (☑250-489-3918; www.trainsdeluxe.com; 57 Van Horne St S, Hwy 3/95; adult $14-22, child $1-6; ☉10am-6pm). It has some fine examples of classic Canadian trains, including the luxurious 1929 edition of the Trans-Canada Limited, a legendary train that ran from Montréal to Vancouver.

Cranbrook to Rossland

Hwy 3 twists and turns its way 300km from Cranbrook to Osoyoos at the south end of the Okanagan Valley. Along the way it hugs the hills close to the US border and passes eight border crossings. As such, it's a road of great usefulness, even if the sights never quite live up to the promise.

Creston, 123km west of Cranbrook, is known for its many orchards and as the home of Columbia Brewing Co's Kokanee

BRITISH COLUMBIA KIMBERLEY

ℹ CHECK YOUR WATCH

It is a constant source of confusion that the East Kootenays lie in the mountain time zone along with Alberta, unlike the rest of BC, which falls within the Pacific time zone. West on Hwy 1 from Golden, the time changes at the east gate of Glacier National Park. Going west on Hwy 3, the time changes between Cranbrook and Creston. Mountain time is one hour ahead of Pacific time.

True Ale. But both of these products are mostly shipped out, so you should do the same. Hwy 3A heads north from here for a scenic 80km to the free **Kootenay Lake Ferry**, which connects to Nelson. This is a fun and scenic journey.

The **Creston Valley Wildlife Management Area** (☑250-402-6900; www.creston-wildlife.ca; Hwy 3; ☺dawn-dusk), 11km west of Creston, is a good place to spot oodles of birds, including blue herons, from the 1km boardwalk.

Some 85km west of Creston, **Salmo** is notable mostly as the junction with Hwy 6, which runs north for a bland 40km to Nelson. The Crowsnest Hwy splits 10km to the west. Hwy 3 bumps north through **Castlegar**, which is notable for having the closest large airport to Nelson and a very large pulp mill. Hwy 3B dips down through the cute little cafe-filled town of **Fruitvale** and industrial **Trail**.

Rossland

POP 3700

About 10km west of Trail, Rossland is a world apart. High in the Southern Monashee Mountains (1023m), this old mining village is one of Canada's best places for mountain biking. A long history of mining has left the hills crisscrossed with old trails and abandoned rail lines, all of which are perfect for riding.

The **visitors center** (☑888-448-7444, 250-362-7722; www.rossland.com; 1100 Hwy 3B; ☺9am-5pm May-Sep) is located in the **Rossland Museum** building, at the junction of Hwy 22 (from the US border) and Hwy 3B.

Mountain biking is the reason many come to Rossland. Free riding is all the rage as the ridgelines are easily accessed and there are lots of rocky paths for plunging downhill. The **Seven Summits & Dewdney Trail** is a 35.8km single track along the crest of the Rossland Range. The **Kootenay Columbia Trails Society** (www.kcts.ca) has tons of info, including downloadable maps.

Good in summer for riding, **Red Mountain Ski Resort** (☑250-362-7384, 800-663-0105, snow report 250-362-5500; www.redresort.com; Hwy 3B; 1-day lift pass adult/child $72/36) draws plenty of ski bums in winter. Red, as it's called, includes the 1590m-high Red Mountain and 2040m-high Granite Mountain, for a total of 1085 hectares of challenging, powdery terrain.

Hwy 3B curves through awesome alpine scenery before rejoining Hwy 3 28km northwest of Rossland. The road then wends its way 170km west to Osoyoos through increasingly arid terrain.

Nelson

POP 10,300

Nelson is reason enough to visit the Kootenays and should be on any itinerary in the region. Tidy brick buildings climb the side of a hill overlooking the west arm of deep-blue Kootenay Lake, and the waterfront is lined with parks and beaches. The thriving cafe, culture and nightlife scene is simply a bonus. However, what really propels Nelson over the top is its personality: a funky mix of hippies, characters, creative types and rugged individualists. You can find all these along Baker St, the pedestrian-friendly main drag where wafts of patchouli mingle with hints of fresh-roasted coffee.

Born as a mining town in the late 1800s, in 1977 a decades-long heritage-preservation project began. Today there are more than 350 carefully preserved and restored period buildings. Nelson is an excellent base for hiking, skiing and kayaking the nearby lakes and hills.

⊙ Sights

Almost a third of Nelson's **historic buildings** have been restored to their high- and late-Victorian architectural splendor. Pick up the superb *Heritage Walking Tour* from the visitors center. It gives details of over two dozen buildings in the center and offers a good lesson in Victorian architecture.

Touchstones Nelson (☑250-352-9813; 502 Vernon St; adult/child $8/4; ☺10am-5pm Mon-Wed, Fri & Sat, to 8pm Thu, noon-4pm Sun) combines engaging historical displays with art in Nelson's grand old city hall (1902).

By the iconic Nelson Bridge, **Lakeside Park** is both a flower-filled, shady park and a beach, with a great summer cafe. From the center, follow the **Waterfront Pathway**, which runs all along the shore – its western extremity passes the airport and has a remote river vantage. You could walk one way to the park and ride **Streetcar 23** (adult/child $3/2; ☺11am-4:30pm Sat & Sun Jun-Oct) the other way. It follows a 2km track from Lakeside Park to the wharf at Hall St.

🏃 Activities

Kayaking

The natural (meaning undammed) waters of Kootenay Lake are a major habitat for kayaks. **ROAM** (☑250-354-2056; www.roam-shop.com; 639 Baker St; ☺8am-7pm Mon-Sat, to 5pm Sun) sells gear, offers advice and works with the noted **Kootenay Kayak Company** (☑250-505-4549; www.kootenaykayak.com; kayak rentals per day $40-50, tours from $80). Kayaks can be picked up at ROAM or Lakeside Park.

Hiking

Great hikes starfish out from Nelson, especially in the Selkirk Mountains north of town.

★**Kokanee Glacier Provincial Park** HIKING (☑trail conditions 250-825-3500; www.bcparks.ca; Kokanee Glacier Rd) This park boasts 85km of some of the area's most superb hiking trails. The fantastic summer-only 2.5km (two hour) round-trip hike to **Kokanee Lake** on a well-marked trail can be continued to the treeless, boulder-strewn expanse around the glacier. Turn off Hwy 3A 20.5km northeast of Nelson, then it's another 16km on Kokanee Glacier Rd.

Along the way at the 11.4km mark, look for the **Old Growth Trail**, a 3km walk through 500-year-old trees.

Burlington Northern Rail Trail HIKING
Extending 42km from Nelson to Salmo along an old rail line, this trail has stunning views amid thick forest. Turn back when you want, but the first 6km has many highlights. The trailhead is at the corner of Cherry and Gore Streets.

Pulpit Rock HIKING
(www.pulpitrocknelson.com) The two-hour climb to Pulpit Rock, just across the lake, affords fine views of Nelson and Kootenay Lake. The trailhead starts at the parking lot on John-stone Rd.

Mountain Biking

Mountain-bike trails wind up from Kootenay Lake along steep and challenging hills, followed by vertigo-inducing downhills. Pick up *Nelson Mountain Bike Guide* ($20), which details 105 trails, from **Sacred Ride** (☑250-362-5688; www.sacredride.ca; 213B Baker St; bicycle rentals per day $45-95; ☺9am-5:30pm Mon-Sat).

Skiing & Snowboarding

Known for its heavy powdery snowfall, **Whitewater Winter Resort** (☑250-354-4944, 800-666-9420, snow report 250-352-7669; www.skiwhitewater.com; off Hwy 6; 1-day lift ticket adult/child $68/34), 12km south of Nelson off Hwy 6, has the same small-town charm as Nelson. Lifts are few, but so are the crowds, who enjoy a drop of 623m on 78 runs.

🛏 Sleeping

By all means stay in the heart of Nelson so you can fully enjoy the city's beat. The visitors center has lists of B&Bs in heritage homes near the center.

★**WhiteHouse Backpacker Lodge** HOSTEL $
(☑250-352-0505; www.white-house.ca; 816 Vernon St; dm $25-30, r $50-65; @☏) Relax on the broad porch overlooking the lake at this comfy heritage house, which has a cool book collection, a fireplace and more. You'll get all the pancakes you can cook yourself for breakfast.

HI Dancing Bear Inn HOSTEL $
(☑877-352-7573, 250-352-7573; www.dancing-bearinn.com; 171 Baker St; dm/r from $24/52; ☺@☏) ✐ The brilliant management here offers advice and smoothes the stay of guests in the 14 shared and private rooms, all of which share bathrooms. There's a gourmet kitchen and a library.

City Tourist Park CAMPGROUND $
(☑250-352-7618; campnels@telus.net; 90 High St; campsites from $20; ☺May-Sep) Just a five-minute walk from Baker St, this small municipal campground has 43 shady sites.

★**Hume Hotel** HOTEL $$
(☑250-352-5331; www.humehotel.com; 422 Vernon St; r $100-200; @☏) This 1898 classic hotel maintains its period grandeur. The 43 rooms vary in quality – beware of air-less ones overlooking the kitchen on sultry

nights. Ask for the huge corner rooms with views of the hills and lake. Rates include a delicious breakfast. It has several appealing nightlife venues.

Cloudside Inn INN $$
(☑800-596-2337, 250-352-3226; www.cloudside.
ca; 408 Victoria St; r $100-200; ❈@🐾🛜) Live like a silver baron at this vintage mansion, where the seven rooms are named after trees. Luxuries abound, and a fine patio looks over the terraced gardens and town.

Mountain Hound Inn GUESTHOUSE $$
(☑866-452-6490, 250-352-6490; www.mountain-
hound.com; 621 Baker St; r $70-120; ❈@🛜) The 19 rooms are small, but have an industrial edge – to go with the cement-block walls. It's ideally located in the center and is a good, no-frills choice.

Victoria Falls Guest House INN $$
(☑250-505-3563; www.victoriafallsguesthouse.
com; cnr Victoria & Falls Sts; r $105-135; 🛜🍽) The wide porch wraps right around this festive yellow renovated Victorian. The five suites have sitting areas and cooking facilities. Decor ranges from cozy antiques to family-friendly bunk beds.

✗ Eating & Drinking

Stroll the Baker St environs and you'll find a vibrant mix of eateries. Look for Nelson Brewing Co's organic beers on tap; we swoon for the intense Full Nelson IPA and the Hopgood Session Ale.

★Cottonwood Community Market MARKET $
(Cottonwood Falls Park; ⏰9:30am-3pm Sat May-Oct) Close to downtown and next to the surging Cottonwood waterfall, this market encapsulates Nelson. There's great organic produce; fine baked goods, many with heretofore unheard of grains; and various craft items with artistic roots in tie-dyeing. A second event, the **Downtown Market** (400 block Josephine St; ⏰10am-4pm Wed Jun-Sep), also has live music.

★Kootenay Bakery Cafe BAKERY $
(☑250-352-2274; www.kootenaybakerycafe.com; 377 Baker St; mains from $6; ⏰7:30am-6pm Mon-Sat; 🍴) 🌿 Organic ingredients and locally sourced foods come together in this bustling bakery with an excellent cafe. Sandwiches, soups, salads, breakfasts and more can be enjoyed while customers cart spelt loafs out the door by the bushel.

Oso Negro CAFE $
(☑250-532-7761; 604 Ward St; coffee from $2; ⏰7am-5pm) This local favorite corner cafe roasts its own coffee. Outside there are tables in a garden that burbles with water features amid statues.

Bibo FUSION $$
(☑250-352-2744; www.bibonelson.ca; 518 Hall St; mains $19-30; ⏰5pm-late) Bibo is all exposed brick inside, while outside a hillside terrace looks down to the lake. Small plates celebrate local produce: enjoy a meze or cheese and charcuterie plate with flights of wine. The short list of upscale mains includes burgers and seafood.

Cantina del Centro MEXICAN $$
(☑250-352-3737; 561 Baker St; small mains $6-10; ⏰11am-late) Bright and vibrant, it gets jammed with diners. The superfresh tacos and other small plates reflect the vivid colors of the Mexican tile floor. You can watch your meal grill up behind the counter while you chill with a margarita.

★All Seasons Cafe FUSION $$$
(☑250-352-0101; www.allseasonscafe.com; 620 Herridge Lane; mains $20-32; ⏰5-10pm) Sitting on the patio under the little lights twinkling in the huge maple above is a Nelson highlight; in winter, candles provide the same romantic flair. The eclectic menu changes with the seasons but always celebrates BC foods. The wine list is iconic.

Library Lounge LOUNGE
(☑250-352-5331; Hume Hotel, 422 Vernon St; ⏰11am-late) This refined space in a classic hotel has some good sidewalk tables where you can ponder the passing parade. There's live jazz most nights. The adjoining **Mike's Place Pub** bustles and has a great beer selection plus fine chow (mains from $12).

🛍 Shopping

Otter Books BOOKS
(☑250-352-7525; 398 Baker St; ⏰9:30am-5:30pm Mon-Sat, 11am-4pm Sun) Books and maps.

Isis Essentials ACCESSORIES
(☑250-352-0666; www.isis.ca; 582 Ward St; ⏰11am-6pm Mon-Sat) The place to feel the local vibe: sex toys and oils in a feminist setting. Sniff out their line of Dungeon Sense scents.

ℹ Information

The **visitors center** (☑877-663-5706, 250-352-3433; www.discovernelson.com; 225 Hall

St; ⏲8:30am-6pm daily May-Oct, 8:30am-5pm Mon-Fri Nov-Apr) contains good information about the region.

Listen to the Nelson beat on **Kootenay Co-Op Radio** (93.5FM).

ℹ Getting There & Around

Castlegar Airport (YCG; www.wkrairport.ca; Hwy 3A) The closest airport to Nelson is 42km southwest.

Greyhound Canada (☎250-352-3939; Chahko-Mika Mall, 1128 Lakeside Dr) Buses serve Fernie ($65, 5½ hours, one daily) and Kelowna ($65, 5½ hours, one daily).

Nelson Transit System (☎250-352-8201; www.bctransit.ca; fare $2) Buses 2 and 10 serve Chahko-Mika Mall and Lakeside Park. The main stop is at the corner of Ward and Baker Sts.

Queen City Shuttle (☎250-352-9829; www.kootenayshuttle.com; one-way adult/child $25/10) Links with Castlegar Airport (one hour); reserve in advance.

Nelson to Revelstoke

Heading north from Nelson, there are two options, both scenic, for reaching Revelstoke. Hwy 6 heads west for 16km before turning north at South Slocan. The road eventually runs alongside pretty Slocan Lake for about 30km before reaching New Denver. It's 97km between Nelson and New Denver.

Going north and east from Nelson on Hwy 3A is the most interesting route. After 34km there's the dock for the free **Kootenay Lake Ferry** at Balfour. This ride is worth it even if you're not going anywhere, because of the long lake vistas of blue mountains rising sharply from the water.

At Balfour the road becomes Hwy 31 and follows the lake 34km north to Kaslo, passing cute little towns along the way.

Kaslo

A cute little lake town that's a good stop, Kaslo is a low-key gem. Don't miss the restored 1898 **SS Moyie** (324 Front St; adult/child $10/4; ⏲10am-5pm May-Oct). It has tourist info on the myriad ways to kayak and canoe the sparkling blue waters right outside.

There's a range of accommodations in and around town including the appealing downtown **Kaslo Hotel** (☎250-353-7714; www.kaslohotel.com; 430 Front St; r $120-200; @📶), which has lake views and a brewery.

New Denver

Wild mountain streams are just some of the natural highlights on Hwy 31A, which goes up and over some rugged hills. At the end of this twisting 47km road, you reach New Denver, which seems about five years away from ghost-town status. But that's not bad as this historic little gem slumbers away peacefully right on the clear waters of Slocan Lake.

The **Silvery Slocan Museum** (☎250-358-2201; www.newdenver.ca; 202 6th Ave; adult/child $4/free; ⏲9am-4pm Jun-Aug) is also home to the helpful visitors center. Housed in the 1897 Bank of Montreal building, it features well-done displays from the booming

INLAND FERRIES

The long Kootenay and Upper and Lower Arrow Lakes necessitate some scenic travel on **inland ferries** (www.th.gov.bc.ca/marine/ferry_schedules.htm; free). On busy summer weekends, you may have to wait in a long line for a sailing or two before you get passage.

Kootenay Lake Ferry (☎250-229-4215) sails between Balfour on the west arm of Kootenay Lake (34km northeast of Nelson) and Kootenay Bay, where you can follow Hwy 3A for the pretty 80km ride south to Creston. It is a 35-minute crossing. In summer the ferry leaves Balfour every 50 minutes between 6:30am and 9:40pm, and Kootenay Lake from 7:10am to 10:20pm.

Needles Ferry (☎250-837-8418) crosses Lower Arrow Lake between Fauquier (57km south of Nakusp) and Needles (135km east of Vernon) on Hwy 6. The trip takes five minutes and runs every 30 minutes in each direction. This is a good link between the Okanagan Valley and the Kootenays.

Upper Arrow Lake Ferry (☎250-837-8418) runs between Galena Bay (49km south of Revelstoke) and Shelter Bay (49km north of Nakusp) on Hwy 23. The trip takes 20 minutes and runs from 5am to midnight every hour from Shelter Bay and every hour between 5:30am and 12:30am from Galena Bay.

OFF THE BEATEN TRACK

BOWRON LAKE PROVINCIAL PARK

The place heaven-bound canoeists go when they die, **Bowron Lake Provincial Park** (www.bcparks.ca; canoe circuit permit $30-60, campsite $16; ☺ May-Sep) is a fantasyland of 10 lakes surrounded by snowcapped peaks. Forming a natural circle with sections of the Isaac, Cariboo and Bowron Rivers, its 116km canoe circuit is one of the world's finest. There are eight portages, with the longest (2km) over well-defined trails.

The whole circuit takes between six and 10 days, and you'll need to be completely self-sufficient. September is a good time to visit, both for the bold colors of changing leaves and lack of summertime crowds. The park website has maps and details everything you'll need to know for planning your trip, including mandatory reservations, which book up months in advance.

If you'd rather leave the details to others, **Whitegold Adventures** (☎250-994-2345; www.whitegold.ca; Hwy 26, Wells) offers four- to eight-day guided paddles of Bowron Lake. A full circuit costs $1800 per person.

To get to the park by car, turn off Hwy 26 just before Barkerville and follow the 28km gravel Bowron Lake Rd.

Sleeping

There are various options before you paddle out. Reserve park campsites in advance. **Bowron Lake Lodge** (☎800-519-3399, 250-992-2733; www.bowronlakelodge.com; Bowron Lake; campsites $28, r $60-80; ☺May-Sep) is picture-perfect and right on the lake. It has cabins and motel rooms, and rents canoes and gear.

---

mining days, a tiny vault and an untouched tin ceiling.

Both New Denver and the equally sleepy old mining town of **Silverton**, just south, have fine cafes.

Making the loop from Nelson via Hwys 6 and 31 through New Denver is a great day trip. Otherwise, if you're headed to Revelstoke, continue north 47km on Hwy 6 from New Denver to Nakusp through somewhat bland rolling countryside.

Nakusp

Right on Upper Arrow Lake, both Nakusp and the chain of lakes were forever changed by BC's orgy of dam building in the 1950s and 1960s. The water level here was raised and the town had to be moved, which is why it now has a sort of 1960s-era look. It does have some attractive cafes and a tiny **museum**.

Nakusp Hot Springs (☎250-265-4528; www.nakusphotsprings.com; 8500 Hot Springs Rd; adult/child $9.50/8.50; ☺9:30am-9:30pm), 12km northeast of Nakusp off Hwy 23, feel a bit artificial after a revamp. However, you'll forget this as you soak away your cares amid an amphitheater of trees.

From Nakusp you could head west on Hwy 6 to Vernon in the Okanagan Valley, a 245km drive that includes the Needles Ferry.

Or head north 55km on Hwy 23 to the Upper Arrow Lake Ferry and the final 48km to Revelstoke.

CARIBOO, CHILCOTIN & COAST

This vast and beautiful region covers a huge swath of BC north of the Whistler tourist hordes. It comprises three very distinct areas. The **Cariboo** region includes numerous ranches and terrain that's little changed from the 1850s when the 'Gold Rush Trail' passed through from Lillooet to Barkerville.

Populated with more moose than people, the **Chilcotin** lies to the west of Hwy 97, the region's north–south spine. Its mostly wild, rolling landscape has a few ranches and some aboriginal villages. Hwy 20 travels west from Williams Lake to the spectacular Bella Coola Valley, a bear-and-wildlife-filled inlet along the **coast**.

Much of the region can be reached via Hwy 97 and you can build a circle itinerary to other parts of BC via Prince George in the north. The Bella Coola Valley is served by ferry from Port Hardy on Vancouver Island, which makes for even more cool circle-route itineraries.

There is a twice-daily **Greyhound Canada** (☑ 800-661-8747; www.greyhound.ca) service along Hwy 97 (Cache Creek to Prince George takes six hours).

Williams Lake to Prince George

Cattle and lumber have shaped **Williams Lake**, the hub for the region. Some 206km north of the junction of Hwys 1 and 97, this small town has a pair of museums and numerous motels. The best reason to stop is the superb **Discovery Centre** (☑ 250-392-5025; www.williamslake.ca; 1660 Broadway S, off Hwy 97; ☺9am-5pm), a visitors center in a huge log building. It has full regional info and the lowdown for trips west to the coast on Hwy 20. Avoid the smear of fast fooderies along Hwy 97 and get a good sandwich and coffee from **Bean Counter Bistro** (180 3rd St; mains from $5; ☺7:30am-5:30pm Mon-Sat; ☎).

Quesnel, 124km north of Williams Lake on Hwy 97, is all about logging. There are some good motels and cafes in the tidy, flower-lined center. From Quesnel, Hwy 26 leads east to the area's main attractions, Barkerville Historic Park and Bowron Lake Provincial Park.

North of Quesnel it's 116km on Hwy 97 to Prince George.

Barkerville & Around

In 1862 Billy Barker, previously of Cornwall, struck gold deep in the Cariboo. Soon Barkerville sprung up, populated by the usual fly-by-night crowds of whores, dupes, tricksters and just plain prospectors. Today you can visit more than 125 restored heritage buildings in **Barkerville Historic Town** (☑ 888-994-3332; www.barkerville.ca; Hwy 26; adult/child $14/4.50; ☺8am-6pm May-Sep). In summer, people dressed in period garb roam through town and, if you can tune out the crowds, it feels more authentic than forced. It has shops, cafes and a couple of B&Bs. At other times of year, you can visit the town for free, but don't expect to find much open.

Near Barkerville, quirky **Wells** has accommodations, restaurants and a general store. The **visitors center** (☑ 877-451-9355, 250-994-2323; www.wellsbc.com; 11900 Hwy 26; ☺9am-6pm May-Sep) has details.

Barkerville is 82km east of Quesnel.

Wells Gray Provincial Park

Plunging 141m onto rocks below, **Helmcken Falls**, Canada's fourth highest, is but one of the undiscovered facets of **Wells Gray Provincial Park** (www.bcparks.ca; Wells Gray Rd), itself an under-appreciated gem.

BC's fourth-largest park is bounded by the Clearwater River and its tributaries, which define the park's boundaries. Highlights for visitors include five major lakes, two large river systems, scores of waterfalls and most every kind of BC land-based wildlife.

Most people enter the park via the town of **Clearwater** on Hwy 5, 123km north of Kamloops. From here, a 36km paved road runs to the park's south entrance. Part gravel, Wells Gray Rd then runs 29km into the heart of the park. Many hiking trails and sights, such as Helmcken Falls, are accessible off this road, which ends at Clearwater Lake.

You'll find opportunities for **hiking**, **cross-country skiing** and **horseback riding** along more than 20 trails of varying lengths. Rustic backcountry campgrounds dot the area around four of the lakes. **Clearwater Lake Tours** (☑ 250-674-2121; www.clearwaterlaketours.com; canoes per day from $50) rents canoes and leads treks.

Of the three vehicle-accessible yet simple **campgrounds** (☑ 250-674-2194; campsites $16) in the park, woodsy **Pyramid Campground** is just 5km north of the park's south entrance and is close to Helmcken Falls. There's plenty of **backcountry camping**, which costs $5 per person per night.

Clearwater has stores, restaurants and a slew of motels, including **Dutch Lake Resort** (☑ 888-884-4424, 250-674-3351; www.dutchlake.com; 361 Ridge Dr, Clearwater; campsites from $35, r $120-190), which has cabins, motel units and 65 campsites. Rent a canoe and practice for greater fun in the park.

Wells Gray Guest Ranch (☑ 866-467-4346, 250-674-2792; www.wellsgrayranch.com; Clearwater Valley Rd; campsites from $25, r $90-180) has cabins and cozy rooms in the main lodge building. It's inside the park, 27km north of Clearwater.

The Clearwater **visitors center** (☑ 250-674-2646; www.wellsgray.ca; 425 E Yellowhead Hwy, cnr Clearwater Valley Rd; ☺9am-6:30pm May-Oct; ☎) is a vital info stop for the park. It books rooms and fun-filled white-water-rafting trips.

Chilcotin & Highway 20

Meandering over the lonely hills west of the Chilcotin, Hwy 20 runs 450km from Williams Lake to the Bella Coola Valley. Long spoken about by drivers in the sort of hushed tones doctors use when describing a worrisome stool specimen, the road has been steadily improved and is now more than 90% paved. However, the section that's not is a doozy: the Hill is a 30km stretch of gravel that's 386km west of Williams Lake. It descends 1524m from Heckman's Pass to the valley, nearly at sea level, through a series of sharp switchbacks and 11% grades. But by taking your time and using low gear, you'll actually enjoy the stunning views. It's safe for all vehicles – tourists engorged with testosterone from their SUVs are humbled when a local in a Chevy beater zips past.

Driving the road in one go will take about six hours. You'll come across a few aboriginal villages, as well as gravel roads that lead off to the odd provincial park and deserted lake. Check with the visitors center at Williams Lake for details and available services.

Bella Coola Valley

Leaving the dry expanses of the Chilcotin, you're in for a surprise when you reach the bottom of the hill. The verdant Bella Coola Valley is at the heart of Great Bear Rainforest, a lush land of huge stands of trees, surging white water and lots of bears. It's a spiritual place: Nuxalk First Nation artists are active here and, for many creative types from elsewhere, this is literally the end of the road.

The valley stretches 53km to the shores of the North Bentinck Arm, a deep, glacier-fed fjord that runs 40km inland from the Pacific Ocean. The two main towns, Bella Coola on the water and Hagensborg 15km east, almost seem as one, with most places of interest in or between the two.

☉ Sights & Activities

Spanning the Chilcotin and the east end of the valley, the southern portion of Tweedsmuir Provincial Park (☑ 250-398-4414; www.bcparks.ca; off Hwy 20) is the second-largest provincial park in BC. It's a seemingly barely charted place, perfect for challenging backcountry adventures. Day hikes off Hwy 20 in the valley follow trails into lush and untouched coastal rainforest.

Walk amid 500-year-old cedars just west of Hagensborg at Walker Island Park on the edge of the wide and rocky Bella Coola River floodplain.

There's really no limit to your activities here. You can hike into the hills and valleys starting from roads (consider Odegaard Falls) or at points only reachable by boat along the craggy coast.

Kynoch Adventures (☑ 250-982-2298; www.bcmountainlodge.com; Hwy 20, Hagensborg; tours from adult/child $80/40) specializes in critter-spotting trips down local rivers and wilderness hikes. Highly recommended float trips to spot the valley's renowned grizzly bear population run from late August into October ($125 per person).

🛏 Sleeping & Eating

There are a dozen B&Bs and small inns along Hwy 20. Many offer evening meals; otherwise, there are a couple of cafes and restaurants.

Rip Rap Camp CAMPGROUND $
(☑ 250-982-2752; www.riprapcamp.com; 1854 Hwy 20, Hagensborg; campsites $17-25, cabins $60-125; ☺ May-Oct; ☎) A much-lauded campground, Rip Rap has plenty of services and a great viewing deck overlooking the river.

★ **Bella Coola Mountain Lodge** INN $$
(☑ 250-982-2298; www.bcmountainlodge.com; 1900 Hwy 20, Hagensborg; r $90-125; @☎) The 14 rooms, many with kitchen facilities, are huge and there's an excellent restaurant (mains $20-30; ☺ 5:30-8:30pm Wed-Sun). The owners also run Kynoch Adventures, and guests can rent minivans and SUVs (from $65 per day).

Tallheo Cannery GUESTHOUSE $$
(☑ 604-992-1424; www.bellacoolacannery.com; campsite $15, r incl transport $125) One of BC's most unusual places to stay is 3km across the inlet from Bella Coola in an old cannery. On approach by boat, you may have misgivings, as large portions of the cannery are collapsing over the water. But fear not, for the rooms in an old 1920s bunkhouse are on solid ground. Transport for campers is $10; tours for day-trippers cost $50.

The adventurous will find that the views (stunning), explorations (it's an entire village with its own beach) and mystery (abandoned detritus of an old cannery) make this a fascinating stay.

❶ Information

Both the visitors center and your accommodations can point you to guides and gear for skiing, mountain biking, fishing, rafting and much more. Car repair, ATMs, laundry and groceries are available. Most tourist services are closed October to April.

Oodles of info and advice, including trail guides, is available at the volunteer-run **visitors center** (☑ 250-982-0092; www.bellacoola.ca; 1881 Hwy 20, Hagensborg; ⊙10am-4pm Jun-Sep) in an atmospheric 1903 house.

❶ Getting There & Away

BC Ferries (☑ 888-223-3779; www.bcferries. com; adult/child $193/97, car from $386) runs the Discovery Coast route, which links Bella Coola and Port Hardy on Vancouver Island a couple of times per week in summer. The journey takes from 13 to 34 hours, depending on stops. Best are the weekly direct 13-hour trips as the usual boat, the *Queen of Chilliwack*, does not have cabins.

There are no buses along Hwy 20 to Williams Lake, although you can go by charter plane. **Pacific Coastal Airlines** (☑ 800-663-2872; www. pacificcoastal.com; one-way $175-340; ⊙ daily) has one-hour flights from Vancouver.

NORTHERN BRITISH COLUMBIA

Northern BC is where you will truly feel that you've crossed that ethereal border to some place different. Nowhere else are the rich cultures of Canada's Aboriginal people so keenly felt, from the Haida on Haida Gwaii to the Tsimshian on the mainland. Nowhere else does land so exude mystery, whether it's the storm-shrouded coast and islands or the silent majesty of glaciers carving passages through entire mountain ranges.

And nowhere else has this kind of promise. Highways like the fabled Alaska or the awe-inspiring Stewart-Cassiar encourage adventure, discovery or even a new life. Here, your place next to nature will never be in doubt; you'll revel in your own insignificance.

Prince Rupert

POP 12,600

People are always 'discovering' Prince Rupert, and what a find it is. This intriguing city, with a gorgeous harbor, is not just a transportation hub (ferries go south to Vancouver Island, west to Haida Gwaii and north to Alaska), but a destination in its own right. It has two excellent museums, fine restaurants and a culture that draws much from its aboriginal heritage. Yet the city struggles to attract the huge cruise ships plying the Inside Passage.

It may rain 220 days a year, but that doesn't stop the drip-dry locals enjoying activities in the misty mountains and waterways. Originally the dream of Charles Hays, who built the railroad here before going to a watery grave on the *Titanic*, Rupert always

---

THE GREAT BEAR RAINFOREST

It's the last major tract of coastal temperate rainforest left on the planet. The Great Bear Rainforest is a wild region of islands, fjords and towering peaks. Covering 64,000 sq km (7% of BC), it stretches south from Alaska along the BC coast and Haida Gwaii to roughly Campbell River on Vancouver Island (which isn't part of the forest). The forests and waters are remarkably rich in life: whales, salmon, eagles, elk, otter and more thrive. Remote river valleys are lined with forests of old Sitka spruce, Pacific silver fir and various cedars that are often 100m tall and 1500 years old.

As vast as it is, however, the Great Bear is under great threat. Less than 50% is protected and industry and government keep missing deadlines for protection plans. Meanwhile mineral and logging companies are eyeing the forest, while others want to build the huge Northern Gateway Pipelines project that would bring supertankers to the coast. Among the many groups fighting to save this irreplaceable habitat is the Raincoast Conservation Foundation; see www.raincoast.org. The website www.savethegreatbear.org is a good source of info.

From Bella Coola, you can arrange boat trips and treks to magical places in the Great Bear, including hidden rivers where you might see a rare Kermode bear, a white-furred offshoot of the black bear known in tribal legend as the 'spirit bear' and the namesake of the rainforest.

seems one step behind a bright future. But its ship may finally have come in, or at least anchored offshore: the city's expanding container port speeds cheap tat from China to bargain-desperate Americans.

⊙ Sights

A short walk from the center, **Cow Bay** is a delightful place for a stroll. The eponymous spotted decor is everywhere, but somehow avoids seeming clichéd. There are shops, cafes and a good view of the waterfront, especially from the cruise ship docks at the Atlin Terminal.

You'll see **totem poles** all around town; two flank the statue of Charlie Hays beside City Hall on 3rd Ave. Also watch around town for more than 30 huge **murals** adorning buildings. Noted artist Jeff King paints history and nature.

★ Museum of Northern BC   MUSEUM

(☑250-624-3207; www.museumofnorthernbc. com; 100 1st Ave W; adult/child $6/2; ☉9am-5pm) Don't miss the Museum of Northern BC, which resides in a building styled after an aboriginal longhouse. The museum shows how local civilizations enjoyed sustainable cultures that lasted for thousands of years – you might say they were ahead of their time. The displays include a wealth of excellent Haida, Gitksan and Tsimshian art and plenty of info on totem poles. The bookshop is excellent.

☀ Activities

Among the many local walks, a good place to start is the **Butze Rapids Trail**, a 4.5km loop starting 3km south of town. It has interpretive signs.

Further afield, **Khutzeymateen Grizzly Bear Sanctuary** is home to more than 50 of the giants.

Skeena Kayaking   KAYAKING

(☑250-624-5246; www.skeenakayaking.ca; kayak rentals per 4hr $50, tours from $80) Skeena Kayaking offers both rentals and custom tours of the area, which has a seemingly infinite variety of places to put in the water.

⌒ Tours

★ Prince Rupert Adventure Tours WILDLIFE

(☑250-627-9166; www.adventuretours.net; Atlin Terminal; bear tours adult/child $225/200, whale tours $115/100) Excellent boat tours include the Khutzeymateen grizzly-watching trips

(mid-May to early August) and whale tours (August to September). Voyages can last many hours as you track the region's rich wildlife.

🛏 Sleeping

Rupert has a range of accommodations, including more than a dozen B&Bs. When all three ferries have pulled in, competition gets fierce, so book ahead.

Pioneer Hostel   HOSTEL $

(☑888-794-9998, 250-624-2334; www.pioneerhostel.com; 167 3rd Ave E; dm $25-30, r $60-80; ☻@☎) Located in a residential neighborhood behind downtown, spotless compact rooms are accented with vibrant colors and there's a small kitchen and BBQ facilities out back. Ferry and train pickups are provided.

Black Rooster Guesthouse   GUESTHOUSE $

(☑250-627-5337; www.blackrooster.ca; 501 6th Ave W; dm $30, r $50-150; @☎) This renovated house just up the hill from the center has a patio and a bright common room. Rooms range from spartan singles to large apartments. Call for shuttle pickup.

Prince Rupert RV Campground   CAMPGROUND $

(☑250-624-5861; www.princerupertrv.com; 1750 Park Ave; campsites/RV sites from $21/33; @☎) Located near the ferry terminal, this somewhat barren campground has 77 sites, hot showers, laundry facilities and a small playground.

Crest Hotel   HOTEL $$

(☑800-663-8150, 250-624-6771; www.cresthotel.bc.ca; 222 1st Ave W; r $120-300; ✳@☎) Prince Rupert's premier hotel has harbor-view rooms that are worth every penny, right down to the built-in bay-window seats with loaner binoculars. Avoid the smallish rooms overlooking the parking lot. Suites are opulent.

Inn on the Harbour   MOTEL $$

(☑250-624-9107, 800-663-8155; www.innontheharbour.com; 720 1st Ave W; r incl breakfast $120-260; ☎) Sunsets may dazzle you to the point that you don't notice the humdrum exterior at this modern, harbor-view motel. The 49 rooms have a plush, modern look.

Eagle Bluff B&B   B&B $$

(☑250-627-4955; www.eaglebluff.ca; 201 Cow Bay Rd; r $65-145; @) Ideally located on Cow Bay, this B&B on a pier is in a heritage building

NORTH PACIFIC CANNERY

The **North Pacific Cannery National Historic Site** (☑ 250-628-3538; www.northpacificcannery.ca; 1889 Skeena Dr; adult/child $12/6; ☉ 10am-5pm), about 20km south of Prince Rupert, near the town of Port Edward, explores the early history of fishing and canning along the Skeena River. The fascinating all-wood complex was really a small town on stilts. It was used from 1889 to 1968. Exhibits document the miserable conditions of the workers; tours cover the industrial process and cannery life. Prince Rupert Transit (p244) has a bus service to the site.

that has a striking red and white paint job. Inside, however, the seven rooms have decor best described as homey; some share bathrooms.

 Eating

Watch for halibut and salmon fresh from the fishing fleet.

Cowpuccino's CAFE $
(☑ 250-627-1395; 25 Cow Bay Rd; coffee $2; ☉ 7am-8pm; 🛜) The coffee at this funky local cafe will make you forget the rain.

★**Charley's Lounge** PUB $$
(☑ 250-624-6771; Crest Hotel, 222 1st Ave W; mains $8-20; ☉ noon-late) Locals flock to trade gossip while gazing out over the harbor from the heated patio. The pub menu features some of Rupert's best seafood. The more formal **Waterfront Restaurant** (mains $12-35; ☉ 6.30am-9pm Mon-Fri, 7am-9pm Sat & Sun) adjoins; it has a changing menu of dishes created in an open kitchen.

Opa Sushi JAPANESE $$
(☑ 250-627-4560; www.opasushi.com; 34 Cow Bay Rd; mains $12-25; ☉ 11:30am-2pm & 5-9pm Mon-Fri, noon-3pm & 5-9pm Sat, 1-8pm Sun) Super sushi is served in a renovated net loft, with easygoing style. Good wine selection.

Smiles Seafood SEAFOOD $$
(☑ 250-624-3072; www.smilesseafoodcafe.ca; 113 Cow Bay Rd; mains $7-30; ☉ 11am-9pm) Since 1934 Smiles has served classic, casual seafood meals. Slide into a vinyl booth or sit out on the deck. Enjoy a shrimp club sandwich or a fresh halibut steak.

Cow Bay Café ITALIAN $$
(☑ 250-627-1212; 205 Cow Bay Rd; mains $10-20; ☉ 11:30am-9pm) Now serving a heavy-on-the-red-sauce menu, this well-known bistro is right in Cow Bay and has wraparound water views.

🛍 Shopping

The smattering of boutiques at Cow Bay makes for the most interesting shopping.

Ice House Gallery GALLERY
(☑ 250-624-4546; Atlin Terminal; ☉ noon-5pm Tue-Sun) See the bounty of Rupert's vibrant creative community at this artist-run gallery.

Rainforest Books BOOKS
(☑ 250-624-4195; www.rainforestbooks.net; 251 3rd Ave W; ☉ 10am-6pm Mon-Sat) Good selection of new and used books.

ℹ Information

Javadotcup (☑ 250-622-2822; 516 3rd Ave W; internet access per hr $3; ☉ 7:30am-9pm; 🛜) This decent cafe has internet access and a couple of rooms upstairs for $60.

Visitors Center (☑ 250-624-5637, 800-667-1994; www.visitprincerupert.com; Museum of Northern BC, 100 1st Ave W; ☉ 9am-5pm) Visitor services are limited to a rack of brochures and the front desk at the museum (p242).

ℹ Getting There & Away

The ferry and train terminals are 3km southwest of the center.

AIR

Prince Rupert Airport (YPR; ☑ 250-622-2222; www.ypr.ca) is on Digby Island, across the harbor from town. The trip involves a bus and ferry; pickup is at the Highliner Hotel (815 1st Ave) about two hours before flight time. Confirm all the details with your airline or the airport.

Air Canada Jazz (☑ 250-624-9633; www.aircanada.com) and **Hawkair** (☑ 250-624-4295; www.hawkair.ca) both serve Vancouver. Check in for the former is at the airport; for the latter, at Highliner Hotel.

BUS

Greyhound Canada (☑ 800-661-8747; www.greyhound.ca; 112 6th St) buses depart for Prince George ($160, 10½ hours) once a day in summer, possibly less often other times.

FERRY

Alaska Marine Highway System (☑ 250-627-1744, 800-642-0066; www.ferryalaska.com; passenger/car $160/356, cabins from $156) One or two ferries each week ply to the Yukon

BRITISH COLUMBIA PRINCE RUPERT

gateways of Haines and Skagway in Alaska via the spectacular Inside Passage.

BC Ferries (☑250-386-3431; www.bcferries. com) The **Inside Passage** run to Port Hardy (adult $115 to $195, child fare 50%, car $250 to $445, cabin from $85, 15 to 25 hours) is hailed for its amazing scenery. There are three services per week in summer and one per week in winter on the *Northern Expedition*. The **Haida Gwaii** service goes to Skidegate Landing (adult $37 to $45, child fare 50%, car $132 to $160, six to seven hours) six times per week in summer and three times a week in winter on the *Northern Adventure*.

TRAIN

VIA Rail (www.viarail.ca; BC Ferries Terminal) operates triweekly services from Prince George (12½ hours) and, after an overnight stop, Jasper in the Rockies.

🛈 Getting Around

Prince Rupert Transit (☑250-624-3343; www.bctransit.com; adult/child $1.75/1.50) Infrequent services run to the ferry port and North Pacific Historic Fishing Village ($2.75). The main bus stop is at the ratty Rupert Square Mall on 2nd Ave.

Skeena Taxi (☑250-624-2185) From the ferries to the center is about $15.

Haida Gwaii

Haida Gwaii, which means 'Islands of the People,' offers a magical trip for those who make the effort. Attention has long focused on the many unique species of flora and fauna to the extent that 'Canada's Galápagos' is a popular moniker. But each year it becomes more apparent that the real soul of the islands is the Haida culture itself. Long one of the most advanced and powerful First Nations, the Haida suffered terribly after Westerners arrived.

Now, however, their culture is resurgent and can be found across the islands in myriad ways beyond their iconic totem poles. Haida reverence for the environment is protecting the last stands of superb old-growth rainforests, where the spruce and cedars are some of the world's largest. Amid this sparsely populated, wild and rainy place are bald eagles, bears and much more wildlife. Offshore, sea lions, whales and orcas abound; in 2013 rare right whales and sea otters were spotted.

In 2010 the name used by Europeans since their arrival in the 18th century, Queen Charlotte Islands, was officially ditched; and the federal government moved forward with its plans to make the waters off Haida Gwaii a marine preserve. In 2013 the magificent Gwaii Haanas Legacy Pole was raised at Windy Bay, the first new pole in the protected area in 130 years.

A visit to the islands rewards those who invest time to get caught up in their allure, their culture and their people – plan on a long stay. The number-one attraction here is remote **Gwaii Haanas National Park Reserve**, which makes up the bottom third of the archipelago. Named the top park in North America by *National Geographic Traveler* for being 'beautiful and intact,' it is a lost world of Haida culture and superb natural beauty.

Haida Gwaii forms a dagger-shaped archipelago of some 450 islands lying 80km west of the BC coast, and about 50km from the southern tip of Alaska. Mainland ferries dock at Skidegate Landing on Graham Island, which houses 80% of the 5000 residents. The principal town is Queen Charlotte (previously Queen Charlotte City and still known by its old QCC acronym), 7km west of Skidegate. The main road on Graham Island is Hwy 16, which is fully paved. It links Skidegate with Masset, 101km north, passing the small towns of Tlell and Port Clements.

Graham Island is linked to Moresby Island to the south by a ferry from Skidegate Landing. The airport is in Sandspit on Moresby Island, 12km east of the ferry landing at Aliford Bay. The only way to get to the park reserve, which covers the south part of Moresby Island, is by boat or floatplane.

⊙ Sights & Activities

The Haida Gwaii portion of the **Yellowhead Hwy** (Hwy 16) heads 110km north from QCC past Skidegate, Tlell and Port Clements. The last was where the famous golden spruce tree on the banks of the Yakoun River was cut down by a demented forester in 1997. The incident is detailed in the best-selling *The Golden Spruce* by John Vaillant, an excellent book on the islands and Haida culture.

All along the road to **Masset**, look for little seaside pullouts, oddball boutiques and funky cafes that are typical of the islands' character.

★**Gwaii Haanas National Park Reserve, National Marine Conservation Area Reserve & Haida Heritage Site** PARK
(☑250-559-8818; reservations 877-559-8818; www.parkscanada.ca/gwaiihaanas) This huge Unesco World Heritage site, with a name that's a mouthful, encompasses Moresby and 137 smaller islands at its southern end. It combines a time-capsule look at

abandoned Haida villages, hot springs, amazing natural beauty and some of the continent's best kayaking.

Archaeological finds have documented more than 500 ancient Haida sites, including villages and burial caves throughout the islands. The most famous village is **SGang Gwaay (Ninstints)** on Anthony Island, where rows of weathered **totem poles** stare eerily out to sea. Other major sights include the ancient village of **Skedans**, on Louise Island, and **Hotspring Island**, whose natural springs disappeared, possibly temporarily, as a result of the October 2012 earthquakes. The sites are protected by Haida Gwaii watchmen, who live on the islands in summer.

Access to the park is by boat or plane only. A visit demands a decent amount of advance planning and usually requires several days. From May to September, you must obtain a reservation, unless you're with a tour operator.

Contact **Parks Canada** (☑ 250-559-8818; www.parkscanada.ca/gwaiihaanas; Haida Heritage Centre at Kay Llnagaay, Skidegate; ⊙ 8:30am-noon & 1-4:30pm Mon-Fri) with questions. The website has links to the **essential annual trip planner**. Any visitor not on a guided tour and who has not visited the park during the previous three years must attend a free orientation at the park office. All visitors must register.

The number of daily **reservations** is limited: plan well in advance. There are user fees (adult/child $20/10 per night). Nightly fees are waived if you have a Parks Canada Season Excursion Pass. A few much-coveted standby spaces are made available daily: call Parks Canada.

The easiest way to get into the park is with a tour company. Parks Canada can provide you with lists of operators; tours last from one day to two weeks. Many can also set you up with **rental kayaks** (average per day/week $60/300) and gear for independent travel.

Moresby Explorers (☑ 800-806-7633, 250-637-2215; www.moresbyexplorers.com; Sandspit) has one-day zodiac tours from $185, including the Louise Island trip that takes in Skedans and its totem poles, as well as much longer trips. It rents kayaks and gear.

Queen Charlotte Adventures (☑ 800-668-4288, 250-559-8990; www.queencharlotte-adventures.com) offers lots of one- to 10-day trips using boats and kayaks, including a

HAIDA HERITAGE CENTRE AT KAY LLNAGAAY

One of the top attractions in the north is this marvelous **cultural center** (☑ 250-559-7885; www.haidaheritage-centre.com; Hwy 16, Skidegate; adult/child $15/5; ⊙ 10am-6pm Sun-Wed, to 9pm Thu-Sat). With exhibits on history, wildlife and culture, it would be enough reason to visit the islands just by itself. The rich traditions of the Haida are fully explored in galleries, programs and work areas, where contemporary artists create works such as the totem poles lining the shore.

three-day kayak trip to the remote south for $550. It rents kayaks and gear.

Naikoon Provincial Park PARK
(☑ 250-626-5115; www.bcparks.ca; off Hwy 16; campsites $16) Much of the island's northeastern side is devoted to the beautiful 726-sq-km Naikoon Provincial Park, which combines sand dunes and low sphagnum bogs, surrounded by stunted and gnarled lodgepole pine, and red and yellow cedar. The **beaches** on the north coast feature strong winds, pounding surf and flotsam from across the Pacific. They can be reached via the stunning 26km-long Tow Hill Rd, east of Masset. A 21km loop **trail** traverses a good bit of the park to/from Fife Beach at the end of the road.

New steps and a boardwalk make visiting the **Tow Hill Lookout** and **Blow Hole** near the end of Tow Hill Rd easy. Allow about one hour for a looping walk with many steps.

Yakoun Lake HIKING
(☑ 250-557-6810) Hike 20 minutes through ancient stands of spruce and cedar to pristine **Yakoun Lake**, a large wilderness lake towards the west side of Graham Island. A small beach near the trail is shaded by gnarly Sitka alders. Dare to take a dip in the bracing waters or just enjoy the sweeping views.

The trailhead to the lake is at the end of a rough track off a branch from the main dirt and gravel logging road between QCC and Port Clements – watch for signs for the lake, about 20km north of QCC. It runs for 70km. On weekdays check in by phone for logging trucks.

BRITISH COLUMBIA HAIDA GWAII

🛏 Sleeping

Small inns and B&Bs are mostly found on Graham Island. There are numerous choices in QCC and Masset, with many in between and along the spectacular north coast. Naikoon Provincial Park has two **campgrounds**, including a dramatic windswept one on deserted Agate Beach, 23km east of Masset.

★ Premier Creek Lodging   INN $

(☑888-322-3388, 250-559-8415; www.qcislands. net/premier; 3101 3rd Ave, QCC; dm from $25, r $45-140; @☎) Dating from 1910, this friendly lodge has eight beds in a hostel building out back and 12 rooms in the main building, ranging from tiny but great-value singles to spacious rooms with views and porches.

North Beach Cabins   CABIN $$

(☑250-557-2415; www.northbeachcabins.com; 16km marker Tow Hill Rd; cabins $85-100) 🍴 Tucked into the dunes of beautiful North Beach are four cozy cabins. You're totally off the grid but, thanks to propane, you can cook, which will be about the only diversion from the fabulous views and endless sandy strolls.

Copper Beech House   B&B $$

(☑250-626-5441; www.copperbeechhouse.com; 1590 Delkatla Rd, Masset; r $100-160) This legendary B&B in a rambling old house on Masset Harbor is owned by poet Susan Musgrave. It has three unique rooms and there's always something amazing cooking in the kitchen.

✕ Eating

The best selection of restaurants is in QCC, although there are also a few in Skidegate and Masset. Ask at the visitors centers about local Haida feasts, where you'll enjoy the best salmon and blueberries you've ever had. Good supermarkets are found in QCC and Masset.

Queen B's   CAFE $

(☑250-559-4463; 3201 Wharf St, QCC; mains $3-10; ☺9am-5pm) This funky place excels at baked goods, which emerge from the oven all day long. There are tables with water views outside and lots of local art inside.

Moon Over Naikoon   BAKERY $

(☑250-626-5064; 17km marker Tow Hill Rd; snacks from $3; ☺8am-5pm Jun-Aug) Embodying the spirit of this road to the end of everything, this tiny community center–cum–bakery has a kaleidoscopic collection of artworks and stuff found on the beach.

Ocean View Restaurant   SEAFOOD $$

(☑250-559-8503; Sea Raven Motel, 3301 3rd Ave, QCC; mains $10-25; ☺11am-9pm) Good fresh seafood (try the halibut) is the specialty at this casual dining room, where some tables look out to the harbor.

Haida House   SEAFOOD $$

(☑855-557-4600; www.haidahouse.com; 2087 Beitush Rd, Tlell; mains $20-30) This seasonal restaurant has excellent and creative seafood and other dishes with island accents. Also rents plush rooms.

❶ Information

Either download or pick up a free copy of the encyclopedic annual *Guide to Haida Gwaii* (www. guidetohaidagwaii.com). A good website for information is www.gohaidagwaii.ca. Parks Canada also has much information online.

The **QCC visitors center** (☑250-559-8316; www.qcinfo.ca; 3220 Wharf St, QCC; ☺8:30am-9pm) is handy and can make advance excursion bookings, although there's been a recent encroachment of gift items. Get a free copy of *Art Route*, a guide to more than 30 studios and galleries.

❶ Getting There & Away

AIR

The main airport for Haida Gwaii is at **Sandspit** (YZP; ☑250-559-0052) on Moresby Island. Note that reaching the airport from Graham Island is time consuming: if your flight is at 3:30pm, you need to line up at the car ferry at Skidegate Landing at 12:30pm (earlier in summer). There's also a small airport at **Masset** (YMT; ☑250-626-3995).

Air Canada Jazz (☑888-247-2262; www. aircanada.com) Flies daily between Sandspit and Vancouver.

Pacific Coastal Airlines (☑800-663-2872; www.pacificcoastal.com) Flies Masset to Vancouver daily.

FERRY

The **BC Ferries** (☑250-386-3431; www.bcferries. com) service from Prince Rupert is the most popular way to reach the islands. Services ply from Prince Rupert to Skidegate Landing (adult $37 to $45, child fare 50%, car $132 to $160, six to seven hours) six times per week in summer and three times a week in winter on the *Northern Adventure*. Cabins are useful for overnight schedules (from $90).

❶ Getting Around

Off Hwy 16, most roads are gravel or worse.
BC Ferries (adult/child $10/5, cars from $23, 20 minutes, almost hourly 7am to 10pm) links

the two main islands at Skidegate Landing and Alliford Bay. Schedules seem designed to inconvenience air passengers.

Eagle Transit (☏877-747-4461; www.eagle-transit.net; adult/child $27/21) buses meet Sandspit flights and serve Skidegate and QCC.

Renting a car can be as expensive ($60 to $100 per day) as bringing one over on the ferry. **Budget** (☏250-637-5688; www.budget.com) is at the Sandspit airport, but may close permanently. **Rustic Car Rentals** (☏877-559-4641, 250-559-4641; citires@qcislands.net; 605 Hwy 33, QCC) is also in Masset.

Prince Rupert to Prince George

You can cover the 725km on Hwy 16 between BC's Princes in a day or a week. There's nothing that's an absolute must-see, but there's much to divert and cause you to pause if so inclined. Scenery along much of the road (with the notable exception of Skeena River) won't fill your memory card, but it is a pleasing mix of mountains and rivers.

Prince Rupert to Smithers

For the first 150km, Hwy 16 hugs the wide and wild **Skeena River**. This is four-star scenic driving and you'll see glaciers and jagged peaks across the waters. However, tatty **Terrace** is nobody's idea of a reward at the end of the stretch.

From Terrace, Hwy 16 continues 93km east to Kitwanga, where the **Stewart-Cassiar Hwy** (Hwy 37) strikes north towards the Yukon and Alaska.

Just east of Kitwanga is the **Hazelton** area (comprising New Hazelton, Hazelton and South Hazelton), the center of some interesting aboriginal sites, including '**Ksan Historical Village & Museum** (☏250-842-5544; www.ksan.org; off Hwy 16; admission $2; ⊙9am-5pm). This re-created village of the Gitksan people features longhouses, a museum, various outbuildings and totem poles. The narrated tour ($10) is a must.

Smithers

Smithers, a largish town with a cute old downtown, is roughly halfway between the

---

ONE TALL TALE

Though most Aboriginal groups on the northwest coast lack formal written history as we know it, centuries of traditions manage to live on through artistic creations such as totem poles.

Carved from a single cedar trunk, totems identify a household's lineage in the same way a family crest might identify a group or clan in Britain, although the totem pole is more of a historical pictograph depicting the entire ancestry.

Two excellent places both to see totem poles and learn more are the Haida Heritage Centre at Kay Llnagaay (p245) at Skidegate and the Museum of Northern BC (p242) in Prince Rupert.

Unless you're an expert, it's not easy to decipher a totem. But you can start by looking for the creatures that are key to the narrative. Try to pick out the following:

Beaver Symbolizes industriousness, wisdom and determined independence.

Black bear Serves as a guardian and spiritual link between humans and animals.

Eagle Signifies intelligence and power.

Frog Represents adaptability, the ability to live in both natural and supernatural worlds.

Hummingbird Embodies love, beauty and unity with nature.

Killer whale Symbolizes dignity and strength; often depicted as a reincarnated spirit of a great chief.

Raven Signifies mischievousness and cunning.

Salmon Typifies dependable sustenance, longevity and perseverance.

Shark Exemplifies an ominous and fierce solitude.

Thunderbird Represents the wisdom of proud ancestors.

Watchmen The village watchmen, who warned of danger.

NORTH TO THE YUKON

From BC, there are three main ways to go north by vehicle. All are potentially good choices, so you have several ways of creating a circle itinerary to the Yukon and possibly Alaska.

Alaska Highway

Fabled and historic, the Alaska Hwy, from its start point in Dawson Creek (364km northeast of Prince George) through northeast BC to Watson Lake (944km), is being somewhat eclipsed by the Stewart-Cassiar Hwy. Still, it's an epic drive, even if the sections to Fort Nelson are bland. It's most convenient for those coming from Edmonton and the east.

Stewart-Cassiar

The Stewart-Cassiar (Hwy 37) runs 700km through wild scenery from the junction with Hwy 16, 240km east of Prince Rupert and 468km west of Prince George. A side trip to the incomparable glaciers around Stewart is essential and easy. This route is convenient for people from most of BC, Alberta and the western US. It ends at the Alaska Hwy, near Watson Lake, in the Yukon.

Alaska Marine Highway System

We love Alaska's car ferries (www.ferryalaska.com) that sail the **Inside Passage**. Free of frills, they let you simply relax and view one of the world's great shows of marine life while enjoying the same scenery cruise-ship passengers spend thousands more to see. You can take a three-day ride on boats from Bellingham (north of Seattle), Washington, to Haines and Skagway in southeast Alaska, on the Yukon border. Or catch the ferries in Prince Rupert for service to the same two towns; you could link this to the BC Ferries route from Port Hardy. The ferries, especially cabins, fill up fast in summer, so reserve.

Princes. The **visitors center** (☑ 800-542-6673, 250-847-5072; www.tourismsmithers.com; 1411 Court St; ☺ 9am-6pm; ☎) can steer you to excellent mountain biking, white-water rafting and climbing. Great hiking is found at nearby **Babine Mountains Provincial Park** (☑ 250-847-7329; www.bcparks.ca; Old Babine Lake Rd; backcountry cabins per person $5) a 324-sq-km park with trails to glacier-fed lakes and subalpine meadows.

Stork Nest Inn (☑ 250-847-3831; www.storknestinn.com; 1485 Main St; r $85-100; ☒☎) is a good choice among many. Main St has several good cafes including **Bugwood Bean** (www.bugwoodbean.com; 2nd & Main Sts; coffee $2; ☺ 8am-5:30pm Mon-Sat; ☎). **Mountain Eagle Books & Bistro** (☑ 250-847-5245; 3775 3rd St; ☺ 9am-6pm Mon-Sat; ☎) has books and info on the area's thriving folk-music scene; the tiny cafe has veggie soup and lunches.

Smithers to Prince George

South and east of Smithers, after 146km you pass through **Burns Lake**, the center of a popular fishing district. After another 128km, at **Vanderhoof**, Hwy 27 heads 66km north to **Fort St James National Historic** Site (☑ 250-996-7191; www.pc.gc.ca; Kwah Rd; adult/child $8/4; ☺ 9am-5pm May-Sep), a former Hudson's Bay Company trading post that's on the tranquil southeastern shore of Stuart Lake and has been restored to its 1896 glory.

From Vanderhoof, the 100km to Prince George passes through a region filled with the dead trees seen across the north. These dark grey specimens are victims of mountain pine beetles, whose explosive population growth is linked to comparatively mild winters due to climate change. Note the many sawmills processing the dead trees.

Prince George

POP 72,200

In First Nations times, before outsiders arrived, Prince George was called Lheidli T'Enneh, which means 'people of the confluence,' an appropriate name given that the Nechako and Fraser Rivers converged here. Today the name would be just as fitting, although it's the confluence of highways that matters most. A mill town since 1807, it is a vital BC crossroads and you're unlikely to visit the north without passing through at least once.

Hwy 97 from the south cuts through the center of town on its way north to Dawson Creek (360km) and the Alaska Hwy. Hwy 16 becomes Victoria St as it runs through town westward to Prince Rupert (724km), and east to Jasper (380km) and Edmonton. The downtown, no beauty-contest winner, is compact and has some good restaurants.

◎ Sights

Exploration Place   MUSEUM
(📋 250-562-1612; www.theexplorationplace.com; Fort George Park, 333 Becott Pl; adult/child $10/7; ⊙9am-5pm) Exploration Place, southeast of downtown (follow 20th Ave east of Gorse St), has various kid-friendly galleries devoted to science, plus natural and cultural history.

Prince George Railway & Forestry Museum   MUSEUM
(📋 250-563-7351; www.pgrfm.bc.ca; 850 River Rd; adult/child $6/3; ⊙10am-5pm) **Cottonwood Island Nature Park** has walks alongside the river and is home to the Prince George Railway & Forestry Museum, which honors choo-choos, the beaver and local lore.

🛏 Sleeping

Hwy 97 (Central St) makes an arc around the center, where you'll find legions of motels and big-box stores. The **Bed & Breakfast Hotline** (📋 877-562-2626; www.princegeorgebnb.com) arranges bookings in your price range (from $70 to $135). Most provide transportation from the train or bus station.

Economy Inn   MOTEL $
(📋 888-566-6333, 250-563-7106; www.economy-inn.ca; 1915 3rd Ave; r $65-95; ❋ 🏠) Close to the center, this simple blue-and-white motel has 30 clean rooms and a whirlpool. Celebrate your savings with a Dairy Queen dip cone from across the street.

Bee Lazee Campground   CAMPGROUND $
(📋 866-679-6699, 250-963-7263; www.beelazee.ca; 15910 Hwy 97 S; campsites $25-28; ⊙May-Sep; 🏠 ⛱) About 15km south of town, this RV-centric place features full facilities, including free hot showers, fire pits and laundry.

Travelodge Prince George   MOTEL $$
(📋 800-663-8239, 250-563-0666; www.trav-elodgeprincegeorge.com; 1458 7th Ave; r $80-130; ❋ @ 🏠) A real barker in the beauty department, the Travelodge is nicer on the inside – isn't everything? The 77 rooms are large and

have an easy-on-the-eyes motif. Better yet, it's steps from good restaurants and bars.

97 Motor Inn   MOTEL $$
(📋 250-562-6010; www.97motorinn.ca; 2713 Spruce St; r $70-100; ❋ 🏠) Near the junction with Hwy 16, this modern motel is on – wait, you guessed it – Hwy 97. Some of the 19 basic rooms have balconies and kitchens. The noted Thanh Vu Vietnamese restaurant is out front.

✗ Eating

The **farmers market** (www.farmersmarketpg.ca; cnr George St & 3rd Ave; ⊙8:30am-2pm Sat May-Oct) is a good place to sample some of the array of local foods and produce.

★Nancy O's   PUB $$
(📋 250-562-8066; www.nancyos.ca; 1261 3rd Ave; mains $10-25; ⊙11am-late Mon-Fri, from 10am Sat & Sun) Nancy O's may make you want to spend two nights in Prince George. Locally sourced ingredients are combined for fabulous food: burgers, veggie specials, a great avocado salad and a truly amazing *steak frites*. The beer selection is fab and there's live music and DJs many nights. The vibe is hipster-comfy.

Cimo   MEDITERRANEAN $$
(📋 250-564-7975; 601 Victoria St; mains $12-29; ⊙11:30am-2pm & 5-9:30pm Mon-Sat) The pesto and other excellent Mediterranean dishes never disappoint. Dine or just enjoy a glass of BC wine in the stylish interior or out on the patio. Much of the produce comes from the kitchen garden. Great BC wine list.

🛍 Shopping

Books & Company   BOOKS
(📋 250-563-6637; 1685 3rd Ave; ⊙7am-7pm Mon-Wed, to 9pm Thu, to 10pm Fri, to 6pm Sat, 10am-5pm Sun; 🏠) The best bookstore in northern BC, it has a great cafe with a deck.

ℹ Information

The excellent **visitors center** (📋 250-562-3700; www.tourismpg.com; VIA Rail Station, 1300 1st Ave; ⊙8am-8pm; 🏠) can make bookings, such as ferry tickets, and loans out free bikes and fishing rods.

ℹ Getting There & Away

Prince George Airport (YXS; 📋 250-963-2400; www.pgairport.ca; 4141 Airport Rd) is off Hwy 97. **Air Canada Jazz** (www.aircanada.com) and **Westjet** (www.westjet.com) serve Vancouver.

Greyhound Canada (☑ 800-661-8747; www. greyhound.ca; 1566 12th Ave) service may be less than daily in winter. Routes include Dawson Creek ($80, six hours), Jasper ($70, five hours), Prince Rupert ($160, 10½ hours) and Vancouver ($95, 12 to 13 hours).

VIA Rail (www.viarail.ca; 1300 1st Ave) heads west three times a week to Prince Rupert (12½ hours) and east three times a week to Jasper (7½ hours) and beyond, through passengers must overnight in Prince George.

❶ Getting Around

Major car- rental agencies have offices at the airport.

Prince George Transit (☑ 250-563-0011; www.transitbc.com; fare $2.25) Operates local buses.

Emerald Taxi (☑ 250-563-3333)

Prince George to Alberta

Look for lots of wildlife along the 380km stretch of Hwy 16 that links Prince George with Jasper, just over the Alberta border. About 113km east of Prince George, the **Ancient Forest Trail** (www.ancientcedar.ca; Hwy 16) leads 1km to some real behemoths of the temperate inland rainforest: old-growth red cedars and hemlocks that reach heights of 60m and more.

The route's major attraction abuts Jasper National Park, but on the BC side of the border. **Mt Robson Provincial Park** (Map p92; ☑ 250-964-2243; www.bcparks.ca; off Hwy 16; campsites $16) has steep glaciers, prolific wildlife and backcountry hiking that is unfortunately overshadowed by its famous neighbor. **McBride** is good for a pause.

Stewart-Cassiar Highway

Much improved, the 700km Stewart-Cassiar Hwy (Hwy 37) is a viable and ever-more-popular route between BC and the Yukon and Alaska. But it's more than just a means to get from Hwy 16 (Meziadin Junction) in BC to the Alaska Hwy in the Yukon (7km west of Watson Lake), it's a window onto one of the largest remaining wild and woolly parts of the province. And it's the road to Stewart, the near-mandatory detour to glaciers, and more.

Except for areas of construction, the road is sealed throughout and is suitable for all vehicles. At any point, you should not be surprised to see bears, moose and other large mammals. Note that the region's untouched status is waning as projects like the invasive Northwest Transmission Line are carved across the wilderness.

There's never a distance greater than 150km between gas stations and you'll find the occasional lodge and campground. But note that many places keep erratic hours and are only open in summer. BC provides **road condition reports** (☑ 800-550-4997; www.drivebc.ca). When it's dry in summer, people drive from Stewart or even Smithers to Watson Lake in a single day, taking advantage of the long hours of daylight. But this a real haul, so prepare.

Gitanyow, a mere 15km north of Hwy 16, has an unparalleled collection of totem poles and you can often see carvers creating another.

Dease Lake, 488km north of Meziadin Junction, is the largest town and has year-round motels, stores and services.

Boya Lake Provincial Park (☑ 250-771-4591; www.bcparks.ca; Hwy 37; campsites $16) is less than 90km from the provincial border. This serene little park surrounds Boya Lake, which seems to glow turquoise. You can camp on the shore.

Alaska Highway

As you travel north from Prince George along Hwy 97, the mountains and forests give way to gentle rolling hills and farmland. Nearing Dawson Creek (360km), the landscape resembles the prairies of Alberta. There's no need to dawdle.

From **Chetwynd** you can take Hwy 29 along the wide vistas of the Peace River valley north via Hudson's Hope to join the Alaska Hwy north of Fort St John.

Dawson Creek is notable as the starting point (Mile 0) for the Alaska Hwy and it capitalizes on this at the **Alaska Highway House** (☑ 250-782-4714; 10201 10th St; admission by donation; ☺ 9am-5pm), an engaging museum in a vintage building overlooking the milepost. The nearby downtown blocks make a good stroll and have free wi-fi, and there's a walking tour of the old buildings. The **visitors center** (☑ 866-645-3022, 250-782-9595; www.tourismdawsoncreek.com; 900 Alaska Ave; ☺ 8am-5:30pm; ☎) has the usual listings of accommodations. Note that this corner of BC stays on Mountain Standard Time year-round. So in winter, the time is the same as Alberta, one hour later than

WORTH A TRIP

STEWART & HYDER

Awesome. Yes, it's almost an automatic cliché, but when you gaze upon the **Salmon Glacier**, you'll understand why it was coined in the first place. This horizon-spanning expanse of ice is more than enough reason to make the 67km detour off Hwy 37; the turnoff is 158km north of Meziadin Junction. In fact, your first confirmation comes when you encounter the iridescent blue expanse of the **Bear Glacier** looming over Hwy 37A.

The sibling border towns of Stewart and Hyder, Alaska, perch on the coast at the head of the Portland Canal. **Stewart**, the much more businesslike of the pair, has the **visitors center** (📞 250-636-9224; www.stewart-hyder.com; 222 5th Ave; ⊙ 9am-6pm) and excellent places to stay and eat.

Among several campgrounds and motels, the real star is **Ripley Creek Inn** (📞 250-636-2344; www.ripleycreekinn.com; 306 5th Ave, Stewart; r $55-140; @ 🛜). The 40 rooms in various heritage buildings are stylishly decorated with new and old items and there's a huge collection of vintage toasters.

Hyder ekes out an existence as a 'ghost town.' Some 40,000 tourists come through every summer, avoiding any border hassle from US customs officers because there aren't any, although going back to Stewart you'll pass through beady-eyed Canadian customs. It has muddy streets and two businesses of note: the **Glacier Inn**, a bar you'll enjoy if you ignore the touristy 'get Hyderized' shot-swilling shtick; and **Seafood Express** (📞 250-636-9011; mains $12-20; ⊙ noon-8pm Jun-Sep), which has the tastiest seafood ever cooked in a school bus. *This* is Hyder.

The enormous, horizon-filling Salmon Glacier is 33km beyond Hyder, up a winding dirt road that's OK for cars when it's dry. Some 3km into the drive, you'll pass the **Fish Creek viewpoint**, an area alive with bears and doomed salmon in late summer.

BC. In summer, the time is the same as Vancouver.

Now begins the big drive. Heading northwest from Dawson Creek, Fort St John is a stop best not started. In fact, the entire 430km to **Fort Nelson** gives little hint of the wonders to come.

Fort Nelson's **visitors center** (📞 250-774-6400; www.tourismnorthernrockies.ca; 5500 Alaska Hwy; ⊙ 7:30am-7:30pm) has good regional information for the drive ahead. The town itself is in the midst of the oil boom brought on by fracking. This is the last place of any size on the Alaska Hwy until Whitehorse in the Yukon – most 'towns' along the route are little more than a gas station and motel or two.

Around 140km west of Fort Nelson, **Stone Mountain Provincial Park** (📞 250-427-5452; www.bcparks.ca; off Hwy 97; campsites $16) has hiking trails with backcountry camping and a campground. The stretches of road often have dense concentrations of wildlife: moose, bears, bison, wolves, elk and much more. From here, the Alaska Hwy rewards whatever effort it took getting this far.

A further 75km brings you to **Muncho Lake Provincial Park** (www.bcparks.ca; off Hwy 97; campsites $16), centered on the emerald-green lake of the same name and boasting spruce forests, vast rolling mountains and some truly breathtaking scenery. There are two campgrounds by the lake, plus a few lodges scattered along the highway.

Finally, **Liard River Hot Springs Provincial Park** (📞 250-427-5452; www.bcparks.ca; off Hwy 97; day use adult/child $5/3, campsite $16-21) has a steamy ecosystem that allows a whopping 250 species of plants to thrive. After a long day in the car, you'll thrive, too, in the soothing waters. From here it's 220km to Watson Lake and the Yukon.

Yukon Territory

Best Places to Eat

➡ Drunken Goat Taverna (p274)

➡ Klondike Kate's (p274)

➡ Klondike Rib & Salmon (p259)

➡ Burnt Toast (p259)

Best Places to Stay

➡ Coast High Country Inn (p258)

➡ Robert Service Campground (p258)

➡ Bombay Peggy's (p273)

➡ Klondike Kate's (p273)

Why Go?

This vast and thinly populated wilderness, where most four-legged species far outnumber humans, has a grandeur and beauty only appreciated by experience. Few places in the world today have been so unchanged over the course of time as has the Yukon. Aboriginal people, having eked out survival for thousands of years, hunt and trap as they always have. The Klondike gold rush of 1898 was the Yukon's high point of population, yet even its heritage is ephemeral, easily erased by time.

Any visit will mean much time outdoors. Canada's five tallest mountains and the world's largest ice fields below the Arctic are all within Kluane National Park. Canoe expeditions down the Yukon River are epic. You'll appreciate the people; join the offbeat vibe of Dawson City and the bustle of Whitehorse.

When to Go
Dawson City

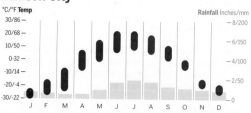

Nov–Apr Days of snowy winter solitude end when the river ice breaks up.

Jun–Aug Summers are short but warm, with long hours of daylight.

Sep You can feel the north winds coming. Trees erupt in color, crowds thin and places close.

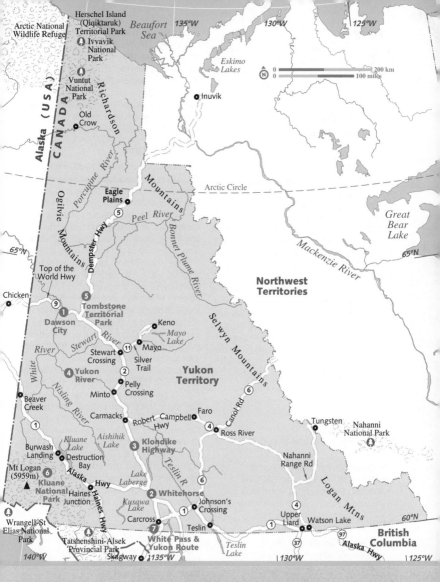

Yukon Territory Highlights

❶ Get caught up in the modern vibe of **Dawson City** (p269), Canada's funkiest historic town.

❷ Spend an extra day in surprising **Whitehorse** (p255), where culture abounds.

❸ Count moose on the **Klondike Highway** (p266) – they may outnumber cars.

❹ Live the dream of kayakers and canoeists by paddling the legendary **Yukon River** (p272).

❺ Lose yourself – not literally! – in **Tombstone Territorial Park** (p276), where the grandeur of the north envelops you.

❻ Find and name one of the 100 unnamed glaciers in **Kluane National Park** (p263).

❼ Sit back and enjoy the ride on the fabled **White Pass & Yukon Route** (p260).

History

There's evidence that humans were eating animals in the Yukon some 15,000 to 30,000 years ago, depending on your carbon-dating method of choice. However, it's widely agreed that these people were descended from those who crossed over today's Siberia while the land bridge was in place. There's little recorded history otherwise, although it's known that a volcanic eruption in AD 800 covered much of the southern Yukon in ash. Similarities to the Athapaskan people of the southwest US have suggested that these groups may have left the Yukon after the volcano ruined hunting and fishing.

In the 1840s Robert Campbell, a Hudson's Bay Company explorer, was the first European to travel the district. Fur traders, prospectors, whalers and missionaries all followed. In 1870 the region became part of the Northwest Territories (NWT). But it was in 1896 when the Yukon literally hit the map, after gold was found in a tributary of the Klondike River, near what was to become Dawson City. The ensuing gold rush attracted upwards of 40,000 hopefuls from around the world. Towns sprouted overnight to support the numerous wealth-seekers, who were quite unprepared for the ensuing depravities.

EXTREME YUKON

Tough conditions spawn tough contests.

➜ **Yukon Quest** (www.yukonquest.com; ☺ Feb) This legendary 1600km dogsled race goes from Whitehorse to Fairbanks, Alaska, winter darkness and -50°C temperatures. Record time: 9 days, 26 minutes.

➜ **Yukon River Quest** (www.yukonriverquest.com; ☺ late Jun) The world's premier canoe and kayak race, which covers the classic 742km run of the Yukon River from Whitehorse to Dawson City in June. Record times include team canoe (39 hours, 32 minutes) and solo kayak (42 hours, 49 minutes).

➜ **Klondike Trail of '98 Road Relay** (www.klondikeroadrelay.com; ☺ early Sep) Some 100 running teams of 10 each complete the overnight course from Skagway to Whitehorse.

In 1898 the Yukon became a separate territory, with Dawson City as its capital. Building the Alaska Hwy (Hwy 1) in 1942 opened up the territory to development. In 1953 Whitehorse became the capital, because it had the railway and the highway. Mining continues to be the main industry, followed by tourism, which accounts for over 310,000 visitors a year.

Local Culture

The 33,000-plus hardy souls who live in the Yukon Territory take the phrase 'rugged individualist' to heart. It's safe to say that the average Yukoner enjoys the outdoors (in all weather conditions!), relishes eating meats seldom found on menus to the south and has a crack in their truck's windshield (caused by one of the many dodgy roads).

More than 70% of the territory's annual revenue each year comes from the federal government and it has been used to fund all manner of services at relatively comfortable levels. Whitehorse, for instance, has a range of cultural and recreational facilities that are the envy of southern Canadian communities many times its size. More than 5000 people have government jobs.

Thanks to the Yukon's long isolation before WWII, the 14 First Nations groups have maintained their relationship to the land and their traditional culture, compared to groups forced to assimilate in other parts of Canada. They can be found across the territory and in isolated places like Old Crow, living lives not fundamentally changed in centuries. It's not uncommon to hear various aboriginal dialects spoken by elders.

Light – or the lack thereof – does play an important role in local life. Many people adjust to the radical variations in daylight through the year, but others do not. Every year you hear of longtime residents and newcomers alike who one day (often in February) announce enough is enough and move south for good.

Parks

The Yukon has a major Unesco World Heritage site in raw and forbidding Kluane National Park which sits solidly within the Yukon abutting Tatshenshini-Alsek Provincial Park in British Columbia (BC). Glacier Bay and Wrangell-St Elias National Parks are found in adjoining Alaska.

The Yukon has a dozen parks and protected areas (www.yukonparks.ca), but much of the territory itself is parklike and government campgrounds can be found throughout. Tombstone Territorial Park is remote, yet accessible via the Dempster Hwy, so you can absorb the horizon-sweeping beauty of the tundra and majesty of vast mountain ranges.

ℹ️ Information

There are excellent visitor information centers (VICs) covering every entry point in the Yukon: Beaver Creek, Carcross, Dawson City, Haines Junction, Watson Lake and Whitehorse.

The Yukon government produces enough literature and information to supply a holiday's worth of reading. Among the highlights are *Camping on Yukon Time, Art Adventures on Yukon Time* and lavish walking guides to pretty much every town with a population greater than 50. Start your collection at the various visitors centers online (www.travelyukon.com). Another good internet resource is www.yukoninfo.com.

A great way to get a feel for the Yukon and its larger-than-life stories is to read some of the vast body of Yukon novels. Start with Jack London – *Call of the Wild* is free online at www.online-literature.com.

ℹ️ Getting There & Around

Whitehorse is linked by air to Vancouver, Calgary and Edmonton. There are even flights nonstop to Germany during summer. Dawson City has flights to Whitehorse, Inuvik in the NWT and to Fairbanks, Alaska.

There are three major ways to reach the Yukon by road: first by ferry to the entry points of Skagway and Haines, Alaska; by the Alaska Hwy from Dawson Creek, BC, and by the Stewart-Cassiar Hwy from northwest BC that joins the Alaska Hwy near Watson Lake.

You can reach Whitehorse from BC by bus. From there a patchwork of companies provides links to Alaska and Dawson. Rental cars and RVs are expensive and only available in Whitehorse. The Alaska and Klondike Hwys are paved and have services every 100km to 200km.

To check road conditions in the Yukon call 📞511 or visit www.511yukon.ca.

WHITEHORSE

POP 26,100

The leading city and capital of the Yukon, Whitehorse will likely have a prominent role in your journey. The territory's two great highways, the Alaska and the Klondike, cross here; it's a hub for transportation (it was a terminus for the White Pass &

YUKON TERRITORY FAST FACTS

➡ Population: 33,900

➡ Area: 483,450 sq km

➡ Capital: Whitehorse

➡ Quirky fact: Home to Robert Service, the poet who immortalized the Yukon through works like *The Shooting of Dan McGrew* and *The Cremation of Sam McGee*.

Yukon Route railway from Skagway in the early 1900s, and during WWII was a major center for work on the Alaska Hwy). You'll find all manner of outfitters and services for explorations across the territory. Most of its residents have government-related jobs, but they escape for the outdoors no matter what the season.

Not immediately appealing, Whitehorse rewards the curious. It has a well-funded arts community (with an especially vibrant visual arts community), good restaurants and a range of motels. Exploring the sights within earshot of the rushing Yukon River can easily take a day or more. Look past the bland commercial buildings and you'll see a fair number of heritage ones awaiting discovery.

In 1953, Whitehorse was made the capital of the territory, to the continuing regret of much smaller and isolated Dawson City.

◉ Sights

You can explore Whitehorse's main sights in a day, mostly on foot.

⭐ **SS Klondike** HISTORIC SITE
(📞867-667-4511; South Access Rd & 2nd Ave; ⏰9:30am-5pm May-Aug) **FREE** Carefully restored, this was one of the largest sternwheelers used on the Yukon River. Built in 1937, it made its final run upriver to Dawson in 1955 and is now a national historic site. Try not to wish it was making the run now.

Waterfront NEIGHBORHOOD
One look at the majestic Yukon River and you'll want to spend time strolling its bank. The beautiful **White Pass & Yukon Route Station** (1109 1st Ave) has been restored and anchors an area that's in the midst of a revitalization. **Rotary Peace Park** at the south end is a great picnic spot.

Whitehorse

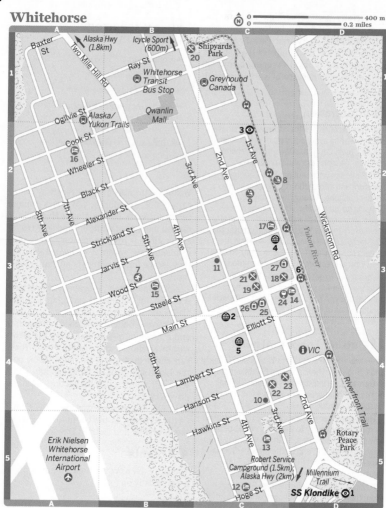

The new **Kwanlin Dün Cultural Centre** (www.kwanlinunculturalcentre.com; 1171 1st Ave; ⊕9:30am-4pm) has changing exhibits and plans a museum showing how local First Nations groups used the river.

At the north end of the waterfront, **Shipyards Park** has a growing collection of historic structures gathered territory-wide and a skateboard track and toboggan hill. Linking it all is a cute little **waterfront trolley** (www.yukonrails.com; one-way $2; ⊕10am-6pm Jun-Aug) which runs all the way from the *SS Klondike* north to Quartz Rd north of Shipyards Park.

MacBride Museum MUSEUM

(☑867-667-2709; www.macbridemuseum.com; cnr 1st Ave & Wood St; adult/child $10/5; ⊕9:30am-5pm) The Yukon's attic covers the gold rush, First Nations, intrepid Mounties and more. Old photos vie with old stuffed critters; daily special events like gold-panning are fun.

Old Log Church HISTORIC BUILDING

(☑867-668-2555; www.oldlogchurchmuseum.ca; 303 Elliott St; adult/child $6/5; ⊕10am-6pm May-Aug) The only log-cabin-style cathedral in the world is a 1900 downtown gem. Displays include the compelling story of Rev Isaac Stringer, who boiled and ate his boots while

Whitehorse

lost in the wilderness for 51 days. Fittingly, all that's left is his sole.

Yukon Beringia Interpretive Centre
MUSEUM

(☑867-667-8855; www.beringia.com; Km 1473 Alaska Hwy; adult/child $6/4; ☺9am-6pm) This place focuses on Beringia, a mostly ice-free area that encompassed the Yukon, Alaska and eastern Siberia during the last ice age. Engaging exhibits re-create the era, right down to the actual skeleton of a 3m-long giant ground sloth.

Yukon Transportation Museum
MUSEUM

(☑867-668-4792; www.goytm.ca; 30 Electra Circle; adult/child $10/5; ☺10am-6pm May-Aug) Find out what the Alaska Hwy was really like back in the day; let's just say mud was a dirty word. Exhibits cover planes, trains and dogsleds. The museum is near the Beringia Centre. Look for the iconic **DC-3 weather vane** (yes, it spins!) out front.

Whitehorse Fishway
LANDMARK

(☑867-633-5965; Nisutlin Dr; admission by donation; ☺9am-7pm Jun-Aug) Stare down a salmon at the Whitehorse Fishway, a 366m wooden fish ladder (the world's longest) past the hydroelectric plant south of town. Large viewing windows let you see chinook salmon swim past starting in late July (before that it's grayling).

The fishway is easily reached on foot via the Millennium Trail.

Arts Underground
GALLERY

(☑867-667-4080; Hougen Centre lower level, 305 Main St; ☺10am-5pm Tue-Sat) Operated by the Yukon Arts Society. There are carefully selected and well-curated rotating exhibits.

Yukon Artists@Work
GALLERY

(☑867-393-4848; 120 Industrial Rd; ☺noon-5pm) Operated by local artists, some of whom may be busily creating when you visit. It's situated just north of the big box shopping area.

🏃 Activities

The visitor information center can guide you to numerous local hikes and activities. Otherwise, Whitehorse is a major outfitting center for adventures on Yukon waterways.

Canoeing & Kayaking

Whitehorse is the starting place for popular canoeing and kayaking trips to Carmacks or on to Dawson City. It's an average of eight days to the former and 16 days to the latter. Outfitters offer gear of all kinds (canoes and kayaks are about $40 per day), guides, tours, lessons and planning services and can arrange transportation back to Whitehorse. Most paddlers use the map *The Yukon River: Marsh Lake to Dawson City* available at www.yukonbooks.com.

Kanoe People
CANOEING

(☑867-668-4899; www.kanoepeople.com; cnr 1st Ave & Strickland St) Can arrange any type of trip including paddles down Teslin and Big Salmon Rivers. Gear, maps and guides for sale; bikes for rent. Half-day paddles around Whitehorse are $60.

Up North Adventures CANOEING
(☎867-667-7035; www.upnorthadventures.com; 103 Strickland St) Offers rentals and transport on the major rivers. Also paddling lessons, guided mountain-bike trips and winter sports.

Cycling
Whitehorse has scores of bike trails along the Yukon River and into the surrounding hills. The visitor information center has maps.

Cadence Cycle CYCLING
(☎867-633-5600; 508 Wood St; rental per day from $35; ⊙10am-6pm Mon-Sat) Sells and rents good used mountain bikes and does repairs.

Icycle Sport CYCLING
(www.icyclesport.com; 9002 Quartz Rd; rental per day from $45; ⊙10am-6pm Mon-Sat) Rents top-end mountain bikes and skis (in winter).

Walking & Hiking
You can walk a scenic 5km loop around Whitehorse's waters that includes a stop at the fishway. From the SS *Klondike* go south on the **Millennium Trail** until you reach the Robert Service Campground and the Rotary Centennial Footbridge over the river. The fishway is just south. Head north along the water and cross the Robert Campbell Bridge and you are back in the town center.

☞ Tours

★**Yukon Historical & Museums Association** WALKING TOUR
(☎867-667-4704; 3126 3rd Ave; admission $6; ⊙11am-6pm Mon-Sat Jun-Aug) Offers quirky and interesting downtown walking tours four times daily. Meet at its office in the 1904 Donneworth House. Ask your guide to show you the WWII-era American latrine that's still not winning any hearts and minds.

Boréale Mountain Biking BIKE TOUR
(☎867-336-1722; www.borealebiking.ca; tours from $60) Highly regarded bike tours cover Whitehorse in a family-friendly half day. More-adventurous options include the 800km of trails in the region, which *Outside* magazine has named among the world's best.

Yukon Conservation Society HIKING TOUR
(☎867-668-5678; www.yukonconservation.org; 302 Hawkins St; ⊙Tue-Sat Jun-Aug) **FREE** Discover the natural beauty all around Whitehorse with a free Yukon Conservation Society nature hike. There are various itineraries ranging from easy to hard.

⌫ Sleeping

Whitehorse can get almost full during the peak of summer, so book ahead. The visitor information center has lists of B&Bs. Whitehorse has a lot of midrange motels that earn the sobriquet 'veteran.' Check a room first before you commit.

★**Robert Service Campground** CAMPGROUND $
(☎867-668-3721; www.robertservicecampground. com; Robert Service Way; campsites $21; ⊙May-Sep; @🛜) It's a pretty 15-minute walk from town on the Millennium Trail to the 70 sites at this tents-only campground on the river 1km south of town. Excellent coffee, baked goods and ice cream in the cafe.

Beez Kneez Bakpakers HOSTEL $
(☎867-456-2333; www.bzkneez.com; 408 Hoge St; dm/r $30/65; @🛜) Like the home you've left behind, this cheery hostel has a garden, deck, grill and bikes. Two cabins ($75) are much in demand.

Hi Country RV Park CAMPGROUND $
(☎867-667-7445; www.hicountryrvyukon.com; 91374 Alaska Hwy; sites $27-40; @🛜) At the top of Robert Service Way, this woodsy campground offers hookups, showers, laundry and a playground.

Coast High Country Inn HOTEL $$
(☎800-554-4471, 867-667-4471; www.highcountry inn.yk.ca; 4051 4th Ave; r $100-220; ❉@🛜) Towering over Whitehorse (four stories!), the High Country is popular with business travelers and high-end groups. The 84 rooms are large – some have huge whirlpools right in the room. The pub is popular.

Historical House B&B B&B $$
(☎867-668-2526; www.yukongold.com; cnr 5th Ave & Wood St; r $95-120; ❉@) A classic wooden home from 1907 with three guestrooms. Top-floor ones have individual bathrooms down the hall and angled ceilings. A larger unit has a huge kitchen. Rooms have high-speed internet and a nice garden.

Midnight Sun Inn   B&B $$
(☑800-284-4448, 867-667-2255; www.midnight-sunbb.com; 6188 6th Ave; r $110-145; ✳@📶) A modern B&B in a sort of overgrown suburban-style house with five themed rooms. The Sun has a loyal following, is downtown and serves big breakfasts.

Edgewater Hotel   HOTEL $$
(☑877-484-3334, 867-667-2572; www.edgewaterhotelwhitehorse.com; 101 Main St; r $100-200; ✳@📶) Much updated, the Edgewater has a dash of style. The 30 rooms are smallish (some lack air-con); better rooms have river views, some have kitchens.

River View Hotel   MOTEL $$
(Canada's Best Value Inn; ☑888-315-2378, 867-667-7801; www.riverviewhotel.ca; 102 Wood St; r $90-150; @📶) The floors sound hollow here but many of the 53 rooms have the views implied by the name (ask for one) and all are very large. It's close to everything, yet on a quiet street.

✕ Eating & Drinking

Ignore the influx of chain eateries and enjoy one of Whitehorse's excellent downtown restaurants. There's a great range; look for fresh Yukon salmon in season and the tasty brews of the local Yukon Brewing Co year-round.

Fireweed Community Market   MARKET
(Shipyards Park; ☉3-8pm Thu May-Sep) draws vendors from the region; the berries are fabulous.

Yukon Meat & Sausage   DELI $
(☑867-667-6077; 203 Hanson St; sandwiches $7; ☉9am-5:30pm Mon-Sat) The smell of smoked meat wafts out to the street and you walk right in; there's a huge selection of prepared items and custom-made sandwiches. Great for picnics, or eat in.

Baked Café   CAFE $
(☑867-633-6291; 100 Main St; snacks $4; ☉7am-7pm; 📶) In summer, the outdoor tables at this buzzing cafe are packed. Smoothies, soups, daily lunch specials, baked goods and more. Don't miss the raspberry pecan scones.

★Klondike Rib & Salmon   CANADIAN $$
(☑867-667-7554; 2116 2nd Ave; mains $12-25; ☉4-9pm May-Sep) It looks touristy and it seems touristy and it *is* touristy, but the food is excellent at this sprawling casual place with two decks. Besides the namesakes (the salmon kebabs are tops), there are other local faves.

★Burnt Toast   BISTRO $$
(☑867-393-2605; 2112 2nd Ave; mains $10-25; ☉9am-9pm) The food is far better than the coy name suggests! Brunch is excellent at this smart bistro (try the French toast) and lunch and dinner specials abound. Food is local and seasonal; just consult the blackboard. Good salads, sandwiches and Yukon meats.

Deck   PUB $$
(Coast High Country Inn; 4051 4th Ave, ; mains $10-20; ☉noon-midnight) The eponymous covered deck here draws crowds of locals, tourists and guides ('and when you see the whites of his eyes...') through the season. Backed by a huge bar with a good draft beer selection, diners choose from huge burgers, salads and fresh Yukon fish (the Arctic char is sublime).

Sanchez Cantina   MEXICAN $$
(☑867-668-5858; 211 Hanson St; mains $14-24; ☉11:30am-3pm & 5-9:30pm) You have to head south across two borders to find Mexican this authentic. Burritos are the thing – get them with the spicy mix of red and green sauces. Settle in for what may be a wait on the broad patio.

Dirty Northern Public House   PUB
(103 Main St; ☉noon-late) There are hints of style at this upscale pub which has a great draft beer selection and makes excellent mixed drinks. Grab a booth and chase the booze with a wood-fired pizza.

🔒 Shopping

The galleries listed in Sights are excellent sources of local items.

★Mac's Fireweed Books   BOOKS
(☑867-668-2434; www.yukonbooks.com; 203 Main St; ☉8am-midnight) Mac's stocks an unrivaled selection of Yukon titles. It also has topographical maps, road maps and periodicals.

Midnight Sun Gallery & Gifts   ARTS & CRAFTS
(☑867-668-4350; 205C Main St; ☉9am-8pm) Has a good selection of Yukon arts, crafts and products.

North End Gallery   ARTS & CRAFTS
(☑867-393-3590; 1116 1st Ave; ☉10am-6pm Mon-Sat) High-end Canadian art.

❶ Information

Yukon News Feisty local newspaper

What's Up Yukon (www.whatsupyukon.com) Source for entertainment listings.

Visitor Information Center (☑867-667-3084; 100 Hanson St; ☉8am-8pm) Essential; has territory-wide information.

Whitehorse General Hospital (☑867-393-8700; 5 Hospital Rd; ☉24hr)

❶ Getting There & Away

Whitehorse is the transport hub of the Yukon.

AIR

Erik Nielsen Whitehorse International Airport (☑867-667-8440; www.gov.yk.ca/yxy/airports/yxy) Five minutes west of downtown off the Alaska Hwy.

Air Canada (☑888-247-2262; www.aircanada.com) Serves Vancouver.

Air North (☑800-661-0407; www.flyairnorth.com) Locally owned; serves Dawson City (with flights on to Inuvik, NWT and Fairbanks, Alaska) plus Vancouver, Kelowna, Edmonton and Calgary.

Condor (☑800-364-1667, in Germany 01805 707 202; www.condor.com) Weekly summer flights to/from Frankfurt.

Westjet (☑888-937-8538; www.westjet.com) Seasonal service to/from Vancouver.

BUS

Bus services, er, come and go; check the latest with the visitor information center.

Alaska/Yukon Trails (☑907-479-2277; www.alaskashuttle.com; ☉Jun–mid-Sep) Service (three times weekly) to Fairbanks (US$365) via a Dawson City overnight stop (stopovers only, trips must start/end in Alaska).

Greyhound Canada (☑800-661-8747, 867-667-2223; www.greyhound.ca; 2191 2nd Ave) Service south along the Alaska Hwy to Dawson Creek (from $250, 20 hours, three times per week); connects with buses for the rest of BC and Canada.

White Pass & Yukon Route (☑867-633-5710; www.wpyr.com; Whitehorse ticket office, 1109 1st Ave; ☉9am-5pm Mon-Sat mid-May–mid-Sep) Offers a jaw-dropping scenic 10-hour rail and bus connection to/from Skagway via Carcross, BC (one-way to Skagway adult/child $185/92.50). Service is not daily. Also offers one-day tours from Whitehorse that include a train ride.

❶ Getting Around

TO/FROM THE AIRPORT

Yellow Cab (☑867-668-4811) About $20 from the center for the 10-minute ride.

BUS

Whitehorse Transit System (☑867-668-7433; $2.50; ☉Mon-Sat) Main transfer point at the Qwanlin Mall. Route 3 serves the airport, Route 5 passes the Robert Service Campground.

CAR & RV

Check your rate very carefully as it's common for a mileage charge to be added after the first 100km, which will not get you far in the Yukon. Also understand your insurance coverage and whether damage from Yukon's rugged roads is covered.

Budget (☑867-667-6200; www.budget.com) At the airport.

Fraserway RV Rentals (☑867-668-3438; www.fraserwayrvrentals.com; 9039 Quartz Rd) Rents all shapes and sizes of RV from $100 per day depending on size (it matters) and season. Mileage extra; rates can quickly add up.

Whitehorse Subaru (☑867-393-6550; www.whitehorsesubaru.com; 17 Chilkoot Way) Good rates; most cars have manual transmissions.

ALASKA HIGHWAY

It may be called the Alaska Hwy but given that its longest stretch is in the Yukon (958km) perhaps another name is in order...

Roughly 2450km in length from Dawson Creek, BC, to Delta Junction, far inside Alaska, the Alaska Hwy has a meaning well beyond just a road; it's also a badge, an honor, an accomplishment. Even though today it's a modern road, the very name still evokes images of big adventure and getting away from it all.

As you drive the Alaska Hwy in the Yukon, you're on the most scenic and varied part of the road. From little villages to the city of Whitehorse, from meandering rivers to the upthrust drama of the St Elias Mountains, the scenery will overwhelm you.

British Columbia to Whitehorse

You'll never be far from an excuse to stop on this stretch of the highway. Towns, small parks and various roadside attractions appear at regular intervals. None are a massive draw, but overall it's a pretty drive made all the more compelling by the locale.

Watson Lake

Originally named after Frank Watson, a British trapper, Watson Lake is the first town in the Yukon on the Alaska Hwy and is just over the border from BC. It's a good rest stop with a superb **visitor information center** (☑867-536-7469; www.watsonlake. ca; Alaska Hwy; ⊙8am-8pm May-Sep), which has a good museum about the highway and a passel of territory-wide info. The town offers campgrounds, motels, services and a Greyhound Canada stop.

The town is famous for its **Sign Post Forest** just outside the visitor center. The first signpost, 'Danville, Illinois,' was nailed up in 1942. Others were added and now there are 72,000 signs, many purloined late at night from municipalities worldwide. The **Air Force Lodge** (☑867-536-2890; www. airforcelodge.com; Alaska Hwy; s/d $75/85) has spotless rooms with shared bathrooms in a historic 1942 barracks for pilots.

Twenty-six kilometers west of Watson Lake is the junction with the Stewart-Cassiar Hwy (Hwy 37), which heads south into BC.

Just west of the junction, family-run **Nugget City** (☑888-536-2307, 867-536-2307; www.nuggetcity.com; Alaska Hwy; campsites from $20, r from $65; ☎) has accommodations and food that's three cuts above the Alaska Hwy norm. Stop just for the baked goods, especially the berry pie.

Another 110km west, past the 1112km marker, look for the **Rancheria Falls**

HISTORY OF THE HIGHWAY

Nowadays the aura of the Alaska Hwy is psychological rather than physical. In every way it's a modern two-lane road, with smooth curves, broad sight lines and paving from one end to another, but that has not always been the case. A famous 1943 photo shows a jeep seemingly being sucked down to China through a morass of mud while soldiers look on helplessly.

With the outbreak of WWII, Canada and the US decided that years of debate should end and that a proper road was needed to link Alaska and the Yukon to the rest of Canada and the US.

That a road – any road – could be carved out of the raw tundra and wilderness of the north in a little over a year was a miracle, although unlimited money and manpower (US soldiers and Canadian civilians, including Aboriginal people) helped. The 2450km gravel highway ran between Dawson Creek in British Columbia and Fairbanks in Alaska. The route chosen for the highway followed a series of existing airfields – Fort St John, Fort Nelson, Watson Lake and Whitehorse – known as the Northwest Staging Route.

In April 1946 the Canadian section of the road (1965km) was officially handed over to Canada. In the meantime, private contractors were busy widening, graveling and straightening the highway, leveling its steep grades and replacing temporary bridges with permanent steel ones – a process that has continued since, creating the modern road you drive today.

Known variously as the Alaskan International Hwy, the Alaska Military Hwy and the Alcan (short for Alaska-Canada) Hwy, it's now called the Alaska Hwy. It has transformed both the Yukon and Alaska, opening up the north to year-round travel and forever changing the way of life of the aboriginal populations along the route.

The Alaska Hwy begins at 'Mile 0' in Dawson Creek in northeastern BC and goes to Fairbanks, Alaska, although the official end is at Delta Junction, about 155km southeast of Fairbanks.

Mileposts long served as reference points, but improvements shortening the road and Canada's adoption of the metric system have made mileage references archaic. Historic numbers persist in the names of some businesses and attractions.

For more on the Alaska Hwy and its harrowing past, check out the Watson Lake visitor information center, the Yukon Transportation Museum (p257) in Whitehorse, the Soldier's Summit Trail (p783) in Kluane National Park and the Alaska Highway House (p250) in Dawson Creek, BC.

For a detailed guide to every feature, including seemingly every pothole and moose turd, look for the *Milepost,* a legendary annual publication.

WORTH A TRIP

ROBERT CAMPBELL HIGHWAY

To get right off the beaten path, consider this lonely gravel road (Hwy 4) which runs 588km from Watson Lake north and west to Carmacks, where you can join the Klondike Hwy for Dawson City. Along its length, the highway parallels various rivers and lakes. Wilderness campers will be thrilled.

At 373km from Watson Lake at the junction with the Canol Rd (Hwy 6) is **Ross River**, home to the Kaska First Nation and a supply center for the local mining industry. There are campgrounds and motels in town.

Recreation Site. A boardwalk leads to powerful twin waterfalls. It's an excellent stop.

Teslin

Teslin, on the long, narrow lake of the same name, is 272km west of Watson Lake and has long been a home to the Tlingits (lin-*kits*). As elsewhere the Alaska Hwy brought both prosperity and rapid change to this aboriginal population. The engrossing **George Johnston Museum** (☑867-390-2550; www.gjmuseum.yk.net; Km 1294 Alaska Hwy; adult/child $5/2.50; ☺9am-6pm May-Aug) details the life and culture of a 20th-century Tlingits leader through photographs, displays and artifacts.

Johnson's Crossing

Some 53km north of Teslin is Johnson's Crossing, at the junction of the Alaska Hwy and Canol Rd (Hwy 6). During WWII the US army built the Canol pipeline at tremendous human and financial expense to pump oil from Norman Wells in the NWT to Whitehorse. It was abandoned after countless hundreds of millions of dollars (in 1943 money, no less) were spent.

Whitehorse to Alaska

For long segments west of Whitehorse, the Alaska Hwy has been modernized to the point of blandness. Fortunately, this ends abruptly in Haines Junction. From here the road parallels legendary Kluane National Park and the St Elias Mountains. The 300km to Beaver Creek is the most scenic part of the entire highway.

Haines Junction

It's goodbye flatlands when you reach Haines Junction and see the sweep of imposing peaks looming over town. You've reached the stunning Kluane National Park and this is the gateway. The town makes an excellent base for exploring the park or staging a serious four-star mountaineering, backcountry or river adventure.

The magnificent Haines Hwy heads south from here to Alaska.

Activities

Even the spectacular ridges surrounding Haines Junction don't begin to hint at the beauty of Kluane National Park. Although the park should be your focus, there are some good activities locally.

For a hike after much of driving, there's a pretty 5.5km **nature walk** along Dezadeash River where Hwy 3 crosses it at the south end of town.

Tatshenshini Expediting (☑867-393-3661; www.tatshenshiniyukon.com; per person from $135) leads white-water rafting trips on the nearby Tatshenshini River, which has rapids from grade II to grade IV. Trips leave from Haines Junction and Whitehorse.

🛏 Sleeping & Eating

There's a cluster of motels and RV parks in Haines Junction. There's a beach and shade at **Pine Lake**, a territorial campground 6km east of town on the Alaska Hwy. Cerulean waters are a highlight at **Kathleen Lake** (campsites $16), a Parks Canada campground 24km south of Haines Junction off the Haines Hwy.

For most groceries, you'll need to stock up in Whitehorse.

Alcan Motor Inn   MOTEL **$$**
(☑888-265-1018, 867-634-2371; www.alcanmotorinn.com; Alaska Hwy; r $110-170; ✳🐾) The modern two-story Alcan has 23 large rooms with great views of the jagged Auriol Range. Some have full kitchens; the on-site cafe, **Northern Lights** (mains $13-20; ☺7am-9pm), has hearty fare.

Raven Motel   INN **$$**
(☑867-634-2500; www.ravenhotelyukon.com; 181 Alaska Hwy; r $125-150; ☺May-Sep; ✳🐾) There are 12 comfortable motel-style rooms here

and guests can partake of a German-style breakfast buffet.

★ **Village Bakery & Deli** BAKERY $

(☑ 867-634-2867; cnr Kluane & Logan Sts; mains $6-11; ⊙ 7am-9pm May-Sep; 🐾) The bakery here turns out excellent goods all day, while the deli counter has tasty sandwiches you can enjoy on the huge deck. On Friday night there's a popular barbecue with live folk music. It has milk and other very basic groceries.

Frosty Freeze BURGERS $

(☑ 867-634-7070; Alaska Hwy; mains $7-11; ⊙ 11am-9pm May-Sep) What looks like a humdrum fast-food joint is several orders of magnitude better. The shakes are made with real ice cream, the sundaes feature fresh berries and the burgers (try the mushroom-Swiss number) are huge and juicy.

❶ Information

The **visitor information center** (☑ 867-634-2345; www.hainesjunctionyukon.com; Alaska Hwy; ⊙ 8am-8pm Jun–mid-Sep) shares space with **Parks Canada** (☑ 867-634-7250; www.parkscanada.gc.ca/kluane; ⊙ 9am-5pm) in the new First Nations **Dä Ku Cultural Centre** (Alaska Hwy). There are excellent films about the park as well as engrossing exhibits on the park and aboriginal life. And that thing that looks like an acid-trip cupcake? It's a sculpture meant to be a winsome tableau of local characters and critters.

Kluane National Park & Reserve

Unesco-recognized as an 'empire of mountains and ice,' Kluane National Park and Reserve looms south of the Alaska Hwy much of the way to the Alaska border. This rugged and magnificent wilderness covers 22,015 sq km of the southwest corner of the territory. Kluane (kloo-wah-neee) gets its far-too-modest name from the Southern Tutchone word for 'lake with many fish.'

With British Columbia's Tatshenshini-Alsek Provincial Park to the south and Alaska's Wrangell-St Elias National Park to the west, this is one of the largest protected wilderness areas in the world. Deep beyond the mountains you see from the Alaska Hwy are over 100 named glaciers and as many unnamed ones.

Winters are long and harsh. Summers are short, making mid-June to early September the best time to visit. Note that winter conditions can occur at any time, especially in the backcountry. See Kathleen Lake (p262) for the park's campground.

❂ Sights

The park consists primarily of the **St Elias Mountains** and the world's largest non-polar **ice fields**. Two-thirds of the park is glacier interspersed with valleys, glacial lakes, alpine forest, meadows and tundra. The **Kluane Ranges** (averaging a height of 2500m) are seen along the western edge of the Alaska Hwy. A greenbelt wraps around the base where most of the animals and vegetation live. Turquoise **Kluane Lake** is the Yukon's largest. Hidden are the immense ice fields and towering peaks, including **Mt Logan** (5959m), Canada's highest mountain, and **Mt St Elias** (5488m), the second highest. Partial glimpses of the interior peaks can be found at the Km 1622 **viewpoint** on the Alaska Hwy and also around the Donjek River Bridge, but the best views are from the air.

In Haines Junction, **Kluane Glacier Air Tours** (☑ 867-634-2916; www.kluaneglacierairtours.com; Haines Junction Airport; tours from $250) offers flight-seeing of Kluane and its glaciers that will leave you limp with amazement. Options begin with a one-hour tour.

⛷ Activities

There's excellent **hiking** in the forested lands at the base of the mountains, along either marked trails or less-defined routes. There are about a dozen in each category, some following old mining roads, others traditional aboriginal paths. Detailed trail guides and topographical maps are available at the information centers. Talk to the rangers before setting out. They will help select a hike and can provide updates on areas that may be closed due to bear activity. Overnight hikes require backcountry permits ($10 per person per night).

A good pause during your drive is the **Soldier's Summit Trail**, an easy 1km hike up from the Tachal Dhal information center. It has views across the park and plaques commemorating the inauguration of the Alaska Hwy at this point on November 20, 1942. You can listen to the original CBC broadcast of the opening.

The Tachal Dhal information center is also the starting point for **Slims West**, a popular 60km round-trip trek to **Kaskawulsh Glacier** – one of the few that can be reached on foot. This is a difficult route that takes from three to five days to complete and includes sweeping views from Observation Mountain (2114m). An easy overnight trip is the 15km **Auriol** loop, which goes from spruce forest to subalpine barrens and includes a wilderness campground. It's 7km south of Haines Junction.

Fishing is good and **wildlife-watching** plentiful. Most noteworthy are the thousands of Dall sheep that can be seen on Sheep Mountain in June and September. There's a large and diverse population of grizzly bear, as well as black bear, moose, caribou, goats and 150 varieties of birds, among them eagles and the rare peregrine falcon.

Many enjoy **skiing** or **snowshoeing**, beginning in February.

ℹ️ Information

Parks Canada has two information centers. One is in Haines Junction, and the other at **Tachal Dhal** (Sheep Mountain; Alaska Hwy; ⊙9am-4pm Jun-Aug), 130km west of Haines Junction. Get a copy of the park guide, which shows the scope of the park (and how little is actually easily accessible). The map shows hikes ranging from 10 minutes to 10 days.

Destruction Bay

This small village on the shore of huge Kluane Lake is 107km north of Haines Junction. It was given its evocative name after a storm tore through the area during construction of the highway. Most of the residents are First Nations, who live off the land through the year. **Congdon Creek** is 17km east of town on the Alaska Hwy and has an 81-site territorial campground and a fine lakeside setting.

Burwash Landing

Commune with an enormous, albeit stuffed, moose at the excellent **Kluane Museum** (☎867-841-5561; Alaska Hwy; adult/child $4/2; ⊙9am-6:30pm May-Aug). Enjoy intriguing wildlife exhibits and displays on natural and aboriginal history.

Beaver Creek

Wide-spot-in-the-road Beaver Creek is a beacon for sleepy travelers or those who want to get gas – certainly its lackluster eateries will ensure the latter. The Canadian border checkpoint is just north of town;

the US border checkpoint is 27km further west. Both are open 24 hours.

The **visitor information center** (☎867-862-7321; Km 1202 Alaska Hwy; ⊙8am-8pm May-Sep) has information on all of the Yukon. A strange **sculpture garden** just north tempts the silly (or intoxicated) into unnatural acts.

Of the four motels in town, the **1202 Motor Inn** (☎800-661-0540, 867-862-7600; www.1202motorinn.ca; 1202 Alaska Hwy; r from $80; ❄ 🐾 🐕) is the most appealing. The 30 rooms are basic and functional. Get one away from the idling trucks.

Alaska

The incredible scenery of the Alaska Hwy dims a bit once you cross into its namesake state. The Alaska Hwy department leaves the road much more despoiled than the pristine road conditions in the Yukon.

From the US border, it's 63km (39 miles) to **Tetlin National Wildlife Refuge** (http://tetlin.fws.gov) on the Alaska Hwy. About 117km past Tetlin, you'll reach the junction with the Taylor Hwy (Hwy 5) which connects north with the Top of the World Hwy to Dawson City.

HAINES HIGHWAY

If you're doing only a short loop between Haines and Skagway via Whitehorse, this 259km road might be the highlight of your trip. In fact, no matter what length your Yukon adventure, the Haines Hwy (Hwy 3) might be the high point. In a relatively short distance you see glaciers, looming snow-clad peaks, lush and wild river valleys, windswept alpine meadows and a bald-eagle-laced river delta.

Heading south of Haines Junction, look west for a close-up of the St Elias Mountains, those glaciers glimpsed at the top stretch all the way to the Pacific Ocean. About 80km south, look for the **Tatshenshini River viewpoint**. This white-water river flows through protected bear country and a valley that seems timeless.

About 10km further, look for **Million Dollar Falls**. For once the sight lives up to the billing, as water thunders through a narrow chasm. Let the roar lull you to sleep at the nearby territorial **campground**.

The highway crosses into BC for a mere 70km but you'll hope for more as you traverse high and barren alpine wilderness,

SPRUCE BEETLES?

Even as beetles wreak havoc on forests across British Columbia and the Rockies, the forests of the Yukon are recovering. The millions upon millions of trees killed by the spruce beetle since 1994 have shed their brown needles and are now a ghostly gray. Meanwhile fast-growing opportunists are adding a bright green hue to the tableaux.

Many reasons for the tree deaths center on climate change, including warmer winters, allowing far more beetles than usual to survive from one year to the next.

In recent years, however, several factors have been working against the beetles: dead trees mean less food, a very cold winter killed many beetles and there is now a population explosion of beetle-eaters. Meanwhile, nature has opened the door to other trees, including birch and alder, which grow relatively quickly.

To get a sense of the devastation caused by beetles in the last two decades stop at the short **Spruce Beetle Loop**, 17km northwest of Haines Junction, just off the highway. It has interpretive signs.

where sudden snow squalls happen year-round. At the 1070m Chilkat Pass, an ancient aboriginal route into the Yukon, the road suddenly plunges down for a steep descent into Alaska. The US border is 72km north of Haines, along the wide **Chilkat River Delta**.

The delta is home to scores of **bald eagles** year-round; the handsome birds flock like pigeons each fall when they mass in the trees overlooking the rivers, drawn by the comparatively mild weather and steady supply of fish.

Pullouts line the Haines Hwy (Hwy 7 in Alaska), especially between mileposts 19 and 26. Take your time driving and find a place to park. Just a few feet from the road it's quiet, and when you see a small tree covered with 20 pensive – and sizable – bald eagles, you can enjoy your own raptor version of *The Birds*.

Haines (Alaska)

Unlike Skagway across the Lynn Canal, Haines has escaped the cruise-ship mobs and it's all the better for it. It's a real community with an appealing downtown close to the working waterfront. There are good shops, a couple of small museums and a historic fort. You can easily walk around much of the town in a few scenic hours.

Coming from the south on the Alaska Marine Highway ferries, Haines is definitely the port of choice for accessing the Yukon.

Prices are in US dollars. Haines is on Alaska time, one hour earlier than the Yukon. For more coverage of Haines and southeast Alaska, see Lonely Planet's *Alaska*.

◉ Sights & Activities

Walk the center and waterfront and then amble over to **Fort Seward**, an old army post dating back 100 years. Now a national historic site, the many mannered buildings have been given a range of new uses from art galleries to funky stores and B&Bs.

Haines makes the most of its feathered residents and has an annual **eagle festival** (www.baldeagles.org/festival; ☉ mid-Nov) in their honor. Numerous local guides will take you to see the birds in ways you can't do from the side of the Haines Hwy.

🛏 Sleeping & Eating

The Haines Convention & Visitors Bureau has oodles of choices in all price ranges.

Portage Cove State Recreation Site   CAMPGROUND $
(Beach Rd; campsites US$5; ☉ mid-May–Aug) It's worth losing your car so you can stay at this cyclist- and backpacker-friendly campground on the water 1.6km south of town. Light a campfire and let the mist roll in.

Captain's Choice Motel   MOTEL $$
(☏ 907-766-3111; www.capchoice.com; 108 2nd Ave N; s/d US$127/137; @ ☂) Haines' largest motel has the best view of the Chilkat Mountains and Lynn Canal and a huge sundeck to enjoy it.

Mountain Market & Spirits   MARKET $
(☏ 907-766-3340; 151 3rd Ave; meals US$4-10; ☉ 7am-7pm; ☂) Get your Haines Hwy or Alaska ferry picnic here. Treats include excellent coffee, baked goods, big sandwiches and lots of organic prepared foods.

★**Fireweed Restaurant** BISTRO $$
(37 Blacksmith St; mains US$9-20; ⊙11:30am-3pm Wed-Sat & 4:30-9pm Tue-Sat; ♠) In Fort Seward, Fireweed is an oasis of organic and creative cuisine. Enjoy the excellent pizzas, salads, chowders and seafood out on the deck overlooking the Lynn Canal. We swoon over the Haines Brewing Spruce Tip Ale.

❶ Information

Haines Convention & Visitors Bureau (✆907-766-2234; www.haines.ak.us; 122 2nd Ave; ⊙8am-5pm Mon-Fri, 9am-4pm Sat & Sun) Collect information here.

❶ Getting There & Away

There's no public transportation from Haines into the Yukon.

Alaska Marine Highway System (✆800-642-0066; www.ferryalaska.com) Superb service links Haines and the Yukon to BC and the US. Car ferries serve Skagway, the Inside Passage and, importantly, Prince Rupert in BC (p243); also Bellingham, Washington in the US. The ferry terminal is 6.5km south of town.

Haines–Skagway Fast Ferry (✆888-766-2103, 907-766-2100; www.hainesskagway-fastferry.com; one-way adult/child $35/18; ⊙Jun-Sep) Carries passengers only (45 minutes, one to seven per day) and docks near the center.

KLONDIKE HIGHWAY

Beginning seaside in Skagway, Alaska, the 716km Klondike Hwy climbs high to the forbidding Chilkoot Pass before crossing into stunning alpine scenery on the way to Carcross. For much of its length the road generally follows the **Gold Rush Trail**, the route of the Klondike prospectors. You'll have a much easier time of it than they did.

North of Whitehorse, the road passes through often-gentle terrain that has been scorched by wildfires through the years. Signs showing the dates let you chart nature's recovery.

Skagway (Alaska)

Skagway has been both delighting and horrifying travelers for over 100 years. In 1898 rogues of all kinds preyed upon arriving miners bound for Dawson. Today it's T-shirt vendors preying on tourists. When several huge cruise ships show up at once, the streets swarm with day-trippers.

However, behind the tat there's a real town that has many preserved attractions. At night, after the cruise ships have sailed, Skagway has its own quiet charm. Although it's in the US, it can only be reached by car on the Klondike Hwy from the Yukon (with a short stretch in BC). It's the starting point for the famed Chilkoot Trail and the White Pass & Yukon Route.

Skagway is the last stop on the Alaska Marine Highway System's inland passage service from the south and as such is an important entry point for the Yukon. Lonely Planet's *Alaska* has extensive coverage of Skagway and the rest of southeast Alaska.

Prices are in US dollars. Skagway is on Alaska time, one hour earlier than the Yukon. Most places close outside of summer.

❂ Sights & Activities

A seven-block corridor along Broadway, part of the **Klondike Gold Rush National Historical Park**, is home to restored buildings, false fronts and wooden sidewalks from Skagway's gold-rush era. The Park Service has tours, a museum and info.

★**White Pass & Yukon Route Railroad** RAILROAD
(✆800-343-7373; www.wpyr.com; 231 2nd Ave; adult/child from US$115/57.50; ⊙May-Sep) The White Pass & Yukon Route is the stunning reason most people visit Skagway (other than T-shirts). The narrow-gauge line twists up the tortuous route to the namesake White Pass, tracing the notorious White Pass trail used during the Klondike gold rush. The three-hour Summit Excursion is the most popular ride, but longer trips are worth the time and money.

🛏 Sleeping & Eating

Reservations are strongly recommended during July and August. The Convention & Visitors Bureau has comprehensive accommodations lists.

Pullen Creek RV Park CAMPGROUND $
(✆907-983-2768, 800-936-3731; www.pullencreekrv.com; 501 Congress St; campsites/RV sites US$22/36) This park is right next to the ferry terminal.

Sgt Preston's Lodge MOTEL $$
(✆866-983-2521, 907-983-2521; http://sgt-prestons.eskagway.com; 370 6th Ave; s US$97-115,

THE YUKON IS MELTING, MELTING...

The Yukon could serve as exhibit one in the case confirming climate change. Every corner of the territory is experiencing rapid changes in the environment because it's getting warmer a lot quicker than anybody ever imagined. In the far north, Herschel Island is literally dissolving as the permafrost thaws. One gruesome sign: long-buried coffins floating to the surface of the melting earth. Unesco has listed it as one of the world's most threatened historic sites.

In Dawson City locals have for decades bet on the day each spring when the Yukon River suddenly breaks up and begins flowing. Detailed records show that the mean date for this has moved one week earlier in the last century to May 5, with the pace accelerating.

Preparing the Yukon for a radically different and warmer future is now a major political topic, even if nobody has the answers.

d US$119-151; @ 🛜) This motel is the best bargain in Skagway and just far enough from Broadway St to escape most of the cruise-ship crush.

★**Stowaway Café** CAJUN **$$**
(🖉 907-983-3463; www.stowawaycafe.com; 205 Congress Way; mains US$11-24; ⊙ 10am-9pm May-Sep) Near the Harbor Master's office, this funky and fantastic cafe serves excellent fish and Cajun-style steak dinners. Make sure you try the wasabi salmon.

❶ Information

Chilkoot Trail Centre (cnr Broadway & 2nd Ave; ⊙ 8am-5pm Jun-Aug), run by **Parks Canada** (🖉 800-661-0486; www.pc.gc.ca/chilkoot) and the **US National Park Service** (🖉 907-983-3655; www.nps.gov/klgo), provides advice, permits, maps and a list of transportation options to/from the Chilkoot Trail.

Skagway Convention & Visitors Bureau (🖉 907-983-2854; www.skagway.com; cnr Broadway St & 2nd Ave; ⊙ 8am-6pm Mon-Fri, to 5pm Sat & Sun) In the can't-miss Arctic Brotherhood Hall (think driftwood).

US National Park Service (🖉 907-983-2921; cnr Broadway & 2nd Ave; ⊙ 8am-6pm May-Sep) Pick up the *Skagway Trail Map* for area hikes; has full details on the Klondike Gold Rush National Historical Park and a small museum.

❶ Getting There & Away

From Skagway to Whitehorse on the Klondike Hwy (Hwy 2) is 177km. Customs at the border usually moves fairly quickly.

BOAT

Alaska Marine Highway System (🖉 800-642-0066; www.ferryalaska.com) These great voyages link Skagway and the Yukon to BC and the US. The car ferries serve Haines, the Inside Passage, and Prince Rupert in BC (p243); also Bellingham, Washington in the US. The ferry terminal is right in the center.

Haines–Skagway Fast Ferry (🖉 888-766-2103, 907-766-2100; www.hainesskagwayfastferry.com; one-way adult/child $35/18; ⊙ Jun-Sep) Carries passengers only (45 minutes, one to seven per day) and docks near the center.

TRAIN & BUS

White Pass & Yukon Route Railroad (🖉 907-983-2217; www.wpyr.com; 231 2nd Ave; ⊙ Jun-Aug) Offers a jaw-dropping scenic 10-hour rail and bus connection to/from Whitehorse via Carcross, BC (one-way to/from Whitehorse adult/child US$185/92.50). Service is not daily.

Chilkoot Trail

Arduous at best and deadly at worst in 1898, the Chilkoot Trail was the route most prospectors took to get over the 1110m Chilkoot Pass from Skagway and into the Yukon. Today, hikers reserve spots months in advance to travel the same route.

The well-marked 53km trail begins near **Dyea**, 14km northwest of Skagway, and heads northeast over the pass. It then follows the Taiya River to Lake Bennett in BC, and takes three to five days to hike. It's a hard route in good weather and often treacherous in bad. You must be in good physical condition and come fully equipped. Layers of warm clothes and rain gear are essential.

Hardware, tools and supplies dumped by the prospectors still litter the trail. At several places there are wooden shacks where you can put up for the night, but these are usually full, so a tent and sleeping bag are required.

There are 10 designated campgrounds along the route, each with bear caches.

At the Canadian end you can either take the White Pass & Yukon Route train from Bennett back to Skagway or further up the line to Fraser in BC, where you can connect with a bus for Whitehorse.

The Chilkoot Trail is a primary feature of the **Klondike Gold Rush International Historical Park**, a series of sites managed by both Parks Canada and the US National Park Service that stretches from Seattle, Washington, to Dawson City. Each Chilkoot hiker must obtain one of the 50 permits available for each day in summer; reserve well in advance. Parks Canada/US National Park Service charge $50 for a permit plus $12 for a reservation. Each day eight permits are issued on a first-come, first-served basis. For information, contact the **Chilkoot Trail Centre** in Skagway or go online. Necessary preplanning includes determining which campsites you'll use each night.

Carcross

Long a forgotten gold rush town, cute little Carcross, 74km southeast of Whitehorse, is on a roll. There are two to three trains in summer from Skagway on the **White Pass & Yukon Route** (www.wpyr.com; train/bus tour adult/child from $169/134.50; ☉Jun-Aug). Some old buildings are being restored and the site on Lake Bennett is superb. (Although Klondike prospectors who had to build boats here to cross the lake didn't think so.)

The **visitor information center** (☏867-821-4431; ☉8am-8pm May-Sep) is in a new complex with seasonal shops and cafes. Get the excellent walking tour brochure. The old **train station** has good displays on local history.

Carcross Desert, the world's smallest desert, is the exposed sandy bed of a glacial lake. It's 2km north of town.

Whitehorse to Carmacks

Leaving Whitehorse by the Klondike Hwy is none too exciting. There's land with low trees and a few cattle ranches. After about 40km, however, look for serene **Lake Laberge**, which has a beach, followed by **Fox Lake**, 24km further north, and **Twin Lakes**, 23km south of Carmacks. Each has a government campground with shelters and pump water.

Carmacks

This village of 400 sits right on the Yukon River and is named for one of the discoverers of gold in 1896, George Washington Carmacks. A rogue seaman wandering the Yukon, it was almost by luck that Carmacks (with Robert Henderson, Tagish Charlie and Keish – aka Skookum Jim Mason) made their claim on Bonanza Creek. Soon he was living the high life and it wasn't long before he abandoned his First Nations family and headed south to the US.

Given his record as a husband and father, it's fitting that Carmacks be honored by this uninspired collection of gas stations and places to stay. The main reason to stop is the excellent **Tagé Cho Hudän Interpretive Centre** (☏867-863-5830; admission by donation; ☉9am-4pm May-Sep). Volunteers explain aboriginal life past and present. Like elsewhere in the territory, residents here are keenly attuned to the land, which supplies them with game and fish throughout the year. A pretty 15-minute interpretive walk by the river provides a glimmer of insight into this life.

This is also the junction with the **Robert Campbell Hwy** (p262).

About 25km north of Carmacks, the **Five Finger Recreation Site** has excellent views of the treacherous stretch of the rapids that tested the wits of riverboat captains traveling between Whitehorse and Dawson. There's a steep 1.5km walk down to the rapids.

Minto

Easily missed – unless you're toting a canoe or kayak – Minto is where the Klondike Hwy leaves the route of the Gold Rush Trail. This is a popular place to put in for the four- to five-day trip down the Yukon River to Dawson City. It's about 72km north of Carmacks.

Stewart Crossing

Another popular place to get your canoe wet, Stewart Crossing is on the Stewart River, which affords a narrow and somewhat more rugged experience before it joins the Yukon to the west for the trip to Dawson.

Otherwise unexceptional, the village is the junction of the Klondike Hwy (Hwy 2) and the **Silver Trail** (Hwy 11).

North of Stewart Crossing the Klondike Hwy continues for 139 bland kilometers to

---

the junction with the Dempster Hwy. From here it's only 40km to Dawson City.

DAWSON CITY

If you didn't know its history, Dawson would be an atmospheric place to pause for a while, plunging into its quirky culture and falling for its seductive, funky vibe. That it's one of the most historic and evocative towns in Canada is like gold dust on a cake: unnecessary but damn nice.

Set on a narrow shelf at the confluence of the Yukon and Klondike Rivers, a mere 240km south of the Arctic Circle, Dawson City was the center of the Klondike gold rush.

Today you can wander the dirt streets of Dawson, passing old buildings with dubious permafrost foundations leaning on each other for support. There's a rich cultural life, with many people finding Dawson the perfect place for free expression (that person downing a shot on the next bar stool may be a dancer, filmmaker, painter or miner).

Dawson can be busy in the summer, especially during its festivals. But by September the days are getting short, the seasonal workers have fled south and the 1300 year-round residents (professionals, miners, First Nations, dreamers, artists and those who aren't sure where they fit) are settling in for another long and quiet winter.

History

In 1898 more than 30,000 prospectors milled the streets of Dawson – a few newly rich, but most without prospects and at odds with themselves and the world. Shops, bars and prostitutes relieved these hordes of what money they had, but Dawson's fortunes were tied to the gold miners and, as the boom ended, the town began a decades-long slow fade.

The territorial capital was moved to Whitehorse in 1952 and the town lingered on, surviving on the low-key but ongoing

KLONDIKE GOLD RUSH

The Klondike gold rush continues to be the defining moment for the Yukon. Certainly it was the population high point. Some 40,000 gold seekers washed ashore (some literally) in Skagway, hoping to strike it rich in the gold fields of Dawson City, some 700km north.

To say that most were ill-prepared for the adventure is an understatement. Although some were veterans of other gold rushes, a high percentage were American men looking for adventure. Clerks, lawyers and waiters were among those who thought they'd just pop up North and get rich. The reality was different. Landing in Skagway, they were set upon by all manner of flimflam artists, most working for the incorrigible Soapy Smith. Next came dozens of trips hefting their 1000lb of required supplies over the frozen Chilkoot Pass. Then they had to build boats from scratch and make their way across lakes and the Yukon River to Dawson. Scores died trying.

Besides more scamsters, there was another harsh reality awaiting in Dawson: by the summer of 1897 when the first ships reached the west coast of the US with news of the discoveries on Dawson's Bonanza Creek, the best sites had all been claimed. The Klondike gold rush mobs were mostly too late to the action by at least a year. Sick and broke, the survivors glumly made their way back to the US. Few found any gold and most sold their gear for pennies to merchants who in turn resold it to incoming gold seekers for top dollar. Several family fortunes in the Yukon today can be traced to this trade.

Today, even the hardiest folk seem like couch potatoes when compared to the protagonists of these harrowing stories. The deprivation, disease and heartbreak of these 'dudes' of the day make for fascinating reading. Among the many books about the Klondike gold rush, the following are recommended (and easily found in the Yukon):

➡ *The Klondike Fever* by Pierre Berton is the classic on the gold rush.

➡ *Sailor on Snowshoes* by Dick North traces Jack London's time in the Yukon and the hunt for his cabin. London's stories of the gold rush made his name as a writer.

➡ *Soapy Smith* by Stan Sauerwein is a delightful tale about the Skagway scalawag for whom the word incorrigible was invented.

Dawson City

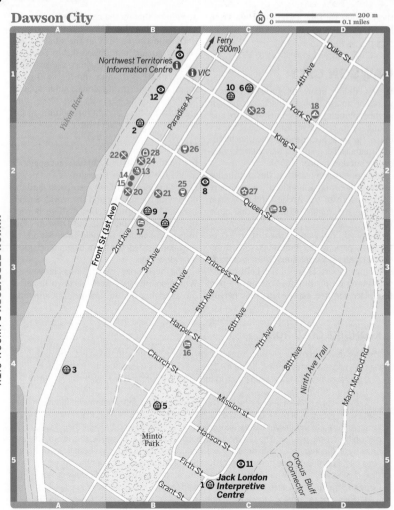

gold-mining industry. By 1970 the population was under 900. But then a funny thing happened on the way to Dawson's demise: it was rediscovered. Improvements to the Klondike Hwy and links to Alaska allowed the first major influx of summertime tourists, who found a charmingly moldering time capsule from the gold rush. Parks Canada designated much of the town as historic and began restorations.

⊙ Sights

Dawson is small enough to walk around in a few hours, but you can easily fill three or more days with the many local things to see and do. If the summertime hordes get you down, head uphill for a few blocks where you'll find timeless old houses and streets.

Like a gold nugget on a tapped-out creek, street numbers are a rarity in Dawson. Unless noted otherwise, opening hours and times given here cover the summer. For the rest of the year, most sights, attractions and many businesses are closed.

Government budget cuts mean Parks Canada's sites and programs are currently in flux; it may require some dexterity to see

Dawson City

some of the world-class sites due to very limited opening hours.

★ Klondike National Historic Sites
HISTORIC SITE

(www.pc.gc.ca/dawson; passes adult $7-32) It's easy to relive the gold rush at myriad preserved and restored places. Parks Canada tries its best with limited resources. Various restored buildings such as the **Palace Grand Theatre** (King St) are open on a sporadic and rotating basis, usually from 10am to 1pm.

Robert Service Cabin
HISTORIC SITE

(cnr 8th Ave & Hanson St; admission $7; ☉reading 1pm May-Aug) The 'Bard of the Yukon,' poet and writer Robert W Service, lived in this typical gold rush cabin from 1909 to 1912. Don't miss the dramatic readings.

Commissioner's Residence
HISTORIC SITE

(Front St; admission $7; ☉2:30-4:30pm) Built in 1901 to house the territorial commissioner, this proud building was designed to give potential civic investors confidence in the city. The building was the longtime home of Martha Black, who came to the Yukon in 1898, owned a lumberyard and was elected to the Canadian Parliament at age 70. (*Martha Black* by Flo Whyard is a great book about this remarkable woman.)

SS Keno
HISTORIC SITE

(Front & Queen Sts; admission $7; ☉9:30am-noon May-Aug) The SS *Keno* was one of a fleet of paddle wheelers that worked the Yukon's rivers for more than half a century. Grounded along the waterfront, the boat re-creates a time before any highways.

Harrington's Store
HISTORIC SITE

(cnr 3rd Ave & Princess St; ☉9am-8:30pm) FREE This old shop has historic photos from Dawson's heyday.

★ Jack London Interpretive Centre
MUSEUM

(Firth St; adult/child $5/free; ☉11am-6pm May-Aug) In 1898 Jack London lived in the Yukon, the setting for his most popular stories, including *Call of the Wild* and *White Fang*. At the writer's cabin there are daily interpretive talks. A labor of love by historian Dick North, Dawne Mitchell and others, this place is a treasure trove of stories – including the search for the original cabin.

Dawson City Museum
MUSEUM

(☎867-993-5291; 5th Ave; adult/child $9/free; ☉10am-6pm May-Aug) Make your own discoveries among the 25,000 gold rush artifacts at this museum. Engaging exhibits walk you through the grim lives of the miners. The museum is housed in the landmark 1901 Old Territorial Administration building.

Dänojà Zho Cultural Centre   CULTURAL BUILDING

(☑867-993-6768; www.trondekheritage.com; Front St; adult $5; ☺10am-5pm Mon-Sat) Inside this impressive riverfront wood building there are displays and interpretative talks on the Tr'ondëk Hwëch'in (River People) First Nations. The collection includes traditional artifacts and a re-creation of a 19th-century fishing camp.

CIBC Building   HISTORIC BUILDING

(Front St) The city of Dawson has started a long-term restoration of this derelict, riverfront bank building that dates to the gold rush. Note how tin was molded to look like stone. Poet Robert Service was once a teller here.

Midnight Dome   LOOKOUT

The slide-scarred face of this hill overlooks the town to the north, but to reach the top you must travel south of town about 1km, turn left off the Klondike Hwy onto New Dome Rd, and continue for about 7km. The Midnight Dome, at 880m above sea level, offers great views of the Klondike Valley, Yukon River and Dawson City. There's also a steep **trail** that takes 90 minutes from Judge St in town; maps are available at the visitor center.

Cemeteries   CEMETERY

(Mary McLeod Rd) A 15-minute walk up King St and Mary McCloud Rd near town leads to 10 cemeteries that are literally filled with characters. Among them: Joe Vogler, who fought to have Alaska secede from the US. He was buried here in 1993, having vowed not to be buried in an Alaska that wasn't free. Todd Palin (husband of Sarah) is among his acolytes.

Crocus Bluff   LOOKOUT

(off Mary McLeod Rd) Near Dawson's cemeteries, a short path out to pretty Crocus Bluff has excellent views of Dawson and the Klondike and Yukon Rivers. If driving, take New Dome Rd and turn at Mary McLeod Rd (ignoring the 'No Exit' signs). It is a short walk up King St from town. You can also take the 400m **Crocus Bluff Connector** path off of the **Ninth Avenue Trail**, which intersects with numerous streets along its 2.5km.

Klondike Institute for Art & Culture   CULTURAL BUILDING

(KIAC; ☑867-993-5005; www.kiac.org; cnr 3rd Ave & Queen St) The Klondike Institute for Art & Culture is part of Dawson's thriving arts community. It has an impressive studio building, galleries and educational programs.

ODD Gallery   GALLERY

(☑867-993-5005; cnr 2nd Ave & Princess St) The exhibition space of the Klondike Institute for Art & Culture, this gallery has regular shows.

Fortymile Gold Workshop/Studio   GALLERY

(☑867-993-5690; 3rd Ave btwn York & King Sts; ☺9am-6pm May-Sep) Watch as jewelry is made from local refined gold, which is silky and has a rich yellow color, as opposed to the bling you see peddled on late-night TV. Examples of gold from various local claims and locations shows how old miners could tell where gold originated.

Mines

The deeply scarred valleys around Dawson speak of the vast amounts of toil that went into the gold hunt. Bike or drive Bonanza Rd to pass some of the earliest gold rush sites along Bonanza Creek.

★ Dredge No 4   HISTORIC SITE

(Bonanza Rd) Some 13km off the Klondike Hwy, this massive dredging machine tore up the Klondike Valley and left the tailings, which remain as a vast, rippled blight on the landscape. Budget cuts to Parks Canada have put its preservation in doubt.

Bonanza Creek Discovery Site   HISTORIC SITE

(Bonanza Rd) Some 1.5km up the valley from Dredge No 4, this national historic site is roughly where gold was first found in 1897. It's a quiet site today with a little water burbling through the rubble.

🏃 Activities

Besides arriving by **canoe** or **kayak**, many people also exit Dawson via the Yukon River. A popular trip good for novices goes from Dawson for three days and 168km downstream to Eagle, Alaska.

A three-hour **hike to Moosehead**, an old First Nations village, is popular. The trail follows hillsides above the river north of town. Be sure to get a map at the visitor center..

You can explore much of the Dawson area by bike, including the **Ridge Road Heritage Trail**, which winds through the gold fields south of town.

Dawson City River Hostel
CANOEING, CYCLING

(www.yukonhostels.com; bike rental per day from $25; ☺May-Sep) Arranges all manner of canoe rentals, trips and transportation from Whitehorse and points further downstream to Dawson and from Dawson to the Alaskan towns of Eagle and Circle.

Dawson Trading Post
CANOEING

(☑867-993-3618; Front St; canoe rental per day $35; ☺9am-5pm Jun-Aug) Dawson Trading Post rents out canoes and can arrange trips.

☞ Tours

★ Parks Canada Walking Tours
WALKING TOUR

(tours $7; ☺May-Aug) Parks Canada docents, often in period garb, lead excellent walking tours. Learn about individual buildings and the many characters that walked the streets (many of whom could be called 'streetwalkers'). There are also self-guided 90-minute audio tours (adult $7, 9am to 5pm).

★ Goldbottom Tours
GOLD RUSH TOUR

(☑867-993-5750; www.goldbottom.com; ticket office Front St; tours with/without transportation from Dawson $55/45; ☺May-Sep) Run by the legendary Millar mining family. Tour their placer mine 15km up Hunker Creek Rd, which meets Hwy 2 just north of the airport. The three-hour tours include a gold-panning lesson; you get to keep what you find. You can also just pan for gold on their site for $20 or spend the night in a cabin for $100.

Husky Bus
BUS TOUR

(☑867-993-3821; www.huskybus.ca; Front St; tours $25-60; ☺May-Aug) Runs various tours that include Midnight Dome (two hours), the Goldfields (three hours) and Tombstone Park (six hours). The latter is highly recommended.

Klondike Spirit Tickets
BOAT TOUR

(☑867-993-5323; www.klondikespirit.com; tickets Triple J Hotel, cnr 5th Ave & Queen St; tours from $55; ☺May-Sep) This faux old stern-wheeler cruises the river on various tours.

★✦ Festivals & Events

Dawson City Music Festival
MUSIC

(☑867-993-5384; www.dcmf.com; ☺mid-Jul) Popular – tickets sell out months in advance and the city fills up; reservations are essential.

Discovery Days
CULTURE

(☺3rd Mon in Aug) Celebrates the you-know-what of 1896 with parades and picnics. Events begin days before, including an excellent art show.

🛏 Sleeping

Reservations are a good idea in July and August, although the visitor information center can help. Many places will pick you up at the airport; ask in advance. Unless otherwise stated, the following are open all year.

Dawson City River Hostel
HOTEL $

(☑867-993-6823; www.yukonhostels.com; dm $20-22, r from $48; ☺May-Sep) 🌿 This delightfully eccentric hostel is across the river from town and five minutes up the hill from the ferry landing. It has good views, cabins, platforms for tents and a communal bathhouse. Tent sites are $14. Owner Dieter Reinmuth is a noted Yukon author.

Yukon River Campground
CAMPGROUND $

(campsites $12; ☺May-Sep) On the western side of the river about 250m up the road to the right after the ferry; has 98 shady sites.

Gold Rush Campground RV Park
CAMPGROUND $

(☑866-330-5006, 867-993-5247; www.goldrushcampground.com; cnr 5th Ave & York St; RV sites $24-44; ☺May-Sep; 🛜) Convenience trumps atmosphere at this 83-site gravel parking lot for RVs.

★ Bombay Peggy's
INN $$

(☑867-993-6969; www.bombaypeggys.com; cnr 2nd Ave & Princess St; r $95-210; ☺Mar-Nov; ❄🛜) A renovated former brothel with alluring period furnishings and spunky attitude. Budget 'snug' rooms share bathrooms. Rooms are plush in a way that will make you want to wear a garter. The bar is a classy oasis.

Klondike Kate's
LODGE $$

(☑867-993-6527; www.klondikekates.ca; cnr King St & 3rd Ave; cabins $140-200; ☺Apr-Sep; @🛜) 🌿 The 15 cabins behind the excellent restaurant of the same name are rustic without the rusticisms. High-speed internet, microwaves and fridges ensure comfort. The porches are perfect for decompressing. Green practices are many.

Aurora Inn
INN $$

(☑867-993-6860; www.aurorainn.ca; 5th Ave; r $130-210; @) All 20 rooms in this European-style inn are large and comfortable. And if there's such a thing as old-world cleanliness, it's here: the admonishments to remove your (invariably) muddy shoes start at the entrance.

Triple J Hotel
HOTEL **$$**

(☎867-993-5323; www.triplejhotel.com; cnr 5th Ave & Queen St; r $100-180; ☎) The 47 rooms in this modern motel with a throw-back look are in a new wing, in the renovated main building or in a cabin. It's a good mainstream choice.

✖ Eating

Picnickers, hikers and backcountry campers will find two good grocery stores in town. A **farmers market** (Front St; ◷11am-5pm May-Sep) thrives by the iconic waterfront gazebo. The sweet-as-candy carrots are the product of very cold nights. Try some birch syrup.

Most of the motels have a restaurant serving burgers etc; few places stay open outside summer.

Cheechako's Bake Shop
BAKERY **$**

(☎867-993-6590; cnr Front & Princess Sts; mains $4-8; ◷7am-4pm Mon-Sat) A real bakery and a good one, on the main strip. Muffins, cookies and treats vie for your attention while sandwiches made on homemade bread.

River West
CAFE **$**

(☎867-993-6339; near cnr Front & Queen Sts; meals $4-7; ◷7am-7pm Mar-Oct) Busy throughout the day, this fine coffeehouse, bakery and cafe looks out on the Front St action. Grab an outside table.

★ Drunken Goat Taverna
GREEK **$$**

(☎867-993-5800; 2nd Ave; mains $14-25; ◷noon-9pm) Follow your eyes to the flowers, your ears to the Aegean music and your nose to the excellent Greek food, run 12-months-a-year by the wonderful Tony Dovas.

★ Klondike Kate's
CANADIAN **$$**

(☎867-993-6527; cnr King St & 3rd Ave; mains $8-25; ◷11am-9pm Mon-Sat, 8am-9pm Sun Apr-Sep) Two ways to know spring has arrived: the river cracks up and Kate's reopens. Locals in the know prefer the latter. The long and inventive menu has fine sandwiches, pastas and fresh Yukon fish. Look for great specials.

● Drinking & Nightlife

The spirit(s) of the prospectors lives on in several saloons. On summer nights the action goes on until dawn, which would mean something if it weren't light all night.

★ Bombay Peggy's
PUB

(☎867-993-6969; cnr 2nd Ave & Princess St; ◷11am-11pm Mar-Nov) There's always a hint of pleasures to come swirling around the tables of Dawson's most inviting bar. Enjoy good beers, wines and mixed drinks inside or out.

Billy Goat
PUB

(☎867-993-5800; 2nd Ave; ◷5pm-1am) Not a branch of the famed Chicago original but a nice, friendly lounge from Tony of Drunken Goat fame. Serves food from the Drunken Goat menu until late. Note the murals on the walls.

Bars at Westminster Hotel
BAR

(3rd Ave; ◷noon-late) These two legendary bars carry the mostly affectionate monikers 'Snakepit,' 'Armpit' or simply 'Pit.' The places for serious drinkers, with live music many nights.

Downtown Hotel
PUB

(☎867-993-5346; cnr Queen St & 2nd Ave; ◷11am-late) This unremarkable bar comes to life at 9pm in summer for what can best be called the 'Sourtoe Schtick.' Tourists line up to drink a shot of booze ($10) that has a pickled human toe floating in it. It's a long-running gag that's delightfully chronicled in Dieter Reinmuth's *The Saga of the Sourtoe*. (That the toe – it *is* real – looks much like a bit of beef jerky should give pause to anyone used to late-night Slim Jim jonesing...)

☆ Entertainment

★ Diamond Tooth Gertie's Gambling Hall
CASINO

(☎867-993-5575; cnr Queen St & 4th Ave; admission $10; ◷7pm-2am Mon-Fri, 2pm-2am Sat & Sun May-Sep) This popular re-creation of an 1898 saloon is complete with small-time gambling, a honky-tonk piano and dancing girls. The casino helps promote the town and fund culture. Each night there are three different floor shows with singing and dancing, which is often surprisingly contemporary.

🛍 Shopping

Maximilian's
BOOKS

(☎867-993-6537; Front St; ◷8am-8pm) Has an excellent selection of regional books, periodicals, gifts and topographical and river maps.

Dawson Trading Post
GIFTS, OUTDOOR EQUIPMENT

(☎867-993-5316; Front St; ◷9am-7pm) Sells interesting old mining gadgets, bear traps ($500) and old mammoth tusks so you can take up carving. It has a good bulletin board.

❶ Information

Much of Dawson is closed October to May. The biweekly, volunteer-run *Klondike Sun* covers special events and activities.

CIBC ATM (2nd Ave) Near Queen St.

Northwest Territories Information Centre (☑867-993-6167; Front St; ☺9am-7pm May-Sep) Maps and information on the NWT and the Dempster Hwy.

Visitor Information Center (☑867-993-5566; cnr Front & King Sts; ☺8am-8pm May-Sep) Tourist and Parks Canada information.

❶ Getting There & Away

Dawson City is 527km from Whitehorse. Public transport to/from Whitehorse is often in flux. Should you fly in, there are no rental cars.

Dawson City Airport (Klondike Hwy) About 19km east of Dawson.

Air North (☑800-661-0407; www.flyairnorth.com) Serves Whitehorse, Old Crow, Inuvik in the NWT and Fairbanks in Alaska.

Alaska/Yukon Trails (☑907-479-2277; www.alaskashuttle.com; ☺Jun–mid-Sep) Service (three times weekly) between Whitehorse and Fairbanks via a Dawson City overnight stop (stopovers only; trips must start/end in Alaska); to/from Fairbanks US$285.

Husky Bus (☑867-993-3821; www.huskybus.ca; Front St; ☺May-Sep) Much welcome regular bus service (two to three times weekly) to/from Whitehorse (fares from $90). Reserve in advance. Will do pickups of paddlers and canoes with advance arrangement along the Klondike Hwy.

DAWSON CITY TO ALASKA

From Dawson City, the free ferry crosses the Yukon River to the scenic **Top of the World Highway** (Hwy 9). Only open in summer, the mostly paved 106km-long ridge-top road to the US border has superb vistas across the region.

You'll continue to feel on top of the world as you cross the border. The land is barren alpine meadows with jutting rocks and often grazing caribou. The **border crossing** (☺ Yukon time 9am to 9pm, Alaska time 8am to 8pm, 15 May to 15 Sep) has strict hours – if you're late you'll have to wait until the next day.

On the US side, Alaska shows its xenophobic side, as the 19km connection to the Taylor Hwy (Hwy 5) is mostly dirt and often impassable after storms (expect to get dirt in parts of your vehicle and person you didn't think possible). The old gold-mining town of **Eagle** on the Yukon River is 105km north. Some 47km south over somewhat better roads, you encounter **Chicken**, a delightful place of free-thinkers happy to sell you a stupid T-shirt at one of the gas station-cafes or offer their views regarding government bureaucrats. Another 124km south and you reach the Alaska Hwy, where a turn east takes you to the Yukon. Just a tick west, **Tok** has services and motels. Alaska time is one hour earlier than the Yukon.

DEMPSTER HIGHWAY

Rather than name this road for an obscure Mountie (William Dempster), this road should be named the Michelin Hwy or the Goodyear Hwy for the number of tires it's sent to an explosive demise. This 736km thrill ride is one of North America's great adventure roads, winding through stark mountains and emerald valleys, across huge tracts of tundra and passing Tombstone Territorial Park.

The Dempster (Hwy 5 in the Yukon, Hwy 8 in the NWT) starts 40km southeast of Dawson City off the Klondike Hwy and heads north over the Ogilvie and Richardson mountains beyond the Arctic Circle and on to Inuvik in the NWT, near the shores of the Beaufort Sea.

Road Conditions

Built on a thick base of gravel to insulate the permafrost underneath (which would otherwise melt, causing the road to sink without a trace), the Dempster is open most of the year, but the best time to travel is between June and early September, when the ferries over the Peel and Mackenzie Rivers operate. In winter, ice forms a natural bridge over the rivers, which become ice roads. The Dempster is closed during the spring thaw and the winter freeze-up; the timing of these vary by the year and can occur from mid-April to June and mid-October to December, respectively.

Graveled almost its entire length, the highway has a well-deserved reputation for being rough on vehicles. Travel with extra gas and tires and expect to use them. Check road conditions in the **Yukon** (☑511; www.511yukon.ca) and the **NWT** (☑800-661-0750; www.dot.gov.nt.ca); the Northwest

TOMBSTONE TERRITORIAL PARK

Shades of green and charcoal color the wide valleys here and steep ridges are dotted with small glaciers and alpine lakes. Summer feels tentative but makes its statement with a burst of purple wildflowers in July. Clouds sweep across the tundra, bringing squalls punctuated by brilliant sun. Stand amid this and you'll know the meaning of the sound of silence.

Tombstone Territorial Park (www.yukonparks.ca) lies along Dempster Hwy for about 50km. The park's only formal **campground** (campsites $12) has a new and excellent **Interpretive Centre** (⊘ 9am-7pm Jun-Sep), which offers walks and talks. It's 71km from the start of the highway and is set in along the headwaters of the Yukon River just before **Tombstone Mountain**, the point where the trees run out and the truly wild northern scenery begins.

There are good **day hikes** near the campground, as well as longer, more rigorous **treks** for experienced wilderness hikers. Permits are required for backcountry camping, especially at several lakes popular in summer. (The park's backcountry camping guide shows refreshing honesty in its answer to this frequently asked question: 'Will you come looking for me if I don't return?' 'No.')

Tombstone is an easy day trip from Dawson City (112km each way). With preparations, however, a multiday park adventure could be the highlight of your trip.

Territories Information Centre (p275) in Dawson City is a good resource. It takes 10 to 12 hours to drive to Inuvik without stopping for a break. (Given that William Dempster regularly made 700km dogsled journeys in subzero weather, this rugged and challenging road is properly named after all.)

🛏 Sleeping & Eating

Accommodations and vehicle services along the route are few.

The first available services after the Klondike Hwy are 371km north in Eagle Plains. The **Eagle Plains Hotel** (☑ 867-993-2453; eagleplains@northwestel.net; KM 371 Dempster Hwy; r $100-150) is open year-round and offers 32 rooms. The next service station is 180km further at **Fort McPherson** in the NWT. From there it's 216km to Inuvik.

The Yukon government has three campgrounds – at **Tombstone Mountain** (72km from the start of the highway), **Engineer Creek** (194km) and **Rock River** (447km). There's also a NWT government campground at **Nitainlaii Territorial Park**, 9km south of Fort McPherson. Sites at these campgrounds are $12.

ARCTIC PARKS

North of the Arctic Circle, the Yukon's population numbers a few hundred. It's a lonely land with little evidence of humans and only the hardiest venture here during the short summers.

The 280-person village of **Old Crow** (www.oldcrow.ca) is home to the Vuntut Gwitch'in First Nations and is unreachable by vehicle. Residents subsist on caribou from the legendary 130,000-strong Porcupine herd, which migrates each year between the Arctic National Wildlife Refuge in Alaska and the Yukon.

On the Yukon side of this vast flat arctic tundra, a large swath of land is now protected in the adjoining **Vuntut** and **Ivvavik National Parks**. Information on both can be obtained from the Parks Canada office in Inuvik, NWT, where you can get information on the very limited options for organizing visits to the parks (think chartered planes, long treks over land and water, and total self-sufficiency). There are no facilities of any kind in the parks.

The aboriginal name of **Herschel Island (Qiqiktaruk) Territorial Park** means 'it is island' and indeed it is. Barely rising above the waters of Mackenzie Bay on the Beaufort Sea, **Herschel Island** (☑867-667-5648; www.yukonparks.ca) has a long tradition of human habitation. In the late 1800s American whalers set up shop at Pauline Cove. Abandoned in 1907, the whalers left behind several surviving wooden buildings. Today Inuvialuit families use the island for traditional hunting, although climate change is causing the island to dissolve into the sea.

Summer visits to Herschel Island are possible via tours from Inuvik.

Understand BC & the Canadian Rockies

BC & the Canadian Rockies Today

Western Canada has been on a high in recent years. Alberta is enjoying the financial benefits of its giant oilfields, while BC is basking in the light of having Vancouver hovering atop those 'world's most livable cities' surveys. But it's not all sunshine. Southern Alberta had its worst flooding in living memory in 2013, while BC continues precariously balancing wilderness preservation with the need to tap resources.

Best on Film

Mount Pleasant (2007) Gritty drama about family life in Vancouver.
City of Gold (1957) Evocative short film comparing gold rush Dawson City to 60 years later. Narrated by noted Canadian author, Pierre Berton.
Carts of Darkness (2008) Documentary about shopping-cart races among Vancouver's homeless.
Delicate Art of Parking (2003) Comedy documentary about traffic enforcers.

Best in Print

City of Glass (Douglas Coupland, 2000) Vancouver's most celebrated author offers a quirky guide to his hometown.
Craft Beer Nation (Joe Wiebe, 2013) Profiling the lip-smacking breweries and beermakers of BC.
The Call of the Wild (Jack London, 1903) The story of a dog during the Klondike gold rush.
Calgary Stampede: 100 Years of the Greatest Show on Earth (Calgary Herald, 2012) The story of Canada's favorite annual party.

Olympic Legacies

When Vancouver hosted the Olympic and Paralympic Winter Games in 2010, the eyes of the world feasted on British Columbia's snowcapped peaks, endless blue skies and street-partying locals. The province used the event to showcase its billion-dollar looks, aiming to encourage tourism and investment. But since the flame went out, the benefits of the Games have been harder to grasp – an indication that economies need more than mega-sized events to generate development.

Alberta proved this after hosting the Winter Olympics in 1988: the province strutted through the recent global recession better than any region in Canada, due to its reputation as a low taxation–big business capital with an economy centered on its booming oil industry. While BC wrings its hands over exploiting gas reserves in its pristine coastal wilderness, the environmentally controversial northern Alberta oil sands continue to pump out money-spinning black gold.

But BC may have the last laugh: proposals have been put forward for a giant oil pipeline to run from the Alberta oilfields to huge tankers docked on the BC coastline. Communities along the proposed route are up-in-arms about the idea, while BC politicians are mulling over how much they can charge for it.

Leaping Loonie

Constantly hovering around parity with the US dollar like a persistent housefly, the rising Canadian dollar, known as the 'Loonie' because of the loon bird depicted on $1 coins, is a challenge for the regional economy. While the country was not subjected to the bankruptcy-threatening damage that recently afflicted other nations, the fact that the US is by far Canada's main trading partner has serious consequences here. Dollar parity means fewer American tourists traveling north. And while visitors from China, Australia and the UK are rising, they can't fill the massive deficit from what has always been the region's biggest tourist market.

Alberta Flooding Blues

Canadians were glued to their TV screens in June 2013 when weeks of torrential rain caused rivers to burst their banks and widespread flooding to engulf southern Alberta. It was the region's worst flood for more than a century. When the waters eventually subsided, 14,500 homes had been damaged, thousands of locals had been forced into temporary accommodation and the cost to restore damaged infrastructure was placed at more than $5 billion.

But the spectacle of the Calgary Stampede grounds fully submerged in several feet of dirty water two weeks before Canada's largest annual rodeo event was due to kick-off dominated TV screens. It also rallied the locals. Deploying a determined, square-jawed 'cowboy attitude', Calgarians banded together for the cause. The Calgary Stampede opened on time in 2013 and ran for its usual 10-day duration. And while some events were canceled, more than one million visitors came through the gates.

Meanwhile in the Yukon

Although BC and the Yukon share a border, they share little else. The history of the Yukon has always been more closely linked to that of neighboring Alaska. The Yukon remains in many ways as it was 200 years ago: a forbidding wilderness bursting into life during a brief summer. Its politics lean towards the conservative, an outgrowth of the area's popular image of self-reliance. But while the Yukon has for years kept itself quietly under the radar, things may soon change dramatically.

Few doubt that enormous energy and mineral riches lie under the Yukon. The territory's remoteness currently limits efforts to explore further, but that will eventually change. Will the region adopt Alberta's oil sands approach or struggle with environmental considerations as BC has?

POPULATION: **4.58 MILLION**

UNEMPLOYMENT RATE: **6.5%**

GDP: **$219 BILLION**

GDP GROWTH: **2.3%**

if British Columbia were 100 people

74 would be white
20 would be Asian
2 would be Latino

3 would be Aboriginal
1 would be black

ethnic backgrounds
(% of population)

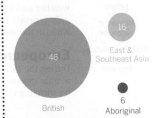

46 British
16 East & Southeast Asia
6 Aboriginal

population per sq km

BC   CANADA   USA

👤 ≈ 4 people

History

Western Canada's human history began 15,000 years ago when thriving Aboriginal communities emerged along the salmon-rich coastline and in the foothills of the Rockies. Everything changed rapidly, though, when the first Europeans arrived in the 1700s. Finding untold abundance and locals without guns, they quickly transformed the area with trade, industry and pioneer settlements. Much of this tumultuous heritage is accessible to visitors, with national historic sites – from forts to famous homes – studding British Columbia, Alberta and the Yukon.

First Peoples Kick Things Off

The ancestors of western Canada's Aboriginal peoples were settlers who showed up in North America at least 15,000 years ago. The most prominent theory is that, after the last Ice Age, they crossed to Alaska on a land bridge over what is now the Bering Strait. Some settled along the Pacific coast, while others found their way to the interior – Alberta, the Yukon and beyond – ultimately populating the rest of North America. This theory is not without its detractors: in recent years archaeologists have discovered the remnants of communities that appear to predate the arrival of the Bering Strait settlers.

Whatever the true story, there is little dispute over who was here first. The Aboriginal peoples of this region, thriving on abundant food and untold resources, developed sophisticated cultures and intricate trade networks over many thousands of years. Coastal peoples dwelled as extended families in large, single-roofed cedar lodges, while inland and mountain communities generally had a tougher time, facing extremes of weather and leading nomadic subsistence lives: in the north they hungrily pursued migratory herds of animals such as moose and caribou, while in the south they chased down bison.

Best Museums

Glenbow Museum, Calgary

Whyte Museum of the Canadian Rockies, Banff

Royal British Columbia Museum, Victoria

Museum of Vancouver

West Coast Railway Heritage Park, Squamish

Europeans Poke Around

During the 18th century, European explorers hungry for new sources of wealth appeared off the west coast as well as in the Rockies region after traveling through the wilderness from eastern Canada. On the coast,

TIMELINE

800	1754	1774
An ash-spewing eruption of the Yukon volcano now known as Mt Churchill causes many to flee to southwest USA, where they may have evolved into the Navajo and Apaches.	The first European fur trader, Anthony Henday, manages to reach Alberta from eastern Canada. He spends the winter living with Aboriginal locals, hunting buffalo alongside them.	Spanish ships gingerly sail northwards along the Pacific Ocean coastline, nosing not very far into what would later become BC. They are the first Europeans to arrive by boat.

Russian Alexsey Chirikov is thought to have been first in 1741, followed by the Spaniards: they sent three expeditions between 1774 and 1779 in search of the fabled Northwest Passage. They ended up by the entrance to Nootka Sound on Vancouver Island but didn't initially venture into the Strait of Georgia.

British explorer Captain James Cook also elbowed in from the South Pacific in 1778. He had a similar Northwest Passage motive, and a similar result: he hit the west coast of Vancouver Island and believed it to be the mainland. It wasn't until 1791 that the mainland-lined Strait of Georgia was properly explored. Spanish navigator José María Narváez did the honors, sailing all the way into Burrard Inlet. He named part of this area Islas de Langara.

Next up was Captain George Vancouver, a British navigator who had previously sailed with Cook. In 1792 he glided into the inner harbor and spent one day there, meeting briefly with Spanish captains Valdez and Galiano who had already claimed the area. Then he sailed away, not thinking twice about a place that would eventually carry his name.

Despite Captain Van's seeming indifference, the Brits' interest in the area grew as its abundant resources became obvious. Finally, a 1794 treaty signed with the Spanish saw war averted and the British assuming control.

Fur: the New Gold

The fur trade was the main lure for the pioneers who followed on the heels of these first European forays, and trade grew rapidly as western Canada's easy prey became clear. Fur trader Anthony Henday was reputedly the first European to arrive in Alberta, exploring the outback areas now known as Edmonton and Red Deer in 1754. The region's Aboriginals – inland and on the coast – soon came into contact with the Europeans.

Legendary trappers like Alexander Mackenzie, Simon Fraser and David Thompson also explored overland routes from the east during this period. At the same time, the Hudson's Bay Company (HBC) rapidly became the catalyst for settler development, building fort communities and fostering trade routes throughout the region.

Of these early explorers, Mackenzie is probably the most interesting. Often compared to the Lewis and Clark expedition in the US, he traversed Canada in 1793, more than 10 years before the Americans crossed their country to the south. Exploring the Rockies, the continental divide and the Fraser River, he later produced a book on his exploits titled *Voyages...to the Frozen and Pacific Oceans*.

By the 1840s the US was making its own claims on the area and the HBC dispatched James Douglas to Vancouver Island, where he established Fort Victoria. A few years later the British and Americans settled

Southern Alberta's ancient Siksika Nation is still renowned for its dancing prowess, especially its celebrated Chicken Dance. Inspired by the courtship moves of a chicken, it's performed by young males in the community. Check out June's World Chicken Dance Championship at the Blackfoot Crossing National Historical Park (www.blackfoot-crossing.ca).

HISTORY FUR: THE NEW GOLD

1792	1805	1827	1866
Captain George Vancouver, of the British Royal Navy, sails in to the same area for one day, little-knowing that the region would eventually take his name. He never returned.	The Northwest Trading Company establishes a fur-trading post at Hudson's Hope in northeast BC. It is later taken over by the Hudson's Bay Company.	The Hudson's Bay Company builds the strategically vital Fort Langley on BC's Fraser River. It's now one of the province's most popular historic attractions.	Mainland BC and Vancouver Island unite, not out of any love but because mainland BC has nowhere to turn after it overspends on infrastructure.

their claims and the border was solidified, ensuring that tourists to Victoria would enjoy high tea as opposed to the mocha-decaf-soy-milk-half-shot lattes found south of the crossing.

Despite it's relative remoteness, the Yukon was also becoming part of the action. The HBC's Robert Campbell became the first European to travel extensively in the region, followed by a ragtag wave of fur traders, prospectors, whalers and – as always – missionaries. Campbell established Fort Selkirk on the Yukon River as a trading post.

Gold: the New Fur

The discovery of gold along BC's Fraser River in 1858 brought a tidal wave of avaricious visitors to the region. A second wave arrived when the yellow stuff was discovered further north in the Cariboo area. Although the gold rush only lasted a few years, many of those who came stayed behind. You can experience a sanitized version of a gold rush town – ie without the effluent, drunkenness and prostitution – at the restored Barkerville Historic Town.

By this stage, desperate travelers were panning and scraping for gold across the region, with large imaginary nuggets forming like misshapen pupils in their eyes. But for every prospector who made his fortune, there were hundreds who failed to find more than a whiff of the elusive treasure.

Of course, that didn't stop people trying. For years, the Yukon became a byword for broken dreams and shattered fortune hunters...right up until 1896, when a discovery on a tributary of the Klondike River near what became Dawson City changed everything. The region's ensuing gold rush attracted hopefuls from around the world – over 99% of whom found no fortune while losing their own.

Rail Link Opens the West

After mainland BC and Vancouver Island were united, Victoria was named BC's new provincial capital in 1868. Meanwhile, in 1867, the UK government had passed the British North American Act, creating the Dominion of Canada. The eastern provinces of Canada united under this confederation, while BC joined in 1871 and Alberta joined in 1905.

But rather than duty to the Crown, it was the train that made them sign on the dotted line. Western Canada remained a distant and forbidding frontier but the fledgling Canadian government promised to build a railway link to the rest of the country within a decade. The Canadian Pacific Railway rolled into Alberta in 1883, nosing into BC four years later.

The construction of the transcontinental railway is one of the most impressive and important chapters in the region's history. The railroad was crucial in unifying the distant east and west wings of the vast coun-

When the Klondike gold rush kicked off in the Yukon, thousands of nugget-eyed prospectors swelled tiny Dawson City to a population above 30,000. Bars, hotels and gambling dens popped up like mushrooms but the boomtown fun only lasted a few years. Many of the old buildings remain to this day.

1871	1876	1886	1896
British Columbia joins the Canadian Confederation and is promised a rail link from eastern Canada to sweeten the deal – it eventually arrives, 16 years later.	American cowboy John Ware brings the first cattle into Alberta from the US, triggering a ranch-based economy that drives the province for decades. Many early ranchers are from England.	The City of Vancouver is incorporated. Within weeks, the fledgling metropolis burns to the ground in the Great Fire. A prompt rebuild ensues, with stone and brick much in evidence.	Sparkly stuff found in Bonanza Creek near today's Dawson City, Yukon, sets off the legendary Klondike gold rush. After three frantic years (and many shattered dreams), the madness subsides.

ALBERTA GETS THE TRAIN... & THE SETTLERS

The transcontinental train line reached Alberta in 1883, triggering a wave of new settlement. In 1881 there were an estimated 1000 settlers in Alberta, but within 10 years this had risen to almost 18,000. Ranchers, attracted by the area's bucolic foothills and wide plains, were the most successful early arrivals, and many of them were Brits – combined with a contingent of American cowboys who had brought the first cattle to Alberta in 1876. There was still plenty of room for development by the end of the century, though, and in the late 1890s a large campaign was launched to encourage more Europeans to start a new life in western Canada. Along with those from the UK, many Germans and Ukrainians answered the call: their cultural influences can still be seen today in the small towns and communities of the region. The campaign to bolster the local population worked: between 1901 and 1921, Alberta's population grew from 73,000 to 584,000.

try in order to encourage immigration and develop business opportunities. But it came with a large price: the much-quoted statistic that a Chinese laborer died for every mile of track built is almost certainly true.

With the train link came a modicum of law and order. Aiming to tame the 'wild west,' the government created the North-West Mounted Police (NWMP) in 1873, which later became the Royal Canadian Mounted Police (RCMP). Nicknamed 'Mounties,' they still serve as the country's national police force.

Also during this period, wealth from gold and revenue from the people looking for it helped the Yukon become a separate territory in 1898, with Dawson City the capital. But the northern party was short-lived: by 1920 economic decline had set in and the population dropped to just 5000, a fraction of its gold-rush heyday. And although the construction of the Alaska Hwy in 1942 opened up the territory to development and provided it with its first tangible link to BC, the glory days were over.

Big Cities Emerge... Then Burn Down

While all this thrusting nation-building was going on, the region's first cities were quietly laying their foundations. And while some – Prince Rupert and New Westminster, for example – were considered as potential regional capitals (New West actually held the position in BC until Victoria took over), it was eventually Vancouver that became western Canada's biggest metropolis. But it's worth remembering that the City of Glass almost didn't make it.

In 1867, near the middle of what's now called Maple Tree Sq, John 'Gassy Jack' Deighton opened a waterfront saloon for thirsty sawmill workers. Attracting an attendant ring of squalid shacks, the ramshackle

Best Historical Sites

Klondike National Historic Sites, Yukon

Fort Langley, BC

Barkerville, BC

Head-Smashed-In Buffalo Jump, Alberta

Gulf of Georgia Cannery, BC

1905	1914	1920	1941
Alberta becomes a province, although it is another 25 years before the federal government allows it to control its own resources. This would prove useful quite a few years later.	The opening of the Panama Canal considerably shortens ocean journeys between BC and Europe. This is particularly good for Vancouver and adds to the port's growth in grain exports.	Having dropped significantly since the turn of the century, the population of the Yukon falls below 5000. It doesn't increase greatly until after the Alaska Hwy is built in 1942–43.	The attack on Pearl Harbor spurs the US into working with Canada to open up the north for their common defense. One of the enduring legacies is the Alaska Hwy.

area around the bar soon became known as Gastown. As the ad hoc settlement grew, the colonial administration decided to formalize it, creating the new town of Granville in 1870. Most people still called it Gastown, especially when Deighton opened a larger saloon nearby a few years later.

In 1886, though, the town's name was officially changed to Vancouver and plans were laid for a much larger city, encompassing the old Gastown/Granville area. But within a few weeks, a giant fire swept rapidly through the fledgling city, destroying around 1000 mostly wooden buildings in less than an hour.

When reconstruction began, stone replaced wood – which explains why this area of Vancouver is now packed with old brick and rock buildings that look like they were constructed to last forever. It's now home to many of Vancouver's best bars – Gassy Jack, now standing atop a whiskey barrel in statue form near the site of his first bar, would be proud.

Aboriginal Turmoil

Many grand municipal buildings around BC were built towards the end of the 1900s by young British architect Francis Rattenbury. But his most famous creations are in Victoria on Vancouver Island: the elegant, dome-topped Parliament Buildings and the iconic ivy-covered Empress Hotel.

Despite the successes of colonization, the Aboriginals, who had thrived here for centuries, were almost decimated by the arrival of the Europeans. Imported diseases – especially smallpox – wiped out huge numbers of people who had no natural immunity or medicines for dealing with them. At the same time, highly dubious land treaties were 'negotiated', which gave the Europeans title to land which had been traditional Aboriginal territory. In exchange, the locals were often reduced to living on small reserves.

But the treatment of the Aboriginals went further than a mere land grab. In what is now regarded as one of the darkest chapters in Canada's history, a process of cultural strangulation took place that ranged from attempting to indoctrinate Aboriginals (especially children) with Christianity to preventing them from practicing certain age-old rites, including the potlatch (gift-giving ceremonial feast). Only in the past 50 years have governments attempted to make amends, launching new treaty negotiations and finally (in 1951) repealing the anti-potlatch laws.

Moving On & Making Amends

After WWII, Western Canada couldn't mine its minerals and chop its trees down fast enough, and a lot of money flowed in. Road and rail links were pushed into all manner of formerly remote places, such as those along the Stewart-Cassiar Hwy. The 1961 Columbia River Treaty with the US resulted in massive dam-building projects that flooded pristine valleys and displaced people. The Americans paid BC to hold back huge amounts of water that could be released to hydroelectric plants south of the border whenever power use demanded.

1947	1960	1964	1964
Alberta makes a major oil discovery at Leduc, not far from Edmonton. As more oil and gas is discovered, the province changes forever, bringing vast wealth into the region.	Aboriginals finally get the right to vote in BC, a key advance in a decades-long initiative to restore the rights of the province's original residents and agree to compensation.	Implementation of the Columbia River Treaty starts the construction of huge dams that forever change the Kootenays. One creates Arrow Lakes, causing Nakusp to be moved, while obliterating other towns.	Canada's gay-rights movement gets off the ground in Vancouver when local feminists and academics create the Association for Social Knowledge, the nation's first gay and lesbian discussion group.

Vancouver hung out the welcome sign to the world in a big way starting in the 1980s, when Expo '86 showcased the city globally. Calgary had its own moment in the spotlight two years later when it became the first city in Canada to host the Winter Olympic Games – Vancouver joined the party in 2010 by hosting it too.

BC has also made progress in making amends for past Aboriginal injustices. The first modern-day treaty – signed with the Nisga'a peoples in 1998 – provided about $200 million and allowed some self-governance. But this new process is highly controversial and not everyone is on board: many non-Aboriginal locals do not want the claims to go too far and only 20% of Aboriginal groups have even begun negotiations.

Making Money & Hosting a Party

Alberta has always been better at making money than BC and the region is currently enjoying a wave of economic success based on the exploitation of its oil sands. Located in northern Alberta, this is a controversial enterprise involving the labor-intensive extraction of bitumen. It has attracted the ire of environmentalists who believe it's one of the dirtiest and most ecologically damaging methods for producing oil. The companies involved – some of the world's biggest petroleum corporations – state that they operate to the highest standards and follow all government guidelines.

Healthy profits of a different kind were enjoyed by suppliers and developers involved with the biggest party to hit Canada in decades: the 2010 Olympic and Paralympic Winter Games, staged in Vancouver and Whistler. Maple leaf flags and face tattoos became the norm as Vancouverites

BC's official coat of arms was unveiled by Queen Elizabeth II in 1987. It is the only coat of arms in the world to incorporate the Queen's own Royal Crest. It also includes the Latin motto 'splendor sine occasu' which is often translated as 'splendor without diminishment.'

HISTORY OF TOTEMS

The artistry of northwest coast native groups – Tsimshian, Haida, Tlingit, Kwakwaka'wakw and Nuxalk – is as intricate as it is simple. One of the most spectacular examples of this is the totem pole, which has become such a symbolic icon that it's part of popular culture, not least because of the entire concept of the low man.

The carving of totem poles was largely quashed after the Canadian government outlawed the potlatch ceremony in 1884. Most totems only last 60 to 80 years, though some on Haida Gwaii are more than 100 years old. When a totem falls, tradition says that it should be left there until another is erected in its place.

Today, totem carving is again widespread, though the poles are often constructed for non-traditional uses, such as public art. Modern totems commissioned for college campuses, museums and public buildings no longer recount the lineage of any one household but instead stand to honor the Aboriginals, their outstanding artistry and their beliefs.

1971	1988	1996	1998
Greenpeace is founded in Vancouver. A small group of activists sets sail in a fishing boat to 'bear witness' to US underground nuclear tests on an island off Alaska.	Calgary hosts the Winter Olympic Games, introducing Eddie 'The Eagle' Edwards to an amused world. Twenty-two years later, he shows up as a commentator at the Vancouver Olympics.	With the Hong Kong handover to China imminent, Vancouver sees a huge increase in Asian immigrants. Many of them fuel the transformation of nearby Richmond into a modern-day Chinatown.	BC, the federal government and the Nisga'a peoples agree on the first modern-day treaty, a huge settlement for the impoverished people living at Nass Camp near the Nisga'a Lava Bed.

BC'S WARTIME SECRET

Among the most intriguing buildings you'll come across as you stroll the boardwalk through the Britannia Shipyard in Steveston – a historic waterfront fishing village in BC's Lower Mainland – is the Murakami House. Originally built over marshland in 1885, it was home to a large Japanese family between 1929 and 1942. Asayo Murakami was brought over from Japan in 1924 to marry a Canadian, but after meeting him for the first time and deciding she didn't like him, she worked independently at the cannery to pay off the amount spent on her passage and free herself from the match.

She later met and married a boat builder and they started a small workshop operation next door. Raising 10 children in the house – the rooms have been recreated and are full of everyday items like toys and books – the entire family was suddenly and unceremoniously moved to Manitoba in 1942 as part of Canada's controversial wartime Japanese internment program. This heavily misguided policy treated Japanese-Canadians as 'threats to national security' due to their Japanese ancestry – despite the fact that many had lived here for decades or were born in Canada.

Many Japanese families in BC and Alberta met a similar fate and after the war only a few returned to their original homes. In 2001, on her 100th birthday, several of Murakami's children came back to the former family residence to plant a garden in her honor. She died in her Alberta home aged 104.

transformed Robson and Granville Sts into a wandering carnival of family-ly-friendly bonhomie. And while national pride is something few Canadians are used to exhibiting in public, the nighttime shenanigans changed all that with rampant flag-waving and regular, heartfelt sing-a-longs of *O Canada*. As a record haul of Canadian medals fueled the crowds, the streets soon became the best place to hang out and catch the Olympic spirit – along with 200,000 of your closest new friends.

When the flame was extinguished at the closing ceremony, the locals wiped off the red face paint and trudged back to their regular lives. But there was a widely held feeling that the province had grown up a little. Western Canada has thousands of years of Aboriginal history but BC, Alberta and the Yukon are still relatively young enterprises at the start of their development. Perhaps the best is yet to come.

2003	2010	2013	2013
BC and Ontario lead the way in North America by making same-sex marriage legal. Many gay and lesbian couples travel from across the continent to Vancouver to be married.	Vancouver hosts the Olympic and Paralymic Winter Games, in front of a global TV audience estimated to be more than two billion. There's plenty of flag-waving and anthem-singing.	Calgary and other areas of southern Alberta receive their worst flooding in living memory, displacing more than 100,000 locals. The region shows its mettle with a giant clean-up drive.	Vancouver's gigantic and much-loved Stanley Park celebrates its 125th birthday with a huge weekend party; thousands attend. It remains the city's oldest and largest park.

Wildlife

British Columbia, Alberta and the Yukon provide a jaw-dropping safari of wildlife sightings. And while the locals are often blasé, visitors frequently rave about the impressive animals they've spotted in Canada's best critter-watching region. Expect a spine-tingling frisson when you see your first bear nonchalantly scoffing berries or watch a bald eagle dive-bombing a salmon-stuffed river. Then there are the whales: boat tours among the orcas are extremely popular on the west coast. The word 'magical' doesn't even come close.

Bears

The number one viewing target for many western Canada visitors, grizzly bears – *ursus arctos horribilis* to all you Latin scholars – are most commonly viewed in the Rockies. Identifiable by their distinctive shoulder hump, they stand up to 3m tall and are solitary mammals with no natural enemies (except humans). While they enjoy fresh-catch meals of elk, moose and caribou, most of their noshing centers on salmon and wild berries. Black bears are also fairly common on the mainland of BC (especially in the north) as well as in the north and west regions of Vancouver Island.

Confusingly, grizzlies are almost black, while their smaller and much more numerous relative, the black bear, is sometimes brown. More commonly spotted in the wild than grizzlies, black bears reside in large numbers in northern BC and in the Banff and Jasper areas, where 'wildlife jams' are a frequent issue among rubbernecking motorists. You may also see these bears as far south as Whistler and in the foothills of North Vancouver.

In 1994, coastal BC's Khutzeymateen Grizzly Bear Sanctuary (near the northern town of Prince Rupert) was officially designated for protected status. Over 50 grizzlies currently live on this 45,000-hectare refuge. A few ecotour operators have permits for viewing these animals if you want to check them out face-to-face. There are also tiny bear sanctuaries in Banff and on Grouse Mountain in North Vancouver.

Kermode bears, sometimes called spirit bears, are a subspecies of the black bear but are whitish in color. They're unique to BC, and are found

The best time to spot grizzlies and black bears in the wild is from mid-April to mid-June, when they've emerged from hibernation and are busy feeding. The much more rare Kermode is best spotted from September to mid-October.

TOP WILDLIFE-WATCHING SPOTS

➡ Maligne Lake Rd – eagles, deer, elk, bighorn sheep and maybe a moose are likely spottings in this Jasper National Park area.

➡ Icefields Parkway – the 230km drive between Banff and Jasper is lined with monumental mountain peaks and a regular chorus of deer, bighorns and black bears.

➡ Khutzeymateen Grizzly Bear Sanctuary – dozens of grizzlies live in this northern BC refuge, and ecotour operators have permits for viewing.

➡ Bella Coola Valley – boat tours along rivers are thick with sightings of grizzly bears wandering the banks.

in the north, from Bella Coola through the Great Bear Rainforest to Stewart, mostly along the lower Skeena River Valley.

Whales

Whale watching is a must-do activity on the west coast and tours (typically up to three hours for around $100 per person) are justly popular. The waters around Vancouver Island, particularly in Johnstone Strait, teem with orcas every summer and tours frequently depart from Tofino, Telegraph Cove, Victoria, Richmond and beyond. The Inside Passage cruise ship and ferry route between Port Hardy and Prince Rupert is also a popular long-haul viewing spot.

This region is home to the grey wolf, also known as the timber wolf. They hunt in packs of up to a dozen strong and mate for life. The females give birth to as many as 11 pups each spring.

While orcas – also known as killer whales – dominate the region's viewing, you might also sight some of the 20,000 Pacific gray whales that migrate along the coastline here twice a year. If you're lucky, you'll also see majestic humpbacks, which average 15m in length.

Orcas get their 'killer' moniker from the fast-paced way they pursue and attack the area's marine life, not from attacks on humans, which are more rare than whale sightings in the Rockies. On your tour you'll likely spot the orcas' preferred nosh languishing on rocks or nosing around your boat – keep your camera primed for porpoises, dolphins, seals, Steller sea lions and sea otters.

Prime orca-viewing season is May to mid-July; for gray whales, it's mid-August to October; and for humpbacks, it's August to October.

Wolves

Wolves, perhaps the most intriguing and mysterious of all Canada's wild animals, hunt cleverly and tenaciously in packs and have no qualms about taking on prey much larger than themselves. Human attacks are extremely rare but you'll nevertheless feel nervous excitement if you're

BEAR AWARE

Bears are rarely in the business of attacking humans but, if provoked, they'll certainly have a go. And it won't be pretty. Most bear attacks on tourists result from ignorance on the part of the visitor, so keep the following points in mind when you're on the road in bear country:

➡ On foot, travel in groups. Consider wearing bear bells as a way to make some noise – bears will generally steer clear of you if they know where you are.

➡ Follow any notices you see about bears in the area and ask park staff about recent sightings.

➡ Keep pets on a leash and do not linger near any dead animals.

➡ Never approach a bear, and keep all food and food smells away from bears; always use bear-resistant food containers.

If the above fails and a bear attacks, do the following:

➡ Don't drop your pack – it can provide protection.

➡ Try to walk backwards slowly without looking the bear in the eye – this is seen as a challenge.

➡ Don't run – a bear will always outrun you.

➡ Try to get somewhere safe, like a car.

➡ If attacked, use bear spray. If this fails, deploy one of the following approaches, depending on the type of bear: for black bears, try to appear larger, shout a lot and fight back; for grizzlies, playing dead, curling into a ball and protecting your head is recommended.

BY THE NUMBERS

This region is home to more than 160 mammal species, 500 bird species, 500 fish species, 20 reptile species and 20 types of amphibians. About 100 species (including most of the whales, the burrowing owl and the Vancouver Island marmot) are considered endangered; another 100 or so are at risk. Ecosystems are at their most diverse in southern BC, but that's also where threats from human pressures are at their greatest.

lucky enough to spot one in the wild – typically in the distance, across the other side of a wide river.

The Rockies are your most likely spot for seeing a wolf. You may also hear them howling at the moon at night if you're camping in the bush.

It's extremely unlikely that you'll be approached by a wolf but they sometimes become habituated to human contact, typically through access to uncovered food on campsites. If a wolf approaches you and seems aggressive or unafraid, wave your arms in the air to make yourself appear larger, reverse slowly and do not turn your back, make noise and throw sticks and/or stones.

Other Local Critters
Coyotes
Raccoon
Skunk
Marmot
Cougar
Porcupine
Beaver
Wolverine

Elk, Caribou & Deer

Although they're usually placid, male elk have sometimes charged into vehicles in the Jasper area after spotting their reflection in the shiny paintwork and believing they've met a rival for their harem of eligible females. They're mostly docile, though, and it's common to see this large deer species wandering around the edges of the townsite for much of the year. November's rut is the best time to visit, though: you'll see the bugling males at their finest, strutting around and taking on their rivals with head-smashing displays of strength.

More common in northern Québec and Labrador, woodland caribou – which have an unfortunate reputation for being far from smart – show up in small groups in BC and the Rockies, although the Jasper population almost wiped itself out a couple of years ago by triggering an avalanche that buried nearly all of them.

Deer are common sights away from the cities in much of BC and beyond. Expect to spot jumpy white-tailed deer and mule deer flitting among the trees and alongside the roads in the Rockies. You might also spot the Columbia black-tailed deer, a small subspecies native to Vancouver Island and BC's west coast.

Moose

Western Canada's postcard-hogging shrub-nibbler is the largest member of the deer family and owes its popularity to a distinctively odd appearance: skinny legs supporting a humungous body and a cartoonish head that looks inquisitive and clueless at the same time. And then there are the antlers: males grow a spectacular rack every summer, only to discard them in November.

You'll spot moose foraging for twigs and leaves – their main diet – near lakes, muskegs and streams, as well as in the mountain forests of the Rockies and the Yukon.

Moose are generally not aggressive, and will often stand stock still for photographs. They can be unpredictable, though, so don't startle them. During mating season (September), the giant males can become belligerent, so keep your distance: great photos are not worth a sharply pronged antler charge from a massive, angry moose.

The Biodiversity Centre for Wildlife Studies (www.wildlifebc.org) has the world's largest wildlife database, with seven million records for BC dating back 120 years. Sources include trappers, birdwatchers, government agencies and loggers.

Bighorn Sheep

The bull moose can grow to almost 3m and weigh as much as 600kg. His spectacular flat antlers, which are shed every year, can be as much as 2m wide with 30 tines (or spikes).

Often spotted clinging tenaciously to the almost-sheer cliff faces overlooking the roads around Banff and Jasper, bighorn sheep are a signature Rockies sight. They're also here in large numbers, so are one of the easiest animals to spot. On the drive between Banff and Jasper via the Icefields Parkway, you'll likely see them: they look like stock-still sculptures standing sentinel on the rocks. The best viewing season is September and October when the rut is on and the males are smashing their heads together to prove their mate-worthy credentials.

Birdlife

Of the region's 500-plus bird species, the black-and-blue Steller's jay is among the most famous; it was named BC's official bird after a government-sponsored contest. Other prominent feathered locals include ravens, great horned owls and peregrine falcons. You don't have to trek into the wilderness for an up-close glimpse: head to Lost Lagoon on the edge of Vancouver's Stanley Park and you'll discover an oasis just a few steps from the city. Look out here for beady-eyed blue herons.

The most visually arresting birds in western Canada are eagles, especially of the bald variety. Their wingspans can reach up to 2m and, like wolves, they are a spine-tingling sight for anyone lucky enough to see one in the wild. Good viewing sites include Brackendale, near Squamish in BC, where up to 4000 eagles nest in winter and an annual bird count lures visitors. Also train your camera lens on Vancouver Island's southern and western shorelines: it won't be long before something awesome sweeps into view.

Sealife

If you photograph one fabled local, you'll likely have an Instagram viral hit on your hands. Bigfoot, or Sasquatch, is said to roam the forests avoiding cameras in this region – keep your eyes peeled in the BC interior and near Tofino, where 'sightings' have been reported.

Divers off the BC coastline can encounter a startling and often bizarre range of aquatic life. The swimming scallop looks like the false teeth your Uncle Ed leaves in a glass by the side of the bed; in fact, it's a fascinating symbiotic creature able to move under its own power, nabbing floating nutrients while a sponge attached to its shell provides protection. Giant Pacific octopuses with tentacles up to 2m in length are found on shallow rocky ocean bottoms. The record weight of one of these creatures is 272kg. Wolf eels are known for darting out of crevices to inspect wetsuit-clad visitors and often snuggling in the crooks of their arms.

Urban Wildlife

You don't always have to travel far into the wilderness to catch sight of Western Canada's multitudinous critters. As cities have expanded outwards, the areas that once teemed with unfettered wildlife have come into direct contact with human habitation. Some animals have responded by retreating further into the wilderness, while others have adapted

SALMON RUNS WILD

After years of depressingly declining returns, the 2010 wild Pacific sockeye salmon run on BC's Fraser River surprised and delighted scientists and local fishing operators by being the largest for almost 100 years. More than 34 million gasping salmon reportedly pushed themselves up the river to lay their eggs and die, a spectacle that turned regional rivers red with the sight of millions of crimson sockeye. However, while restaurants fell over themselves to offer wild salmon dishes for several months, scientists correctly predicted that the record run was a flash-in-the-pan and not an indication of long-term recovery in the salmon sector.

their way of life to co-existing with the two-legged locals. It's not always an easy relationship.

In small towns like Whistler, Dawson City and Tofino, grainy images of bears roaming around people's backyards usually light up social media platforms around the region several times a year. But some creatures have taken it a step further. In metro Vancouver, there are an estimated 3000 coyotes that live and forage in or near populated neighborhoods: it's common to see notices posted around the region during denning season (the time when pups are raised) warning local dog owners to be aware of aggressively protective coyote mothers.

In contrast, the animal-human problem is mostly deer-shaped in the town of Jasper, Alberta. Here, drivers are used to watching the road ahead of them for oblivious road-crossers – they can cause massive damage (to both animals and cars) in a collision. And if you're a gardener in this region, you have to either give up your green-thumbed ways or embark on a serious fortification of your plot: a favorite deer supper here often involves flowers, vegetables and fruit trees.

Salmon are possibly the most important fish in BC. Sacred to many Aboriginal communities, they are also a mainstay of the province's fishing industry. Salmon come in five species: Chinook (also called king), coho, chum, sockeye and pink.

WILDLIFE URBAN WILDLIFE

Artistic Side

It's easy to believe this region doesn't have much of an arts scene. How can mountain bikers or die-hard cowboys be interested in galleries, dance and literature? But in reality, Western Canada is a roiling hotbed of creativity, especially at the grassroots level. The trick is to hit the major cultural attractions first, then latch on to some artsy locals and follow them to the coolest off-the-beaten-path events, exhibitions and happenings. You'll likely be fully rewarded for your efforts.

Visual Arts

Top Art Galleries

....

Vancouver Art Gallery

....

Art Gallery of Alberta, Edmonton

....

Art Gallery of Calgary

....

Art Gallery of Greater Victoria

....

Robert Bateman Centre, Victoria

When JB Harkin, first commissioner of the National Parks Board of Canada, stated that the Rocky Mountains were like priceless works of art, he had a valid point. The challenge for artists in this spectacular region is that whatever they produce, nature will always be ahead of the game. Despite that, some regional artists have risen to the challenge splendidly.

Emily Carr made her name by painting aboriginal villages and swirling forest landscapes on Vancouver Island. She is often referred to as an honorary member of Canada's famous Group of Seven. But she wasn't the only great painter to come from this region. Transforming canvases a few decades later, the rich, stylized work of EJ Hughes vividly depicted coastal life along the West Coast.

In recent years, Vancouver has become Western Canada's contemporary art capital, with photoconceptualism especially revered. Locals Stan Douglas and Rodney Graham (who also works in multimedia) are celebrated but it's Jeff Wall, a photorealist whose large works have the quality of cinematic production, who has attained global recognition, including having his work exhibited at New York's Museum of Modern Art.

But the city's art scene isn't just about hitting the big time. Ask locals what their favorite annual art event is and many will point you to November's weekend-long Eastside Culture Crawl (www.eastsideculture crawl.com), when around 300 East Vancouver artists open their home

---

RIOTOUS ARTWORK

Look for the large London Drugs shop in the Woodwards building on W Hastings St in Vancouver and enter the building's courtyard, carved from what was originally the interior of one of the city's largest department stores. The space is now dominated by the city's most evocative – and perhaps provocative – public artwork.

Measuring 15m by 9m and created by Stan Douglas, *Abbott & Cordova, 7 August 1971* is a mammoth double-sided black-and-white photo montage depicting a key moment in the history of local social protest: the night when police in full riot gear broke up a pro-marijuana smoke-in being staged in the Downtown Eastside.

The action (the image shows mounted police pushing against unarmed locals and miscreants being stuffed into police wagons) soon spiraled out of control, with pitched battles and general chaos triggering a siege-like atmosphere on the area's streets. Later, the event became known as the 'Gastown Riot' and 'The Battle of Maple Tree Square.'

TOP READS

➡ **The Cremation of Sam McGee** (Robert W Service) Written by the renowned Bard of the Yukon, this is a classic of regional prose about two gold miners, the cold and what men will sometimes do. It's Service at its peak.

➡ **Runaway: Diary of a Street Kid** (Evelyn Lau) Tells the true story of the author's dangerous life on the streets of downtown Vancouver.

➡ **Red Dog, Red Dog** (Patrick Lane) Follows two brothers trying to navigate tough times in the 1950s Okanagan Valley. It's a gripping look at heartbreak, corruption and the tough lives of those who settled Canada.

➡ **Stanley Park** (Timothy Taylor) Stirs together a haute-cuisine chef with a park's dark secrets. The result is a story capturing Vancouver's quirky modern ambience.

➡ **Klondike Tales** (Jack London) Draws on the author's first-hand experiences for these 23 stories showing the hardships, triumphs and betrayals of the Yukon gold rush. *The Call of the Wild* wins new fans every year. Learn more about London and his books at the Jack London Interpretive Centre in Dawson City.

---

studios and galleries for a strolling mass of locals to wander around. It's the most enjoyable way to meet the city's grassroots artists and artsy Vancouverites.

If you like the idea of not paying to see art, you'll find a strong commitment to public art across the region. Statues and installations can be found in Calgary and Edmonton as well as British Columbia's Victoria and Richmond. But big-city Vancouver leads the way with hundreds of photogenic installations studding the city.

From Stanley Park and the West End to Gastown and Commercial Dr, you'll find impressive, sometimes challenging, works on many streets. On Main St in East Vancouver, around the intersection with 18th Ave, look out for a giant ceramic poodle on a pedestal. The work, which many locals said was a waste of money, caused great controversy when it was unveiled in 2013 but it has since grown in the affections of many Vancouverites, even sparking its own fake Twitter account.

The free *Van Dop Arts and Cultural Guide* to BC lists galleries, studios and festivals across the province. It's online at www.artbc.com.

Literature

Perhaps due to the long winters in Alberta and the month-long rainfests on the BC coast, western Canadians are big readers. And they don't go short of local tomes to dip into: BC has an estimated 1500 professional authors and dozens of publishers to provide material for the region's insatiable bookworms.

This bulging bookshelf of authors includes WP Kinsella (author of *Shoeless Joe*, the story that became the *Field of Dreams* movie); William Gibson (sci-fi creator of cyberpunk); and Malcolm Lowry, who wrote his *Under the Volcano* masterpiece here.

There's a rich vein of contemporary work, too. One of Canada's most celebrated authors, Douglas Coupland, lives in West Vancouver and has produced genre-defining titles such as *Generation X, Girlfriend in a Coma* and the excellent 'alternative guidebook' *City of Glass*, which showcases his love for Vancouver with quirky mini-essays and evocative photography. Coupland's latest novel is *Worst. Person. Ever.*

A revered nonfiction scene has also developed in this region in recent years, with books from local lads Charles Montgomery and JB Mackinnon winning prestigious national awards. Mackinnon's latest title, *The Once and Future World*, looks at the natural abundance of the past to inspire a new way of looking at our environment today.

The Golden Spruce (2005), by John Vaillant, is a riveting read that tells the astonishing true story of a former logger who felled a protected 300-year-old Sitka spruce tree that was sacred to the Aboriginal people of Haida Gwaii.

While Alberta doesn't reach the heady heights of BC when it comes to literary output, it's nevertheless a great idea to dip into a couple of books before you arrive for a richer understanding of the area. Consider *The Wild Rose Anthology of Alberta Prose,* edited by George Melnyk and Tamara Seiler, or *Writing the Terrain: Travelling Through Alberta with the Poets,* edited by Robert Stamp.

In the Yukon, drop into Dawson City. Bookish-types will love nosing around the Jack London Interpretive Centre, a cabin evoking the time the celebrated author lived in the region. In fact, bring a book along for the trip: preferably *Sailor on Snowshoes* by Dick North, which explores London's time in the area. Alternatively, dip into almost anything written by the legendary Robert W Service during his pioneer-era time here and you'll increase your understanding of this rugged region exponentially.

Theater & Dance

Local theaters can be found throughout BC and beyond, with even the smallest communities providing a venue for grassroots performing troupes and visiting shows. Bigger cities like Vancouver, Victoria, Edmonton and Calgary often have several large auditoria with their own repertory theater companies – Vancouver's Arts Club Theatre Company (www.artsclub.com) is the region's largest, staging shows at three venues around the city. The performance season usually runs from October to April, but there are frequently shows treading the boards outside this period. And, like its visual arts scenes, it pays to dig a little for some hidden gems: there are dozens of smaller venues, with a fringe theater approach, throughout the region.

Which, of course, is a reminder that fans of the small stage may wish to time their visits for the region's wealth of fringe theater events. Edmonton hosts the oldest and biggest fringe festival in North America (www.fringetheatre.ca), while there are also large and popular festivals in Vancouver (www.vancouverfringe.com) and Victoria (www.victoriafringe.com).

Vancouver is also a major Canadian dance capital, second only to Montréal. It hosts frequent annual events, from classical to challenging modern interpretation. If you're a true dance buff, consider picking up a copy of *Dancing Through History: In Search of the Stories that Define Canada* by Vancouver-based author and dancer Lori Henry. The fascinating book explores the nation's culture through its traditional dances.

Cinema & Television

Western Canada is a hot spot for TV producers and moviemakers looking for a handy stand-in for American locations, hence the name 'Hollywood North' used to describe the film sector up here. You probably didn't know it, but blockbusters like *X-Men* and *Superman Returns* were filmed around Vancouver – the center of the region's production – while the bucolic ranchlands of Alberta served as the backdrop for *Brokeback Mountain.*

Launched in 1982, the gargantuan Edmonton International Fringe Festival sells more than 100,000 tickets and hosts more than 1500 shows every year. Spots are highly coveted and an annual lottery is held to determine which performers will appear at the festival.

The website of the National Film Board of Canada (www.nfb.ca) is a treasure trove of north-of-the-border films available for free online viewing. Recommended is *Carts of Darkness,* a riveting exploration of shopping cart races among the homeless in North Vancouver.

ALL THE WORLD'S A STAGE

Vancouver's Bard on the Beach (www.bardonthebeach.org) is a quintessentially west coast way to catch a show. The June-to-September event includes a roster of three or four Shakespeare and Shakespeare-related plays performed in tents on the Kitsilano waterfront, with the North Shore mountains peeking through the back of the stage. It sells almost to capacity every year, making it one of North America's most successful and enduring Shakespeare festivals.

YUKON SHOOTING STAR

Only one Yukoner has a star on the Hollywood Walk of Fame and that's Victor Jory. Like any good northerner, his story is better than the plots of the 200 or so movies and TV shows that have his name in the credits. He was born in 1902 to a single mother who ran a rooming house near Dawson City. Hanging around Hollywood got him his first role in 1930 and over the next 50 years he had parts in big pictures (quarrelsome field boss in *Gone with the Wind*) and small ones (the lead in *Cat-Women of the Moon*). Reflecting the ethos of the Yukon, he never said no to anything that might put food on his plate.

But it's not all about making US-set flicks. Canada has a thriving independent film-making sector and catching a couple of locally made movies before you arrive can provide some handy insights into the differences between the US and Canada. Look out for locally shot indie flicks including *Mount Pleasant* and *Double Happiness*.

The region also has a growing reputation for special effects and post-production work, with *Avatar*, *District 9* and *Life of Pi* using local studios for added visual spectacle.

It's not unusual to spot movie trucks and trailers on your travels here – especially in downtown Vancouver – and you might like to try your hand at becoming an extra on your visit. The website of the BC Film Commission (www.bcfilmcommission.com) gives the lowdown on what's filming and provides contact information for potential 'background performers.'

If you prefer to watch, there are some popular movie, TV and media festivals throughout the year in this region, including the Calgary International Film Festival, Edmonton International Film Festival, Vancouver International Film Festival and Whistler Film Festival.

Music

Ask visitors to name Canadian musicians and they'll stutter to a halt after Celine Dion and Justin Beiber. But ask the locals in BC, Alberta and the Yukon, and they'll hit you with a roster of local performers you've probably never heard of, plus some that you probably thought were American.

Superstars Michael Bublé, Sarah McLachlan, Bryan Adams and Diana Krall are all from BC, and their slightly less stratospheric colleagues include Nelly Furtado and Spirit of the West. For those who like their music with an indie hue, Black Mountain, Dan Mangan and CR Avery are among the area's most popular grassroots performers.

Alberta has also spawned several big names: Joni Mitchell was born there for starters. Fans of indie rock would be familiar with Feist, as well as Tegan and Sarah. Pop and country music singer/songwriter, k.d. lang also hails from Edmonton, Alberta.

Bars are a great place to start if you want to take the pulse of the local music scene: expect to pay anything from zero to $10 for cover. Larger cities like Vancouver, Calgary and Edmonton offer a wide range of dedicated venues for shows, from stadiums to cool-ass underground spaces.

Perhaps even better, the region is bristling with great music festivals. Look out for toe-tapping options like the Vancouver International Jazz Festival and the Calgary Folk Music Festival.

Whatever your musical tastes, the best way to access the live scene on a grassroots level is always to pick up local weekly newspapers and duck into small independent record stores. Cities large and small often have vinyl-hugging shops here and they're frequently staffed by musicians who know all there is to know about who's hot on the local scene.

When Marilyn Monroe filmed *River of No Return* in and around Banff National Park in 1953, many locals fell instantly in love. Star-struck Albertans of the time still fondly recall the actress popping up around the region with her smiling husband-to-be, baseball player Joe DiMaggio.

Vancouver's free *Georgia Straight* weekly newspaper has a great website listing local arts, music and culture happenings in and around the city. Check it out at www.straight.com.

Aboriginal Cultures

Western Canada's original locals have called this region home for thousands of years. While first contact with European explorers ultimately had a hugely detrimental impact on many of these communities, many of whom continue to face severe struggles in a society dominated by non-aboriginals, recent history has been characterized more by reconciliation and a widespread and growing respect for the area's earliest inhabitants. For example, on your travels you'll find fascinating First Nations museums, thriving cultural centers and photo-worthy public art installations that will likely be highlights of your visit.

Early History

The prevailing theory that this region's first human inhabitants arrived many thousands of years ago by crossing a land bridge over the Bering Strait, near what's now known as Alaska, has been seriously challenged (and, in some quarters, discredited) in recent years. Opposing theories have suggested that the earliest residents may have arrived on the east coast via boats from Asia, Polynesia or Siberia. What is known for sure is that the current Aboriginal communities in this region are descendants of the people who called this area home more than 10,000 years ago.

Some of these communities settled the forested foothills of the mountains to the east, while many others stayed on the ocean coastline, reaping the seemingly endless supply of juicy salmon, deer and rich local vegetation. Inland BC didn't provide the same bounty and the Aboriginal Salish people in places such as the Okanagan Valley had to devote much more of their time to subsistence living and surviving the long winters. In the far north, the Tagish, Gwich'in and others depended on migrating moose and caribou.

Bannock, a traditional flat bread originally imported to Canada by Scottish pioneers, is a staple of First Nations dining. There are many recipes, often passed down through generations. Vancouver's Salmon 'n' Bannock restaurant is a good spot to try it.

While a common perception of these people is that they lived in teepees and smoked peace pipes, there was, in fact, a huge variety of groups, each living in distinctly different ways. For example, the first Vancouverites lived in villages of wood-planked houses arranged in rows, often surrounded by a stockade. Nearby, totem poles would be set up as an emblem of a particular family or clan.

The distinct communities that formed in this area at that time included the Musqueam – who mostly populated the area around English Bay, Burrard Inlet and the mouth of the Fraser River – as well as the Squamish, who had villages in what are now called North Vancouver, West Vancouver, Jericho Beach and Stanley Park. Other groups that resided in the area included the Kwantlen, Tsawwassen and Coast Salish peoples.

Early Lifestyle

There is very little evidence today about exactly how these early BC residents went about their daily lives. Most settlements have crumbled into the ground and few have been rediscovered by archaeologists. In addition, these communities mostly deployed oral records, which meant telling each other – often in song – the stories and legends of their ancestors, rather than writing things down. It's important to recall that this method would have been highly successful until the Europeans arrived and generations of locals were quickly wiped out by disease or military attack.

One aspect of these early societies that is universally accepted is that art and creativity were a key presence in many communities. Homes were often adorned with exterior carvings and totem poles, and these illustrated a reverential regard for nature. This suggests that the region's first people enjoyed a symbiotic relationship with their surroundings – in many ways, they were the founding fathers of Western Canada's current green movement.

European Contact

Disease imported by early European visitors, such as Captain Cook, started the long slide for these peoples. Outright racism was rampant as well as official discrimination – perhaps the worst instance of which was the residential school system, which removed Aboriginal children from their families in order to strip them of their language and culture. In 1859 the governor of BC, James Douglas, declared that all the land and any wealth underneath it belonged to the Crown.

Laws enacted during much of the 20th century brutalized Aboriginal culture. A notorious law banned the potlatch, a vital ceremony held over many days by communities to mark special occasions, and establish ranks and privileges. Dancing, feasting and elaborate gift-giving from the chief to his people are features.

In the Rockies region of Alberta, similar devastating challenges were faced by the Sioux, Cree and Blackfoot Aboriginals. This region is also the traditional home of the Métis, which translates from the French word for mixed blood and historically refers to the children born from Cree and French fur traders. It now refers to anyone born of mixed Cree and European ancestry. Métis account for one-third of Canada's Aboriginal population and Edmonton is home to one of the country's largest populations.

It wasn't until 1949 that BC's First Nations were given the right to vote in provincial elections. The legislation, which was highly controversial at the time, also gave the vote to Canadian residents of Chinese and Japanese origin.

Head-Smashed-In Buffalo Jump

Winning kudos among most visitors for having the most eye-poppingly impressive name of any cultural attraction in Canada, this Alberta destination is a celebrated Unesco World Heritage Site. Situated at the junction of the Rocky Mountains and the Great Plains, this archeological destination lures thousands of visitors every year with its evocative exhibits and displays highlighting 6000 years of Aboriginal settlement.

But, like the label says, one aspect of historic life intrigues visitors more than most others. This site was where local Aboriginal people, over many centuries, perfected the buffalo jump method of hunting. The practice involved forcing bison to stampede over a steep precipice, from

---

TOP ABORIGINAL CULTURAL ATTRACTIONS

➡ Museum of Anthropology, Vancouver

➡ Royal British Columbia Museum, Victoria

➡ Haida Heritage Centre at Qay'llnagaay, Haida Gwaii

➡ Museum of Northern British Columbia, Prince Rupert

➡ Head-Smashed-In Buffalo Jump, Fort Macleod

➡ Blackfoot Crossing Historical Park, Canadian Badlands

➡ Squamish Lil'wat Cultural Centre, Whistler

➡ Bill Reid Gallery of Northwest Coast Art, Vancouver

where their carcasses were dragged (relatively easily) to nearby blood-splattered camps for butchering. The name, in fact, tells you all you need to know.

Aboriginal Communities Today

In recent years Aboriginal communities across BC have succeeded in having their own names officially applied to several areas. For example, the former Queen Charlotte Islands is now officially Haida Gwaii and an area of southern BC ocean has been designated as the Salish Sea.

The last 50 years have seen both an effort by governments to reverse the grim course of previous decades and a resurgence of Aboriginal culture. A long and difficult process has begun to settle claims from the 1859 proclamation through negotiations with the various bands. So far, the one treaty signed – with the Nisga'a peoples – provides about $200 million and allows some self-governance. Given the money involved, it's easy to see why the treaty process is one big vat of contention in BC (for eaxample, much of the land under downtown Vancouver is subject to Aboriginal claims). Only 20% of Aboriginal groups have even begun negotiations.

The *Recognition and Reconciliation Act* is BC's effort to literally rewrite all of its laws regarding the Aboriginals. It includes schemes to organize the province's 203 bands into 30 indigenous governments. That, plus provisions that would carve out a big piece of the mineral wealth pie for Aboriginal people, sparked enormous debate through 2009.

Relations in the Yukon have been less contentious as the size of the land has so far overwhelmed the conflicts among the tiny population.

Yukon First Nations

Today, the Yukon region is home to 14 First Nations (sharing eight languages). These include the Kluane, Teslin Tlingit and Ross River Dena communities. An estimated one-quarter of all Yukoners can trace their Aboriginal ancestry.

These communities often work together to share issues and raise concerns. At their annual general assembly in 2013, the Council of Yukon First Nations passed a resolution calling for the Yukon government to ban fracking (a controversial method of oil and gas extraction) throughout the region.

Aboriginal Arts

The Stanley Park Miniature Railway attraction in Vancouver is transformed every summer into the home of Klahowya Village. The family-friendly train trundles through an interpretive Aboriginal landscape while crafts, storytelling and live music animate the rest of the site.

There was formerly little outside recognition of the art produced by Canada's Aboriginal communities. But over the last several decades or so, there's been a strong and growing appreciation of this unique creative force. For most visitors, totem poles are their entry point, but this region's cultural treasures go way beyond totems. Artworks such as masks, drums and paintings feature the distinctive black and red sweeping brush strokes depicting wolves, ravens and other animals from the spirit world.

Though most Aboriginal groups lack formal written history as we know it, centuries of cultural traditions live on. Art has long been a method of expression, intimately linked with historical and cultural preservation, religion and social ceremony.

Today, Lawrence Paul Yuxweluptun explores politics, the environment and Aboriginal issues with his paintings that take inspiration from Coast

VANCOUVER'S POET

Pauline Johnson (1861–1913) was Vancouver's most famous poet. The daughter of a Mohawk chief and a middle class English woman, she recited her works dressed in traditional Aboriginal buckskin. Hugely popular in the city, her funeral was the largest ever held in Vancouver at the time. She is also the only person to be officially buried in Stanley Park.

ABORIGINAL WINERY

Nk'Mip Cellars (it's pronounced 'in-ka-meep') became North America's first Aboriginal owned and operated winery when it opened its doors in Osoyoos, in the heart of BC's winery-heavy Okanagan region. The swanky, state-of-the-art winery was an immediate hit with visitors, many of whom drop by for tours as well as tastings. The winery, which is run by the Osoyoos Band, also has its own vineyard. Varietals currently produced include merlot, chardonnay, pinot noir and riesling ice wine.

Salish mythology. Shuswap actor and writer Darrell Dennis tackles Aboriginal stereotypes head-on in his thrilling one-man show *Tales of an Urban Indian*. Among the memorable lines: 'I can't even make it rain for God sakes.'

Tofino-based Roy Henry Vickers fuses mystical and traditional themes with contemporary approaches, while Lawrence Paul Yuxweluptun and Brian Jungen have gained national and international recognition for their challenging abstract approaches.

Cultural Experiences

It took Canada as a whole many years to realize that international visitors coming to the country were eager to experience Aboriginal culture for themselves – and not just by viewing a dusty diorama of an 'Indian village' in a forgotten corner of a local museum. After wildlife watching and photographing a monumental mountain or two, visitors from Asia, Europe and beyond are keen to encounter and understand the country's first inhabitants.

Large and impressive cultural centers have sprung up in BC and Alberta in recent years. These include the award-winning Blackfoot Crossing Historical Park in Alberta, where you can learn from the locals about the authentic exhibits, watch a spectacular cultural dance display (look out for the Chicken Dance, typically performed by the community's young males), and stay overnight in a woodland teepee, with the sound of area coyotes howling at the moon lulling you to sleep.

In BC, the breathtaking Haida Heritage Centre in Haida Gwaii offers a deep immersion into the history and rich creative impulses of the fascinating Haida people. The archipelego's Gwaii Haanas National Park Reserve also offers the chance to peruse evocative former villages on the southern shoreline, where decaying old totem poles face the mist-streaked ocean as if they're telling a story. This region is not surprisingly viewed as one of BC's most magical and mystical places, with visitors frequently citing the area as one of the unforgettable highlights of their vacation.

If you're not planning to leave the city, Vancouver is also crammed with First Nations encounters. There's Aboriginal art in public buildings and galleries throughout the city. But if you only have time for one spot, make it the University of British Columbia. It's home to the Museum of Anthropology – the city's best museum – and it's teeming with astonishing art and artifacts that illustrate the rich heritage of Aboriginal culture and society throughout this region. The regular (and free) guided tours are recommended.

For a comprehensive introduction to experiences, attractions and activities available for visitors interested in this side of Western Canada's culture, check out the handy website of the Aboriginal Tourism Association of BC (www.aboriginalbc.com). It shows you everything you need to know, from where to take interpretive wildlife tours to how to find traditional First Nations food.

Haida Make History

Hundreds of locals, visitors and dignitaries gathered on Haida Gwaii in mid-2013 to mark a special and highly symbolic event. The first such ceremony in the area for more than a century, a three-storey-high totem pole was manually raised (with ropes) in the Gwaii Haanas National

Park Reserve. The colorful, highly intricate pole took more than a year to carve and its symbols were chosen to show that the islands are protected from harm.

There's more to the pole than its creation – it was carved to mark the two-decade anniversary of a treaty between the Haida and the Canadian government that allows both groups to protect and co-manage this region. It was also sited on Lyell Island, where the Haida protested logging of the area in 1985. The tense stand-off made national headlines and ultimately culminated in the creation of Gwaii Haanas National Park Reserve. That protest is remembered on the pole itself: a carved area showing five men locking arms together in solidarity.

It is estimated that Aboriginal tourism contributes around $50 million to the local economy in BC. The largest part of that money – around a third – is paid by travelers involved in adventure tourism activities.

Operators

On your travels around BC, look out for Aboriginal-themed or led tours and excursions with the following operators. They're often a great way to gain a different perspective on the region:

Haida Expeditions (www.haidaexpeditions.com) for fishing, hikes and whale watching.

Talaysay Tours (www.talaysay.com) for kayak tours.

Spirit Eagles Experiences (www.spiriteagle.ca) for guided canoe and cultural tours.

Tuckkwiowhum Aboriginal Interpretive Village (www.tuckkwiowhum.com) for a heritage sleepover, teepee camping and guided tours.

Aboriginal Journeys (www.aboriginaljourneys.com) for wildlife-watching tours, spotting everything from orcas to grizzlies.

West Coast Cuisine

While dining out here used to mean a choice of doughnuts at the local Tim Hortons outlet, western Canada is now sitting at the grownups table when it comes to great grub. Seafood fans in BC are often stuffed to the gills with aquatic treats, while carnivores in the Rockies region love being in Canada's beef capital. And throughout the west, a new-found love of local ingredients has transformed restaurant menus, many of which already offer Canada's best international dining.

Seafood

Don't tell Atlantic Canada, but the west coast is the country's seafood capital. In fact, a trip here that doesn't include throwing oneself into BC's brimming marine larder is like visiting London without having a cup of tea: you can do it, but it's not advisable.

In Vancouver you'll find an astonishing array of innovative seafood dishes. This is arguably the world's best sushi city outside Japan and there are hundreds of spots to dip into, from slick joints with sake bars to cheap-and-cheerful hole-in-the-walls where you'll be rubbing shoulders with overseas language students.

You'll also find a full table of traditional and innovative dishes in the area's Chinese restaurants, from the chatty dim-sum dining rooms of old Chinatown to the contemporary fusion joints in Richmond, a bustling, Hong Kong–like foodie heaven. If you're feeling adventurous, look out for locally harvested *geoduck* (pronounced 'gooey duck'), a giant saltwater clam. It's a delicacy in Chinese dining and is even shipped from here to chefs across the world.

But it's not just multicultural approaches that bring BC's seafood to local diners. Vancouver's Pacific Northwest eateries almost always feature seasonal fresh catches. As you travel around the region, you'll find the same amazing seafood – at non-city prices – almost everywhere you go. Wild salmon is a signature here and in the fall it dominates menus – do not miss it. Almost as popular is the early-spring spot prawn season when the sweet crustaceans turn up on tables throughout BC.

If you fancy meeting the fishers and choosing some grub straight off the back of their boats, you can also do that. The boats bobbing around the government wharf near Vancouver's Granville Island are a good spot to try, as is the evocative boardwalk area in Steveston. This south Richmond heritage fishing village is an ideal destination for seafood fans: there are two excellent museums recalling the area's days as the center of the once-mighty regional fishing fleet and there are several finger-licking restaurants offering the best fish and chips in BC.

If you're lucky enough to make it to Haida Gwaii, you'll also encounter some of the best seafood you've ever had in your life, typically caught that day and prepared in a simple manner that reveals the rich flavors of the sea. Keep your appetite primed here for halibut, scallops and crab, often plucked from the shallow waters just off the beach by net-wielding locals walking along the sand.

Farmers markets are exploding across the region, bringing home-grown produce to the tables of locals and epicurious visitors. Look out for seasonal fresh-picked peaches, strawberries, blueberries and apples. For BC market locations, see www.bcfarmersmarket.org; for Alberta, check www.albertamarkets.com. In the Yukon, hit Whitehorse's Fireweed Community Market.

Local Flavors

While Vancouver now rivals – and arguably surpasses – Montréal and Toronto as Canada's fine-dining capital, it wins over both those cities with its surfeit of excellent multicultural dining options. You'll be hard-pressed to find a bad Chinese or Japanese restaurant here, while its Pacific Northwest dining choices (usually fused with intriguing international influences) bring the best of the region to tables across the city.

In recent years, some of the country's most innovative chefs have set up shop, inspired by the twin influences of an abundant local larder of unique flavors and the most cosmopolitan – especially Asian – population in Canada. Fusion is the starting point here, but there's also a high level of authenticity in traditional multicultural dining: amazing sushi bars and Japanese *izakayas* jostle for attention with superb Vietnamese and Korean eateries that feel like they've been transported from halfway around the world.

Outside Vancouver, the urban areas of Vancouver Island – especially in downtown Victoria – plus the Okanagan Valley offer additional top-notch eateries. And if you're heading up to Whistler, you can expect plenty of surprisingly gourmet restaurants to restore your energy after an exhilarating day on the slopes.

But eating well is not just about fine dining, and you'll find many welcoming places to nosh in more rustic areas of BC, Alberta and the Yukon, many of them delivering some tastebud-popping surprises. Follow the locals to waterfront seafood diners in coastal communities like Gibsons, Salt Spring Island and Prince Rupert for the kind of freshly caught aquatic treats that would often cost several times as much in the big city.

Even the smallest towns can usually rustle up a decent meal – including those ubiquitous 'Chinese and Canadian' eateries where the menu usually combines deep-fried cheeseburgers with gelatinous sweet-and-sour pork dishes. There are also many family-oriented, mid-priced eateries and chatty diners for those traveling with kids. And unlike pubs in the UK and other countries, bars here are usually just as interested in serving food as they are beer.

This foodie nirvana stretches across the Rockies into Alberta, Canada's cowboy country. It's the nation's beef capital – you'll find top-notch Alberta steak on menus at leading restaurants across the country. But it's not all about steak here: look out for caribou and venison, both rising in popularity in recent years. If you're offered 'prairie oysters,' though, you

---

If you're buying fresh wild salmon in this region, look out for the following signs of freshness: it should not smell 'fishy'; the gills should have a red hue; the eyes should be bright and clear. For more tips and information on the region's tasty salmon, see www.bcsalmon.ca.

Elizabeth Levinson's *An Edible Journey: Exploring the Islands' Fine Food, Farms and Vineyards* is a lip-smacking taste trip around the foodie destinations of Vancouver Island and the Southern Gulf Islands.

DON'T LICK THE PAGES: REGIONAL FOOD MAGAZINES

Writers are increasingly inspired to wax lyrical over the region's foodie fashions. Check out these local magazines for the inside track on local scenes:

Avenue Magazine (www.avenuecalgary.com) Lifestyle publication illuminating the Calgary restaurant scene for hungry locals, with a separate Edmonton edition (www.avenueedmonton.com) also available.

City Palate (www.citypalate.ca) Covering Calgary's food and dining scene.

Eat Magazine (www.eatmagazine.ca) Free mag covering BC food and wine happenings.

Edible Vancouver (www.ediblecommunities.com/vancouver) Free quarterly with an organic and slow-food bent, available at choice local food shops.

Vancouver Magazine (www.vanmag.com) City lifestyle glossy with good coverage of local restaurants and culinary happenings.

BC FOR FARM-HOPPERS

Ask Vancouverites where the food on their tables comes from and most will point vacantly at a nearby supermarket, while others will confidently tell you about the Fraser Valley. This lush interior region starts about 50km from the city and has been studded with busy farms for decades. In recent years, farmers and the people they feed have started to get to know one another on a series of five **Circle Farm Tours**. These self-guided driving tours take you around the communities of Langley, Abbotsford, Chilliwack, Agassiz and Harrison Mills, and Maple Ridge and Pitt Meadows, pointing out recommended pit-stops – farms, markets, wineries and dining suggestions – along the way and adding a cool foodie adventure to your BC trip. The tour maps can be downloaded free at www.circlefarmtour.ca.

might want to know (or maybe you'd prefer not to) that they're bull's testicles prepared in a variety of intriguing ways designed to take your mind off their origin.

Wherever your traveling taste buds take you, try to score some unique local flavors with a sampling of aboriginal food. Canada's Aboriginal people have many fascinating and accessible culinary traditions. Reliant on meat and seafood (try a juicy halibut stew on BC's Haida Gwaii), there's also an aboriginal tradition of bannock bread, imported by the Scots and appropriated by Canada's original locals. And if you think you're an expert on desserts, try some 'Indian ice cream.' Made from whipped soapberries, it's sweetened with sugar to assuage its bitter edge.

Eat Streets

Some thoroughfares in this region are permanently suffused with the aroma of great cooking, as well as a chorus of satisfied-looking diners rubbing their bellies and surreptitiously loosening their straining belts. If you're hungry, heading to these areas is the way to go – you'll meet the locals and have a great taste-of-the-region meal in the bargain.

If you're in Vancouver, there are several tasty options to choose from. Near Stanley Park, the West End's Denman St is teeming with good-value midrange restaurants. There's a huge variety here, from Vietnamese to Ukrainian and pizza to Pacific Northwest. The menu is similarly diverse on adjoining Davie St and on Kitsilano's West 4th Ave. But if fine dining floats your boat, check out Hamilton St and Mainland St in Yaletown: both are lined with fancy joints for that romantic, special-occasion meal.

Across the region, Richmond's 'Golden Village' area is packed with superb Asian dining, while the streets radiating from Chinatown in Victoria house some treats. The city's Johnson St also has a few tempting joints. If you're up north in Prince Rupert, you won't have to go hungry: head to Cow Bay Rd for fish and chips and some great bistro options.

Over in Alberta, the Whyte Ave stretch of Edmonton's Old Strathcona neighborhood offers some excellent independent dining options, including plenty of taste-tripping international eateries. In Calgary – where the dining scene has jumped in quality in recent years – the top dining thoroughfares are downtown's Stephen St as well as in the neighborhoods of Kensington, Mission and Inglewood.

Festivals & Events

Food and drink is the foundation of having a good time in BC, Alberta and the Yukon. Languid summer barbecues, fall's feastlike Thanksgiving Day and winter family get-togethers at Christmas traditionally center on tables groaning with meat and seafood dishes, diet-eschewing fruit desserts and plentiful wine and beer.

Canada is the third-largest beef exporter in the world, with Alberta by far the largest contributor to that figure across the country. The latest figures show that 2.1 million cattle were raised in Alberta in 2009 and exports headed as far as Europe, Taiwan and Japan.

Tasty food blogs

Chow Times (www.chowtimes.com)

Clearly the Place to Eat (www.stomachtreatment.blogspot.ca)

Victorian Food Blog (www.victorianfood.ca)

Urban Diner (www.urbandiner.ca)

Vancouver Foodster (www.vancouverfoodster.com)

In addition, there's a full menu of annual festivals where you can dive into the flavors of the region and bond with the locals over tasty treats.

Recommended events here include:

Dine Out Vancouver (www.dineoutvancouver.com) A three-week-long January event where local restaurants offer great-value two- or three-course tasting menus.

Feast Tofino (www.feasttofino.com) A month-long menu of Tofino events in May focused on local seafood.

Taste of Edmonton (www.tasteofedm.ca) A 10-day outdoor event in July showcasing local eateries and producers. There's also a similar, smaller event in Calgary (www.tasteofcalgary.com) in August.

Taste Festival (www.victoriataste.com) Four-day fiesta of Vancouver Island food and wine treats.

Feast of Fields (www.feastoffields.com) Local produce and top chefs at alfresco party days in Vancouver, the Okanagan and on Vancouver Island.

Cowichan Wine & Culinary Festival (www.wines.cowichan.net) A September celebration of regional treats on Vancouver Island.

Cornucopia (www.whistlercornucopia.com) A baccanalian November food and wine fest in Whistler.

Vegetarians & Vegans

In urban BC there's a full roster of vegetarian and vegan options for traveling herbivores, with many places also boasting their organic credentials. Vancouver, in particular, has seen a surge in cool new vegetarian restaurants in recent years – the kind of places where even meat-eaters are delighted to dine.

Eat heartily before you leave the city, though, since your options will diminish as the towns shrink in size. In the smaller settlements of BC and the Yukon, vegetarian options can be limited to salads, sandwiches or portobello mushroom burgers, with the occasional veggie-only joint standing out like a beacon – not a bacon – in the carnivorous darkness.

Crossing into the meat-loving Rockies, your choices will diminish. But it's not all doom and gloom: Calgary and Edmonton have their own

Vancouver's downtown convention centre often hosts thousands of visitors at a time. They also need refueling. In one year, the facility estimates it serves seven tonnes of beef and 538,000 cups of coffee. For a recent Buddhist convention, 18,000 meals were served over a three-day period.

STREET EATS

Aiming to emulate Portland's legendary street-food scene, Vancouver's sidewalk-dining revolution started in mid-2010 with the introduction of 17 diverse food carts across the city. Suddenly, barbecued pulled pork, organic tacos and gourmet Korean-fusion takeout were available to hungry locals. Despite a few teething troubles, the network has since rapidly expanded to more than 100 carts. You can grab a pulled-pork-filled bun from a Re-Up BBQ food truck and sit on the sunny steps of the Vancouver Art Gallery to watch the world go by. Or pick-up some spicy duck sliders from Roaming Dragon and decamp to Stanley Park for a picnic. Carts are spread across the city, but you'll usually find several hanging out around downtown's Vancouver Art Gallery. Check out www.streetfoodapp.com/vancouver for the latest on listings and locations. And if you're here in summer, don't miss the the city's weekly Food Cart Fest (www.foodcartfest.com), a gathering of tasty vendors and hundreds of taste-tripping locals.

But while Vancouver kick-started the region's street eats trend, it's not the only city jumping on board. Calgary and Edmonton recently launched their own fledgling scenes and Victoria is also moving in the right direction. Keep your eyes peeled – and your stomach empty – for emerging scenes around the area. If you can't find a cart, just head to Richmond, BC. The city hosts two Asian-style night markets on weekends throughout the summer and they're stuffed with steaming food stands serving everything from spicy fish balls to 'tornado potatoes' – thin-cut spirals of fried potato served on skewers.

dedicated veggie eateries, and you can usually find some meat-free pasta options available in Banff and Jasper restaurants.

Eating With Kids

Children are generally welcome at most dining establishments in BC and beyond, although fine-dining restaurants may sometimes be a little snooty about accommodating junior, especially if he/she noisily wrecks the romantic atmosphere of the joint.

Avoid any possible embarrassments – apparently tantrums and food fights are not acceptable everywhere – by hitting midrange eateries with your sprogs. While some restaurants have kids' menus, others will happily prepare a half-order of a regular dish if you ask nicely. Many chain restaurants will also provide high chairs.

White Spot, BC's very own restaurant chain, is a great place to dine with kids. Its main menu ranges from burgers (with secret 'Triple-O' sauce) to seafood pastas and Asian stir-frys, while its kids' meals are served in cardboard pirate ships that are often eyed enviously by adults at other tables (the chain stages a once-a-year adult version of the 'pirate pack' for charity and it's always a hot seller, reducing some locals to teary-eyed nostalgia).

Culinary Tours

If following your nose is an unreliable method for tapping into the region's culinary scene, consider an escort: BC is especially well served by operators who can guide you through the area's flavors on a tasty tour. Slip into your pants with the elasticized waist and hit the road for what may well be the highlight of your visit.

If you're attracted to Vancouver Island's cornucopia of great produce, consider an educational tour of the verdant Cowichan Valley farm region, offered by **Travel with Taste** (www.travelwithtaste.com). You'll meet and sample from artisan cheese makers and boutique vintners before tucking into a gourmet lunch of wild BC salmon. The company also offers lip-smacking guided tours around Victoria and Salt Spring Island.

Alternatively, if you don't plan to stray far from big city Vancouver, consider a Granville Island Market tour with **Edible Canada** (www.edible canada.com). You'll be guided around the colorful market and shown how to pick ingredients for that perfect meal – there are also samples aplenty. The company also runs a bistro on the island where you can dive into Canadian dishes and pick up some regional foodie treats – from jams to Vancouver-made ice-cream – in the little on-site shop.

Or consider a wander around the city with **Vancouver Foodie Tour** (www.foodietours.ca). Among its offerings is a popular weave around downtown's cool street-food vendors.

Over in Calgary, consider a chef-guided tour of the Calgary Farmers Market with **Calgary Food Tours** (www.calgaryfoodtours.com). The company also offers a full range of taste-tripping tour options around the region, from foraging to supper clubs.

Cooking Courses

If you're inspired by the bounty on offer in this region, consider adding an educational side dish to your trip. Check out the following culinary courses or contact your destination's tourism organization to see what's on offer.

Amateurs and pros alike will find a course to suit their level at Vancouver's popular **Dirty Apron Cooking School** (www.dirtyapron.com). An everchanging smorgasbord of regional cuisines is the approach and the classes – mostly taught by French-influenced chef David Robertson – aim

If you're inspired by the region's local food credentials, pick up a copy of The Zero-Mile Diet: A Year-Round Guide to Growing Organic Food (2010) by BC's Carolyn Herriot. It's packed with ideas for sparking your own foodie revolution.

The Yukon Gold is one of Canada's favorite premium potato varieties. To reflect its yellow color and nugget-sized appearance, it was named after the country's gold rush region. It is popular for boiling, baking and frying, mainly because it retains its distinctive yellow hue.

WEST COAST CUISINE EATING WITH KIDS

to make students feel comfortable about mastering the required skills for a wide array of approaches.

Vancouver's popular cooking-themed bookstore, **Barbara-Jo's Books to Cooks** (www.bookstocooks.com), also stages demonstrations, classes and cookbook launches in its swanky on-site kitchen. Check the website to see what's coming up and book ahead before you leave home.

There's a similar operation in Calgary, where **Cookbook Co Cooks** (www.cookbookcooks.com) offers tomes for sale as well as a diverse menu of workshops and classes for locals and visitors.

When to Eat

You can get virtually anything your belly craves at almost any time of the day in Vancouver, but outside the region's main metropolis restaurants may shut early, even in seemingly hip places like Victoria, Edmonton and Whistler. If it's time for dinner, be at the restaurant by 8pm outside peak summer weekends or you may be out of luck.

Breakfast is usually eaten between 7am and 10am. Many hotels offer at least a continental breakfast (a hot drink, juice, toast, muffins and maybe cereal) during these hours with higher-end joints typically serving cooked options – various varieties of eggs benedict are very popular here (go for the smoked salmon). Most local residents eat breakfast at home on weekdays or grab a quick bite on the run with their morning coffee. But on weekends, a much more leisurely breakfast or brunch at a cafe or restaurant is a favorite pastime – in fact, weekend brunch service often stretches well into the afternoon at restaurants in this region and its one of the most popular ways for locals to socialize, especially in brunch-loving hotspot cities, such as Victoria and Vancouver.

The midday meal is typically taken between 11am and 1pm. It can be as simple as a snack bought from a farmers market or street-food cart, or a picnic taken on your hike. Dinner is served anytime from about 5pm to 8pm, often later on weekends and in large cities, as well as resort areas such as Whistler and Banff.

Dress is casual almost everywhere. In most restaurants, you'll be fine no matter what you're wearing. For more formal places, the clichéd 'smart casual' is perfectly acceptable.

There are more than 70,000 farms in Alberta, accounting for at least 30% of the country's total farm area. The top three crops are wheat, barley and canola. While beef remains the province's top agricultural food export, other popular livestock includes elk, bison and reindeer.

REGIONAL COOKBOOKS

Western Canada's top chefs, food journos and finest restaurants have been sharing their tips and recipes with the locals in book form for years. Pick up one of these unique souvenirs of your visit at bookstores and giftshops across the region:

Foodshed: An Edible Alberta Alphabet (Dee Hobsbawn-Smith, 2012) Local food writer profiles Alberta farm producers and offers a recipe for each letter of the alphabet.

Fresh: Seasonal Recipes Made with Local Foods (John Bishop, 2007) A celebration of BC produce and its dedicated growers, this sumptuous 100-recipe book underlines Bishop's credentials as the city's leading sustainable restaurateur.

Ocean Wise Cookbook (Jane Mundy, 2010) Created by the Vancouver Aquarium, Ocean Wise encourages restaurants and seafood purveyors across Canada to employ sustainable fishing practices. This book showcases great seafood recipes from chefs and eateries in Vancouver and beyond.

Blue Water Cafe Seafood Cookbook (Frank T Pabst and Yoshihiro Tabo, 2009) Learn from a couple of Vancouver culinary masters about how to nail seafood preparation.

Araxi: Seasonal Recipes from the Celebrated Whistler Restaurant (James Walt, 2009) Emulate the sumptuous, regionally focused dishes at this top-notch ski resort restaurant.

Drinking BC & Beyond

The locals in this region once happily downed generic fizzy beers or sipped rocket fuel fruit wines made from foraged berries. But mirroring the recent rise in regional cuisine, Western Canadians have developed one of the nation's tastiest tipple scenes. BC's Okanagan Valley sates most wine fans, but additional wineries have popped up around the region. Beer-wise, BC also leads the way: it's arguably Canada's craft beer capital. And don't miss the lip-smacking craft cideries and distilleries, a more recent trend here.

Wine Regions

Overseas visitors are often surprised to learn that wine is produced here, but their skepticism is usually tempered after a choice drink or two. BC's wines have gained ever-greater kudos in recent years and while smaller-scale production and the industry dominance of wine regions like Napa means they'll never be a global market leader, there are some surprisingly high-quality treats awaiting.

Since the best way to sample any wine is to head straight to the source – where you can taste the region in the glass – consider doing some homework and locating the nearest vineyards on your visit: they'll likely be a lot closer than you think. The following are the region's main wine areas, but there are also wineries – alone or in mini-clusters – in BC's Fraser Valley and on the Southern Gulf Islands. Alberta has far fewer wineries, but keep your eyes peeled while you're on the road: there are a handful of friendly fruit-wine joints worth stopping at.

Wherever your tipple-craving takes you, drink widely and deeply. And make sure you have plenty of room in your suitcase – packing materials are always available, but you may drink everything before you make it to the airport anyway.

For background and further information before you arrive, pour a large glass and peruse the handy regional pages on the Wines of Canada website (www.winesofcanada.com) and the BC Wine Lover blog (www.bcwinelover.com).

The website of the BC Wine Institute (www.winebc.com) is an invaluable resource for planning a vintage trawl around the region. It has route maps for several wine tours around the area.

Okanagan Valley

The rolling hills of this lakeside BC region are well worth the five-hour drive from Vancouver. Studded among the vine-striped slopes are more than 100 wineries enjoying a diverse climate that fosters both crisp whites and bold reds. With varietals including pinot noir, pinot gris, pinto blanc, merlot and chardonnay, there's a wine here to suit almost every palate. Most visitors base themselves in Kelowna, the Okanagan's wine capital, before fanning out to well-known blockbuster wineries like Mission Hill, Quail's Gate, Cedar Creek and Summerhill Pyramid Winery (yes, it has a pyramid). Many of them have excellent vista-hugging restaurants. For more information on Okanagan wines and wineries, visit www.okanaganwines.ca.

John Schreiner's *Okanagan Wine Tour Guide* (2010) is an in-depth tome covering the region for visiting oenophiles. It's packed with great suggestions on how to make the most of a wine-based tour around the region.

Golden Mile

Some of BC's best Okanagan wineries are centered south of the valley around the historic town of Oliver, where the Golden Mile's warm climate fosters a long growing season. Combined with gravel, clay and sandy soils, this area is ideally suited to varietals like merlot, chardonnay, gewürztraminer and cabernet sauvignon. While the 20 or so wineries here are not actually crammed into 1 mile – it's more like 20km – the proximity of celebrated producers like Burrowing Owl, Tinhorn Creek and Road 13 Vineyards makes this an ideal touring area. If you're still thirsty, continue south to Osoyoos and check out Nk'Mip Cellars, a First Nations winery on the edge of a desert.

Vancouver Island & the Gulf Islands

Long-established as a farming area, Vancouver Island's verdant Cowichan Valley is also home to some great little wineries. A short drive from Victoria you'll find Averill Creek, Blue Grouse, Cherry Point Vineyards and Venturi-Schulze. Also consider Merridale Estate Cidery, which produces several celebrated ciders on its gently sloped orchard grounds. For more information on Vancouver Island's wineries, visit www.wineislands.ca.

The website also covers a lesser-known winery region: the bucolic Gulf Islands area is home to several small, island-based wineries, including three that welcome visitors on Salt Spring Island. If you plan to visit Salt Spring on a summer weekend, gather picnic supplies at the Saturday Market before picking up a local bottle to accompany your alfresco feast.

Past Whistler on the Sea to Sky Hwy, the small town of Pemberton has been a potato-growing center for generations. It's also the home of Pemberton Distillery (www.pembertondistill-ery.com), which uses the region's spuds to make its celebrated, multi-award-winning Shramm vodka.

Here for the Beer?

Western Canadians don't only drink wine, of course – beer is arguably an even more important beverage here. And while the usual round of bland factory suds and those international usual suspects (you know the ones we mean) are always available, a little digging – actually, hardly any digging at all – uncovers a thriving regional microbrewing scene that's dripping with distinctive craft beers.

From Tofino to Powell River, BC is packed like a clamorous Friday-night pub with around 50 microbreweries, many of them only established in the past 15 years. On your thirst-slaking travels, look out for taps from celebrated producers like Central City Brewing (Surrey), Phillips Brewing (Victoria), Howe Sound Brewing (Squamish), Parallel 49 Brewing (Vancouver) and the near-legendary Crannóg Ales (Sorrento), which crafts a rich, velvety Back Hand of God stout that few can resist. And while Victoria has led the BC pack for craft-beer making for years, Van-

---

DOWNING ICE WINE IN THE SNOW

There are many good reasons to visit the Winter Okanagan Wine Festival – accessible educational seminars, dinner events, cozy alpine-lodge ambiance and some of BC's best outdoor winter activities – but the evening Progressive Tasting is the best. Twenty wineries set up their stalls and offer more than 100 wines at locations throughout the Christmas-card village, while increasingly tipsy visitors slip, slide and tumble their way between them in an attempt to keep their glasses as full as possible.

Staged in mid-January, the annual festival is particularly renowned for celebrating a distinctive tipple that's become a signature of Canadian wineries. Made from grapes frozen on the vine at −8°C (there are plenty of fakes on the market that don't meet this simple criterion), Canadian ice wine is a premium, uber-sweet dessert drink sold in distinctive slender bottles at upwards of $50 a pop. While Austria, Germany and other countries produce their own ice wines, it's a product that reflects Canada's enduring international image as a snowy winter wonderland.

A SIX-PACK OF TOP BEERS

On your travels around the region, look out for these taste-tested top brews:

Driftwood Brewery's Fat Tug IPA (www.driftwoodbeer.com)

Powell Street Craft Brewery's Old Japloy Pale Ale (www.powellbeer.com)

Central City Brewing's Red Racer ESB (www.centralcitybrewing.com)

Crannóg Ales' Back Hand of God Stout (www.crannogales.com)

Howe Sound Brewing's Father John's Winter Ale (www.howesound.com)

Salt Spring Island Ale's Heather Ale (www.gulfislandsbrewery.com)

couver has suddenly upped its game with several new breweries coming on line around the city, many with tasting bars.

You don't have to go thirsty in the Rockies region either: travelers in Alberta should hunt down local beverages from Calgary's Wild Rose Brewery, Edmonton's Alley Kat Brewing and Yellowhead Brewery, and the popular Jasper Brewing Company brewpub, evocatively located in the heart of the national park. If you're way up north, it has to be Yukon Brewing (start with a pint of Yukon Gold).

The smaller the brewery, the more likely it is to produce tipples that make generic fizzy beers taste like something you'd rather wash your car with. Ales, bitters, lagers, pilsners, bocks, porters, stouts and even hemp beers are often available at pubs, bars and restaurants throughout the region. Some bars (notably a handful in downtown Vancouver) host weekly cask nights when they crack open a guest keg of something special: check ahead to find out what's available during your visit.

If you want to see how it's all done – and stoke your thirst in the process – Granville Island Brewing in Vancouver and Big Rock Brewery in Calgary are among those offering short tours coupled with satisfyingly leisurely sample tastings. Cheers!

> The first Okanagan vineyards were planted in the mid-1800s when catholic priests began producing sacramental wine for local services.

Festivals

Time your visit well and you'll be sipping glasses of wine or downing pints of beer (or perhaps the other way around) at a series of regional events. Large or small, they're a great way to hang out with the locals.

Wine lovers are well served in the Okanagan, where there are several events throughout the year. The biggest is the 10-day Fall Wine Festival, while January's Winter Okanagan Wine Festival is evocatively hosted in an icicle-draped ski resort: there's usually plenty of ice wine to go around here. For information on the region's events, see www.thewinefestivals.com.

If you're in Vancouver in March, connect with the Vancouver International Wine Festival (www.vanwinefest.ca). It's the city's largest and oldest wine-based celebration and it focuses on one wine region every year.

Combining drinks and grub, Alberta's Rocky Mountain Wine and Food Festival (www.rockymountainwine.com) takes place on three different dates in Calgary, Edmonton and Banff.

If beer floats your boat, you can sample all those BC microbrews you've been craving at the ever-popular Vancouver Craft Beer Week (www.vancouvercraftbeerweek.com) in late-May. It's the province's biggest beer event but it's not the only one: check out Victoria's Great Canadian Beer Festival (www.gcbf.com) and the Calgary International Beerfest (www.calgarybeerfest.com). If you're looking for something stronger, don't miss the annual Hopscotch Festival (www.hopscotchfestival.com) staged in Vancouver and Kelowna, which focuses on whiskey as well as beer.

> *Craft Beer Revolution* (2013) by Joe Wiebe is an in-depth profile of BC's breweries, with recommendations for where to go and what to drink throughout the region. There's also information on tasting tours and festivals for traveling beer nuts.

CANADA'S COFFEE CAPITAL

If you've explored BC's wine and beer scene a little too enthusiastically, you may need a strong, java-based pick-me-up. Luckily, Vancouver is the country's leading coffee city. On many street corners you'll spot ubiquitous Tim Hortons and Starbucks outlets – Vancouver was the location for the first non-US Starbucks in 1987 – but follow the locals and you'll uncover a rich, aromatic venti-sized cup of great independent coffee shops. The Kitsilano, Commercial Drive and Main St neighborhoods are your best bets for a twitchy afternoon with the locals, and you'll find everything from old-school Italian haunts to slick hipster hangouts.

Where to Drink

You don't have to visit wineries or breweries to find a good drink in this region: BC, Alberta and the Yukon are well stocked with watering holes, from traditional pubs to slick wine bars and cocktail joints, although finding a perfect Moscow Mule in smaller towns may be a little harder. Keep in mind that most bars follow the North American table service approach: unlike other countries, servers come to the table for your order rather than expecting you to hang around trying to get your own drink at the bar. The (potential) downside is that table service means tipping is standard.

While craft beer is taking off across the region, brewpubs are still underrepresented in some areas: you'll find a few in Vancouver and Victoria, and in towns like Banff, Jasper, Kelowna and Nanaimo. A recent rule change in Vancouver has also made it easier to try some beers when you're visiting a working brewery. Among the city's best are 33 Acres and Parallel 49.

If you're looking for some takeout, you'll find two different systems operating in BC and Alberta: while partially deregulated, most booze in BC is sold through government-run liquor stores (see www.bcliquorstores.com for locations), although private beer and wine shops have begun emerging in recent years. Alberta fully privatized its liquor store sector in 1993.

Vancouver Island's Victoria is the tea capital of North America, with tasty traditional offerings as well as Asian-fusion teashops for those who like to push the teabag envelope beyond Earl Grey.

Classes & Tours

If you're jealous of people who confidently swirl their glasses before airily proclaiming their wine is oaky with a hint of pineapple and Old Spice, get your own back by learning some wine-snob tricks of your own. If you have the time and money, you could consider a full-on sommelier course. But if you're looking for something a little less grueling (and expensive), check out some of the short courses staged across the region.

Among the best are those available in Vancouver. The East Vancouver Wine Academy (www.eastvanwineacademy.com) hosts great-value evenings where a different wine region is explored in a chatty atmosphere. One of the city's best liquor stores, Legacy Liquor Store (www.legacyliquorstore.com), offers regular events where you'll learn about and taste a few wines based around a theme – often a country like Spain or Chile.

If you'd rather hit the road and visit the wineries but need a little help finding them, head to Kelowna in the heart of the Okanagan Valley. The downtown visitor center stocks a great wine trails brochure (free) with directions and information on grape-based trails around the region.

Top Cat Tours (www.topcattours.com) has a tempting menu of fully guided options around the Okanagan. These include a South Okanagan Tour that includes the Golden Mile.

If you're in Victoria, consider the guided bike and brewery tour offered by The Pedaler (www.thepedaler.ca), while the mainland's Vancouver Brewery Tours (www.vancouverbrewerytours.com) makes it easier by driving you around several city producers in its minibus.

The legal drinking age in BC and the Yukon is 19, while it's 18 in Alberta. If you 'look young' you should expect to be asked for identification. Canada is very serious about curbing drink-driving, and you may encounter mandatory roadside checkpoints, especially on summer evenings or around winter holidays.

Survival Guide

Directory A-Z

Accommodations

British Columbia and Alberta offer a good range of hotels, B&Bs and hostels. There are plenty of accessible and far-flung campsites. Options are dramatically reduced in northern BC and the Yukon: budget options are often replaced by modest but pricey motels.

Facilities

TYPE	PRICE RANGE
Budget (campsites, hostels and basic hotels and motels, often with shared bathrooms)	$
Midrange (B&Bs, motels and hotels, with private bathrooms)	$$
Top end (quality hotels and resorts and luxury B&Bs; facilities may include spas)	$$$

Booking Ahead

➤ In Rockies hotspots Banff and Jasper, accommodation is severely limited in summer so advance booking is critical. Reserving ahead in summer is also a good idea throughout BC and Alberta, especially in July and August and around holidays. Winter (particularly December to February) is a peak season in ski areas like BC's Whistler and Alberta's Sunshine Meadows, so booking is vital. Due to a limited amount of accommodations, booking ahead is also a good idea for summer trips to the Yukon.

➤ *British Columbia Approved Accommodation Guide,* an extensive annual directory published by the province's official tourism body, details options in all classes of lodgings. It's free and is available at visitor information centers or online from **Destination British Columbia** (www.hellobc. com), where accommodation bookings can also be made.

➤ **Travel Alberta** (☑800-252-3782; www.travelalberta.com) offers a similar downloadable guide via its website.

➤ For the north, check out the online accommodation listings at **Travel Yukon** (☑800-661-0494; www. travelyukon.com).

B&Bs

➤ North American B&Bs are typically more upscale than the casual, family-style pensions found in Europe. There are thousands to choose from – with many unique or romantic options – across the region.

➤ Booking ahead is essential since B&Bs often have only one to three rooms.

➤ Check the rules: many are adult-only and do not accept pets. Others only open seasonally and/or require a two-night minimum stay.

➤ B&B parking is often free.

➤ Local visitor centers usually have good B&B listings for their areas. Also see **Bed and Breakfast Online** (www.bbcanada.com) for listings across the region.

Camping

➤ This region is a campers' paradise with thousands of government-run and private options.

➤ Options range from basic pitches nestled in the remote wilderness to highly accessible, amenity-packed campgrounds popular with families.

➤ Campgrounds are typically open from May to September but dates vary by location.

➤ Some popular sites are sold out months in advance: booking ahead is

BOOK YOUR STAY ONLINE

For more accommodations reviews by Lonely Planet authors, check out http://lonelyplanet.com/hotels/. You'll find independent reviews, as well as recommendations on the best places to stay. Best of all, you can book online.

recommended, especially for holiday weekends and the summer peak season.

➡ Facilities vary widely. Expect little more than pit toilets and a fire ring at backcountry sites, while larger campgrounds may have shower blocks and guided interpretive programs.

➡ Camping in national or provincial parks can cost up to $40 per night, although many are around $25. Private sites may offer more facilities and charge a little more.

➡ For information, listings and bookings for government-run sites in national and local parks, see **Parks Canada** (www.pccamping.ca), **BC Parks** (www.discovercamping.ca) and **Alberta Parks** (www.reserve.albertaparks.ca).

Guest Ranches

BC and Alberta have dozens of enticing guest ranches, the euphemism for horse-centered dude ranches where you can join a trail ride or sit by a mountain lake. The Cariboo-Chilcotin region is a guest ranch hotbed.

Hostels

➡ Independent and Hostelling International (HI) hostels are easy to find in popular visitor destinations, with some areas enjoying healthy competition between several establishments.

➡ Dorms (typically $25 to $40) may be small or sleep up to 20 people and facilities usually include shared bathrooms, kitchen and common areas. Laundry facilities, bike storage and wi-fi (or computer terminals) are also common.

➡ Private rooms in hostels are increasingly popular: they are also the most sought after, so book far ahead.

➡ Many outdoorsy hostels offer extras like bike or kayak hire while city-based hostels often have free/low-cost social programs, such as tours or pub nights.

➡ While city hostels are often open 24 hours, those in other areas may be closed during the day – check ahead.

➡ Booking ahead for hostels in popular destinations like Tofino, Whistler and Banff is essential in summer.

➡ For locations and bookings, see **Hostelling International** (www.hihostels.ca), **SameSun** (www.samesun.com) and **Backpackers Hostels Canada** (www.backpackers.ca).

Hotels & Motels

➡ Hotel rates vary around the region. Plan to spend at least $150 for a basic double room with a private bathroom during summer peaks in Vancouver and Victoria. In less-visited areas, $100 is closer to the norm.

➡ Boutique properties and high-end hotels are available in Vancouver and Victoria, with chateaux-like resorts in Whistler and the Rockies.

➡ Wilderness retreats are dotted around the BC coastline and in some parts of the Rockies, offering spas and top-notch dining packages.

➡ Midrange hotel and motel rooms typically include a private bathroom, one or two large beds, a tea and coffee maker, and free wi-fi.

➡ Your hotel may not include air-conditioning, so check before you book.

➡ In distant areas such as northern BC, the Alberta outback and remote Yukon spots, you'll find hotels folksy at best.

➡ Many motels (and an increasing number of suite-style hotels) offer handy (and money-saving) kitchenettes.

➡ Children can often stay free in the same room as their parents – check if there's a charge for rollaway beds.

Customs Regulations

➡ Check in with the **Canada Border Services Agency** (CBSA; www.cbsa.gc.ca) for the latest customs lowdown.

EXTRA CHARGES

Be aware that there are often extras to pay on your daily hotel room rate. These can include resort fees, parking fees and local hotel taxes. Clarify all these possible extras before you book.

→ The duty-free allowance coming into Canada is 1.14L (40oz) of liquor, 1.5L (or two 750mL bottles) of wine or 24 cans or bottles of beer, as well as up to 200 cigarettes, 50 cigars or 200g of tobacco.

→ You are allowed to bring in gifts up to a total value of $60. Gifts above $60 are subject to duty and taxes on the over-limit value.

→ Fresh and prepared foods are the subject of myriad rules and regulations here. Just buy what you need in Canada.

→ You can bring in or take out up to $10,000 in cash – report larger amounts at the border.

→ Register excessive or expensive sporting goods and cameras with customs, as this will save you time and trouble when leaving, especially if you plan on crossing the Canada–US border.

→ If you are bringing a dog or cat into the country you will need proof that it has had a rabies shot in the past 36 months.

→ Pistols, fully automatic weapons, any firearms less than 66cm (26in) in length and self-defense sprays (like pepper or mace) are not permitted into Canada.

Discount Cards

→ Discounts for seniors, students and families are commonly offered at attractions throughout this region. Students from overseas will usually need a valid **International Student Identity Card** (www.isic.org).

→ A **Parks Canada Discovery Pass** (www.pc.gc.ca/ar-sr/lpac-ppri/ced-ndp.aspx; adult/child/family $68/33/136) is good value if you're planning to visit national parks and historic sites across the region.

Electricity

120V/60Hz

120V/60Hz

Food

For an introduction to the region's thriving food scene, see p301.

Gay & Lesbian Travelers

In BC and Alberta, attitudes toward gays and lesbians are relaxed, especially in urban areas like Vancouver and Calgary where there are dedicated rainbow-hued nightlife scenes.

While you won't find as open a gay and lesbian culture in other parts of the region, throughout the provinces and in the Yukon attitudes are generally tolerant. That said, the lack of prominent gay and lesbian communities outside urban centers tends to mean that most people keep their orientation to themselves.

The following are useful resources for gay travelers:

Gay Canada (www.gaycanada.com) Search by province or city for queer-friendly businesses and resources.

Qmunity (www.qmunity.ca) Online resources for the community throughout BC.

Xtra (www.xtra.ca) Source for gay and lesbian news nationwide.

Health

There's a high level of hygiene in this region, so most common infectious diseases will not be a major concern for travelers. No special vaccinations are required, but all travelers should be up-to-date on standard immunizations, such as tetanus and measles.

Health Insurance

The Canadian healthcare system is one of the best in the world and excellent care is widely available. Benefits are generous for Canadian citizens, but foreigners aren't covered, which can make treatment prohibitively expensive.

Make sure you have travel-health insurance if your regular policy doesn't apply when you're abroad. Find out in advance if your insurance plan will make payments directly to providers or reimburse you later for overseas health expenditures.

Availability & Cost of Health Care

For immediate medical assistance anywhere in BC and Alberta, call ⚡911; in the Yukon, call ⚡867-667-5555, except for Whitehorse, which has ⚡911 service. In general, if you have a medical emergency, it's best to find the nearest hospital emergency room.

If you have a choice, a university hospital can be preferable to a community hospital, although you can often find superb medical care in small local hospitals, and the waiting time is usually shorter. If the problem isn't urgent, you can call a nearby hospital and ask for a referral to a local physician – less expensive than a trip to the emergency room.

Pharmacies are abundantly supplied; however, you may find that some medications that are available over the counter in your home country require a prescription in Canada. In the largest cities you'll be able to find 24-hour pharmacies, although most drugstores typically keep regular store hours.

Importing Medications

Bring medications in their original containers, clearly labeled. A signed, dated letter from your physician describing all medical conditions and medications, including generic names, is also a good idea. If carrying syringes or needles be sure to have a physician's letter documenting their medical necessity.

EATING PRICE RANGES

The following price ranges refer to a standard main course. Taxes and services charges are not included in these prices.

$ less than $12

$$ $12–$25

$$$ more than $25

Infectious Diseases

You need to be aware of the following, particularly if you're traveling in wilderness areas:

➡ **Giardiasis** A parasitic infection of the small intestine. Its symptoms may include nausea, bloating, cramps and diarrhea, and may last for weeks. Avoid drinking directly from lakes, ponds, streams and rivers, which may be contaminated by animal or human feces.

➡ **Lyme Disease** Transmitted by tiny deer ticks and mostly occurring in late spring and summer in southern areas. The first symptom is usually an expanding red rash. Flu-like symptoms, including fever, headache, joint pains and body aches, are also common.

➡ **West Nile Virus** Recently observed in provinces including Alberta, the virus is transmitted by Culex mosquitoes, which are active in late summer and early fall, and generally bite after dusk. Most infections are mild, but the virus may infect the central nervous system, leading to fever, headache, confusion, coma and sometimes death.

Websites

➡ **Public Health Agency of Canada** (www.phac-aspc.gc.ca) General Canadian government health resource.

➡ **MD Travel Health** (www.mdtravelhealth.com) Travel-related health information for countries around the world.

➡ **World Health Organization** (www.who.int) General health information covering all countries.

➡ **Australia** (www.smarttraveller.gov.au) Health advice for Australians traveling abroad.

➡ **United Kingdom** (www.nhs.uk/healthcareabroad) Travel resources for UK citizens traveling overseas.

➡ **United States** (www.cdc.gov/travel/) Health advice for traveling Americans.

Insurance

Make sure you have adequate travel insurance to cover your trip in this region. Luggage theft or loss insurance is handy but health coverage for medical emergencies and treatment is vital: medical treatment for non-Canadians is expensive.

Worldwide travel insurance is available at www.lonelyplanet.com/travel_services. You can buy, extend and claim online anytime – even if you're already on the road.

Internet Access

➡ Wi-fi or wired internet connections are increasingly standard in accommodations across BC, Alberta and the Yukon.

➡ You'll also find wi-fi and internet-access computers in libraries and wi-fi in coffeeshops – these have largely replaced internet cafes for travelers here.

➜ In this guide, the internet icon (@) is used for places with public internet computers. The wi-fi icon (📶) is used for any place with wi-fi access. In accommodations listings, it also means that at least some rooms have wi-fi.

Legal Matters

➜ The Canadian federal government permits the use of marijuana for medicinal purposes, but official prescription cannabis is strictly regulated.

➜ It's illegal to consume alcohol anywhere other than a residence or licensed premises, which puts parks, beaches and other public spaces off limits.

➜ You can incur stiff fines, jail time and penalties if caught driving under the influence of alcohol or any illegal substance. The blood-alcohol limit is 0.08%, which is reached after just two beers. Penalties include being thrown in jail overnight, followed by a court appearance, heavy fine and/ or further incarceration.

➜ Canada has strict regulations banning smoking in all public places. This can include patios and other outdoor spaces. Your best bet is to light up in the middle of a big empty parking lot.

Maps

➜ Members of the Canadian Automobile Association (CAA), American Automobile Association (AAA) or affiliated clubs can get free road maps before leaving home or from offices throughout BC and Alberta.

➜ Bookstores, gas stations and convenience stores usually sell a wide variety of maps ranging from regional overviews to detailed street atlases.

➜ For extended hikes or multiday backcountry treks, it's a good idea to carry a topographic map. The best are the series of 1:50,000 scale maps published by the government's **Centre for Topographic Information** (www.nrcan.gc.ca). These are sold by approximately 900 map dealers around the country; check the website for vendors. You can also download and print maps from www.geobase.ca.

➜ **Gem Trek Publishing** (www.gemtrek.com) offers some of the best Rocky Mountains maps in scales from 1:35,000 to 1:100,000.

Money

➜ All prices in this guide are in Canadian dollars, unless stated.

➜ The Canadian dollar ($) is divided into 100 cents (¢). Coins come in 5¢ (nickel), 10¢ (dime), 25¢ (quarter), $1 (loonie) and $2 (toonie) pieces.

➜ Notes come in $5, $10, $20, $50 and $100 denominations; $100 bills can prove difficult to cash. Canadian bills are all the same size but vary in their colors and images.

ATMs

ATMs are common throughout BC, Alberta and the larger towns of the Yukon. Canadian ATM fees are generally low but your bank at home may charge another fee on top of that.

Credit Cards

Credit and debit cards are almost universally accepted and, in fact, you'll find it hard or impossible to rent a car, book a room or order tickets online or over the phone without one.

Moneychangers

If you're not going to withdraw cash as needed from ATMs, exchange your money when you arrive in Canada. There are currency exchange counters at international airports such as Vancouver and Calgary. Currency exchange offices are also common in the area's bigger towns and cities as well as in tourist destinations like Whistler and Banff. Keep in mind that larger banks may also exchange currency and their rates are usually better. US dollars are often accepted by businesses at larger tourist towns like Victoria and Whistler – especially in gift shops – but keep in mind that the exchange rates they use are typically not favorable.

Taxes & Refunds

BC and Alberta have different consumer tax rates. The federal Goods and Services Tax (GST) adds 5% to nearly every product, service or

---

PRACTICALITIES

➜ **Weights & Measures** The metric system is used throughout Canada, although popular references to the imperial system (as used in the US) still survive.

➜ **DVD & Video** Canada is in DVD region 1. Buy or watch videos on the NTSC system.

➜ **Newspapers** Most towns have a daily or weekly newspaper. The Vancouver Sun and Calgary Herald provide reasonable regional coverage.

➜ **Radio** Signs at the entrances to towns provide local frequencies for CBC Radio One ( ).

➜ **Smoking** Banned inside public buildings across the region.

transaction in Alberta. This is also the case in the Yukon.

In BC, there is a 5% GST levy as well as 7% Provincial Sales Tax (PST). Not all items you pay for will attract both rates, but many do. Some items even attract higher PST rates here: alcohol is 10%, for example.

Almost all tax rebate schemes have been killed, but if you booked your trip as part of a package, you may be able to get a refund on tax paid on accommodations. Check in with the **Canada Revenue Agency** (☎800-668-4748, 902-432-5608; www.cra-arc.gc.ca/E/pbg/gf/gst115) for the latest information.

Tipping

Gratuities are part of the price you'll pay for visiting this part of the world. The following are typical rates:

SERVICE	USUAL TIP
Restaurant wait staff	15%
Bar servers	$1 per drink
Hotel bellhops	$1 to $2 per bag
Hotel room cleaners	$2 per day
Taxi drivers	10–15%

Traveler's Checks

The days of traveler's checks are waning and they're becoming increasingly obsolete as ATMs spread and become more convenient for vacationers. Traveler's checks issued in Canadian dollars are generally treated like cash by most businesses, especially in larger, heavily visited areas like Banff, Jasper, Vancouver, Victoria and Whistler.

Traveler's checks issued in most other currencies must be exchanged for Canadian dollars at a bank or foreign-currency office.

Opening Hours

The following table is a guide to standard opening hours for businesses throughout this region. Reviews in the guide show specific hours, which may differ from these standard hours. Many attractions, for example, reduce their hours during the off-season.

BUSINESS	STANDARD HOURS
Banks	9am or 10am-5pm Mon-Fri; some open 9am-noon Sat
Bars	11am-midnight or later; some only open from 5pm
Post offices	9am-5pm Mon-Fri; some open on Sat
Restaurants	breakfast 7-11am, lunch 11:30am-2pm, dinner 5-9:30pm (8pm in rural areas)
Shops	10am-5pm or 6pm Mon-Sat; noon-5pm Sunday; some (especially in malls) open to 8pm or 9pm Thu and/or Fri
Supermarkets	9am-8pm; some open 24hr

Post

➡ **Canada Post** (www.canadapost.ca) is reliable and easy to use. Look for the red storefronts around towns denoting main branches.

➡ Even more ubiquitous are the full-service Canada Post counters tucked into the back of convenience stores, drug stores and supermarkets. Look for the signs in their windows. They often have longer opening hours.

➡ Your hotel may also sell individual stamps, while books of stamps are available in many convenience stores.

➡ Rates for postcards and letters to the US are $1.10, to the rest of the world $1.85.

Public Holidays

National public holidays are celebrated throughout Canada with BC, Alberta and the Yukon each observing an additional statutory holiday – often called a 'stat' – at separate times of the year. Banks, schools and government offices (including post offices) are closed, and transportation, museums and other services may operate on a Sunday schedule. Holidays falling on a weekend are usually observed the following Monday and long weekends are among the busiest on the region's roads and ferry routes.

New Year's Day January 1

Family Day second Monday in February in BC; third Monday in February Alberta

Easter (Good Friday and Easter Monday) March/April

Victoria Day Monday preceding May 25

Canada Day July 1

BC Day first Monday in August; BC only

Discovery Day third Monday in August; Yukon only

Labour Day first Monday in September

Thanksgiving second Monday in October

Remembrance Day November 11

Christmas Day December 25

LOCAL HOLIDAYS: WHAT THEY MEAN

Aside from the public holidays enjoyed by everyone across the region, BC, Alberta and the Yukon have their own distinctive extra days off when they spend at least a couple of hours phoning their neighbors across the country to brag about not having to go into work. On these days you can expect shops and businesses to be operating on reduced hours (or to be closed), so plan ahead. The region's three separate public holidays:

➜ **BC Day** Officially called British Columbia Day, this welcome August holiday (a trigger for many locals to take a summertime long weekend) was introduced in 1974 and was intended to recognize the pioneers that kick-started the region.

➜ **Discovery Day** The Yukon's mid-August holiday marks the 1896 gold discovery in Bonanza Creek that triggered the Klondike Gold Rush. It starts a week-long Dawson City festival that includes historic re-creations.

➜ **Family Day** This February statutory holiday was instituted in Alberta in 1990 and in BC in 2013. It does not exist (yet) in the Yukon.

Boxing Day December 26; many stores open, other businesses closed

Telephone

➜ If you are calling a number within the same area code here, you still need to dial all 10 digits. If you are dialing long distance within this region or any other region in North America, you need to dial ☑1, then the 10 digits.

➜ For calling outside of North America, dial ☑011 followed by the country code and the number. When calling North America from abroad the country code is ☑1.

➜ Pay phones are increasingly disappearing from sidewalks across the region. If you do find one, you'll need coins or a long-distance phonecard to work them. Phonecards can be purchased in convenience stores, post offices, gas stations etc. Shop around for the best card deals.

➜ Cell (mobile) phones use the GSM and CDMA systems, depending on the carrier. If you have an unlocked GSM phone, you should be able to buy a SIM card for under $50, which will include a bit of talk time. Using your home-country cell-phone service in Canada will be subject to rates much like those of hotel phones: extortionate. And note that much of the backcountry has no cell-phone signal.

➜ Toll-free numbers begin with ☑800, ☑877 or ☑866. However, these numbers do not typically work when calling from overseas.

Time

➜ Most of BC and the Yukon operate on Pacific Time, which is eight hours behind Greenwich Mean Time.

➜ Alberta is on Mountain Time, which is one hour later than Pacific Time.

➜ Clocks are turned forward one hour on the second Sunday in March and are turned back one hour on the first Sunday in November.

➜ Canada's time zones mirror those across the border in the US.

Tourist Information

With tourism such a major part of this region's economy, resources for travelers are excellent: official websites are useful for trip planning and there are hundreds of visitor centers dotted across the area.

Many smaller regions have their own organizations but they usually operate under the umbrella of these larger bodies:

Destination British Columbia (www.hellobc.com)

Travel Alberta (☑800-252-3782; www.travelalberta.com)

Tourism Yukon (☑800-661-0494; www.travelyukon.com)

Travelers with Disabilities

➜ Guide dogs may legally be brought into restaurants, hotels and other businesses.

➜ Many public service phone numbers and some pay phones are adapted for the hearing impaired.

➜ Most public buildings are equipeed for wheelchair accessibility and many parks feature trails that are likewise accessible.

➜ Many newer or renovated hotels also have dedicated accessible rooms.

➜ Public transport is increasingly accessible with all buses in Vancouver, for example, now fully wheelchair accessible.

➜ Start your trip planning at **Access to Travel** (www.accesstotravel.gc.ca), the federal government's dedicated website. It has detailed information on air, bus, rail and ferry transportation.

➜ Other helpful resources:

BC Coalition of People with Disabilities (☎604-875-0188, 800-663-1278; www.bccpd.bc.ca)

Canadian National Institute for the Blind (www.cnib.ca)

Mobility International (www.miusa.org)

Society for Accessible Travel & Hospitality (www.sath.org)

Visas

Visitors from most of the US, Western Europe and many Commonwealth countries normally don't require a visa for a tourist stay of less than 180 days. But citizens of many other countries do. **Citizenship & Immigration Canada** (www.cic.gc.ca) has the latest visa details on its website and it has links to Canadian embassies and consulates worldwide so you can check requirements locally.

Women Travelers

➜ BC, Alberta and the Yukon are generally safe places for women traveling alone, although the usual precautions apply: just use the same commonsense you would at home.

➜ In Vancouver, the Main and Hastings Sts area is best avoided at night and it's not a great idea to go for a walk in Stanley Park on your own after dark. In more remote parts of the province, particularly in Northern BC, women traveling alone will find themselves a distinct minority, although there's no shortage of feisty locals ready to assist a sister in need, especially in the Yukon.

➜ In bars and nightclubs, solo women will probably attract a lot of male attention. If

BORDER CROSSINGS

Many points of entry on the US–Canada border are open 24 hours. The exceptions are some minor ones and those in the Yukon that have limited hours and/or close for the season. Entering Canada by land from the US usually goes smoothly at the dozens of border crossings from the continental US and Alaska. But there may be a wait on weekends – especially holiday weekends – particularly at the I-5/Hwy 99 crossing south of Vancouver, where you may have to wait several hours. Either avoid crossing at these times, or drive to one of the other Lower Mainland crossings such as Aldergrove.

The website www.borderlineups.com has live cameras showing the situation at major crossings as well stats on wait times.

US citizens flying home should note that you must clear US Immigration and Customs at Vancouver and Calgary airports *before* you fly to the US. This means two things: get to those two airports at least an hour earlier than normal as the US lines can be long; and when your plane arrives in the US, you are treated as a domestic passenger, so you're on your way.

you don't want company, a firm 'No thank you' typically does the trick. If you feel threatened in an area where there are other people, protesting loudly will usually bring others to your defense.

➜ Note that carrying mace or pepper spray is illegal throughout Canada.

➜ Attacks are unlikely but if you are assaulted, call the police immediately. Rape crisis hotlines include **Calgary** (☎403-237-5888) and **Vancouver** (☎604-872-8212).

Work

➜ In almost all cases, non-Canadians need a valid work permit to get a job in Canada. Obtaining one may be difficult, as employment opportunities go to Canadians first. Some jobs are exempt from the permit requirement. For full details on temporary work,

check with **Citizenship & Immigration Canada** (www.cic.gc.ca). Those aged 18 to 30 may be able to get work permits as students or as part of a working holiday program. See the CIC website for details.

➜ Don't try to work without a permit: if you're caught, that will be the end of your Canadian dream.

➜ Short-term jobs, such as restaurant and bar work, are generally plentiful in popular tourist spots like Whistler and Banff, where the turnover is predictably high. Often there will be postings on the resort website.

➜ Resources for potential job-seekers:

International Experience Canada (www.international.gc.ca/experience)

Student Work Abroad Program (SWAP; www.swap.ca)

Transportation

GETTING THERE & AWAY

British Columbia and Alberta are directly accessible from international and US destinations, while the Yukon usually requires a plane connection. Flights, tours and rail tickets can be booked online at www.lonelyplanet.com/bookings.

Entering the Region

When flying into Canada, you will be expected to show your passport (plus visa, if required) to an immigration officer and answer a few questions about the duration and purpose of your visit. After clearing customs, you'll be on your way.

Driving across the border from the US can be a little more complex. Questioning is sometimes more intense and, in some cases, your car may be searched.

See **Citizenship and Immigration Canada** (www.cic.gc.ca) for the latest information on entry requirements.

Air

BC-bound travelers typically fly into Vancouver. But if the Rockies is your main attraction, Calgary or Edmonton will be more convenient.

Many visitors fly into one of these Alberta airports, then travel to BC via the Rockies before departing from Vancouver. If you're bound for the Yukon, you'll probably be booking a connecting flight from BC or Alberta on to Whitehorse.

Air Canada and WestJet are the main Canadian airlines serving this region, while many international airlines from Europe, Asia and around the world also fly in.

Airports

Calgary international Airport (YYC; www.calgaryairport.com)

Edmonton International Airport (YEG; www.flyeia.com)

Kelowna International Airport (YLW; www.kelownaairport.com)

Vancouver International Airport (YVR; www.yvr.ca)

Victoria International Airport (www.victoriaairport.com)

Whitehorse Airport (YXY; ☑867-667-8440; www.gov.yk.ca/yxy/airports/yxy)

Land

From the USA

BUS

You can travel from the US to many places in BC and Alberta (plus, non-directly, Whitehorse in the Yukon) with **Greyhound** (☑800-231-2222; www.greyhound.com). You will

---

CLIMATE CHANGE & TRAVEL

Every form of transport that relies on carbon-based fuel generates CO_2, the main cause of human-induced climate change. Modern travel is dependent on airplanes, which might use less fuel per kilometer per person than most cars but travel much greater distances. The altitude at which aircraft emit gases (including CO_2) and particles also contributes to their climate change impact. Many websites offer 'carbon calculators' that allow people to estimate the carbon emissions generated by their journey, and, for those who wish to do so, to offset the impact of the greenhouse gases emitted with contributions to portfolios of climate-friendly initiatives throughout the world. Lonely Planet offsets the carbon footprint of all staff and author travel.

SAMPLE REGIONAL AIRLINE ROUTES & FARES

ROUTE	AIRLINE	DURATION	FREQUENCY	FULL FARE (ONE WAY; EXCLUDING TAXES)
Vancouver-Masset (Haida Gwaii)	Pacific Coastal Airlines	2½hr	1 daily	$346
Vancouver-Whitehorse	Air North	2½hr	2 daily	$451
Vancouver-Dawson Creek	Central Mountain Air	2hr	1 daily	$455
Victoria-Vancouver	Harbour Air	30min	multiple daily services	$185
Vancouver-Tofino	Orca Airways	1hr	3 daily	$190
Edmonton-Vancouver	WestJet	1½hr	10 daily	$256
Prince Rupert-Vancouver	Air Canada Express	2hr	2 daily	$341

have to stop at the border to clear Canadian customs and immigration – which sometimes takes a while, especially on weekends and public holidays – and you may be transferred to a different bus. Order tickets online in advance for the best prices.

Quick Coach Lines (www.quickcoach.com) also runs daily express buses between Seattle, Seattle's Sea-Tac International Airport and downtown Vancouver.

Bolt Bus (www.boltbus.com) operates cross-border services to Vancouver from Portland and Seattle, with bargain prices available if you book far enough in advance.

CAR & MOTORCYCLE

The US highway system connects directly with Canadian roads at numerous points along the BC and Alberta borders. Gas is generally cheaper in the US, so fill up before you head north: Vancouver has a reputation for having some of North America's highest pump prices.

Cars rented in the US can generally be driven over the Canadian border and back, but double-check this on your rental agreement.

The Blaine Peace Arch and Pacific Hwy border crossings near Vancouver are the region's busiest, especially on holiday weekends: consider the quieter Lynden or Sumas crossings instead. This can sometimes save an hour or two in travel time.

TRAIN

Amtrak (www.amtrak.com) trundles into Vancouver from south-of-the-border Bellingham, Seattle and Portland. Be aware that buses are used instead of trains on some runs so check at time of booking. In the US, you can also connect from San Francisco, Los Angeles, Chicago and beyond. Book ahead for the best fares.

Luxury train operator **Rocky Mountaineer** (☑877-460-3200; www.rockymountaineer.com) has also recently launched some new departures from Seattle to its north-of-the-border mountain hotspots. This is the first time the company has moved into the US directly.

From Canada

BUS

Greyhound Canada (☑800-661-8747; www.greyhound.ca) has services into Alberta, BC and the Yukon from points

east across the country. Booking ahead and/or online delivers better prices but the best fares are also non-refundable. Photo ID is required for will-call ticket pick-up.

TRAIN

The **VIA Rail** (☑888-842-7245; www.viarail.ca) Canadian service trundles into Vancouver from Toronto three times a week, with stops in Edmonton and Jasper. It's a slow but highly picturesque trip and there is a wide range of tickets available, from sleeper cabins to regular seats.

Sea

Most ferries into BC from the US terminate in Victoria's Inner Harbour, where you'll be expected to clear Canadian customs and immigration. **Alaska Marine Highway System** (www.ferryalaska.com) ferries roll into northern Prince Rupert from Alaska.

These operators service US routes into Victoria:

Black Ball Ferry Line (☑360-457-4491; www.coho ferry.com)

Victoria Clipper (www.clippervacations.com)

GETTING AROUND

Air

WestJet and Air Canada Express (formerly Air Canada Jazz) are the dominant airlines servicing the larger towns and cities in this region. But there's also an extensive network of smaller operators – often using propeller planes or floatplanes – that provide excellent, although not often cheap, quick-hop services. Keep in mind that reduced fares are typically available for advance booking.

Airlines with regional services in BC, Alberta and the Yukon:

Air Canada Express (☑888-247-2262; www.aircanada.com)

Air North (☑in Canada 867-668-2228, in USA 800-661-0407; www.flyairnorth.com)

Central Mountain Air (☑888-865-8585; www.flycma.com)

Harbour Air (☑800-665-0212; www.harbourair.com)

Orca Airways (☑888-359-6722; www.flyorcaair.com)

Pacific Coastal Airlines (☑800-663-2872; www.pacific-coastal.com)

Salt Spring Air (☑877-537-9880; www.saltspringair.com)

WestJet (☑888-937-8538; www.westjet.com)

Bicycle

If you have the time, cycling is one of the best ways to get around and immerse yourself in this region – so long as you also have the stamina. Cities such as Vancouver and Victoria are especially welcoming, with their ever-increasing bike route networks. At time of research for this book, Vancouver was working towards the introduction of a public bike share scheme.

Helmets are mandatory in BC (and in Alberta for under-18s). Many forms of public transportation – the BC Ferries system and Vancouver's TransLink buses, for example – enable you to take your bike with you.

Off-road mountain biking is also highly popular here, with some ski resorts transforming into bike parks in summer. Bike-rental operators are common, even in smaller towns. You'll likely need a credit card for the deposit, and rental rates are typically around $40 per day.

Area resources:

Alberta Bicycle Association (www.albertabicycle.ab.ca)

British Columbia Cycling Coalition (www.bccc.bc.ca)

HUB (www.bikehub.ca)

Boat

BC Ferries (☑888-223-3779; www.bcferries.com) runs 36 vessels on 25 routes around the province's coastal waters. Its extensive network includes frequent busy runs – with giant 'superferries' – between the mainland and Vancouver Island. There are also dozens of community routes, with much smaller vessels, linking shoreline communities as well as the Gulf Islands. The signature long-haul route is from Port Hardy to Prince Rupert, a day-long glide along the spectacular Inside Passage.

It's one of the world's biggest ferry networks, and well worth scheduling a trip as part of your visit. Many of the routes are vehicle-accessible but walk-on passengers pay much lower fares. Off-season fares are usually cheaper, while the larger vessels are also equipped with restaurants, shops and wi-fi.

Popular routes:

➡ **Lower Mainland to Vancouver Island** The two busiest routes are from Tsawwassen (an hour's drive south of Vancouver) to Swartz Bay (30 minutes north of Victoria), and from Horseshoe Bay (30 minutes north of downtown Vancouver) to Departure Bay near Nanaimo on central Vancouver Island. Vehicle reservations are recommended for summer and weekend travel.

➡ **Inside Passage** Among the most scenic boat trips in the world. In summer the service is scheduled for 15-hour daylight runs between Port Hardy and Prince Rupert, in different directions on alternate days. Sailings between October and May typically include stops in tiny Aboriginal villages and can take up to two days. Reserve ahead, especially in the summer peak, and consider an additional ferry trip to Haida Gwaii when you reach Prince Rupert.

➡ **Discovery Coast Passage** This additional long-haul journey covers the dramatic route between Port Hardy

---

SAILING THE INSIDE PASSAGE

Taking a BC Ferries cruise along the stunning Inside Passage is likely to be the transportation highlight of your trip. Expect to see marine life ranging from whales and dolphins to lazy-looking seals lounging on the rocky shoreline. Look for eagles overhead and bears on the shore as you spend hours passing deserted islands and rocky coasts accented by waterfalls. On these runs, the crews are famously friendly and the captain will slow the ship when, say, a pod of orcas swims past. You'll spend most of your time basking on deck, but consider paying extra for a tiny cabin so you can really chill out.

and Bella Coola on the central BC coast. It's shorter than the Inside Passage route, but equally scenic. Runs from mid-June to mid-September. Reservations necessary.

Bus

Greyhound Canada (☑800-661-8747; www.greyhound.ca) covers much of BC and Alberta and also offers services into the Yukon's Whitehorse via the Alaska Hwy. Booking ahead usually delivers the lower rates. See the table below for sample routes and standard fares.

Additional regional bus operators:

Brewster Transportation (☑866-606-6700; www.brewster.ca) Runs regular services between Jasper, Banff and Lake Louise.

Malaspina Coach Lines (☑877-227-8287; www.malaspinacoach.com) Service between Vancouver and the Sunshine Coast communities of British Columbia.

Moose Travel Network (☑888-816-6673; www.moosenetwork.com) Backpacker bus routes across the region, linking Vancouver, Vancouver Island and the Rockies.

Pacific Coach Lines (☑800-661-1725; www.pacificcoach.com) For services between Whistler, Vancouver and Victoria.

Snowbus (☑888-794-5511; www.snowbus.com) Popular winter-only ski-bus service between Vancouver and Whistler.

Tofino Bus (☑866-986-3466; www.tofinobus.com) Operates Vancouver Island services between Tofino, Ucluelet, Nanaimo and Victoria.

Car & Motorcycle

Although BC, Alberta and the Yukon cover a huge area, driving is the best way to travel here. Generally the highways are excellent.

SAMPLE GREYHOUND BUS ROUTES

ROUTE	DURATION	FREQUENCY	FULL FARE (ONE WAY)
Seattle-Vancouver	4hr	4 daily	US$38
Portland-Vancouver	9hr	3 daily	US$76
Toronto-Calgary	2 days	3 daily	$244
Calgary-Edmonton	4hr	8 daily	$56
Kamloops-Vancouver	5hr	6 daily	$73
Vancouver-Whistler	2.5hr	6 daily	$29
Edmonton-Jasper	5hr	2 daily	$78
Vancouver-Calgary	17hr	5 daily	$110

Automobile Associations

British Columbia Automobile Association (www.bcaa.com) provides its members, and the members of other auto clubs (such as the AAA in the US), with travel information, maps, travel insurance and hotel reservations. It also provides a service in the Yukon. **Alberta Motor Association** (www.ama.ab.ca) operates a similar service further east.

Bring Your Own Vehicle

Cars that are licensed to drive in North America may be driven across the border and into Canada. Make sure you have all your vehicle registration papers, driver's license and proof of insurance.

Car Hire

Major car-rental firms have offices at airports in BC, Alberta and Whitehorse, as well as in larger city centers. In smaller towns there may be independent firms. Clarify your insurance coverage for things like gravel damage if you are going to be driv-ing off major roads that are paved.

Shop around for deals but watch out for offers that don't include unlimited kilometers. Never buy the rental-car company's gas if offered when you pick up your car – it's a bad deal. Buy your own and return it full. If you are considering a one-way rental, be aware of high fees.

You generally have to be aged over 25 years to rent a car here, although some companies will rent to those aged between 21 and 24 for an additional premium. Regular rates for an economy-sized vehicle are typically between $40 and $65 per day.

All the usual rental companies operate here, including the following:

Avis (☑800-230-4898; www.avis.ca)

Budget (☑800-268-8900; www.budget.ca)

Enterprise (☑800-261-7331; www.enterprise.ca)

Hertz (☑800-654-3001; www.hertz.ca)

National (☑877-222-9058; www.nationalcar.ca)

Zipcar (📞866-494-7227; www.zipcar.ca)

RECREATIONAL VEHICLES

Recreational vehicles (RVs) are popular in western Canada, and rentals must be booked well in advance of the summer season. In high season, RVs typically cost $165 to $265 or more a day. One-way rentals are possible, but you'll pay a surcharge. Also budget plenty for fuel as RVs typically get miserable mileage.

Large rental companies have offices in Vancouver, Calgary, Whitehorse and bigger BC towns. Operators include the following:

Canadream Campers (📞403-291-1000, 800-461-7368; www.canadream.com)

Go West Campers (📞800-661-8813; www.go-west.com)

West Coast Mountain Campers (📞888-878-3200; www.wcmcampers.com)

Driver's License

Your home driver's license is valid for up to six months in BC. If you plan to drive here for longer, you'll also need an International Driver's Permit.

Fuel

Gasoline is sold in liters in Canada, where it's typically more expensive than in the US. In Calgary – headquarters of the region's oil sands petroleum business – prices are often among the best in the country. Gas prices are usually much higher in remote areas than in the cities.

Road Hazards

It's best to avoid driving in areas with heavy snow, but if you do, be sure your vehicle has snow tires or tire chains as well as an emergency kit of blankets etc. If you get stuck, don't stay in the car with the engine going: every year people die of carbon monoxide poisoning. A single candle burning in the car will keep it reasonably warm.

Make sure the car you're driving is in good condition and take along some tools, flares, water, food and a spare tire. Rural areas do not often have cell phone service.

Be careful on logging roads as logging trucks always have the right of way and often pay little heed to other vehicles. It's best not to drive on log-ging roads at all during weekday working hours.

Gravel roads of all kinds – such as those in the Yukon – can take a toll on windshields and tires. Keep a good distance from the vehicle in front, and when you see an oncoming vehicle (or a vehicle overtaking you), slow down and keep well to the right.

Wild animals are another potential hazard. Most run-ins with deer, moose and other critters occur at night when wildlife is active and visibility is poor. Many areas have roadside signs alerting drivers to possible animal crossings. Keep scanning both sides of the road and be prepared to stop or swerve. A vehicle's headlights will often mesmerize an animal, leaving it frozen in the middle of the road.

For handy updates on driving conditions around the region, peruse these useful online resources:

➜ **BC** www.drivebc.ca

➜ **Alberta** www.amaroadreports.ca

➜ **Yukon** www.511yukon.ca

Road Rules

North Americans drive on the right-hand side of the road. Speed limits, which are posted in kilometers per hour in Canada, are generally 50km/h in built-up areas and 90km/h on highways. A right turn is permitted at a red light after you have come to a complete stop, as is a left turn from a one-way street onto another one-way street. U-turns are not allowed. Traffic in both directions must stop when stationary school buses have their red lights flashing – this means that children are getting off and on. In cities with pedestrian crosswalks, cars must stop to allow pedestrians to cross.

Seat belt use is compulsory in Canada. Children under the age of five must be in a restraining seat. Motorcyclists must use lights and wear helmets. The blood-alcohol limit when driving is 0.08% (about two drinks) and is

SAMPLE DRIVING DISTANCES

ROUTE	DISTANCE	DURATION
Banff-Fernie	360km	4hr
Calgary-Edmonton	300km	3½hr
Edmonton-Jasper	365km	4hr
Jasper-Banff	290km	4hr
Kelowna-Banff	480km	6hr
Prince George-Prince Rupert	705km	8½hr
Prince Rupert-Whitehorse (via Stewart-Cassiar Hwy)	1375km	19hr
Vancouver-Kelowna	390km	4hr
Vancouver-Prince George	790km	9hr
Whitehorse-Dawson City	530km	7hr

strictly enforced with heavy fines, bans and jail terms.

Hitchhiking

Hitchhiking is not common in BC, Alberta and the Yukon, except in more remote smaller communities. It's never entirely safe in any country in the world, and is not recommended. Travelers who decide to hitchhike (or pick up hitchhikers) should understand that they are taking a risk. If you do choose to hitchhike, do it only in pairs. Hitching on the Trans-Canada Hwy is illegal until 40km past the Vancouver city limits.

Local Transportation

BC has excellent local public transportation in Vancouver and Victoria. Similarly, Calgary and Edmonton have good transit systems. Outside of these areas, service can be sparse, erratic or infrequent.

Most places have taxi companies, but some can be very expensive, so check the rates before you hop in.

In the Yukon, public transit in Whitehorse will suffice for getting around town but you'll have a hard time traveling further around this region without a car.

Tours

There are lots of options for traveling with company around this region, and tours range from backpacker level to high-end luxe.

Backroads (☑510-527-1555, 800-462-2848; www.backroads.com) Guided cycling, walking and/or paddling tours in the Rockies, Nova Scotia and Québec.

Hammerhead Scenic Tours (☑403-590-6930; www.hammerheadtours.ca) Calgary-based bus tour company offering excursions to Banff, Drumheller, Head-Smashed-In Buffalo Jump and beyond.

Harbour Air (☑800-665-0212; www.harbour-air.com) Spectacular floatplane tours over BC's Lower Mainland coast and mountain region.

Just Dive In Adventures (☑250-816-2241; www.justdiveinadventures.com) Guided underwater excursions on the east coast of Vancouver Island, including a popular scuba-with-the-seals package.

Moose Travel Network (☑in eastern Canada 888-816-6673, in western Canada 888-244-6673; www.moosenetwork.com) Operates backpacker-type tours in buses throughout British Columbia, Alberta and beyond.

Mountain High River Adventures (☑877-423-4555; www.raftfernie.com) Fernie-based operator offering adrenalin-pumping rafting trips in the region.

Nahanni River Adventures (☑800-297-6927; www.nahanni.com) Operates rafting and kayaking expeditions in the Yukon, British Columbia and Alaska, including trips on the Firth, Alsek and Babine Rivers, as well as down the Tatshenshini-Alsek watershed.

Prince Rupert Adventure Tours (☑800-201-8377; www.adventuretours.net) Grizzly-bear-watching boat tours are the highlight, as well as its whale-watching excursions.

Up North Adventures (☑867-667-7035; www.upnorthadventures.com) Whitehorse-based company offers a plethora of services including guided kayak, fishing and snowmobile tours.

Train

Passenger train services are limited in BC and virtually nonexistent in Alberta. The national carrier, **VIA Rail** (☑888-842-7245; www.viarail.ca), has only one route from Vancouver. The *Canadian* departs a paltry three times a week and makes a few stops in BC before reaching Jasper, Alberta. The 18½-hour trip takes in some beautiful scenery. You can alight in Jasper and maybe pick-up the connecting train to Prince Rupert, or continue on the *Canadian* through Alberta, the Prairies and on to Toronto (it takes about 3½ days from Vancouver to Toronto).

Fares from Vancouver to Jasper start at $162 and rise exponentially if you'd like a private sleeping cabin with gourmet meals and access to the dome car.

VIA also runs a lovely route between Jasper and Prince Rupert. It's a daytime-only trip with an overnight stay in Prince George, plus stops in Terrace, New Hazelton, Smithers, Houston and Burns Lake. You have to find your own lodgings in Prince George. Fares from Jasper to Prince Rupert start at $113, and there's a deluxe service with observation car available in the summer.

Vancouver Island recently lost its VIA Rail service between Victoria and Courtenay but there is talk of restoring it in the coming years.

Book ahead for all VIA services: advance tickets offer the best deals.

In addition to the older trains of the government-run VIA system, this region is also home to two major players in the luxury train travel market.

Rocky Mountaineer (☑877-460-3200; www.rockymountaineer.com) runs lovely, half-day trips between North Vancouver and Whistler as well as even more luxurious multiday services from Vancouver through the Rocky Mountains into Alberta. The trains travel at 'Polaroid speed' so you can be sure to get all the photos you need.

Even higher-end is the exclusive **Royal Canadian Pacific** (☑877-665-3044; www.royalcanadianpacific.com), an uber-luxe trip of a lifetime which loops through the mountains of Alberta via Calgary and includes posh dining along with wildlife-watching and golf packages. It markets itself as the world's finest luxury train.

Behind the Scenes

SEND US YOUR FEEDBACK

Things change – prices go up, schedules change, good places go bad and bad places go bankrupt. So if you find things better or worse, recently opened or long since closed, or you just want to tell us what you loved or loathed about this book, please get in touch and help make the next edition even more accurate and useful. We love to hear from travelers – your comments keep us on our toes and our well-traveled team reads every word. Although we can't reply individually to postal submissions, we always guarantee that your feedback goes straight to the appropriate authors, in time for the next edition. Each person who sends us information is thanked in the next edition – the most useful submissions are rewarded with a selection of digital PDF chapters.

Visit **lonelyplanet.com/contact** to submit your updates and suggestions or to ask for help. Our award-winning website also features inspirational travel stories, news and discussions.

Note: We may edit, reproduce and incorporate your comments in Lonely Planet products such as guidebooks, websites and digital products, so let us know if you don't want your comments reproduced or your name acknowledged. For a copy of our privacy policy visit lonelyplanet.com/privacy.

OUR READERS

Many thanks to the travelers who used the last edition and wrote to us with helpful hints, useful advice and interesting anecdotes:

Caroline Helbig, Catherine Heintz, Geneviève Wilshire, John Hoffmann, Lieke Sauer and Sandra Theimer, Stevens Quilliou, Ted Brooks, Yinna Harold

AUTHOR THANKS

John Lee

John would like to thank the too-numerous-to-mention visitor center staff as well as the hundreds of locals he met en route for their friendly tips and advice for places to check out. He'd also especially like to thank his father – William Lee – for first bringing him to Vancouver for a visit from the UK during the Expo '86 world exposition all those years ago.

Brendan Sainsbury

Thanks to all the bus drivers, tourist info volunteers, Parks Canada guides, restaurateurs, coffee baristas, theatrical performers and indie punk rockers who helped me during my research. Special thanks to my wife Liz and seven-year-old son Kieran for their company on the road, and to my sis-in-law Tina Varughese for putting me up in Calgary.

Ryan Ver Berkmoes

The number of folks to thank outnumber Kermode bears, but here's a few: Russ Lester, my fearless co-pilot, the opinionated Susan Clarke, the organized Karla Zimmerman and the pinch-hitting Korina Miller. It's always good to share BC with John Lee. At LP, I am deeply indebted to the indefatigable Mark Griffiths, Martine Power and Saralinda Turner, who showed incredible understanding when I needed it. And while there may not be golden bears, there is the golden Alexis Averbuck, who discovered and shared my love for this beautiful part of the world.

ACKNOWLEDGMENTS

Climate map data adapted from Peel MC, Finlayson BL & McMahon TA (2007) 'Updated World Map of the Köppen-Geiger Climate Classification', *Hydrology and Earth System Sciences*, 11, 1633¬44.

Transit map: Vancouver TransLink Map © TransLink 2013.

Cover photograph: Banff National Park, Alberta, Stefan Damm/4Corners

THIS BOOK

This 6th edition of Lonely Planet's *British Columbia & the Canadian Rockies* guidebook was researched and written by John Lee, Ryan Ver Berkmoes and Brendan Sainsbury. This guidebook was commissioned in Lonely Planet's Oakland office, and produced by the following:

Commissioning Editors Jennye Garibaldi, Korina Miller

Coordinating Editor Alison Ridgway

Senior Cartographer Mark Griffiths

Book Designer Lauren Egan

Managing Editors Martine Power, Angela Tinson

Assisting Editors Paul Harding

Cover Researcher Naomi Parker

Thanks to Ryan Evans, Larissa Frost, Genesys India, Jouve India, Indra Kilfoyle, Chad Parkhill, Trent Paton, Tracy Whitmey

Index

Map Pages **000**
Photo Pages **000**

NOTES

Map Legend

Sights
- Beach
- Bird Sanctuary
- Buddhist
- Castle/Palace
- Christian
- Confucian
- Hindu
- Islamic
- Jain
- Jewish
- Monument
- Museum/Gallery/Historic Building
- Ruin
- Sento Hot Baths/Onsen
- Shinto
- Sikh
- Taoist
- Winery/Vineyard
- Zoo/Wildlife Sanctuary
- Other Sight

Activities, Courses & Tours
- Bodysurfing
- Diving
- Canoeing/Kayaking
- Course/Tour
- Skiing
- Snorkeling
- Surfing
- Swimming/Pool
- Walking
- Windsurfing
- Other Activity

Sleeping
- Sleeping
- Camping

Eating
- Eating

Drinking & Nightlife
- Drinking & Nightlife
- Cafe

Entertainment
- Entertainment

Shopping
- Shopping

Information
- Bank
- Embassy/Consulate
- Hospital/Medical
- Internet
- Police
- Post Office
- Telephone
- Toilet
- Tourist Information
- Other Information

Geographic
- Beach
- Hut/Shelter
- Lighthouse
- Lookout
- Mountain/Volcano
- Oasis
- Park
- Pass
- Picnic Area
- Waterfall

Population
- Capital (National)
- Capital (State/Province)
- City/Large Town
- Town/Village

Transport
- Airport
- BART station
- Border crossing
- Boston T station
- Bus
- Cable car/Funicular
- Cycling
- Ferry
- Metro/Muni station
- Monorail
- Parking
- Petrol station
- Subway/SkyTrain station
- Taxi
- Train station/Railway
- Tram
- Underground station
- Other Transport

Note: Not all symbols displayed above appear on the maps in this book

Routes
- Tollway
- Freeway
- Primary
- Secondary
- Tertiary
- Lane
- Unsealed road
- Road under construction
- Plaza/Mall
- Steps
- Tunnel
- Pedestrian overpass
- Walking Tour
- Walking Tour detour
- Path/Walking Trail

Boundaries
- International
- State/Province
- Disputed
- Regional/Suburb
- Marine Park
- Cliff
- Wall

Hydrography
- River, Creek
- Intermittent River
- Canal
- Water
- Dry/Salt/Intermittent Lake
- Reef

Areas
- Airport/Runway
- Beach/Desert
- Cemetery (Christian)
- Cemetery (Other)
- Glacier
- Mudflat
- Park/Forest
- Sight (Building)
- Sportsground
- Swamp/Mangrove

OUR STORY

A beat-up old car, a few dollars in the pocket and a sense of adventure. In 1972 that's all Tony and Maureen Wheeler needed for the trip of a lifetime – across Europe and Asia overland to Australia. It took several months, and at the end – broke but inspired – they sat at their kitchen table writing and stapling together their first travel guide, *Across Asia on the Cheap*. Within a week they'd sold 1500 copies. Lonely Planet was born.

Today, Lonely Planet has offices in Melbourne, London, Oakland and Delhi, with more than 600 staff and writers. We share Tony's belief that 'a great guidebook should do three things: inform, educate and amuse'.

OUR WRITERS

John Lee

Coordinating Author, British Columbia Originally from the UK, John moved to British Columbia to study at the University of Victoria in the 1990s. Eventually staying and moving to Vancouver, he started a freelance travel-writing career in 1999. Since then, he's been covering the region and beyond for Lonely Planet plus magazines, newspapers and online outlets around the world. Winner of numerous writing awards, very active on Twitter and a weekly columnist for Canada's the *Globe and Mail* national newspaper, catch up with him at www.johnleewriter.com.

Brendan Sainsbury

Alberta An expat Brit from Hampshire, England, Brendan first came to Canada in 2004 in pursuit of a woman he had met in Spain (they married and are currently living happily ever after in White Rock, BC). He has covered Alberta numerous times for Lonely Planet both for this book and for a separate LP guide to Banff, Jasper and Glacier National Parks. He has a special affection for the province's national parks, particularly Lake Louise and the Lake Agnes Teahouse.

Read more about Brendan at:
lonelyplanet.com/members/brendansainsbury

Ryan Ver Berkmoes

British Columbia, Yukon Territory Ryan's been bouncing around BC, the Yukon and Manitoba for more than two decades. As always he revelled in critter-spotting, whether from car, ferry, train or plane. It's fitting given Ryan's back-ground with moose. At his first newspaper job he was tasked with placing random moose jokes in the classifieds to pique reader interest (What's a moose's favorite condiment? Moose-turd). For better jokes than that, surf over to ryanverberkmoes.com or follow him: @ryanvb.

Read more about Ryan at:
lonelyplanet.com/members/ryanverberkmoes

Published by Lonely Planet Publications Pty Ltd
ABN 36 005 607 983
6th edition – April 2014
ISBN 978 1 74220 7452
© Lonely Planet 2014   Photographs © as indicated 2014
10 9 8 7 6 5 4 3 2 1
Printed in China

Although the authors and Lonely Planet have taken all reason-able care in preparing this book, we make no warranty about the accuracy or completeness of its content and, to the maxi-mum extent permitted, disclaim all liability arising from its use.